WORLD MILITARY LEADERS

WORLD MILITARY LEADERS

Paul Martell and **Grace P. Hayes**
Editors

Trevor N. Dupuy
Executive Editor

R. R. Bowker Company
New York

T. N. Dupuy Associates
Dunn Loring, Virginia

Published by T. N. DUPUY ASSOCIATES,
Dunn Loring, Virginia, in association with
R. R. BOWKER CO. (a Xerox company), New York, N.Y.
Library of Congress Catalog Card Number: 74-78392 ISBN: 0-8352-0785-4
Copyright © 1974 by Trevor N. Dupuy

Printed and bound in the United States of America

PREFACE

This book is designed to supply a long-felt need for a biographical directory of military and civilian personnel in senior positions in military establishments in all nations of the world. While recognizing that some nations publish little information on senior military officers, the editors have sought to assemble as complete and as balanced a collection of biographies as possible.

The major portion of the information contained in this book was provided by defense departments or ministries, and the editors are gratified by the substantial cooperation they have received. Additional material was gathered from a variety of open, published sources, including official personnel lists, newspapers and other periodicals, and various biographical publications. The editors recognize that imbalances in coverage have resulted and are hopeful that readers will assist by supplying additional entries and by correcting inaccuracies for inclusion in the next edition.

Compilation of such a book as this is faced with the problem of trying to keep abreast of changes in rank and assignment in a highly transient population. During the year that it has been in preparation changes have been entered as they have been reported. Unfortunately not all such changes are published or are as readily available as the original information. Moreover, changes in political and military situations in several areas have resulted in sudden shifts of personnel which have been incompletely reported in the press and impossible to verify from official sources. Wherever possible personnel changes under these conditions have been recorded to the extent the available information will permit.

Preparing biographies of military leaders of the People's Republic of China involves some unique uncertainties. Not only is information officially limited, but the political roles of senior officers in recent years has involved them in purges, losses, and sudden changes in status. Moreover, the shifts resulting from such internal processes as the Great Proletarian Cultural Revolution are only partly discernible to the outside observer. Within such limitation, the best available information on these leaders has been used. Although ranks in the Peoples' Liberation Army have been abolished, ranks as known to have existed prior to the abolition have been given the officers included here. Because of uncertainties about dates, those given for the Peoples' Republic of China are dates on which a position is known to have been held.

The first section of the book contains the biographies in alphabetical order. The second section lists the entries under the name of the nation which they serve. Each listing includes as many as are available of the following items of information: name, rank, current position or assignment, date of assuming position, date of birth, place of birth, education and professional training, date of commissioning, experience in active theaters of war, recent positions and assignments, most important honors, decorations, and awards, professional affiliations, dates of promotion to senior grades, publications, and other pertinent data. Except when translation is impractical, information is given in English. The use of abbreviations is minimal, and has been limited to those readily found in standard reference works or previously spelled out within an entry.

The editors wish to express thanks to those in official positions, in government defense establishments and in embassies, who have provided biographical sketches and responded to numerous questions as we have sought to verify information.

The assistance of Billie P. Davis, who prepared the manuscript for publication and provided intelligent and observant editorial help throughout the process of compilation, has been invaluable.

Comments on this publication and suggestions for additions and corrections will be welcomed. A tear sheet is provided for the convenience of readers who wish to suggest new listings or to point out errors or changes in rank or assignment for inclusion in the next edition.

To the Military Biography Editors
T. N. Dupuy Associates
P.O. Box 157
Dunn Loring, Virginia 22027

Gentlemen:

I recommend that you add biographical sketches of the following to your publication:

Name:

Rank:

Present Position:

Address:

To the Military Biography Editors
T. N. Dupuy Associates
P.O. Box 157
Dunn Loring, Virginia 22027

Gentlemen:

The following corrections and additions should be made to the biography of

WORLD MILITARY LEADERS

A

Aaron, Harold Robert. Major General, United States Army; Deputy Chief of Staff, Intelligence, US Army, Europe, and Seventh Army, 1972- . Born June 21, 1921, in Kokomo, Indiana. Attended US Military Academy; Infantry School, Basic and Advanced Courses; Artillery School, Advanced Course; Command and General Staff College; Armed Forces Staff College; National War College, 1963-64; Georgetown University, MA and PhD, International Relations. Commissioned Second Lieutenant, June 1, 1943. Served in WW II and the Vietnam War. Member, Joint Actions Division, Office of Special Activities, Joint Staff, Joint Chiefs of Staff Organization, 1965-67; Commanding Officer, 1st Special Forces Group (Airborne), 1st Special Forces, US Army, Pacific-Okinawa, 1967-68; Commanding Officer, 5th Special Forces Group (Airborne), 1st Special Forces, US Army, Pacific-Vietnam, 1968-69; Chief, Force Analysis Group, Force Plans Analysis Directorate, Office of the Assistant Vice Chief of Staff, US Army, 1969; Assistant Division Commander, 8th Infantry Division, US Army, Europe, 1969-71; Chief of Staff, Headquarters V Corps, US Army, Europe, 1971-72. Distinguished Service Medal; Legion of Merit with Oak Leaf Cluster; Bronze Star Medal with V Device and two Oak Leaf Clusters. Promoted to Brigadier General June 1, 1970; Major General February 1, 1973.

Abbot, James Lloyd, Jr. Rear Admiral, United States Navy, Retired; Director of Educational Development, Staff of the Chief of Naval Training, Naval Air Station, Pensacola, Florida, 1972- . Born June 26, 1918, in Mobile, Alabama. Spring Hill College; US Naval Academy, 1935-39; Flight Training Course, 1941; Armed Forces Staff College, 1952-53; George Washington University, MS, Business Administration, 1964; National War College, 1963-64. Commissioned Ensign, US Navy, 1939; designated Naval Aviator, 1941. Served in the Pacific Theater in WW II. Commanding Officer, USS *Intrepid* (CVA-11), 1961-63; Director for Mid-Range Studies, Office of the CNO, 1964-65; Deputy Director of Naval Warfare Analyses, 1965-66; Director of Naval Warfare Analyses, 1966-67; Commander, US Naval Support Force, Antarctica, 1967-69; Commander, Antisubmarine Warfare Group FOUR, 1969-70; Inspector General, US Atlantic Fleet, 1970-72; transferred to retired list, July 1, 1972; returned to active duty, November 1972. Legion of Merit with Gold Star; Air Medal; Navy Commendation Medal; and other medals and awards. Promoted to Rear Admiral, May 30, 1967.

Abhany, Kouprasith. General, Royal Army of Laos; Commander in Chief, Royal Lao Armed Forces.

Abraham, Sutton Martin O'Heguerty. Major-General, British Army; Chief, Joint Services Liaison Organization, British Army of the Rhine, 1971- . Born January 26, 1918. Trinity College, Cambridge, BA, Modern Languages; Staff College, 1948; Imperial Defence College, 1967. Commissioned, General List, Territorial Army, 1939; transferred to 12th Royal Lancers, 1941. Served in North African and Italian Theaters, WW II. Recent positions: Commander, Royal Armoured Corps (Brigadier), 1st British Corps, Germany, 1964-66; Director, Combat Development (Army), Ministry of Defence, 1968-71. Military Cross and Bar.

Abramov, K. Colonel General, USSR Army; Commandant, Rear Services (Logistics) and Transport College. Served on the Soviet-German Front in WW II. Member of Communist Party of the Soviet Union.

Abrams, Creighton Williams. General, United States Army; Chief of Staff, US Army, Washington, D.C., 1972- . Born September 15, 1914, Springfield, Massachusetts. Attended US Military Academy; The Armored School, Advanced Course; US Army Command and General Staff College; US Army War College. Commissioned Second Lieutenant, 1936. Served in WW II, and Vietnam War. Commanding General, V Corps, US Army, Europe, 1963-64; Vice Chief of Staff, US Army, Washington, D.C., 1964-67; Deputy Commander, US Military Assistance Command, Vietnam, 1967-68; Commander, US Military Assistance Command Vietnam, and Commanding General, US Army, Vietnam, 1968-72. Distinguished Service Cross with Oak Leaf Cluster; Defense Distinguished Service Medal; Distinguished Service Medal with three Oak Leaf Clusters; Silver Star with Oak Leaf Cluster; Legion of Merit with Oak Leaf Cluster; Bronze Star Medal with V Device; and other medals and awards. Promoted to Brigadier General, February 17, 1956; Major General, June 1, 1960; Lieutenant General, August 1, 1963; General, September 4, 1964.

1

Abu-Taleb, Fathi. Colonel, Armed Forces of the Hashemite Kingdom of Jordan; Military, Naval and Air Attache, Embassy of Jordan, Washington, D.C., USA, 1971- . College Graduate; took various Military Courses, including Tank and Technical Courses, in England; attended Joint Services Staff College, India. Commander, Tank Battalion; Chief of Staff, Armored Division; Commandant, Army Armor School; Assistant Military, Naval and Air Attache, London, England.

Acheampong, Ignatius K. Colonel, Army of the Republic of Ghana; Head of State and Chairman of the National Redemption Council, Commissioner for Defence and Commissioner for Finance and Economic Planning, 1972- . Born September 23, 1931, Kumasi, Ashanti. Diploma Certificate in Commerce; General Certificate of Education (Ordinary Level); Officer Cadet Training School, Mons, Aldershot, England; Personnel Administration Course; US Army Command and General Staff College, Fort Leavenworth, Kansas, USA. Commissioned Second Lieutenant in 1959. Has held several positions in Ghana's Army, which include Commanding Officer of the Fifth and Sixth Battalions; Chairman of the Western Region of Administration, 1966-c. 1970; Commander First Infantry Brigade Group, Accra, c. 1970-72.

Adams, Andrew Joseph. Major General, United States Army; Secretary, American Battle Monuments Commission, Washington, D.C., 1968- . Born August 29, 1909, Andalusia, Alabama. Attended US Military Academy; US Army Command and General Staff College; Air Command and Staff College; Industrial College of the Armed Forces. Commissioned Second Lieutenant, 1931. Served in WW II. Commanding General, XIX US Army Corps, and Fort Chaffee, Arkansas, 1962-63; Assistant Chief of Staff, G-4, US Army, Pacific, Fort Shafter, Hawaii, 1963-66; Deputy Chief of Staff for Logistics, US Continental Army Command, Fort Monroe, Virginia, 1966-67; Assistant to Secretary, American Battle Monuments Commission, Washington, D.C., 1967-68. Distinguished Service Medal; Silver Star; Legion of Merit with Oak Leaf Cluster; Bronze Star Medal; and other medals and awards. Promoted to Brigadier General, December 1, 1956; Major General, October 1, 1961.

Adams, Arthur Harvey. Major General, United States Marine Corps; Deputy Chief of Staff to the Commander in Chief, Atlantic, 1972- . Born April 16, 1915, Jasper, Minnesota. University of Minnesota, 1934-38; Flight Training Course, 1938-39; Junior Course, Marine Corps Schools, 1947; Air War College, 1958-59. Commissioned Second Lieutenant, USMCR, Naval Aviator, 1939. Served in Pacific Theater, WW II; Korean War; Vietnam War. Director of Information, HQMC, 1963-66; Commanding General, Marine Air Reserve Training Command, Glenview, Illinois, and Commanding General, 4th Marine Aircraft Wing, 1966-68; Commanding General, Third Marine Aircraft Wing, Fleet Marine Force, Pacific, 1968-69; Senior Member, United Nations Command Component, Military Armistice Commission, Korea, 1969-70; Deputy Commander, Fleet Marine Force, Pacific, 1970-72. Legion of Merit with Gold Star; Distinguished Flying Cross with two Gold Stars; Bronze Star Medal with Combat "V"; and other medals and awards. Promoted to Brigadier General, July 1964; Major General, November 6, 1967.

Adamson, Robert E., Jr. Vice Admiral, United States Navy; Deputy Chief of Naval Operations (Surface Warfare), 1972- . Born December 28, 1920, Chicago, Illinois. Columbia University, New York, 1939-40; US Naval Academy, 1940-43; Postgraduate School, Ordnance Engineering Course, Annapolis, 1947-48; Massachusetts Institute of Technology, MS, Physics, 1948-50; Army Command and General Staff College, 1958-59. Commissioned Ensign, US Navy, in 1943. Served in the Pacific Theater, WW II; Korean War; Vietnam War. Commanding Officer USS *Wiltsie* (DD-716), 1961-62; Commanding Officer USS *Mullany* (DD-528), 1962-63; Commander Destroyer Division ONE HUNDRED FIFTY-TWO, 1963-64; Assistant Chief of Staff for Operations and Plans to Commander Cruiser-Destroyer Force, Pacific Fleet, 1964-65; Commanding Officer USS *Galveston* (CLG-3), 1965-67; Head, General Purpose Objective Forces Strategic Plans Division, Office of CNO, 1967; Deputy Commander Naval Ship Systems Command for Maintenance and Logistic Support, 1967-69; Commander US Naval Support Activity, Danang, and later Saigon, Vietnam, 1969-70; Commander South Atlantic Force, US Atlantic Fleet, 1971-72. Distinguished Service Medal; Legion of Merit with Gold Star; and other US and foreign medals and awards. Promoted to Vice Admiral, June 22, 1972.

Adebayo, Robert. Brigadier, Nigerian Army; Commandant, Nigerian Defense Academy, 1971- . Born in 1928. Attended Christ School, Lagos; Military Academy, England; Imperial Defence College, England. Commissioned in England, 1953; served in Nigeria from 1954. Aide de Camp to the Governor General, 1957-58; Nigerian Contingent, UN Peacekeeping Force, Congo, 1961-63; Chief of Staff, Nigerian Army, 1964-65; Military Governor, Western Nigeria, 1966-71; Member, Supreme Military Council. Promoted to Major, 1960; Lieutenant Colonel, 1962; Colonel, 1964.

Adriazola Valda, Oscar. Brigadier General, Bolivian Air Force; Commander of the Bolivian Air Force, 1971- . Attended Military Academy, 1950; Pilot Training, 1951-53; Squadron Officers School, Montgomery, Alabama, USA, 1960; Command and General Staff School, Argentina, 1963. Commissioned in 1950. Assistant Air Attache, Bolivian Embassy, Buenos Aires, Argentina, 1962; Chief of Transport Operations, 1963; Squadron Commander, 1964; Air Attache, Bolivian Embassy, Washington, D.C., USA, 1965-68; Commander, Air Academy, 1968; Chief of the Military Household, 1969; Mayor of Santa-Cruz, 1970; Air Force Chief of Staff, 1971. Legion of Merit (USA); and other medals and awards. Promoted to Brigadier General, 1972.

Aeberhard, Alfred. Brigadier General, Swiss Army; Chief of Transport Service and Repair Troops. Born in 1913.

Aganov, S. K. Lieutenant General, USSR Army; Deputy Commander, Railway Troops. Served on the Soviet-German Front in WW II. Member of Communist Party of the Soviet Union.

Agosti, Orlando Ramon. Brigadier, Argentine Air Force; Air Attache, Embassy of Argentina, Washington, D.C.; Chief of Delegation, Inter-American Defense Board. Date of Rank: December 31, 1971.

Aguirre Obarrio, Eduardo. Minister of National Defense, Argentina, 1973-   .

Ahmad, Hasan Hafeez. Vice Admiral, Navy of Pakistan; Chief of the Naval Staff, 1972-   . Born in 1926. Attended Britannia Royal Naval College, United Kingdom, 1945-47; Technical Naval Courses, United Kingdom, 1947-49; Joint Services Staff Course, Latimer, United Kingdom, 1964-65. Joined the Royal Indian Navy in 1945. Commissioned Sub-Lieutenant, 1947. Served in the India-Pakistan War, 1965, 1971. Former Director, Pakistan Navy Tactical School; Commandant, Naval Academy; Director of Naval Operations, 1965-66; Military Attache, Pakistan Embassy, Paris, France, 1966-71; Commander, PNS *Babub,* 1971; Acting Commander in Chief, Pakistan Navy, 1971-72. Tamgha-e-Quaid-e-Azam; Commandeur de l'Ordre Nationale du Merite (France); Grand Officier de l'Ordre Nationale du Merite (France); and other honors and awards. Promoted to Rear Admiral, December 30, 1971; Vice Admiral, March 3, 1972.

Ahmad, Mohammed al-Baqir. Major General, Sudanese Army; Minister of Interior, Sudan, 1971-   . Born in 1927, in El Sofi. Attended Commercial School, Khartoum; Military College; Cairo University. Commissioned Second Lieutenant in 1950. Military Governor, Upper Nile Province, 1959-60; Military Attache, Sudanese Embassy, London, 1960-67; Director of Training and Chief of Staff, Southern Command, 1968; Commandant, Military College, 1968-69; Under Secretary, Ministry of Defense, 1969; First Deputy Chief of Staff of the Armed Forces, 1969-70; Chief of Staff of the Armed Forces, 1970-71.

Ahmed, Aziz. Minister of State for Defence and Foreign Affairs, Pakistan, 1973-   . Born June 1906, in Lahore (Punjab). Chief Secretary to the Government of East Pakistan, 1947-52; Secretary to the Cabinet, Central Government, 1952-56; Secretary in Charge of the Ministry of Commerce, 1956-58; Secretary, Ministry of Refugees and Rehabilitation, 1958; Secretary General to the Government of Pakistan, 1958-59; Ambassador of Pakistan to the United States, 1959-63; Foreign Secretary, 1963-66; Chairman, National Press Trust, 1967-70; Minister of State, Foreign Affairs, 1971-73. Hilal-i-Pakistan; Hilal-i-Quaid-i-Azam; Sitara-i-Pakistan; OBE (British); and other honors and awards.

Ahmed, Rashid. Rear Admiral, Navy of Pakistan; Naval Chief of Staff. Served in India-Pakistan War, 1972.

Ahmed, Syed Ghias Uddin. Secretary General, Defence, Government of Pakistan, 1972-   . Born June 1, 1915, in Abbaspur, Lyallpur District. Attended Government College, Lyallpur; Government College, Lahore; Magdalene College, Cambridge (England). Joined Indian Civil Service in 1939. Commissioner, Rawalpindi Division, 1958-63; Additional Chief Secretary to the Government of West Pakistan, 1963-66; Director, Civil Service Academy, April-June 1966; Secretary to Government of Pakistan, Ministry of Home and Kashmir Affairs, July 1966-February 1967; Defence Secretary, Government of Pakistan, December 1966-September 1967; Adviser In Charge, Ministry of Defence, September-December 1971; Defence Secretary, December 1971-May 1972.

Ahnfelt, Sigmund. Major General, Swedish Royal Army; Commander in Chief, Military Command Bergslagen, 1973-   . Born November 28, 1915. Attended Royal Army Staff College; US Army Command and General Staff College, USA, 1949-50. Commissioned in the Royal Army in 1938. Commanding Officer, Infantry Regiment I 15, 1962-66; Chief of Staff, Military Command South, 1966-73. Commander of the Royal Order of the Sword; and other medals and awards. Member, Royal Academy of Military Sciences. Promoted to Major General, 1966.

Aiken, Sir John (Alexander Carlisle). Air Marshal, British Royal Air Force; Head of Economy Project Team, 1972-   . Born December 22, 1921. Attended Central Flying School, 1948; Staff College, 1953; Joint Services Staff College 1958; Imperial Defence College, 1968. Commissioned in 1941. Served with fighter squadrons in Europe and Far East, WW II. Duty in the Air Ministry, 1960-63; Station Commander, RAF, Finningley, 1963-64; Air Commodore, Intelligence, Ministry of Defence, 1965-67; Deputy Commander, RAF, Germany, 1969-71; Director-General of Training, RAF, 1971-72. KCB.

Akin, Veichi. General, Turkish Army; Commander, Military District 1973.

Akinci, Esref. General, Turkish Army; Commander, Turkish Land Forces Command, 1973-   . Studied at Military Academy; Infantry School; War College. Formerly Director of Mapping Service; Division Commander; Assistant Chief of Staff for Logistics, to Chief of General Staff; Assistant Chief of Staff to the Land Forces Commander; Commander, Army Corps; Member, Supreme Military Council; Army Commander; Counselor to the Minister of Defense. Distinguished Unit Award; Distinguished Courageous Service; and other medals and awards. Promoted to General, August 30, 1969.

Alba, Jorge. Brigadier General, Colombian Army; Military Attache, Embassy of Colombia, Washington, D.C., 1971-73.

Albert y Correia, Joae. Brigadier, Portuguese Army; Secretary of State for Army 1973.

Albright, Jack Alvin. Major General, United States Army; Commanding General, US Army Strategic Communications Command, Fort Huachuca, Arizona, 1971-   . Born January 10, 1921, Memphis, Tennessee. University of Maryland, BS Degree, Military Science; Signal School, Advanced Course; US Army Command and General Staff College; Armed Forces Staff College; Industrial College of the Armed Forces; George Washington University, MBA Degree, Business Administration. Commissioned Second Lieutenant, US Army, 1942. Served in WW II, and Vietnam War. Commanding Officer, White House Communications Agency, Washington, D.C., 1965-69; Deputy Commanding General, 1st Signal Brigade, US Army Strategic Communications Command, Southeast Asia, US Army, Pacific-Vietnam, 1969-70; Deputy Commanding General, US Army Strategic Communications Command, Fort Huachuca, Arizona, 1971. Distinguished Service Medal; Legion of Merit; Bronze Star Medal with Oak Leaf Cluster; and other medals and awards. Promoted to Brigadier General, September 1, 1969; Major General, August 1, 1971.

Albrittain, John Warren. Rear Admiral, Medical Corps, United States Navy; Deputy Chief, Bureau of Medicine and Surgery, Navy Department, 1969-   . Born April 30, 1911, La Plata, Maryland. University of Maryland, MD. Commissioned Lieutenant (j.g.), Medical Corps, US Naval Reserve, 1939; transferred to US Navy, 1941. Commanding Officer US Naval Hospital, St. Albans, New York, 1965-66; Commanding Officer, US Naval Hospital and Naval Hospital School, Great Lakes, Illinois, and District Medical Officer, Ninth Naval District, 1966-69. Various medals and awards. Promoted to Rear Admiral, July 1, 1965.

Alcantara, Francisco Augusto Simas de. Fleet Admiral, Brazil; Chief of the Navy General Staff and Chief of Naval Operations, 1972-   . Attended Naval School; Armament Course, Naval War College; Antisubmarine Warfare Course (USA); Senior War College. Combat duty in World War II. Recent duty includes Director-General of Naval Materiel; Director-General of Naval Personnel; Director of Hydrography and Navigation; Director, Naval War College; Commandant, 2d Naval District; Director, Admiral Wandenkolk Instruction Center; Commander, Naval Base, Natal; Member of Staff, Naval Ministry; Secretary-General of the Brazilian Loide, 1950-51. Medalha Estácio de Sá; Medalha do Mérito Aeronáutico; Medalha da Junta Interamericana de Defesa; Medalha do Mérito Tamandaré; Medalha da Ordem do Rio Branco; Medalha da Ordem Militar; Medalha do Mérito Naval; Medalha da Força Naval do Sul. Promoted to Fleet Admiral, November 20, 1969.

Alcoreza Melgarejo, Carlos. Brigadier General, Bolivian Army; Commander of the Bolivian Army, 1973-   . Attended Military Academy, 1947; School of Arms, 1953; Senior War College, Argentina, 1958; School of Advanced Military Studies, 1970. Commissioned in 1947. Army G-3, 1960-62; Chief of Studies, School of Arms, 1962-63; Instructor, Command and General Staff School, 1963-64; Minister of Finance, 1964-67; Army G-1, 1967-70; Chief of Staff, 3d Division, 1971-72; Commander, 1st Division,

1972; Army Chief of Staff, 1973. "Piloto Honoris Causa"; and other medals and awards. Promoted to Brigadier General, 1972.

Alekseyev, N. N. Colonel General, Engineer, USSR Army; Deputy Minister of Defense, and Chief of Weapons Development, 1970-   . Served on the Soviet-German Front in WW II. Member of Communist Party of the Soviet Union.

Alekseyev, Vladimir Nikolayevich. Vice Admiral, USSR Navy; First Deputy Chief of Staff, Main Naval Staff, 1968-   . Born in 1912 in Kimilty, Irkutsk Oblast. Drafted into the Navy, 1933. Attended Special Naval Commanders' Courses, c. 1938; Naval War College, 1943; General Staff War College, 1953. Commissioned in middle 1930s. Served in the Soviet-German War (WW II). Assigned to the Staff, Northern Fleet, 1943; Commander, 3rd Torpedo Boat Squadron, 1944; Commanded large naval unit in the late 1940s and early 1950s; Commander, Naval Base, 1953-57; Chief of Staff, Baltic Fleet, 1958-67. Member of Communist Party of the Soviet Union, 1941-   . Decorations include: Hero of the Soviet Union; Order of Lenin; Five Orders of Red Banner; and Order of the Fatherland War.

'Ali, Ahmad Isma'il. General, Army of the Arab Republic of Egypt; Commander in Chief of Egyptian Armed Forces and Minister of War, 1972-   . Born October 14, 1917. Attended Royal Military Academy; Military Staff College, MS, Military Science, 1950; Military training course, UK; Frunze Military Academy, USSR, 1957; Nasir Military Science University, 1965. Commissioned Second Lieutenant in 1938. Served as intelligence officer in the Western Desert in WW II; in front lines in 1948 Arab-Israeli War. Instructor, Military Staff College, 1950-53; Military adviser in the Congo (Kinshasa), 1961; Chief of Staff to United Arab Command Commander in Chief 'Ali 'Ali 'Amir, 1965; Chief of Staff to Commander of Egyptian Land Forces, 1966; Commander Eastern Command Forces, Ismailia, 1967; Chief of "B" Field Army, 1967-68; Deputy Chief of Staff of the Armed Forces, then Chief of Staff, 1968-69, with additional duty as Assistant Secretary General of the Arab League for Military Affairs; Director of General Intelligence, 1971-72. Liberation Order; Anniversary Order of the Establishment of the UAR; Military Pendant of Evacuation; Military Pendant of Independence; Victory Pendant; Order of the People's Army of Yugoslavia; and other medals and awards.

Alibert, Pierre Leon Antoine. Major General, French Air Force; Commander of Air Engineers, 1968-   ; Administrator of Airport of Paris, 1965-   . Born December 23, 1920. Attended Air Academy in Salon-de-Provence; Advanced School of Electricity; Air Senior War College. Commissioned in 1940. Served in World War II and in Indochina. Commander Francezal Air Base at Toulouse, 1963-65. Commandeur, Légion d'Honneur; Croix de Guerre; Médaille de la Résistance; and Médaille de l'Aéronautique.

Allen, James R. Major General, United States Air Force; Assistant Deputy Chief of Staff, Operations, Strategic Air Command, 1972-   . Born November 17, 1925, in Louisville, Kentucky. US Military Academy, 1944-48; Flying Training School, 1949; Army Command and General Staff College, 1959-60; Industrial College of the Armed Forces, 1964-65; George Washington University, MS, Business Administration, 1965. Commissioned in 1948; received pilot wings in 1949. Served in the Korean War; Vietnam War. Deputy Commander, Operations, 12th Tactical Fighter Wing, Vietnam, 1965-66; Deputy Commander, Operations, 3615th Pilot Training Wing, 1967-68; Assistant Deputy Director of Plans, Directorate of Plans, Deputy Chief of Staff, Plans and Operations, 1968-69; Deputy Director, Plans and Policy, Directorate of Plans, Deputy Chief of Staff, Plans and Operations, 1969-71; Commander, Nineteenth Air Division, 1972. Legion of Merit with two Oak Leaf Clusters; Distinguished Flying Cross with one Oak Leaf Cluster; Bronze Star Medal; and other medals and awards. Promoted to Major General, June 5, 1972.

Allen, Joseph P. United States; NASA Scientist-Astronaut, 1967-   . Born June 27, 1937, Crawfordsville, Indiana. Depauw University, Greencastle, Indiana, BA, 1959; Yale University, New Haven, Connecticut, MS, 1961, PhD, 1965; Flight Training, Vance Air Force Base. Research Associate, Nuclear Physics Laboratory, University of Washington, 1967; Staff Physicist, Nuclear Structure Lab, Yale University, 1965-66; Guest Research Associate, Brookhaven National Laboratory, 1963-67. NASA experience: Mission Scientist Member of the Support Crew for Apollo 15.

Allen, Lew, Jr. Major General, United States Air Force; Director, National Security Agency, Fort Meade, Maryland, 1973-   . Born September 30, 1925, Miami, Florida. US Military Academy, 1943-46; Advanced Pilot Training, 1946; University of Illinois, MS, Nuclear Physics, 1952, PhD, 1954. Commissioned Second Lieutenant, US Army, 1946. Deputy Director, Advanced Plans, Directorate of Special Projects, Office of the Secretary of the Air Force, 1965-68; Deputy Director, Office of Space Systems, Office of the Secretary of the Air Force, 1968-69; Director, Office of Space Systems, Office of the Secretary of the Air Force, 1969-70; Assistant to Director, Special Projects, Office of the Secretary of the Air Force, 1970-71; Director, Special Projects, Office of the Secretary of the Air Force, and Deputy Commander, Satellite Programs, Space and Missile Systems Organization (SAMSO), 1971-73. Legion of Merit with two Oak Leaf Clusters; Joint Service Commendation Medal; and other medals and awards. Promoted to Brigadier General, November 1, 1969; Major General, 1972.

Allerton, Ord Denny. Air Commodore, British Royal Air Force; Director of Movements, Air Ministry. CB; CBE.

Allison, Royal Bertram. Lieutenant General, United States Air Force; Assistant to Chairman, Joint Chiefs of Staff, for Strategic Arms Negotiations, and Principal Military Member on US Delegation to Strategic Arms Limitations Talks,

1969-   . Born April 22, 1919, in Harlan, Oregon. Oregon State College, 1938-41; Army Air Corps Flying School, 1941-42; Command and General Staff School, 1945. Commissioned Second Lieutenant, US Army Air Corps, 1942. Served in the Mediterranean Theater, WW II. Director of Plans, Deputy Chief of Staff, Operations, Headquarters USAF, Europe, 1961-63; Assistant Deputy Chief of Staff, Operations, Headquarters USAF, Europe, 1963-64; Deputy Chairman, Chairman's Special Studies Group, Joint Chiefs of Staff, 1964-67; Deputy Chief of Staff, Plans and Operations, Commander in Chief, Pacific, 1967-69. Distinguished Service Medal; Silver Star; Legion of Merit; Distinguished Flying Cross; Soldier's Medal; and other medals and awards. Promotions: Brigadier General, December 29, 1963; Major General, September 1, 1966; Lieutenant General, November 14, 1969.

Almgren, Carl Eric. Lieutenant General, Swedish Royal Army; Commander in Chief, Swedish Army, 1969-   . Royal Army Staff College, 1941-43; Royal National Defense College, 1951. Assistant Defense Attache, Tallin and Riga, 1939-40; Commanding Officer, Infantry Regiment I 5, 1960-61; Major General and Chief, Defense Staff, 1961-67; Commander in Chief, Military District East, and Commandant General, Stockholm, 1967-69. Knight Grand Cross of the Royal Order of the Sword; Knight Grand Cross of the Royal Order of Wasa; Order of the White Rose (Finland); Order of St. Olav (Norway); and other medals and awards. Member and Chairman of the Royal Academy of Military Sciences. Promoted to Lieutenant General, 1966.

Almquist, Elmer Hugo. Lieutenant General, United States Army; Assistant Chief of Staff for Force Development, US Army, Washington, D.C., 1972-   . Born May 17, 1919, Louisville, Kentucky. Attended Alabama Polytechnic Institute, BS Degree, Mechanical Engineering; The Field Artillery School, Basic Course; US Army Command and General Staff College; Armed Forces Staff College; US Army War College. Commissioned Second Lieutenant, US Army Reserve, 1940. Served in WW II. Assistant Division Commander, 7th Infantry Division, US Army, Pacific-Korea, 1964-65; Deputy Director, later Director of Operations, Office, Deputy Chief of Staff for Military Operations, US Army, Washington, D.C., 1965-67; Commanding General, US Army Southern European Task Force, 1967-68; Deputy Chief of Staff for Military Operations, US Army, Europe and Seventh Army, 1968-69; Chief of Staff, US Army, Europe and Seventh Army, 1970-72. Distinguished Service Medal with Oak Leaf Cluster; Legion of Merit with Oak Leaf Cluster; Bronze Star Medal with V Device and two Oak Leaf Clusters; and other medals and awards. Promoted to Brigadier General, May 1, 1964; Major General, July 1, 1967; Lieutenant General, October 1, 1972.

Alpsu, Osman. Lieutenant General, Hellenic Air Force, Commander Second Tactical Air Force, 1973.

Altunin, Aleksandr T. Colonel General, USSR Army; Deputy Minister of Defense, and Chief, Civil Defense,

1972- . Born in 1921. Combat duty on the Soviet-German Front in WW II. Deputy Commander, later Commander, Kaliningrad Military Garrison, c. 1964-68; Commander, North Caucasus Military District, 1968-70; Chief, Main Directorate for Personnel, Ministry of Defense, 1970-72; Member, Communist Party of Soviet Union. Hero of the Soviet Union; Order of Lenin; and other orders and medals. Promotions: Major General, 1960; Lieutenant General, 1968; Colonel General, 1970.

Alvares, Carlos. Rear Admiral, Argentine Navy; Commander in Chief, Argentine Navy, 1972- . Formerly Naval Attache, Embassy of Argentina, Washington, D.C.

Alvarez, Gregorio. General, Uruguayan Army; Chief of Staff, Joint Staff; Secretary General, National Security Council.

Alvarez, José Angel. Rear Admiral, Argentine Navy; Naval Attache, Embassy of Argentina, Washington, D.C.; Delegate, Inter-American Defense Board.

Alvarez Penaranda, Raul. Colonel, Bolivian Army; Chief of Staff, Bolivian Army, 1973- .

Amat Y Leon Mujica, Manuel. Rear Admiral, Peruvian Navy; Commander in Chief of the Fleet.

Ambaryan, Kh. Colonel General, USSR Army; Deputy Commander, Soviet Ground Forces, Combat Training. Served on the Soviet-German Front in WW II. Member, Communist Party of the Soviet Union.

Amel'ko, Nikolay Nikolayevich. Admiral, USSR Navy; Deputy Commander, Soviet Navy, 1970- . Born November 22, 1914, in Leningrad. Attended Frunze Naval Academy, 1932-36; General Staff War College, 1956; awarded degree of Doctor of Naval Sciences, 1966. Drafted into the Navy in 1931; commissioned in 1936. Served in the Soviet-German War (WW II). Squadron Commander, Baltic Fleet, 1941; Chief of Staff, Marine Brigade, Leningrad Front, 1941 - c. 1943; Commander of various naval units, 1945 - c. 1954; Chief of Staff, Pacific Fleet, 1956-62; Commander, Pacific Fleet, 1962-69. Member of Communist Party of the Soviet Union, 1944- ; Candidate Member, Communist Party Central Committee; Deputy to the USSR Supreme Soviet, 1966- . Order of Lenin; Order of Red Banner; and other Soviet and foreign orders and medals.

Amiama Castillo, Francisco A. Commodore, Navy of the Dominican Republic; Under Secretary for the Navy.

Amin, Idi. Major General, Ugandan Army; President of Uganda, Minister of Defence, and Commander in Chief, Ugandan Armed Forces, 1971- . Born in 1925. Joined King's African Rifles, 1946, and served as NCO with British forces until Uganda was granted independence; Commander, Ugandan Army, 1964-71; Leader of military coup d'etat, 1971.

Anderson, Andrew B., Jr. Major General, United States Air Force; Assistant Deputy Chief of Staff, Operations, Strategic Air Command, Offutt Air Force Base, Nebraska, 1973- . Born April 14, 1926, in Rocky Mount, North Carolina. US Military Academy, 1944-48; Pilot Training Course, 1948-49; Air Force Institute of Technology, BS, Aerospace Engineering, 1955; Industrial College of the Armed Forces, 1965-66; University of Nebraska, MA, History. Commissioned Second Lieutenant, US Army, 1948. Served in the Korean War. Executive Assistant to the Military Advisor to the Personal Representative of the President of the United States at the Paris Peace Talks on Vietnam, Paris, France, 1968-69; Special Assistant, Joint Matters, Office of the Director, Joint Chiefs of Staff, Washington, D.C., 1969-70; Vice Commander, 93d Bombardment Wing, Castle Air Force Base, California, 1970; Commander, 410th Bombardment Wing, K. I. Sawyer Air Force Base, Michigan, 1970-71; Chief of Staff, Second Air Force, Barksdale Air Force Base, Louisiana, 1971-73. Legion of Merit; Air Medal; and other medals and awards. Promoted to Brigadier General, September 1971; Major General, 1973.

Anderson, Earl Edward. General, United States Marine Corps; Assistant Commandant, United States Marine Corps, 1972- . Born June 24, 1919, Morgantown, West Virginia. University of West Virginia, BS, 1940; Marine Corps Officers Basic School, 1940-41; Flight Training Course, 1943; Command and Staff School, Quantico; Army War College, 1959-60; George Washington University, JD. Commissioned 1940; designated Naval Aviator, 1943. Served in Pacific Theater, WW II; Korean War; Vietnam War. Commander, Marine Aircraft Group 36, 1961-63; Chief of Staff, Military Assistance Advisory Group, Vietnam, 1963-64; Program coordinator, Marine Tactical Data System, Headquarters Marine Corps, 1964-66; Deputy Chief of Staff (Research, Development and Studies), Headquarters Marine Corps, 1966-67; Chief of Staff, III Marine Amphibious Force, Vietnam, 1967-69; Deputy Director of Personnel, Headquarters Marine Corps, 1969-70; Marine Corps Member, Board of Directors, US Olympic Committee, 1970; US Member, Executive Committee, Conseil International du Sports Militaire, 1971; Commanding General, Fleet Marine Force, Atlantic, 1971-72. Distinguished Service Medal with Gold Star; Legion of Merit with Combat "V" and two Gold Stars; Distinguished Flying Cross with Gold Star; Bronze Star Medal with Combat "V"; and other US and foreign medals and awards. Promoted to Brigadier General, January 3, 1966; Major General, September 1, 1968; Lieutenant General, June 1971; General, March 31, 1972.

Anderson, Herbert Henry. Rear Admiral, United States Navy; Director of Policy Plans and National Security Council Affairs, Office of the Assistant Secretary of Defense, 1971- . Born November 21, 1918, in Campbell, New York. Bucknell University, Lewisburg, Pennsylvania, 1936-37; US Naval Academy, 1937-41; Graduate School of Business Administration, Harvard University, MBA, 1951-53; National War College, 1957-58. Commissioned Ensign, US Navy, 1941. Served in the Pacific

Theater in WW II; Vietnam War. Commander Destroyer Squadron SEVENTEEN, 1964-65; Director, Program Change Control Division, Office of the CNO, 1965-67; Assistant Chief Bureau of Naval Personnel for Education and Training, 1967-69; Commander Cruiser-Destroyer Flotilla ELEVEN, 1969-70; Commander South Atlantic Force, 1970-71. Legion of Merit with two Gold Stars; Navy Commendation Medal with Gold Star; and other US and foreign medals and awards. Promoted to Rear Admiral, July 1, 1967.

Anderson, Roy Gene. Rear Admiral, United States Navy; Commandant, Fifth Naval District, Norfolk, Virginia, 1972-   . Born December 24, 1915, Neosho, Missouri. Kansas State Teachers College, 1935-36; US Naval Academy, 1936-40; Submarine School, New London, Connecticut, 1942-43; Postgraduate School, Annapolis, 1945-46; California Institute of Technology, MS, Aeronautical Engineering, 1946-47; Industrial College of the Armed Forces, 1962-63. Commissioned Ensign, US Navy, 1940. Served in the Pacific Theater in WW II. Commanding Officer USS *Taconic* (AGC-17), 1964-65; Commander Amphibious Group FOUR, 1965-67; Senior Navy Member, Military Studies and Liaison Division, Weapons Systems Evaluation Group, Office of the Secretary of Defense, 1967-70; Director of the Systems Analysis and Long Range Objectives Division, Office of the CNO, 1970-71; Commander Service Force, US Atlantic Fleet, 1971-72. Legion of Merit with three Gold Stars; Bronze Star Medal with Gold Star and Combat "V"; Navy Commendation Medal with Gold Star and Combat "V"; and other medals and awards. Promoted to Rear Admiral, December 1, 1965.

Andersson, Sven Olof Morgan. Minister of National Defense, Sweden, 1957-   . Born April 5, 1910, in Gothenburg. Attended People's High School, Geneva, 1931. Swedish Politician; Carpenter. General Secretary of Social-Democratic Party, 1945-48; Minister without portfolio, 1948-51; Minister of Communications, 1951-57; Member of Parliament, Second Chamber, 1940-44; Member of Parliament, First Chamber, 1948-   . Member of the Social-Democratic Party.

Andrews, Burton Howell. Rear Admiral, United States Navy; Deputy Commander for Research and Development, Naval Ship Systems Command, 1972-   . Born July 14, 1916, Los Angeles, California. US Naval Academy, 1936-41; Submarine School, 1942; Naval Postgraduate School, MS, Electronics Engineering, 1945-49. Commissioned Ensign, US Navy, in 1941. Served in the Pacific Theater in WW II. Commanding Officer and Director, Naval Underwater Sound Laboratory, 1960-64; Director of Exploratory Development Division, Office of Naval Material, 1964-66; Office of Director of Defense Research and Engineering, 1966; Deputy Director of Laboratory Programs, Naval Material Command, and Deputy Director of Laboratories, 1966-68; Vice Commander, Naval Electronic Systems Command, 1968-71; Deputy Director for Tactical Electromagnetic Programs,

Office of the CNO, 1971-72. Legion of Merit; Bronze Star Medal with Gold Star and Combat "V"; Navy Commendation Medal with Gold Star; and other medals and awards. Promoted to Rear Admiral, March 1, 1969.

Andryushchenko, V. K. Lieutenant General, USSR Army; Chief of Staff, Transcaucasus Military District, 1968-   . Served on the Soviet-German Front in WW II. Member, Communist Party of the Soviet Union.

Angarita, Agustin. Brigadier General, Colombian Army; Military Attache, Embassy of Colombia, Washington, D.C., 1973-   .

Angelis, Odysseus. General, Hellenic Army; Commander in Chief, Hellenic Armed Forces, 1969-   . Born February 3, 1912, Steni of Chalkis, Greece. Attended Military Academy, 1934; Higher War College; National Defense College. Commissioned Second Lieutenant (Artillery), Hellenic Army, 1934. Served in Albanian Campaign, 1940-41; Greece and Middle East, WW II; Anticommunist War, 1946-49. Chief of Staff, IX Division, 1958; Commandant Artillery School; Chief, Intelligence Division, Army General Staff, 1960; Chief of Staff of Higher Military Command, Attica and Islands, 1963-65; Commanding General, V Division, Crete, 1965; Assistant Chief of Army Staff for Intelligence, Plans, and Operations; Deputy Chief of Hellenic National Defense General Staff, 1967; Chief of the Hellenic Army General Staff, 1967-68; Chief of the National Defense General Staff, 1968-69. Golden Medal of Gallantry; Commander of the Royal Order of King George I; Golden Cross of the Royal Order of King George I, with Swords; Grand Commander of the Royal Order of the Phoenix; Military Cross; Military Merit Medal; Distinguished Service Order; Legion of Merit (USA); Grand Cross of the Order of Military Valor with White Ribbon (Spain); and other medals and awards. Promoted to Brigadier General, 1963; Major General, 1965; Lieutenant General, 1967; General, 1970.

Anishchyk, G. S. Lieutenant General, USSR Army; First Deputy Commander, North Caucasus Military District, 1969-   . Served on the Soviet-German Front in WW II. Member, Communist Party of the Soviet Union.

Anson, Sir Peter, 7th Baronet. Rear Admiral, British Royal Navy; Assistant Chief, Defence Staff (Signals), 1972-   . Born July 31, 1924. Attended Royal Naval College, Dartmouth. Served on HMS *Prince of Wales* and HMS *Exeter* in WW II. Commanding Officer, HMS *Broadsword*, 1961-62; Deputy Director, *then* Director, Weapons, Radio (Naval), 1963-66; Commanding Officer, HMS *Naiad*, and Captain (D) Londonderry Squadron, 1966-68; Captain, Commanding HMS *Mercury* and HM Signal School, 1968-70; Commander, Naval Forces Gulf, 1970-72. Promoted to Captain, 1963, Rear Admiral, 1972.

Anthis, Rollen Henry. Major General, United States Air Force; Assistant to Commander, Air Force Logistics Command, 1973-   . Born December 4, 1915, in Navina,

Oklahoma. University of Oklahoma, Law School; Army Air Corps Flying School, 1938-39; Air War College, 1948-49; National War College, 1958-59. Commissioned Second Lieutenant, US Army Air Corps, in 1939. Served in the Mediterranean Theater, WW II; Vietnam War. Commander, 2d Air Division, and Chief, Air Force Section, Military Assistance Advisory Group, Vietnam, 1961-64; Special Assistant, Counterinsurgency and Special Activities (SACSA), Joint Chiefs of Staff, 1964-66; Commander, Headquarters Command, US Air Force, 1966-67; Commander, Seventeenth Air Force, US Air Forces, Europe, Germany, 1967-69; Chief of Staff, Combined Military Planning Staff, Central Treaty Organization, Turkey, 1969-71; Assistant Commander, Air Force Logistics Command (AFLC), 1971-72; Senior Member, United Nations Command, Military Armistice Commission, Korea, 1972-73. Distinguished Service Medal; Legion of Merit with three Oak Leaf Clusters; Air Medal; Wings of the Air Forces of France, Thailand, Republic of Vietnam, and Republic of Korea; Legion of Honor of International Supreme Council, Order of DeMolay, 1964; Citation of Honor Award of the Air Force Association; and other US and foreign medals and awards. Promoted to Major General, August 1, 1963.

Antipov, A. Major General, USSR Air Force; Deputy Chief, Political Directorate, Belorussian Military District. Served on the Soviet-German Front in WW II. Member, Communist Party of the Soviet Union.

Antipov, P. Lieutenant General, USSR Army; Deputy Commander, Siberian Military District (Combat Training). Served on the Soviet-German Front in WW II. Member, Communist Party of the Soviet Union.

Antonelli, Theodore. Major General, United States Army; Deputy Commanding General for Logistics Support, US Army Materiel Command, Washington, D.C., 1972-   . Born January 6, 1920, New Haven, Connecticut. University of Connecticut, BS Degree, Government and Economics; The Transportation School, Advanced Course; US Army Command and General Staff College; US Army War College; US Industrial College of the Armed Forces; George Washington University, MA Degree, International Affairs. Commissioned Second Lieutenant, US Army Reserve, 1941. Served in WW II, and Vietnam War. Vice Director, Defense Communications Planning Group, Defense Communications Agency, US Naval Observatory, Washington, D.C., 1968-69; Special Assistant for Post Hostilities Logistic Operations, US Army Materiel Command, Washington, D.C., 1969; Director of Distribution and Transportation, US Army Materiel Command, Washington, D.C., 1969-71; Deputy Chief of Staff, Logistics, US Army, Vietnam, 1971-72; Chief of Staff, US Army, Vietnam, 1972. Distinguished Service Medal; Silver Star with Oak Leaf Cluster; Legion of Merit with Oak Leaf Cluster; Bronze Star Medal; and other medals and awards. Promoted to Brigadier General, August 18, 1967; Major General, July 1, 1970.

Antos, Stanislaw. Major General, Polish Army; Chief, Inspectorate of Training, Ministry of National Defense. Commissioned Second Lieutenant, Polish Army, 1946. Attended Armor Officers School, Modlin, 1945-46; General Staff War College. Commanding General, 12th Mechanized Division, Szczecin, 1964-68; Chief of Staff, Pomeranian Military District, 1968-71. Member of Polish United Workers Party. Cross of Grunwald; Cross of Merit; and other orders and medals.

Anwar, Mohammed. Major General, Indonesian Marine Corps; Commander of Navy Marine Corps.

Appel, John Glenn. Major General, United States Army; Director of Logistics, J-4, US European Command, 1973-   . Born June 4, 1918, Terre Haute, Indiana. Attended Rose Polytechnic Institute, BS Degree, Chemical Engineering; US Army Command and General Staff College; The Chemical Corps School, Advanced Course; US Air Command and Staff College; US Armed Forces Staff College; US Army War College. Commissioned Second Lieutenant, US Army Reserve, 1941. WW II. Commanding General, Desert Test Center, Fort Douglas, Utah, 1966-69; Director of Plans, Office, Deputy Chief of Staff for Logistics, US Army, Washington, D.C., 1969-70; Director of Chemical and Nuclear Operations, Office, Assistant Chief of Staff for Force Development, US Army, Washington, D.C., 1970-72. Legion of Merit with Oak Leaf Cluster; and other medals and awards. Promoted to Brigadier General, August 1, 1967; Major General, November 1, 1970.

Arapakis, Peter. Rear Admiral, Hellenic Navy; Chief, Hellenic Navy, 1973-   . Born 1923, Callithea-Attica, Greece. Attended Officers Submarine School; Air Force-Army-Navy Cooperation School; Artillery School, USA; Amphibious Warfare Training School, USA; Naval War College, USA; Special Weapons College, Federal Republic of Germany; Naval War College. Commissioned Ensign, Hellenic Navy, 1944. Participated in WW II; Antiguerrilla War, 1946-49. Commanding Officer, HS *King George II;* Aide-de-Camp to the Minister of National Defense; Commanding Officer, HS *Ierax;* Director, G-5 Branch, Naval General Staff; Commanding Officer, HS *Aspis;* Staff Officer NMR (Greece), Paris; Senior Naval Officer, Southern Aegean; Commanding Officer, Destroyer Squadron; Director, Division "A", Hellenic Navy Command; Commander, Hellenic Fleet. Commander of Royal Order of George I; Grand Commander of Royal Order of the Phoenix; Commander of Royal Order of the Phoenix; Golden Cross of the Royal Order of the Phoenix; War Cross "C" Class; Royal Navy Campaign Cross; Medal of Outstanding Acts; and other medals and awards. Promoted to Captain, August 24, 1967; Commodore, June 29, 1970; Rear Admiral, June 29, 1971.

Araripe Macedo, Joelmir Campos de. Engineer Lieutenant Brigadier, Brazil; Minister of Aeronautics. Born February 16, 1909, in Guanabara. Studied at Military College, Rio de Janeiro (Agronomy), 1924; Military School, Realengo, 1925-28; Army Technical School, 1941; War College.

Commissioned August 9, 1928. Director of Aeronautical Engineering, 1955-57; Director of Aeronautical Materiel, 1958-60; Director of Air Courses, 1961-67; Air Inspector General, 1967; President of the Coordinating Commission of the International Airport Project, 1967-71. Medalha Militar de Ouro com Passadeira de Platina; Cruz de Aviação, fita "B" (South Atlantic Patrol); Ordem de Mérito Aeronáutico, grau de Grã-Cruz; Mérito Santos-Dumont; and other medals and awards of Brazil and other nations. Promoted to Air Brigadier, November 2, 1954; Major Brigadier, December 19, 1958; Lieutenant Brigadier, August 7, 1965.

Arce, Jóse L. Vice Admiral, Peruvian Navy, Naval Attaché, Embassy of Peru, Washington, D.C. Born October 28, 1917, in Salaverry. Attended Peruvian Naval Academy, 1934-39; Navy Superior War College; Army Superior War College; Center of Superior Military Studies; Peruvian Diplomatic Academy. Commissioned in 1940. Formerly Commander in Chief of Fluvial Force of the Amazon and Chief of Fifth Naval Zone; Commander, Auxiliary Fleet; Commander, C.BAP. *Almirante Grau;* Sub-Director and Chief of Studies, Superior Naval War College; Inspector General of the Navy; Chief, Naval General Staff; Peruvian Navy Delegate to the Inter-American Defense Board; Naval Attaché to the Organization of American States. Cruz Peruana al Mérito Naval; Orden Militar de Ayacucho; Estrella Negra (France); Tamandaré (Brazil); Condor de los Andes (Bolivia).

Archer, Arthur John. Major-General, British Army; Commander 2d Division, 1972- . Born February 12, 1924. Attended St. Catherine's College, Cambridge; Staff College, 1956; Joint Services Staff College, 1959; Imperial Defence College, 1970. Entered Army, 1943; commissioned, 1944; received regular commission in the Dorset Regiment, 1946. Commander Land Force Gulf, 1968-69; Director of Public Relations (Army), 1970-72. Promoted to Brigadier in 1968; Major-General in 1972.

Ariko, G. I. Colonel General, USSR Army; Chief of Staff, Belorussian Military District, 1966- . Served on the Soviet-German Front in WW II. Member, Communist Party of the Soviet Union.

Armstrong, Alan James. Major General, United States Marine Corps; Assistant Chief of Staff, G-4, Headquarters, US Marine Corps, 1971- . Born April 18, 1920, Garland, Nebraska. University of Nebraska, 1937-40; Flight Training Course, 1941; Amphibious Warfare School, Junior Course, Quantico, 1946; Armed Forces Staff College, 1956-57; Army War College, 1962-63. Commissioned Second Lieutenant, USMCR, Naval Aviator, 1941. Served in Pacific Theater, WW II; Korean War; Vietnam War. Assistant Chief of Staff, G-3, 1st Marine Aircraft Wing, Japan, 1963-64; Member, Joint Planning Group, Office of Deputy Chief of Staff (Plans and Programs), Headquarters Marine Corps, 1964-65; Assistant Deputy Chief of Staff (Air), HQMC, 1965-68; Director, Development Center, Marine Corps Development and Education Command, 1968-70; Commanding General, 1st Marine Aircraft Wing,

Vietnam, 1970-71; Commanding General, III Marine Amphibious Brigade, Vietnam, 1971. Distinguished Service Medal; Legion of Merit with one Gold Star; Distinguished Flying Cross with one Gold Star; and other US and foreign medals and awards. Promoted to Brigadier General, September 3, 1966; Major General, September, 1969.

Armstrong, Parker Broadhurst. Rear Admiral, United States Navy; Commander, Service Force, US Pacific Fleet, 1972- . Born November 13, 1918, in Hartford, Connecticut. US Naval Academy, 1938-41; Naval Postgraduate School, MS, Electrical Engineering, 1948; Industrial College of the Armed Forces, 1958-59. Commissioned Ensign, US Navy, in 1941. Served in the Atlantic Theater in WW II. Commander USS *Norfolk* (CL-1), 1964-65; Commander Destroyer Squadron THIRTY-SIX, 1965-66; Deputy Assistant Director (Seawarfare Systems), Office of Defense Research and Engineering, Office of the Secretary of Defense, 1966-67; Director, Undersea Warfare and Strategic Warfare Development Division, Office of the CNO, 1967-69; Commander Cruiser-Destroyer Flotilla TEN, 1969-70; Commander Antisubmarine Warfare Systems Project Office, Naval Material Command, 1970-72. Legion of Merit with Gold Star; and other medals and awards. Promoted to Rear Admiral, August 1, 1968.

Arrisueno, Alfredo C. Major General, Peruvian Army; Peruvian Delegate, Inter-American Defense Board. Date of Rank: January 1, 1971.

Arsiyev, Nikolay Aleksandrovich. Lieutenant General, USSR Army; Chief of Staff, Moscow Air Defense District, 1968- . Born in 1921. Drafted into Soviet Army, 1939. Trained at Smolensk Artillery Academy, 1939-40. Commissioned in Artillery, 1940. Served on the Soviet-German Front in WW II. Commander, Artillery Battery and later Artillery Battalion, Volkhov Front, 1941-42; Chief of Staff, Artillery, Infantry Division, 1943; Chief of Staff, Corps Artillery, 1944; Chief of Staff, Army Artillery, 1945; Assigned to the General Staff, Soviet Armed Forces, c. 1946 - c. 1966; Assigned to the Moscow Air Defense District, c. 1966-68; Member, Communist Party of the Soviet Union, 1941- . Order of Red Banner; Order of Red Star; and other orders and medals.

Artigas Fernandez, Mario. Rear Admiral, Mexican Navy. Director of Services, Mexican Navy.

Arvas, Dag Gustaf Christer. Rear Admiral, Swedish Royal Navy; Chief of the Military Office of the Royal Ministry of National Defense, 1970- . Royal Navy Staff College, 1940-42; Royal National Defense College, 1963, 1969. Commander, Coastal Fleet, 1966-70. Commander of the Royal Order of the Sword; Commander of the Order of Dannebrog. Member of the Royal Academy of Military Sciences; Member of the Royal Society of Naval Sciences. Promoted to Rear Admiral in 1966.

Ascani, Fred J. Major General, United States Air Force; Senior Air Force Member, Weapons Systems Evaluation

Group, Office of the Deputy Director, Research and Engineering, Office of the Secretary of Defense, 1970-   . Born May 29, 1917, in Beloit, Wisconsin. Beloit College, 1935-37; US Military Academy, 1937-41; Army Air Corps Flying School, 1941-42; Air War College, 1953-54; University of Southern California, MS, Systems Management, 1971. Commissioned Second Lieutenant, US Army, 1941; received pilot wings, 1942. Served in the North African Theater, WW II. Commander, Systems Engineering Group, and Deputy Commander, Research and Technology Division, Wright-Patterson Air Force Base, 1964-65; Vice Commander, Fifth Air Force, Pacific Air Forces, Fuchu Air Station, Japan, 1965-67; Director of Operations, Air Force Logistics Command, 1967-70. Distinguished Service Medal; Legion of Merit with one Oak Leaf Cluster; Distinguished Flying Cross with one Oak Leaf Cluster; Croix de Guerre with Palm; and other US and foreign decorations. MacKay and Thompson Trophies. Established world's speed record of 635 miles per hour in an F86-E. Promoted to Major General, September 24, 1964.

Ashmore, Sir Edward (Beckwith). Admiral, British Royal Navy; Commander-in-Chief, Fleet, Allied Commander in Chief, Channel, and Commander in Chief, Eastern Atlantic Area, 1971-   . Born December 11, 1919. Attended Royal Naval College, Dartmouth. Served in the Home Fleet and the British Pacific Fleet in WW II. Director of Naval Plans and Defence Plans, 1961-62; Commander, British Forces Caribbean Area, 1963-64; Assistant Chief, Defence Staff, Signals, 1965-67; Flag Officer, Second-in-Command, Far East Fleet, 1967-68; Vice-Chief, Naval Staff, 1969-71; Commander-in-Chief, Western Fleet, 1971. KCB; DSC. Promoted to Rear-Admiral, 1965; Vice-Admiral, 1968; Admiral, 1970.

Ashmore, Peter William Beckwith. Vice-Admiral, British Royal Navy; Chief of Allied Staff, NATO Naval Headquarters, Southern Europe, 1970-72. Born February 4, 1921. Attended Royal Naval College, Dartmouth; Imperial Defence College, 1962. Commissioned in 1941. Served on destroyers in WW II. Director of Naval Plans, Admiralty, 1963-66; Flag Officer, Admiralty Interview Board, 1966-67; Chief of Staff to Commander-in-Chief, Western Fleet, 1967-69 and Commander, Allied Naval Forces Europe, 1969-70. CB; MVO (4th Class); DSC. Promoted to Captain, 1957; Rear-Admiral, 1966. Master of Her Majesty's Household; Extra Equerry to the Queen.

Atanasov, Nikola. General, Bulgarian Army; Deputy Chief, General Political Directorate.

Aubiniere Lippmann, Robert Joseph. General, French Air Force; Director General, National Center for Space Studies, 1962-   . Member of the Administrative Council of the National Office of Aerospace Studies and Research. Born September 24, 1912, Paris, France. Ecole Polytechnique, 1933. Commissioned in 1935. Served in WW II in North Africa and in the French resistance. Assistant Chief of Staff, 5th Aerial Region, 1950-53; Commander, Base

School 721, Rochefort, 1954-57; Director, Inter-Army Special Materiel Testing Center, Colomb-Bechar, 1957-58; Technical and Industrial Director of Aeronautics, 1960-62. Grand Officer, Légion d'Honneur; Croix de Guerre; Médaille de l'Aéronautique; and other medals and awards. Promoted to Brigadier General, 1958; Major General, 1961.

Aulestia, Victor. General, Ecuadorean Army (Retired); Minister of National Defense, Ecuador, 1973-   .

Aurora, Jagjit Singh. General, Army of India; General Officer Commanding in Chief, Indian and Bangladesh Forces, Eastern Command, 1972-   .

Auswöger, Otto. Major General, Austrian Army; Commanding General, Group II, 1973-   . Born January 25, 1914. Studied at the Austrian Military Academy, in Wiener Neustadt, 1934-37. Commissioned Second Lieutenant, Austrian Army, in 1937. Chief of Staff, 4th and later 6th Infantry Brigade, 1956-57; Chief of Staff, Headquarters, Group II, 1957-62; Commander, 5th Infantry Brigade, 1962-66; Deputy Commander, Group II, 1966-73. Goldenes Ehrenzeichen; and other decorations and awards. Promoted to Colonel, 1961; Brigadier, 1966; Major General, February 21, 1973.

Avon, Maurice Antoine. Major General, French Air Force; Commander of Southern Air Defense Zone and Director of Military Air Traffic, 1968-   . Born September 6, 1918. Attended Senior Air War College. Commissioned Sub-lieutenant, 1939. Served in France and with the Free French in WW II, and in Algeria. Assistant Chief of Staff for Operations in Algeria, 1958-60; Commander, 9th Fighter Brigade, and Commander Metz Air Base, 1960-64; Head, G-3, Air Force General Staff, 1964-66. Commandeur, Légion d'Honneur; Croix de Guerre; Croix de Valeur Militaire.

Avseyenko, V. Lieutenant General, Engineer, USSR Army; Commandant, Military Engineering College. Served on the Soviet-German Front in WW II. Member of the Communist Party of the Soviet Union.

Axtell, George Clifton. Lieutenant General, United States Marine Corps; Commanding General, Fleet Marine Force, Atlantic, 1972-   . Born November 29, 1920, Ambridge, Pennsylvania. University of Alabama, 1939-40; Flight Training Course, 1940-41; Naval Postgraduate School, Meteorological Engineering Course, 1942-43; Marine Corps School, Junior Course, 1947; National War College, 1963-64; George Washington University, LLB, MA (Comptroller). Commissioned USMC, Naval Aviator, 1941. Served in Pacific Theater, WW II; Korean War; Vietnam War. Chief of Staff, Fleet Marine Force, Pacific, 1964-65; Chief of Staff, III Marine Amphibious Force, 1965-66; Commander, Force Logistics Command, Fleet Marine Force, Pacific, 1966; Assistant Chief of Staff, G-4, Headquarters, Marine Corps, 1966-70; Commanding General, 2d Marine Aircraft Wing, 1970-72. Navy Cross; Legion of Merit with Combat "V" and two Gold Stars;

Distinguished Flying Cross with Gold Star; and other medals and awards. Promoted to Brigadier General, December, 1966; Major General, August 7, 1969; Lieutenant General, April 1, 1972.

Ayan, Ethem R. Brigadier General, Turkish Air Force; Commander First Tactical Air Force, 1973.

Azimi, Reza. General, Imperial Iranian Army; Minister of War, Iran, 1971-   . Born in 1913. Attended Military Academy, Teheran, 1929; War College, 1940. Recent assignments: Commander, Central Army No. 1; Deputy Commander, Ground forces; Commander, Western Army; Commanding General, Ground Forces, 1960-66; Adjutant General to the Shahanshah. More than 15 medals and awards.

B

Babadzhanyan, A. Kh. Marshall of Armored Forces, USSR Army; Commander, Armored Forces, 1969-   . Born in 1903. Served on the Soviet-German Front in WW II. Corps Commander, First Guard Tank Army, 1945; First Deputy Commander, Carpathian Military District; Commander, Odessa Military District, 1959; Commandant, Armored Forces War College, 1967-69. Member, Communist Party of the Soviet Union. Promoted to Major General, 1945; Marshal of Armored Forces, 1969.

Bacalis, Paul N. Major General, United States Air Force; Deputy Chief of Staff for Plans, Strategic Air Command, and Commander in Chief Strategic Air Command Representative to Joint Strategic Target Planning Staff, 1970-   . Born November 24, 1919, in Norfolk, Virginia. Army Air Corps Flying School, 1941-42; Royal Canadian Air Force Staff College, 1951-52; Air Command and Staff School, 1952. Commissioned Second Lieutenant, US Army Air Corps, 1942. Served in the China Theater, WW II. Chief, Safety Division, Directorate of Operations, Strategic Air Command, 1965-66; Director, Special Projects, Headquarters USAF, 1966-68; Commander, 14th Strategic Aerospace Division, 1968-70; Assistant Deputy Chief of Staff, Materiel, Strategic Air Command, 1970. Distinguished Service Medal; Silver Star; Legion of Merit; Distinguished Flying Cross with one Oak Leaf Cluster; and other US and foreign medals and awards. Promoted to Major General, February 24, 1970.

Bachri, Samsjul. Vice Admiral, Indonesian Navy; Commander in Chief, Indonesian Fleet.

Badcock, John Michael Watson. Major-General, British Army; Director of Manning (Army), 1972-   . Born November 10, 1922. Attended Worcester College, Oxford; Staff College; Joint Services Staff College; Imperial Defence College. Enlisted in the Army in 1941; commissioned in Royal Corps of Signals, 1942. Served in the UK and Northern Europe in WW II. Commander 2d

Infantry Brigade and Deputy Constable of Dover Castle, 1969-71; Military Secretary, 1971-72. Promoted to Brigadier, 1968; Major-General, 1972.

Baer, Robert Jacob. Major General, United States Army; Project Manager, XMI Tank System, US Army Materiel Command, Warren, Michigan, 1972-   . Born August 12, 1924, in Jamestown, Missouri. Attended US Military Academy; The Ground General School; The Armored School, Basic and Advanced Courses; US Army Command and General Staff College; Armed Forces Staff College; Army War College, 1966-67. Commissioned Second Lieutenant in 1947. Served in the Vietnam War. Plans Officer, Revolutionary Development Support Branch, Plans and Programs Division, later Deputy Chief, Civil Operations and Revolutionary Support Directorate, US Military Assistance Command, Vietnam, 1967-68; Commanding Officer, 1st Brigade, 1st Cavalry Division (Airmobile), US Army, Pacific-Vietnam, 1968-69; Chief, later Division Chief, Combat Vehicles Office, Office of the Assistant Chief of Staff for Force Development, 1969-70; Acting Deputy Director, Doctrine and Systems Directorate, Office of the Assistant Chief of Staff for Force Development, 1970-71; Chief, Firepower Systems Division, Systems Directorate, Office of the Assistant Chief of Staff for Force Development, 1971; Director of Development, Office of Chief of Research and Development, 1971-72; Deputy Chairman, Wheeled Vehicle Study Group, 1972. Silver Star; Legion of Merit with Oak Leaf Cluster; and other medals and awards. Promoted to Brigadier General, November 1, 1971; Major General, 1973.

Bagley, David Harrington. Vice Admiral, United States Navy; Deputy Chief of Naval Operations (Manpower and Naval Reserve) and Chief of Naval Personnel, 1972-   . Born December 7, 1920, Raleigh, North Carolina. US Naval Academy, 1940-43; Naval War College, Command and Staff Course, 1953-54; Naval War College, Naval Warfare Course, 1959-60. Commissioned Ensign, US Navy, in 1943. Served in the Pacific Theater in WW II; Korean War; Vietnam War. Executive Assistant and Naval Aide to the Under Secretary of the Navy, 1964-66; Commanding Officer, USS *Oklahoma City* (CLG-5), 1966-68; Commander Cruiser-Destroyer Flotilla NINE, 1968-69; Commander Cruiser-Destroyer Group, Seventh Fleet, 1968-69; Chief, Studies, Analysis and Gaming Agency, Joint Chiefs of Staff, 1969-70; Assistant Deputy Chief of Naval Operations for Personal Services and Assistant Chief of Naval Personnel (Personal Affairs), 1970-72. Legion of Merit with three Gold Stars; and other medals and awards. Promoted to Rear Admiral, 1968; Vice Admiral, 1972.

Bagley, Worth Harrington. Vice Admiral, United States Navy; Commander in Chief, US Naval Forces Europe, 1973-   . Born July 29, 1924, in Annapolis, Maryland. US Naval Academy, 1943-46; Air Observer Course, 1946; Naval Mine Warfare School, 1946-47; Command and General Staff College, Intelligence Course, 1950; Naval Intelligence School, 1950-51; Naval War College, 1960-61.

Commissioned Ensign, US Navy, in 1946. Served in Vietnam War. Commanding Officer USS *Lawrence* (DDG-4), 1963-65; Readiness and Training Officer, Staff of Commander Cruiser-Destroyer Force, US Pacific Fleet, 1965-66; Executive Assistant and Naval Aide to the Secretary of the Navy, 1966-68; Commanding Officer USS *Canberra* (CA-70), 1968-69; Commander Cruiser-Destroyer Flotilla SEVEN, 1969-70; Director, General Planning and Programming Division, Naval Operations, 1970-71; Director, Navy Program Planning, Office of the Chief of Naval Operations, 1971-73. Legion of Merit with Gold Star; Navy Commendation Medal; and other medals and awards. Promoted to Vice Admiral, May 14, 1971.

Bailey, James A. Major General, United States Air Force; Deputy Chief of Staff, Comptroller, Air Force Logistics Command, 1971-   . Born December 23, 1920, Rock Hill, South Carolina. Civilian Pilot's License, 1940; University of South Carolina, BS, Business Administration; US Air Force Institute of Technology, Industrial Administration; Harvard Graduate School of Business Administration, MA, 1963. Commissioned Second Lieutenant, US Army Air Corps, 1944. Chief, Aerospace Support Division, Deputy Chief of Staff, Systems and Logistics, Headquarters, USAF, 1963-67; Director, Materiel Management, Warner Robins Air Materiel Area, 1967-68; Vice Commander, Warner Robins Air Materiel Area, 1968-69; Commander, Pacific Exchange System, Honolulu, Hawaii, 1969-71.

Bailey, Mildred Caroon. Brigadier General, United States Army; Director, Women's Army Corps, Office, Deputy Chief of Staff for Personnel, US Army, 1971-   . Born April 18, 1919, Fort Barnwell, North Carolina. Attended Women's College, University of North Carolina, BA; Berlitz School of Language; Strategic Intelligence School. Commissioned Third Officer, Women's Army Auxiliary Corps, September 26, 1942. Commanding Officer, Headquarters Company, US Army Women's Army Corps, 1961-63; Officer in Charge Women's Army Corps Exhibit, US Army Troop Information Support Unit, Office, Chief of Information, 1963-68; Congressional Liaison Officer, Senate Liaison Division, Office, Chief of Legislative Liaison, 1968-70; Deputy Commander, US Women's Army Corps Center, Fort McClellan, Alabama, 1970-71. Legion of Merit; Meritorious Service Medal; Army Commendation Medal. Promoted to Brigadier General, August 1, 1971.

Baird, James Parlane. Major-General, British Army; Director General, Army Medical Services, 1973-   . Born May 12, 1915. Attended Bathgate Academy; University of Edinburgh. Doctor of Medicine, 1958. Commissioned in the Army Medical Corps, 1939. Professor of Military Medicine, Royal Army Medical College, 1965-67; Consulting Physician, British Army of the Rhine, 1967; Director of Army Medicine and Consulting Physician to the Army, 1969-71; Commandant and Director of Studies, Royal Army Medical College, 1971-73. Queen's Honorary Physician; Fellow of the Royal College of Physicians of Edinburgh, 1952; Fellow of the Royal College of

Physicians, London, 1959. Publication: *Tropical Diseases Supplement* to *Principles and Practice of Medicine*, 1968.

Baker, Royal Newman. Major General, United States Air Force; Vice Commander, Headquarters, Aerospace Command. Born November 27, 1918, in Corsicana, Texas. North Texas State Teachers College, Denton, Texas, BS, Industrial Arts, 1941; Army Air Corps Flying School, 1941-42; Air Command and Staff School, 1950; National War College, 1960-61. Commissioned Second Lieutenant, US Army Air Corps, 1942. Served in the European Theater, WW II; Korean War; Vietnam War. Chief, Regional Division I, Plans and Policy Directorate, Joint Chiefs of Staff, 1964-66; Vice Commander, Twelfth Air Force, 1966-68; Assistant Chief of Staff for Plans, J-5, Military Assistance Command, Vietnam, 1968; Vice Commander, Seventh Air Force, Vietnam, 1968-69; Commander, Seventeenth Air Force, Ramstein Air Base, Germany, 1969. Distinguished Service Cross; Distinguished Service Medal; Silver Star; Legion of Merit with three Oak Leaf Clusters; Distinguished Flying Cross with two Oak Leaf Clusters; Air Medal with 39 Oak Leaf Clusters; and other US and foreign medals and awards.

Balakirev, V. Colonel, USSR Army; Deputy Chief, Political Directorate, Odessa Military District. Served on the Soviet-German Front in WW II. Member, Communist Party of the Soviet Union.

Baldwin, Clarke Tileston, Jr. Major General, United States Army; Chief, Military Assistance Advisory Group, Spain, 1972-   . Born February 27, 1923, Newton, Massachusetts. US Military Academy; The Armored School, Basic and Advanced Courses; US Army Command and General Staff College; The National War College. Commissioned Second Lieutenant, 1943. Served in WW II. Commanding Officer, 2d Armored Cavalry Regiment, US Army, Europe, 1967-68; Assistant Division Commander, 4th Armored Division, US Army, Europe, 1968-69; Deputy Director of International and Civil Affairs, Office, Deputy Chief of Staff for Military Operations, US Army, Washington, D.C., 1969-70; Director of International and Civil Affairs, Office, Deputy Chief of Staff for Military Operations, US Army, Washington, D.C., 1970-72. Legion of Merit with three Oak Leaf Clusters; Bronze Star Medal with V Device; and other medals and awards. Promoted to Brigadier General, August 20, 1969; Major General, August 1, 1971.

Ball, Alfred Henry Wynne. Air Vice-Marshal, British Royal Air Force; Director General of Organisation (RAF), 1971-   . Born January 18, 1921. Attended Campbell College, Belfast; Royal Air Force College, Cranwell; Staff College; Joint Services Staff College; Imperial Defence College, 1967. Commissioned in 1939. Served in North Africa, UK, and France in WW II. Group Captain, Washington, 1959-62; Air Commodore, Aden, 1964-67; Director of Operations (RAF), Ministry of Defence, 1967-68; Assistant Chief of Staff, Automatic Data Processing Division, SHAPE, 1969-71. CB; DSO; DFC; Air

Medal (USA). Promoted to Group Captain, 1959; Air Commodore, 1964.

Balla, Arabe Chawey. Major, Army of Niger; Chief of General Staff, Army of Niger. Born July 25, 1925, in Niamey, Niger. Attended Military School, Senegal; Non-commissioned Officers School, France. Served in French Army, Madagascar, Algiers and other posts, 1946-57; since independence of Niger, 1960, advanced through ranks to Major. Order of Merit (Egypt); and other medals and awards.

Ballenger, Felix Pettey. Rear Admiral, Medical Corps, United States Navy; Commanding Officer, National Naval Medical Center, Bethesda, Maryland, 1969-   . Born June 4, 1914, in Lubbock, Texas. Texas Technological College, BA, 1934; University of Texas Medical School, Galveston, MD, 1938. Commissioned Lieutenant (j.g.), Medical Corps, US Naval Reserve, 1942; transferred to US Navy, 1943. Served at sea and in North Africa in WW II; at sea in the Korean War. Commanding Officer, US Naval Hospital, Yokosuka, Japan, 1965-67. Inspector General, Medical, Bureau of Medicine and Surgery, Navy Department, 1967-69. Promoted to Rear Admiral, 1967.

Balluku, Beqir. Minister of People's Defense, Albania, 1973-   .

Bamrungphong, Boonchai. General, Royal Thai Army. Chief of Staff, Royal Thai Army.

Bandaranaike, Sirimavo Ratwatte Dias. Prime Minister and Minister of Defense, Sri Lanka.

Banza, Alexandre. Colonel, Army of the Central African Republic; Commander Para-Commandos. Born in 1932, in Carnot, French Equatorial Africa. Attended Officers School. Commissioned Second Lieutenant, ca. 1962. Served with 1st Battalion, Congo-Gabon Rifles; transferred to Central African Republic Army, 1962; Minister of State in Charge of Finance and Ex-Servicemen, 1966; Minister of State for Finance and National Economy, 1967.

Baranov, N.M. Vice Admiral, USSR Navy; First Deputy Commander in Chief, Black Sea Fleet, 1969-   . Served in the Soviet-German War (WW II). Formerly Chief of Staff, Northern Fleet, 1967-69. Member of Communist Party of the Soviet Union.

Baranski, Wojciech. Lieutenant General, Polish Army; Commanding General, Pomeranian Military District. Attended Infantry Officers School; General Staff War College. Served in the Polish-German War, 1943-45. Formerly Staff Member Silesian Military District; Deputy Chief of General Staff. Member of Polish United Workers Party. Polonia Restituta; Cross of Grunwald; Cross of Merit; and other orders and awards. Promoted to Major General, 1966; Lieutenant General, 1972.

Barbudo Duarte, Excmo. Sr. Don Enrique. Admiral, Spanish Navy; Chief of the Naval Staff.

Barfield, Thomas Harwell. Major General, United States Army: Commander 23rd NORAD/CONAD Region, and Commanding General, 2d Region, US Army Air Defense Command, Duluth, Minnesota, 1969-   . Born January 20, 1917, Thomasville, Alabama. University of Alabama, AB Degree, History; The Coast Artillery School, Basic and Advanced Courses; US Army Command and General Staff College; National War College; George Washington University, MA Degree, International Affairs. Commissioned Second Lieutenant, US Army Reserve, 1938. Served in WW II. Commanding General, 38th Artillery Brigade (Air Defense), USArmy, Pacific-Korea, 1966-67; Chief, Requirements and Development Division, J-5, Joint Staff, Organization, Joint Chiefs of Staff, Washington, D.C., 1967-68; Deputy Chief of Staff, Operations, US Army Air Defense Command, Ent Air Force Base, Colorado Springs, Colorado, 1968-69. Legion of Merit with three Oak Leaf Clusters; Bronze Star Medal with Oak Leaf Cluster; and other medals and awards. Promoted to Brigadier General, September 1, 1966; Major General, January 1, 1970.

Barnard, Lance H. Deputy Prime Minister and Minister for Defence, Navy, Army, Air and Supply, Australia, 1972-   . Born May 1, 1919, Launceston, Tasmania. WW II Service in the Middle East. Member of Parliament for Bass in Northeastern Tasmania since 1954. State President, Tasmanian Branch of Australian Labor Party, 1966-67 and 1970-73; Deputy Leader, Federal Parliamentary Labor Party, 1967-   ; Deputy Leader of the Opposition, 1967-72; Member, ALP Federal Conference, ALP Federal Executive, all Federal Labor Party policy committees; Commonwealth Labor Advisory Council.

Barnes, John Winthrop. Major General, United States Army; Chief, Military Assistance Advisory Group, China, 1971-   . Born March 6, 1921, El Paso, Texas. US Military Academy; The Engineer School, Basic and Advanced Courses; The Armored School, Advanced Course; US Army Command and General Staff College; US Armed Forces Staff College; US Naval War College; California Institute of Technology, MS Degree, Aero Engineering (Jet Propulsion). Commissioned Second Lieutenant, 1942. Served in WW II and in Vietnam War. Deputy Senior Advisor, II Corps Tactical Zone, US Military Assistance Command, Vietnam, 1967-68; Commanding General, 173d Airborne Brigade, US Army, Pacific-Vietnam, 1968-69; Director of Development Office, Chief of Research and Development, US Army, Washington, D.C., 1969-71; Director of Plans and Programs and Deputy Chief of Research and Development for International Programs, Office, Chief of Research and Development, US Army, Washington, D.C., 1971. Distinguished Service Medal; Legion of Merit with Oak Leaf Cluster; Soldier's Medal; Bronze Star Medal; and other medals and awards. Promoted to Brigadier General, July 3, 1968; Major General, March 1, 1971.

Barraclough, Sir John. Air Chief Marshal, British Royal Air Force; Air Secretary, 1972-   . Born May 2, 1918.

Attended Harvard Business School (USA), 1967. Commissioned in 1938. Served in Europe in WW II. Director, Public Relations, Air Ministry, 1961-64; Air Officer Commanding, No. 19 Group, Coastal Command, 1964-67; Air Officer in Charge of Administration, Bomber Command, 1967-68; Air Officer in Charge of Administration, Strike Command, 1968-70; Vice-Chief, Defence Staff, 1970-72. KCB; CBE; DFC; AFC.

Barrett, John Michael. Rear Admiral, United States Navy; Deputy Chief, Naval Material (Programs and Financial Management), Naval Material Command, 1970-   , and Director of Fiscal Management Division, Office of CNO, 1972-   . Born March 14, 1920, in Cedar Rapids, Iowa. US Naval Academy, 1939-42; Naval Submarine School, 1942; Naval War College, Senior Course, 1957-58. Commissioned Ensign, US Navy, in 1942. Served in submarines in the Atlantic and Pacific Theaters, WW II; in submarines in the Korean War. Commander Submarine Squadron SIXTEEN, 1966-67; Commander Submarine Flotilla ONE, 1967-68; Chief, Navy Section, Joint US Military Mission for Aid, Turkey, 1968-70. Silver Star Medal; Legion of Merit; Bronze Star Medal with Gold Star and Combat "V"; Navy and Marine Corps Medal; and other medals and awards. Promoted to Rear Admiral, July 1, 1969.

Barrow, Robert H. Major General, United States Marine Corps; Commanding General, Marine Corps Recruit Depot, Parris Island, South Carolina, 1972-   . Born February 5, 1922, Baton Rouge, Louisiana. Louisiana State University; Amphibious Warfare School, Junior Course, Quantico, 1948-49; Senior Course, 1963; National War College, 1967-68; University of Maryland, BS, 1956; Tulane University, MS; Commissioned USMCR, 1943. China Theater, WW II; Korean War; Vietnam War. Deputy Assistant Chief of Staff, G-3, Headquarters, Fleet Marine Force, Pacific, 1964-67; Commanding Officer, Ninth Marines, 3d Marine Division, and Deputy G-3, II Marine Amphibious Force, Vietnam, 1968-69; Special Assignment at Camp Smedley D. Butler, Okinawa, 1969-72. Silver Star Medal; Navy Cross; Distinguished Service Cross; Legion of Merit with one Gold Star and Combat "V". Promoted to Brigadier General, August 23, 1969; Major General, September 5, 1972.

Barthélemy, Maurice Louis. General, French Army; Commander, 32d Military Division, Caen, 1970-   . Born March 24, 1914, in Saint Quentin. Attended Military Academy at Saint Cyr, 1933-35; General Staff School; US Command and General Staff College. Commissioned in 1935. Served in France and with the Free French in WW II, and in Indochina. Commander, 152d Mechanized Infantry Regiment, 1960-62; Assistant to Military Governor General of Paris, 1963-68; Chief of French Mission to NATO, 1968-70. Commandeur, Légion d'Honneur; Crois de Guerre; Médaille de la Résistance; Croix de Valeur Militaire; Silver Star (US); King's Medal for Courage (GB); and other medals and awards.

Baryla, Jozef. Major General, Polish Army; First Deputy Chief, Main Political Directorate, 1973-   . Attended Officers School; Military-Political College. Department Chief, Main Political Directorate, Polish Armed Forces, 1967-70; Deputy Commander for Political Affairs, Pomeranian Military District, 1970-73. Cross of Grunwald, Cross of Merit, and other orders and awards. Member, Polish United Workers Party.

Bashtanikov, N. Lieutenant General, USSR Army; First Deputy Commander, Central Group of Soviet Forces, Czechoslovakia, 1970-   . Served on the Soviet-German Front in WW II. Member, Communist Party of the Soviet Union.

Bate, William. Major-General, British Army; Director of Movements (Army), Ministry of Defence, 1971-   . Born June 6, 1920. Attended Staff College, 1954; Joint Services Staff College, 1957; Imperial Defence College, 1969. Commissioned in 1941. Served in Burma in WW II. Assistant Adjutant and Quartermaster General, Operations and Plans, Headquarters, British Army of the Rhine, 1961-63; Commanding Officer, 2 Division Column, British Army of the Rhine, 1963-65; Staff Officer, Staff College, Camberley, 1965-67; Director of Quartering (Maintenance), Ministry of Defence, 1967-68; Director of Administrative Planning (Army), 1970. OBE; Aide de Camp to the Queen, 1969. Promotions; Brigadier, 1967; Major General, 1970.

Batitskiy, Pavel Fyodorovich. Marshal of the Soviet Union, USSR Army; Commander in Chief, Air Defense Forces, 1966-   . Born July 27, 1910, in Kharkov. Attended Frunze War College; Voroshilov General Staff War College. Joined the Soviet Army, 1924. Served on the Soviet-German Front, WW II, as Chief of Staff, Infantry Division, Later Commander, Infantry Division and Corps, 1941-45. Commanding General, Military District, 1948-50; First Deputy Commander Anti-aircraft Defense, 1953-54; Commander, Moscow District Air Defense Forces, 1954-65; First Deputy Chief of the General Staff, 1965-66; Member of CPSU and its Central Committee; Deputy to USSR Supreme Soviet. Hero of the Soviet Union; four orders of Lenin; two Orders of Kutuzov; Order of Suvorov; four Orders of Red Banner; Order of the October Revolution; three Orders of Red Star; and other orders and medals. Promoted to rank of Marshal of the Soviet Union, April 1968.

Batur, Mushin. General, Turkish Air Force; Commander, Turkish Air Force Command, 1969-   . Studied at Military Academy; Air Training School; Air War College. Formerly Commander, Tactical Air Force; Assistant Chief of Staff for Logistics to Chief of General Staff; Member, Supreme Military Council. Distinguished Courageous Service Award; Flying Cross with one, two and three Stars; and other medals and awards. Promoted to General, August 30, 1969.

Baturone Colombo, Excmo. Sr. Don Adolfo. Admiral, Spanish Navy; Minister of Marine.

Baturov, N. Rear Admiral, USSR Navy; First Deputy Chief, Political Directorate, Northern Fleet, 1971-   . Served in the Soviet-German War (WW II). Member of the Communist Party of the Soviet Union.

Baughan, Robert Louis, Jr. Rear Admiral, United States Navy; Project Manager of Major Combatant Ships Project, 1972-   . Born September 6, 1919, in Huntington, West Virginia. US Naval Academy, 1937-41; Naval Postgraduate School, Ordnance Engineering Course, 1946-47; Massachusetts Institute of Technology, MS, 1947-49; Industrial College of the Armed Forces, 1965-66. Commissioned Ensign, US Navy, in 1941. Served in the Atlantic and Pacific Theaters, WW II; Korean War. Commander USS *Leahy* (DLG-16), 1962-64; Commander Destroyer Squadron SIX, 1964-65; Staff Officer, Pacific Division, Operations Directorate, Joint Chiefs of Staff Organization, 1966-68; Deputy Director for Operations, National Military Command Center, 1968-69; Commander Cruiser-Destroyer Flotilla NINE, 1969-70; Vice Commander Naval Ordnance Systems Command, 1970-71; Project Manager, General Purpose Amphibious Ship/Destroyer 963 Class Project, 1971-72. Legion of Merit with two Gold Stars; Bronze Star Medal with three Gold Stars and Combat "V"; Navy Commendation Medal; and other US and foreign medals and awards. Promoted to Rear Admiral, March 1, 1969.

Baumann, Hans. Major General, Swiss Army; Commandant, Central War College. Born in 1914.

Baumberger, Walter Harlen, Vice Admiral, United States Navy; Commander, United States Taiwan Defense Command, 1970-   . Born January 27, 1912, McMechen, West Virginia. US Naval Academy, 1930-34; Naval War College, 1954-55. Commissioned Ensign, US Navy, in 1934. Served in both Atlantic and Pacific Theaters in WW II. Commanding Officer USS *Canberra*, 1960; Chief of Staff and Aide to Commander Cruiser-Destroyer Force, Pacific, 1960-62; Commander Cruiser-Destroyer Flotilla THREE, 1962-63; Director, Ships Material Readiness Division, Office of the CNO, 1963-65; Commander Cruiser-Destroyer Force, Pacific Fleet, 1965-67; Deputy Commander in Chief, US Pacific Fleet, and Chief of Staff and Aide to Commander in Chief, US Pacific Fleet, 1967-70. Distinguished Service Medal; Legion of Merit with Gold Star; Navy and Marine Corps Medal; Bronze Star Medal with Combat "V"; and other medals and awards. Promoted to Vice Admiral, March 17, 1967.

Bautz, Edward, Jr. Major General, United States Army; Deputy Chief of Staff for Military Operations and Reserve Forces, Continental Army Command, Fort Monroe, Virginia, 1971-   . Born April 2, 1920, Union City, New Jersey. Rutgers University, BS Degree, Business Administration; US Army Command and General Staff College; US Army War College. Commissioned Second Lieutenant, US Army Reserve, 1941. Served in WW II; Vietnam War. Deputy Director, Enlisted Personnel Directorate, Office of Personnel Operations, US Army,

Washington, D.C., 1966; Deputy Director for Reserve Officers Training Corps Affairs, Directorate of Individual Training, Office, Deputy Chief of Staff for Personnel, US Army, Washington, D.C., 1966-67; Director, Military Personnel Policies, Office, Deputy Chief of Staff for Personnel, US Army, Washington, D.C., 1967-69; Assistant Chief of Staff, Operations, J-3, US Military Assistance Command, Vietnam, 1969-70; Commanding General, 25th Infantry Division, US Army, Pacific-Vietnam, 1970. Distinguished Service Medal with Oak Leaf Cluster; Silver Star; Legion of Merit with Oak Leaf Cluster; Bronze Star Medal with V Device and two Oak Leaf Clusters; and other medals and awards. Promoted to Brigadier General, 1966; Major General, 1969.

Bayer, Kenneth Howard. Major General, United States Army; Chief of Staff, North American Air Defense Command/Continental Air Defense Command, Ent Air Force Base, Colorado, 1969-   . Born April 16, 1918, New York, New York. University of Alabama, BS Degree, Electrical Engineering; The Coast Artillery School, Basic Course; US Army Command and General Staff College; Armed Forces Staff College; The National War College; University of Pennsylvania, MS Degree, Electrical Engineering. Commissioned Second Lieutenant, US Army Reserve, 1940. Served in WW II. Assistant Division Commander, 7th Infantry Division, US Army, Pacific-Korea, 1963-64; Commanding General, III Corps Artillery, Fort Chaffee, Arkansas, 1964; Deputy Director for Operations, Directorate of Research and Development, US Army Materiel Command, Washington, D.C., 1964-66; Director, Directorate of Development, US Army Materiel Command, Washington, D.C., 1966-67; Commanding General, 32d Army Air Defense Command, US Army, Europe, 1967-69. Distinguished Service Medal; Legion of Merit; Bronze Star; and other medals and awards. Promoted to Brigadier General, August 1, 1963; Major General, September 1, 1966.

Bayne, Marmaduke Gresham. Rear Admiral, United States Navy; Commandant, National War College, 1972-   . Born May 2, 1920, in Norfolk Virginia. University of Tennessee, Knoxville, BA, 1938-42; Naval Training School, 1942; Naval Submarine School, 1944; General Line School, 1946-47; Armed Forces Staff College, 1957. Commissioned Ensign, US Naval Reserve, 1942; transferred to US Navy, 1946. Served in the Pacific Theater in WW II. Assistant Chief of Staff, Polaris, to Commander Submarine Force, Atlantic Fleet, 1963-65; Commander Submarine Flotilla EIGHT, 1965-67; Assistant Director, Politico-Military Policy Division, Office of the CNO, 1967-68; Deputy Chief of Staff and Assistant Chief of Staff for Plans, Policy and Operations, to Supreme Allied Commander, Atlantic, 1968-70; Commander, Middle East Force, 1970-72. Legion of Merit with two Gold Stars; and other medals and awards. Promoted to Rear Admiral, July 1, 1969.

Bays, Marcel. Major General, Swiss Army; Commander of Infantry. Born in 1914.

Beach, W.G.H. Major General, British Army; Director of Army Staff Studies, 1971- . Born May 20, 1923. Attended Winchester College; Peterhouse, Cambridge, MA; Defence Fellow, Edinburgh University, 1971. Served in France in WW II. Commander 2 Division RE, 1965-67; Commander 12th Infantry Brigade, 1969-70. OBE; MC.

Beamish, Cecil Howard. Air Vice-Marshal, British Royal Air Force; Director, Dental Services, RAF, 1969- . Born March 31, 1915. Attended Queen's University, Belfast. Joined the RAF in 1936. Served in Europe in WW II. CB; Queen's Honorary Dental Surgeon, 1969. Fellow in Dental Surgery, Royal College of Surgeons.

Bean, Alan L. Captain, US Navy; NASA Astronaut, 1963- . Born March 15, 1932, Wheeler, Texas. University of Texas, BS, Aeronautical Engineering, 1955; Navy Test Pilot School, Patuxent River, Maryland; School of Aviation Safety, University of Southern California. Commissioned Ensign, 1955. Member, Attack Squadron 44, 1955-59; Test Pilot, Naval Air Test Center; Member, Attack Squadron 172. NASA experience: Backup Command Pilot, Gemini 10; Backup Lunar Module Pilot, Apollo 9; Lunar Module Pilot, Apollo 12, November 14-24, 1969; Commander, Second Skylab mission; assigned as Backup Commander of US Flight Crew for Apollo-Soyuz Test Project, July 1975. NASA Distinguished Service Medal; Navy Astronaut Wings; Navy Distinguished Service Medal; Texas Press Association's Man of the Year Award, 1969; Rear Admiral William S. Parsons Award for Scientific and Technical Progress, 1970; University of Texas Distinguished Engineering Graduate Award, 1970; Distinguished Alumnus Award, 1970; Godfrey L. Cabot Award, 1970; National Academy of Television Arts and Sciences Special Trustees Award, 1970; Honorary ScD, Texas Wesleyan College, 1972.

Beatty, George Samuel, Jr. Major General, United States Army; Director, Inter-American Defense College, Washington, D.C., 1972- . Born October 26, 1917, Clinton, North Carolina. Presbyterian College, BA, Mathematics and History; US Army Command and General Staff College; Naval War College. Commissioned Second Lieutenant, US Army Reserve, 1938. Served in WW II and in Vietnam War. Deputy Chief of Legislative Liaison, Office, Secretary of the Army, Washington, D.C., 1966-67; Commanding General, 4th Brigade, 6th Infantry Division, US Army, Pacific-Hawaii, 1968; Deputy Commanding General, US Army Training Center, Infantry, and Fort Lewis, Washington, 1968-69; Deputy Commandant, US Army Aviation School, Fort Rucker, Alabama, and Commanding General, US Army Flight Training Center, Fort Stewart, Georgia, 1969-70; Chairman, US Delegation, Joint United States/Brazil Military Commission, and Commander, US Military Group, Brazil, 1970-72. Distinguished Service Medal; Legion of Merit with two Oak Leaf Clusters; Bronze Star Medal; and other medals and awards. Promoted to Brigadier General, August 18, 1967; Major General, October 1, 1969.

Beckington, Herbert L. Major General, United States Marine Corps; Assistant Deputy Chief of Staff (Plans), and Director, Joint Planning Group, Headquarters US Marine Corps, 1972- . Born October 3, 1920, Rockford, Illinois. The Citadel, BA, 1943; Reserve Officer's Class, Marine Corps Schools, 1943; Officer's Base Defense School, 1943; Sea School, San Diego; Catholic University, 1950-53, LLB, 1953; Amphibious Warfare School, Junior Course, Quantico, 1957-58. Commissioned Second Lieutenant, USMCR, 1943; transferred to USMC, 1946. Served in Pacific Theater, WW II; Vietnam War. Commanding Officer Seventh Marines, 1st Marine Division, Vietnam, 1968-69; Chief, Academic Department, Education Center, Quantico, 1969; Assistant, then Deputy Director, Personnel, HQMC, 1969-71; Assistant Division Commander, 2nd Marine Division, 1971-72. Legion of Merit with Combat "V" and three Gold Stars; and other medals and awards. Promoted to Brigadier General, August 15, 1969; Major General, August 1972.

Bednyagin, A. Lieutenant General, USSR Army; Chief Political Directorate, Kiev Military District. Served on the Soviet-German Front in WW II. Member, Communist Party of the Soviet Union.

Beetham, Michael James. Air Vice-Marshal, British Royal Air Force; Assistant Chief of Staff (Plans and Policy) SHAPE, 1972- . Born May 17, 1923. Attended Flying Training Course, 1941-42; Royal Air Force Staff College, 1952; Imperial Defence College, 1967. Commissioned in 1942. Served in Bomber Command in WW II. Group Captain Operations, Headquarters Bomber Command, 1962-64; Commanding Officer, RAF Khormaksar, Aden, 1964-66; Director of Operations, RAF, Ministry of Defence, 1968-70; Commandant, Royal Air Force Staff College, 1970-72. CBE; DFC; AFC. Promoted to Group Captain, 1962; Air Commodore, 1966; Air Vice-Marshal, 1970.

Begg, Sir Varyl (Cargill). Admiral of the Fleet, British Royal Navy; Governor and Commander-in-Chief, Gibraltar, 1969- . Born October 1, 1908. Attended Malvern College; Imperial Defence College, 1954; Entered Royal Navy, 1926 (special entry). Served at sea and in the Admiralty, WW II, Korean War. Lord Commissioner of the Admiralty, and Vice-Chief of Naval Staff, 1961-63; Commander-in-Chief, British Forces, Far East, and United Kingdom Military Adviser to SEATO, 1963-65; Commander-in-Chief, Portsmouth, and Allied Commander-in-Chief, Channel, 1965-66; Chief, Naval Staff, and First Sea Lord, 1966-68. GCB; DSO; DSC; Panglima Mangku Negara (Malaysia); Knight of Order of St. John of Jerusalem, 1969. Promoted to Rear-Admiral 1957; Vice-Admiral, 1960; Admiral, 1963; Admiral of the Fleet, 1968.

Behrens, William Wohlsen, Jr. Vice Admiral, United States Navy; Associate Administrator for Inter-Agency Relations and Naval Deputy to Administrator, National Oceanic and Atmospheric Administration, Department of Commerce,

1972-   . Born in 1922 in Newport, Rhode Island. US Naval Academy, 1940-43; Submarine School, 1943-44; National War College, 1963-64; George Washington University, MA, International Relations. Commissioned Ensign, US Navy, in 1943. Served in submarines in the Pacific Theater in WW II; amphibious operations in the Vietnam War. Chief, NATO Nuclear Planning Section, Strategic Plans Division, Office of the CNO, 1964-66; Member, Policy Planning Council, Department of State, 1966-67; Commander US Seventh Fleet Amphibious Force/Amphibious Group ONE, 1967-69; Director, Politico-Military Policy Division, Office of the CNO, 1969-70; Oceanographer of the Navy, 1970-72, and Federal Coordinator for Ocean Mapping and Prediction, 1971-72. Silver Star Medal; Legion of Merit with three Gold Stars and Combat "V"; Bronze Star with Combat "V" and Oak Leaf Cluster; and other US and foreign medals and awards. Promoted to Vice Admiral, February 18, 1972.

Belik, P.A. General of the Army, USSR Army; Commander, Transbaikal Military District, 1966-   . Served on the Soviet-German Front in WW II. Formerly First Deputy Commander, Group of Soviet Forces in Germany. Member, Communist Party of the Soviet Union.

Beling, John Kingsman. Rear Admiral, United States Navy; Commander Iceland Defense Force and Commander Fleet Air, Keflavik, 1970-   . Born October 29, 1919, in New York, New York. Stevens Institute of Technology, BS, Mechanical Engineering, 1937-41; Massachusetts Institute of Technology, Ph.D, Physics, 1951; Flight Training Course, 1942-43; Naval Postgraduate School, 1946-47; Naval War College, 1960-61. Commissioned Ensign, US Naval Reserve, in 1943; designated Naval Aviator in 1943; transferred to US Navy in 1946. Served in the Pacific Theater in WW II; Vietnam War. Head, Technical Branch, Atomic Energy Division, Office of the CNO, 1962-64; Commanding Officer, USS *Alstede* (AF-48), 1964-65; Training Officer, Staff of Naval Air Force, Atlantic Fleet, 1965-66; Commanding Officer, USS *Forrestal* (CVA-59), 1966-67; Director of Air, Surface and Electronics Warfare Division, Office of the CNO, 1967-70. Legion of Merit; Distinguished Flying Cross; Air Medal with two Gold Stars; and other medals and awards. Promoted to Rear Admiral, August 1, 1968.

Bell, Clarence Edwin. Vice Admiral, United States Navy; Commander, Amphibious Force, US Atlantic Fleet, and Commander Amphibious Operations Support Command, US Atlantic Fleet, 1971-   . Born July 25, 1916, in Hamlet, North Carolina. Maryland University, 1934-35; US Naval Academy, 1935-39; Submarine School, 1941; Armed Forces Staff College, 1950-51; National War College, 1959-60. Commissioned Ensign, US Navy, in 1939. Served in submarines in the Pacific Theater in WW II. Commanding Officer USS *Little Rock* (CLG-4), 1963-64; Deputy Director for Inspection Services, Office of the Assistant Secretary of Defense (Administration), 1964-67; Commander Amphibious Group FOUR, 1967-68; Director, General Planning and Programming Division, Office of the

CNO, 1968-69; Director, Navy Program Planning, Office of the CNO, 1969-71. Silver Star Medal with Gold Star; Distinguished Service Medal; Legion of Merit; and other medals and awards. Promoted to Vice Admiral, July 16, 1969.

Bellamy, Jack. Major General, United States Air Force; Assistant Chief of Staff, Operations (J-3), US Support Activities Group, Thailand, 1973-   . Born July 16, 1924, in Gate City, Virginia. Pilot Training Course, 1943-44; Aircraft Maintenance Officer School, Chanute Air Force Base, Illinois, 1948-49; Air Tactical School, 1949; Air Command and Staff College, 1959-60. Commissioned Second Lieutenant, US Army Air Corps, in April 1944. Served in the European Theater, WW II; Korean War; Vietnam War. Chief, Tactical Division, and later Deputy Director of Requirements, Directorate of Operational Requirements, Headquarters, Pacific Air Forces (PACAF), Hickam Air Force Base, Hawaii, 1966-67; Deputy Director, then Director, Operational Plans, Deputy Chief of Staff for Operations, Headquarters, Pacific Air Forces, Hickam Air Force Base, Hawaii, 1967-69; Vice Commander, 479th Tactical Fighter Wing, George Air Force Base, California, 1969-70; Commander, 49th Tactical Fighter Wing, Holloman Air Force Base, New Mexico, 1970-72; Assistant Deputy Chief of Staff, Logistics, Tactical Air Command, Langley Air Force Base, Virginia, 1972; Deputy Chief, Directorate of Operations, Military Assistance Command, Vietnam (MACV), and Assistant Director of Operations, Seventh Air Force, Tan Son Nhut Airfield, Vietnam, 1972-73. Decorations include Legion of Merit, Distinguished Flying Cross with Oak Leaf Cluster, Meritorious Service Medal, Air Medal with seven Oak Leaf Clusters. Promoted to Brigadier General, November 1, 1971; Major General, 1973.

Bellis, Benjamin N. Major General, United States Air Force; Deputy for F-15, Aeronautical Systems Division, Air Force Systems Command, 1969-   . Born February 4, 1924, in Wheatland, Wyoming. US Military Academy, 1942-46; University of Michigan, MS, Aeronautical Engineering, 1952; Air Command and Staff College, 1957-58; Industrial College of the Armed Forces, 1964-65; George Washington University, MS, Business Administration, 1965; Executive Program, Graduate School of Business, University of California, Berkeley. Commissioned Second Lieutenant, US Army Air Corps, in 1946. Deputy System Program Director, and subsequently System Program Director, F-12/SR-71, Systems Program Office, 1965-68; Deputy, Reconnaissance and Electronic Warfare, Aeronautical Systems Division, 1968-69. Legion of Merit with one Oak Leaf Cluster; Air Force Commendation Medal with one Oak Leaf Cluster; and other medals and awards. Promoted to Major General, May 1, 1972.

Beloborodov, Afanasiy Pavlovich. General of the Army, USSR Army. Born in 1903. Attended Nizhny Novgorod Infantry Academy, 1924-26; General Staff War College, 1936. Volunteered for military service, 1923; commissioned in 1926. Participated in Chinese Eastern

Railway incident, 1929; Soviet-German War, 1941-45; Soviet-Japanese War, 1945. Commander, 78th Rifle Division and later 9th Guard Division, Moscow Front, 1941; Commander, 5th Guard Rifle Division, 1942-43; Commander, 43d Army, 1st Baltic Front, 1944-45; **Commander First Red Banner Army, 1st Far East Front,** 1945; Deputy Commander in Chief, Central Army Group; Army Commander; Military Attache in Czechoslovakia; Commander, Voronezh Military District; Chief, Main Personnel Directorate; Commander, Moscow Military District. Member, Communist Party of the Soviet Union, 1926-   ; Member, Communist Party Central Committee; Deputy of the Supreme Soviet, USSR. Twice Hero of the Soviet Union; two Orders of Lenin; four Orders of Red Banner; two Orders of Suvorov; Order of Kutuzov. Promotions: Major General, 1941; Lieutenant General, 1943; Colonel General, 1945; General of the Army, 1963.

Belonozhko, S. Ya. Colonel General, USSR Army; Commander, Turkestan Military District, 1969-   . Served on the Soviet-German Front in WW II. Member, Communist Party of the Soviet Union.

Belonsov, G. Lieutenant General, USSR Army; Chief, Political Directorate Rear Services (Logistics), Ministry of Defense. Served on the Soviet-German Front in WW II. Member, Communist Party of the Soviet Union.

Belser, Joseph H. Major General, United States Air Force; Deputy Chief of Staff, Plans, Headquarters Aerospace Defense Command, 1971-   . Born November 22, 1921, Santa Anna, Texas. Oklahoma State University; Army Air Corps Flying School, 1942; University of Texas, Austin, Texas, BS, Chemistry, 1950. Commissioned Second Lieutenant, US Army Air Corps, 1942. Served in the European and Pacific Theaters, WW II; Korean War. Commander, 35th Air Division, North American Air Defense, 1967-68; Vice Commander, First Air Force, 1968-69; Director, Operations, North American Air Defense Command/Continental Air Defense Command, 1969-70; Chief, Western Hemisphere Division, Director, J-5 (Plans and Policy), The Joint Staff, Organization of the Joint Chiefs of Staff, 1970-71. Legion of Merit with two Oak Leaf Clusters; Distinguished Flying Cross with two Oak Leaf Clusters; and other medals and awards. Promoted to Major General, February 26, 1971.

Belyayev, Pavel Ivanovich. Colonel, USSR Air Force; Cosmonaut, 1960-   . Born June 26, 1925, in the **Vologda District.** Attended Air Force Pilot School; Air Force War College. Commissioned Second Lieutenant, Soviet Air Force, 1944. Fighter Pilot on the Soviet-German Front, WW II. Recently Commander, Voskhod-2 Spaceship, 1965. Member Communist Party of the Soviet Union.

Benade, Leo Edward. Lieutenant General, United States Army; Deputy Assistant Secretary of Defense (Military Personnel Policy), Office, Assistant Secretary of Defense (Manpower and Reserve Affairs), Washington, D.C.,

1968-   . Born July 29, 1916, Dubuque, Iowa. University of Chicago, BA Degree, English; US Army Command and General Staff College; US Army War College; University of Chicago, LLB Degree, Law; The American University, JSD Degree, Law. Commissioned Second Lieutenant, US Army Reserve, 1942. Served in WW II. Deputy Adjutant General, later Adjutant General, US Army, Europe and Seventh Army, 1966-67; Director of Personnel Systems, Office, Deputy Chief of Staff for Personnel, US Army, Washington, D.C., 1967-68. Distinguished Service Medal with Oak Leaf Cluster; Legion of Merit with two Oak Leaf Clusters; and other medals and awards. Promoted to Brigadier General, August 18, 1967; Major General, June 1, 1970; Lieutenant General, June 22, 1972.

Bender, Chester R. Admiral, United States Coast Guard; Commandant, US Coast Guard, 1970-   . Born March 19, 1914, Burnsville, West Virginia. US Coast Guard Academy, 1932-36; Navy Flight Training Courses, 1939. Commissioned Ensign, 1936; Received Aviator's Wings, 1940. Served in Asiatic-Pacific Theater in WW II. Chief, Administrative Management Division, later Chief, Program Analysis Division, Coast Guard Headquarters, 1962-64; Commander, 9th Coast Guard District, Cleveland, Ohio, 1964-65; Superintendent, Coast Guard Academy, 1966-67; Commander, 12th Coast Guard District and Western Area, San Francisco, California, 1967-70. Bronze Star; Legion of Merit; Distinguished Service Medal; and other medals and citations. Promoted to Rear Admiral, 1964; Admiral, 1970.

Benjelloun, Muhammad. Secretary General of National Defense, Morocco.

Benkert, William Michael. Rear Admiral, United States Coast Guard; Chief, Office of Marine Environment and Systems, 1971-   . Born April 24, 1923, Chicago, Illinois. US Coast Guard Academy, 1940-43. Commissioned Ensign, 1943. Served in Pacific Theater, WW II. Commander, Polar Icebreaker *Eastwind,* 1965-67; Chief Merchant Marine Inspection Office, New York, 1967-70; Deputy Chief, Office of Merchant Marine Safety, Headquarters, US Coast Guard, 1970-71. WW II Campaign service medals and ribbons. Promoted to Captain, July 1, 1965; Rear Admiral, October 4, 1971.

Bennecke, Jürgen. General, Army of the Federal Republic of Germany; Staff, Ministry of Defense. Born September 12, 1912, Halberstadt, Germany. Attended Military Academy. Commissioned Second Lieutenant, 1933; joined West German Armed Forces, 1952. Served on Western front, in the Balkans, and on the Eastern front in WW II; POW two years. Commander, 16th Motorized Infantry Brigade, Flensburg, 1958-60; Commander, 7th Motorized Infantry Division, Unna, 1963-64; Commandant, General Staff College, Hamburg, 1964-66; Commanding General, I Corps, 1966-68; Commander in Chief, Allied Forces, Central Europe, 1968-70.

Bennett, Charles I., Jr. Major General, United States Air Force; Vice Commander, Eighth Air Force, Strategic Air

Command, Guam, 1972-   . Born December 21, 1922, in Chattanooga, Tennessee. Army Air Corps Flying School, 1941-42; Canal Zone College, Republic of Panama, 1949; University of Pittsburgh, Pennsylvania, Air Force Advanced Management Course, 1953-54; United Kingdom Joint Services Staff College, London, England, 1958; National War College, 1964-65; George Washington University, 1965. Commissioned Second Lieutenant, US Army Air Corps, 1942. Served as transport pilot, WW II; Vietnam War. Deputy Assistant Director of Plans, National Security Council Affairs, Deputy Chief of Staff, Plans and Operations, 1965-66; Executive to the Chief of Staff, USAF, 1966-69; Chief of Staff, Seventh Air Force, Vietnam, 1969-71; Commander, 47th Air Division, Strategic Air Command, 1971; Commander, 93d Bombardment Wing, Strategic Air Command, 1971-72. Distinguished Service Medal; Legion of Merit with one Oak Leaf Cluster; and other US and foreign medals and awards. Promoted to Major General, April 1, 1972.

Bennett, Donald Vivian. General, United States Army; Commanding General, Eighth US Army; Commander in Chief, United Nations Command; Commander, US Forces, Korea, 1972-   . Born May 9, 1915, Lakeside, Ohio. US Military Academy; Field Artillery School, Basic Course; US Army Command and General Staff College; US Army War College. Commissioned Second Lieutenant, 1940. Served in WW II. Director, Strategic Plans and Policy, Office, Deputy Chief of Staff for Military Operations, US Army, Washington, D.C., 1963-66; Superintendent, US Military Academy, West Point, New York, 1966-68; Commanding General, VII Corps, US Army, Europe, 1968-69; Director, Defense Intelligence Agency, Washington, D.C., 1969-72. Distinguished Service Cross; Distinguished Service Medal with two Oak Leaf Clusters; Legion of Merit with three Oak Leaf Clusters; Bronze Star Medal; and other medals and awards. Promoted to Brigadier General, September 24, 1962; Major General, December 1, 1965; Lieutenant General, August 1, 1968; General, September 1, 1972.

Bennett, Fred G. Vice Admiral, United States Navy; Commander Antisubmarine Warfare Force, US Atlantic Fleet, and Commander Ocean Sub Area, Western Atlantic Area, 1971-   . Born in Yazoo City, Mississippi. US Naval Academy, 1932-36; Ordnance Engineering Course, Naval Postgraduate School, 1942-43; Massachusetts Institute of Technology, MS, 1943-44; Naval War College, 1953-54. Commissioned Ensign, US Navy, in 1936. Served in the Pacific Theater, WW II. Director of Budget and Reports, Office of the Comptroller, 1963-65; Commander Cruiser-Destroyer Flotilla EIGHT, 1965-66; Director of General Planning and Programming Division, Office of the CNO, 1966-68; Director of Navy Program Planning and Scientific Officer for the Center of Naval Analyses, Office of the CNO, 1968-69; Chief of Staff to the President, Naval War College, 1969-71. Promotions: Rear Admiral, 1963; Vice Admiral, January 17, 1968.

Bennett, Warren Kennedy. Major General, United States Army; Chief of Staff, Third US Army, Fort McPherson,

Georgia, 1972-   . Born February 6, 1919, Buffalo, Missouri. Southwest Missouri State College, BS Degree, Business Administration; US Army Command and General Staff College; US Armed Forces Staff College; US National War College. Commissioned Second Lieutenant, US Army Reserve, 1942. WW II; Vietnam War. Deputy, later Director, International and Civil Affairs, Office, Deputy Chief of Staff for Military Operations, US Army, Washington, D.C., 1967-68; Deputy Chief of Staff for Plans, III Marine Amphibious Force, US Military Assistance Command, Vietnam, 1968-69; Commanding General, 199th Infantry Brigade (Light), US Army, Pacific-Vietnam, 1969; Director of International and Civil Affairs, Office, Deputy Chief of Staff for Military Operations, US Army, Washington, D.C., 1969-70; Secretary of the General Staff, Office, Chief of Staff, US Army, Washington, D.C. 1970-72. Distinguished Service Medal with Oak Leaf Cluster; Silver Star; Legion of Merit with Oak Leaf Cluster; Bronze Star Medal with three Oak Leaf Clusters; and other medals and awards. Promoted to Brigadier General, April 1, 1966; Major General, November 1, 1969.

Bentes Monteiro, Euler. Major General, Brazilian Army; Chief of Army Financial Management, 1968-   . Attended Brazilian Military Academy, 1936; Command and General Staff School; Superior War School. Previous assignments include Commander of Engineer units; Deputy Chief of Engineering Department; Superintendent, Agency for the Development of Northeast Brazil. Promoted to Major General, July 25, 1969.

Beregovoy, Georgij Timofeyevich. Major General, USSR Air Force; Cosmonaut, 1964-   . Born April 15, 1921, in Fedorovka, Poltava Oblast. Attended Lugana Military Pilots Academy, 1938-41; Advance Officers Flight Tactics courses, 1945; Test Pilot courses, 1948; Air Force College, correspondence course, graduated, 1956. Volunteered for military service, 1938; commissioned in 1941. Fighter Pilot and subsequently Flight and Squadron Commander, Soviet-German War, 1941-45. Test Pilot, Air Force Research Institute, 1948-64. Member, Communist Party of the Soviet Union, 1943-   . Twice Hero of the Soviet Union; two Orders of Lenin; Order of Red Banner; Order of Red Star.

Beregovoy, Mikhail Timofeyevich. Lieutenant General, USSR Army; Chief, Soviet Antiaircraft Defense System's Radio Engineering Corps, 1969-   . Born in 1919 in Fedorovka, Poltava Oblast. Military Academy, c. 1941; Govorov Antiaircraft Military Radio Engineering College. Commissioned c. 1941. Served on the Soviet-German Front in WW II. After war held staff and command posts in a number of antiaircraft defense districts. Member, Communist Party of the Soviet Union. Decorations include two Orders of Red Banner; Order of Red Star; and other orders and medals.

Berg, William W. Major General, United States Air Force; Assistant Deputy Chief of Staff, Programs and Resources, Headquarters US Air Force, 1972-   . Born March 14,

1918, in Logansport, Indiana. University of Maryland, BS; George Washington University, MA; Officer Candidate School, 1942-43; Air Force Advanced Management Course, Graduate School of Business Administration, University of Pittsburgh, 1951-52; Industrial College of the Armed Forces, 1961-62. Enlisted in the US Army, 1936. Commissioned Second Lieutenant, US Army, 1943. Served in the Mediterranean Theater, WW II. Deputy Assistant Secretary of Defense, Military Personnel Policy, 1962; Director, Manpower and Organization, Office, Deputy Chief of Staff, Programs and Resources, 1968-72. Distinguished Service Medal; Legion of Merit; and other US and foreign medals and awards. Promoted to Major General, May 1, 1968.

Bergin, Daniel Edward. Rear Admiral, United States Navy; Deputy Director for Intelligence, Headquarters Commander in Chief, US Naval Forces, Europe, 1972- . Born December 10, 1919, New York, New York. Manhattan College, 1937-38; US Naval Academy, 1938-41; National War College, 1963-64; George Washington University, Postgraduate Course, International Affairs, 1964. Commissioned Ensign, US Navy, in 1941. Served in Atlantic and Pacific Theaters in WW II; Vietnam War. Commander Destroyer Squadron THREE, 1965-66; Chief of Staff and Aide to Commander Cruiser-Destroyer Force, US Pacific Fleet, 1966-68; Deputy Assistant Director for Intelligence Production, Defense Intelligence Agency, 1968-71; Commander, Cruiser-Destroyer Flotilla THREE, 1971-72. Legion of Merit with two Gold Stars and Combat "V"; Bronze Star Medal; and other medals and awards. Promoted to Rear Admiral, July 1, 1969.

Berkhan, Karl Wilhelm. Parliamentary Under Secretary, Federal Ministry of Defense, Federal Republic of Germany, 1969- . Born April 8, 1915, Hamburg. School of Engineering, Mechanical Engineer; University of Hamburg, Teaching Institute, 1945-47 and 1953-55. Served in German Armed Forces, 1939-45. Member of Federal Parliament.

Berry, Sidney Bryan. Major General, United States Army; Commanding General, US Army Military Personnel Center since 1973, and Chief, Office of Personnel Operations, US Army, Washington, D.C., 1972- . Born February 10, 1926, Hattiesburg, Mississippi. US Military Academy; The Ground General School, Basic Course; The Infantry School, Basic and Advanced Courses; The Marine Corps School; US Army War College; Columbia University, MA Degree, International Relations. Commissioned Second Lieutenant, 1948. Served in Vietnam War. Assistant Commandant, US Army Infantry School, Fort Benning, Georgia, 1968-70; Assistant Division Commander, 101st Airborne Division (Airmobile), US Army, Vietnam, 1970-71; Deputy Chief, Office of Personnel Operations, US Army, Washington, D.C., 1971-72. Distinguished Service Medal; Silver Star with three Oak Leaf Clusters; Legion of Merit with three Oak Leaf Clusters; Distinguished Flying Cross; Bronze Star Medal with V Device; and other medals and awards.

Promoted to Brigadier General, August 1, 1968; Major General, October 1, 1971.

Beshany, Philip Arthur. Vice Admiral, United States Navy; Commander United States Taiwan Defense Command, 1972- . Born July 3, 1914, in Jamaica, Long Island, New York. Brooklyn College; US Naval Academy, 1934-38; Submarine Training Course, 1940; Naval Postgraduate School; Industrial College of the Armed Forces, 1959-60. Commissioned Ensign, US Navy, in 1938. Served in submarines in the Pacific Theater, WW II. Commander Second Polaris Squadron, Submarine Squadron SIXTEEN, 1963-64; Assistant Chief of Staff for Logistics, Commander in Chief Allied Forces, Southern Europe, 1964-66; Director, Submarine Warfare Division, Office of the CNO, 1966-69; Commander Amphibious Group FOUR, 1969-70; Assistant Deputy Chief of Naval Operations for Fleet Operations and Readiness, 1970-71; Deputy Chief of Naval Operations (Submarine Warfare), 1971-72. Silver Star Medal with Gold Star; Legion of Merit with Gold Star; Bronze Star Medal with Combat "V"; and other medals and awards. Promoted to Vice Admiral, June 1971.

Betts, Charles Stephen. Air Vice-Marshal, British Royal Air Force; Air Officer Commanding No. 24 Group, RAF, Rudloe Manor, 1972- . Born April 8, 1919. Attended Sidney Sussex College, Cambridge. Joined the Royal Air Force in 1941. Assistant Commandant (Engineering), RAF College, Cranwell, 1971-72. Promotions: Air Commodore, 1966; Air Vice-Marshal, 1972.

Bevz, S. Rear Admiral, USSR Navy; Chief, Political Directorate, Pacific Fleet, 1971- . Served in the Soviet-German War, (WW II). Member of Communist Party of the Soviet Union.

Bewoor, Gopal Gurunath. General, Army of India; Army Chief of Staff, 1973- .

Bhutto, Zulfikar Ali. President of Pakistan and Minister of Defence and Foreign Affairs. Born January 1928, in Larkana. Attended University of California, Berkeley, USA, BA Degree, Political Science, 1950; Oxford University, England, BA Degree, Jurisprudence, 1952. Minister for Commerce, 1958; Minister of Foreign Affairs, 1963-66; Deputy Prime Minister and Minister of Foreign Affairs, 1971; Head of Pakistan Delegations to the United Nations, 1959, 1960, 1963, 1964, 1965; Member of the Pakistan National Assembly, 1970; Founder of the "Pakistan People's Party" in 1967, and its Chairman. Decorations: Hilal-e-Pakistan; Doctorate of Law conferred by the University of Sind, 1966; and numerous other honors and awards, Pakistani and foreign.

Biermann, H. H. Admiral, South African Navy; Commandant General, South African Defence Force. SSA; OBE.

Biermann, S. C. Rear Admiral, South African Navy; Chief of the Naval Staff.

Bigeard, Marcel Maurice. General, French Army; Staff of Chief of Army General Staff, 1970- . Born February 14, 1916, in Toul. Attended Senior Staff College, Paris, 1955; Senior War College. Served in WW II, POW; Indochina War, 1945-54, POW; Algeria. Chief, Operational Sector, Algeria, 1959-60; Commander, 6th Overseas Inter-arms Regiment, 1960-63; Commander, 25th Parachute Brigade, 1966-68; Technical Advisor to Central African Government; Commander of the 20th Airborne Brigade, 1966-68; Assistant to Commanding General, French Forces, Dakar Base, 1968-70. Grand Officier, Légion d'Honneur; Distinguished Service Order (GB); Médaille de la Résistance; and other medals and awards. Promoted to Brigadier General, 1967.

Binns, George Augustus. Surgeon Rear-Admiral, British Royal Navy; Medical Officer in Charge, RN Hospital, Plymouth, and Command Medical Officer, 1972- . Born January 23, 1918. Trained at St. Bartholomew's Hospital. Joined Royal Naval Volunteer Reserve in 1942. Served in WW II. Senior Specialist in Ophthalmology, 1962. Queen's Honorary Surgeon; Member of the Royal College of Surgeons; Licentiate of the Royal College of Physicians; Fellow of the Royal Society of Medicine. Cross of St. John, 1972.

Bird, Frank Ronald. Air Vice-Marshal, British Royal Air Force; Assistant Chief of Staff (Automatic Data Processing), SHAPE, 1971- , . Born November 18, 1918. Attended Royal Air Force College, Cranwell; Royal Air Force Staff College, Andover, 1950-51; Canadian National Defence College, Kingston, Ontario, 1963-64. Commissioned in 1939. Served in Flying Training and Bomber Command, WW II. Deputy Director of Operations (Bomber), Air Ministry, 1960-63; Commandant, Aircraft and Armament Experimental Establishment, Boscombe Down, 1964-68; Director General of Organisation (RAF), 1968-71. CB; DSO; DFC; AFC. Fellow of the Royal Aeronautical Society.

Bird-Wilson, Harold Arthur Cooper. Air Vice-Marshal, British Royal Air Force; Air-Officer-Commanding, No. 23 Group, 1970- . Born November 20, 1919. Attended Liverpool College; Command and General Staff School, Fort Leavenworth, Kansas (USA), 1944; Royal Air Force Staff College, Bracknell, 1949; Royal Air Force Flying College, Manby, 1951. Commissioned in 1937. Served at Dunkirk and in the Battle of Britain, WW II. Staff Intelligence, Air Ministry, 1961-63; Air-Officer-Commanding and Commandant, Central Flying School, 1963-65; Air-Officer-Commanding, Hong Kong, 1965-67; Director of Flying (Research and Development), Ministry of Technology, 1967-70. CBE; DSO; DFC and Bar; AFC and Bar; DFC (Dutch); Medal of Merit (Czechoslovakian).

Birindelli, Gino. Admiral, Italian Navy; Commander, Allied Naval Forces Southern Europe and Commander Navy, South Malta.

Blacker, Sir Cecil (Hugh). Lieutenant General, British Army; Adjutant General, Ministry of Defence, 1973- . Born June 4, 1916. Attended Wellington College. Served in European Theater in WW II. Assistant Commandant, Royal Military Academy, Sandhurst, 1960-62; Commander, 39 Infantry Brigade Group, 1962-64; General Officer Commanding, 3d Division, 1964-66; Director, Army Staff Duties, Ministry of Defence, 1966-69; General Officer Commanding-in-Chief, Northern Command, 1969-70; Vice Chief of the General Staff, 1970-73. Represented Great Britain in World Modern Pentathlon Championship, 1951; Represented Great Britain in Showjumping, 1959-61. KCB, OBE, MC. Publications: *The Story of Workboy,* 1960; *Soldier in the Saddle,* 1963.

Blair, Chandos. Major-General, British Army; General Officer Commanding, Scotland, and Governor of Edinburgh Castle, 1972- . Born February 25, 1919. Attended Royal Military College, Sandhurst. Commissioned in 1939, in the Seaforth Highlanders. Served with them in WW II. Commander, 39th Brigade Radfan and North Ireland; General Officer Commanding, 2d Division, British Army of the Rhine, 1968-70; Defence Services Secretary, Ministry of Defence, 1970-72. MBE; MC and Bar.

Blakefield, William Henry. Major General, United States Army; Deputy Commanding General, First United States Army, Fort George G. Meade, Maryland, 1973- . Born December 28, 1917, Sturgeon Bay, Wisconsin. Ripon College, BA Degree, Pre-medicine; US Army Command and General Staff College; Armed Forces Staff College; The National War College. Commissioned Second Lieutenant, US Army Reserve, 1939. Served in WW II. Chief, Army Section, Joint US Military Mission for Aid to Turkey, 1964-66; Assistant Division Commander, 3d Infantry Division, US Army, Europe, 1966-67; Commanding General, US Army Intelligence Command, Fort Holabird, Maryland, 1967-70; Chief, Korea Military Advisory Group, 1970; Chief of Staff, Eighth US Army, Korea, 1970-73. Distinguished Service Medal; Silver Star; Legion of Merit; Bronze Star Medal with V Device and Oak Leaf Cluster; and other medals and awards. Promoted to Brigadier General, August 1, 1964; Major General, September 1, 1969.

Blanchard, George Samuel, Jr. Major General, United States Army; Director of Plans, Programs (MVA), and Budget, Office, Deputy Chief of Staff for Personnel, US Army, Washington, D.C., 1972- . Born April 3, 1920, Washington, D.C. US Military Academy; The Infantry School, Basic and Advanced Courses; US Army Command and General Staff College; US Armed Forces Staff College; US National War College; Syracuse University, MS Degree, Public Administration. Commissioned Second Lieutenant, 1944. Served in WW II and in Vietnam War. Assistant Division Commander, 1st Cavalry Division (Airmobile), US Army, Pacific-Vietnam, 1966-67; Chief of Staff, I Field Force, US Army, Pacific-Vietnam, 1967-68; Director of Plans and Programs, Office, Assistant Chief of Staff for Force Development, US Army, Washington, D.C. 1968-69; Director, Vietnam Task Force, East Asia, and Pacific

Affairs, Office, Assistant Secretary of Defense (International Security Affairs), Washington, D.C., 1969-70; Commanding General, 82d Airborne Division, Fort Bragg, North Carolina, 1970-72. Distinguished Service Medal with two Oak Leaf Clusters; Silver Star with Oak Leaf Cluster; Legion of Merit with Oak Leaf Cluster; Distinguished Flying Cross; Bronze Star Medal with Oak Leaf Cluster; and other medals and awards. Promoted to Brigadier General, September 21, 1966; Major General, September 1, 1970.

Blanco-Peyrefitte, J. Rear Admiral, Mexican Navy; Naval Attache, Embassy of Mexico, London.

Blank, Jonas L. Major General, United States Air Force; Assistant Deputy Chief of Staff, Systems and Logistics, Headquarters, US Air Force, 1972-   . Born April 9, 1921, in Greensburg, Pennsylvania. US Military Academy, 1939-43; Harvard University Graduate School of Business Administration, 1949-51; Air Command and Staff College, 1954-55; Industrial College of the Armed Forces, 1962-63. Commissioned Second Lieutenant, US Army Air Corps, 1943. Served in the European Theater, WW II, POW. Chief, Plans and Policy Branch, Logistics Division, Supreme Headquarters Allied Powers, Europe (SHAPE), France, 1963-66; Chief, Procurement and Comptroller Division, Director of Inspection, Headquarters, 1002d Inspector General Group, 1966-67; Chief, Resources Management Division, Director of Inspection, Headquarters, 1002d Inspector General Group, 1967; Commandant, Squadron Officers School, 1967-68; Commandant, Air Command and Staff College, Air University, 1968-70; Director, Supply and Services, Office, Deputy Chief of Staff, Systems and Logistics, Headquarters USAF, 1970-72. Legion of Merit; Distinguished Flying Cross; and other medals and awards.

Blesse, Frederick C. Major General, United States Air Force; Deputy Chief of Staff for Operations, Headquarters, Pacific Air Forces, Hawaii, 1971-   . Born August 22, 1921, Colon, Panama Canal Zone. US Military Academy, 1941-45; National War College, 1965-66; George Washington University, MA, International Relations, 1966. Commissioned Second Lieutenant, US Army Air Corps, 1945. Served in the Korean War; Vietnam War. Director of Operations, 366th Tactical Fighter Wing, Vietnam, 1967-68; Director of Operations, 474th Tactical Fighter Wing, 1968-69; Commander, 474th Tactical Fighter Wing, 1969-70; Commander, 831st Air Division, 1970; Assistant Director of Operations, Seventh Air Force, Vietnam, 1970-71. Silver Star with two Oak Leaf Clusters; Legion of Merit with one Oak Leaf Cluster; Distinguished Flying Cross with five Oak Leaf Clusters; Bronze Star Medal with V device; and other US and foreign medals and awards. Promotions: Brigadier General, October 1, 1970; Major General, December 1, 1972. Publications: *No Guts, No Glory* (fighter tactics book).

Blixenkrone-Moller, Otto. Lieutenant General, Royal Danish Army; Commanding General of the Army, 1967-   . Born April 27, 1912, Agersφ, Denmark.

Attended Army Officer School, 1936-38; Geodetic Courses, 1940-41; General Staff School, 1946-47. Military Attache, Danish Embassies in Washington, D.C., USA, and Ottawa, Canada, 1953-56; Commander, Infantry Battalion, 1956-59; Chief, Staff Operations Division, Danish Army, 1959-61; Commander, Region IV and Corps Regiment of Funen, 1961-63; Chief of Staff, Army, 1963-67. Promoted to Major General, 1963; Lieutenant General, 1967.

Bliznyuk, I. Major General, USSR Army; Chief, Political Directorate, Airborne Forces, 1972-   . Served on the Soviet-German Front in WW II. Member, Communist Party of the Soviet Union.

Blocher, Rudolf. Major General, Swiss Army; Commanding General, 7th Border Division. Born in 1920.

Blood, Gordon F. Major General, United States Air Force; Commander, US Air Force Tactical Fighter Weapons Center, 1973-   . Born September 30, 1919, in Washington, D.C. Army Air Corps Flying School, 1940-41; Command and General Staff School, 1943-44; Air Command and Staff School, 1949; Air War College, 1958-59; University of Maryland, BS, 1962. Served in the US Marine Corps Reserve, 1937-40. Commissioned Second Lieutenant, US Army Air Corps, 1941. Served in Alaska, WW II; Korean War; Vietnam War. Commander, 36th Tactical Fighter Wing, Germany, 1963-64; Deputy for Operations, Fourth Allied Tactical Air Force (NATO Command), Germany, 1964-66; Chief, Objectives, Plans and Programs Division, Office of the Joint Chiefs of Staff, 1966-67; Deputy Chief of Staff, Operations, Seventh Air Force, Vietnam, 1967-68; Commander, Twelfth Air Force, Tactical Air Command, 1970-72. Silver Star; Legion of Merit with three Oak Leaf Clusters; Distinguished Flying Cross with one Oak Leaf Cluster; and other medals and awards.

Bloxom, Elliott. Rear Admiral, Supply Corps, United States Navy; Fleet Supply Officer, and Assistant Chief of Staff for Supply, Commander in Chief, US Atlantic Fleet, 1970-   . Born January 17, 1916, in Hampton, Virginia. College of William and Mary, Williamsburg, Virginia, BS, 1937; Naval Supply Corps School, 1947; Naval War College, 1960-61. Commissioned Ensign, US Naval Reserve, in 1940; transferred to Supply Corps, US Navy, in 1946. Served in the Atlantic and Pacific Theaters in WW II. Executive Assistant to Assistant Chief of the Bureau for Transportation and Facilities, Navy Department, 1963-65; Commander Naval Supply Center, Pearl Harbor, Hawaii, 1965-67; Deputy Commander, Military Traffic Management and Terminal Service, 1967-70. Legion of Merit; and other medals and awards. Promoted to Rear Admiral, December 15, 1967.

Blundell, Daphne Mary. Commandant, British Royal Navy; Director, Women's Royal Naval Service, 1970-   . Born August 19, 1916. Attended Bedford College, London. Commissioned in the Women's Royal Naval Service in 1943. Served in the Orkneys, Ceylon, East Africa and Malta in WW II. Staff of Flag Officer, Naval Air Command, 1964-67; Staff of Commander-in-Chief, Portsmouth, 1967-69; Superintendent, WRNS Training and Drafting, 1969-70. Promoted to Commandant in 1970. CB; Honorary Aide de Camp to the Queen, 1970-   .

Bobko, Karol J. Lieutenant Colonel, US Air Force; NASA Astronaut, 1969-   . Born New York, New York, December 1937. US Air Force Academy, 1955-59; University of Southern California, MS, Aerospace Engineering, 1970; Aerospace Research Pilots Schools, Edwards Air Force Base, California. Commissioned Second Lieutenant, USAF, 1959; received pilots wings, 1960. Member, 523d Tactical Fighter Squadron, and 336th Tactical Fighter Squadron, 1961-65; Manned Orbiting Laboratory Program, 1966-69. NASA experience: Crew Member of Skylab Medical Experiments Altitude Test; assigned to Support Crew for Apollo-Soyuz Test Project, July 1975. NASA Exceptional Service Medal.

Bobylev, S. Major General, USSR Army; Chief, Political Directorate, Leningrad Military District, 1970-   . Served on the Soviet-German Front in WW II. Member, Communist Party of the Soviet Union.

Bochkarev, M. Rear Admiral, USSR Navy; Chief, Black Sea Fleet Logistics, 1972-   . Served on the Soviet-German Front in WW II. Promoted to Rear Admiral, 1972. Member of the Communist Party of the Soviet Union.

Boissieu Dean De Luigné, Alain De. General, French Army; Chief of Staff of the Ground Forces, 1971-   ; Member of Senior War Council, 1971-   . Born July 5, 1914, in Chartres. Attended Saint Cyr, 1936-38; General Staff School, 1945; War College, 1953; Center for Advanced Military Studies, 1961; Institute of National Defense, 1961. Commissioned Sub-lieutenant, Cavalry, 1938. Served in France, Middle East, and East Africa in WW II, POW 1940-41; Algeria, 1956-59. Commander, 2d Armored Brigade, 1962-64; Commandant, Special Military School, Saint Cyr, and Interservice Military School, Coetquidan, 1964-67; Commander, 7th Division, Mobile Forces, Mulhouse, 1967-69; Inspector of Armored Forces and Cavalry, 1969-71. Grand Officier, Légion d'Honneur; Compagnon de la Libération; Croix de Guerre; Médaille de la Résistance; and other medals and awards. Promoted to Brigadier General, 1964; Major General, 1968; Lieutenant General, 1970.

Bokassa, Jean Bedel. General, Army of the Central African Republic; President, Prime Minister, Minister of Defense, and Commander in Chief, Central African Republic Armed Forces, 1966-   . Born February 22, 1921. Attended Ecole Sainte Jeanne d'Arc, M'Baiki; Ecole Missionnaire, Bangui; Ecole Missionnaire, Brazzaville. Joined the French Army in 1939; rose to Captain, 1961. Organized Army of the Central African Republic and became its commander. Légion d'Honneur (France); Croix de Guerre (France); and other medals and awards.

Bolliger, Kurt. Lieutenant General, Swiss Air Force; Commanding General Air and Antiaircraft Defense. Born in 1919. Previous Assignment: Chief, Command and Control.

Bolling, Alexander Russell, Jr. Major General, United States Army; Commander, US Military Group, Brazil, 1972-   . Born September 11, 1922, Fort McPherson, Georgia. US Military Academy; The Infantry School, Basic and Advanced Courses; US Army Command and General Staff College; US Army War College. Commissioned Second Lieutenant, 1943. Served in WW II and in Vietnam War. Commanding Officer, 3d Brigade, 82d Airborne Division, Fort Bragg, North Carolina, later US Army Pacific-Vietnam, 1966-68; Chief of Staff, XXIV Corps, US Army, Pacific-Vietnam, 1969; Director, Organization, Unit Training and Readiness, Office, Assistant Chief of Staff for Force Development, US Army, Washington, D.C., 1969-71; Commanding General, US Army Training Center (Infantry) and Fort Lewis, Washington, 1971-72. Distinguished Service Medal; Silver Star with two Oak Leaf Clusters; Legion of Merit with four Oak Leaf Clusters; Bronze Star Medal with V Device and Oak Leaf Cluster; and other medals and awards. Promoted to Brigadier General, October 1, 1968; Major General, August 1, 1970.

Bolt, Jones E. Major General, United States Air Force; Inspector General, Headquarters Air Training Command, 1971-   . Born June 16, 1921, in Ware Shoals, South Carolina. Clemson University, 1938-42, BS, Engineering, 1942; Basic and Advanced Flying Schools, 1942-43; Aircraft Engineering School, 1945-46; Air Command and Staff College, 1953. Commissioned Second Lieutenant, USAR, 1942; received pilot wings, 1943. Served in the European Theater, WW II, POW; Vietnam War. Director of Safety, Twelfth Air Force, 1964-65; Commander, 12th Tactical Fighter Wing, Vietnam, 1966-67; Commander, 366th Tactical Fighter Wing, Vietnam, 1967; Director, Tactical Air Control Center, Headquarters Seventh Air Force, 1967-68; Deputy Director, Strike Forces, Directorate of Operations, Deputy Chief of Staff, Plans and Operations, Headquarters USAF, 1968-70; Deputy Chief of Staff, Plans and Operations, Headquarters USAF, 1968-70; Deputy Chief of Staff for Operations, Headquarters US Air Forces, Europe, Germany, 1970-71. Distinguished Service Medal; Distinguished Flying Cross with two Oak Leaf Clusters; and other US and foreign medals and awards. Promoted to Major General, February 24, 1970.

Bolton, Donnelly Paul. Major General, United States Army, Deputy Chief of Staff for Military Operations, US Army Pacific, Fort Shafter, Hawaii, 1973-   . Born May 9, 1919, Chicago, Illinois. US Military Academy; The Infantry School, Basic Course; US Army Command and General Staff College; British Joint Services Staff College; US Army War College. Commissioned Second Lieutenant, 1942. WW II; Vietnam War. Assistant Division Commander, 25th Infantry Division, US Army, Pacific-Vietnam, 1966-67; Assistant Chief of Staff for Military Assistance, US Military Assistance Command, Vietnam, 1967-68; Deputy Director of Operations, Office, Deputy Chief of Staff for Military

Operations, US Army, Washington, D.C., 1968-70; Director of Operations, Office Deputy Chief of Staff for Military Operations, US Army, Washington, D.C., 1970-73. Distinguished Service Medal; Silver Star; Legion of Merit; Distinguished Flying Cross; Bronze Star Medal with V Device and two Oak Leaf Clusters; and other medals and awards. Promoted to Brigadier General, February 1, 1967; Major General, October 1, 1970.

Bondarenko, F. M. Lieutenant General, Artillery, USSR Army; Commander, Missile Forces, Air Defense Command, 1968- . Served on the Soviet-German Front in WW II. Member, Communist Party of the Soviet Union.

Bondarenko, G. A. Vice Admiral, USSR Navy; Chief of Staff, Pacific Fleet, 1967- . Served in the Soviet-German War (WW II). Member of the Communist Party of the Soviet Union.

Borel, Denis. Major General, Swiss Army; Deputy Chief of General Staff, Logistics. Born in 1917.

Borisov, G. Lieutenant General, USSR Army; Chief, Political Directorate, Northern Group of Soviet Forces, Poland, 1969- . Served on the Soviet-German Front in WW II. Member, Communist Party of the Soviet Union.

Bornes Fortes, Breno. General, Brazilian Army; Chief of Staff, Brazilian Army, 1972- . Attended Brazilian Military Academy, 1929; Command and General Staff School; Superior War School; US Army Field Artillery School, Advanced Course. Previous positions include Commanding General, 6th Infantry Division; Deputy Chief of Staff of the Army; Vice Chief of Staff of the Army; Commanding General, II Army. Several Brazilian decorations; awards from Paraguay and Portugal.

Borovykh, A. G. Colonel General, USSR Air Force; Commander, Fighter Aviation/Air Defense Command, 1969- . Served on the Soviet-German Front in WW II. Member, Communist Party of the Soviet Union.

Borzov, Ivan Ivanovich. Colonel General, USSR Naval Air Force; Commander in Chief, Naval Air Force, 1962- . Born in 1915 in Yegor'yevsk County, Moscow Oblast. Attended Naval Air Force Academy, 1935 c. 1938; Naval War College, c. 1945-48. Drafted into Air Force in 1935. Commissioned c. 1938. Served in the Soviet-German War (WW II). Squadron Commander, 1st Aerial Torpedo Regiment, Baltic Fleet Air Force, 1941; Commander, 1st Aerial Torpedo Regiment, 1942-45; Commander, Air Force Division, 1948 c. 1950; Chief of Staff and Deputy Commander, Fifth Fleet Air Force, Pacific Fleet, c. 1950 - c. 1953; Commander, Air Force, Northern and Baltic Fleets, 1953-57; First Deputy Commander, Soviet Naval Air Force, 1957-62. Member, Communist Party of the Soviet Union, 1942- . Hero of the Soviet Union; Two Orders of Lenin; Five Orders of Red Banner; Order of Ushakov; Order of Red Star.

Boswell, Marion L. Major General, United States Air Force; Director, Legislative Liaison, Office of the Secretary of the Air Force, 1972- . Born October 1, 1923, in Louisville, Kentucky. William Jewell College, Missouri, BA, 1946; Army Air Corps Flying School, 1943-44; National War College, 1965-66; George Washington University, MA, 1966. Commissioned Second Lieutenant, US Army Air Corps, 1944. Served in the European Theater, WW II; Vietnam War. Deputy Commander, Operations, 49th Tactical Fighter Wing, Germany, 1966-68; Vice Commander, 366th Tactical Fighter Wing, Vietnam, 1968-69; Commander, 4th Tactical Fighter Wing, 1969-70; Deputy Director, Legislative Liaison, Office of the Secretary of the Air Force, 1970-72. Legion of Merit; Distinguished Flying Cross with one Oak Leaf Cluster; and other US and foreign medals and awards. Promoted to Brigadier General, August 1, 1970; Major General, September 20, 1972.

Botha, Peter W. Minister of Defense, Republic of South Africa.

Botzer, A. Rear Admiral, Israeli Navy; Commander in Chief of the Israeli Navy.

Boumedienne, Houari. Colonel, Algerian Army; Chairman of the Revolutionary Council, and Prime Minister, 1965- ; Minister of Defense, 1962- . Born in 1927. Studied at Islamic Institute, Cairo, Egypt. Chief of Staff, National Liberation Front, 1960-62; First Deputy Prime Minister, 1963-65.

Boustany, Emile Georges. General, Lebanese Army; Commander in Chief, Lebanese Armed Forces, 1965- . Born in 1909 in Jounieh, Kesrouan, Lebanon. Attended Military Officers School, 1933-34. Director, Engineering Corps, 1954; Commander Northern Region, 1959-64; Chief, Inspection and Training, 1964-65. National Order of Cedar; Gold Medal of Lebanese Order of Merit; Military Cross; Order of the Throne (Morocco); Order of Merit (Syria); Order of Military Merit (Brazil); Order of Phoenix (Greece); Legion of Merit (USA); and other medals and awards. Promoted to General, 1965.

Bowers, Verne Lyle. Major General, United States Army; The Adjutant General, US Army, Washington, D.C., 1971- . Born December 23, 1919, Webb, Iowa. University of Maryland, BS Degree, Military Science; The Adjutant General's School, Officer Advanced Course; US Army Command and General Staff College; US Army War College; George Washington University, MA Degree, International Affairs; Harvard Business School, Advanced Management Program. Commissioned Second Lieutenant, US Army Reserve, 1943. Served in WW II and in Vietnam War. Deputy, later Adjutant General, Headquarters, US Army, Europe and Seventh Army, 1966-68; Deputy Chief of Staff for Personnel, US Continental Army Command, Fort Monroe, Virginia, 1968-69; Deputy Chief of Staff (Personnel and Administration), US Army, Vietnam, 1969-70; Deputy The Adjutant General, Office of the

Adjutant General, US Army, Washington, D.C., 1970-71. Distinguished Service Medal; Legion of Merit with two Oak Leaf Clusters; and other medals and awards. Promoted to Brigadier General, August 1, 1968; Major General, August 1, 1970.

Bowes-Lyon, (Francis) James (Cecil). Major-General, British Army; General Officer Commanding, London District, and Major General Commanding the Household Division, 1971-   . Born September 19, 1917. Attended Royal Military College, Sandhurst. Commissioned in the Grenadier Guards, 1938. Served in the Guards Armoured Division in WW II. Commander, 157th Lowland Brigade (Scotland) 1963; General Officer Commanding, 52d Lowland Division District, 1966-68; General Officer Commanding, Berlin (British Sector), 1968-70. CB; OBE; MC and Bar.

Boychenko, I. Lieutenant General, USSR Army; Chief, Political Directorate, Siberian Military District. Served on the Soviet-German Front in WW II. Member, Communist Party of the Soviet Union.

Boyko, V. P. Lieutenant General, USSR Army; Chief Political Directorate, General Staff War College. Served on the Soviet-German Front in WW II. Member of Communist Party of the Soviet Union.

Boylan, George S., Jr. Lieutenant General, United States Air Force; Deputy Chief of Staff, Programs and Resources, Headquarters, US Air Force, 1969-   . Born December 3, 1919, in Wilmington, North Carolina. Lees-McRae Junior College, Banner Elk, North Carolina, 1937-39; Flying Schools, 1940-41; Command and General Staff College; University of North Carolina, Chapel Hill, BS, Commerce, 1950; Air War College, 1954-55. Commissioned Second Lieutenant, US Army Air Corps, 1941. Served in the North Atlantic and European Theaters, WW II. Deputy Director of Aerospace Programs, and later Deputy Director of Resources, Aerospace Programs, Deputy Chief of Staff, Programs and Resources, Headquarters USAF, 1963-64; Commander, US Forces, Azores, and Commander, 1605th Air Base Wing, Lajes Field, Azores, 1964-65; Deputy Chief of Staff, Plans, and Vice Commander, Military Airlift Command, 1965-68; Director of Aerospace Programs, Deputy Chief of Staff, Programs and Resources, Headquarters USAF, 1968-69. Distinguished Service Medal; Legion of Merit with one Oak Leaf Cluster; Distinguished Flying Cross with one Oak Leaf Cluster; and other medals and awards. Promoted to Brigadier General, October 11, 1963; Major General, December 1, 1965; Lieutenant General, August 1, 1969.

Boyle, Douglas Seaman. Rear-Admiral, Canadian Armed Forces; Commander, Canadian Maritime Command, Halifax, N.S., 1973-   . Born November 20, 1923, in Revelstoke, British Columbia. Attended Navigation-Direction Course, 1946-47; Naval Advanced Course, 1951; Imperial Defence College (UK), 1969-70. Commissioned in the Royal Canadian Navy, 1943. Combat

duty in WW II. Director, Senior Appointments, Canadian Forces Headquarters, Ottawa, 1964-66; Director, General Postings and Careers, Canadian Forces Headquarters, Ottawa, 1966-69; Commander, NATO Standing Naval Force, Atlantic, 1970-71; Director General, Plans Requirements and Production, Canadian Forces Headquarters, Ottawa, 1971-72; Chief of Personnel, Canadian Armed Forces, Ottawa, 1972-73. Promoted to Commodore, August 1966; Rear-Admiral, May 1, 1972.

Boylingui, Nazaire. Brigadier General, Gabonese Army; Commander of the Army, Republic of Gabon.

Braadland, Magne. Rear Admiral, Norwegian Navy; Defense and Naval Attache, Embassy of Norway, Washington, D.C.

Brabec, Antonin. Major General, Army of Czechoslovakia; Chief, Political Directorate of the Western Military District, 1973-   . Born c. 1924. Attended military-political school, Bohosudov, 1951; Klement Gottwald Military Political Academy, Prague, 1956-59; Voroshilov General Staff College, Moscow, 1967-68. Joined Czechoslovak Army, 1949. Served as political officer, 1951-55; Defense Ministry Staff, 1959-61; Staff of Antonin Zapotocky Military Academy, Brno, 1962-66, 1969-70; Staff of Main Political Directorate, Ministry of National Defense, 1968-69; Deputy Chief, Main Political Directorate, Ministry of National Defense, 1970-71. Member of Czechoslovak Communist Party; Deputy to People's Chamber, 1972-   . Promoted to Major General, October 1969.

Bradley, Omar Nelson. General of the Army, United States Army; assigned to the Office, Chief of Staff, Department of the Army, Washington, D.C., 1953-   . Born February 12, 1893, in Clark, Missouri. US Military Academy; Infantry School, Advanced Course; Command and General Staff School, Army War College. Commissioned Second Lieutenant, US Army, 1915. Served in WW I and WW II. Assistant Secretary, Army General Staff, 1940-41; Commander, Infantry School, Fort Benning, Georgia, 1941-42; Commander, 28th Division, 1942-43; Commander II Corps, 1943; Commander First Army, 1943-44; Commander 12th Army Group, 1944-45; Head, Veterans Administration, 1945-48; Chief of Staff, US Army, 1948-49; Chairman, Joint Chiefs of Staff, 1949-53. Distinguished Service Medal with three Oak Leaf Clusters; Distinguished Service Medal (Navy); Silver Star; Bronze Star Medal; and other medals and awards. Promoted to Brigadier General, February 24, 1941; Major General, February 18, 1942; Lieutenant General, June 9, 1943; General, March 29, 1945; General of the Army, September 22, 1950. Author of *A Soldier's Story*.

Bramall, Edwin Noel Westby. Major-General, British Army; General Officer Commanding 1st Division, British Army of the Rhine, 1972-   . Born December 18, 1923. Attended Staff College, 1952; Imperial Defence College, 1970. Served in northwestern Europe in WW II; Malaysia-Indonesia confrontation, 1965-66. Commander 5th Airportable Brigade, 1968-69. OBE; MC.

Brand, Vance DeVoe. United States; NASA Astronaut, 1966-   . Born in Longmont, Colorado, May 9, 1931. University of Colorado, BS, Business, 1953, BS, Aeronautical Engineering, 1960; University of California at Los Angeles, MBA, 1964; Naval Test Pilot School, 1963. Commissioned Second Lieutenant, US Marine Corps Reserve, 1953; released from active duty, 1957; Marine Corps Reserve and Air National Guard, 1957-64; holds commission in Air Force Reserve. Flight Test Engineer and Experimental Test Pilot, Lockheed Aircraft Corporation, 1960-66. NASA experience: Crew Member, thermal vacuum testing of prototype command module; Support Crewman for Apollo 8 and 13; Backup Commander, Skylab 2 and 3; assigned as Command Module Pilot for Apollo-Soyuz Test Project, 1975. MSC Certificate of Commendation.

Brasseur-Kermadec. Vice Admiral, French Navy; Commander in Chief Mediterranean Theater and Prefet Maritime of the Third Region.

Braswell, Arnold W. Major General, United States Air Force; Commander, United States Logistics Group, Ankara, Turkey, 1973-   . Born October 3, 1925, in Minden, Louisiana. Louisiana State University, 1942-44; US Military Academy, 1944-48; Flying Training Course, 1949; Air Command and Staff College, 1961-62; National War College, 1966-67; George Washington University, MBS, 1967. Commissioned Second Lieutenant, US Air Force, in 1948. Served in the Korean War and the Vietnam War. Director of Plans, Headquarters Seventh Air Force, Saigon, Vietnam, 1967-68; Director of Operations, 4th Tactical Fighter Wing, Seymour Johnson Air Force Base, North Carolina, 1968-69; Air Staff Planning Representative in Joint Staff Planning Conferences, Office of Deputy Chief of Staff, Plans and Operations, Headquarters US Air Force, Washington, D.C., 1969-70; Deputy Director for Force Development, Directorate of Plans, Headquarters US Air Force, Washington, D.C., 1970-73. Legion of Merit; Distinguished Flying Cross; Air Medal with four Oak Leaf Clusters; and other US and foreign medals and awards. Promoted to Major General, April 2, 1973.

Bravo Carrera, Luis M. Admiral, Mexican Navy; Secretary of the Navy.

Bray, Leslie W., Jr. Major General, United States Air Force; Director of Doctrine, Concepts and Objectives, Deputy Chief of Staff, Plans and Operations, Headquarters US Air Force, 1970-   . Born May 28, 1921, in Wichita Falls, Texas. Arlington State University, Arlington, Texas; Army Air Corps Flying School, 1942; University of Maryland, BS, 1958; Air War College, 1958-59. Commissioned Second Lieutenant, US Army Air Corps, 1942. Served in the China-Burma-India Theater, WW II. Assistant Deputy Director of Plans for War Plans, Deputy Chief of Staff, Plans and Operations, 1963-64; Assistant, Personnel Analysis, US Air Force Military Personnel Center, Randolph Air Force Base, Texas, 1964-66; Deputy Assistant, Joint Matters, Directorate of Plans, Deputy Chief of Staff, Plans and Operations, 1966-67; Assistant Director of Plans for Joint and National Security Council Matters, 1967-69; Deputy Director of Plans, 1969-70. Legion of Merit; Distinguished Flying Cross; and other medals and awards. Promoted to Major General, May 1, 1920.

Breedlove, James M. Major General, United States Air Force; Deputy Director, Defense Mapping Agency, 1973-   . Born September 8, 1922, in Franklin, Kentucky. Attended University of Louisville, 1942-43; US Military Academy, 1943-47; Pilot Training Course, 1947-48; Armed Forces Staff College, 1962; Imperial Defence College, London, England, 1966. Commissioned Second Lieutenant, US Army Air Corps, in June 1947. Served in the Korean War and the Vietnam War. Special Assistant to the Deputy Chief of Staff, Operations, Headquarters Third Air Force, South Ruislip, England, 1967; Deputy Commander for Operations, 81st Tactical Fighter Wing, Bentwaters, England, 1967-68; Director of Readiness Inspection, Headquarters US Air Force, Europe, Lindsey Air Station, Germany, 1968-69; Vice Commander, then Commander, 388th Tactical Fighter Wing, Korat Royal Thai Air Force Base, Thailand, 1969-70; Vice Commander, then Commander, 3500th Pilot Training Wing, Reese Air Force Base, Texas, 1970-71; Deputy Chief of Staff for Operations, Air Training Command, Randolph Air Force Base, Texas, 1971-73. Legion of Merit; Distinguished Flying Cross; Bronze Star Medal; Air Medal with nine Oak Leaf Clusters; and other US and foreign medals and awards. Promoted to Major General, May 1, 1973.

Brett, Devol. Major General, United States Air Force; Chief, Military Assistance Advisory Group, Teheran, Iran, 1972-   . Born August 1, 1923, in San Francisco, California. US Military Academy, 1941-45; Army Air Forces Junior Officers Course, 1946; Air Tactical School, 1948-49; Royal Air Force Staff College, Bracknell, England, 1953-54; National War College, 1964-65; George Washington University, MA, International Affairs, 1966. Commissioned Second Lieutenant, US Army Air Corps, 1945. Served in the Korean War; Vietnam War. Vice Commander, 12th Tactical Fighter Wing, Vietnam, 1967-68; Deputy Director, Tactical Air Control Center, Seventh Air Force, Vietnam, 1968; Commander, 81st Tactical Fighter Wing, England, 1968-69; Inspector General, Headquarters, United States Air Forces, Europe, Germany, 1969-70; Director, Near East and South Asia Region, Office of the Assistant Secretary of Defense (International Security Affairs), 1970-72. Silver Star; Legion of Merit with three Oak Leaf Clusters; Distinguished Flying Cross with two Oak Leaf Clusters; Bronze Star Medal; and other US and foreign medals and awards. Promoted to Major General, December 1, 1971.

Bringle, William Floyd. Admiral, United States Navy; Commander in Chief, US Naval Forces, Europe, and Naval Component Commander of the US European Command with additional duty as United States Commander Eastern Atlantic, 1971-   . Born April 23, 1913, Covington, Tennessee. US Naval Academy, 1933-37; Flight Training Course, 1940; Naval War College, 1952-53. Commissioned Ensign, US Navy, in 1937; designated Naval Aviator, in

1940. Served in the Atlantic and Pacific Theaters in WW II. Commanding Officer USS *Kitty Hawk*, 1961-62; Assistant Director, then Director Aviation Plans Division, Office of CNO, 1962-64; Commander Carrier Division SEVEN, 1964-65; Deputy Chief of Staff for Plans and Operations to Commander in Chief, US Pacific Fleet, 1965-67; Commander Seventh Fleet, 1967-70; Commander Naval Air Force, US Pacific Fleet, 1970-71. The Navy Cross; Distinguished Service Medal with Gold Star; Legion of Merit with two Gold Stars and Combat "V"; Distinguished Flying Cross with five Gold Stars; Air Medal with sixteen Gold Stars; and other US and foreign medals and awards. Promoted to Rear Admiral, January 1, 1964; Vice Admiral, November 6, 1967; Admiral, July 1, 1971.

Britten, Robert Wallace Tudor. Major-General, British Army; General Officer Commanding West Midland District, 1973-   . Born February 28, 1922. Attended Wellington College; Trinity College, Cambridge; Imperial Defence College, 1969. Commissioned Second-Lieutenant, Royal Engineers, in 1941. Served in India and Burma in WW II. Staff Member, War Office, 1958-61; Staff Member, 1st British Corps, British Army of the Rhine, 1961-64; Commander, 1st Training Regiment, Royal Engineers, 1964-65; GSO-1, Directing Staff, Joint Services Staff College, 1965-67; Commander, 30 Engineer Brigade and Chief Engineer Western Command, 1967-68; Director of Equipment Management, Ministry of Defence, Army, 1970-71; Deputy Quartermaster-General, 1971-73. Military Cross. Promoted to Brigadier in 1967; Major-General, 1971.

Brodie, Harry B. Brigadier-General, Canadian Armed Forces; Canadian Forces Attache (Army), Embassy of Canada, Washington, D.C., 1971-73.

Brogan, Mervyn Francis. Lieutenant General, Royal Australian Army; Chief, General Staff and First Member Military Board, 1971-   . Born January 10, 1915, Sydney, Australia. Attended Royal Military College, Duntroon; Staff College; Joint Services Staff College; Imperial Defence College; Wesley College, Sydney University. Commissioned in 1935. Served in 1st Australian Corps and Headquarters New Guinea Forces, WW II. Commanding General, Northern Command, Queensland and Papua-New Guinea, 1962-65; Director, Joint Service Plans, and Chairman Joint Planning Committee, Department of Defence, 1965-66; Quartermaster General and Third Member Military Board, 1966-68; Commanding General, East Command, 1968-71. CB; CBE. Member, Australian Institute of Engineering; Fellow of the Australian Institute of Management.

Broom, Ivor Gordon. Air Vice-Marshal, British Royal Air Force; Air Officer Commanding, No. 11 (Fighter) Group, Strike Command, 1970-   . Born June 2, 1920, in Cardiff. Attended Central Flying School, 1942; Royal Air Force Staff College, Bracknell, 1949; No. 3 Flying College Course, Manby, 1952-53; Imperial Defence College, 1965-66. Commissioned in 1941. Served in fighter units in WW II. Commander, Royal Air Force, Brüggen, 1962-64; Director of Organisation (Establishments), 1966-68;

Commandant, Central Flying School, 1968-70. CB; CBE; DSO; DFC with two Bars; AFC.

Brown, Charles Pershing. Major General, United States Army; Commanding General, US Army Test and Evaluation Command, Aberdeen Proving Ground, Maryland, 1971-   . Born January 11, 1918, McAlester, Oklahoma. University of Oklahoma, BS Degree, Business Administration; Field Artillery School, Basic Course; US Army Command and General Staff College; US Army War College; New York University, MBA Degree, Business Administration. Commissioned Second Lieutenant, US Army Reserve, 1940. Served in WW II and in Vietnam War. Deputy Chief of Staff, Comptroller, US Continental Army Command, Fort Monroe, Virginia, 1965-66; Director of the Army Budget, Office, Comptroller of the Army, Washington, D.C., 1966-67; Commanding General, US Army Artillery and Missile Center, and Commandant, US Field Artillery Center and School, Fort Sill, Oklahoma, 1967-70; Deputy Commanding General, I Field Force, Vietnam, 1970-71; Commanding General, Second Regional Assistance Command, US Army, Pacific-Vietnam, 1971; Senior US Representative, United States/Vietnam Peace Delegation, Paris, France, 1971. Distinguished Service Medal; Legion of Merit with two Oak Leaf Clusters; Bronze Star Medal; and other medals and awards. Promoted to Brigadier General, May 1, 1963; Major General, July 1, 1966.

Brown, George Scratchley. General, United States Air Force; US Air Force Chief of Staff, 1973-   . Born August 17, 1918, Montclair, New Jersey. University of Missouri, 1936-37; US Military Academy, 1937-41; Primary and Advanced Flying Schools, 1941-42; National War College, 1956-57. Commissioned in 1941; received pilot wings, 1942. Served in the European Theater, WW II; Korean War; Vietnam War. Military Assistant to the Secretary of Defense, 1959-63; Commander, Eastern Transport Air Force, 1963-64; Commander, Joint Task Force II, Sandia Base, New Mexico, 1964-66; Assistant to the Chairman Joint Chiefs of Staff, 1966-68; Commander, Seventh Air Force, and Deputy Commander, Air Operations, US Military Assistance Command, Vietnam, 1968-70; Commander, Air Force Systems Command, Andrews Air Force Base, Maryland, 1970-73. Distinguished Service Cross; Distinguished Service Medal with one Oak Leaf Cluster; Silver Star; Legion of Merit with two Oak Leaf Clusters; Distinguished Flying Cross with one Oak Leaf Cluster; Bronze Star Medal; and other US and foreign medals and awards. Promoted to Brigadier General, August 1, 1959; Major General, April 1, 1963; Lieutenant General, August 1, 1966; General, August 1, 1968.

Brown, I. G. Major General, United States Air Force; Director, Air National Guard, 1970-   . Born June 11, 1915, in Hot Springs, Arkansas. Entered civilian aviation field as Federal Aviation Administration licensed instructor and commercial operator. Commissioned First Lieutenant, US Army Air Corps, 1942; transferred to Arkansas Air National Guard, 1946; recalled to active duty during Korean War. Assistant Chief, National Guard Bureau for Air

National Guard, 1962-69. Distinguished Service Medal; Legion of Merit; and other medals and awards. Promoted to Major General, April 20, 1970.

Brown, Leslie E. Major General, United States Marine Corps; Commanding General, 1st Marine Aircraft Wing, 1972-   . Born July 7, 1920, Yakima, Washington. Compton Junior College, 1938-40; Flight Training Course, 1945-46; Naval Justice Course, Port Hueneme; Naval War College, 1958-59; Oklahoma State University, 1962-63, BS. Enlisted in 1940; received field commission as Second Lieutenant, USMC, 1942. Served in Pacific Theater, WW II; Korean War; Vietnam War. Assistant Chief of Staff, G-4 (Logistics), Marine Air Reserve Training Command, 1966-67; Chief of Staff, Marine Air Reserve Training Command, 1967-68; Deputy Chief of Staff, J-3 (Operations), Headquarters, US European Command, 1968-70; Assistant Wing Commander, 3d Marine Aircraft Wing, 1970-71; Commander, 3d Marine Aircraft Wing, 1971-72. Silver Star Medal with Gold Star; Legion of Merit with Combat "V" and Gold Star; Distinguished Flying Cross; Bronze Star Medal with Combat "V"; and other medals and awards. Promoted to Brigadier General, 1967; Major General, August, 1971.

Browne, Charles Duncan Alfred. Air Commodore, British Royal Air Force; Air Officer in Charge, Central Tactics and Trials Organisation, RAF, High Wycombe, 1971-   . Born July 8, 1922. Attended Staff College, Andover, 1956-57. Joined RAF Volunteer Reserve, 1940; Permanent Commission, 1945. Served in the Western Desert, and Southern Europe in WW II. Member of Administration, Staff College, Henley, 1964; Deputy Director, Air Staff Plans, Ministry of Defence (Air), 1964-66; Commanding Officer, Royal Air Force Brüggen, Germany, 1966-68; Commandant, Aircraft and Armament Experimental Establishment, 1968-71. CB; DFC. Member of British Institute of Management.

Brunner, Horst. Major General, National People's Army, Democratic Republic of Germany; Deputy Chief, Main Political Directorate.

Bryan, William E., Jr. Major General, United States Air Force; Deputy Chief of Staff, Operations and Intelligence, Allied Forces Central Europe, and Senior United States Representative, 1972-   . Born October 5, 1921, in Flint, Michigan. Army Air Corps Flying School, 1942-43; Armed Forces Staff College, 1955; National War College, 1962-63. Commissioned Second Lieutenant, US Army Air Corps, 1942. Served in the European Theater, WW II; Korean War; Vietnam War. Commander, 4th Tactical Fighter Wing, 1965-66; Commander, 831st Air Division, 1966-67; Deputy Chief of Staff, United States Military Assistance Command, Vietnam, 1967-69; Chief of Staff, Headquarters Tactical Air Command (TAC), 1969-70; Commander, Nineteenth Air Force, TAC, 1970-72. Distinguished Service Cross; Distinguished Service Medal; Legion of Merit; Distinguished Flying Cross with four Oak Leaf Clusters; Bronze Star Medal; and other medals and awards. Promoted to Major General, May 1, 1970.

Buchenko, V. I. Major General, USSR Army; Chief, Political Directorate, Baku Air Defense District, 1968-   . Served on the Soviet-German Front in WW II. Member, Communist Party of the USSR.

Buckland, Ronald John Denys Eden. Major-General, British Army; Major-General in charge of Administration, Headquarters United Kingdom Land Forces, 1972-   . Born July 27, 1920. Attended New College, Oxford, MA Degree; Staff College; Imperial Defence College, 1968; Joint Services Staff College. Commissioned in the Coldstream Guards, 1940. Served in Northwest Europe in WW II; Malaya. GSO 1, 4th Division, British Army of the Rhine, 1963-65; Commander, 133 Infantry Brigade (Territorial Army), 1966-67; Assistant Chief of Staff, Joint Exercises Division, Headquarters, ALFCE, Holland, 1967; Deputy Adjutant and Quartermaster General, 1st British Corps, British Army of the Rhine, 1969-70; Chief of Staff, Headquarters, Strategic Command, 1970-72. MBE.

Bugayev, Boris Pavlovich. Lieutenant General, USSR Air Force; Minister of Civil Aviation, USSR, 1970-   ; Deputy to USSR Supreme Soviet, 1970-   . Born July 29, 1923, in Cherkassy, Ukraine. Studied at School of Civil Aviation; Air Force Officers School. Commissioned Second Lieutenant, USSR Air Force, in 1943. Served on the Soviet-German Front in WW II. First Deputy Minister of Civil Aviation, 1966-70. Hero of Socialist Labor; two Orders of Lenin; two Orders of Red Banner; Order of Red Star.

Bulkeley, John Duncan. Rear Admiral, United States Navy; President of Board of Inspection and Survey, 1967-   . Born August 19, 1911, New York, New York. US Naval Academy, 1929-33; Armed Forces Staff College, 1949-50. Commissioned Ensign, US Navy, 1934. Served in PT boats in the Philippines and in the Atlantic and Pacific Theaters in WW II; commanded a destroyer division in the Korean War. Commander Naval Base, Guantanamo Bay, Cuba, 1963-66; Commander Cruiser-Destroyer Flotilla EIGHT, 1966-67. Medal of Honor; Navy Cross; Silver Star Medal with Gold Star (Army); Silver Star Medal (Navy); Legion of Merit with Combat "V"; Army Distinguished Service Cross with Oak Leaf Cluster; French Croix de Guerre with Star; and other US and foreign medals and awards. Promoted to Captain, July 1, 1952; Rear Admiral, February 1, 1964.

Bullard, Ross P. Rear Admiral, United States Coast Guard; Commander, 5th Coast Guard District, Portsmouth, Virginia 1971-   . Born March 26, 1914, Decatur, Illinois. US Coast Guard Academy, 1935-39; US Navy Post Graduate School of Communications, 1952-53. Commissioned Ensign, 1939. Served in Atlantic and Pacific Theater, WW II. Chief Mobilization and Planning Officer, Staff, Coast Guard Commander, Western Area, San Francisco, California, 1965-66; Chief, Operations Division, 12th Coast Guard District, San Francisco, California, 1966-67; Commander, 8th Coast Guard District, New Orleans, Louisiana, 1967-71. WW II campaign medals and ribbons; and other medals and citations. Promoted to Captain, July 1, 1960; Rear Admiral, July 1, 1967.

Bullen, Reginald. Air Vice-Marshal, British Royal Air Force; Air Officer in Charge of Administration, Headquarters Training Command, RAF Brampton, 1972-   . Born October 19, 1920. Attended RAF College, Cranwell, 1952-54; Air Staff College, 1955; RAF Staff College, Bracknell, 1959-61; NATO Defence College, 1965; Imperial Defence College, 1970. Served with Royal Air Force and Royal Australian Air Force squadrons in WW II. Staff member, Headquarters Allied Forces Central Europe, 1965-68; Director of Personnel, Ministry of Defence, 1968-69; Deputy Air Officer in Charge of Administration, Headquarters Maintenance Command, 1971-72.

Bumba. Major General, Army of Zaire; Commanding General, Zairian Armed Forces. Born in 1930, Alberta. Attended Ecole Mferien d'Agricole; Ecole de Cinema, Belgium; EA/SCG, Luluabourg (now Kananga), 1952; Ecole Central de la Force Publique. Joined Public Force, 1950; Lieutenant, Congolese Army, 1960; Commander, 1st Paratroop Battalion, 1964; Commander, Airborne Brigade (BAR), 1967; Commander, Airborne Attack Troops, 1972.

Burdett, Allen Mitchell, Jr. Major General, United States Army; Commanding General, US Army Aviation Center, and Commandant, US Army Aviation School, Fort Rucker, Alabama, 1970-   . Born August 25, 1921, Washington, D.C. US Military Academy; The Infantry School, Basic and Advanced Courses; US Army Command and General Staff College; US Armed Forces Staff College; US Army War College; George Washington University, MA Degree, International Affairs. Commissioned Second Lieutenant, 1943. Served in WW II and in Vietnam War. Military Assistant to Deputy Director (Tactical Warfare Programs), Office, Director of Defense Research and Engineering, Office, Secretary of Defense, Washington, D.C. 1966-68; Assistant Division Commander, 101st Airborne Division (Airmobile), US Army Vietnam, 1968-69; Commanding General, 1st Aviation Brigade, and Aviation Officer, US Army, Vietnam, 1969-70; Director, Army Aviation, Office, Assistant Chief of Staff for Force Development, US Army, Washington, D.C. 1970. Distinguished Service Medal; Silver Star with Oak Leaf Cluster; Legion of Merit with two Oak Leaf Clusters; Distinguished Flying Cross with Oak Leaf Cluster; Bronze Star Medal with two Oak Leaf Clusters; and other medals and awards. Promoted to Brigadier General, October 27, 1966; Major General, February 1, 1970.

Burke, Julian Thompson, Jr. Rear Admiral, United States Navy; Commander US Naval Forces, Japan, 1970-   . Born April 24, 1918, in Alexandria, Virginia. US Naval Academy, 1936-40; Submarine School, 1943; Naval War College, 1957-58. Commissioned Ensign, US Navy, in 1940. Served in the Pacific Theater in WW II and amphibious operations in the Vietnam War. Commanding Officer USS *Fremont*, 1963-64; Commander Amphibious Squadron SIX, 1964-65; Head, Navy Plans Branch, Office of the CNO, 1965-66; Commander Amphibious Group THREE, 1966-67; Commander Amphibious Group ONE, 1967-68; Assistant Deputy Chief of Naval Operations (Naval Reserve), 1968-70. Silver Star Medal; Legion of Merit with Gold Star and Combat "V"; Bronze Star Medal with

Combat "V"; Navy Commendation Medal with Combat "V" and Gold Star; and other US and foreign medals and awards. Promoted to Rear Admiral, July 1, 1967.

Burke, William Alden. Major General, United States Army; Deputy Assistant Chief of Staff for Force Development, US Army, Washington, D.C.; 1972-   . Born February 8, 1921, Muskogee, Oklahoma. George Washington University, BA Degree, Social Science; The Cavalry School, Advanced Course; The Armored School, Advanced Course; US Army Command and General Staff College; US Army War College. Commissioned Second Lieutenant, US Army Reserve, 1942. Served in WW II and in Vietnam War. Chief, Army Section, Joint US Military Mission to Turkey, 1966-68; Assistant Division Commander, 1st Armored Division, Fort Hood, Texas, 1968-69; Deputy Chief of Staff for Operations, III Marine Amphibious Force, US Military Assistance Command, Vietnam, 1969; Commanding General, 1st Brigade, 5th Infantry Division (Mechanized), US Army, Pacific-Vietnam, 1969-70; Commanding General, 4th Infantry Division, US Army, Pacific-Vietnam, 1970; Director of Systems, Office, Assistant Chief of Staff Force Development, US Army, Washington, D.C., 1971-72. Distinguished Service Medal; Silver Star with two Oak Leaf Clusters; Legion of Merit with Oak Leaf Cluster; Distinguished Flying Cross; Bronze Star Medal with Oak Leaf Cluster; and other medals and awards. Promoted to Brigadier General, July 1, 1966; Major General, August 1, 1970.

Burlachenko, P. D. Rear Admiral, USSR Navy; Chief, Political Directorate, Caspian Flotilla. Served in the Soviet-German War, 1941-45. Member Communist Party of the Soviet Union.

Burnett, Edward John Sidney. Major-General, British Army; Major-General, Brigade of Gurkhas, Hong Kong, 1971-   . Born February 8, 1921. Attended Kelly College, Tavistock. Commissioned into Indian Army, 1941; transferred to 10th PMO Gurkha Rifles in 1948. Served in Burma-India in WW II. Commander 48 Gurkha Infantry Brigade, Hong Kong, 1968-70; Commander Gurkha L. of C. in Nepal, 1970-71. DSO; OBE; MC; Star of Nepal.

Burns, John J. Major General, United States Air Force; Commander, 12th Air Force, 1973-   . Born June 28, 1924, in Jersey City, New Jersey. Army Air Corps Flying School, 1942-43; University of Omaha, BS, Mathematics, 1964. Commissioned Second Lieutenant, US Army Air Corps, 1943. Served in the European Theater, WW II; Korean War; Vietnam War. Deputy Commander, Operations, 8th Tactical Fighter Wing, Thailand, 1967; Vice Commander, 8th Tactical Fighter Wing, Thailand, 1967-68; Commander, 4525th Fighter Weapons Wing, 1968-69; Commander, 4510th Combat Crew Training Wing, 1969-70; Deputy Director, General Purpose Forces, Directorate of Operational Requirements and Development Plans, Office of Deputy Chief of Staff, Research and Development, 1970-72; Director, Operational Requirements and Development Plans, Deputy Chief of Staff, Research and Development, Headquarters US Air Force, 1972-73. Silver

Star; Legion of Merit with one Oak Leaf Cluster; Distinguished Flying Cross with two Oak Leaf Clusters; Bronze Star Medal; and other medals and awards. Promoted to Major General, August 1, 1972.

Burton, Jonathan Rowell. Major General, United States Army; Commanding General, 3d Armored Division, US Army, Europe, 1973-   . Born October 27, 1919, in Berwyn, Illinois. Attended Michigan State College; Cavalry School; Armored School, Advanced Course; Army War College; Army Aviation School, 1963-64; George Washington University, MA, International Relations. Commissioned Second Lieutenant (ORC) in 1942. Served in WW II and the Vietnam War. Commanding Officer, Division Support Command, later Commander, 3d Brigade, 1st Cavalry Division, US Army, Vietnam, 1966-67; Director, Department of Tactics, US Army Aviation School, Fort Rucker, Alabama, 1967-68; Chief, Force Planning Division, then Deputy Director of Plans, Office of the Deputy Chief of Staff for Logistics, 1968-69; Deputy Director, J-4, Joint Chiefs of Staff Organization, 1969-70; Assistant Division Commander, then Commanding General, 3d Brigade (Separate), 1st Cavalry Division, US Army, Vietnam, 1970-71; Deputy Commander, Army and Air Force Exchange Service, Dallas, Texas, 1972-73. Distinguished Service Medal; Silver Star; Legion of Merit with Oak Leaf Cluster; Distinguished Flying Cross; Bronze Star Medal with two Oak Leaf Clusters; and other medals and awards. Promoted to Brigadier General May 1, 1970; Major General February 1, 1973.

Butler, Hew Dacres George. Major-General, British Army; General Officer Commanding Near East Land Forces, 1972-   . Born March 12, 1922. Attended Staff College, 1951; Imperial Defence College, 1969. Commissioned in 1941. Served in North Africa in WW II, POW, 1943-45. Commander 24 Infantry Brigade, Aden, 1966-67. Assistant Chief of Staff G3 Northag, 1970-72.

Butler, Sir Mervyn (Andrew Haldane). Lieutenant-General, British Army; Commandant, Royal College of Defence Studies, 1972-   . Born July 1, 1913. Attended St. Columba's College, Rathfarnham, Eire; Royal Military College, Sandhurst. Commissioned in the South Lancashire Regiment, 1933; transferred to the Suffolk Regiment, 1945. Served in the European and African Theater, WW II; Suez Operation, 1956. General Officer Commanding, 2 Division, 1962-64; Assistant Chief of the Defence Staff (Joint Warfare), Ministry of Defence, 1964-66; Commandant, Staff College, Camberley, 1966-67; General Officer Commanding 1st British Corps, 1968-70; General Officer Commanding-in-Chief, Army Strategic Command, 1970-71. KCB; CBE; DSO and Bar; MC; Croix de Guerre (French). Promoted to Brigadier, 1951; Major-General, 1961; Lieutenant-General, 1968.

Button, Arthur Daniel. Air Vice-Marshal, British Royal Air Force; Director of RAF Educational Services, 1972-   . Born May 26, 1916. Attended University College, Southampton, BS; RAF Staff College, 1953. Joined the RAF Educational Service in 1938; transferred to General Duties Branch in 1941; Education Branch, 1946. Served in instructional duty in WW II. Deputy Director of RAF Educational Services, 1964-66; Command Education Officer, Near East Air Force, 1966-68; Command Education Officer, Strike Command, 1968-72. OBE. Chartered Engineer; Associate Fellow of the Royal Aeronautical Society.

Bykovsky, Valery Fyodorovich. Colonel, USSR Air Force; Cosmonaut, 1960-   . Born August 2, 1934. Attended Katcha Air Force Pilot School, 1954; Zhukovsky Air Force Engineering College; Cosmonaut Training Course, 1960. Commissioned Second Lieutenant, USSR Air Force, in 1954. Jet pilot, 1954-59; Chief Assistant for Major Andrian Nikolayev's space flight, 1962; space flight, June 14-19, 1963; Member, Communist Party of the Soviet Union. Hero of Soviet Union; Order of Lenin; Order of Red Banner; Order of Red Star; and other orders and awards.

C

Cabello, Leodegar. Major General, Paraguayan Army (Retired); Secretary of State for National Defense, 1962-   . Born October 2, 1911, in Carapegua. Attended Paraguayan Military Academy, 1929-33; Advanced War School, Staff Officer Course, 1945. Commissioned Second Lieutenant, Infantry, 1933. Served in the Chaco War (1932-35). Permanent Military Delegate to the Inter-American Defense Board, 1950; General Staff Member of the Inter-American Defense Board, 1951; Acting Commander of the Military Region of the Chaco, 1955; Acting Commander of the 1st Military Region, 1956; Chief of the General Staff, 1956; Commander, 1st Military Region, 1957; Acting Commander in Chief of the Armed Forces, 1957, 1958, 1967, 1972; Commander, 1st Cavalry Division, "General Bernadino Caballero," 1961. Medalla Commemorativa de la Victoria de Boqueron; Medalla al Merito de la Asociación de Mutilados y Lisiados de la Guerra del Chaco; Medalla de Caballeria; Medalla de Transmisiones; and various foreign medals and awards.

Caceres, Juan Antonio. Major General, Paraguayan Army; Chief of the General Staff, Paraguayan Armed Forces, 1970-   ; and Commander, 1st Infantry Division, 1958-   . Born May 16, 1916, in Villa Florida. Attended Paraguayan Military Academy, 1934-37; Advanced War School, Staff Officer Course, 1952; Post Graduate Course 1954; National War College, 1969. Commissioned Second Lieutenant, Engineer branch, 1937. Commander of the 1st Military Region, 1958; Acting Commander of Air Forces, 1959; Director of Cadre Maneuvers, 1964; Acting Chief of the General Staff, 1969-70; President of the Directive Council of the Loan Fund of the Ministry of National Defense, 1970; Acting Commander, 1st Cavalry Division, "General Bernardino Caballero," 1970. Promoted to Major General, May 14, 1958.

Cagle, Malcolm Winfield. Vice Admiral, United States Navy; Chief of Naval Training, and Director of Naval Education and Training, Office of the Chief of Naval Operations, 1971- .Born September 26, 1918, Grand Junction, Colorado. US Naval Academy, 1937-41; Flight Training Course, 1943; National War College, 1957-58. Commissioned Ensign, US Navy, 1941; designated Naval Aviator, 1943. Served in the Atlantic and Pacific Theaters, WW II; the Korean War; and the Vietnam War. Commanding Officer USS *Suribachi* (AE-21) 1963-64; Commanding Officer USS *Franklin D. Roosevelt* (CVA-42), 1964-65; Director, Aviation Programs Division, Office of the Deputy CNO (Air), 1965-68; Commander Carrier Division ONE, 1968-69; Director, General Planning and Programming Division, Office of the CNO, 1969-70; Assistant Deputy Chief of Naval Operations for Air, 1970-71. Navy Cross; Distinguished Service Medal; Legion of Merit; Distinguished Flying Cross; Air Medal; 1957 US Naval Institute Prize Essay Award; 1957 Alfred Thayer Mahan Award (Navy League Winner); and other medals and awards. Promoted to Vice Admiral, July 22, 1971. Publications: *Battle Report*, Volume VI (with Captain Walter Karig); *The Sea War in Korea* (with Captain Frank Manson); *Naval Aviation Guide*; *Flying Ships*; *Hovercraft and Hydrofoils*; *A Pilot's Meteorology*; various essays and television scripts.

Calderon Molano, José Ramon. Major General, Colombian Air Force; Commandant of the Air Force, 1970- . Born August 18, 1923, Tunja (Boyacá). Advanced Military Studies, War College; Navigation Instruction (USA); Command and Staff School (USA). Commissioned October 16, 1944. Orden de Boyacá (Gran Oficial); Orden al Merito Aeronautica Antonio Ricaurte (Comendador); Orden al Mérito Naval Almirante Padilla (Comendador); Orden al Mérito Militar Antonio Nariño (Gran Oficial); Orden al Mérito Militar José Maria Cordoba (Comendador). Promoted to Brigadier General, December 16, 1968; Major General, December 16, 1971.

Caldwell, Frank Griffiths. Major-General, British Army; Assistant Chief of General Staff (Operational Requirements), 1972- . Born February 26, 1921. Attended Elizabeth College, Guernsey. Commissioned in the Royal Engineers in 1940. Served in North Africa and northwest Europe in WW II; Malaya, 1951-53. Commander Royal Engineers, 2 Division, British Army of the Rhine, 1961-63; Corps Commander Royal Engineers, 1 (BR) Corps, 1967-68; Director of Defence Operational Plans, Ministry of Defence, 1970; Engineer in Chief (Army), 1970-72. OBE; MC and Bar; Belgian Croix de Guerre and Croix Militaire.

Caldwell, William Burns, III. Major General, United States Army; Deputy Director, Security Assistance Plans, Policy, and Programs, Office of the Assistant Secretary of Defense (International Security Affairs), 1973- . Born July 20, 1925, in Fort Moultrie, South Carolina. Attended US Military Academy; The Infantry School, Basic and Advanced Courses; Command and General Staff College; UK Joint Services Staff College; US National War College, 1963-64; George Washington University, MA, International Affairs. Commissioned Second Lieutenant in 1948. Served

in the Vietnam War. Military Senior Advisor, CORDS, III Corps Tactical Zone, II Field Force, Vietnam, 1967-68; Commanding Officer, 2d Regiment, US Corps of Cadets, US Military Academy, West Point, 1968; Chief, Strategic Plans Branch, Plans and Policy Division, Supreme Headquarters Allied Powers Europe, 1968-70; Assistant Division Commander, 4th Armored Division, US Army, Europe, 1971-72; Chief of Staff, VII Corps, US Army, Europe, 1972-73. Silver Star with two Oak Leaf Clusters; Legion of Merit with three Oak Leaf Clusters; Distinguished Flying Cross; Bronze Star Medal with V Device and two Oak Leaf Clusters; Air Medal, 16 awards. Promoted to Brigadier General, October 1, 1969; Major General, July 14, 1973.

Callaway, Howard H. United States Secretary of the Army, 1973- . Born April 2, 1927, LaGrange, Georgia. US Military Academy, 1949. Commissioned Second Lieutenant, 1949; discharged, 1952. Served in Korean War. Member of Congress, 1965-66; President, Interfinancial, Inc., Atlanta, Georgia; Chairman, Council of Trustees, Freedoms Foundation, Valley Forge; participant in numerous business, political, educational and civic enterprises.

Calvert, James Francis. Vice Admiral, United States Navy; Commander First Fleet, 1972- . Born September 8, 1920, in Cleveland, Ohio. Oberlin College, Oberlin, Ohio, 1937-39; US Naval Academy, 1939-42; Submarine School, 1942; National War College, 1961-62. Commissioned Ensign, US Navy, in 1942. Served in submarines in the Pacific Theater in WW II; Vietnam War. Commanding Officer, USS *Skate*, 1956-59; Commander Submarine Division ONE HUNDRED TWO, 1959-61; Head, Europe and NATO Branch, Politico-Military Policy Division, Office of CNO, 1962-64; Director, Politico-Military Policy Division, Office of the CNO, 1965-67; Commander Cruiser-Destroyer Flotilla EIGHT, 1967-68; Superintendent, US Naval Academy, 1968-72. Superintendent, US Naval Academy, 1968-72. Distinguished Service Medal; Silver Star Medal with Gold Star; Legion of Merit with three Gold Stars; Bronze Star Medal; and other US and foreign medals and awards. Promotions: Rear Admiral, July 2, 1965; Vice Admiral, July 31, 1970.

Cam, Tran Van. Brigadier General, Army of the Republic of South Vietnam; Commander 23rd Infantry Division.

Cameron, Neil. Air Vice-Marshal, British Royal Air Force; Deputy Commander, RAF Germany, 1972- . Born July 8, 1920. Attended Royal Air Force Staff College, 1949; Imperial Defence College, 1963. Served in Fighter and Fighter Bomber Squadrons, WW II. Principal Staff Officer, Deputy Supreme Commander, SHAPE, 1964; Assistant Commandant, Royal Air Force College, Cranwell, 1965; Programme Evaluation Group, Ministry of Defence, 1965-66; Assistant Chief, Defence Staff (Policy), 1968-70; Senior Air Staff Officer, Air Support Command, 1970-72. CB; CBE; DSO; DFC.

Camm, Frank Ambler. Major General, United States Army; Assistant General Manager (Military Application), Atomic Energy Commission, Germantown, Maryland, 1972-   . Born March 13, 1922, Fort Knox, Kentucky. US Military Academy; The Engineer School, Basic, Advanced, and Field Grade Officer Courses; US Army Command and General Staff College; The National War College; Harvard University, MS Degree, Civil Engineering; George Washington University, MA Degree, International Affairs. Commissioned Second Lieutenant, 1943. Served in WW II and in Vietnam War. Deputy Director, Special Projects Office, later Director, Special Operations Directorate, US Military Assistance Command, Vietnam, 1967-68; Chief, Force Development Plans Division, Plans and Programs Directorate, Office, Assistant Chief of Staff for Force Development, US Army, Washington, D.C., 1968-69; Division Engineer, US Army Engineer Division, South Pacific, San Francisco, California, 1969-72. Legion of Merit with two Oak Leaf Clusters; Bronze Star Medal with three Oak Leaf Clusters; and other medals and awards. Promoted to Brigadier General, November 26, 1969; Major General, December 1, 1971.

Campbell, Ian Robert. Air Vice-Marshal, British Royal Air Force; Director of Management and Support Intelligence, Ministry of Defence, 1970-   . Born October 5, 1920. Attended Royal Air Force College, Cranwell; Royal Air Force Flying College, 1957. Served in WW II, anti-shipping operations;POW, Italy and Germany. Officer Commanding, RAF Marham, 1961-63; Ministry of Defence (Air) DASB, 1964; Senior Air Staff Officer, Headquarters No. 1 Group, 1965-68; Air Attache, Bonn, Federal Republic of Germany, 1968-70. CBE; AFC.

Campbell, Roland A. Major General, United States Air Force; Commander, Twenty-first Air Force, Military Airlift Command, 1971-   . Born September 20, 1917, in Persia, Iowa. Spokane Junior College, 1935-37; Eastern Washington College of Education, Cheney, Washington, 1937-39; Army Air Corps Flying School, 1939-40; Air War College, 1956-57. Commissioned Second Lieutenant, US Army Air Corps, 1940; regular Air Force Commission, 1947. Served in the Southwest Pacific Area, WW II; Korean War. Commander 72d Bombardment Wing, Puerto Rico, 1964-65; Assistant Deputy Chief of Staff, Materiel, Strategic Air Command, 1966-68; Deputy Chief of Staff, Materiel, Strategic Air Command, 1968-69; Deputy Chief of Staff, Materiel, Headquarters, Pacific Air Forces, 1969-70; Chief of Staff, Pacific Air Forces, Hawaii, 1970-71. Legion of Merit with two Oak Leaf Clusters; Distinguished Flying Cross; Bronze Star Medal; and other medals and awards. Promoted to Major General, June 1, 1968.

Campbell, William Beverly. Major General, United States Air Force; Commander Army and Air Force Exchange Service (AAFES), 1970-   . Born May 21, 1916, in Carrollton, Georgia. West Georgia College, 1934-36; US Military Academy, 1936-40; Army Air Corps Flying School, 1942; Industrial College of the Armed Forces, 1955-56. Commissioned Second Lieutenant, US Army

Quartermaster Corps, 1940; received pilot wings, 1942. Served in the European Theater, WW II. Commander, 4th Strategic Aerospace Division, 1960-64; Deputy Inspector General, Headquarters, US Air Force, 1964-68; Director, Manpower and Organization, Deputy Chief of Staff, Programs and Resources, 1968; Assistant Deputy Chief of Staff, Programs and Resources, 1968-70. Distinguished Service Medal; Legion of Merit; Distinguished Flying Cross with one Oak Leaf Cluster; Croix de Guerre with Palm; and other medals and awards. Promoted to Major General, August 1, 1964.

Can, Vu Van. Senior Colonel, People's Army of Vietnam; Vice Minister of Public Health, 1960-   ; Deputy Chief, General Directorate of Rear Services, People's Army of Vietnam, 1950-   . Formerly Member of Preparatory Committee, Vietnam-Soviet Friendship Association; Chief of Medical Bureau, People's Army of Vietnam, 1950-64; Member, Department of Medical Science, State Science Committee, 1960; elected Deputy to Third National Assembly, 1964; acting Minister of Public Health, 1968; elected Deputy to Fourth National Assembly, 1971. Promoted to Senior Colonel, 1955.

Cang, Chung Tan. Vice Admiral, Navy of the Republic of South Vietnam; Commander of Capital Military District and Governor of Saigon/Gia Dinh.

Cantarel, Emile Pierre Adrien Clement. General of the Army, French Army; Chief of Staff, Army, and Vice President, Senior War Councils, 1965-   . Born August 10, 1909, Fler-de-l'Orme, Orme. Served in France and North Africa in WW II; Indochina. Commander, 5th Armored Division, North Oran Zone, 1959-61; Commander, Senior War College, 1961-62; Commander, Oran Army Corps, 1962-63; Inspector General, Ground Forces, 1963-65. Légion d'Honneur; and other medals and awards. Promoted to General of the Army, 1964.

Cantlay, George Gordon. Major General, United States Army; Commanding General, 2d Armored Division, Fort Hood, Texas, 1971-   . Born August 2, 1920, Honolulu, Hawaii. US Military Academy; Armored School, Basic and Advanced Courses; US Army Command and General Staff College; US Army War College; George Washington University, MA Degree, International Affairs. Commissioned Second Lieutenant, 1943. WW II; Vietnam War. Assistant Division Commander, 1st Infantry Division, US Army, Pacific-Vietnam, 1968-69; Deputy Commanding General, Delta Military Assistance Command, US Military Assistance Command, Vietnam, 1969-70; Commanding General, US Army Training Center (Armor), Fort Knox, Kentucky, 1970; Deputy Commanding General, US Army Armor Center, Fort Knox, Kentucky, 1970-71. Distinguished Service Medal; Silver Star; Legion of Merit with two Oak Leaf Clusters; Distinguished Flying Cross with Oak Leaf Cluster; Bronze Star Medal with V Device and Oak Leaf Cluster; and other medals and awards. Promoted to Brigadier General, August 1, 1969; Major General, August 1, 1971.

Carcagno, Jorge Paul. General, Argentine Army; Commander in Chief, Argentine Army, 1973-   .

Cardenas Ramirez, Lucio. Brigadier General, Venezuelan Army; Commanding General, Venezuelan National Guard (Fuerzas Armadas de Cooperacion, FAC), 1969-   . Born October 29, 1915, in Capacho, Tachira State. Attended Infantry Course and Civil Guard Course, Madrid, Spain, 1950-51; Command and General Staff College, US Army School of the Americas, Canal Zone, 1959. Commissioned Second Lieutenant, National Guard, in 1945. Director, National Guard Enlisted Training School, 1962-64; Aide to the Commanding General, National Guard, 1964-65; Director General of Administration, National Guard, 1965-68; Chief of Staff, National Guard, 1968-69. Order of Liberator, Caballero grade; Order of Liberator, officer grade; Order of General Rafael Urdaneta, second and third class; Order of General Francisco de Miranda, second class; Cross of the National Guard, first and third class; and other medals and awards. Promotions: Colonel, July 5, 1965; Brigadier General, December 30, 1969.

Carlton, Paul K. General, United States Air Force; Commander, Military Airlift Command, Scott Air Force Base, Illinois, 1972-   . Born April 14, 1921, in Manchester, New Hampshire. University of Pittsburgh, 1939-40; Ohio University, 1940-41; Flying School, 1941-42; George Washington University, 1961; National War College, 1961-62. Commissioned Second Lieutenant, US Army Air Corps, 1942. Served in the China-Burma-India Theater, WW II. Commander, 305th Bombardment Wing, 1963-65; Chief, Single Integrated Operational Plans Division, Directorate of Operations, Strategic Air Command, 1965-67; Assistant Deputy Chief of Staff, Operations, Headquarters Strategic Air Command, 1967-68; Commander, 1st Strategic Aerospace Division, 1968-69; Deputy Chief of Staff, Operations, Headquarters Strategic Air Command, 1969; Commander, Fifteenth Air Force (SAC), 1969-72. Distinguished Service Medal; Silver Star; Legion of Merit with one Oak Leaf Cluster; Distinguished Flying Cross; and other medals and awards. Promotions: Brigadier General, June 1, 1965; Major General, November 1, 1967; Lieutenant General, August 1, 1969; General, October 9, 1972.

Carmody, Martin Doan. Rear Admiral, United States Navy; Commander Operational Test and Evaluation Force, and Assistant Director of Operational Test and Evaluation, Office of the CNO, 1971-   . Born October 27, 1917, in Indian Harbor, Indiana. San Jose State College (California), BA; Flight Training Course, 1941; General Line School, 1948-49. Commissioned Ensign, US Naval Reserve, in 1941; designated Naval Aviator in 1941; transferred to US Navy in 1944. Served in the Pacific Theater in WW II; Korean War; Vietnam War. Director, Air Planning Requirements Branch, Office of the CNO, 1962-63; Commanding Officer, USS *Zelima* (AF-49), 1963-65; Commanding Officer, USS *Kitty Hawk* (CVA-63), 1965-66; Project Manager, Reconnaissance Electronic Warfare Special Operations and Naval Intelligence Processing Systems Project, Naval Material Command, 1966-67; Director of the Electronic Warfare and Tactical Command Systems Division, Office of the CNO, 1967-69; Commander Carrier Division ONE, 1969-70. Legion of Merit with two Gold Stars; Distinguished Flying Cross with two Gold Stars; Bronze Star Medal with Combat "V"; Air Medal with eight Gold Stars; and other medals and awards. Promoted to Rear Admiral, June 1, 1968.

Carpenter, V.H.J. Major General, British Army; Transport Officer in Chief (Army), 1973.

Carr, Gerald Paul. Lieutenant Colonel, US Marine Corps; NASA Astronaut, 1966-   . Born Denver, Colorado, August 22, 1932. University of Southern California, BS, Mechanical Engineering, 1954; US Naval Postgraduate School, BS, Aeronautical Engineering, 1961; Princeton University, MS, Aeronautical Engineering, 1962; US Marine Corps Officers' Basic School. Commissioned Second Lieutenant, US Marine Corps, 1954. Marine All-Weather-Fighter Squadron 114; Marine All-Weather-Fighter Squadron 122, 1962-65. NASA experience: Member, Support Crew of Apollo 8 and 12; Commander, Skylab 4 mission. National Defense Service Medal; Armed Forces Expeditionary Medal; Marine Corps Expeditionary Medal; NASA Group Achievement Award.

Carr, William K. Major-General, Canadian Armed Forces; Chief of Air Operations, National Defence Headquarters, Ottawa, 1973-   . Born in March 1923 in Grand Banks, Newfoundland. Studied at Mount Allison University, Sackville, New Brunswick; Institute of Technology, Rochester, New York (USA); Royal Canadian Air Force Staff College, Toronto, 1953; National Defence College, Kingston, Ontario, 1964. Commissioned in the Royal Canadian Air Force, 1941. Combat duty in WW II. Director General, Canadian Air Forces, Canadian Forces Headquarters, Ottawa, 1966-68; Director General, Forces Objectives, Canadian Forces Headquarters, Ottawa, 1968; Commander, Canadian Forces Training Command, Winnipeg, 1968-72; Deputy Chief of Staff, Operations, Headquarters, North American Air Defence Command, Ent Air Force Base, Colorado, 1972-73. Distinguished Flying Cross; and other medals and awards. Promoted to Major-General, September 1968.

Carrasco Riveros, José. Brigadier General, Bolivian Air Force; Chief of Delegation, Inter-American Defense Board. Date of Rank: December 31, 1968.

Carroll, Derek Raymond. Major-General, British Army; Chief Engineer, British Army of the Rhine, 1970-   . Born January 2, 1919. Studied at Royal Institute of British Architects, 1936-39; Staff College, 1945; Imperial Defence College, 1968. Enlisted in the Territorial Army, 1939. Commissioned in the Royal Engineers, 1943. Served in the Western Desert and Italy in WW II. Commander Royal Engineers 4 Division, 1962-64; Malaya, 1965-66; Commander, 12 Engineer Brigade, 1966-67; Ministry of Defence, 1969-70. OBE.

Carson, Charles William, Jr. Major General, United States Air Force; Commander, Alaskan Air Command, 1973- . Born September 13, 1921, in Coalgate, Oklahoma. US Military Academy, 1939-43; Specialized Pilot Training Course, 1943; Air Force Institute of Technology, 1947-49, BA equivalent, Industrial Engineering, 1947. Commissioned Second Lieutenant, US Army Air Corps, 1943. Served in the European Theater, WW II; Vietnam War. Assistant to the Commander, Ninth Air Force, 1966; Commander, 833d Air Division, Tactical Air Command, 1966-68; Chief, Air Force Advisory Group, US Military Assistance Command, Vietnam, 1968-69; Commander, US Air Force Recruiting Service, 1969-70; Deputy Chief of Staff for Technical Training, Headquarters Air Training Command, 1970-71; Commander, Air Training Command's Lackland Military Training Center, 1971-73. Distinguished Service Medal; Legion of Merit; Distinguished Flying Cross; and other US and foreign medals and awards. Promoted to Major General, February 24, 1970.

Carvajal Prado, Patricio. Minister of Defense, Chile, 1973.

Carver, Sir (Richard) Michael (Power). General, British Army; Chief of the General Staff, 1971- . Born April 24, 1915. Attended Winchester College; Royal Military Academy, Sandhurst; Joint Services Staff College. Commissioned Second Lieutenant, Royal Tank Corps, 1935. Served in armored units in WW II. General Officer Commanding 3d Division, 1962-64; Commander, Joint Truce Force, Cyprus, and Deputy Commander, United Nations Force, Cyprus, 1964; Director, Army Staff Duties, Ministry of Defence, 1964-66; Commander, Far East Land Forces, 1966-67; Commander in Chief, Far East, 1967-69; General Officer Commanding-in-Chief, Southern Command, 1969-71. GCB, CBE, DSO and Bar, MC. Promotions: Major General, 1962; Lieutenant General, 1966; General, 1967. Publications: *Second to None*, 1954; *El Alamein*, 1962; *Tobruk*, 1964.

Cary, Freeman Hamilton. Rear Admiral, Medical Corps, United States Naval Reserve; Attending Physician at US Capitol, and Staff Member, National Naval Medical Center, Bethesda, Maryland, 1973- . Born September 14, 1926, in LaGrange, Georgia, Georgia Institute of Technology, Atlanta, Georgia, 1943-45; Emory University, Atlanta, BS, 1946, MD, 1950. Commissioned Lieutenant, Medical Corps, US Naval Reserve in 1954; inactive from 1958-1971. Senior Assistant to the Attending Physician at the US Capitol, 1971-73. National Defense Service Medal; Fellow of the American College of Physicians, the American Heart Association's Council of Clinical Cardiology, and of the American College of Chest Physicians. Promoted to Rear Admiral, January 3, 1973.

Casey, Maurice F. Major General, United States Air Force; Deputy Director, J-4, Office, Joint Chiefs of Staff,

1973- . Born June 3, 1920, in Chicago, Illinois. University of Chicago, Illinois; University of Miami, Florida; Army Air Corps Flying School, 1942-43; Air Command and Staff School, 1948; National War College, 1961-62. Commissioned Second Lieutenant, US Army Air Corps, 1943. Served in the European Theater, WW II; Korean War. Deputy Director of Information, Office of the Secretary of the Air Force, 1962-65; Commander, 60th Military Airlift Wing, 1965-68; Director, Transportation, Deputy Chief of Staff, Systems and Logistics, Headquarters USAF, 1968-73. Legion of Merit with three Oak Leaf Clusters; Distinguished Flying Cross with two Oak Leaf Clusters; Bronze Star Medal; and other US and foreign medals and awards. Promoted to Major General, February 20, 1970.

Cassell, George Louis. Rear Admiral, United States Navy; Commander Fleet Air, Quonset, and Commander Hunter-Killer Force, US Atlantic Fleet, 1972- . Born June 3, 1918, Dallas, Texas. Texas Agricultural and Mechanical University; Southern Methodist University, Dallas, BBA, 1941; Flight Training Course, 1941-42; General Line School, 1948-49; Armed Forces Staff College, 1955-56. Commissioned Ensign, US Naval Reserve, 1942; designated Naval Aviator, 1942; transferred to US Navy, 1945. Served in the Pacific Theater in WW II; Korean War; Vietnam War. Commanding Officer USS *Nitro* (AE-23), 1963-65; Commanding Officer USS *Coral Sea* (CVA-43), 1965-66; Assistant Chief of Staff for Operations, Commander in Chief, US Pacific Fleet, 1966-68; Deputy Commander, Naval Striking and Support Forces, Southern Europe, 1968-71; Commander Antisubmarine Warfare Group TWO, 1971-72; Commander Antisubmarine Warfare Group FOUR, 1972. Legion of Merit with two Gold Stars and Combat "V"; Distinguished Flying Cross; and other US and foreign medals and awards. Promoted to Rear Admiral, July 1, 1969.

Cassidy, Patrick Francis. Lieutenant General, United States Army; Commanding General, Fifth United States Army, Fort Sam Houston, Texas, 1971- . Born March 22, 1915, Pendleton, Oregon. University of Oregon, BS Degree, Business Administration; U.S. Army Command and General Staff College; U.S. Army War College. Commissioned Second Lieutenant, U.S. Army Reserve, 1937. WW II. Chief of Staff, VII Corps, U.S. Army, Europe, 1964-66; Commanding General, 8th Infantry Division, U.S. Army Europe, 1966-68; Chief, Office of Personnel Operations, U.S. Army, Washington, D.C., 1968-69; Commanding General, I Corps (Group), U.S. Army, Pacific-Korea, 1969-70; Deputy Commanding General, Eighth U.S. Army, U.S. Army, Pacific-Korea, 1970-71. Distinguished Service Cross; Distinguished Service Medal; Silver Star; Legion of Merit with Oak Leaf Cluster; Bronze Star Medal with Oak Leaf Cluster, and other medals and awards. Promoted to Brigadier General, November 11, 1962; Major General, March 1, 1966; Lieutenant General, August 29, 1969.

Cassidy, Richard Thomas. Lieutenant General, United States Army; Commanding General, US Army Air Defense Command, Ent Air Force Base, Colorado, 1971-   . Born August 16, 1916, Camp Keathley, Philippine Islands. US Military Academy; The Antiaircraft Artillery School, Advanced Course; US Army Command and General Staff College; US Army War College. Commissioned Second Lieutenant, US Army, 1940. WW II. Commanding General, 4th Region, US Army Air Defense Command, Richards-Gebaur Air Force Base, Missouri, 1963; Commanding General, 32d Artillery Brigade (Air Defense), US Army, Europe, 1963-66; Commanding General, 2d Region, US Army Air Defense Command, Richards-Gebaur Air Force Base, Missouri, 1966; Director, Air Defense, Office, Assistant Chief of Staff for Force Development, US Army, Washington, D.C., 1966-68; Commanding General, US Army Air Defense Center, and Commandant, US Army Air Defense School, Fort Bliss, Texas, 1968-71. Legion of Merit; Bronze Star Medal; and other medals and awards. Promoted to Brigadier General, April 8, 1963; Major General, September 1, 1966; Lieutenant General, April 27, 1971.

Castañon de Mena, Don Juan. Lieutenant General, Army of Spain; Minister of the Army, 1969-   . Geographical Engineer; Doctor of Architecture; attended General Staff Course in Senior War College. Professor, General Staff School, 1946-51; Aide de Camp to the Chief of State and Generalissimo of the Armed Forces, 1951-62; Brigadier General of the General Staff; Professor of the Army Senior School, 1959-62; Military Governor General of Madrid, 1962-63; Commanding General of the 11th Infantry Division, "Guadarrama," 1963-65; Chief of the Military Household of the Chief of State and Generalissimo of the Armed Forces, 1965-69. Cruz, Placa y Gran Cruz de la Real y Militar Orden de San Hermenegildo; Cruz de la Orden Militar de tercera clase con distintivo blanco; Gran Cruz de la Orden del Mérito Militar con distintivo blanco; Gran Cruz del Mérito Naval con distintivo blanco; Gran Placa de Honor y Mérito de la Cruz Roja Española; Gran Cruz de la Orden del Mérito Civil; Gran Cruz de Isabel la Catolica; Cross of the Order of the Eagle (German); Grand Cross of the Order of Boyacá (Colombia); Grand Cross of the Peruvian Order; Legion of Merit (USA); Cross of the Ground Forces of Venezuela.

Castles, Bryan J. Rear Admiral, Royal Australian Navy; formerly Third Naval Member and Chief of Naval Technical Services.

Castro Ruz, Raul. Major, Cuban Army; First Vice Premier and Minister of the Armed Forces, Cuba, 1960-   . With brother, Fidel Castro, planned and executed insurrection in Cuba, 1958-59; Chief of the Armed Forces, 1959-60.

Catledge, Richard C. Major General, United States Air Force; Commander, US Air Force Tactical Air Warfare Center, 1971-   . Born in Shawnee, Oklahoma. Army Air Corps Flying School, 1942-43; Naval War College, 1959-60. Commissioned Second Lieutenant, US Army Air Corps, 1943. Served in the Mediterranean Theater, WW II; Vietnam War. Commander, 3d Tactical Fighter Wing, Vietnam, 1966-67; Wing Commander, Luke Air Force Base, Arizona, 1967-69; Inspector General, Tactical Air Command, 1969-70; Deputy Chief of Staff, Requirements, 1970. Legion of Merit with one Oak Leaf Cluster; Distinguished Flying Cross; and other medals and awards. Promoted to Major General, August 1, 1971.

Cattanach, Helen. Brigadier, British Army; Matron-in-Chief, Queen Alexandra's Royal Army Nursing Corps, 1973-   . Born June 21, 1920. Trained at Woodland Hospital, Aberdeen. Served in hospitals in Hong Kong and UK, 1963-64; Matron, British Military Hospital, Munster, 1968; Cambridge Military Hospital, Aldershot, 1969-71; Director of Studies, Queen Alexandra's Royal Army Nursing Corps, 1971-72. RRC.

Catton, Jack J. General, United States Air Force; Commander, Air Force Logistics Command, Wright-Patterson Air Force Base, Ohio, 1972-   . Born February 5, 1920, Berkeley, California. Santa Monica Junior College, 1937-39; Loyola University Law School, Los Angeles, California, 1939-40; Pilot Training Course, 1940-41; Commander's Class, Air Force Manpower Management Training Program, George Washington University, 1952. Commissioned Second Lieutenant, US Army Air Corps, 1941. Served in the Pacific Theater, WW II; Korean War. Commander 817th Air Division, Pease Air Force Base, New Hampshire, 1959-61; Commander 822d Air Division, Turner Air Force Base, Georgia, 1961-62; Commander, 823d Air Division, Homestead Air Force Base, Florida, 1962-63; Commander, 821st Strategic Aerospace Division, Ellsworth Air Force Base, South Dakota, 1963-64; Director, Operational Requirements and Development Plans, Deputy Chief of Staff, Research and Development, 1964-66; Director, Aerospace Programs, Deputy Chief of Staff, Programs and Resources, Headquarters USAF, 1966-67; Deputy Chief of Staff, Programs and Resources, Headquarters USAF, 1967-68; Commander, Fifteenth Air Force, 1968-69; Commander, Military Airlift Command, 1969-72. Distinguished Service Medal with one Oak Leaf Cluster; Legion of Merit with one Oak Leaf Cluster; Distinguished Flying Cross with one Oak Leaf Cluster; and other medals and awards. Promotions: Brigadier General, August 1, 1959; Major General, May 16, 1963; Lieutenant General, August 1, 1967; General, August 1, 1969.

Cepicky, Josef. Major General, Army of Czechoslovakia; Chief of Staff, Western Military District 1969-   . Born c. 1920 in Pilsen. Attended military-political school, Bohosudov, 1950-51; Klement Gottwald Military Political Academy, 1953-55; Voroshilov General Staff College, Moscow, 1961-63. Joined Czechoslovak Army, 1949. Member of division staff in Eastern Military District in Slovakia, 1955-61, Staff of Directorate of Induction and Security, Central Committee, Czechoslovak Communist

Party, 1961; Chief of Staff, Eastern Military District, 1965-66; Assistant to Chief, Main Political Directorate, Ministry of National Defense, 1966-67; Assistant to Chief of General Staff, Ministry of National Defense, 1968; Member of Staff of Minister of Defense, 1968-69. Member, Czechoslovak Communist Party. Promoted to Major General, 1966.

Cernan, Eugene A. Captain, US Navy; NASA Astronaut, 1963-   . Born Chicago, Illinois, March 14, 1934. Purdue University, BS, Electrical Engineering; US Naval Postgraduate School, MS, Aeronautical Engineering. Commissioned Ensign, 1956. Served with Attack Squadrons 126 and 113. NASA Experience: Pilot, Gemini 9, 1966; Backup Pilot, Gemini 12; Backup Lunar Module Pilot, Apollo 7; Lunar Module Pilot, Apollo 19, May 18-26, 1969; Backup Spacecraft Command, Apollo 14; Spacecraft Commander, Apollo 17, December 6-19, 1972. NASA Distinguished Service Medal; NASA Exceptional Service Medal; Manned Spacecraft Center Superior Achievement Award; Navy Distinguished Service Medal; Navy Astronaut Wings; Navy Distinguished Flying Cross; National Academy of Television Arts and Sciences Special Trustees Award, 1969; Honorary Lifetime Membership in American Federation of Radio and Television Artists; Honorary LLD, Western State University College of Law, 1969; Honorary EngD, Purdue University, 1970.

Cha, Su-Kap. Rear Admiral, Navy of the Republic of Korea; Vice Chief of Naval Operations.

Chairsell, William S. Major General, United States Air Force; Commander, US Air Force Tactical Fighter Weapons Center. Born July 12, 1919, in Birmingham, Alabama. Virginia Polytechnical Institute, 1937-41, BS, Electrical Engineering, 1941; Army Air Corps Flying School, 1941-42; Air Command and Staff College, 1950; Industrial College of the Armed Forces, 1961-62; George Washington University, MA, Business Administration, 1963. Commissioned Second Lieutenant, US Army Air Corps, 1942. Served in the Vietnam War. Commander, 49th Tactical Fighter Wing, Germany, 1964-66; Commander, 388th Tactical Fighter Wing, Thailand, 1966; Vice Commander, Ninth Air Force, 1970. Distinguished Service Medal; Legion of Merit with one Oak Leaf Cluster; Distinguished Flying Cross with one Oak Leaf Cluster; and other US and foreign medals and awards. Promoted to Major General, February 24, 1970.

Chaloryoo, Sa-Ngad. Admiral, Royal Thai Navy. Deputy Commander in Chief, Royal Thai Navy.

Chamot Biggs, Jorge. Lieutenant General, Peruvian Air Force; Chief of Peruvian Delegation, Inter-American Defense Board. Date of Rank: January 1, 1970.

Chandrubeksa, Boonchoo. Air Chief Marshal, Royal Thai Air Force. Commander in Chief, Royal Thai Air Force.

Chang, Bong Chun. Brigadier General, Army of the Republic of Korea; Defense and Military Attache, Embassy of Korea, Washington, D.C.

Chang Kuo-ying. General, Army of Republic of China; Deputy Commander in Chief, Army, 1968-   . Born January 20, 1916, Anhwei. Central Military Academy; Army College; Institute of Revolutionary Reconstruction; Army Command and General Staff College; Command and General Staff College, USA; National War College; Armed Forces University. Participated in Sino-Japanese War; Chinese Civil War. Division Commander, 1949-55; Corps Commander, 1957-60; Commander, 2d Field Army, 1961-65; Deputy Minister, Ministry of National Defense, 1965-67; Deputy Chief of General Staff, 1967-68.

Chang Ta-chih. Lieutenant General, People's Liberation Army, People's Republic of China; Vice Chairman, Military Commission of the Chinese Communist Party Central Committee. Born in 1911, Feng-Hsiang Hsien, Shensi. Red Army Academy (student), 1936. Joined Communist guerrilla units, North Shensi, c. 1932; fought in the Sino-Japanese War and the Civil War. Political Commissar, Cavalry Unit, Inner Mongolia, 1942; Army Commander, Northwest China, 1950; Director, Public Security Department, Northwest Military and Administrative Committee, 1952-53; Member of National Defense Council, 1954; Commander, Lanchow Military Region, 1956-   ; Communist Party Member, c. 1932; Alternate Member of CCP Central Committee, 1956-69, Member, 1969; Member, Standing Committee, 1968; Leader, People's Liberation Army Forces in Kansu, 1963; Member of Kansu Revolutionary Committee, 1968-   . Member of Tenth CCP Central Committee, 1973; Member of the Presidium, Tenth National Party Congress, 1973. Decorations: Order of August First, 1st Class; Order of Independence and Freedom, 1st Class; Order of Liberation, 1st Class.

Chang T'i-hsueh. People's Republic of China; Political Commissar, Hupeh Military District, 1963-   . Fought in the Sino-Japanese War and the Civil War. Commander, Red 5th Battalion, 1938; Commander, 14th Brigade, 5th Division, New Fourth Army, Hupeh-Honan-Anhwei Military Region, c. 1944; Commander, East Hupeh Military District, and Commander, 2d Brigade, c. 1946 - c. 1949; First Deputy Secretary, Hupeh Provincial Committee, 1954-56, then Secretary of Secretariat and Party Secretary, 1956; Vice Governor, later Governor, Hupeh Province, 1955; Deputy to National People's Congress, 1954. Communist Party Member; Vice Chairman, Hupeh Revolutionary Committee, 1968; Member of Central Committee, 1969; Member of Tenth CCP Central Committee, 1973; Member of the Presidium, Tenth National Party Congress, 1973.

Chao Kwei-sun. Lieutenant General, Army of Republic of China; Deputy Secretary General, Planning Commission for Recovery of the Mainland, 1969-   . Born in 1912 in Kiangsu. Military Academy; Army War College; Armed Forces Staff College; Command and General Staff College,

USA. Served in Sino-Japanese War; Chinese Civil War. Highlights of career include Commander, 20th Division, 1943-44; Deputy Commanding General, 89th Army Corps, 1944-45; Member, United Nations Military Staff Committee, 1946; Chief of Staff, Combined Service Forces, 1946-48; Chief, Transportation Service, Combined Service Forces, 1948-49; Director, G-4, Ministry of National Defense, 1949-50; Personal Assistant to the President, 1951-55; Deputy Commander in Chief, Combined Service Forces, 1955-57; Strategic Adviser to the President, 1968-69. Publications: *An Analysis of the Communist International Strategy of Sovietization of the World; A Study of the Combined Service of Chinese Armed Forces.*

Chapman, Curtis Wheaton, Jr. Major General, United States Army; Deputy Commanding General, US Army, Combat Developments Command, Fort Belvoir, Virginia, 1971-   . Born August 30, 1918, Huntington, West Virginia. US Military Academy; The Engineer School, Basic Course; US Army Command and General Staff College; Industrial College of the Armed Forces; University of Hartford, BS Degree, Business Administration; California Institute of Technology, MS Degree, Civil Engineering. Commissioned Second Lieutenant, 1941. Served in WW II and in Vietnam War. Commanding General, 20th Engineer Brigade, US Army, Vietnam, 1967-68; Division Engineer, US Army Engineer Division, Pacific Ocean, Honolulu, Hawaii, 1968-70; Director of Military Engineering, Office, Chief of Engineers, US Army, Washington, D.C., 1970-71. Distinguished Service Medal; Silver Star; Legion of Merit with Oak Leaf Cluster; Bronze Star Medal; and other medals and awards. Promoted to Brigadier General, June 1, 1967; Major General, September 1, 1971.

Chapman, Kenneth R. Major General, United States Air Force; Deputy Chief of Staff, Development Plans, Air Force Systems Command, 1970-   . Born July 30, 1923, in Summerfield, Kansas. Kansas State University, Manhattan, Kansas, 1941-43; US Military Academy, 1943-46; Advanced Pilot Training, 1946; University of California, Berkeley, MS, Nuclear Chemistry, 1954; Armed Forces Staff College, 1963; Industrial College of the Armed Forces, 1965-66. Commissioned Second Lieutenant, US Army Air Corps, 1946. Deputy Branch Chief, Space Nuclear Auxiliary Power Program, Reactor Branch, Division of Reactor Developments, Atomic Energy Commission, 1963-65; Chief Nuclear Ordnance Group, then Deputy Director for Research and Development Analysis, and later Deputy Director for Requirements, Plans, and Analysis, Directorate of Operational Requirements and Development Plans, Office, Deputy Chief of Staff, US Air Force, 1966-70. Legion of Merit; Air Commendation Medal with two Oak Leaf Clusters; and other medals and awards. Promoted to Major General, September 1, 1972.

Charbonnet, Pierre Numa, Jr. Rear Admiral, United States Navy; Commander Fleet Air, Mediterranean, Commander Antisubmarine Warfare Force, Sixth Fleet, and Commander Maritime Air Forces, Mediterranean, 1971-   . Born December 22, 1919, in San Francisco, California. US Naval Academy, 1937-41; Flight Training Course, 1943-44; National War College, 1959-60; Harvard Graduate School of Business Administration, Advanced Management Program, 1963-64. Commissioned Ensign, US Navy, in 1941; designated Naval Aviator in 1944. Served in the Pacific Theater, WW II; Vietnam War. Commanding Officer, USS *Coral Sea*, 1964-65; Chief of Staff and Aide to Commander, Carrier Division Seven, and Commander Attack Carrier Striking Force, Seventh Fleet, 1965; Commandant, Eighth Naval District, 1965-68; Commander Carrier Division Six, 1968-69; Director, Fleet Operations Division, 1969-71. Legion of Merit with Gold Star; Distinguished Flying Cross with Gold Star; Air Medal with six Gold Stars; and other medals and awards. Promoted to Rear Admiral, November 30, 1965.

Charusathiara, Prapass. Field Marshal, Royal Thai Army, Air Chief Marshal, Admiral; Deputy Prime Minister, Minister of Interior, Acting Director-General of the Police, 1972-   ; Deputy Supreme Commander of the Armed Forces, 1964-   . Born December 5, 1912, in the Province of Udornthani, Thailand. Attended Chulachomklao Royal Military Academy, Royal Thai Army, 1929-33; National Defence College, 1956. Commissioned Second Lieutenant in 1933. Served in the Military Campaign in the Shan States, 1941. Commanding General, 1st Army Area, 1957-60; Assistant Commander in Chief, Royal Thai Army, 1960-63; Assistant Supreme Commander of the Armed Forces, 1963-64; Commander in Chief, Royal Thai Army, 1964. Minister of Interior, 1957, 1959; Deputy Prime Minister and concurrently Minister of Interior, 1958, 1963, 1969, 1972; Deputy Chairman, National Executive Council, 1971. Knight Grand Cross (First Class) of the Most Illustrious Order of Chula Chom Klao; Knight Grand Cross (Special Class) of the Most Exalted Order of the White Elephant; Knight Grand Cordon (Special Class) of the Most Noble Order of the Crown; Mahayothin (Second Class) of the Honorable Order of Rama; Ratanaporn (Second Class — Rama 9); Ratanaporn (Third Class — Rama 8); and numerous other medals and decorations, Thai and foreign. Promotions: Major General, 1952; Lieutenant General, 1957; General, 1959; Admiral, Air Chief Marshal, 1963.

Chase, Levi R. Major General, United States Air Force; Vice Commander, Ninth Air Force, Tactical Air Command, 1971-   . Born December 23, 1917, in Cortland, New York. Syracuse University, New York, 1937-40; Army Air Corps Flying School, 1941; Albany Law School, Albany, New York, 1946-49; Air War College, 1959-60. Commissioned Second Lieutenant, US Army Air Corps, 1941. Served in North Africa and the China-Burma-India Theater in WW II; Korean War; Vietnam War. Commander, 15th Tactical Fighter Wing, 1964-65; Commander, 12th Tactical Fighter Wing, Vietnam, 1965-66; Vice Commander, 313th Air Division, Okinawa, 1966-67; Commander, 327th Air Division, and Chief, Air Section, Military Assistance Advisory Group, China, Taiwan, 1967-69; Assistant Deputy Chief of Staff, Operations, Headquarters, Tactical Air Command, 1969-70; Deputy Chief of Staff, Personnel, Headquarters, Tactical Air

Command, 1970-71. Silver Star with two Oak Leaf Clusters; Legion of Merit with two Oak Leaf Clusters; Distinguished Flying Cross with five Oak Leaf Clusters; Bronze Star Medal; and other US and foreign medals and awards. Promoted to Major General, July 1, 1971.

Chasha, I. Major General, USSR Army; Military Commissar, Latvia. Served on the Soviet-German Front in WW II. Member, Communist Party of the Soviet Union.

Chaudhry, Zafar Ahmad. Air Marshal, Air Force of Pakistan; Chief of the Air Staff, 1972-   . Born August 19, 1926, in Sialkot, Pakistan. Attended Punjab University; RAF Staff College, Andover, United Kingdom; Joint Services Staff College, Latimer, United Kingdom; Imperial Defence College, United Kingdom. Commissioned in the Royal Indian Air Force in 1945. Commanded a Fighter Squadron, a Fighter/Bomber Wing, The Pakistan Air Force Academy, Pakistan Air Force Base at Sargodha. Director of Plans and Policy, and of Training and Operations, Air Headquarters; Assistant Chief of Air Staff (Operations), 1971. Decorations Sitara-i-Qaid-i-Azam, and other honors and awards. Promotions: Air Vice Marshal, 1971; Air Marshal, 1972.

Chazaro Lara, Ricardo. Rear Admiral Engineer, Mexican Navy; Under Secretary of the Navy.

Chen Chang-feng. Lieutenant General, People's Liberation Army, People's Republic of China; Commander, Kiangsi Military Region and Secretary, Kiangsi Provincial Party Committee, 1973-   . Member, Chinese Communist Party.

Chen Ching-kun. Vice Admiral, Navy of the Republic of China; Commander, Fleet Command.

Chen Ta-ching. General, Army of Republic of China; Minister of National Defense, 1972-   . Born October 8, 1905, Kiangsi. Whampoa Military Academy. Served in Sino-Japanese War; Chinese Civil War. Deputy Commander in Chief and later Commander in Chief, Army Group, 1941-46; Deputy Commander, 1st Pacification Area and Capital Garrison Command, 1946-48; Commander, Chuchow Pacification Command, 1948; Commander, Woosung-Shanghai Garrison Command, 1948-49; Deputy Director, National Security Bureau, 1954-59; Director, National Security Bureau, 1959-64; Commander in Chief, General Headquarters, Taiwan Garrison, 1962-67; and concurrently, Commander, Taiwan Corps Control Area, 1964-67; Commander in Chief, Chinese Army, 1967-69; Governor, Taiwan Provincial Government, 1969-72; Member, Central Committee, Kuomintang. Author of *To Be Good and To Do Good.*

Chen I-fan. General, Air Force of Republic of China; Commander in Chief, Chinese Air Force, 1970-   . Born October 18, 1914, Liaoning. Air Force Academy; Air Command and Staff College; Senior Course, Yuanshan Officer's Corps; Shih Chien Institute, Joint Operations Course; Amphibious Warfare Training Course, US Navy; US Manpower Management Course; Armed Forces War College.

Served in Sino-Japanese War; Chinese Civil War. Career: Commander, 1st Bombardment Group, 1945-52; Chief, Combat Intelligence Branch, A-2, Chinese Air Force, 1952-53; Military Attache, Chinese Embassy, Manila, Republic of the Philippines, 1953-55; Chief of Staff, Air Training Command, 1957-58; Assistant Deputy Chief of Staff, Operations, Headquarters, Chinese Air Force, 1958-61; Assistant Deputy Chief of the General Staff, Planning, Ministry of National Defense, 1961-63; Deputy Chief of Staff, Personnel, Headquarters, Chinese Air Force, 1964; Director, Manpower Department, Ministry of National Defense, 1964-67; Chief of Staff, Chinese Air Force, 1967-69; Commanding General, Combat Air Commander, 1969-70

Ch'en Hsi-lien. General, People's Liberation Army, People's Republic of China; Commander, Shenyang Military Region, 1959-   . Born in 1913 in Huangan, Hupeh. Attended Red Army Academy, Yenan, 1931. Joined the Communist forces in Hupeh-Honan-Anhwei Area in the late 1920's; Fought in the Sino-Japanese War, the Civil War and the Korean War; took part in the Long March. Commander, Company to Division, 1933-35; Commander, 769th Regiment, 129th Division, Eighth Route Army, 1937 - c. 1939; Commander of Brigade, 129th Division, c. 1939 - c. 1944; Commander of Column (combat group), 129th Division, Shansi-Hopeh-Shantung-Honan Military Region, c. 1944 - c. 1945; Commander, Third Column, Central Plains People's Liberation Army, and the West Anhwei Military District, c. 1946 - c. 1948; Commander, Third Army Corps, Second Field Army, Central-South China and later Southwest China, c. 1948-49; Vice Chairman, Chungking Military Control Commission, and Mayor of Chungking, 1949-51; Member of Southwest Military and Administrative Committee, 1950-56; Commander, Artillery Forces, People's Liberation Army, 1951-59; Member of National Defense Council, 1954; Deputy to National People's Congress, 1954-59; Communist Party Member, c. 1930; Alternate Member of CCP Central Committee, 1956-63, Member, 1963-   ; Secretary, Northeast Party Bureau, Shenyang, 1961-   ; Chairman, Liaoning Revolutionary Committee, 1968; First Secretary, Provincial Party Committee, 1971; Member of Politburo, 1969; Member of Tenth CCP Central Committee, 1973; Member of the Presidium, Tenth National Party Congress, 1973.

Ch'en Jen Chi. Lieutenant General, People's Liberation Army, People's Republic of China; Political Commissar, Headquarters, Artillery Force, 1961-   . Participated in anti-Japanese guerrilla warfare, 1937-45; fought in the Civil War. Political Commissar, People's Liberation Army, Hainan Military District, 1954; Chief, Political Department, Canton Military Region, 1955; Member of Chinese Communist Party; Alternate Member of Central Committee, 1969. Order of August 1.

Ch'en K'ang. Lieutenant General, People's Liberation Army, People's Republic of China; Vice Chairman, Yunnan Provincial Revolutionary Committee, 1968-   . Participated in anti-Japanese guerrilla warfare, 1937-45; and the Civil War. Head, Kunming Military Region, 1956;

Deputy Commander, Yunnan Military District, 1957-59; Deputy Commander, Kunming Military Region, 1959; Member of Chinese Communist Party; Member of Central Committee, 1969; Member of Tenth CCP Central Committee, 1973. Order of August 1; Order of Liberation.

Ch'en Shih-ch'u. Colonel General, People's Liberation Army, People's Republic of China; Commander, Engineer Corps, People's Liberation Army, 1952-   . Born in 1909, Ching-Men hsien, Hupeh. Attended Anti-Japanese Military and Political Academy, 1937. Served in the Sino-Japanese War and the Civil War; took part in the Long March. Joined the Red Army in 1927. Battalion Commander, Kiangsi, c. 1932 - c. 1934; Commander, Special Training Battalion, First Army Corps, c. 1934 - c. 1936; Chief of Staff, 343d Brigade, 115th Division, 8th Route Army, 1937 - c. 1940; Chief of Staff, 115th Division, Commission, 1949 - c. 1952; Member, East China Military Military Region, c. 1944-46; Chief of Staff, New Fourth Army and Shantung Military District, 1946-47; Member of the Communist Mission at the Executive Headquarters, Peking, to supervise the truce between Nationalists and Communists; Chief of Staff, East China People's Liberation Army (later known as Third Field Army), and Commander of 11th Army Corps, 1947-49; Commander, Nanking Garrison, and Member of Nanking Military Control Commission, 1949 c. 1952; Member, East China Military and Administrative Council, 1950-52; Member, National Defense Council, 1954; Deputy to the National People's Congress, 1954; Communist Party Member, c. 1927; Member of Central Committee, 1969; Member of Tenth CCP Central Committee, 1973. Order of Independence and Freedom, 1st Class; Order of Liberation, 1st Class.

Ch'en Tsai-tao. Lieutenant General, People's Liberation Army, People's Republic of China; Commander, Foochow Military Region, 1973-   . Formerly Commander, Wuhan Military Region. Member, Chinese Communist Party.

Cheney, James Spiers. Major General, United States Air Force; The Judge Advocate General, US Air Force, 1969-   . Born August 13, 1918, Tucson, Arizona. Young L.G. Harris Junior College, Georgia, 1938-39; Atlanta Law School, 1939-40, LLB, 1950; Army Air Corps Flying School, 1941-42. Commissioned Second Lieutenant, US Army Air Corps, 1942. Served in the Euopean Theater, WW II; Korean War. Deputy Staff Judge Advocate, US Air Forces, Europe, 1962-64; Director, Military Justice, Office, Judge Advocate General, Headquarters, USAF, 1964-67; Staff Judge Advocate, Headquarters Pacific Air Forces, Hawaii, 1967-69; Assistant Judge Advocate General, USAF, 1969. Legion of Merit with two Oak Leaf Clusters; Distinguished Flying Cross; and other US and foreign medals and awards. Promoted to Major General, September 30, 1969.

Ch'eng Shih-ch'ing. Major General, People's Liberation Army, People's Republic of China; First Political Commissar, Kiangsi Military District, 1967-   , Chairman, Kiangsi Provincial Revolutionary Committee, 1968-   . Born in 1918, Kuochiaho, China. Participated in

anti-Japanese guerrilla warfare, 1937-45; Civil War. Chief, Political Division, Headquarters, People's Liberation Army, 1961; Political Commissar, Yentai Army, Tsinan Forces, 1965-67; Deputy Political Commissar, Fuchow, Military Region, 1967. Member of Chinese Communist Party; Communist Youth League, 1932; First Secretary, Provincial Party Committee, 1970; Member of Central Committee, 1969. Order of August 1.

Cheng Wei-shan. Lieutenant General, People's Liberation Army, People's Republic of China; Commander, Peking Military Region, 1968-   , and Member of Municipal Committee, 1967-   . Born in 1914, in Macheng, Hupeh. Studied at Red Army Military Academy. Joined the Chinese Red Army, 1935. Participated in anti-Japanese guerrilla warfare, 1937-45, and the Civil War. Deputy Commander, Peking-Tientsin Garrison, 1955; Commander, People's Liberation Army Units, Peking Area, 1959. Member of Chinese Communist Party since 1932; Deputy to the National Congress. Order of August 1; Order of Liberation.

Cheng Wei-yuan. General, Army of Republic of China; Commander in Chief, Combined Service Forces, 1972-   . Born 1913 in Anhwei. Military Academy, 1930-33; Infantry School, Italy, 1938-39; Light Infantry School, Italy, 1939; Armed Forces Staff College, 1953; Command and Staff College, USA, 1957. Served in Sino-Japanese War and Chinese Civil War. Military Attache, Chinese Embassy, Rome, Italy, 1947-49; Commanding General, Infantry Division, 1953-54; Chief of Staff, Field Army, 1954-55; Commanding General, Army Corps, 1955-57; G-3 and G-1, Ministry of National Defense, 1957-59; Chief of Staff of Army of Republic of China, 1958-60; Commandant, Marine Corps, 1961-64; Commanding General, 1st Field Army, 1964-66; Vice Chief of the General Staff, Ministry of National Defense, 1966-67; Deputy Commander in Chief, Chinese Army, 1967-69; Vice Chief of the General Staff, Ministry of National Defense, 1969-72.

Chernobay, G. K. Vice Admiral, USSR Navy; Commander, Caspian Flotilla, 1969-   . Served in the Soviet-German War, 1941-45. Formerly Chief of Staff, Black Sea Fleet. Member, Communist Party of the Soviet Union.

Chiang Kai-shek (Chiang Chung-cheng). Generalissimo, Armed Forces of Republic of China; President, Republic of China, and Commander in Chief, Armed Forces. Born October 31, 1887, Fenghua, Chekiang Province. Military education: National Military Academy, Paoting, China; Military Academy, Tokyo, Japan. Joined Chinese Revolutionary Army, 1911. Sino-Japanese War: Supreme Commander, Allied Forces, China Theater, WW II; Chinese Civil War. Earlier career: Staff, General Headquarters, Canton, 1917-20; Founder and Commandant, Whampoa Military Academy, Canton, 1924; Commander in Chief, Northward Expeditionary Forces, 1926; Chairman, State Council, and Generalissimo of Chinese Armed Forces, 1928-   ; Chairman, National Military Affairs Council, 1932-46; Director General, Kuomintang Party, Republic of

China, 1938-   . Author of *China's Destiny*, 1943; *Collected Wartime Messages of Generalissimo Chiang Kai-shek; Soviet Russia in China*, 1957.

Chiang Wego Wei-kuo. Lieutenant General, Army of Republic of China; Commandant, War College, Armed Forces University, and concurrently, Deputy Commanding General, Armed Forces University, 1969-   . Born October 6, 1916, Shanghai. Education and training: College of Science, Soochow University; Military Academy, Munich, Germany, 1937-39; US Army Air Corps Tactical School, Maxwell Field, Alabama, USA, 1939-40; Armor School, Chinese Army, Ramgar, India; Command and General Staff College, Fort Leavenworth, Kansas, USA, 1953-55; US Army Air Defense School, Fort Bliss, USA, 1959; Advanced Course, Yuanshan Officers Training Course; National War College. Service in Sino-Japanese War; Chinese Civil War. Executive Officer and Commander, 1st Tank Regiment, 1945-48; Chief of Staff and then Commanding General, Armor Command, 1948-50; Commanding General, Armored Forces, Taiwan, 1950-53; Deputy Director, later Director, G-3, Operations, Ministry of National Defense, 1955-58; Commanding General, Armored Forces, General Headquarters, Chinese Army, 1958-63; Commandant, Chinese Army Command and General Staff College, 1963-68; Vice Commandant, Armed Forces War College, 1968-69.

Chiappe Posse, Hugo. General, Uruguayan Army; Commander in Chief, Uruguayan Army.

Chiem, Vu Xuan. Senior Colonel, People's Army of Vietnam; Deputy Chief, General Directorate of Rear Services, People's Army of Vietnam, 1963-   ; elected Deputy to Fourth National Assembly, 1971; Member, National Assembly National Reunification Committee, 1971. Promoted to Senior Colonel, 1963.

Ch'in Chi-wei. Lieutenant General, People's Liberation Army, People's Republic of China; Commander, Chengtu Military Region, 1973-   . Born Hungan, Hupei Province, 1911. Participated in anti-Japanese guerrilla warfare, 1937-45 and Civil War; took part in the Long March. Member of guerrilla force which was later incorporated into 31st Division, Worker's and Peasant's Red Army, 1927-31; Commander, 2d Company, Pistol Battalion, 4th Front Army, 1931; Section Chief, 4th Bureau, Headquarters Forces, 4th Front Army, 1936; Staff Officer, 129th Division, 8th Route Army, 1937; Commander, 9th Column, Shansi-Hopei-Shantung-Honan Military Area, 1948; Commander, 15th Army, 4th Army Corps, 2d Field Army, 1949; Deputy Commander, Yunnan Military District, People's Liberation Army, 1954; Member, Yunnan Provincial People's Council, 1955; Deputy Commander, Kunming Military Region, People's Liberation Army, 1955-58; Commander, Kunming Military Region, People's Liberation Army, 1957-67; Member, National Defense Council, 1965; Member of Tenth CCP Central Committee, 1973; Member of the Presidium, Tenth National Party Congress, 1973. Promoted to Lieutenant General, September 1955.

Ch'iu Hui-tso. Lieutenant General, People's Liberation Army, People's Republic of China; Deputy Chief of Staff, People's Liberation Army, 1969-   . Participated in anti-Japanese guerrilla warfare, 1937-45, and the Civil War. Director, Political Department, Honan Military District, 1949; Council Member, Kwangsi Provincial People's Government, 1950-52; Deputy Director, Political Department, South China Military Area, 1952-54, Deputy Political Commissar, and Director of Political Department, Kwangtung Military District, 1953-54; Director-General, Rear Service Department, 1959; Member of National Defense Council, 1965; Member, Chinese Communist Party; Member, Central Committee, 1969; whereabouts since September 1971 unknown. Order of Liberation, 1st Class; and other medals and awards. Promoted to Lieutenant General, 1955.

Chizh, V. F. Colonel General, USSR Army; Staff, Civil Defense. Served on the Soviet-German Front in WW II. First Deputy Commander, Kiev Military District, 1963. Member, Communist Party of the Soviet Union.

Chocha, Boleslaw. Lieutenant General, Polish Army; Chief of General Staff, and Deputy Minister of National Defense, 1968-   . Born August 6, 1923, Grodno, Poland (now USSR). Attended Officers School, 1943; Higher Officers School, Ryazan, USSR, 1944; General Staff War College, Warsaw, 1948-51. Commissioned Second Lieutenant, Polish Army, 1943. In Polish-German War, 1943-45, served with 1st Polish Army in the USSR. Formerly Instructor, General Staff War College, Warsaw; Deputy Chief, General Tactics and Operational Science Department, General Staff War College, Warsaw; Commander, 6th Airborne Division; Deputy Chief of General Staff, 1965-68. Decorations include Polonia Restituta, Cross of Grunwald, and Cross of Valor. Member, Polish United Workers Party and its Central Committee.

Choi, Hyon. General, Democratic People's Republic of Korea, Army; Minister of National Defense.

Chon, Tran Van. Rear Admiral, Navy of the Republic of South Vietnam; Commander in Chief, Vietnamese Navy, and Chief of Naval Operations.

Christman, Thomas Jackson. Rear Admiral, United States Navy; Vice Commander, Naval Ordnance Systems Command, 1971-   . Born March 6, 1922, in Seattle, Washington. University of Florida, Gainesville, 1939-40; US Naval Academy, 1940-43; Naval Postgraduate School, Physics Electronics Course, 1947-48; Massachusetts Institute of Technology, MS, Electrical Engineering, 1948-50, MS, Industrial Management, 1958-59. Commissioned Ensign, US Navy, 1943. Served in the Pacific Theater in WW II. Head, Missile Branch, and Deputy Director, Technical Division, Special Projects Office, 1962-67; Commander, Naval Ammunition Depot, Crane, Indiana, 1967-68; Deputy Commander for Plans and Resources, Naval Ordnance Systems Command, 1968-70; Deputy Commander for Logistics Support, Naval Ordnance

Systems Command, 1970-71. Various medals and citations. Promoted to Rear Admiral, July 1, 1969.

Chung Han-hua. Lieutenant General, People's Liberation Army, People's Republic of China; Commander, Canton Military Region. Formerly Political Commissar, Wuhan Military Region. Member of Chinese Communist Party.

Chursin, Serafim Evgenevich. Admiral, USSR Navy; Professor, Naval War College, 1968-   . Born January 9, 1906, in Voronezh. Studied at Naval Academy; Frunze Higher Naval School; General Staff College. Commissioned in 1927. Duty in submarines in WW II. Formerly Commander, Danube Flotilla; Commander, Caspian Sea Flotilla; Chief of Staff, then Deputy Fleet Commander; First Deputy Fleet Commander; Commander, Black Sea Fleet, 1962-68; Deputy to the USSR Supreme Soviet; Member, Communist Party of the Soviet Union, since 1929. Order of Lenin; Order of Red Banner; Order of Red Star; and other medals and awards.

Christe, Robert. Major General, Swiss Army; Commanding General, 2d Border Division. Born in 1917.

Ciarlini, Giannetto. Brigadier General, Italian Air Force; Defense and Air Attache, Embassy of Italy, Washington, D.C.

Cieslik, Jan. Major General, Polish Army; Deputy Commanding General for Political Affairs, Air Defense Forces. Born in 1925. Attended Political Officers Military School, Lodz, 1945; Military-Political College. Commissioned Second Lieutenant, Polish Army, 1945. Participated in anti-German guerrilla operations in Poland, 1942-45. Secretary, Polish United Workers Party, at the Main Political Directorate, Polish Armed Forces, 1964-66; Deputy, and later Secretary, Polish United Workers Committee, Ministry of National Defense. Member of Polish United Workers Party. Virtuti Militari; Polonia Restituta; the Partisan Cross; Cross of Grunwald; and other orders and medals. Promoted to Major General, 1970.

Cincar, Jozef. Lieutenant General, Army of Czechoslovakia; Chief of Air and Air Defense Forces, and Deputy Minister of National Defense, 1969-   . Born November 14, 1921, in Topolany, Slovakia. Attended Zhukovskiy Military Air Engineering Academy, Moscow, 1946-49; Czechoslovak military college, 1950-55; Voroshilov General Staff College, Moscow, 1960-65. Served in 1st Czechoslovak Army Corps, then as aircraft gunner, and with the 3d Air Force Regiment, 1st Czechoslovak Combined Division, WW II. Member, Staff of Air Defense Department, Ministry of National Defense, 1958-60; Chief of the Military Office, Czechoslovak Government Presidium, 1968-69. Member of Czechoslovak Communist Party, 1946-   .

Clancy, Albert Harrison, Jr. Rear Admiral, United States Navy; Force Material Officer, Staff, Commander Naval Air Force, US Pacific Fleet, 1972-   . Born August 2, 1919, in Santa Fe, New Mexico. University of New Mexico; US

Naval Academy, 1936-40; Flight Training Course, 1942-43; Naval Postgraduate School, Annapolis, 1946-47; California Institute of Technology, MS, Aeronautical Engineering, 1947-49. Commissioned Ensign, US Navy, in 1940; designated Naval Aviator, in 1943. Served in the Pacific Theater in WW II. Commander, Naval Air Engineering Center, 1965-67; Navy Deputy, F-111 System Program Director, US Air Force Aerospace System Division, 1967-68; Program Manager of the Reconnaissance, Electronic Warfare, Special Operations and Naval Intelligence Processing Systems Project Office, 1968-71; Assistant Commander for Material Acquisition, Naval Air Systems Command Headquarters, 1971-72. Legion of Merit; Distinguished Flying Cross with Gold Star; Air Medal with six Gold Stars; and other medals and awards. Promoted to Rear Admiral, November 1, 1967.

Clarey, Bernard Ambrose. Admiral, United States Navy; Commander in Chief, US Pacific Fleet, with additional duty as Naval Component Commander, US Pacific Command, 1970-   Born May 4, 1912, in Oskaloosa, Iowa. William Penn College, Oskaloosa, Iowa, 1929-30; US Naval Academy, 1930-34; Submarine School, 1937; National War College, 1955-56. Commissioned Ensign, US Navy, in 1934. Served in the Pacific Theater, WW II; Korean War. Chief of Staff and Aide to Commander Submarine Force, Pacific Fleet, 1956-58; Command Officer USS Hassayampa (AO-145), 1958; Director, Military Personnel Policy Division, 1959-61; Director for Military Personnel, Office of the Assistant Secretary of Defense (Manpower), 1961-62; Commander Submarine Force, Pacific Fleet, 1962-64; Deputy Commander and Chief of Staff and Aide to Commander in Chief, Pacific Fleet, 1964-66; Commander Second Fleet, 1966-67; Director, Navy Program Planning, Office of the CNO, 1967-68; Vice Chief of Naval Operations, 1968-70. Navy Cross with two Gold Stars; Distinguished Service Medal with three Gold Stars, Silver Star Medal; Legion of Merit; Bronze Star Medal with Combat "V"; and other US and foreign medals and awards. Promotions: Rear Admiral, July 1, 1959; Vice Admiral, June 5, 1964; Admiral, January 17, 1968.

Clark, Albert P. Lieutenant General, United States Air Force; Superintendent, United States Air Force Academy, 1970-   . Born August 27, 1913, at Schofield Barracks, Hawaii. US Military Academy, 1932-36; Flying School, 1936-37; Army Air Force Gunnery School, 1946; Armed Forces Staff College, 1947; National War College, 1951-52. Commissioned Second Lieutenant, US Army, 1936; received pilot wings, 1937. Served in the European Theater, WW II, POW. Chief of Staff, US Air Force, Europe, 1956-57; Commander, 2d Air Division, and Chief, US Military Training Mission, Saudi Arabia, 1957-59; Director of Military Personnel, Deputy Chief of Staff, Personnel, Headquarters USAF, 1959-63; Commander, 313th Air Division, Kadena Air Base, Okinawa, 1963-65; Vice Commander, Tactical Air Command, 1965-68; Commander, Air University, 1968-70. Distinguished Service Medal; Legion of Merit with one Oak Leaf Cluster; Air Medal; Air Force Commendation Medal; and other medals and awards. Promotions: Brigadier General, October 24, 1956; Major

General, June 30, 1959; Lieutenant General, August 1, 1965.

Clarke, Frederick James. Lieutenant General, United States Army; Chief of Engineers, U.S. Army, Washington, D.C., 1969- . Born March 1, 1915, Little Falls, New York. U.S. Military Academy; U.S. Army Command and General Staff College; Armed Forces Staff College; The National War College; Cornell University, MS Degree—Civil Engineering. Commissioned Second Lieutenant, 1937. Served in WW II. Director of Military Construction, Office, Chief of Engineers, U.S. Army, Washington, D.C., 1963-65; Commanding General, U.S. Army Engineer Center and Fort Belvoir, and Commandant, U.S. Army Engineer School, Fort Belvoir, Virginia, 1965-66; Deputy Chief of Engineers, U.S. Army, Washington, D.C., 1966-69. Distinguished Service Medal; Legion of Merit, and other medals and awards. Promoted to Brigadier General, December 1, 1960; Major General, May 1, 1964; Lieutenant General, August 1, 1969.

Clay, Frank Butner. Major General, United States Army; Chief, US Army Audit Agency, Washington, D.C., 1972- . Born February 26, 1921, Auburn, Alabama. US Military Academy; The Armor School, Advanced Course; US Army Command and General Staff College; US National War College. Commissioned Second Lieutenant, 1942. Served in WW II, and in Vietnam War. Assistant Division Commander, 101st Airborne Division, Fort Campbell, Kentucky, later US Army, Pacific-Vietnam, 1967-68; Assistant Chief of Staff for Personnel, J-1, US Military Assistance Command, Vietnam, 1968-69; Deputy Commandant, US Army Command and General Staff College, Fort Leavenworth, Kansas, 1969-70; Deputy Director, Joint Staff, Organization, Joint Chiefs of Staff, Washington, D.C., 1970-71; Military Advisor to the Chairman, US Delegation, United States/Vietnam Peace Negotiations, Paris, France, 1971-72. Distinguished Service Medal; Silver Star with two Oak Leaf Clusters; Legion of Merit; Distinguished Flying Cross; Bronze Star Medal with V Device and two Oak Leaf Clusters; and other medals and awards. Promoted to Brigadier General, May 1, 1967; Major General, October 19, 1970.

Clay, Lucius D., Jr. General, United States Air Force; Commander in Chief, North American Air Defense Command, Headquarters Ent Air Force Base, Colorado Springs, Colorado, 1973- . Born July 6, 1919, in Alexandria, Virginia. U.S. Military Academy, 1939-42; Officers Flying School, 1942. Commissioned Second Lieutenant US Army, 1942; received pilot wings, 1942. Served in the European Theater, WW II; Vietnam War. Deputy Director, Operations, J-3, Joint Staff, Joint Chiefs of Staff, 1962-64; Vice Commander, and Commander, Twelfth Air Force, Tactical Air Command, 1964-66; Director, Plans, Deputy Chief of Staff, Plans and Operations, Headquarters USAF, 1966-67; Director, Aerospace Programs, Deputy Chief of Staff, Programs and Resources, Headquarters USAF, 1967-68; Deputy Chief of Staff, Programs and Resources, Headquarters USAF,

1968-69; Deputy Chief of Staff, Plans and Operations, Headquarters USAF, 1969-70; Vice Commander in Chief, Pacific Air Forces, Hickam Air Force Base, Hawaii, 1970; Commander, Seventh Air Force, and Deputy Commander, Air Operations, US Military Assistance Command, Vietnam, 1970-71; Commander in Chief, Pacific Air Forces, Hickam Air Force Base, Hawaii, 1971-73. Distinguished Service Medal with two Oak Leaf Clusters; Legion of Merit; Distinguished Flying Cross; Bronze Star Medal; and other US and foreign medals and awards. Promotions: Brigadier General, August 1, 1962; Major General, August 1, 1964; Lieutenant General, August 1, 1968; General, September 1, 1970.

Cleland, John Robin Davis, Jr. Major General, United States Army; Chief, Military Equipment Delivery Team, Cambodia, 1972- . Born July 5, 1925, in Washington, D.C. Attended University of Omaha, BGE, History; George Washington University, MS, International Affairs; Infantry School, Advanced Course; Command and General Staff College; Armed Forces Staff College; Army War College, 1965-66. Commissioned Second Lieutenant (OCS) November 8, 1944; permanent commission March 1947. Served in the Vietnam War. Commanding Officer, 3d Battalion, 503d Infantry, 82d Airborne Division, Fort Bragg, North Carolina, and later US Army, Pacific-Vietnam, 1967-68; Deputy Commander, 173d Airborne Brigade, US Army, Pacific-Vietnam, 1968; Commanding Officer, Task Force South (Provisional), 173d Airborne Brigade, 1968; Military Staff Officer, Office of the Special Assistant for Counterinsurgency, US Embassy/US Military Assistance Command, Thailand/Joint US Military Advisory Group, Thailand, 1969-70; Assistant Chief of Staff for Operations, J-3, US Military Assistance Command, Thailand, 1970-71; Deputy Director of International and Civil Affairs, Office of the Deputy Chief of Staff for Military Operations, 1971-72. Silver Star; Legion of Merit with three Oak Leaf Clusters; Bronze Star Medal; Air Medal (18 awards). Promotions: Brigadier General, December 1, 1971; Major General, 1973.

Cleary, Colin Garfield. Air Vice Marshal, Royal Australian Air Force; Air Member for Supply and Equipment, 1968- . Born August 18, 1913, in Melbourne. Commissioned in 1936. Director, Equipment Requirements, 1958-60; Controller of Equipment, RAAF, 1961-68. CBE.

Clemedson, Carl-Johan. Major General, Swedish Royal Army; Surgeon General, 1966- . Born April 30, 1918. Doctor of Medicine, 1947; Assistant Professor, 1956; Professor, 1959. Chief of the Medical Division, National Defense Research Institute, 1949-59; Professor of Public Health, University of Gothenburg, 1959-64. Commander of the Royal Order of the North Star. Promoted to Major General, 1964.

Clementi, Cresswell Montagu. Air Vice-Marshal, British Royal Air Force; Air Officer in Charge of Administration, Air Support Command, RAF, Uxbridge, 1972- . Born

December 30, 1918. Magdalen College, Oxford, MA Degree; Royal Air Force Staff College, 1949; Joint Service Staff College, Latimer, 1955; Imperial Defence College, 1964. Commissioned in the Royal Air Force Volunteer Reserve in 1938. Flew with Bomber Command in WW II. Group Captain, Operations/Plans/Training, Near East Air Force, Cyprus, 1961-63; Director, Air Staff Plans, Ministry of Defence (Air Force Department), 1965-67; Air Officer Commanding, No. 19 Group, Royal Air Force, Mount Batten, Plymouth, 1968-69; Senior RAF Member, Royal College of Defence Studies, 1969-72. CB; CBE.

Clements, William P., Jr. United States Deputy Secretary of Defense, 1973-   . Born Dallas, Texas, April 13, 1917. Attended Southern Methodist University. Chairman of the Board, SEDCO, Inc.; Member, Department of Defense Blue Ribbon Panel, 1969-70; Chairman, Board of Governors, Southern Methodist University, 1965-73; Trustee, Southwestern Medical School, University of Texas; Trustee, Texas Research Foundation; Member, National Executive Board, Boy Scouts of America, 1969-   ; and participant in numerous other civic and educational organizations.

Clotteau. Vice Admiral, French Navy; Prefet Maritime of the First Region.

Cloutier, Sylvain. Deputy Minister of National Defence, Canada, 1971-   . Born in 1929 in Trois-Rivieres, Quebec. Attended Ottawa University, BA and BPh, 1949; University of Montreal, MS (Commerce and Accounting), 1953; Harvard University (USA), MA (Business Administration), 1955. Member, Public Service Commission of Canada, 1965-67; Deputy Secretary of the Treasury Board of Canada, 1967-70; Deputy Minister for Taxation, Department of National Revenue, 1970-71.

Coats, Wendell John. Major General, United States Army; Chief of Staff, US Readiness Command, MacDill Air Force Base, Florida, 1971-   . Born July 28, 1915, Sterling, Colorado. US Military Academy; The Artillery School, Basic Course; US Army Command and General Staff College; US Army War College; University of Wisconsin, MA Degree, Journalism; Georgetown University, PhD Degree, International Relations. Commissioned Second Lieutenant, 1940. Served in WW II. Deputy Director, Logistics, J-4, US European Command, 1964-67; Deputy Commanding General, US Army Training Center (Infantry), Fort Polk, Louisiana, 1967; Chief of Public Information, Office, Secretary of the Army, and Chief of Information, US Army, Washington, D.C., 1967-69; Commanding General, 2d Armored Division, Fort Hood, Texas, 1969-71. Distinguished Service Medal; Silver Star; Legion of Merit with two Oak Leaf Clusters; Bronze Star Medal; and other medals and awards. Promoted to Brigadier General, August 1, 1964; Major General, February 1, 1968.

Cobb, James Outterson. Rear Admiral, United States Navy; Commandant Fifth Naval District and Commander Naval Base, Norfolk, Virginia, 1970-   . Born January 9, 1910, Albany, New York. US Naval Academy, 1929-33; Flight Training Course, 1936-37. Commissioned Ensign, US Navy,

in 1933; designated Naval Aviator in 1937. Served in the Pacific Theater in WW II. Assistant Chief of Naval Personnel, for Personnel Control, 1962-64; Deputy Chief of Naval Personnel, and Assistant Chief of the Bureau of Naval Personnel, 1964-65; Commander Carrier Division TWO, 1965-67; Vice Director, Joint Staff Office, Joint Chiefs of Staff, 1967-68; Chief, Joint US Military Group/US Military Assistance Advisory Group, Spain, 1968-70. Distinguished Flying Cross; Legion of Merit; Distinguished Service Medal; and other medals and awards. Promoted to Rear Admiral, July 1, 1961.

Cobb, William Warren. Major General, United States Army; United States Commander, Berlin, US Army, Europe, 1971-   . Born August 15, 1917, Dallas, Texas. University of Kansas, AB Degree, History; The Armored School, Advanced Course; US Army Command and General Staff College; US Army War College. Commissioned Second Lieutenant, Army National Guard, 1941. Served in WW II and in Vietnam War. Assistant Commandant, US Army Armor School, Fort Knox, Kentucky, 1967-69; Assistant Division Commander, 4th Armored Division, US Army, Europe, 1969-70; Commanding General, 4th Armored Division, US Army, Europe, 1970-71. Silver Star; Legion of Merit with two Oak Leaf Clusters; Distinguished Flying Cross; Bronze Star Medal with two Oak Leaf Clusters; and other medals and awards. Promoted to Brigadier General, August 1, 1968; Major General, August 1, 1970.

Cody, Joseph Julius, Jr. Major General, United States Air Force; Deputy Director, Contract Administration Services, Defense Supply Agency, 1971-   . Born February 13, 1918, in San Antonio, Texas. St. Mary's University, 1936-40, BS, Physics, 1940; Army Air Corps Flying School, 1940-41; Air War College, 1956-67. Commissioned Second Lieutenant, US Army Air Corps, 1941. Served in the European Theater, WW II. Vice Commander, Space Systems Division, 1963-64; Chief of Staff, Headquarters Air Force Systems Command, 1964-65, and 1967-68; Deputy Chief of Staff, Systems, 1965-67; Commander, Electronic Systems Division, L.G. Hanscom Field, Massachusetts, 1968-71. Distinguished Service Award; Legion of Merit with three Oak Leaf Clusters; Bronze Star Medal; and other US and foreign medals and awards. Promoted to Major General, September 1, 1965.

Coffin, Robert Edmondston. Lieutenant General, United States Army; Deputy Director (Engineering and Management), Office, Director of Defense Research and Engineering, Office, Secretary of Defense, Washington, D.C., 1971-   . Born June 15, 1917, Bellingham, Washington. Stanford University, BA Degree, Economics and History; The Field Artillery School, Basic Course; US Army Command and General Staff College; Armed Forces Staff College; The National War College. Commissioned Second Lieutenant, US Army Reserve, 1939. Served in WW II. Assistant Division Commander, 2d Infantry Division, Fort Benning, Georgia, 1963-65; Chief, Nuclear Activities Branch, Operations Division, Supreme Headquarters Allied Powers Europe, 1965-67; Deputy Chief of Research and Development, US Army, Washington, D.C.,

1967-69; Commanding General, US Army Southern European Task Force, US Army, Europe, 1969-71. Distinguished Service Medal; Legion of Merit with Oak Leaf Cluster; Bronze Star Medal with two Oak Leaf Clusters; and other medals and awards. Promoted to Brigadier General, August 1, 1963; Major General, August 1, 1967; Lieutenant General, July 9, 1971.

Colbert, Richard G. Admiral, United States Navy; Commander in Chief Allied Forces, Southern Europe, 1972- . Born February 12, 1915, in Brownsville, Pennsylvania. US Naval Academy, 1933-37; Naval War College, 1955-56. Commissioned Ensign, US Navy, 1937. Served in the Atlantic and Pacific Theaters, WW II. Commanding Officer USS *Boston* (CAG-1), 1961-62; Member Policy Planning Council, the Department of State, 1962-65; Commander Cruiser Destroyer Flotilla SIX, 1965-66; Deputy Chief of Staff and Assistant Chief of Staff for Policy, Plans and Operations to the Supreme Allied Commander, Atlantic, 1966-68; President, Naval War College, 1968-71; Chief of Staff, Supreme Allied Commander, Atlantic, 1971-72. Legion of Merit and other medals and awards. Promotions: Vice Admiral, 1968: Admiral, 1972.

Cole, Philip Patten. Rear Admiral, United States Navy; Commander Service Group THREE and Commander Service Squadron THREE, 1970- , . Born December 16, 1919, in Pittsburgh, Pennsylvania. US Naval Academy, 1938-41; Submarine School, 1944; Naval Postgraduate School, MS, 1947-50; Naval War College, 1963-64; George Washington University, MA, International Affairs, 1964. Commissioned Ensign, US Navy, in 1941. Served at sea in the Pacific Theater in WW II; Vietnam War. Commanding Officer USS *Canisteo*, 1964-65; Commander Submarine Squadron SIX, 1965-66; Chief of Staff and Aide to Commander Submarine Force, US Pacific Fleet, 1966-68; Commander US Naval Forces, Marianas, 1968-69; Commander Military Sealift Command, Pacific, 1969-70. Promoted to Rear Admiral, July 1, 1969.

Cole, Ray M. Major General, United States Air Force; Commander, 21st Air Force, 1973- . Born April 15, 1923, in Trumann, Arkansas. Arkansas State College, 1940-42; Army Air Corps Flying School, 1942-43; Air Force Institute of Technology, BS, Industrial Engineering; Northwestern University, MS, Business Administration, 1950; Industrial College of the Armed Forces, 1963-64; Advanced Management Program, Harvard University Graduate School of Business Administration, 1969. Commissioned Second Lieutenant, US Army Air Corps, 1943. Served in the China-Burma-India Theater, WW II; Korean War. Assistant Deputy Director, Operations, J-3, Organization, Joint Chiefs of Staff, 1964-67; Executive Officer and Assistant Deputy Chief of Staff, Personnel, US Air Force, 1967-69; Vice Commander, Twenty-second Air Force, 1969-71; Deputy Chief of Staff for Plans, Headquarters Military Airlift Command, 1971-72; Chief of Staff, Headquarters Military Airlift Command, 1972-73. Legion of Merit; Distinguished Flying Cross; Bronze Star Medal; and other

medals and awards. Promoted to Major General, August 1, 1971.

Coleman, William Smith. Major General, United States Army; Commanding General, Army Readiness Region, Fort Knox, Kentucky, 1973- . Born January 29, 1919, Iva, South Carolina. Clemson Agricultural and Mechanical College, BS, Agriculture; The Infantry School, Advanced Course; US Army Command and General Staff College; US Army War College; George Washington University, MS, International Affairs. Commissioned Second Lieutenant, US Army Reserve, 1940. Served in WW II and in Vietnam War. Director, International Relations Studies, US Army War College, Carlisle Barracks, Pennsylvania, 1966-67; Assistant Division Commander, 1st Infantry Division, US Army, Vietnam, 1967-68; Deputy Assistant Chief of Staff, J-3, for Army of the Republic of Vietnam, and Regional Force/Popular Force Affairs, US Military Assistance Command, Vietnam, 1968; Assistant Division Commander, 1st Infantry Division, US Army, Vietnam, 1968; Deputy Commanding General, US Army Training Center, Infantry, and Fort Jackson, South Carolina, 1969-70; Commanding General, US Army Training Center, Infantry and Fort Jackson, South Carolina, 1970-72; Chief, Army Advisory Group, US Military Assistance Command, Vietnam, 1972-73. Distinguished Service Medal; Silver Star with three Oak Leaf Clusters; Legion of Merit with Oak Leaf Cluster; Distinguished Flying Cross with Oak Leaf Cluster; Bronze Star Medal; and other medals and awards.

Colladay, Martin G. Major General, United States Air Force; Vice Director, Joint Staff, Organization of the Joint Chiefs of Staff, 1972- . Born October 5, 1925, in Hutchinson, Kansas. US Military Academy, 1942-46; Air Training Command School, 1952-53; Industrial College of the Armed Forces, 1963-64; George Washington University, MA, International Affairs, 1964. Commissioned Second Lieutenant, US Army Air Corps, 1946. Deputy Director of Materiel, 1st Strategic Aerospace Divsion, 1965-66; Assistant, General Officer Matters, Deputy Chief of Staff, Personnel, Headquarters, USAF, 1966-69; Vice Commander, Twenty-first Air Force, Military Airlift Command, 1969-70; Assistant Chief of Staff, J-3, United Nations Command/US Forces Korea and Director, United States/Republic of Korea Operational Planning Staff Korea, 1970. Legion of Merit with one Oak Leaf Cluster; Air Force Commendation Medal; and other medals and awards. Promoted to Major General, February 1, 1972.

Collin, Geoffrey de Egglesfield. Major-General, British Army; General Officer Commanding North Eastern District, 1973- . Born July 18, 1921. Attended Wellington College, Crowthorne, Berks; Staff College, Camberley, 1951; Imperial Defence College, 1968. Commissioned in the Royal Artillery, 1941; qualified as an Army Pilot, 1946. Served in India and Burma in WW II. Instructor, Staff College, Camberley, 1960-62; Commander, 50 Missile Regiment. Royal Artillery, 1962-64; Commander, Royal Artillery, 4th Division, 1966-67; Commandant, Royal School of Artillery, 1969-71; Major-General, Royal

Artillery, Headquarters, British Army of the Rhine, 1971-73. MC.

Collins, Arthur Sylvester, Jr. Lieutenant General, United States Army; Deputy Commander in Chief, US Army, Europe and Seventh Army, 1971-   . Born August 6, 1915, Boston, Massachusetts. US Military Academy; The Infantry School, Battalion Command and Staff Course; US Army War College; George Washington University, MA Degree, International Affairs. Commissioned Second Lieutenant, 1938. Served in WW II and in Vietnam War. Director of Officer Personnel, Office of Personnel Operations, US Army, Washington, D.C., 1963-64; Assistant Deputy Chief of Staff for Military Operations (Plans and Operations), US Army, Washington, D.C., 1964-65; Commanding General, 4th Infantry Division and Fort Lewis, Washington, 1965-66; Commanding General, 4th Infantry Division, US Army, Pacific-Vietnam, 1966-67; Assistant Chief of Staff for Force Development, US Army, Washington, D.C., 1967-70; Commanding General, I Field Force, Vietnam, US Army, Pacific-Vietnam, 1970-71. Distinguished Service Medal with two Oak Leaf Clusters; Silver Star; Legion of Merit with Oak Leaf Cluster; Bronze Star Medal with V Device and two Oak Leaf Clusters; and other medals and awards. Promoted to Brigadier General, April 17, 1962; Major General, September 1, 1963; Lieutenant General, January 6, 1967.

Collins, Harold Edward. Major General, United States Air Force; Director, Development and Acquisition, Deputy Chief of Staff, Research and Development, Headquarters US Air Force, 1972-   . Born November 10, 1924, in Port Arthur, Texas. Lamar Institute of Technology, 1941-42; Army Air Corps Flying School, 1943-44; Air Command and Staff College, 1956-57; National War College, 1964-65; Advanced Management Program, Harvard Graduate School of Business, 1966. Commissioned in 1944. Served in the European Theater, WW II; Korean War. Deputy Chief, Aeronautical Systems Division, Directorate of Development, Office of the Deputy Chief of Staff, Research and Development; Headquarters USAF, 1965-67; Chief, Aeronautical Systems Division, 1967-69; US Defense Representative to Pakistan, US Strike Command, 1969-70; Inspector General, Air Force Systems Command, 1970-72. Legion of Merit with two Oak Leaf Clusters; Fellow of the Society of Experimental Test Pilots; and other medals and citations. Promoted to Major General, May 1, 1972.

Conrad, Charles, Jr. Captain, US Navy; NASA Astronaut, 1962-   . Born June 2, 1930, Philadelphia, Pennsylvania. Princeton University, BS, Aeronautical Engineering, 1953; Navy Test Pilot School. Commissioned Ensign, 1953. Project test pilot, Armaments Test Division, Flight Instructor, and Performance Engineer, Navy Test Pilot School. NASA experience: Pilot, Gemini 5, August 1965; Command Pilot, Gemini 11, September 12-15, 1966; Backup Spacecraft Commander, Apollo 9; Spacecraft Commander, Apollo 12; Commander, Skylab 2. NASA Distinguished Service Medal; two NASA Exceptional Service Medals; Navy Astronaut Wings; Navy Distinguished Service Medal; two Distinguished Flying Crosses;

Distinguished Alumnus Award, Princton University, 1965; US Jaycees' 10 Outstanding Young Men Award, 1965; American Astronautical Society Flight Achievement Award, 1966; Pennsylvania's Award for Excellence in Science and Technology, 1967, 1969; Rear Admiral William S. Parsons Award for Scientific and Technical Progress, 1970; Godfrey L. Cabot Award, 1970; Silver Medal of the Union League of Pennsylvania, 1970; FAI Yuri Gagarin Gold Space Medal; De La Vaulx Medal; National Academy of Television Arts and Sciences Special Trustees Award, 1970; Honorary MA, Princeton University, 1966; Honorary LLD, Lincoln-Wesleyan University, 1970; Honorary ScD, Kings College, Wilkes-Barre, Pennsylvania, 1971.

Conroy, Raymond Chandler. Major General, United States Army; Chief of Staff, US Army, Europe and Seventh Army, 1972-   . Born January 17, 1916, Chicago, Illinois. University of Oregon, BS Degree, Water Transportation; US Army Command and General Staff College; Armed Forces Staff College; Industrial College of the Armed Forces; University of Southern California, MBA Degree, Business Administration. Commissioned Second Lieutenant, US Army Reserve, 1942. Served in WW II and in Vietnam War. Commanding General, US Army Terminal Command, Pacific (also Deputy Commanding General, US Army Materiel Command for Western Operations, 1963-65; and Commanding General Joint Army-Navy Ocean Terminal, Pacific, 1964-65), Western Area, Military Traffic Management and Terminal Service, Oakland Army Base, California, 1963-66; Assistant Deputy Chief of Staff for Logistics (Plans, Doctrines and Systems), later Assistant Deputy Chief of Staff for Logistics, US Army, Washington, D.C., 1966-69; Assistant Chief of Staff, Logistics, J-4, US Military Assistance Command, Vietnam, 1969-70; Deputy Chief of Staff for Logistics, US Army, Europe and Seventh Army, 1970-72. Distinguished Service Medal with Oak Leaf Cluster; Legion of Merit with Oak Leaf Cluster; Bronze Star Medal; and other medals and awards; Promoted to Brigadier General, August 1, 1963; Major General, October 1, 1966.

Cook, Ralph Edward. Rear Admiral, United States Navy; Chief, National Security Agency/Central Security Service, Pacific, 1971-   . Born December 8, 1915, in Butte, Montana. Montana State College, BS, Electrical Engineering, 1934-38. Commissioned Ensign, US Naval Reserve, in 1941; transferred to US Navy in 1946. Combat duty in the Pacific Theater in WW II. Deputy Director, Naval Communications/Director, Naval Security Group, 1963-67; Deputy for Cryptology, Office of the Assistant CNO (Communications), Deputy Commander for Cryptology, and Director of the Naval Security Group, Naval Communications Command, 1967-68; Commander Naval Security Group Command and Executive Assistant for Cryptology, 1968-71. Legion of Merit with Gold Star; Letter of Commendation from the Royal Australian Navy; and other medals and awards. Promoted to Rear Admiral, February 1, 1968.

Cooke, Edward William. Rear Admiral, United States Navy; Director, Budget and Reports, Office of the Comptroller, Navy Department, 1972-   . Born August 9, 1921, in

Fonda, Iowa. US Naval Academy, 1942-45; Naval Submarine School, 1947; Electronics School, 1950-51; Naval War College, 1966-67; George Washington University, MS, International Affairs, 1969. Commissioned Ensign, US Navy, 1945. Served in the Pacific Theater in WW II; submarine in the Korean War. Executive Assistant and Naval Aide to Assistant Secretary of the Navy (Installations and Logistics), 1967-69; Commander, Submarine Squadron FIVE, 1969-71; Commander, Submarine Flotilla ONE, 1971-72. Legion of Merit; Navy Commendation Medal; and other medals and awards. Promoted to Rear Admiral, February 1, 1972.

Cooksey, Howard Harrison. Major General, United States Army; Deputy Commander, US Support Activities Group, 1973-   . Born June 21, 1921, Brentsville, Virginia. Virginia Polytechnic Institute, BS, Business Administration; The Armored School, Advanced Course; US Army Command and General Staff College; US Armed Forces Staff College; US National War College; George Washington University, MA, International Affairs. Commissioned Second Lieutenant, US Army Reserve, 1943. Served in WW II and in Vietnam War. Assistant Division Commander, 23d Infantry Division (Americal), US Army, Pacific-Vietnam, 1968-69; Deputy Chief of Staff for Plans and Operations, US Army, Pacific-Vietnam, 1969; Commanding General, US Army Training Center, Infantry and Fort Dix, New Jersey, 1970-72; Commanding General, First Regional Assistance Command and Senior Advisor, Military Region 1, US Military Assistance Command, Vietnam, 1972-73; Acting Chief of Staff, US Military Assistance Command, Vietnam, 1973. Distinguished Service Medal; Silver Star; Legion of Merit with Oak Leaf Cluster; Bronze Star Medal with two Oak Leaf Clusters; and other medals and awards. Promoted to Brigadier General, February 1, 1968; Major General, August 1, 1970.

Cooper, Damon Warren. Vice Admiral, United States Navy; Commander Attack Carrier Striking Force, Seventh Fleet/Commander Carrier Division FIVE, 1971-   . Born April 27, 1919, in Elizabethtown, Kentucky. Western Kentucky State Teachers College; US Naval Academy, 1937-41; Naval Intelligence School, 1946-47; Naval War College, 1957-58; National War College, 1960-61. Commissioned Ensign, US Navy, in 1941; designated Naval Aviator in 1943. Served in the Pacific Theater in WW II; Korean War; Vietnam War. Commanding Officer USS *Pine Island* (AV-12), 1963-64; Commanding Officer USS *Ticonderoga* (CVA-14), 1964-65; Assistant Director for Captain Detail (Aviation), Bureau of Naval Personnel, briefly Deputy Assistant Chief for Personnel Control, 1965-66; Commander Patrol Force, Seventh Fleet/Taiwan Patrol Force/Fleet Air Wing ONE, 1966-68; Assistant Chief of Naval Personnel for Personnel Control, 1968-70; Commander Carrier Division NINE, 1970-71. Legion of Merit with Gold Star; Distinguished Flying Cross with two Gold Stars; Bronze Star Medal; Air Medal with twelve Gold Stars; and other US and foreign medals and awards. Promotions: Rear Admiral, July 1, 1967; Vice Admiral, August 16, 1972.

Cooper, Kenneth Banks. Major General, United States Army; Director of Installations, Office of the Deputy Chief of Staff, Logistics, 1972-   . Born November 12, 1923, Fort Leavenworth, Kansas. Attended US Military Academy; Engineer School, Basic and Advanced Courses; Command and General Staff College; Army War College, 1964-65; Massachusetts Institute of Technology, MS, Civil Engineering. Commissioned June 6, 1944. Served in WW II and the Vietnam War. Research and Technical Operations Officer, later Assistant Deputy Director for Engineering, Defense Communications Planning Group, Defense Communications Agency, 1966-68; Executive to the Secretary of the Army, 1968-70; Deputy Commanding General, US Army Engineer Command, Vietnam (Provisional), US Army, Pacific-Vietnam, 1970; Commanding General, 20th Engineer Brigade, US Army, Pacific-Vietnam, 1970-71; Deputy Commanding General, US Army Engineer Command, Vietnam (Provisional), US Army, Pacific-Vietnam, 1971; Deputy Director of Civil Works, Office of the Chief of Engineers, 1971-72. Distinguished Service Medal with Oak Leaf Cluster; Legion of Merit with Oak Leaf Cluster; and other medals and awards. Promoted to Brigadier General July 1, 1970; Major General March 1, 1973.

Cooper, William Frank. Major-General, British Army; Director, Military Assistance Office, 1972-   . Born May 30, 1921. Attended Royal Military Academy, Woolwich. Commissioned in Royal Engineers, 1940. Served in North Africa and Italy in WW II; Malaya, 1956-58; Chief Engineer Far East Land Forces, 1968-70; Deputy Director of Army Staff Duties, Ministry of Defence, 1970-72. CBE; MC.

Corbin, Thomas G. Major General, United States Air Force; Air Deputy, Headquarters Allied Forces Northern Europe (NATO), 1968-   . Born January 14, 1917, in Fremont, North Carolina. Davidson College, North Carolina, BS, 1937; US Military Academy, 1937-41; Army Air Corps Flying School, 1941-42; Royal Air Force Staff College, Bracknell, England, 1950; National War College, 1956-57. Commissioned in 1941. Served in the European Theater, WW II. Commander 818th Strategic Aerospace Division, 1958-62; Deputy Director, Legislative Liaison, Office of the Secretary of the Air Force, 1962-65; Director, Legislative Liaison, Office of the Secretary of the Air Force, 1965-66; Commander, US Air Force Special Air Warfare Center, 1966-68. Silver Star Medal; Legion of Merit; Distinguished Flying Cross with one Oak Leaf Cluster; and other US and foreign medals and awards. Promoted to Major General, July 1, 1965.

Corcoran, Charles Allen. Lieutenant General, United States Army; Chief of Staff, U.S. Pacific Command, 1970-   . Born September 16, 1914, Laredo, Texas. Armed Forces Staff College; The National War College. Commissioned Second Lieutenant, Army National Guard, 1939. Served in WW II and in Vietnam War. Director of Coordination and Analysis, Office, Chief of Staff, U.S. Army, Washington, D.C., 1963-65; Secretary of the General Staff, Office, Chief of Staff, U.S. Army, Washington, D.C., 1965-66; Commanding General, 5th Infantry Division (Mechanized) and Fort Carson, Colorado, 1966-68; Assistant Chief of Staff, Operations, J-3, U.S. Military Assistance Command, Vietnam, 1968; Chief of Staff, U.S. Military Assistance Command, Vietnam, 1968-69; Commanding General, I Field Force, U.S. Army, Pacific-Vietnam, 1969-70. Distinguished Service Medal with Two Oak Leaf Clusters; Legion of Merit; Bronze Star Medal, and other medals and awards. Promoted to Brigadier General, December 20, 1963; Major General, October 27, 1966; Lieutenant General, March 15, 1969.

Correa, Samuel Augusto Alves. Brigadier General, Brazilian Army; Military Attache, Embassy of Brazil, Washington, D.C.; Delegate, Inter-American Defense Board; Chairman, Joint Brazil-United States Defense Commission. Date of Rank: August 25, 1968.

Cosgrove, Paul F., Jr. Rear Admiral, Supply Corps, United States Navy; Executive Director for Supply Operations, Defense Supply Agency, 1972-   . Born July 14, 1918, in Augusta, Georgia. Georgia School of Technology, Atlanta, BA, Industrial Management, 1939; Supply Corps School, 1940; Naval War College, 1954-55. Commissioned Ensign, Supply Corps, US Navy, in 1940. Served in the Pacific Theater in WW II. Commanding Officer, Navy Fleet Material Support Office, and Commander Naval Supply Center, Mechanicsburg, Pennsylvania, 1965-67; Deputy Commander for Supply Operations, Naval Supply Systems Command Headquarters, 1967-70; Force Supply Officer, Staff of Commander, Service Force, US Pacific Fleet, 1970-72. Legion of Merit; and other medals and awards. Promoted to Rear Admiral, July 1, 1967.

Coulthard, Colin Weall. Air Vice-Marshal, British Royal Air Force; Military Deputy to Head of Defence Sales, Ministry of Defence, 1973-   . Born February 27, 1921. Attended De Havilland Aeronautical Technical School; RAF Staff College, 1950. Commissioned in 1941. Served in fighters in WW II. Station Commander, Gutersloh, 1961-64; Deputy Director Operations Establishment (RAF) Ministry of Defence, 1964-66; Staff Officer (Air), Army Headquarters Malta, 1966-67; Director of Operational Requirements (RAF), Ministry of Defence, 1967-69; Air Attache, British Embassy, Washington, D.C., 1970-72. AFC and Bar.

Cousins, Ralph Wynne. Admiral, United States Navy; Commander in Chief, Atlantic/US Atlantic Fleet and Supreme Allied Commander, Atlantic, with additional duty as Commander in Chief Western Atlantic Area, 1972-   . Born July 24, 1915, in Eldorado, Oklahoma. Ironwood Junior College, Ironwood, Michigan, 1932-33; US Naval Academy, 1933-37; Test Pilot School, 1950; National War College, 1962-63. Commissioned Ensign, US Navy, in 1937; designated Naval Aviator in 1940. Served in the Pacific Theater, WW II; Vietnam War. Commanding Officer USS *Nantahala* (AO-60), 1959-60; Commanding Officer, USS *Midway* (CVA-41), 1960-61; Assistant Director of Captain Detail (Aviation), Bureau of Naval Personnel, 1961-62; Military Assistant to Deputy Secretary of Defense, 1963-65; Commander Carrier Division NINE, 1965-66; Assistant Chief of Staff (Plans), Commander in Chief,

Pacific, 1966-67; Commander Attack Carrier Striking Force, Seventh Fleet, and Commander Carrier Division FIVE, 1967-69; Deputy Chief of Naval Operations (Fleet Operations and Readiness), 1969-70; Vice Chief of Naval Operations, 1970-72. Navy Cross; Distinguished Service Medal with two Gold Stars; Legion of Merit with Gold Star; and other US and foreign medals and awards. Promotions: Rear Admiral, December 7, 1964; Vice Admiral, July 3, 1968; Admiral, October 30, 1970.

Cowles, Donald Harry. Lieutenant General, United States Army; Deputy Chief of Staff for Military Operations, US Army, Washington, D.C., and Senior US Army Member of the Military Staff Committee of the United Nations, 1972-   . Born September 10, 1917, Westfield, Massachusetts. Massachusetts State College, BS Degree, Biological Science; The Cavalry School, Advanced Course; The Armored School, Advanced Course; US Army Command and General Staff College; US Army War College; Yale University, MF Degree, Forestry Economics. Commissioned Second Lieutenant, US Army Reserve, 1939. Served in WW II and in Vietnam War. Deputy Assistant for Strategic Mobility, Organization, Joint Chiefs of Staff, Washington, D.C., 1966-67; Military Assistant to the Assistant Secretary of Defense (Public Affairs), Washington, D.C., 1967-68; Commanding General, 3d Armored Division, US Army, Europe, 1968-69; Deputy Chief of Staff for Personnel, US Army Europe and Seventh Army, 1969-70; Assistant Chief of Staff, Operations, J-3, US Military Assistance Command, Vietnam, 1970-71; Chief of Staff, US Military Assistance Command, Vietnam, 1971-72; Director of Procurement, Training and Distribution, Office, Deputy Chief of Staff for Personnel, US Army, Washington, D.C., 1972. Distinguished Service Medal; Silver Star; Legion of Merit with two Oak Leaf Clusters; Bronze Star Medal with Oak Leaf Cluster; and other medals and awards. Promoted to Brigadier General, September 17, 1965; Major General, November 1, 1967; Lieutenant General, October 1, 1972.

Cowtan, Frank Willoughby John. Major-General, British Army; Commandant, Royal Military College of Science, 1971-   . Born February 10, 1920. Attended Wellington College; Royal Military Academy, Woolwich; Staff College, 1951; National Defence College (Canada), 1967-68. Commissioned in the Royal Engineers, 1939. Served in northwest Europe and North Africa in WW II. Commanding Officer, Victory College, Royal Military Academy, Sandhurst, 1962-65; Commander, 11 Engineer Brigade, British Army of the Rhine, 1965-67; Director, Quartering (Army), 1968-70; Deputy Quartermaster General, Ministry of Defence (AD), 1970-71. CBE; MC and Bar.

Crabb, Gordon John Branstone. Rear Admiral, Royal Australian Navy; Fourth Naval Member and Chief of Supply and Works, 1972-   . Born July 5, 1917, in London. Australian Administrative Staff Course, 1963; attended Imperial Defence College. Head, Australian Joint Services Staff, Washington, D.C., 1966-68; Flag Officer Commanding HMA Fleet, 1968-69; Flag Officer Commanding East Australian Area, 1970-72. CBE; DSC.

Cragg, Ernest T. Major General, United States Air Force; Vice Commander, Second Air Force, Strategic Air Command, 1972-   . Born January 19, 1922, in Mount Vernon, New York. US Military Academy, 1940-43; University of Michigan, Graduate Course, Electrical Engineering, 1947-49; National War College, 1962-63; George Washington University, MA, International Affairs, 1963. Commissioned Second Lieutenant, US Army Air Corps, 1943. Served in the European Theater, WW II. Commander, 20th Tactical Wing, England, 1965-66; Commander, 3500th Pilot Training Wing, Air Training Command (ATC), 1966-67; Deputy Chief of Staff, Operations, Headquarters ATC, 1967-69; Deputy Director, and later Director, Aerospace Programs, Office, Deputy Chief of Staff, Programs and Resources, 1969-71; Assistant Deputy Chief of Staff, Programs and Resources, Headquarters USAF, 1971-72. Distinguished Service Medal; Legion of Merit with two Oak Leaf Clusters; Distinguished Flying Cross; and other US and foreign medals and awards. Promoted to Major General, May 1, 1970.

Cramer, Shannon Davenport, Jr. Rear Admiral, United States Navy; Deputy Director, J-5 (Strategic), the Joint Staff, Office of the Joint Chiefs of Staff, 1972-   . Born September 18, 1921, in Washington, D.C. US Naval Academy, 1940-43; Submarine School, 1946-47. Commissioned Ensign, US Navy, 1943. Served in the Atlantic Theater in WW II. Commanding Officer, Submarine Squadron FIFTEEN, 1966-67; Deputy Director, National Military Command Systems, J-3, Joint Chiefs of Staff, 1967-68; Military Assistant to Assistant Secretary of Defense (Public Affairs), 1968-70; Commander, Submarine Flotilla SIX, 1970-72. Legion of Merit with three Gold Stars; and other medals and awards. Promoted to Rear Admiral, August 1, 1968.

Crawford, Albert Benjamin, Jr. Major General, United States Army; Project Manager, Army Tactical Data Systems, US Army Electronics Command, Fort Monmouth, New Jersey, 1971-   . Born February 3, 1928, in Tucson, Arizona. Attended US Military Academy; Signal School, Advanced Course; Command and General Staff College; Army War College; Stanford University, MS Degrees in Electrical Engineering and Industrial Engineering. Served in the Vietnam War. Chief, Communications System Engineering Management Agency, US Army Strategic Communications Command, US Army, Pacific-Vietnam, 1968-69; Commanding Officer, I Corps Tactical Force Signal Group, US Army, Pacific-Vietnam, 1969; Commanding Officer, 12th Signal Group, US Army, Pacific-Vietnam, 1969; Chief, Information Sciences Group, Management Information Systems Directorate, Office of the Assistant Vice Chief of Staff, 1969-70; Deputy Director of Management Information Systems, Office of the Assistant Vice Chief of Staff, 1970-71. Legion of Merit with Oak Leaf Cluster; Bronze Star Medal; and other medals and awards. Promoted to Brigadier General June 1, 1972; Major General, 1973.

Crawford, Earl Russell. Rear Admiral, United States Navy; Deputy Chief of Staff to Commander in Chief, United States European Command, 1971-   . Born May 2, 1913, in Peru, Indiana. US Naval Academy, 1932-36; Naval Submarine School, 1939; Naval War College, 1954-55. Commissioned Ensign, US Navy, in 1936. Served in the Pacific Theater in WW II. Commander Amphibious Squadron ONE, 1962-63; Member of Joint Staff and Executive Officer, J-5, Joint Staff, Joint Chiefs of Staff, 1963-64; Commander Amphibious Training Command, US Atlantic Fleet, 1964-65; Commander Amphibious Group TWO, 1965-66; Commander Naval Base, Guantanamo Bay, Cuba, 1966-68; Commander Training Command, US Atlantic Fleet, 1968-69; Assistant Deputy Chief of Naval Operations (Logistics), 1969-71. Legion of Merit with Gold Star; and other medals and awards. Promoted to Rear Admiral, July 1, 1964.

Creasey, Timothy May. Major-General, British Army; Commander, Sultan of Muscat's Armed Forces, 1972-   . Born September 21, 1923. Attended Clifton College; Imperial Defence College, 1971. Commissioned in the Baluch Regiment, Indian Army, 1942; transferred to Royal Norfolk Regiment in 1946. Served in Italy, Greece, and the Far East in WW II. Instructor, Royal Military Academy, Sandhurst, 1963-64; Commander, 1 Royal Anglian, in Aden and British Army of the Rhine, 1965-67; Commander, 11th Armoured Brigade, 1969-70. OBE.

Creech, Wilbur L. Major General, United States Air Force; Deputy Chief of Staff for Operations, United States Air Forces, Europe, Ramstein Air Base, Germany, 1973-   . Born March 30, 1927, in Argyle, Missouri. Aviation Cadet Training Course, 1948-49; University of Maryland, BS; National War College, 1965-66; George Washington University, MS, International Relations, 1966. Commissioned Second Lieutenant, US Air Force, September 1949. Served in the Korean War and Vietnam War. Staff Assistant, Office of Assistant Secretary of Defense, 1966-68; Deputy Commander for Operations, 37th Tactical Fighter Wing, Phu Cat Air Base, Vietnam, 1968-69; Assistant Deputy Chief of Staff for Operations, Headquarters, Seventh Air Force, Tan Son Nhut Airfield, Vietnam, 1969; Commander, 86th Tactical Fighter Wing, Zweibrucken Air Base, Germany, 1970; Commander, 401st Tactical Fighter Wing, Torrejon Air Base, Spain, 1970-71; Deputy Chief of Staff for Operations, Headquarters, US Air Forces, Europe, Lindsey Air Station, Wiesbaden, Germany, 1971-73. Decorations include Legion of Merit with two Oak Leaf Clusters; Distinguished Flying Cross with three Oak Leaf Clusters; Silver Star; Air Medal with nineteen Oak Leaf Clusters. Promotions: Brigadier General, December 1, 1971; Major General, 1973.

Crekillie, Armand Francois Emile. Lieutenant-General, Belgian Air Force; Chief of the Belgian General Staff. Born in 1921, in Ostende. Enlisted in Belgian Forces in Great Britain in 1941; transferred to Belgian Section, British Royal Air Force, 1942. Commissioned Sub-lieutenant, 1943. Flew 95 missions in WW II. Director of Operations, Air Force Staff, 1963-64; Chief of Staff, Tactical Air Force, 1964-68; Deputy Chief of Staff, Air Force, 1968-71;

Commander, Tactical Air Force, 1971-72. Aiguillette, 1940; Croix de Guerre 40 avec Palme; Médaille du Voluntaire de Guerre 40-45; Médaille de France Libérée; Médaille Commemorative 40-45 with two Crossed Sabres and three Barrettes.

Crippen, Robert L. Lieutenant Commander, US Navy; NASA Astronaut, 1969-   . Born September 11, 1937, Beaumont, Texas. University of Texas, BS, Aerospace Engineering, 1960; US Air Force Aerospace Research Pilot School, Edwards Air Force Base. Commissioned Ensign, through Aviation Officer Program, Pensacola, Florida. Fleet Squadron VA-72, USS *Independence*, 1962-64; Instructor, Air Force Aerospace Research Pilot School; USAF Manned Orbiting Laboratory Program, 1966-69. NASA experience: Crew Member on Skylab Medical Experiments Altitude Test; Member Support Crew for Apollo-Soyuz Test Project Mission, July 1975. NASA Exceptional Service Medal.

Cristi, Esteban. General, Uruguayan Army; Commanding General, Military Region I.

Crittenberger, Willis Dale, Jr. Major General, United States Army; Deputy Director for Plans and Policy (International Negotiations); J-5, Organization, Joint Chiefs of Staff, Washington, D.C., 1971-   . Born January 10, 1919, Baltimore, Maryland. US Military Academy; The Field Artillery School, Basic Course; US Army Command and General Staff College; US Armed Forces Staff College; US National War College. Commissioned Second Lieutenant, 1942. Served in WW II and in Vietnam War. Commanding General, II Field Force Artillery, US Army, Pacific-Vietnam, 1966; Military Assistant to Deputy US Ambassador, Saigon, Vietnam, 1966-67; Commanding General, II Field Force Artillery, US Army, Pacific-Vietnam, 1967; Assistant Division Commander, 2d Armored Division, Fort Hood, Texas, 1967-68; Deputy, later Director of Plans, Office, Deputy Chief of Staff for Military Operations, US Army, Washington, D.C., 1968-69; Deputy Chief of Staff for Operations, US Army Europe and Seventh Army, 1969-71. Legion of Merit with four Oak Leaf Clusters; Bronze Star Medal with V Device and two Oak Leaf Clusters; Air Medal (four awards); Army Commendation Medal; and other medals and awards. Promoted to Brigadier General, April 1, 1966; Major General, August 1, 1969.

Crizer, Pat William. Major General, United States Army; Director of Systems, Office of the Assistant Chief of Staff for Force Development, US Army, 1972-   . Born September 29, 1924, in Appalachia, Virginia. Attended US Military Academy; Infantry School, Basic and Advanced Courses; Command and General Staff College; Army War College, 1964-65; Syracuse University, MBA, Comptrollership. Commissioned in 1946. Commanding Officer, 3d Brigade, and temporarily Assistant Division Commander, 5th Infantry Division (Mechanized), Fort Carson, Colorado, 1967-69; Chief of the Coordination Division, Office of the Deputy Secretary of the General Staff (Coordination and Reports), Office of the Chief of Staff, US Army, 1969-70; Deputy Chairman, Special

Review Panel, Office of the Chief of Staff, 1970; Executive-Assistant Secretary of the General Staff, 1970-71; Assistant Division Commander, 2d Infantry Division, US Army, Pacific-Korea, 1971-72. Silver Star with Oak Leaf Cluster; Legion of Merit with two Oak Leaf Clusters, and other medals and awards. Promoted to Brigadier General, February 1, 1971; Major General, 1973.

Crompton, Roy Hartley. Air Commodore, British Royal Air Force; Air Officer Commanding and Commandant, RAF Central Flying School, 1972-   . Born April 24, 1921. Attended University College, London; Flying Training School, South Africa, 1942; Air Staff College, 1952; Joint Services Staff College, 1962; Naval War College, Greenwich, 1967. Commissioned in 1942. Served in India-Burma Theater in WW II. Chief of Staff Secretariat, 1962-64; Station Commander No. 1 Flying Training School, 1965-67; Deputy Director of Defence Policy Staff, 1968-70; Group Director, RAF Staff College, 1970; Project Officer, National Defence College, 1970-71. OBE. Member, British Institute of Management.

Cross, Richard G., Jr. Major General, United States Air Force; Deputy Director for Plans, Deputy Chief of Staff, Plans and Operations, Headquarters US Air Force, Washington, D.C., 1973-   . Born June 4, 1920, in St. Louis, Missouri. Aviation Cadet Training Course, 1942-43; University of Maryland, 1949-52; Armed Forces Staff College, 1958-59; Port Huron College, Michigan, 1964; National War College, 1965-66. Commissioned Second Lieutenant, US Army Air Corps, in 1943. Served in the European Theater, WW II, and in the Vietnam War. Assistant Deputy Commander for Operations, 401st Tactical Fighter Wing, Torrejon Air Base, Spain, 1966-67; Chief, Operational Readiness Inspection Team for the US Air Forces in Europe, Lindsey Air Station, Germany, 1967-68; Commander, 36th Tactical Fighter Wing, Bitburg Air Base, Germany, 1968-69; Assistant Deputy Chief of Staff, Operations, Headquarters, Aerospace Defense Command, Ent Air Force Base, Colorado, 1969-70; Inspector General, Headquarters, Aerospace Defense Command, Ent Air Force Base, Colorado, 1970; Commander, 26th North American Air Defense (NORAD) Region/Air Division, Luke Air Force Base, Arizona, 1970-71; Assistant Deputy Chief of Staff, Operations, Seventh Air Force, Vietnam, 1971-72; Chief, Air Operations Division, Military Assistance Command, Vietnam, (MACV), 1972-73; Deputy Director of Plans for Force Development, Deputy Chief of Staff, Plans and Operations, Headquarters US Air Force, Washington, D.C., 1973. Silver Star; Legion of Honor; Distinguished Flying Cross with Oak Leaf Cluster; and other medals and awards. Promotions: Brigadier General, November 1, 1969; Major General, 1973.

Crow, Duward Lowery. Lieutenant General, United States Air Force; The Comptroller of the Air Force, Headquarters USAF, 1969-   . Born June 26, 1919, in Fort Payne, Alabama. University of Alabama, 1936-37; US Military Academy, 1937-41; US Army Command and General Staff College, 1946; Harvard University, Graduate School of

Business Administration, MBA, 1948; Air War College, 1958. Commissioned Second Lieutenant, US Army, 1941. Served in the China-Burma-India Theater, WW II; Korean War. Comptroller, Air Force Systems Command, 1963-64; Director of Budget, Office of the Comptroller, Headquarters USAF, 1964-69. Distinguished Service Medal (Air Force); Legion of Merit; Bronze Star; and other medals and awards. Promotions: Brigadier General, January 30, 1962; Major General, February 1, 1965; Lieutenant General, March 17, 1969.

Crowley-Milling, Sir Denis. Air Marshal, British Royal Air Force; Air Officer Commanding, No. 38 Group, Royal Air Force, Odiham, 1970-   . Born March 22, 1919. Attended Malvern College, Worcester; Flying College, RAF, Manby, 1957-58. Joined RAF Volunteer Reserve in 1937. Served in fighters and fighter bombers in WW II. Group Captain Operations, Central Fighter Establishment, 1959-62; Station Commander, Royal Air Force, Leconfield, 1962-64; Air Officer Commanding, Royal Air Force, Hong Kong, 1964-66; Director of Operational Requirements, Ministry of Defence (Air), 1966-67; Commander, Royal Air Force Staff, and Principal Air Attache, Washington, D.C., USA, 1967-70. KCB; CBE; DSO; DFC and Bar.

Cruddas, Thomas Rennison. Rear-Admiral, British Royal Navy; Deputy Controller Aircraft B, Procurement Executive, Ministry of Defence, 1973-   . Born February 6, 1921. Attended Royal Navy Engineering College, Keyham. Served at sea in the Mediterranean and East Indies in WW II. Staff of Flag Officer Aircraft Carriers, 1961-63; Assistant Director of Ship Production, 1964-66; served with US Navy as Program Manager, UK Phantom Aircraft, Washington, D.C., 1967-69; Command Engineer Officer, Staff Flying Officer, Naval Air Command, 1970-72; Rear-Admiral Engineering Naval Air Command, 1972. Member, Institute of Mechanical Engineering; Fellow of the Royal Aeronautical Society. Promoted to Rear-Admiral, 1972.

Csémi, Károly. Lieutenant General, Hungarian Army; First Deputy Minister of Defense, Hungarian People's Republic, 1973-   . Born in 1922 in Tany, Hungary. Attended Academy for Armored Troops. Chief of Staff, Hungarian People's Army, 1963-73; Member Hungarian Socialist Workers' Party, Member of Central Committee, 1966-   . Order of the Red Star, Grand Cross of Commanders; and other Hungarian and foreign orders and medals.

Cuadra Medina, Mariano. Lieutenant General, Spanish Air Force; Chief of Staff, Spanish Air Force, 1972-   . Diplomate of Air Force Staff, 1945. Commander of 4th Squadron of Spanish Volunteers in German-Soviet War, WW II. Formerly Commander, Joint Torrejon Air Force Base; Air Attache, Spanish Embassy, London; Director, Air Force War College; Deputy Chief of Air Force Staff; Director, Center of Studies for National Defense. Military Medal (Individual); Great Crosses: Army, Navy and Air Force Merit, and Saint Hermenegild Royal and Military Order; and other medals and awards. Promoted to Lieutenant General, October 23, 1970.

Cucino, Andrea. General, Italian Army; General Secretary for Defense, 1972-   . Born July 23, 1914, in Montecorvino Rovella (Salerno). Attended Military Academy and Artillery School; Staff College; Joint Staff School; NATO Defense College. Combat duty in WW II. Commanding Officer, 132d Artillery Regiment, 1959-60; Military Adviser for Disarmament Problems, Ministry of Foreign Affairs, and Member, NATO Standing Group, Washington, D.C., USA, 1960-62; Commanding Officer, III Armored Brigade "Ariete", 1962-64; Assistant Chief of General Staff, 1964-65; Director for Planning and Operation, Defense Staff, 1965; General Officer Commanding, "Ariete" Armored Division, 1967; Director of Artillery, Ministry of Defense, 1968-72. Silver Medal; Bronze Medal for Military Galantry; two Promotions for War Merit; and other medals and awards.

Cuenca Diaz, Hermenegildo. Major General, Mexican Army; Secretary for National Defense, 1970-   . Born April 13, 1902, in Mexico City, Mexico. Attended Mexican Military College. Chief of Staff, Ministry of National Defense, 1951-58; Senator, State of Lower California, 1964-70. Promoted to Major General, 1958.

Cunningham, Hubert Summers. Major General, United States Army; Chief, Joint US Military Assistance Group, Korea, 1972-   . Born July 3, 1921, Enterprise, Oregon. The Infantry School, Advanced Course; US Army Command and General Staff College; US Army War College; Harvard University, MBA Degree, Business Administration; George Washington University, MA Degree, International Affairs. Commissioned Second Lieutenant, 1943. Served in WW II and Vietnam War. Assistant Division Commander (Support), 101st Airborne Division (Airmobile), US Army, Pacific-Vietnam, 1968; Director, Training Directorate, US Military Assistance Command, Vietnam, 1968-69; Commanding General, 173d Airborne Brigade, US Army, Pacific-Vietnam, 1969-70; Director of Operations, J-3, US Readiness Command, MacDill Air Force Base, Florida, 1970-72. Distinguished Service Medal; Legion of Merit with Oak Leaf Cluster; Distinguished Flying Cross; Bronze Star Medal with two Oak Leaf Clusters; and other medals and awards. Promoted Brigadier General, August 1, 1969; Major General, July 1, 1971.

Cunningham, Hugh Patrick. Major-General, British Army; General Officer Commanding South West District, 1971-   . Born November 4, 1921. Commissioned Second Lieutenant, Royal Engineers, 1942. Served in India-Burma and Southwest Pacific in WW II; Greece, 1950-51. Commander, Royal Engineers, 3 Division, Cyprus and Aden, 1963-66; Commander, 11 Engineer Brigade, British Army of the Rhine, 1967-69; Commander, Mons OCS, 1969-70; British Staff in Canada, 1970-71. OBE.

Currea Cubides, Hernando. General, Colombian Army; Minister of Defense, 1970-   . Born October 7, 1919, Bogota. Attended Military Cadet School; General Staff Course; Advanced Studies Course; Artillery Officers' School (USA); Command and Staff School (USA). Commissioned December 14, 1939. Brigade Commander; Chief of the

Joint General Staff, 1968-69; Commanding General of the Armed Forces, 1969-70. Orden de Boyacá (Gran Oficial); Antonio Ricaurte (Gran Oficial); Almirante Padilla (Gran Oficial); Orden del Mérito Militar Antonio Nariño (Gran Oficial); and other medals and awards. Promoted to Brigadier General, December 1, 1965; Major General, December 16, 1968; General, December 16, 1971.

Curtis, Gilbert L. Major General, United States Air Force; Chief of Staff, Headquarters Military Airlift Command, 1971-   . Born August 29, 1917, in Bridgeport, Connecticut. Lehigh University, Bethlehem, Pennsylvania; Army Air Corps Flying School, 1940; Air Command and Staff School, 1949-50; Industrial College of the Armed Forces, 1959-60. Commissioned Second Lieutenant, US Army Air Corps, 1940. Commander, 63d Troop Carrier Wing, 1964-66; Commander, 63d Military Airlift Wing, 1966-68; Deputy Chief of Staff, Plans, Headquarters Military Airlift Command, 1968-69; Commander, Twenty-first Air Force, 1969-71. Legion of Merit with two Oak Leaf Clusters; Air Force Commendation Medal; and other medals and awards. Promoted to Major General, August 1, 1968.

Cushman, John Holloway. Major General, United States Army; Commanding General, 101st Airborne Division (Airmobile) and Fort Campbell, Kentucky, 1972-   . Born October 3, 1921, Tientsin, China. US Military Academy; Engineer School, Basic and Advanced Courses; Infantry School, Advanced Course; US Army Command and General Staff College; The National War College; Massachusetts Institute of Technology, MS Degree, Civil Engineering. Commissioned Second Lieutenant, 1944. Served in WW II and Vietnam War. Commanding Officer, 2d Brigade, 101st Airborne Division (Airmobile), Fort Campbell, Kentucky, later US Army, Pacific-Vietnam, 1967-68; Commanding General, Fort Devens, Massachusetts, 1968-70; Deputy Commanding General, later Commanding General, Delta Military Assistance Command, US Military Assistance Command, Vietnam, 1970-72; Commanding General, US Army Training Center (Infantry) and Fort Campbell, Kentucky, 1972. Distinguished Service Medal; Silver Star with Oak Leaf Cluster; Legion of Merit with Oak Leaf Cluster; Distinguished Flying Cross; Bronze Star Medal with V Device; and other medals and awards. Promoted to Brigadier General, November 1, 1968; Major General, April 1, 1971.

Cushman, Robert Everton, Jr. General, United States Marine Corps; Commandant, Marine Corps, 1972-   . Born December 24, 1914, St. Paul, Minnesota. US Naval Academy, 1931-35; Marine Corps Officers Basic School, 1935; Marine Corps Senior School, 1945. Commissioned 1935. Served in Pacific Theater, WW II; Vietnam War. Assistant Chief of Staff, G-2 (Intelligence), and Assistant Chief of Staff, G-3 (Plans, Operations, Training), 1962-64; Commanding General, Marine Corps Base, Camp Pendleton, California, and Commanding General 4th Marine Division Headquarters Nucleus, 1964-66; Commanding General, 5th Marine Division, 1966; Commanding General, III Marine Amphibious Force, Vietnam, 1967-69; Senior Advisor, I

Corps Tactical Zone, and I Corps Coordinator for United States/Free World Military Assistance Forces, 1968-69; Deputy Director, Central Intelligence Agency, 1969-71. Navy Cross; Distinguished Service Medal with Gold Star; Legion of Merit with Combat "V"; Bronze Star Medal with Combat "V"; and other US and foreign medals and awards. Promoted to Brigadier General, July 1958; Major General, August 1961; Lieutenant General, June 1, 1967; General, 1971.

Czinege, Lajos. General, Hungarian Army; Minister of Defense, Hungarian People's Republic, 1960-   . Born in 1924 in Karcag, Hungary. Attended Military Political College. Prior to present assignment held high political offices in National and Provincial organizations; Member, Hungarian Socialist Workers' Party, Member of Central Committee, 1959-   . Order of the Red Banner for Labor; Order of the Red Star; Order of the Hungarian People's Republic; and other Hungarian and foreign medals and orders.

Czubinski, Lucjan. Major General, Polish Army; Chief Military Prosecutor, Polish Armed Forces, 1968-   . Born 1930, Dobrzelin, Kutno County. Educated at Poznan University, Law School, LLD. Previously Prosecutor, Office of the Chief Military Prosecutor. Cross of Grunwald; Cross of Merit; and other medals and awards. Promoted to Major General, 1970. Member, Polish United Workers Party.

Czyzewski, Waclaw. Lieutenant General, Polish Army; Deputy Chief, Main Inspectorate of Training, Ministry of National Defense, 1969-   . Born 1917. Attended General Staff War College. Served in anti-German guerrilla warfare in Poland, WW II. Commander, Infantry Battalion, and later Infantry Regiment, 1945-48; Chief of Staff, Infantry Division, 1956-58; Commander, Infantry Division, 1958; Director, Office of Military History, 1959-63; Deputy Commander, Military Technical College, 1964-68; Chief, Polish Contingent, Neutral Nations Supervisory Commission, Korea, 1968-69. Cross of Grunwald; The Partisan Cross; Polonia Restituta; Cross of Valor; and other medals and awards. Promoted to Major General, 1957; Lieutenant General, 1970. Member, Polish United Workers Party.

D

D'Ambrosio, Eugene Joseph. Major General, United States Army; Director of Maintenance, US Army Materiel Command, 1971-   . Born April 13, 1921, in Yonkers, New York. Attended Ordnance School, Basic and Advanced Courses; US Army Command and General Staff College; Army War College, 1967-68. Commissioned Second Lieutenant (ORC) in 1944; transferred to Regular Army 1958. Chief of Equipment Maintenance and Readiness Division, and Director of Materiel Readiness and Support Services, Office of the Assistant Secretary of the Army (Installations and Logistics), 1968-70; Assistant for Maintenance Management and Deputy for Supply, Maintenance, and Transportation, then Chief of the Logistics Management Systems Division, Office of the Assistant Secretary of the Army (Installations and

Logistics), 1970; Commanding Officer, Red River Army Depot, Texarkana, Texas, 1970-71. Legion of Merit with Oak Leaf Cluster; Bronze Star Medal with Oak Leaf Cluster; Air Medal; and other medals and awards. Promoted to Brigadier General, September 1, 1971; Major General, 1973.

Dan, Thaung. Brigadier, Burmese Army; Chief of the Burmese Air Force, 1972-   , and Minister of Culture, Information and Social Welfare. Born c. 1920. Attended Rangoon University. Served in the Burma Independence Army in WW II. Held various staff and command positions. Member of the Secretariat of the Central Committee of the Burma Socialist Program Party.

Daniel, Charles Dwelle, Jr. Major General, United States Army; Director of Army Research, Office of the Chief of Research and Development, US Army, 1972-   . Born on October 30, 1925, in San Antonio, Texas. Attended US Military Academy; Field Artillery School; Antiaircraft and Guided Missile School; Artiilery School, Advanced Course; Command and General Staff College; Industrial College of the Armed Forces, 1967-68; Tulane University, MS, Nuclear Physics, and PhD, Physics. Commissioned Second Lieutenant, June 1946. Chief of the Nuclear, Chemical and Biological Division, then Director of Missiles and Space, Office of the Chief of Research and Development, US Army, 1968-71; Commanding General, I Corps (Group) Artillery, US Army, Pacific-Korea, 1971; Deputy Commanding General, Korea Support Command, US Army, Pacific-Korea, 1971-72. Silver Star; Legion of Merit with two Oak Leaf Clusters; Distinguished Flying Cross; Bronze Star Medal with four Oak Leaf Clusters; Air Medal (17 awards); and other medals and awards. Promoted to Brigadier General July 1, 1971; Major General August 1, 1973.

Danilov, W. A. Major General, USSR Army; Deputy Commanding General, Northern Group of Soviet Forces in Poland, for Political Affairs.

Dankevich, P. Colonel General, USSR Army; Deputy Commander, Strategic Missile Forces. Served on the Soviet-German Front in WW II. Member, Communist Party of the Soviet Union.

Dantas Torres, Mauricio. Fleet Admiral, Brazilian Navy; Director-General of Navigation, 1971-   . Attended Naval School; Armament Course; Officers School for Improvement and Specialization; Naval War College; Escort Command Course and Antisubmarine Warfare Course (Miami and Key West, Florida, USA). Combat duty in WW II. Recent duty: Commander in Chief, Squadron; Commandant, 1st Naval District; Staff Chief, Atlantic Defense Zone Command (EMFA); Director, Center of Naval Armament; Captain of the Ports of the State of Bahia; Director, Merchant Marine School, Rio de Janeiro; Commander, Navy Central Radio Station. Medalha Militar de Ouro; Medalha do Mérito Tamandaré; Ordem do Mérito Aeronautico; Ordem do Mérito Militar; Ordem do Mérito Naval; Medalha da Forca Naval do Sul; Medalha da Forca Naval do Nordeste; and other medals and awards from Brazil and other nations. Promoted to Fleet Admiral, 13 January, 1971.

Dao, Le Minh. Brigadier General, Army of the Republic of South Vietnam; Commander 18th Infantry Division.

Dao, Le Quang. Major General, People's Army of Vietnam; Deputy Chief, General Political Directorate, People's Army of Vietnam, 1956-   ; Alternate Member Lao Dong Party Central Committee, 1960; Member Central Military Party Committee. Delegate to Mixed Central Armistice Commission of Hanoi, 1954-55; Member Central Organizing Committee for celebration of 40th Anniversary of October Revolution, 1957; in charge of public facilities in Hanoi and mobilization and organization of the masses, 1960; Commanding General, Lao War Front, 1971; Member of Presidium, Vietnam Fatherland Front, Third Congress. Promotions: Senior Colonel, 1954; Major General, April 1960.

Daoudou, Sadou. Minister of State for Armed Forces, Cameroon.

Darmstandler, Harry M. Major General, United States Air Force; Assistant Deputy Chief of Staff, Plans, Strategic Air Command, Offutt Air Force Base, Nebraska, 1973-   . Born August 9, 1922, Indianapolis, Indiana. Aviation Cadet Training Course, 1942-43; Naval War College, Command and Staff School, 1955-56; University of Omaha, BS, Military Science; 1964; National War College, 1964-65; George Washington University, MS, International Affairs, 1965. Commissioned Second Lieutenant, US Army Air Corps, in 1943. Combat duty in the European Theater, WW II; Korean War. Special Assistant, then Executive Assistant, later Military Assistant to the Chief of Staff, Supreme Headquarters Allied Powers Europe, 1969-70; Commander, 12th Missile Division, Strategic Air Command, Davis-Monthan Air Force Base, Arizona, 1972-73; Inspector General, Strategic Air Command, Offutt Air Force Base, Nebraska, 1973. Decorations include Legion of Merit with Oak Leaf Cluster, Distinguished Flying Cross, and Air Medal with two Oak Leaf Clusters. Promotions: Brigadier General, December 1, 1971; Major General, 1973.

da Silva, Paulo Victor. Brigadier General, Brazilian Air Force; Air Attache, Embassy of Brazil, Washington, D.C.; Delegate, Inter-American Defense Board; Member, Brazil-United States Joint Defense Commission, 1973-   .

David, Bert Alison. Major General, United States Army; Commanding General, US Army Training Center (Infantry) and Fort Dix, New Jersey, 1972-   . Born July 4, 1924, Palmerton, Pennsylvania. US Military Academy; The Infantry School, Basic Course; The Armored School, Advanced Course; US Army Command and General Staff College; Armed Forces Staff College; Industrial College of the Armed Forces; George Washington University, MS Degree, Business Administration. Commissioned Second Lieutenant, 1946. Served in Vietnam War. Assistant Deputy Chief of Staff for Logistics, US Army, Europe and Seventh Army, 1968-69; Assistant Division Commander, 3d Infantry Division, US Army, Europe, 1969-70; Commanding General, First Republic of Korea Army Detachment, US Army Advisory Group, Korea, 1970-71;

Chief, Army Section, Joint US Military Assistance Group, Korea, 1971-72. Silver Star; Legion of Merit with three Oak Leaf Clusters; Bronze Star Medal; and other medals and awards. Promoted to Brigadier General, September 1, 1969; Major General, November 1, 1971.

Davidenko, V.I. Lieutenant General, USSR Army; Deputy Chief, Main Directorate of Combat Training, Soviet Ground Forces. Served on the Soviet-German Front in WW II. Member, Communist Party of the Soviet Union.

Davidson, Phillip Buford, Jr. Lieutenant General, United States Army; Deputy Assistant Secretary of Defense (Resources and Management), Office Assistant Secretary of Defense (Intelligence), Washington, D.C., 1972-   . Born November 26, 1915, Hachita, New Mexico. US Military Academy; US Army Command and General Staff College; US Army War College; The National War College. Commissioned Second Lieutenant, 1939. Served in WW II and Vietnam War. Deputy Commanding General, US Army Training Center (Infantry) and Fort Dix, New Jersey, 1964-65; Assistant Chief of Staff, G-2, US Army, Pacific-Hawaii, 1965-67; Assistant Chief of Staff, Intelligence, J-2, US Military Assistance Command, Vietnam, 1967-69; Commanding General, US Army Training Center, Infantry and Fort Ord, California, 1969-71; Assistant Chief of Staff for Intelligence, US Army, Washington, D.C., 1971-72. Distinguished Service Medal; Silver Star; Legion of Merit with three Oak Leaf Clusters; Bronze Star Medal; and other medals and awards. Promoted to Brigadier General, September 4, 1964; Major General, July 28, 1968; Lieutenant General, October 1, 1972.

Davies, Alan Cyril. Air Vice-Marshal, British Royal Air Force; Assistant Chief of Air Staff (Policy), Ministry of Defence, 1972-   . Born March 31, 1924. Attended Air Warfare College, 1962; Imperial Defence College, 1969. Enlisted in the Royal Air Force in 1941; commissioned in 1943. Combat duty in WW II. Commander, No. 201 Squadron, 1959-61; Deputy Director, Operational Requirements, Ministry of Defence, 1964-66; Commander, Royal Air Force, Stradishall, Suffolk, 1967-68; Director, Air Plans, Ministry of Defence, 1969-72. CBE.

Davies, Thomas Daniel. Rear Admiral, United States Navy; Deputy Chief of Naval Material for Development, and Chief of Naval Development and Assistant Oceanographer for Ocean Engineering and Development, 1969-   . Born November 3, 1914, in Cleveland, Ohio. Case Institute of Technology, 1931-33; US Naval Academy, 1933-37; Flight Training Course, 1942; National War College, 1961-62. Commissioned Ensign, US Navy, in 1937; designated Naval Aviator in 1942. Served in the Atlantic Theater in WW II. Commanding Officer USS *Caliente* (AO-53), 1960-61; Commander Fleet Air Wing THREE, 1962-63; Commander Naval Air Station, Norfolk, Virginia, 1963-64; Director of Department of the Navy Program Appraisal Office, 1965-67; Commander Carrier Division TWENTY, 1967-69. Legion of Merit with Gold Star; Distinguished Flying Cross with Gold Star; Thurlow Award of the Institute of

Navigation, 1949; Comte de la Vaulx Medal; and other US and foreign medals and awards. Formerly held the world distance record for aircraft and the transcontinental East to West speed record. Promoted to Rear Admiral, July 1, 1965.

Davis, Franklin Milton, Jr. Major General, United States Army; Commandant, US Army War College, and Commanding General, Carlisle Barracks, Pennsylvania, 1971-   . Born July 19, 1918, Malden, Massachusetts. University of Massachusetts, BA Degree, Economics; The Cavalry School, Basic Course; The Signal School, Advanced Course; The Armored School, Advanced Course; US Army Command and General Staff College; US Armed Forces Staff College; US Army War College; George Washington University, MA Degree, International Affairs. Commissioned Second Lieutenant, US Army Reserve, 1940. Served in WW II and Vietnam War. Chief of Staff, V Corps, US Army, Europe, 1966-67; Assistant Chief of Staff, Personnel, J-1, US Military Assistance Command, Vietnam, 1967-68; Commanding General, 199th Light Infantry Brigade, US Army, Pacific-Vietnam, 1968; Director of Personnel Studies and Research, later Director of Military Personnel Policies, Office, Deputy Chief of Staff for Personnel, US Army, Washington, D.C. 1968-71. Distinguished Service Medal; Legion of Merit with Oak Leaf Cluster; Distinguished Flying Cross; Bronze Star Medal with V Device and Oak Leaf Cluster; and other medals and awards. Promoted to Brigadier General, July 1, 1967; Major General, June 1, 1970.

Davis, George Monroe, Jr. Vice Admiral, Medical Corps, United States Navy; Surgeon General of the Navy and Chief, Bureau of Medicine and Surgery, 1969-   . Born June 6, 1916, in Bixby, Oklahoma. Northeastern State Teachers College of Oklahoma; University of Oklahoma, MD, 1939; Postgraduate Course, Internal Medicine, Northwestern School of Medicine, Chicago, Illinois, 1946-47. Commissioned Lieutenant (j.g.), Medical Corps, US Navy, in 1939. Served in the Pacific Theater, WW II; Korean War. Commanding Officer Naval Hospital Yokosuka, Japan, 1962-65; Commanding Officer Naval Hospital, Bethesda, Maryland, 1965-66; Commanding Officer National Naval Medical Center, Bethesda, Maryland, 1966-68; Deputy Surgeon General, US Navy, 1968-69. Distinguished Service Medal; two Navy Commendation Medals; and other medals and awards. Promotions: Rear Admiral, 1965; Vice Admiral, 1969.

Davis, John Blount, Jr. Rear Admiral, United States Navy; Staff Duty, Commander Amphibious Force, US Pacific Fleet, 1972-   . Born February 13, 1919, in Athens, Georgia. Georgia School of Technology; US Naval Academy, 1938-41; Naval Postgraduate School, Ordnance Engineering Course, Annapolis, 1945-46; Cornell University, MS, Engineering, 1946-48; Naval War College, Command and Staff Course, 1952-53; National War College, 1963-64; George Washington University, MA, International Affairs, 1962-64. Commissioned Ensign, US Navy, in 1941. Served in the Atlantic and Pacific Theaters, WW II. Commanding Officer, USS *Prairie* (AD-15),

1964-65; Commander Destroyer Squadron SEVEN, 1965-66; Aide and Executive Assistant to Commander in Chief, Atlantic Fleet, 1966-67; Commander Cruiser-Destroyer Flotilla NINE, 1967-68; Director Systems Analysis Division, Office of the CNO, 1968-70; Commander Amphibious Operations Support Command, Pacific, 1970-72. Legion of Merit with Gold Star; and other medals and awards. Promoted to Rear Admiral, August 1, 1968.

Davis, Woodard E., Jr. Major General, United States Air Force; Commander, US Air Force Tactical Air Warfare Center, 1973-   . Born September 17, 1921, in Riderwood, Alabama. Alabama Polytechnic Institute, 1939-42; Army Air Corps Flying School, 1942-43; Air Tactical School, 1950; Air War College; University of Maryland; University of Florida. Commissioned Second Lieutenant, US Army Air Corps, 1943. Served in the European Theater, WW II; Vietnam War. Commander, 3510th Flying Training Wing and Base Commander, Randolph Air Force Base, Texas, 1965-67; Commander, 12th Tactical Fighter Wing, Vietnam, 1967-68; Commander, 835th Air Division, 1968-69; Deputy Chief of Staff, Operations, Fourth Allied Tactical Air Force, SHAPE, Germany, 1969; Deputy Chief of Staff, Operations and Intelligence, Allied Forces Central Europe, The Netherlands, 1971-72; Commander, Nineteenth Air Force, Tactical Air Command, 1972-73. Silver Star with one Oak Leaf Cluster; Legion of Merit with two Oak Leaf Clusters; Distinguished Flying Cross with two Oak Leaf Clusters; and other US and foreign medals and awards. Promoted to Major General, August 1, 1971.

Davison, Frederic Ellis. Major General, United States Army; Commanding General, 8th Infantry Division, US Army, Europe, 1972-   . Born September 28, 1917, Washington, D.C. Howard University, BS Degree, Zoology and Chemistry; The Infantry School, Basic and Advanced Courses; US Army Command and General Staff College; US Army War College; Howard University, MS Degree, Zoology and Chemistry; George Washington University, MA Degree, International Affairs. Commissioned Second Lieutenant, US Army Reserve, 1939. Served in WW II and Vietnam War. Deputy Commander, later Commanding General, 199th Infantry Brigade (Light), US Army, Pacific-Vietnam, 1967-69; Director, Enlisted Personnel Directorate, Office of Personnel Operations, US Army, Washington, D.C., 1969-71; Deputy Chief of Staff for Personnel, US Army, Europe, and Seventh Army, 1971-72. Distinguished Service Medal; Legion of Merit with Oak Leaf Cluster; Bronze Star Medal; and other medals and awards. Promoted to Brigadier General, October 1, 1968; Major General, April 1, 1971.

Davison, Michael Shannon. General, United States Army; Commander in Chief, US Army, Europe and Seventh Army, and Commander, Central Army Group, North Atlantic Treaty Organization, 1971-   . Born March 21, 1917, San Francisco, California. US Military Academy; The Cavalry School, Basic Course; US Army Command and General Staff College; The National War College; Harvard University, MPA Degree, Public Administration. Commissioned Second Lieutenant, 1939. WW II; Vietnam

War. Director of Doctrine and Systems, later Deputy Assistant Chief of Staff for Force Development, US Army, Washington, D.C., 1965-66; Commandant, US Army Command and General Staff College, and Commanding General, US Army Combat Developments Command, Institute of Combined Arms and Support, Fort Leavenworth, Kansas, 1966-68; Deputy Commander in Chief and Chief of Staff, US Army, Pacific-Hawaii, 1968-69; Chief of Staff, US Pacific Command, 1969-70; Commanding General, II Field Force, Vietnam, US Army, Pacific-Vietnam, 1970-71. Distinguished Service Medal with Oak Leaf Cluster; Silver Star; Legion of Merit with Oak Leaf Cluster; Bronze Star Medal with V Device and two Oak Leaf Clusters; and other medals and awards. Promoted to Brigadier General, September 1, 1962; Major General, July 1, 1965; Lieutenant General, October 1, 1968; General, May 26, 1971.

Dawee, Chullasapya. Air Chief Marshal, Royal Thai Air Force; Assistant Supreme Commander of the Armed Forces, 1973-   . Born August 8, 1914, in Thonburi. Attended Chulachomklao Military Academy, 1935; Flying Training School, 1936; Air Tactical School, Advanced Tactical Operation Course, USA. Commissioned Second Lieutenant, Thai Army, 1935; transferred to Air Force, 1936. Chief of the Air Staff, 1955; Chief of Staff, Supreme Command and Military Adviser to SEATO, 1961; Deputy Minister of War, 1963; Chief of Staff, Supreme Command, Thailand, 1969-73; and SEATO Military Adviser for Thailand, 1961-73. Medal of Freedom with Palms; Legion of Merit (USA); and other Thai and foreign medals and awards. Promoted to Air Chief Marshal, 1957.

Dayan, Moshe. Lieutenant General (Reserve), Israel Defense Forces; Minister of Defense, Israel, 1967-   . Born May 20, 1915, in Degania. Attended Girls Agricultural College, Nahalal; Tel-Aviv University Law School, LLB, 1959; Staff College, Camberley, United Kingdom; University of Jerusalem, Political and Middle Eastern Sciences. Served in the Middle East Theater in WW II; Israeli-Arab Wars, 1948-49, 1956, 1967, 1973. Commander, Southern Region Command, 1950; Commander, Northern Region Command, 1951-52; Chief of Staff, Defense Forces, 1953-58; Minister of Agriculture, 1959-64; Member of Knesset. Promotions: Colonel, 1945; Major General, 1950. Author of Diary of the Sinai Campaign.

Deane, John Russell, Jr. Lieutenant General, United States Army; Deputy Director, Defense Intelligence Agency, Washington, D.C., 1972-   . Born June 8, 1919, San Francisco, California. US Military Academy; Infantry School, Basic and Advanced Courses; US Army Command and General Staff College; Armed Forces Staff College; The National War College; George Washington University, MBA Degree, Business Administration. Commissioned Second Lieutenant, 1942. Served in WW II and Vietnam War. Commanding General, 173d Airborne Brigade, US Army, Pacific-Vietnam, 1966-67; Director of Doctrine, Office, Assistant Chief of Staff for Force Development, US Army, Washington, D.C., 1967-68; Commanding General, 82d

Airborne Division, Fort Bragg, North Carolina, 1968-70; Vice Director, later Director, Defense Communication-Planning Group, Washington, D.C., 1970-71; Director, Defense Special Projects Group, Washington, D.C., 1971-72; Deputy Assistant Chief of Staff for Force Development, US Army, Washington, D.C., 1972. Distinguished Service Cross with Oak Leaf Cluster; Distinguished Service Medal with Oak Leaf Cluster; Silver Star with two Oak Leaf Clusters; Legion of Merit with three Oak Leaf Clusters; Distinguished Flying Cross; Bronze Star Medal with Oak Leaf Cluster; and other medals and awards. Promoted to Brigadier General, August 1, 1965; Major General, November 1, 1967; Lieutenant General, September 27, 1972.

Debalyuk, A. Major General, USSR Army; Chief, Political Directorate, Belorussian Military District, 1971-   . Duty on the Soviet-German Front, WW II. Chief, Political Directorate, Turkestan Military District, 1966-71. Member, Communist Party of the Soviet Union.

Debeche, Albert. Lieutenant General, Belgian Air Force; Chief of Belgian Air Force General Staff. Born May 19, 1919, in Viviere. Attended Ecole Royale Militaire, 1938-40; Instruction Center for Artillery Sub-Lieutenants, 1940. Commissioned Acting Pilot Officer, British Royal Air Force, 1942. Served in Belgium, France, and in Belgian section of the British Royal Air Force in WW II. Director of Planning, Air Force General Staff, 1962-64; Aide de Camp to the King, 1964; Chief of Staff to Inspector General of the Air Force, 1964-65; Commander, Air Force Instruction and Training Division, 1965-68; Inspector General of the Air Force, 1968-71. Croix de Chevalier de l'Ordre de la Couronne; Lion de Bronze sur la Médaille Commemorative, 40-45.

Debré, Michel. Minister of National Defense, France, 1969-   . Born January 15, 1912, in Paris. Attended Cavalry School, Saumur, 1931-32; Faculté de Droit, Doctor of Law degree, 1934; Ecole Libre des Sciences Politiques; Concours de l'Auditorat au Conseil d'Etat, 1934. Commissioned Sub-Lieutenant, 11th Cuirassier Regiment, 1932. Served in WW II, POW, 1940; participated in French Resistance. Minister of Economy and Finance, 1966-68; Minister of Foreign Affairs, 1968-69; Mayor of Amboise, 1966; Deputy, 1963. Officier de la Légion d'Honneur a titre militaire; Croix de Guerre, 1939-45; Rosette de la Résistance; Médaille des Evadés; Grand Cross of the American Legion.

de Chastonay, Bernard. Major General, Swiss Army; Commanding General, 10th Mountain Division. Born in 1922.

de Courten, Harald. Major General, Swiss Army; Commander Artillery Forces. Born in 1913.

De Giorgi, Gino. Admiral, Italian Navy; Chief of Naval Staff, 1973-   . Born July 17, 1914, in Florence. Attended Naval Academy; Naval Command Course; Naval War College, Newport, Rhode Island, USA. Combat duty in WW II. Chief of Staff, Headquarters, 1st Naval Division, 1963; Commanding Officer, 2d Naval Division, 1968; Deputy Chief of Naval Staff, 1970-72; Commander in Chief Italian Fleet, 1972-73. Two Silver Medals; two Crosses for Military Gallantry; two Crosses for War Merit; and other medals and awards. Promotions: Commodore, 1964; Rear Admiral, 1968; Admiral, 1972.

Delahouse, Paul. Rear Admiral, French Navy. Naval Attache, Embassy of France, London.

DeLonga, Peter R. Major General, United States Air Force; Director of Maintenance Engineering and Supply, Deputy Chief of Staff, Systems and Logistics, 1973-   . Born February 11, 1921, in Beadling, Pennsylvania. Slippery Rock College, Pennsylvania, BS, 1943; Royal Air Force Flying Training School, 1943-44; Air Force Institute of Technology, 1946-48, BS, Industrial Engineering and Logistics, 1948; Air Command and Staff School, Logistics Course, 1953-54; Advanced Management Course, Harvard University, 1964. Commissioned Second Lieutenant, US Army Air Corps, 1944. Served in the China-Burma-India Theater, WW II; Vietnam War. Chief, Operations Division, Office, Deputy Chief of Staff, Systems and Logistics, 1967-68; Chairman, Long Range Logistics Manpower Task Force, Office, Secretary of Defense, 1968-69; Assistant, Logistics Planning, 1969-70; Deputy Chief of Staff, Materiel, Headquarters Seventh Air Force, Vietnam, 1970-72; Deputy Chief of Staff, Logistics, Headquarters Pacific Air Forces, Hawaii, 1972-73. Distinguished Service Medal; Legion of Merit with two Oak Leaf Clusters; Distinguished Flying Cross with one Oak Leaf Cluster; and other US and foreign medals and awards. Promoted to Major General, March 1, 1972.

DeLuca, Joseph R. Major General, United States Air Force; Director of Budget, Office of the Comptroller, Headquarters US Air Force, 1971-   . Born September 3, 1918, in Greenville, Pennsylvania. Professional School of Accounting and Finance, Cleveland, Ohio; Army Air Corps, Officers Candidate School, 1942; Cleveland College, Western Reserve University, Cleveland, Ohio, 1946; Aviation Ordnance Course, 1947; Air War College, 1956-57; University of Maryland, BS, Business Administration, 1962; George Washington University, MA, International Affairs, 1963. Commissioned Second Lieutenant, US Army Air Corps Reserve, 1942. Served in the European Theater, WW II. Deputy Commander, Ogden Air Materiel Area, 1964-65; Deputy Director of Supply, Headquarters Air Force Logistics Command, 1965-67; Deputy Chief of Staff, Supply, Air Force Logistics Command, 1967-69; Commander, Advanced Logistics System Center, 1969-70; Deputy Chief of Staff, Comptroller, 1970-71. Distinguished Service Medal; Legion of Merit; Eugene M. Zuckert Management Award; and other medals and awards. Promoted to Major General, November 1, 1967.

de Magalhaes, Gualter Maria Menezes. Vice Admiral, Brazilian Navy; Commander in Chief of the Fleet. Born January 12, 1918, in Rio de Janeiro. Naval Academy; Naval War College; Senior War College, Command and General

Staff Course; US Naval Fleet Sound School; US Naval Diesel Training School. Commissioned Guarda-Marinha, April 1, 1937. Combat duty in World War II. Commanding Officer, submarine chasers *Jacui* and *Guaiba,* tug *Triunfo,* light cruiser Tamandaré; Commandant of the Center for Instruction of Naval Reserve Officers; Director of the Naval Sports Center; Captain of the Ports of the State of Pará e Amapá; Deputy Chief of Staff of the Naval Ministry; Commandant of the "Almirante Wandenkolk" Instruction Center; Chief of Staff of the Naval Ministry; Commandant, 3d Naval District. Medalha de Serviço de Guerra with three starts; Medalha da Força Naval do Nordeste with silver leaf; Ordem do Mérito Naval, Gráu de Comendador; Medalha Mérito Tamandaré; Medalha da Campanha do Atlantico Sul; Medalha Militar de Ouro; and other medals and awards from Brazil and other nations. Promoted to Rear Admiral, September 6, 1966; Vice Admiral, December 9, 1969.

de Maiziere, Ulrich Karl Ernst. General, Army of the Federal Republic of Germany; Chief of Staff of the Armed Forces, 1966- . Born February 24, 1912, Stade, Germany. Attended Military Academy, 1930-33. Commissioned Second Lieutenant, German Army, 1933. Participated in German-Polish and German-Soviet Campaigns, WW II. Chief of Operations Branch, Armed Forces Staff, 1955-57; Commander, Combat Team and later Brigade, Hannover, 1958-59; Deputy Commander, 1st Armored Infantry Division, 1959-60; Commandant, Armed Forces Leadership and Character Guidance School, Koblenz, 1960-62; Commandant, Armed Forces Command and Staff College, Hamburg, 1962-64; Chief of Army Staff, 1964-66. Iron Cross, 1st and 2d Class; and other medals and awards. Promoted to General, 1966.

Dement'ev, V. T. Major General, USSR Army; Chief, Political Directorate, North Caucasus Military District, 1969- . Duty on the Soviet-German Front in WW II. Member, Communist Party of the Soviet Union.

Dempster, Kenneth C. Major General, United States Air Force; Director, Plans, Programs and Systems, Defense Supply Agency, 1970- . Born September 25, 1917, Gardnerville, Nevada. San Mateo Junior College, San Mateo, California, 1935-37; University of California, Berkeley, California, 1937-40; Army Air Corps Flying School, 1940; Air Command and Staff School, 1949; Army War College, 1954-55. Commissioned Second Lieutenant, US Army Air Corps, 1940. Served in the Pacific and European Theaters, WW II; Korean War; Vietnam War. Deputy Director, Operational Requirements, Deputy Chief of Staff, Programs and Resources, Headquarters USAF, 1964-66; Director, Operational Requirements and Development Plans, Deputy Chief of Staff, Programs and Resources, Headquarters USAF, 1966-67; Vice Commander, Thirteenth Air Force, Clark Air Base, Philippines, 1967-70. Legion of Merit with three Oak Leaf Clusters; Distinguished Flying Cross; Bronze Star Medal; and other US and foreign medals and awards. Promotions: Brigadier General, June 1, 1964; Major General, September 15, 1966.

de Oliveira Figueiredo, João Baptista. Major General, Brazilian Army; Chief of Presidential Military Household, 1969- . Born January 15, 1918, in Rio de Janeiro. Attended Military Academy, Rio de Janeiro; Military School of Realengo; School for Officers' Advanced Training; Army Command and Staff School; Senior War College. Member, Military Mission to Paraguay, 1955-56; Commander, Força Publica of São Paulo State, 1966; Commander, 1st Regiment Guards' Cavalry, 1967-69; Chief of Staff, 3d Army, 1969; Secretary General, Council of National Security. Medalha Militar; Medalha de Guerra; Medalha Honorifica (Paraguay); and other medals and awards. Promoted to Major General, 1969.

de Poix, Vincent Paul. Vice Admiral, United States Navy; Director, Defense Intelligence Agency, 1972- . Born August 13, 1916, Los Angeles, California. Lafayette College, Easton, Pennsylvania, 1934-35; US Naval Academy, 1935-39; Flight Training Course, 1941; Ordnance Engineering (Aviation) Course, Postgraduate School, 1944-45; Massachusetts Institute of Technology, MS, Aeronautical Engineering, 1945-46; National War College, 1963-64. Commissioned Ensign, US Navy, in 1939; designated Naval Aviator in 1941. Served in the Pacific Theater, WW II; Korean War; Vietnam War. Prospective, then actual Commanding Officer USS *Enterprise* (CVA(N)65), 1960-63; Assistant Director for Administration and Management, Defense Research and Engineering, Office of the Secretary of Defense, 1964-66; Assistant Director, Operational Test and Evaluation, Defense Research and Engineering, 1966; Commander Carrier Division SEVEN, 1966-67; Assistant Deputy Chief of Naval Operations (Development), 1967-69; Deputy Director of Defense Research and Engineering (Administration, Evaluation and Management), Office of Secretary of Defense, 1969-71; Commander Second Fleet, 1971-72. Distinguished Service Medal with Gold Star; Legion of Merit; Air Medal with Gold Star; and other US and foreign medals and awards. Promoted to Vice Admiral, February 14, 1969.

DePuy, William Eugene. Lieutenant General, United States Army; Assistant Vice Chief of Staff, US Army, Washington, D.C., 1969- . Born October 1, 1919, Jamestown, North Dakota. South Dakota State College, BS Degree, Economics; US Army Command and General Staff College; Armed Forces Staff College; British Imperial Defense College. Commissioned Second Lieutenant, US Army Reserve, 1941. Served in WW II and Vietnam War. Director, Plans and Programs, Office, Assistant Chief of Staff for Force Development, US Army, Washington, D.C., 1963-64; Assistant Chief of Staff for Operations, J-3, US Military Assistance Command, Vietnam, 1964-66; Commanding General, 1st Infantry Division, US Army, Pacific-Vietnam, 1966-67; Special Assistant for Counterinsurgency and Special Activities, Organization, Joint Chiefs of Staff, Washington, D.C., 1967-68; Acting Assistant Vice Chief of Staff, US Army, Washington, D.C., 1969. Distinguished Service Cross with Oak Leaf Cluster; Distinguished Service Medal, with two Oak Leaf Clusters; Silver Star with two Oak Leaf Clusters; Legion of Merit; Distinguished Flying

Cross; Bronze Star Medal; and other medals and awards. Promoted to Brigadier General, July 1, 1963; Major General, April 1, 1966; Lieutenant General, March 10, 1969.

de SaVianna Rebelo, Horacio Jose. General Portuguese Army; Minister of Defense and Army.

Deslandes, Venancio. General, Portuguese Air Force; Chief of General Staff of the Armed Forces, 1968-   . Born May 8, 1909, in Lisbon, Portugal. Attended Portuguese Military Academy. Comissioned Second Lieutenant (Cavalry), Portuguese Army, in 1928; transferred to the Air Force, 1935. Commanding Officer, 2d Air Base, 1951-53; Professor, Institute of Higher Military Studies; Ambassador to Spain, 1959-61; Govenor-General and Supreme Commander, Angola, 1961-62; Deputy Chief of Staff of the Armed Forces, 1963-68. Deputy in the National Assembly. Promoted to General in 1958.

Desobry, William Robertson. Major General, United States Army; Commanding General, US Army Armor Center, Commandánt, US Armor School, and Commanding General US Army Training Center (Armor), Fort Knox, Kentucky, 1971-   . Born September 11, 1918, Manila, Philippine Islands. Georgetown University, BS Degree, Foreign Service; The Infantry School, Basic Course; US Army Command and General Staff College; The National War College. Commissioned Second Lieutenant, US Army Reserve, 1941. Served in WW II and Vietnam War. Director, Department of Strategy, US Army War College, Carlisle Barracks, Pennsylvania, 1965; Deputy Senior Advisor, IV Corps Advisory Group, US Military Assistance Command, Vietnam, 1965-66; Senior Advisor, IV Corps Advisory Group, US Military Assistance Command, Vietnam, 1966-68; Deputy Director of Plans, Office, Deputy Chief of Staff for Military Operations, US Army, Washington, D.C., 1968; Director of Operations, Office, Deputy Chief of Staff for Military Operations, US Army, Washington, 1968-70; Commanding General, 1st Armored Division, Fort Hood, Texas, 1970-71. Distinguished Service Medal; Silver Star; Legion of Merit with two Oak Leaf Clusters; Bronze Star Medal; and other medals and awards. Promoted to Brigadier General, September 1, 1966; Major General, September 18, 1968.

De Souza, Paul Emile. Lieutenant Colonel, Army of Dahomey; Chief of Staff, Dahomeyan Army, 1970-   . Formerly Chief of Military Cabinet of the President; Head of State and Minister of Defense, 1969-70.

Desta, Iskender. Admiral, Imperial Ethiopian Navy; Deputy Commander in Chief, Imperial Ethiopian Navy. Born July 7, 1935, Addis Ababa.

Dettre, Rexford H., Jr. Major General, United States Air Force; Deputy Director, Plans and Policy, J-5, The Joint Staff, Organization of the Joint Chiefs of Staff, 1971-   . Born March 21, 1920, Philadelphia, Pennsylvania. US Military Academy, 1939-43; University of California, Graduate Studies, Mechanical Engineering, 1945-49; Air

Command and Staff College, 1952. Commissioned Second Lieutenant, US Army Air Corps, 1943. Served in the European Theater, WW II, POW; Korean War; Vietnam War. Commander, 4780th Air Defense Wing, 1966-67; Commander, 30th Air Division, 1967-68; Assistant Deputy Chief of Staff, Plans, and later Deputy Chief of Staff, Plans, Headquarters Aerospace Defense Command, 1968-70; Assistant Chief of Staff, Plans, J-5, US Military Assistance Command, Vietnam, 1970-71. Distinguished Service Medal; Legion of Merit; Distinguished Flying Cross; and other medals and awards. Promoted to Major General, July 1, 1970.

Dextraze, Jacques Alfred. General, Canadian Armed Forces; Chief of the Defence Staff, Canadian Armed Forces, 1972-   . Born August 15, 1919, Montreal, Quebec. St. Joseph's College, Berthierville, Quebec; Officer Cadet Training Unit; Canadian Army Staff College, Kingston, Ontario, 1952. Enlisted in Les Fusiliers Mont-Royal, 1940; commissioned, 1941. Served in northern Europe in WW II; inactive 1945-50; served in the Korean War. Commander, Eastern Quebec Area, Quebec City, 1962-63; Chief of Staff, United Nations Forces, Congo, 1963-64; Commander, 2d Infantry Brigade Group, Camp Petawawa, Ontario, 1964-66; Chief of Staff for Operations and Training, Mobile Command Headquarters, Montreal, 1966-67; Deputy Commander for Operations, Mobile Command Headquarters, Montreal, 1967-68; Deputy Chief of Personnel for Policy and Resource Management, Canadian Forces Headquarters, Ottawa, 1968-69; Deputy Chief of Personnel (Military), and Chief of Personnel, Canadian Forces Headquarters, Ottawa, 1969-72; Special Assistant to the Chief of the Defence Staff, Canadian Armed Forces, 1972. CBE; CMM; DSO with Bar; CD. Promoted to Brigadier, February 1962; Major-General, September 1967; Lieutenant-General, December 1970; General, September 1, 1972.

Dhenin, Geoffrey Howard. Air Vice-Marshal, British Royal Air Force; Principal Medical Officer, Strike Command, Royal Air Force, 1971-   . Born April 2, 1918. St. John's College, Cambridge; Guy's Hospital, London; degrees: MA, MD, Diploma in Public Health; Pilot Training, 1945-46; Staff College, Bracknell, 1958-59. Served in Bomber Command in WW II. Commander, Princess Mary's RAF Hospital, Akrotiri, Cyprus, 1960-63; Commander, RAF Hospital, Ely, 1963-66; Principal Medical Officer, Air Support Command, 1966-68; Director, Health and Research, RAF, 1968-70; Deputy Director General, Medical Services, RAF, 1970-71. AFC and Bar; GM; Queen's Honorary Physician, 1970.

Dhiradhamrong, Abhichart. Major General, Royal Thai Army; Chief of Military Planning Office, SEATO, 1966-   . Born March 1, 1922, in Bangkok, Thailand. Chulachomklao Royal Military Academy, 1942; Thammasart University, Masters Degree, Public Administration; Infantry School, Fort Benning, Georgia, USA; Royal Thai Army Command and General Staff College; Command and General Staff College, USA; Royal Thai Army Armed Forces Staff College; National Defense

College. Commissioned Second Lieutenant, Royal Thai Army, 1942. Served in the Korean War. Formerly Staff Member, Headquarters, Supreme Command, Bangkok, 1960-66.

Di, Tran Ba. Brigadier General, Army of the Republic of South Vietnam; Commander 9th Infantry Division.

Diagana, Sidi Mohamed. Minister of National Defense, Islamic Republic of Mauritania.

Diaz Osorio, Alfonso. Rear Admiral, Colombian Navy; Chief of the Naval Staff.

Dickel, Friedrich. Colonel General, National People's Army, Democratic Republic of Germany; Minister of the Interior and Chief of German People's Police, 1963-   . Born December 9, 1913, in Wuppertal-Vohwinkel. Joined German Young Communist League, 1928; joined German Communist Party, 1930. Left Germany in 1933. Served in Spanish Civil War with the International Brigade and in the USSR in World War II. Joined German People's Police, 1946, and later transferred to Mobile People's Police. Head of People's Police Political School, 1948; Deputy Chief of Mobile People's Police; Chief of Political Administration, Mobile People's Police; First Deputy Minister for National Defense, 1956-57, 1959-63. Member of Central Committee, Socialist Unity Party, 1967-   ; Member of People's Chamber, 1967-   .

Dickman, Joseph Lawrence. Major General, United States Air Force; Deputy Director (Operations and Administration), Defense Nuclear Agency, 1971-   . Born March 23, 1917, in Tampa, Florida. United States Military Academy, 1935-39; Army Air Corps Flying School, 1939; Air Command and Staff College, 1947-48; Air War College, 1951; National War College, 1955-56. Commissioned Second Lieutenant, US Army Air Corps, 1939. Served in the European Theater, WW II. Executive Assistant to the Secretary of the Air Force, 1961-63; Commander, Duluth Air Defense Sector, 1963-64; Director of Operations, Deputy Chief of Staff, Operations, Headquarters North American Air Defense Command/Continental Air Defense Command (NORAD/CONAD), 1964-65; Director, Combat Operations Center, Headquarters NORAD/CONAD Region, 1965-67; Commander, Eastern NORAD/CONAD and First Air Force (ADC), 1967-70; Deputy Chief of Staff, Operations, Aerospace Defense Command, 1970-71. Legion of Merit; Distinguished Flying Cross with one Oak Leaf Cluster; and other medals and awards. Promoted to Major General, August 20, 1965.

Diete-Spiff, Alfred Papapreye. Lieutenant Commander, Nigerian Navy; Military Governor, Rivers District, 1967-   . Born July 30, 1942, in Nembe. Attended St. Joseph's College, Sassie-Buea, West Cameroon; Britannia Royal Naval College, Dartmouth, England, 1962-66. Commissioned in the Nigerian Navy, 1966.

Dietrich, William Allen. Major General, United States Air Force; Vice Commander, Twenty-second Air Force, Travis Air Force Base, California, 1971-   . Born November 12, 1923, in Oklahoma City, Oklahoma. Aviation Cadet Training Course, 1942; Air Force Advanced Management School, 1955-56; George Washington University, BA, Business Management and Administration, 1956; Command and General Staff College, 1959-60. Commissioned Second Lieutenant, US Army Air Corps, 1942. Served in the China-Burma-India Theater, WW II, and in the Vietnam War. Special Plans Officer, and later, Deputy Secretary of the Joint Staff, US Military Assistance Command, Vietnam (MACV), 1965-66; Deputy Commander for Operations, and later Vice Commander, 516th Tactical Airlift Wing, Dyess Air Force Base, Texas, 1966-68; Commander, 313th Tactical Airlift Wing, Forbes Air Force Base, Kansas, 1968-70; Commander, US Air Force Tactical Airlift Center and the 839th Air Division, Pope Air Force Base, North Carolina, 1970-71. Decorations include Legion of Merit with Oak Leaf Cluster, Distinguished Flying Cross with Oak Leaf Cluster, Air Medal with two Oak Leaf Clusters, Breast Order of Yun Hui (Republic of China). Promotions: Brigadier General, August 1, 1970; Major General, 1973.

Dillon, John G. Rear Admiral, Civil Engineer Corps, United States Navy; Assistant for Construction Operations, Office of the Deputy Assistant Secretary of Defense (Installations and Housing), 1971-   . Born December 11, 1919, in Tacoma, Washington. College of Puget Sound; Washington State College, Pullman, BS, Civil Engineering, 1941; Naval War College, Newport, Rhode Island, 1959-60. Commissioned Ensign, Civil Engineer Corps, US Naval Reserve, in 1942; transferred to US Navy, 1946. Served in the Pacific Theater, WW II; Vietnam War. Director, then Commanding Officer Southeast Division, Naval Facilities Engineering Command/District Civil Engineer and Officer in Charge of Construction, Sixth Naval District, 1965-67; Special Assistant for Management Studies to Vice Commander, Naval Facilities Engineering Command, 1967-68; Deputy Commander for Planning, Naval Facilities Engineering Command, 1968-69; Commander Third Naval Construction Brigade, 1969-70; Commanding Officer, Northern Division Naval Facilities Engineering Command, Philadelphia, 1970-71. Distinguished Service Medal; Legion of Merit; Navy Commendation Medal; Moreell Medal of Society of American Military Engineers; Award for Outstanding Achievement in the Field of Engineering (Wahington State University); and other US and foreign medals and awards. Promotions: Captain, March 1, 1963; Rear Admiral, July 1, 1969.

Dinca, Ion. Lieutenant General, Romanian Army; Member of Staff of Central Committee, Romanian Communist Party.

Dixon, Robert James. Lieutenant General, United States Air Force; Deputy Chief of Staff, Personnel, Headquarters, US Air Force, 1970-   . Born April 9, 1920, in New York, New York. Dartmouth College, AB, 1941; Pilot Training, Royal Canadian Air Force, 1941-42; Air War College, 1959. Commissioned Pilot Officer (Second Lieutenant), Royal

Canadian Air Force, 1942; transferred to the US Army Air Forces, 1943. Served in the European Theater, WW II, POW; Korean War; Vietnam War. Commander, 45th Air Division, 1965-67; Assistant Deputy Chief of Staff, Personnel, for Military Personnel, and Commander, USAF Military Personnel Center, Randolph Air Force Base, Texas, 1967-69; Vice Commander, Seventh Air Force, Vietnam, 1969-70. Distinguished Service Cross; Distinguished Service Medal with one Oak Leaf Cluster; Legion of Merit with one Oak Leaf Cluster; Distinguished Flying Cross; Bronze Star Medal; and other US and foreign medals and awards. Promotions: Brigadier General, June 16, 1965; Major General, December 1, 1967; Lieutenant General, August 1, 1970.

Do, Tran. Major General, People's Army of Vietnam; Deputy Commander, People's Liberation Armed Forces, 1963-   ; Alternate Member Lao Dong Party Central Committee; Chairman Political Directorate, Central Office for South Vietnam; Member, Central Office for South Vietnam Military Party Committee, 1963. Born in 1922 in North Vietnam. Member, Revolutionary Youth Movement, 1930; Arrested and deported to Son La, 1941; held high party and military posts in Viet Minh movement, 1945-55; Commander, 312th Division, 1958; may have been killed during Tet Offensive, February 1968.

Dobrev, Khristo. Colonel General, Bulgarian Army; Deputy Minister of Defense; Commander in Chief, Bulgarian Air Defense and Air Forces.

Dodd, Frank Leslie. Air Vice-Marshal, British Royal Air Force; Director General, Linesman Project, 1970-   . Born March 5, 1919. Attended Reading University; Central Flying School Course, 1940; Royal Air Force Flying College, 1952-53; Staff College, 1955; Imperial Defence College, 1964. Joined Royal Air Force Volunteer Reserve, 1938; commissioned in 1940. Flying instructor and photo reconnaissance pilot in WW II. Commanding Officer, Royal Air Force, Coningsby, 1961-63; Air Officer Commanding and Commandant, Central Flying School, 1965-68; Ministry of Defence, Director of Establishments, 1968-70. CBE; DSO; DFC; AFC and two Bars.

Dolvin, Welborn Griffin. Lieutenant General, United States Army; Commanding General, IX Corps, US Army, Japan, 1972-   . Born February 8, 1916, Siloam, Georgia. US Military Academy; The Infantry School, Basic Course; US Army Command and General Staff College; US Army War College. Commissioned Second Lieutenant, 1939. Served in WW II and Vietnam War. Commanding General, 3d Armored Division, US Army, Europe, 1966-68; Chief of Staff, Central Army Group, and Commanding General, US Army Element, Headquarters, Central Army Group, Europe, 1968-70; Special Assistant to the Commander, US Military Assistance Command, Vietnam, 1970; Chief of Staff, US Military Assistance Command, Vietnam, 1970-71; Commanding General, XXIV Corps, US Army, Pacific-Vietnam, 1971-72. Distinguished Service Cross; Distinguished Service Medal with two Oak Leaf Clusters; Silver Star with three Oak Leaf Clusters; Legion of Merit

with two Oak Leaf Clusters; Bronze Star Medal; and other medals and awards. Promoted to Brigadier General April 1, 1961; Major General, September 1, 1963; Lieutenant General, August 1, 1971.

Don, Nguyen. Major General, People's Army of Vietnam; Deputy Chief of General Staff, 1969; Vice Minister of National Defense, 1967; alternate Member, Lao Dong Party Central Committee, 1960; Member Central Military Party Committee. Born in 1914 in Son Tinh District, Quang Ngai Province. Joined Indochina Communist Party, arrested and deported to Ba To (Quang Ngai) prison by French, 1940; escaped, assisted in organization of guerrilla unit in Ba To, 1943; held important political and military posts in Viet Minh movement, 1945-54; Commander 305th and 324th Divisions and Fourth Military Region, 1955-60; returned to South, 1961; Commander and Secretary of Fifth Military Region Committee, and Deputy Commander Central Office for South Vietnam, 1962-67; recalled to North, 1967; Chief of General Department of Rear Services, 1969; Member, Secretariat of Vietnam and Federation of Youth, 1970; elected Deputy to Fourth National Assembly, 1971. Promoted to Major General, 1958.

Donaldson, James Carmichael, Jr. Rear Admiral, United States Navy; Study Director, Fleet Reorganization Study, Office of the Chief of Naval Operations, 1972-   . Born December 11, 1921, in Bessemer, Alabama. US Naval Academy, 1939-43; Naval War College, 1952; Industrial College of the Armed Forces, 1962; George Washington University, MBA, 1962. Commissioned Ensign, US Navy, in 1943; designated Naval Aviator in 1944. Served in the Pacific Theater in WW II; Vietnam War. Commanding Officer, USS *Hermitage* (LSD-34), 1964-65; Commanding Officer, USS *Hancock* (CVA-19), 1965-66; Director, Fleet Operations Division, and Director, Naval Reconnaissance Center, Office of the CNO, 1967-69; Commander Carrier Division THREE, 1969-70; Deputy Director for Operations (Reconnaissance and Electronic Warfare), Organization of the Joint Chiefs of Staff, 1970-72. Distinguished Service Medal; Legion of Merit with two Gold Stars; and other US and foreign medals and awards. Promoted to Rear Admiral, 1968.

Donegan, Patric. Minister of Defense, Ireland, 1973-   .

Donley, Edwin I. Major General, United States Army; Commanding General, US Army Missile Command, Redstone Arsenal, Alabama, 1969-   . Born May 9, 1918, Buchanan, Michigan. US Naval Academy; US Army Command and General Staff College; Industrial College of the Armed Forces; University of Michigan, MBA Degree, Industrial Management. Commissioned Second Lieutenant, US Army Reserve, 1941. Served in WW II. Deputy Commanding General, Land Combat Systems, US Army Missile Command, Redstone Arsenal, Alabama, 1966-67; Commanding General, US Army Mobility Equipment Command, St. Louis, Missouri, 1967-68; Deputy Commanding General for Supply and Maintenance, US Army Communications Zone Europe, and Chief, US Army

Communications Zone Europe Supply and Maintenance Agency, US Army, Europe, 1968-69; Commanding General, US Army Materiel Command, Europe, 1969. Legion of Merit with two Oak Leaf Clusters; Bronze Star Medal; and other medals and awards. Promoted to Brigadier General, April 1, 1966; Major General, December 1, 1969.

Donnet, Baron M. Lieutenant General Aviator, Belgian Army; Naval, Military and Air Attache, Embassy of Belgium, London.

Dorinin, M. Major General, USSR Army; Deputy Chief, Political Directorate, Carpathian Military District. Served on Soviet-German Front in WW II. Member of the Communist Party of the Soviet Union.

Dorj, B. Colonel General, Mongolian Army; Minister of Defense, Mongolian People's Republic.

Dougherty, Russell Elliott. General, United States Air Force; Chief of Staff, Supreme Headquarters, Allied Powers, Europe, Belgium, 1972-   . Born November 15, 1920, in Glasgow, Kentucky. Western Kentucky University, BA, 1941; Flying Training Course, 1943; University of Louisville Law School, JD, 1948; National War College, 1959-60. Commissioned in the Army Air Corps Reserve, 1943; transferred to US Air Force, 1947. Served in the Korean War. Assistant Director of Plans for Joint National Security Council Matters, 1963-64; Deputy Director, Plans, J-3, Headquarters US European Command, France, 1964-65; Director, European Region, Office of the Secretary of Defense (International Security Affairs), 1965-67; Director, J-5, Plans and Policy, Headquarters US European Command, Germany, 1967-69; Assistant Deputy Chief of Staff, Plans and Operations, Headquarters USAF, 1969-70; Deputy Chief of Staff, Plans and Operations, Headquarters USAF, 1970-71; Commander, Second Air Force, 1971-72. Distinguished Service Medal with one Oak Leaf Cluster; Legion of Merit with two Oak Leaf Clusters; Bronze Star Medal; and other medals and awards. Promotions: Brigadier General, January 5, 1964; Major General, November 1, 1966; Lieutenant General, February 6, 1970; General, May 1, 1972.

Douglas, Desmond Lloyd George. Air Vice Marshal, Royal Australian Air Force; Senior Defence Whip. Born May 5, 1917, Sandgate, Queensland. Attended Royal Australian Air Force Cadet College, 1937; Imperial Defence College, 1964. Commissioned in 1937. Served in the European Theater in WW II. Officer Commanding, RAAF, Richmond, N.S.W., 1965-67; Director General, Plans and Policy, Department of Air, 1967-70; Head, Australian Joint Services Staff, Washington, D.C., USA, 1970-72. OBE; DFC. Member of the Australian Institute of Mechanical Engineering.

Douglas-Withers, John Keppel Ingold. Major-General, British Army; Assistant Chief of Personnel and Logistics, Ministry of Defence, 1972-   . Born December 11, 1919. Attended Christ Church, Oxford; University of Poitiers, France, 1938; Staff College, Camberley, 1950; Imperial Defence College, 1965. Commissioned in 1940. Served in Middle East, Africa and Europe in WW II. Commander, 47 Field Regiment, British Army of the Rhine and Hong Kong, 1962-64; Commander, 6th Infantry Brigade, British Army of the Rhine, 1966-67; Chief of Staff, 1st British Corps, 1968-69; General Officer Commanding, South West District, 1970-72. CBE; MC. Associate of Institute of Linguists (French and German), 1939-   .

Doukara, Kissima. Captain, Army of Mali; Minister of Defense, Security and Interior, Mali.

Dovers, William John. Rear Admiral, Royal Australian Navy; Deputy Chief, Naval Staff, 1972-   . Born February 12, 1918, in Eastwood, N.S.W. Attended Royal Australian Naval College; Imperial Defence College. Commissioned Sub-Lieutenant in 1939. Served in the Atlantic, Mediterranean, and with the Eastern Fleet in WW II. Deputy Chief, Naval Personnel, 1966-67; Second Naval Member, 1967; Director, Joint Staff, Department of Defence, 1968-71; Flag Officer Commanding Australian Fleet, 1971-72. CBE; DSC. Promoted to Rear Admiral in 1967.

Dowd, Wallace Rutherford, Jr. Rear Admiral, Supply Corps, United States Navy; Commander Naval Supply Systems Command, and Chief of Supply Corps of the Navy, 1972-   . Born July 1, 1921, in Cambridge, Massachusetts. University of Washington, BA, 1942; Naval Supply Corps School, 1942; Stanford University, Graduate School of Business Administration, MBA, 1949; Naval War College, 1954-55. Commissioned Ensign, Supply Corps, US Navy, in 1942. Served in the Pacific Theater, WW II; Korean War; Vietnam War. Head of Material Management Branch, Office of the CNO, 1965-66; Assistant Fleet and Force Supply Officer, Staff of Commander Service Force, US Pacific Fleet, 1966-68; Commander Naval Supply Center, Charleston, South Carolina, 1968-70; Vice Commander, Naval Supply Systems Command, 1970-71; Commander Naval Supply Center, Oakland, 1971-72. Distinguished Service Medal; Legion of Merit with Gold Star; Navy Commendation Medal; and other medals and awards. Promoted to Rear Admiral, July 1, 1969.

Downey, John Chegwyn Thomas. Air Vice-Marshal, British Royal Air Force; Senior RAF Member, Royal College of Defence Studies, 1972-   . Born November 26, 1920. Attended Imperial Defence College, 1968. Joined Royal Air Force in 1939. Served in Coastal Command in WW II. Head, Near East Defence Secretariat, Cyprus, 1960-62; Commander, Royal Air Force, Farnborough, 1962-64; Director, Operational Requirements (RAF), Ministry of Defence, 1965-67; Commandant, Royal Air Force College of Air Warfare, Manby, 1969; Commander, Southern Maritime Air Region, 18 (M) Group, Strike Command, with NATO responsibilities as Air Commander Central Sub-Area, Eastern Atlantic Command and Plymouth Sub-Area, Channel Command, 1969-72. DFC; AFC. Associate Fellow Royal Aeronautical Society.

Dragunskiy, David Abramovich. Lieutenant General, USSR Army; Commandant, Senior Officers Courses "Vystrel", 1971-   . Born in 1910, in Svyatsk, Bryansk Oblast. Drafted into Army, 1933. Served in undeclared Soviet-Japanese War, 1938; Soviet-German War, 1941-45. Commander, Separate Tank Battalion, Smolensk and Moscow Fronts, 1941; Chief of Staff, Tank Brigade, 1st Tank Army, 1942; Commander, 55th Tank Brigade, 3d Tank Army, 1943-45; after the War commanded Tank Division in Soviet Far East; Commander, Soviet Forces, Armenia, 1961-65; Deputy Commander, Transcaucasian Military District, 1965-70. Member, Communist Party of the Soviet Union, 1931-   ; Member, Presidium of the Armenian Communist Party, 1961-65; twice elected Deputy to the Armenian Supreme Soviet; Deputy to the Georgian Supreme Soviet, 1967-69. Twice Hero of the Soviet Union, two Orders of Lenin; Order of Red Banner; Order of Red Star; and other USSR and foreign orders and medals.

Dreiseszun, Abraham J. Major General, United States Air Force; Commander, Defense Personnel Support Center, Defense Supply Agency, 1972-   . Born October 2, 1920, in Kansas City, Missouri. Army Air Force Flying School, 1941-42; Armed Forces Staff College, 1956-57; Industrial College of the Armed Forces, 1962-63; Advance Management Program, Harvard University, 1965. Commissioned Second Lieutenant, US Army Air Corps, 1942. Served in the European and North African Theaters, WW II. Deputy Commander and later Commander, San Bernardino Air Materiel Area (SBAMA), Director, Procurement and Production, Oklahoma City Air Materiel Area (OCAMA), 1966-67; Director, Materiel Management, Oklahoma City Air Materiel Area, 1967-68; Deputy Chief of Staff, Procurement and Production, Headquarters Air Force Logistics Command, 1968-72. Legion of Merit; Distinguished Flying Cross; and other medals and awards. Promoted to Major General, Ausust 1, 1971.

Druzhinin, M. Major General, USSR Army; First Deputy Chief, Political Directorate, Kiev Military District. Duty on the Soviet-German Front in WW II. Member, Communist Party of the Soviet Union.

Druzhinin, V. V. Colonel General, USSR Army; Deputy Chief of the General Staff, 1968-   . Duty on the Soviet-German Front in WW II. Chief, Air Defense Forces Radio Engineering Service, 1961-67. Promoted to Lieutenant General in 1961. Member, Communist Party of the Soviet Union.

Ducat-Amos, Barbara Mary. Air Commandant, British Royal Air Force; Matron-in-Chief, Princess Mary's Royal Air Force Nursing Service, 1972-   . Born February 9, 1921. Trained at St. Thomas's Hospital, London, SRN, 1943. Joined Princess Mary's Royal Air Force Service, 1944; served in UK and Aden until 1947; rejoined in 1952. Service in various RAF hospitals. Matron, 1967; Senior Matron, 1968; Principal Matron, 1970.

Dudur, I. Lieutenant General, USSR Army; First Deputy Commander, Turkestan Military District. Duty on the Soviet-German Front in WW II. Member, Communist Party of the Soviet Union.

Duerk, Alene Bertha. Rear Admiral, Nurse Corps, United States Navy; Director, Navy Nurse Corps, Bureau of Medicine and Surgery, 1970-   . Born March 29, 1920, in Defiance, Ohio. Toledo (Ohio) Hospital School of Nursing, Diploma, 1941; Western Reserve University, BS, Ward Management and Teaching, Medical and Surgical Nursing, 1948. Commissioned Ensign, Nurse Corps, US Naval Reserve, January 23, 1943; transferred to US Navy, 1953; inactive, 1946-51. In WW II served in Naval Hospitals at Portsmouth, Virginia, and Bethesda, Maryland; USS *Benevolence* (AH-13), Pacific Theater. Senior Nurse Corps Officer, Naval Station Dispensary, Long Beach, California, 1963-65; Chief of Nursing Branch, Naval Hospital Corps School, San Diego, California, 1965-66; Assistant for Nurse Recruitment, Office of Deputy Assistant Secretary of Defense (Health and Medical), 1966-67; Assistant Head of Medical Placement Liaison (Nurse Corps), Bureau of Naval Personnel, 1967-68; Chief of Nursing Service, Naval Hospital, Great Lakes, 1968-70. Naval Reserve Medal; American Campaign Medal; Asiatic-Pacific Campaign Medal with Bronze Star; Navy Occupation Service Medal, Asia Clasp; National Defense Service Medal with Bronze Star. Promoted to Rear Admiral, June 1, 1972.

Duke, Charles Moss, Jr. Colonel, US Air Force; NASA Astronaut, 1966-   . Born October 3, 1935, Charlotte, North Carolina. US Naval Academy, 1953-57; Flight Training, 1957-58; Massachusetts Institute of Technology, MS, Aeronautics and Astronautics, 1964; Aerospace Research Pilot School, 1965. Commissioned Second Lieutenant, US Air Force, 1957. 526th Fighter Interceptor Squadron, three years; Instructor, Air Force Aerospace Research Pilot School. NASA experience: Member, Support Crew, Apollo 10; Backup Lunar Module Pilot, Apollo 13, Lunar Module Pilot, Apollo 16, April 16-27, 1972. Backup Lunar Module Pilot, Apollo 17. NASA Distinguished Service Medal; Manned Spacecraft Center Certificate of Commendation; Air Force Distinguished Service Medal; Air Force Senior Pilot Astronaut Wings; Society of Experimental Test Pilots' Ivan C. Kinchloe Award, 1972.

Dulacki, Leo J. Major General, Unites States Marine Corps; Director of Personnel, Deputy Chief of Staff, Manpower, 1973-   . Born 1919, Omaha, Nebraska. Creighton University, BS, 1941; Amphibious Warfare School, Marine Corps, 1947; Army Language School, 1948-49; Strategic Intelligence School, 1949-50; Marine Corps Command and Staff College, 1953-54; Naval War College, 1964-65; George Washington University, MA, International Affairs, 1965. Commissioned Second Lieutenant, USMC, 1941. Served in Pacific Theater, WW II; Korean War; Vietnam War. Director, Marine Corps Command Center, Headquarters Marine Corps, 1966-67; Assistant Director, Personnel, Headquarters Marine Corps, 1967-68; Commanding General, 5th Marine Division, 1968-69; Chief of Staff, III Marine Amphibious Force, Vietnam, 1969-70; Commanding General, 4th Marine Division, 1970-73. Distinguished Service Medal; Legion of Merit with three

Gold Stars; Bronze Star Medal with Gold Star; and other US and foreign medals and awards. Promoted to Brigadier General, August 1967; Major General, August 17, 1970.

Dume, Petrit. General, Albanian Army; Chief of General Staff, Albanian Army, 1973-   , and First Deputy Minister of Defense.

Dunbar, Charles Whish. Major-General, British Army; Director of Infantry, 1970-   . Born June 2, 1919. Attended Glasgow University; Staff College, 1949; Imperial Defence College, 1966. Commissioned in the Royal Northumberland Fusiliers, 1940; transferred to Royal Artillery, 1945; transferred to Highland Light Infantry, 1946. Served in Maritime Royal Artillery and a paratroop regiment in WW II. Commander, Infantry Brigade Group, Germany, 1962-65; Brigadier, General Staff, Headquarters, Middle East Land Forces, Aden, 1967; General Officer Commanding, North West District, 1968-70. CBE. Member, Royal Company of Archers (Queen's Body Guard for Scotland).

Dung, Van Tien. Lieutenant General, People's Army of Vietnam; Alternate Member, Lao Dong Politburo, 1960; Chief of the General Staff, People's Army of Vietnam, 1953; Member Lao Dong Party Central Committee, 1960; Member National Defense Council, 1960; Vice Secretary, Central Military Party Committee. Born in 1917 in Co Nhue Village, Ha Dong Province. Worked in textile mill, Hanoi, 1936; joined Indochina Communist Party, 1937; Chairman of Military Political Department and Deputy Secretary of Military Current Affairs Committee, 1946; Commander, 320th Division, 1950-51; Alternate Member, Lao Dong Party Central Committee, 1951; elected Deputy to Third National Assembly, 1964; elected Deputy to Fourth National Assembly, 1971. Promotions: Major General, 1947; Lieutenant General, 1959.

Dunlop, Colin Charles Harrison. Rear-Admiral, British Royal Navy; Flag Officer, Medway, and Admiral Superintendent, HM Dockyard, Chatham, 1971-   . Born March 4, 1918. Attended Marlborough College. Joined the Royal Navy in 1935. Served at sea in WW II. Secretary to 1st Sea Lord, 1960-63; Commander, HMS *Pembroke*, 1964-66; Programmed Evaluation Group, Ministry of Defence, 1966-68; Director, Defence Policy (A), Ministry of Defence, 1968-69; Commander, British Navy Staff, Washington, D.C., USA, 1969-71; Chief, Naval Supply, and Secretariat Officer, 1970-71. CB: CBE.

Dunn, Carroll Hilton. Lieutenant General, United States Army; Director, Defense Nuclear Agency, Washington, D.C., 1971-   . Born August 11, 1916, Lake Village, Arkansas. University of Illinois, BS Degree, Mechanical Engineering; US Army Command and General Staff College; Industrial College of the Armed Forces; University of Iowa, MS Degree, Civil Engineering. Commissioned Second Lieutenant, US Army Reserve, 1938. Served in WW II; Vietnam War. Deputy Chief of Staff, Eighth US Army, Korea, 1964-66; Director of Construction, US Military Assistance Command, Vietnam, 1966; Assistant Chief of Staff, Logistics, J-4, US Military Assistance Command, Vietnam, 1966-67; Director of Military Construction, Office, Chief of Engineers, US Army, Washington, D.C., 1967-69; Deputy Chief of Engineers, US Army, Washington, D.C., 1969-71. Distinguished Service Medal; Silver Star; Legion of Merit with Oak Leaf Cluster; Bronze Star Medal with V Device and two Oak Leaf Clusters; and other medals and awards. Promoted to Brigadier General, April 17, 1962; Major General, August 1, 1966; Lieutenant General, August 1, 1971.

Dunn, John Murphy. Major General, United States Army; Assistant to the Vice President for Foreign and Military Affairs, 1969-   . Born July 22, 1925, in Los Angeles, California. Attended Harvard University; Armored School; Field Artillery School, Artillery and Guided Missile School, Advanced Course; Command and General Staff College; National War College, 1966-67; Princeton University, MPA, Public Affairs, MA, Politics, and PhD, International Relations, Political Science and Economics. Commissioned Second Lieutenant (ORC), August 2, 1947; commissioned in National Guard, September 2, 1947; Regular Army, June 13, 1951. Served in the Korean War. Special Assistant to US Ambassador and then to Director, US Operations Mission, Vietnam, 1964; Project Officer, Studies Branch, then Deputy Chief, Organization and Doctrine Division, US Army Combat Developments Command Combined Arms Group, Fort Leavenworth, Kansas, 1964-66; Commanding Officer, 2d Armored Division Artillery, Fort Hood, Texas, 1967-69. Silver Star; Legion of Merit; Bronze Star Medal; and other medals and awards. Promoted to Brigadier General August 1, 1970; Major General March 1, 1973.

Dunstan, Donald Beaumont. Major General, Royal Australian Army; Director, Materiel, 1972-   . Born February 18, 1923. Studied at Prince Alfred College, Adelaide; Royal Military College, Duntroon; Staff College, Queenscliff, 1958; Staff College, Camberley, England, 1959-60. Commissioned in 1942. Served in Pacific Theater in WW II; Korean War; Vietnam War. Deputy Commander, 1st Australian Task Force, Vietnam, 1969; Commander, Australian Forces, Vietnam, 1971. CBE.

Dupont, Rene G. Major General, United States Air Force; Assistant Deputy Chief of Staff, Personnel, Headquarters United States Air Force, 1972-   . Born November 21, 1919, in Los Angeles, California. Army Air Forces Officer Candidate School, 1941-42; Air Tactical School, 1948; Air Command and Staff School, 1951; National War College, 1962-63. Commissioned Second Lieutenant, US Army Air Corps, 1942. Served in the European Theater, WW II. Assistant Director, Plans, for Joint Chiefs of Staff Matters, Headquarters, USAF, 1965-67; Secretary of the Staff, Supreme Headquarters Allied Powers Europe, 1967-69; Assistant Deputy Chief of Staff, Personnel, for Military Personnel, Headquarters USAF, and Commander, USAF Military Personnel Center, Randolph Air Force Base, Texas, 1969-72. Distinguished Service Medal; Legion of Merit with two Oak Leaf Clusters; and other medals and awards. Promoted to Major General, August 1, 1969.

Duquemin, Gordon James. Major General, United States Army; Commanding General, 1st Infantry Division (Mechanized), and Fort Riley, Kansas, 1973-   . Born January 3, 1924, in Milwaukee, Wisconsin. Attended US Military Academy; Ground General School; Infantry School, Basic and Advanced Courses; Command and General Staff College; Naval War College, 1965-66; George Washington University, MS, International Relations. Commissioned June 3, 1947. Served in the Vietnam War. Assistant Chief of Staff, G-3, 4th Infantry Division, US Army, Pacific-Vietnam, 1966; Commanding Officer, 2d Battalion, 8th Infantry, then Executive Officer, 2d Brigade, 4th Infantry Division, US Army, Pacific-Vietnam, 1966-67; Executive Officer, J-5, Joint Chiefs of Staff Organization, 1967-68; Commanding Officer, 2d Brigade, then Chief of Staff, 4th Infantry Division, US Army, Pacific-Vietnam, 1968-69; Deputy Senior Advisor, II Corps Tactical Zone, US Military Assistance Command, Vietnam, 1969-70; Deputy Commanding General, US Army Training Center (Infantry), and Fort Jackson, South Carolina, 1970-71; Assistant Deputy Chief of Staff for Individual Training, then Special Assistant to the Chief of Staff, Continental Army Command, Fort Monroe, Virginia, 1971-72. Distinguished Service Medal; Silver Star with two Oak Leaf Clusters; Legion of Merit with two Oak Leaf Clusters; Distinguished Flying Cross; Bronze Star Medal with V Device with three Oak Leaf Clusters; Air Medal (18 awards); and other medals and awards. Promoted to Brigadier General, January 1, 1970; Major General October 1, 1972.

Durkin, Herbert. Air Vice-Marshal, British Royal Air Force; Air Officer Commanding, No. 90 (Signals) Group, RAF, 1971-   . Born March 31, 1922. Emmanuel College, Cambridge, MA Degree; Royal Air Force Staff College, 1953; Joint Services Staff College, 1961; Imperial Defence College, 1970. Commissioned in the Technical Branch, Royal Air Force, 1941. Served in Europe in WW II. Headquarters 2 Allied Tactical Air Force, 1961-63; Senior Technical Staff Officer, Headquarters, Signal Command, 1964-65; Commandant, No. 2 School of Technical Training, Cosford, 1965-67; Director, Engineering (Policy), Ministry of Defence, 1967-69. CB. Chartered Engineer; Fellow of the Institute of Electrical Engineers; Fellow of the Royal Aeronautical Society; Member of the British Institute of Management. Promotions: Group Captain, 1962; Air Commodore, 1967.

Dwyer, Ross T. Major General, United States Marine Corps; Deputy Director, Joint Staff, Office of the Joint Chiefs of Staff, 1972-   . Born July 20, 1919, Honolulu, Hawaii. Stanford University, BA, Economics, 1942; Amphibious Warfare School, Junior Course, Quantico, 1938; Armed Forces Staff College, 1960-61; National War College, 1967-68. Commissioned USMCR, 1942. Served in Atlantic and Pacific Theaters, WW II; Korean War; Vietnam War. Marine Corps Aide to the Secretary of the Navy, 1965-67; Commander, 1st Marines, 1st Marine Division, Vietnam, 1968; Assistant Division Commander, 1st Marine Division, Vietnam, 1968-69; Chief of Staff, G-3, III Marine Amphibious Force, Vietnam, 1969; Commanding General,

Fifth Marine Division, Fifth Marine Amphibious Brigade, First Marine Division and I Marine Amphibious Force, 1969-72. Distinguished Service Medal; Legion of Merit with Gold Star; Bronze Star Medal with Combat "V"; and other medals and awards. Promoted to Brigadier General, August 14, 1968; Major General, August 17, 1971.

Dyatlenko, V. K. Lieutenant General, USSR Army; First Deputy Commander, Moscow Military District, 1969-   . Duty on the Soviet-German Front, WW II. Member, Communist Party of the Soviet Union.

Dye, Jack Bertie. Major-General, British Army; Director, Volunteers, Territorials and Cadets, 1971-   . Born in 1919. Attended Staff College. Combat duty in WW II. Commander, South Arabian Army, 1966-68; General Officer Commanding, Eastern District, 1969-71. Colonel Commandant, The Queen's Division, 1970-   . CBE; MC.

Dymoke, Lionel Dorian. Rear Admiral, British Royal Navy; Director of Engineering (Ships). Chartered Engineer; Fellow of the Institute of Mechanical Engineering; Member of the Institute of Marine Engineering.

Dysko, Edward. Major General, Polish Army; Commander, 1st Mechanized Division.

Dzhurov, Dobri Marinov. General, Bulgarian Army; Minister of Defense, Bulgarian People's Republic, 1962-   . Born January 5, 1916, in Vrabevo, Lovech District. Studied at Frunze Military College, USSR. Served in the Chavdar Partisan Brigade (anti-German), in WW II. Recent Positions: Commander of an Army; Deputy Minister of Defense, 1956-62. Member of Bulgarian Communist Party since 1938 and member of its Central Committee since 1958. Order of Georgi Dmitrov; Order of the People's Republic of Bulgaria, first class; Order of 9 September 1944, first and second class; Order of Liberation; Order of Red Flag; and other Bulgarian and foreign medals and awards.

Dziekan, Tadeusz. Major General, Polish Army; Deputy Commanding General for Political Affairs, Pomeranian Military District. Attended Political Officers Military School; Military-Political College. Formerly Deputy Chief, Political Directorate Pomeranian Military District. Member of Polish United Workers Party. Cross of Grunwald; Cross of Merit; and other orders and medals.

Dzur, Martin. Colonel General, Czechoslovak Army; Minister of National Defense, Czechoslovakia, 1969-   . Born July 12, 1919, at Plostin, Czechoslovakia. Attended V.M. Molotov Military Academy of Rear Echelon Services, Kalinin, USSR; War College of the Armed Forces, USSR. Commissioned Second Lieutenant, 1943. Served in Czechoslovak Brigade in the USSR in WW II. Formerly on the Staff, Ministry of National Defense and General Staff, 1954-58; Deputy Minister of National Defense, 1958-68. Order of Labor; and other medals and awards. Member of Communist Party of Czechoslovakia and of its Central Committee; Deputy, Federal Parliament of Czechoslovakia.

E

Eade, George J. Lieutenant General, United States Air Force; Deputy Commander in Chief US European Command, Vaihingen, Germany, 1973- . Born October 27, 1921, in Lockney, Texas. Illinois Institute of Technology; Basic and Advanced Flying Schools, 1942. Commissioned Second Lieutenant, US Army Air Corps, 1942. Served in the European Theater, WW II. Chief, Control Division, Strategic Air Command, 1965-67; Director of Operations Plans, Office, Deputy Chief of Staff, Operations, Strategic Air Command, 1967-70; Director of Plans, Office, Deputy Chief of Staff, Plans and Operations, Headquarters USAF, 1970-71; Assistant Deputy Chief of Staff, later Deputy Chief of Staff, Plans and Operations, Headquarters, US Air Force, 1971-73. Distinguished Service Medal; Legion of Merit; Air Force Commendation Medal with two Oak Leaf Clusters; and other medals and awards. Promoted to Brigadier General, September 1, 1966; Major General, August 1, 1969; Lieutenant General, April 23, 1971.

Easton, Ian. Rear-Admiral, British Royal Navy; Head, British Defence Staff, Washington, D.C., 1973- . Born November 27, 1917. Attended Royal Naval College, Dartmouth; Naval Staff College, 1953; Joint Services Staff College, 1959. Joined the Royal Navy, 1931; commissioned, 1939; qualified as Naval Pilot, 1939. Served as Naval Pilot in WW II. Assistant Director, Tactical and Weapons Policy Division, 1960-62; Commanding Officer, HMAS *Watson* (exchange service with Royal Australian Navy), 1962-64; Naval Assistant to Naval Member of Templer Committee, 1965-66; Director, Naval Tactical and Weapons Policy Division, 1966-68; Commanding Officer, HMS *Triumph*, Far East, 1968-69; Assistant Chief of Naval Staff (Policy), 1969-71; Flag Officer, Admiralty Interview Board, 1971-73. DSC. Promoted to Vice Admiral, September 1972.

Eaton, Brian Alexander. Air Vice-Marshal, Royal Australian Air Force; Air Officer Commanding Operational Command. Born December 15, 1916, in Launceston, Tasmania. Attended Royal Australian Air Force College, Pt. Cook; Imperial Defense College, 1961. Served in the African-European Theater, WW II. Deputy Chief, Air Staff, 1966; Air Officer Commanding, Headquarters 224 Mobile Group (RAF), Far East Air Force, Singapore, 1967-68; Chief of Staff, Headquarters Far East Air Force, 1968-69; Member for Personnel, Department of Air, 1969-71. CB; CBE; DSO and Bar; DFC; Silver Star (USA).

Eberhard, Luis. Rear Admiral, Chilean Navy; Naval Attache, Embassy of Chile, Washington, D.C.; Chief of Delegation, Inter-American Defense Board. Date of Rank; February 28, 1973.

Eberle, James Henry Fuller. Rear-Admiral, British Royal Navy; Assistant Chief of Fleet Support, Ministry of Defence (Royal Navy), 1971- . Born May 31, 1927. Attended Clifton College; Royal Naval College Dartmouth and Greenwich. Served in WW II. Executive Officer, HMS *Eagle*,

1963-65; Commanding Officer, HMS *Intrepid*, 1968-70. Member of the Council, Royal United Services Institute for Defence Studies, 1972. Promoted to Rear-Admiral in 1971.

Edmundson, James Valentine. Lieutenant General, United States Air Force; Deputy Commander in Chief, US Readiness Command, 1972- . Born June 18, 1915, in Hollywood, California. Santa Monica Junior College, AA, 1934; Pilot Training, 1938; Air War College, 1948-49; George Washington University, Manpower and Management Course, 1953. Commissioned Second Lieutenant, US Army Air Corps, 1938. Served in the Pacific, China-Burma-India, and European Theaters, WW II; Korean War. Commander, 36th Air Division, Strategic Air Command, 1955-57; Deputy Director of Operations, Strategic Air Command, 1957-58; Director of Operations, Strategic Air Command, 1958-60; Director, Personnel Procurement and Training, Deputy Chief of Staff, Personnel, Headquarters USAF, 1960-62; Commander, Seventeenth Air Force, USAF, Europe, 1962-64; Director for Inspection Services, Office, Assistant Secretary of Defense (Administration), 1964-67; Vice Commander in Chief, Pacific Air Forces, 1967-70. Distinguished Service Medal (Air Force design); Distinguished Service Medal (Army design); Silver Star; Legion of Merit with two Oak Leaf Clusters; Distinguished Flying Cross with six Oak Leaf Clusters; Bronze Star Medal; and other medals and awards. Promotions: Brigadier General, December 15, 1953; Major General, March 10, 1958; Lieutenant General, February 17, 1965.

Edwards, G. J. J. Brigadier-General, Canadian Armed Forces; Canadian Forces Attache (Air), Embassy of Canada, Washington, D.C. Decorations: DFC; CD.

Eggert, Folke Gustaf. Brigadier General, Swedish Royal Army; Chief Quartermaster Materiel Department, Defense Materiel Administration, 1971- . Royal National Defense College, 1963. Commander of the Royal Order of the Sword; and other medals and awards. Promoted to Brigadier General, 1971.

Ehm, Willi. Vice Admiral, People's Navy, Democratic Republic of Germany; Commander in Chief, People's Navy.

Ejoor, David Akpode. Colonel, Nigerian Army; Military Governor, Mid Eastern Nigeria. Born January 10, 1934. Attended Royal Military Academy, Sandhurst, England, 1954-56. Commissioned Second Lieutenant, Nigerian Army, in 1956. Served as member of the Nigerian Contingent, United Nations Peacekeeping Force, Congo; Staff and Command Positions, Nigerian Army.

Eklund, Carl Gunnar. Lieutenant General, Swedish Royal Coast Artillery; Chief, Defense Staff, 1972- . Attended Royal Navy Staff College, 1947-49; Royal National Defense College, 1959, 1966. Chief of Staff, Military Command Lower Norrland, 1966-70; Chief, Naval Staff, 1970-72. Commander of the Royal Order of the Sword; and other medals and awards. Member of the Royal Academy of

Military Sciences; Member of the Royal Society of Naval Sciences. Promoted to Lieutenant General, 1972.

Elazar, David. Lieutenant General, Israeli Defense Forces: Chief of Staff and Commander in Chief Israeli Army, 1971-   . Born in 1925, in Sarajevo, Yugoslavia; immigrated to Palestine in 1940. Attended Hebrew University; Israeli Military College. Joined Palmah, 1946. Fought in the War of Independence, 1948-49; Israeli-Egyptian War, 1956; Six Day War, June 1967; October War, 1973. Staff Member, Operations Department, General Headquarters, 1952-53; Commanding Officer, Infantry School, 1956-   ; Deputy Commander, and later Commander, Armoured Corps, 1961; Officer in Charge, Northern Command, 1964; Commanding Officer, Northern Command, Six Day War, 1967; Chief, General Staff Branch, 1969.

Elder, John Howard, Jr. Major General, United States Army; Assistant Deputy Chief of Staff for Military Operations, US Army, Washington, D.C., 1973-   . Born June 14, 1920, Richmond, Virginia. Virginia Polytechnic Institute, BS Degree, Civil Engineering; The Engineer School, Advanced Course; US Army Command and General Staff College; US Army War College. Commissioned Second Lieutenant, US Army Reserve, 1941. Served in WW II and Vietnam War. Commanding General, 18th Engineer Brigade, US Army, Pacific-Vietnam, 1968-69; Chief, Objective Plans and Programs Division, later Objective Plans and Military Assistance Division, Plans and Policy Directorate, J-5, Organization, Joint Chiefs of Staff, Washington, D.C., 1969-70; Deputy Director, J-5, Organization, Joint Chiefs of Staff, Washington, D.C., 1971-72; Director of Plans, Office, Deputy Chief of Staff for Military Operations, US Army, Washington, D.C. 1972. Distinguished Service Medal with Oak Leaf Cluster; Legion of Merit with Oak Leaf Cluster; Bronze Star Medal with V Device and four Oak Leaf Clusters; and other medals and awards. Promoted to Brigadier General, April 1, 1969; Major General, August 1, 1970.

Elliott, Frank W., Jr. Major General, United States Air Force; Commander, Chanute Technical Training Center, 1972-   . Born December 2, 1924, in Statesville, North Carolina. San Diego State College, California, 1941; Lenoir Rhyne College, Hickory, North Carolina, 1942; Army Air Corps Flying School, 1943-44; Navigator Bombardier and Radar Bombardier School, 1951-52; National War College, 1964-65. Commissioned Second Lieutenant, US Army Air Corps, 1944. Served in the European Theater, WW II; Vietnam War. Executive Office of the Vice Chief of Staff, USAF, 1968-69; Commander, 92d Strategic Aerospace Wing, 1969-70; Commander, 14th Strategic Aerospace Division, 1970-71; Commander, 307th Strategic Wing, Thailand, 1971-72. Legion of Merit; Distinguished Flying Cross; and other medals and awards. Promotions: Brigadier General, May 1, 1970; Major General, 1972.

Ellis, Billy J. Major General, United States Air Force; Commander, 17th Air Division (Provisional), Strategic Air Command, U-Tapao Airfield, Thailand, 1973-   . Born December 11, 1928, in De Quincy, Louisiana. Louisiana State University, 1946-47; US Military Academy, 1947-51; Basic and Advanced Pilot Training, 1951-52; Air Command and Staff College, 1963-64; Industrial College of the Armed Forces, 1967-68; George Washington University, MBA, 1968. Commissioned Second Lieutenant, US Air Force, in 1951; received Pilot Wings in 1952. Served in the Korean War and Vietnam War. F-105 Weapons Project Officer, Directorate of Operations, Headquarters Tactical Air Command, Langley Air Force Base, Virginia, 1965-66; Chief, Combat Crew Training Branch, Tactical Air Command, Langley Air Force Base, Virginia, 1966-67; Chief, Combat Operations, and later, Assistant Deputy Commander for Operations, 388th Tactical Fighter Wing, Korat, Thailand, 1968-69; Assistant for General Officer Matters, Office of Deputy Chief of Staff, Personnel, Headquarters US Air Force, Washington, D.C., 1969-72; Commander, 40th Air Division, Strategic Air Command, Wurtsmith Air Force Base, Michigan, 1972-73. Decorations include Legion of Merit with Oak Leaf Cluster, Distinguished Flying Cross with two Oak Leaf Clusters, Bronze Star Medal, and Air Medal with ten Oak Leaf Clusters. Promotions: Brigadier General, March 1, 1972; Major General, 1973.

Ellis, Richard H. Lieutenant General, United States Air Force; Commander, Sixteenth Air Force, Torrejon Air Base, Spain, 1973-   . Born July 19, 1919, in Laurel, Delaware. Dickinson College, Carlisle, Pennsylvania, AB, 1941; Dickinson School of Law, JD, 1949; Flight Training Course, 1941-42. Commissioned Second Lieutenant, US Army Air Corps, 1942. Served in the Southwest Pacific Theater, WW II; Korean War. Commander, 315th Air Division, Tachikawa Air Base, Japan, 1963-65; Deputy Director, J-5 (Plans and Policy), Joint Staff, Office, Joint Chiefs of Staff, 1965-67; Director of Plans, Deputy Chief of Staff, Plans and Operations, Headquarters USAF, 1967-69; Assistant Deputy Chief of Staff, Plans and Operations, Headquarters USAF, 1969; Commander, Ninth Air Force, 1969-70; Vice Commander in Chief, US Air Force Europe, Germany, 1970-71; Commander, Sixth Allied Tactical Air Force, Izmir, Turkey, 1971-72; Commander, Allied Air Forces, Southern Europe, Naples, Italy, 1972-73. Distinguished Service Cross; Distinguished Service Medal; Silver Star; Legion of Merit with two Oak Leaf Clusters; Distinguished Flying Cross; and other medals and awards. Promoted to Brigadier General, August 13, 1962; Major General, January 5, 1966; Lieutenant General, September 1, 1970.

Ellis, Vincent Henry. Major General, United States Army; Deputy for Materiel Acquisition, Office, Assistant Secretary of the Army (Installations and Logistics), Washington, D.C., 1972-   . Born November 9, 1920, Del Rio, Texas. Kansas State College, BS Degree, Mechanical Engineering; The Artillery School, Advanced Course; The Ordnance School, Advanced Course; US Army Command and General Staff College; US Air War College; Cornell University, MS Degree, Mechanical Engineering. Commissioned Second Lieutenant, US Army Reserve, 1942. Served in WW II.

Deputy Commanding General, US Army, Tank-Automotive Command, Warren, Michigan, 1967-68; Senior Logistical Advisor to Republic of Korea Army, US Army Advisory Group, Korea, 1968-69; Commanding General, Eighth US Army Depot Command, Korea, 1969; Deputy Commanding General, Eighth US Army Support Command, Eighth US Army Rear, Korea, 1969-70; Deputy for Procurement, Office, Assistant Secretary of the Army (Installations and Logistics), Office, Secretary of the Army, Washington, D.C., 1970-72. Legion of Merit with two Oak Leaf Clusters; and other medals and awards. Promoted to Brigadier General, June 19, 1968; Major General, April 1, 1971.

Elwood, Hugh McJunkin. Lieutenant General, United States Marine Corps; Deputy Chief of Staff (Plans and Programs), Headquarters, US Marine Corps, 1971- . Born November 14, 1915, Pittsburgh, Pennsylvania. US Naval Academy, 1935-38; Marine Corps Officers Basic School, 1938; Flight Training Course, 1940-41; Command and Staff School, Quantico, 1944-45; Naval War College, Strategy and Logistics Course, 1952-53. Enlisted in US Marine Corps, 1932; commissioned, 1938; designated Naval Aviator, 1941. Served in Pacific Theater, WW II; Korean War; Vietnam War. Commanding General, Marine Air Reserve Training Command, Glenview, Illinois, 1963-65; Assistant Wing Commander, 1st Marine Aircraft Wing, Fleet Marine Force, Pacific, 1966-67; Commanding General, 2d Marine Aircraft Wing, 1967-68; Assistant Chief of Staff (J-3), Operations, Staff, Commander in Chief, Pacific, 1968-71. Legion of Merit; Distinguished Flying Cross; Air Medal with three Gold Stars; and other medals and awards. Promoted to Brigadier General, February 1963; Major General, March 20, 1967; Lieutenant General, May 1, 1971.

Emerson, Henry Everett. Major General, United States Army; Commanding General, 2d Infantry Division, US Army, Pacific-Korea, 1973- . Born May 28, 1925, in Washington, D.C. Attended US Military Academy; Ground General School; Infantry School, Basic and Advanced Courses; Naval War College; Armed Forces Staff College; Army War College, 1964-65. Commissioned Second Lieutenant, June 3, 1947. Served in the Korean War and the Vietnam War. Chief, Schools and Education Division, Office of the Deputy Chief of Staff for Personnel, US Army, 1966-68; Commanding Officer, 1st Brigade, 9th Infantry Division, US Army, Pacific-Vietnam, 1968; Commanding Officer, 12th Support Brigade, then Assistant Division Commander, 82d Airborne Division, Fort Bragg, North Carolina, 1969-70; Camp Commander, Third US Army ROTC Summer Camp, Fort Bragg, North Carolina, 1970; Special Assistant to the Commanding General, then Acting, then Commanding General, John F. Kennedy Center for Military Assistance, and Commandant, US Army Institute for Military Assistance, Fort Bragg, North Carolina, 1970-73. Distinguished Service Cross with Oak Leaf Cluster; Distinguished Service Medal with Oak Leaf Cluster; Silver Star with four Oak Leaf Clusters; Legion of Merit with Oak Leaf Cluster; Distinguished Flying Cross; Bronze Star Medal with V Device and two Oak Leaf Clusters; Air Medal with V Device (14 awards); and other

medals and awards. Promoted to Brigadier General January 1, 1970; Major General December 1, 1972.

Empson, Sir (Leslie) Derek. Vice-Admiral, British Royal Navy; Second Sea Lord and Chief of Naval Personnel, 1971- . Born October 29, 1918. Attended Eastbourne College; Clare College, Cambridge University (BA, 1940); Imperial Defence College, 1966. Commissioned Sub-Lieutenant (A) Royal Naval Volunteer Reserve, 1940; Permanent Commission in Royal Navy, 1944. Fleet Air Arm pilot in WW II. Commander, HMS *Eagle*, 1963-65; Flag Officer, Aircraft Carriers, 1967-68; Assistant Chief of Naval Staff (Operations and Air), 1968-69; Commander, Far East Fleet, 1969-71. KCB. Promotions: Captain, 1957; Rear-Admiral, 1967; Vice-Admiral, 1970; Admiral, 1972.

Enger, Walter Melvin. Rear Admiral, Civil Engineer Corps, United States Navy; Commander Naval Facilities Engineering Command, and Chief of Civil Engineers of the Navy, 1969- . Born May 1, 1914, in Urbana, Illinois. University of Illinois, BS, Civil Engineering, 1935. Commissioned Lieutenant (j.g.), Civil Engineer Corps, US Naval Reserve, 1941; transferred to US Navy, 1943. Served in the Pacific Theater, WW II. Director, Chesapeake Division, Bureau of Yards and Docks, 1964-65; Deputy Chief, Bureau of Yards and Docks/Deputy of Civil Engineers, 1965-66; Vice Commander, Naval Facilities Engineering Command, and Deputy Chief of Civil Engineers of the Navy, 1966-69. Legion of Merit; Navy Commendation Medal; and other medals and awards. Promoted to Rear Admiral, August 10, 1965.

Engel, Benjamin Franklin. Vice Admiral, United States Coast Guard; Commander, Atlantic Area and 3d Coast Guard District, New York, 1970- . Born May 1, 1914, Grand Rapids, Michigan. US Coast Guard Academy, 1934-38; Navy Flight Training Course, 1942-53; Naval War College, 1957-58. Commissioned Ensign, 1938; designated Coast Guard Aviator, 1943. Served in Atlantic Theater, WW II. Chief, Aviation Units Division, Headquarters, US Coast Guard, 1963-65; Deputy Chief, Office of Operations, Headquarters, US Coast Guard, 1965-66; Chief, Operations, 14th Coast Guard District, Honolulu, Hawaii, 1966-67; Commander, 14th Coast Guard District, 1967-70. Legion of Merit; and other medals and citations. Promoted to Rear Admiral, May 1, 1967; Vice Admiral, October 14, 1972.

England, Anthony Wayne. United States; NASA Scientist-Astronaut, 1967- . Born May 15, 1942, Indianapolis, Indiana. Masachusetts Institute of Technology, BS and MS, Geology and Physics, 1965; PhD, Earth and Planetary Sciences, 1970; Flight Training Course. Graduate Fellow, Massachusetts Institute of Technology, 1964-67. NASA experience: Member Support Crew, Apollo 16. Manned Spacecraft Center Superior Achievement Award, 1970; National Science Foundation Fellowship.

Engle, Joe Henry. Colonel, US Air Force; NASA Astronaut, 1966- . Born August 26, 1932, Abilene, Kansas. University of Kansas, BS, Aeronautical Engineering, 1955;

US Air Force Experimental Test Pilot School; Air Force Aerospace Research Pilot School. Commissioned Second Lieutenant, US Air Force, 1955. 474th Fighter Day Squadron; 309th Tactical Fighter Squadron; Test Pilot, Fighter Test Group, Edwards Air Force Base; Aerospace Flight Test Pilot, X-15 Research Program, Edwards Air Force Base. NASA experience: Member, Support Crew, Apollo 10; Backup Lunar Module Pilot, Apollo 14; Design and Development of Space Shuttle Vehicle. Air Force Astronaut Wings; Distinguished Flying Cross; Air Force Association's Outstanding Young Officer, 1964; US Jaycee's List of Ten Outstanding Young Men in America, 1964; Lawrence Sperry Award of the American Institute of Aeronautics and Astronautics, 1966; Manned Spacecraft Center Superior Achievement Award, 1970.

Enrile, Juan Ponce. Secretary of National Defense, Republic of the Philippines. Born February 14, 1924, in Gonzaga, Cagayan. Ateneo de Manila, Associate in Arts, 1949; University of the Philippines, Bachelor of Laws, 1953; Harvard Law School (USA), 1954-55. Former Professor of Taxation, Corporation Law, and Political Law, College of Law, Far Eastern University; Acting Chairman, Monetary Board, Central Bank; Acting Secretary of Finance; Acting Insurance Commissioner; Acting Commissioner of Customs; Under Secretary of Finance.

Eoannides, George. Minister of Defense and Interior, Cyprus.

Erly, Robert Broussard. Rear Admiral, United States Navy; Chief, Military Assistance Advisory Group, Portugal, and Commander, Iberian Command, 1970-   . Born June 12, 1914, Washington, D.C. US Naval Academy, 1933-37; Armed Forces Staff College, 1952-53; National War College, 1962-63; Defense Intelligence School, East Coast. Commissioned Ensign, US Navy, 1937. Served in destroyers in the Atlantic and Pacific Theaters, WW II and the Korean War; amphibious operations in the Vietnam War. Commander Amphibious Squadron FIVE, 1961-62; Chief of Staff and Aide to Commander Amphibious Force, US Pacific Fleet, 1963-65; Commander Amphibious Group THREE/Commander, River Coastal Warfare Group, 1965-67; Inspector General US Atlantic Fleet, 1968-69; Deputy Chief of Staff and Deputy Chief of Staff for Plans and Operations, Commander in Chief, US Atlantic Fleet. Legion of Merit with Gold Star; Bronze Star Medal with Combat "V"; and other US and foreign medals and awards. Promoted to Rear Admiral, July 1, 1965.

Esch, Arthur Gerald. Rear Admiral, United States Navy; Commandant, Naval District, Washington, Navy Yard, Washington, D.C., 1971-   . Born January 31, 1917, in Washington, Illinois. Eureka (Illinois) College; US Naval Academy, 1936-40; George Washington University, LLB, 1949; National War College, 1963-64. Commissioned Ensign, US Navy, 1940. Served in the Pacific Theater, WW II. Director, Policy Division, Bureau of Naval Personnel, 1960-63; Commander Destroyer Squadron TWO, 1964-65; Assistant for Joint Chiefs of Staff Matters—Objective Plans, Strategic Plans Division, Office of the CNO, 1965-68;

Assistant Chief of Staff Logistics, Commander in Chief Allied Forces Southern Europe, 1968-70; Commander Cruiser-Destroyer Flotilla ELEVEN, 1970-71. Legion of Merit with Gold Star; Bronze Star Medal with Combat "V"; Navy Commendation Medal with Combat "V"; and other medals and awards. Promoted to Rear Admiral, January 1, 1969.

Espellet, Eddy Sampaio. Vice Admiral, Brazilian Navy; Vice Chief of Naval Operations, 1973-   . Naval Attache, Embassy of Brazil, Washington, D.C., 1971-73.

Espino, Romeo C. General, Philippine Army; Chief of Staff, Armed Forces of the Philippines, 1972-   . Born December 20, 1914, in Los Baños, Laguna. Studied at University of the Philippines, College of Agriculture, 1933-37, BS Degree, Agriculture, and 1942-44, BS Degree, Plant Pathology; MLQ College of Law, LLB Degree, 1948-52; University of the Philippines, Institute of Public Administration Executive Development, 1953; Commonwealth Infantry, GSS, Baguio, 1939-41; The Infantry School, Fort Benning, Georgia, USA, 1945; Command and General Staff Course No. 6, Command and General Staff School, Fort McKinley, Rizal, 1959-60; and other special schools and courses. Commissioned Second Lieutenant, in 1937. Served in the Philippines in WW II. Vice Commander, Philippine Army, 1964-65; Commanding General, 1st Military Area, 1965-66; Commanding General, 1st Infantry Division, PA, 1966-67; Commanding General, Philippine Army, 1967-68; Commanding General, Philippine Defense Forces, 1968-70; Vice Chief of Staff, 1970-72. Distinguished Service Star with one Bronze Anahaw Leaf; Gold Cross; Silver Star (USA); and other medals and awards.

Essoussi, Mohamed el Habib Ben Mohamed Ben Brahim. Major General, Tunisian Army; Chief of Staff, Tunisian Army, 1967-   . Attended French Staff School; French Senior War College. Formerly G-4, Tunisian Army; Chief of Staff, Congo Brigade; Deputy Assistant Chief of Staff, Tunisian Army. Order of the Independence; Order of the Republic (Commander and Grand Officer); Battle of the Evacuation of Bizerte Medal; Légion d'Honneur (France); Croix de Guerre (France); Médaille des Evadés (France); Order of the British Empire; United Nations Congo Medal; National Order of Merit (France) (Grand Officer). Promoted to Major General, June 1, 1972.

Esuene, Udoakaha Jacob. Brigadier, Nigerian Armed Forces; Military Governor, South-Eastern State, 1967-   . Born October 17, 1936, Afaha Eket, Nigeria. Attended Teacher Training College, Uyo; British Royal Military Academy, Sandhurst. Joined the Army in 1958. Staff Member, Nigerian Contingent, United Nations Peacekeeping Force, Congo, 1961-62; Commanding Officer, Air Force Base, Kaduna, 1965-66; Senior Air Operations Officer, Headquarters, Air Force, Lagos, 1966-67. Honorary LLD, University of Nigeria.

Etter, Harry Stough. Rear Admiral, Medical Corps, United States Navy; Assistant Chief, Bureau of Medicine and

Surgery, for Planning and Logistics, Navy Department, 1967-   . Born October 15, 1915, in Shippensburg, Pennsylvania. Duke University, Durham, North Carolina, MD, 1939; Naval War College, Naval Warfare and Senior Courses, 1955-56. Commissioned Lieutenant (j.g.), Medical Corps, US Navy, 1941. Served in the North Atlantic Theater, WW II. Executive Officer, Naval Hospital, Portsmouth, Virginia, 1965-66; Commanding Officer Naval Hospital, Bethesda, Maryland, 1966-67. Various medals and awards. Promoted to Rear Admiral, Medical Corps, US Navy, January 1, 1967.

Eugster, Sir Basil. General, British Army; General Officer Commanding-in-Chief, United Kingdom Land Forces, 1972-   . Born August 15, 1914. Christ Church, Oxford, MA Degree; Joint Services Staff College, 1950; Imperial Defence College, 1959. Commissioned in the Irish Guards, 1935. Served in Narvik, Italy and Northwest Europe, WW II. Commander, 3d Infantry Brigade Group, and Dhekelia Area, Cyprus, 1959-62; Commandant, School of Infantry, Warminster, 1962-63; General Officer Commanding, 4 Division, British Army of the Rhine, 1963-65; General Officer Commanding, London District, and Major-General Commanding Household Brigade, 1965-68; Commander, British Forces, Hong Kong, 1968-70; General Officer Commanding-in-Chief, Southern Command, 1971-72. KCB; KCVO; CBE; DSO; MC and Bar.

Evans, Andrew J., Jr. Major General, United States Air Force; Deputy Chief of Staff, Research and Development, 1973-   . Born November 11, 1918, in Charleston, South Carolina. The Citadel, Charleston, South Carolina; US Military Academy, 1937-41; Army Air Corps Flying School, 1941; Command and General Staff School; Air Command and Staff School, 1947-48; Air War College, 1951-52. Commissioned in 1941. Served in the European Theater, WW II; Korean War; Vietnam War. Director, Development Planning, Deputy Chief of Staff, Research and Development, Headquarters, USAF, 1963-64; Director of Development and Special Assistant, Deputy Chief of Staff, Research and Development, for Counterinsurgency (COIN), 1964-68; Commander, USAF Tactical Air Warfare Center, Eglin Air Force Base, Florida, 1968-70; Deputy Commander Seventh Air Force/Thirteenth Air Force, Thailand, 1970-71; Commander, US Military Assistance Command, Thailand, and Chief, Joint United States Military Advisory Group, 1971-73. Distinguished Service Medal; Silver Star; Legion of Merit; Distinguished Flying Cross with two Oak Leaf Clusters; Croix de Guerre; and other US and foreign medals and orders. Promoted to Major General, September 1, 1966.

Evans, David George. Air Vice-Marshal, British Royal Air Force; Assistant Chief, Air Staff (Operations), 1970-73. Born July 14, 1924, in Windsor, Ontario, Canada. Attended North Toronto Collegiate, Canada; Royal Air Force Staff College, 1955; College of Air Warfare, 1961; Imperial Defence College, 1967. Served in European Theater in WW II. Air Plans Staff Officer, Ministry of Defence (Air), 1962-63; Officer Commanding, RAF Station, Gutersloh, Germany, 1964-66; Air Officer Commanding, RAF Central Tactics and Trials Organisation, 1968-70. CBE; Queen's Commendation for Valuable Service in the Air. Represented Great Britain at Bobsleigh in World Championship and in 1964 Olympic Games.

Evans, Ronald E. Captain, US Navy; NASA Astronaut, 1966-   . Born November 10, 1933, St. Francis, Kansas. University of Kansas, BS, Electrical Engineering, 1956; US Naval Postgraduate School, MS, Aeronautical Engineering, 1964. Commissioned Ensign, USN, 1956; received pilot wings, 1957. Served in Vietnam War. Pilot, VF-142; Flight Instructor, VF-124, 1961-62; Pilot VF-51, on USS *Ticonderoga*. NASA experience: Pilot, Command Module, Apollo 17, December 6-19, 1972; Backup Command Module Pilot, Apollo-Soyuz Test Project, July 1975. Eight Air Medals; Navy Commendation Medal with combat distinguishing device; Manned Spacecraft Center Superior Achievement Award, 1970.

Evans, William John. Major General, United States Air Force; Assistant Deputy Chief of Staff, Research and Development, Headquarters, US Air Force, 1972-   . Born March 4, 1924, in Norwich, Connecticut. Yale University, 1942-43; US Military Academy, 1943-46; Army War College, 1959-60. Commissioned Second Lieutenant, US Army Air Corps, 1946. Served in the Korean War; Vietnam War. Commander, 31st Tactical Fighter Wing, Vietnam, 1967-68; Deputy Director, Concepts and Operational Readiness, Defense Communications Planning Group, 1969-70; Special Assistant, Sensor Exploitation, Headquarters USAF, 1970-71; Director, Operational Requirements and Development Plans, Deputy Chief of Staff, Research and Development, 1971; Director, Development and Acquisition, Deputy Chief of Staff, Research and Development, 1971-72. Silver Star; Legion of Merit; Distinguished Flying Cross with two Oak Leaf Clusters; Bronze Star Medal; Air Medal with 24 Oak Leaf Clusters; and other US and foreign medals and awards. Promoted to Major General, November 1, 1971.

Ewell, Julian Johnson. Lieutenant General, United States Army; Chief of Staff, Allied Forces Southern Europe, 1971-   . Born November 5, 1915, Stillwater, Oklahoma. U.S. Military Academy; The Infantry School, Basic and Advanced Courses; U.S. Army Command and General Staff College; U.S. Army War College; National War College. Commissioned Second Lieutenant, U.S. Army, 1939. Served in WW II and Vietnam War. Assistant Division Commander, 8th Infantry Division, U.S. Army, Europe, 1963-65; Chief of Staff, V Corps, U.S. Army, Europe, 1965-66; Chief of Staff, later Deputy Commanding General and Chief of Staff, U.S. Army Combat Developments Command, Fort Belvoir, Virginia, 1966-68; Commanding General, 9th Infantry Division, U.S. Army, Vietnam, 1968-69; Commanding General, II Field Force, Vietnam, 1969-70; Military Advisor, United States Peace Delegation, Paris, France, 1970-71. Distinguished Service Cross; Distinguished Service Medal with Oak Leaf Cluster; Silver Star with Oak Leaf Cluster; Legion of Merit with Oak Leaf Cluster; Bronze Star Medal, and other medals and awards.

Promoted to Brigadier General, April 8, 1963; Major General, April 1, 1966; Lieutenant General, May 15, 1969.

Eyadema, Etienne Gnassingbe. Major General, Togolese Army; President of Togo and Minister of Defense, 1967-   . Born in 1935, in Pya, Lama Kara District. Commissioned in 1963. Served with French forces as private and NCO in Indochina, Dahomey, Niger and Algeria, 1953-61. Chief of Staff, Togolese Army, 1965-67; assumed power in Togo through coup d'etat, 1967. Grand Officier, Ordre National de Mono; Military Cross; Chevalier, Légion d'Honneur (France); and other medals and awards.

Eyal, S. Major General, Israeli Army. Naval, Military and Air Attachc, Embassy of Israel, London and Paris.

Eyiceoglu, Celal. Senior Admiral, Turkish Navy; Commander in Chief, Turkish Naval Forces.

F

Faglic, Andrej. Major General, Army of Czechoslovakia; Deputy Chief, Personnel Department.

Fairburn, Robert Randell. Major General, United States Marine Corps; Commanding General, Marine Corps Supply Activity, Philadelphia, 1970-   . Born May 9, 1917, Chicago. Chaffey Junior College; University of California, Berkeley, BS, Business Administration, 1939; Officers Candidate School, Marine Corps Schools, 1941-42; Supply School, 1951-52; Amphibious Warfare School, Senior Course, Quantico, 1955; Industrial College of the Armed Forces, 1962-63; George Washington University, MA, Business Administration, 1963. Commissioned USMCR, 1942; transferred to USMC, 1946. Served in Pacific Theater, WW II; Vietnam War. Wing Supply Officer, 1st Marine Aircraft Wing, Vietnam, 1966-67; Commanding General, Marine Corps Supply Center, Albany, Georgia, 1967-70. Bronze Star Medal with Combat "V"; Navy Commendation Medal; and other medals and awards. Promoted to Brigadier General, April 14, 1967; Major General, August 5, 1969.

Falls, Robert Hilborn. Rear Admiral, Canadian Armed Forces; Deputy Chief of the Defence Staff for Operations, 1973-   . Born April 29, 1924, in Welland, Ontario. Joined Royal Canadian Air Force, 1943; commissioned in the Royal Naval Volunteer Reserve, 1945; transferred to Royal Canadian Naval Reserve as sub-lieutenant (pilot), September 1945. Commander Destroyer Escort *Chaudiere*, 1963-65; Commandant, Canadian Maritime Warfare School, Halifax, 1965-66; Commander, Aircraft Carrier *Bonaventure*, 1966-69; Director General, Postings and Careers, Canadian Forces Headquarters, Ottawa, 1969-71; Commander, Canadian Flotilla, Atlantic, 1971-73; Associate Assistant Deputy Minister, National Defense, for Policy, Canadian Forces Headquarters, Ottawa, 1972-73. Promoted to Rear Admiral, September 1972.

Fallu, Sumba. Brigadier General, Army of Zaire; Military, Naval and Air Attache, Embassy of the Republic of Zaire, Washington, D.C.

Farhat, Abdallah. Minister of National Defense, Tunisia, 1972-   . Attended Institute of Higher Studies, Tunis. Inspector, Central Administration, Bureau of Posts, Telegraphs and Telephones; Director of the Presidential Cabinet, 1956-64; President-Director, National Society for Investments, 1964; Secretary of State for Posts, Telegraphs and Telephones, 1964-69; Secretary of State for Agriculture, 1969; Minister of Agriculture, 1969-70; Director of Presidential Cabinet, 1970-72. Grand Sash of the Order of the Republic; Grand Sash of the Order of Independence.

al-Faris, Ibrahim Mohamed. Brigadier General, Army of Saudi Arabia; Armed Forces Attache, Embassy of Saudi Arabia, Washington, D.C., 1971-73.

Farrar-Hockley, Anthony Heritage. Major-General, British Army; General Officer Commanding, 4th Division, 1971-   . Born April 8, 1924. Defence Fellowship, Exeter College, Oxford, 1968-70. Commissioned in the 1st Airborne Division. Served in Greece, Italy and Southern France in WW II; Port Said (Egypt) 1956. Commander, Parachute Battalion, Persian Gulf and Radfan Campaign, 1962-65; Principal Staff Officer to Director of Borneo Operations, 1965-66; Commander, 16 Parachute Brigade, 1966-68; Director of Public Relations (Army), 1970; Commander, Land Forces, North Ireland, 1970-71. DSO and Bar; MBE; MC. Publications: *The Edge of the Sword*, 1954; *The Commander*, 1957; *The Somme*, 1964; *Death of an Army*, 1968; *Airborne Carpet*, 1969; *War in the Desert*, 1969.

Faucett, Ralph Eugene. Rear Admiral, Medical Corps, United States Navy; Commanding Officer, Naval Hospital, Oakland, California, 1972-   . Born July 28, 1916, in Milton, Indiana. Indiana University, BS, 1938, MD, 1942; Earlham College, BA, 1939; University of Pennsylvania Graduate School of Medicine, Internal Medicine, 1947-48; Officers Submarine Course, 1951-52. Commissioned Lieutenant (j.g.), Medical Corps, US Navy, 1943. Served in the Pacific Theater, WW II. Commanding Officer, Naval Hospital, St. Albans, New York, 1967-69; Assistant Chief, Bureau of Medicine and Surgery, for Research and Military Medical Specialties, Navy Department, 1969-72. Promoted to Rear Admiral, August 1, 1968.

Faulkner, Arthur James. Minister of Defence, Minister in Charge of War Pensions, Minister in Charge of Rehabilitation, New Zealand, 1972-   . Born in 1921, in Auckland. Served as Spitfire pilot in North Africa and northern Europe in WW II. Member of New Zealand Parliament (Labour Party), 1957-   ; parliamentary experience before elevation to the Cabinet included service on the Select Committees of Defence, Foreign Affairs, Statutes Revision, Local Government, and others; Convener of Labour Caucus Committees on Defence, Foreign Affairs, the South Pacific Commission and South Pacific Affairs; Member, New Zealand Labour Party, 1936-   .

Fautario, Hector Luis. Brigadier, Argentine Air Force; Commander in Chief, Argentine Air Force, 1973-   .

Faver, Dudley Ervin. Major General, United States Air Force; Director, Secretary of the Air Force Personnel Council, 1971-   . Born August 17, 1916, in Sweetwater, Texas. Abilene Christian College, Abilene, Texas, BA, 1937; Army Air Corps Flying School, 1941; Air Command and Staff School, 1949; Air War College, 1957-58. Commissioned Second Lieutenant, US Army Air Corps, 1941. Commander 3320th Technical School, Amarillo Technical Training Center, 1961-64; Commander, 3500th Pilot Training Wing, 1964-66; Deputy Director, Personnel Training and Education, and Personnel Planning, Deputy Chief of Staff, Personnel, 1966-71. Legion of Merit with two Oak Leaf Clusters; and other medals and awards. Promoted to Brigadier General, April 21, 1966; Major General, February 24, 1970.

Fedayev, N. Lieutenant General, USSR Air Force; Commandant, Zhukovskiy Air Force Engineering War College. Duty on the Soviet-German Front in WW II. Member, Communist Party of the Soviet Union.

Fegan, Joseph Charles, Jr. Major General, United States Marine Corps; Commanding General, Third Marine Division, 1972-   . Born December 21, 1920, Los Angeles, California. Princeton University, BA, Political Science, 1942; Amphibious Warfare School, Quantico, 1954; Vox Institute of Language, and Strategic Intelligence School, 1956-57; Command and Staff College, Atomic Weapons Employment Course, Quantico, 1959-60; National War College, 1965-66. Commissioned USMCR, 1942. Served in Pacific Theater, WW II; Korean War; Vietnam War. Deputy, Combat Operations Center, US Military Assistance Command, Vietnam, 1966-67; Marine Corps Liaison Officer, Joint Chiefs of Staff, 1967; Commanding Officer, Marine Barracks, and Director, Marine Corps Institute, Washington, D.C., 1967-68; Assistant Division Commander, 2d Marine Division, and Commanding General, Force Troops, Fleet Marine Force, Atlantic, 1968-72. Silver Star Medal with Gold Star; Legion of Merit; and other medals and awards. Promoted to Brigadier General, September 27, 1968; Major General, December 15, 1971.

Felices, Salvador E. Major General, United States Air Force; Commander, 1st Strategic Aerospace Division, 1972-   . Born August 13, 1923, Santurce, Puerto Rico. A&M College, University of Puerto Rico; US Military Academy, 1943-46; National War College, 1964-65. Commissioned Second Lieutenant, US Army Air Corps, 1946. Served in the Korean War; Vietnam War. Commander, 416th Bombardment Wing, 1967-68; Commander, 306th Bombardment Wing, Guam, 1968-69; Commander, 823d Air Division, 1969-70; Assistant Deputy Chief of Staff, Materiel, Strategic Air Command, 1970-71; Deputy Chief of Staff, Logistics, Strategic Air Command, 1971-72. Legion of Merit with two Oak Leaf Clusters; Distinguished Flying Cross; and other medals and awards. Promoted to Major General, January 1, 1972.

Fell, Michael Frampton. Vice-Admiral, British Royal Navy; Chief of Staff to Commander Allied Naval Forces Southern Europe, 1972-   . Born January 17, 1918. Attended Flying Training Course; Naval Staff Course. Joined the Royal Navy in 1938. Fleet Air Arm Pilot in WW II; served in Korea. Captain (F), 3d Frigate Squadron, Far East Fleet, Commander, HMS *Loch Hillisport*, 1961-64; Chief of Staff to Commander-in-Chief, Portsmouth, 1963-64; Commander, HMS *Ark Royal*, 1965-66; Flag Officer, Gibraltar, 1966-68; Commander, Carriers and Amphibious Ships, and Commander, 2d Carrier Striking Force, NATO, 1968-70; Flag Officer, Naval Air Command, 1970-72. CB; DSO; DSC and Bar.

Feng Chi-chung. Admiral, Navy of Republic of China; Deputy Minister, Ministry of National Defense, 1972-   . Born January 27, 1914, Canton. Chinese Naval Academy; Chinese War College. Service in Sino-Japanese War; Chinese Civil War. Other Positions: Commander, Amphibious Force Command, 1955-59; Commander, Fleet Command, 1959-61; Deputy Chief of General Staff for Planning, Ministry of National Defense, 1961-65; Deputy Commander in Chief, Chinese Navy, 1965-70; Director, Joint Operations Training Department, Ministry of National Defense, 1970-72.

Ferber, Ernst. General, Army of the Federal Republic of Germany; Commander in Chief, Allied Forces, Central Europe, 1973-   . Born September 27, 1914, Wiesbaden. Attended Officers School. Served in German Armed Forces in WW II. Joined the Armed Forces (Bundeswehr), 1955, with the rank of Lieutenant Colonel; Commander, Panzer Grenadier Division; Deputy Inspector of the Army; Inspector of the Army.

Fingerhut, Helmut. Under Secretary, Federal Ministry of Defense, Federal Republic of Germany, 1970-   . Born November 22, 1921, Frankfurt a.M. Attended Trade School, Frankfurt a.M. Served as German Army NCO, 1940-45. Director, Personnel Division, City of Frankfurt a.M., 1960-70; Head of a Government Department and Chief of a Division, 1970-72.

Firat, Hilmi. Vice Admiral, Turkish Navy; Chief of Staff, Turkish Naval Forces.

Fish, Howard M. Major General, United States Air Force; Deputy Director of Budget, Office of the Comptroller, Headquarters US Air Force, Washington, D.C., 1971-   . Born August 1, 1923, in Melrose, Minnesota. Advanced Navigator Training Course, 1943-44; Air Command and Staff College, 1954; University of Chicago, MBA, 1957; Armed Forces Staff College, 1960; Air War College, 1963-64; George Washington University, MA, International Affairs, 1964. Commissioned Second Lieutenant, US Army Air Corps, in 1944. Served in the European Theater in WW II, POW; in the Korean War; and in the Vietnam War. Plans and Programs Officer, Directorate of Plans, Headquarters US Air Force, Washington, D.C., 1964-67; Assistant for Analysis, Deputy Director of Plans for Force Development, Headquarters US Air Force, Washington, D.C., 1967-69;

Director of Tactical Analysis, Seventh Air Force, Tan Son Nhut Airfield, Republic of Vietnam, 1969-70; Deputy Director of Doctrine, Concepts and Objectives, Deputy Chief of Staff, Plans and Operations, Headquarters US Air Force, 1970-71. Decorations include Legion of Merit with Oak Leaf Cluster, Distinguished Flying Cross with Oak Leaf Cluster, and Air Medal with four Oak Leaf Clusters. Promotions: Brigadier General, August 1, 1971; Major General, June 1, 1973.

FitzPatrick, David Beatty. Air Commodore, British Royal Air Force; Director, Guided Weapons (Trials and Ranges), Ministry of Technology, 1969-   . Born January 31, 1920; Kenilworth College, Exeter; Midhurst; Central Flying School; Royal Air Force Flying College; NATO Defence College, 1960; Joint Services Staff College, 1961. Commissioned in 1938. Served in Atlantic, Mediterranean and Far East Theaters in WW II. Deputy Director (Operations), Air Staff, 1961-64; Commander, Royal Air Force, Akrotiri and Nicosia, 1964-66; Director of (Q) Royal Air Force, Ministry of Defence, 1966-69; attached to NBPI for special duty, 1969. CB; OBE; AFC and Bar. Member, British Institute of Management, 1970; Associate Fellow, Royal Aeronautical Society, 1971.

Fitzpatrick, Sir (Geoffrey Richard) Desmond. General, British Army; Deputy Supreme Allied Commander, Europe, 1970-   . Born December 14, 1912. Attended Royal Military Academy, Sandhurst. Commissioned in the Royal Dragoons, 1932. Served in Middle East, Italy and Northwest Europe in WW II. Assistant Chief of Defence Staff, Ministry of Defence, 1959-61; Director of Military Operations, War Office, 1962-64; Chief of Staff, British Army of the Rhine, 1964-65; General Officer Commanding-in-Chief, Northern Ireland, 1965-66; Vice-Chief of General Staff, 1966-68; Commander-in-Chief, British Army of the Rhine, and Commander, Northern Army Group, 1968-70. GCB; DSO; MBE; MC. Aide-de-Camp (General) to the Queen, 1970-   . Promotions: Major-General, 1959; Lieutenant-General, 1965; General, 1968.

Flanagan, Edward Michael, Jr. Lieutenant General, United States Army; Comptroller of the Army, Washington, D.C., 1973-   . Born July 13, 1921, Saugerties, New York. US Military Academy; The Artillery School, Basic and Advanced Courses; US Army Command and General Staff College; US Armed Forces Staff College; US Army War College; Boston University, MA Degree, Political Science. Commissioned Second Lieutenant, 1943. Served in WW II and Vietnam War. Assistant Division Commander, 25th Infantry Division, US Army, Pacific-Vietnam, 1966-67; Director, Training Directorate, and Special Assistant to the Commander, US Military Assistance Command, Vietnam, 1967-68; Deputy Chief of Staff, Operations, III Marine Amphibious Force, US Military Assistance Command, Vietnam, 1968; Commanding General, US Army John F. Kennedy Center for Special Warfare, and Commandant, US Army Institute for Military Assistance, Fort Bragg, North Carolina, 1968-71; Commanding General, 1st Infantry Division (Mechanized) and Fort Riley, Kansas, 1971-72.

Distinguished Service Medal; Legion of Merit with Oak Leaf Cluster; Bronze Star Medal; and other medals and awards. Promoted to Brigadier General, October 1, 1966; Major General, January 1, 1970; Lieutenant General, January 1, 1973.

Flanagan, William Robert. Rear Admiral, United States Navy; Deputy Chief of Naval Personnel and Assistant Deputy Chief of Naval Operations (Manpower), 1973-   . Born in Athens, Georgia. US Naval Academy, 1940-43; Flight Training Course, 1945-46; Naval War College, 1959-60. Commissioned Ensign, US Navy, 1943; designated Naval Aviator, 1946. Served in the Pacific Theater, WW II; Vietnam War. Commanding Officer USS *Montrose* (APA212), 1964-65; Bureau of Naval Personnel, 1965-67; Commanding Officer USS *Constellation* (CVA-64), 1967-68; Deputy Commander, Naval Forces, Vietnam, and Deputy Chief, Naval Advisory Group, Military Assistance Command, Vietnam, 1969-71; Director, East Asia and Pacific Region, Office of the Secretary of Defense (International Security Affairs), 1971-72; Commander of Carrier Division ONE, 1972-73. Distinguished Service Medal with Gold Star; Legion of Merit with Combat "V"; Air Medal; Navy Commendation Medal; and other US and foreign medals and awards.

Fleming, Lawrence J. Major-General, United States Air Force; Commander, 24th North American Air Defense (NORAD) Region, and 24th Air Division, Aerospace Defense Command, Malmstrom Air Force Base, Montana, 1973-   . Born December 12, 1922, in Green Bay, Wisconsin. Attended St. Norbert's College, West DePere, Wisconsin, 1941-42; Flying Training Course, 1943-44; Air Command and Staff School, 1957-58. Commissioned Second Lieutenant, US Army Air Corps, in 1944. Served in the European Theater, WW II and in the Vietnam War. Director of Tactical Evaluation, 29th Air Division, Richards-Gebaur Air Force Base, Missouri, 1964-65; Commander, 13th Fighter Interceptor Squadron, Glasgow Air Force Base, Montana, 1965-66; Commander, 343d Fighter Group, Duluth International Airport, Minnesota, 1966-68; Advisor to Deputy Chief of Staff, Operations, Vietnamese Air Force, Tan Son Nhut Airfield, Vietnam, 1968-69; Deputy for Operations, Central North American Air Defense Command Region/Tenth Air Force, Aerospace Defense Command, Richards-Gebaur Air Force Base, Missouri, 1969-70; Continental Air Defense Command Liaison Officer to the Organization of the Joint Chiefs of Staff, 1970; Assistant Deputy Chief of Staff, Operations, Headquarters Aerospace Defense Command, Ent Air Force Base, Colorado, 1970-71; Commander, Air Defense Weapons Center, Aerospace Defense Command, Tyndall Air Force Base, Florida, 1971-73. Legion of Merit with Oak Leaf Cluster; Distinguished Flying Cross; Meritorious Service Medal; Air Medal with six Oak Leaf Clusters; and other medals and awards. Promoted to Major General, June 1, 1973.

Fletcher, Robert Rowland. Rear Admiral, United States Public Health Service; Chief Medical Officer, US Coast Guard, 1971-   . Born November 23, 1925, Tampa,

Florida. Riddle Interamerican College, Miami, Florida, AS Degree, 1948; University of Miami, BS Degree, 1949; University of Puerto Rico, School of Medicine, MD Degree, 1955. Commissioned Lieutenant (jg), July 1, 1955. Senior Medical Officer, Coast Guard Academy, 1965-70; Senior Medical Officer, Coast Guard Training and Supply Center, Alameda, California, 1970-71. Promoted to Captain, July 1, 1965; Rear Admiral, July 15, 1971.

Foltin, Ferdinand. Brigadier, Austrian Army; Military and Air Attache, Austrian Embassy, Washington, D.C., USA, 1969-72. Born November 30, 1916. Studied at the Austrian Military Academy, Wiener Neustadt, 1936-38. Commissioned Second Lieutenant, 1938. Served in the German Army in WW II. Section Chief, Ministry of Defense, 1965-67; Commandant, Close Combat School, and Army Physical Education, 1967; Commander, Armored Infantry Brigade, 1967-69. Grosses Ehrenzeichen; Goldenes Verdienstzeichen; and other decorations and awards. Promotions: Colonel, 1965; Brigadier, January 1, 1970.

Formichev, M. G. Lieutenant General, USSR Army; First Deputy Commander, Transbaikal Military District, 1965- . Served on the Soviet-German Front in WW II. Member, Communist Party of the Soviet Union.

Forbes, Robert Charles. Major General, United States Army; Chief of Staff, Allied Land Forces, Southeastern Europe, 1971- . Born July 22, 1917, Camden, New Jersey. University of Pennsylvania, AB Degree, Arts and Sciences; The Infantry School, Advanced Course; US Army Command and General Staff College, US Army War College. Commissioned Second Lieutenant, US Army Reserve, 1939. Served in WW II and Vietnam War. Assistant Division Commander, 9th Infantry Division, Fort Riley, Kansas, 1966-67; Deputy Commanding General/Chief of Staff, II Field Force, US Army, Vietnam, 1967; Commanding General, 199th Infantry Brigade, US Army, Vietnam, 1967-68; Assistant Chief of Staff, Personnel, J-1, US Military Assistance Command, Vietnam, 1968; Director, International Logistics, US Army Materiel Command, Washington, D.C., 1968-69; Director, Materiel Requirements, US Army Materiel Command, Washington, D.C., 1969-71. Distinguished Service Medal; Silver Star with Oak Leaf Cluster; Legion of Merit with Oak Leaf Cluster; Bronze Star Medal with two Oak Leaf Clusters; and other medals and awards. Promoted to Brigadier General, May 1, 1965; Major General, July 1, 1968.

Ford, Robert Cyril. Major-General, British Army; Commandant, Royal Military Academy, Sandhurst, 1973- . Born December 29, 1923. Attended Royal Military Academy, Sandhurst; Staff College, Camberley, 1955. Commissioned in the 4th/7th Royal Dragoon Guards, 1943. Served in Northwest Europe, WW II; Egypt and Palestine, 1947-48. Squadron Leader 4/7 Royal Dragoon Guards, 1962-63; General Staff Officer 1 to Chief of Defence Staff, 1964-65; Commander, 4/7 Royal Dragoon Guards, South Arabia and Northern Ireland, 1966-67; Commander, 7th Armoured Brigade, 1968-69; Principal Staff Officer to the Chief of Defence Staff, 1970-71;

Commander, Land Forces, Northern Ireland, 1971-73. CBE.

Forero, Jose G. Brigadier General, Colombian Army; Assistant Military Attache, Embassy of Colombia, Washington, D.C. Promoted to Brigadier General December 1, 1970.

Forrest Ronald Stephen. Rear-Admiral, British Royal Navy; Defence Services Secretary, 1972- . Born January 11, 1923. Attended Royal Naval College, Dartmouth; Joint Services Staff College, 1963. Commissioned in 1943. Served at sea in WW II. Chief Staff Officer to Admiral Commanding Reserves, 1964; Commander Dartmouth Training Squadron, 1966-68; Director, Seaman Officers Appointments, 1968-70; Commanding Officer, HMS *London*, 1970-72. Naval General Service Medal. Promoted to Rear-Admiral in 1972.

Forrester, Eugene Priest. Major General, United States Army; Director of Plans, Programs, and Budget, Office of the Deputy Chief of Staff for Personnel, US Army, 1973- . Born April 17, 1926, in Watertown, Tennessee. Attended US Military Academy; Ground General School; Infantry School, Basic and Advanced Courses; Command and General Staff College; British Army Staff College; Armed Forces Staff College; National War College, 1966-67; George Washington University, MA, International Affairs. Commissioned Second Lieutenant, June 8, 1948. Served in the Korean War and the Vietnam War. Deputy Chief, later Chief, Force Development Division, and later Assistant Chief of Staff, G-3, Headquarters, US Army, Vietnam, 1967-68; Commanding Officer, 3d Brigade, 4th Infantry Division, US Army, Pacific-Vietnam, 1968; Executive to the Vice Chief of Staff, US Army, 1968-70; Assistant Division Commander, 1st Cavalry Division (Airmobile), US Army, Pacific-Vietnam, 1970; Deputy Assistant Chief of Staff, Civil Operations and Revolutionary Development Support, US Military Assistance Command, Vietnam, 1970-71; Special Assistant to Director of Officer Personnel, then Director of Officer Personnel Directorate, Office of Personnel Operations, 1971-72; Director of Procurement, Training and Distribution, Office of the Deputy Chief of Staff for Personnel, 1972-73. Distinguished Service Medal; Silver Star; Legion of Merit with three Oak Leaf Clusters; Distinguished Flying Cross with Oak Leaf Cluster; Bronze Star Medal with two Oak Leaf Clusters; Air Medal (19 awards). Promoted to Brigadier General August 1, 1970; Major General March 1, 1973.

Fortelia, Eduardo. Brigadier General, Peruvian Army; Military Attache, Embassy of Peru, Washington, D.C., 1971-73.

Foster, Hugh Franklin, Jr. Major General, United States Army; Commanding General, United States Army Electronics Command, Fort Monmouth, New Jersey, 1971- . Born March 2, 1918, Brooklyn, New York. U.S. Military Academy; U.S. Army Command and General Staff College; U.S. Army War College; Purdue University,

MS Degree, Electronic Engineering. Commissioned Second Lieutenant, U.S. Army, 1941. Served in WW II and Vietnam War. Signal Officer, Eighth U.S. Army, Pacific-Korea 1965-67; Commanding General, U.S. Army Communications Systems Agency (Provisional), Fort Monmouth, New Jersey, 1967-69; Commanding General, U.S. Army Strategic Communications Command, Southeast Asia, and Assistant Chief of Staff, Communications-Electronics, U.S. Army, Pacific-Vietnam, 1970-71. Distinguished Service Medal; Legion of Merit with three Oak Leaf Clusters; and other medals and awards. Promoted to Brigadier General, July 1, 1967; Major General, June 10, 1969.

Foster, Ralph Longwell. Major General, United States Army; Secretary of the General Staff, Office, Chief of Staff, US Army, Washington, D.C., 1972- . Born September 19, 1917, Greenfield, Massachusetts. Massachusetts State College, BS Degree, Chemistry; The Cavalry School, Basic Course; US Army Command and General Staff College; US Army War College. Commissioned Second Lieutenant, US Army Reserve, 1939. Served in WW II. Assistant Chief of Staff, G-3, Eighth US Army, Korea, 1963-65; Assistant Division Commander, 1st Armored Division, Fort Hood, Texas, 1965-68; Deputy Commanding General, Seventh Army Support Command, US Army, Europe, 1968-69; Commanding General, V Corps Support Command, US Army, Europe, 1969-70; Deputy Chief of Staff, Intelligence, US Army, Europe and Seventh Army, 1970-72. Legion of Merit with Oak Leaf Cluster; Bronze Star Medal with V Device and Oak Leaf Cluster; and other medals and awards. Promoted to Brigadier General, June 1, 1963; Major General, January 1, 1969.

Foxley-Norris, Sir Christopher (Neil). Air Chief Marshal, British Royal Air Force; Chief of Personnel and Logistics, Ministry of Defence, 1971- . Born March 16, 1917. Attended Trinity College, Oxford; Middle Temple, MA, 1946; Imperial Defence College, 1961. Commissioned in RAF Reserve of Officers, 1936. Served in WW II, Battle of Britain. Director of Organisation and Administration Plans, Air Ministry, 1962; Assistant Chief, Defence Staff, 1963; Air Officer Commanding, 224 Group, Far East Air Force, 1964-67; Director General, RAF Organisation, Ministry of Defence, 1967-68; Commander in Chief, RAF, Germany, and Commander, NATO 2d Tactical Air Force, 1968-70. GCB; OBE; DSO.

Franco Ibarnegaray, Carlos. Major General, Spanish Air Force; Chief, Canary Islands Air Zone, 1970- . Diplomate of Air Force Staff. Formerly Commander, 23d Fighter Group; Chief of 3d Section, Air Force Staff; Chief of Air Branch, Rota Air Force and Naval Base; Commander of 37th Wing; Chief of Staff, 3d Air Region (Valencia); Director, Air Force War College. Great Crosses: Army, Navy and Air Force Merit, and Saint Hermenegild Royal and Military Order; War Cross; Red Cross for Military Merit; Campaign Medal; Military Medal (Collective); Cross and Badge of Saint Hermenegild Royal and Military Order; Cross for Army Merit (1st Class); Cross for Navy Merit (1st Class); Cross of Air Force Merit (1st Class); Cross for

Military Merit (France); Legion of Honor, Official Rank (France); and other medals and awards. Promoted to Major General, August 2, 1970.

Franklin, Wesley Charles. Major General, United States Army; Deputy Commanding General for Reserve Forces, Southern Area, Fifth US Army, Fort Sam Houston, Texas, 1971- . Born March 23, 1917, New York, New York. Cornell University, BS Degree, Chemistry and Biology; Signal School; Education Equivalent to the Signal School, Advanced Course; US Army Command and General Staff College; National War College. Commissioned Second Lieutenant, US Army Reserve, 1938. Served in WW II. Commanding General, US Army Electronics, Materiel Agency, Philadelphia, Pennsylvania, 1963-64; Deputy Commanding General for Operations, US Army Electronics Command, Fort Monmouth, New Jersey, 1964-66; Deputy Commanding General, US Army Security Agency, Arlington Hall Station, Arlington, Virginia, 1966-67; Deputy Assistant Chief of Staff for Intelligence and Deputy for Foreign Intelligence and Security, Office, Assistant Chief of Staff, Intelligence, US Army, Washington, D.C., 1967; Deputy Assistant Chief of Staff for Intelligence, Office, Assistant Chief of Staff, Intelligence, US Army, Washington, D.C., 1967-69; Chief of Staff, US Forces, Japan, 1969-71; Deputy Commanding General for Reserve Forces, Fourth US Army, Fort Sam Houston, Texas, 1971. Legion of Merit with three Oak Leaf Clusters; Bronze Star Medal; and other medals and awards. Promoted to Brigadier General, September 1, 1963; Major General, October 1, 1967.

Frankosky, James O. Major General, United States Air Force; Vice Commander, Thirteenth Air Force, Clark Air Base, Republic of Philippines, 1971- . Born February 6, 1919, Fargo, North Dakota. North Dakota Agriculture College, Fargo, North Dakota, 1938; US Military Academy, 1939-43; Special Weapons Course, 1948; National War College, 1959-60; George Washington University, MS, 1969. Commissioned Second Lieutenant, US Army Air Corps, 1943. Served in the European Theater in WW II. Commander, 509th Bombardment Wing, 1963-67; Deputy Director, Strategic and Defense Forces, Directorate, Operational Requirements and Development Plans, Deputy Chief of Staff, Research and Development, Headquarters USAF, 1967-69; Deputy Director, Operational Requirements, 1969-71. Legion of Merit with two Oak Leaf Clusters; Distinguished Flying Cross with one Oak Leaf Cluster; Croix de Guerre; and other medals and awards. Promoted to Major General, August 1, 1971.

Fraser, Colin Angus Ewen. Major-General, Australian Army; General Officer Commanding, Southern Command, Australia, 1971- . Born September 25, 1918, in Nairobi, Kenya. Attended Royal Military College, Duntroon, 1934-38; Staff College, Camberley, 1946. Commissioned in 1938. Served in the UK, Middle East, and Pacific in WW II; Korean War, Vietnam War. Chief of Staff, Northern Command, Brisbane, 1964-68; Commandant, Royal Military College, Duntroon, 1968-69; Commander, Australian Force, Vietnam, 1970-71. CB; CBE.

Fraser, Sir David (William). Lieutenant-General, British Army; Vice Chief, General Staff, 1973-   . Born December 30, 1920. Attended Christ Church, Oxford. Commissioned in 1941 in the Grenadier Guards. Served in WW II in the European Theater. Commander, 19th Infantry Brigade, 1963-65; Director of Defence Policy, Ministry of Defence, 1966-69; General Officer Commanding 4th Division, 1969-71; Assistant Chief of Defence Staff (Policy), Ministry of Defence, 1971-73. OBE.

Freeman, Mason B. Rear Admiral, United States Navy; Superintendent, Naval Postgraduate School, Monterey, California, 1972-   . Born February 8, 1914, in Chicago, Illinois. US Naval Academy 1931-35; Naval Postgraduate School, Annapolis, General Ordnance Course, 1941-42; Naval War College, 1949-50; National War College, 1956-57. Commissioned Ensign, US Navy, in 1935. Served in the Pacific Theater, WW II; Vietnam War. Commander Destroyer Squadron SIXTEEN, 1960-61; Director, Electronic Warfare Division, Office of CNO, 1961-62; Naval Command and Control Systems Executive, Office of CNO, 1962-63; Commander Cruiser-Destroyer Flotilla TWO, 1963-64; Assistant Chief of Naval Personnel for Education and Training, 1964-67; Commander Cruiser-Destroyer Force, Pacific Fleet, 1967-70; Vice Director, J-3 (Operations), and later of Joint Staff, Joint Chiefs of Staff, 1970-72. Distinguished Service Medal; Bronze Star Medal with Combat "V"; and other medals and awards. Promoted to Rear Admiral, July 1, 1963.

Freer, Robert William George. Air Vice-Marshal, British Royal Air Force; Air Officer Commanding, II Group, RAF, 1972-   . Born September 1, 1923, in Darjeeling. Attended Royal Air Force Staff College, Cranwell, 1947-50; Royal Air Force Flying College, 1960; Imperial Defence College, 1968. Station Commander, Royal Air Force, Seletar, 1963-66; Deputy Director, Defence Plans (Air), Ministry of Defence, 1966-67; Deputy Commandant, Royal Air Force Staff College, 1969-71; Senior Air Staff Officer, Headquarters, Near East Air Force, 1971-72. Air Aide-de-Camp to the Queen, 1969-71. CBE. Member, Royal United Services Institute for Defence Studies.

Fretes Davalos, Carlos J. General, Paraguayan Army; Military Attache, Embassy of Paraguay, Washington, D.C.; Chief of Delegation, Inter-American Defense Board. Date of Rank: December 1, 1966

Fris, Edward Steve. Major General, United States Marine Corps; Deputy Chief of Staff (Air), Headquarters, US Marine Corps, 1972-   . Born September 1, 1921, Orient, Illinois. Missouri School of Mines, BS, Electrical Engineering, 1943; Reserve Officers Course, Marine Corps Schools, 1943; Naval Training School, Harvard University, and Radar Maintenance Course, Camp Murphy; Flight Training Course, 1946-47; Amphibious Warfare School, Junior Course, Quantico, 1950; Naval Postgraduate School, Annapolis, Maryland, 1951-52; Naval Postgraduate School, Monterey, California, 1952-54. Commissioned Second Lieutenant, USMCR, 1943; designated Naval Aviator, 1947. Served in Pacific Theater, WW II; Vietnam War.

Commander, Marine Air Control Group 18, 1st Marine Air Wing, Vietnam, 1968-69; Inspector General, Marine Corps, 1969-70; Assistant Deputy Chief of Staff (Programs), 1970-71; Commander, Marine Corps Air Bases, Western Area, and Commanding General, Marine Corps Air Station, El Toro, California, 1971-72. Promoted to Brigadier General, August 22, 1969; Major General, August 25, 1972.

Frolenkov, M. Colonel General, USSR Army; First Deputy Commander, Siberian Military District, 1970-   . Served on the Soviet-German Front in WW II. Member, Communist Party of the Soviet Union.

Frolov, A.A. Colonel General, USSR Army; Commandant, Communications War College. Served on the Soviet-German Front in WW II. Member, Communist Party of the Soviet Union.

Fuenterrosa, Eugenio. Vice Admiral, Argentine Navy; Chief of the Naval Staff.

Fuller, Lawrence Joseph. Major General, United States Army; Deputy Director for Attache Affairs, Defense Intelligence Agency, Washington, D.C., 1971-   . Born December 20, 1944, Everett, Washington. US Military Academy; The Engineer School; US Army Command and General Staff College; The National War College; Grand Rapids Junior College, AA Degree, Pre-law; University of Michigan, JD Degree; George Washington University, LLM Degree; Stanford University, MA Degree, History; Stanford University, MA Degree, Far Eastern Studies. Commissioned Second Lieutenant, 1940. Served in WW II. Assistant Judge Advocate General for Civil Law, Office of the Judge Advocate General, US Army, Washington, D.C., 1964-67; The Assistant Judge Advocate General, US Army, Washington, D.C., 1967-71. Distinguished Service Medal; Legion of Merit; and other medals and awards. Promoted to Brigadier General, February 27, 1964; Major General, July 1, 1967.

Fullerton, Charles G. Major, US Air Force; NASA Astronaut, 1969-   . Born October 11, 1936, Rochester, New York. California Institute of Technology, BS and MS, Mechanical Engineering, 1957, 1958; Basic and Advanced Flight Training; Air Force Aerospace Research Pilot School, Edwards Air Force Base, 1964-65. Commissioned Second Lieutenant, US Air Force, 1959. Pilot, 303d Bomb Wing, Strategic Air Command; Aeronautical Systems Division, test pilot. NASA Experience: Member, Support Crew, Apollo 14 and 17. Air Force Commendation Medal; Air Force Meritorious Service Medal.

Fulton, William Bennison. Major General, United States Army; Commanding General, 9th Infantry Division and Fort Lewis, Washington, 1972-   . Born October 31, 1919, Berkeley, California. University of California, BA Degree, Political Science; The Infantry School, Basic Course; US Army Command and General Staff College; US Air War College; George Washington University, MA Degree, International Affairs. Commissioned Second Lieutenant, US Army Reserve, 1942. Served in WW II and

Vietnam War. Assistant Division Commander, 9th Infantry Division, US Army, Pacific-Vietnam, 1967-68; Deputy Commanding General, US Army Training Center, Infantry, Fort Polk, Louisiana, 1968-69; Chairman, Defense Communications Planning Group, Integration Committee, Washington, D. C., 1969; STANO Systems Manager, Office, Chief of Staff, US Army, Washington, D.C., 1969-71; Director, Doctrine and Command Systems, and STANO Systems Manager, Office, Assistant Chief of Staff for Force Development, US Army, Washington, D.C., 1971-72. Distinguished Service Cross; Distinguished Service Medal; Silver Star; Legion of Merit with two Oak Leaf Clusters; Bronze Star Medal; and other medals and awards. Promoted to Brigadier General, August 18, 1967; Major General, July 1, 1970.

Furlong, Raymond B. Major General, United States Air Force; Vice Commander, Ninth Air Force, Shaw Air Force Base, South Carolina, 1973-   . Born August 13, 1926 in Saint Marys, Pennsylvania. Ursinus College, Collegeville, Pennsylvania, BS, Chemistry, 1946; Flight Training Course, 1948-49; Harvard University Business School, MBA, 1957; Command and General Staff College, 1961-62; National War College, 1968-69. Commissioned Second Lieutenant, US Air Force, 1949. Served in the Korean War. Operations Office, 772d Troop Carrier Squadron, and Chief, Rated Assignment Branch, Deputy for Personnel, Headquarters Tactical Air Command, Langley Air Force Base, Virginia, 1963-65; Operations Staff Officer, Assistant Chief of Staff for Studies and Analysis, Headquarters, US Air Force, Washington, D.C., 1965-67; Military Assistant to the Deputy Secretary of Defense, Washington, D.C., 1968-73. Legion of Merit; Distinguished Flying Cross; Air Medal with two Oak Leaf Clusters; and other medals and awards. Promotions: Brigadier General, March 1, 1972; Major General, 1973.

Fuson, Jack Carter. Major General, United States Army; Commanding General, US Army Transportation Center and Fort Eustis, and Commandant US Army Transportation School, Fort Eustis, Virginia, 1973-   . Born November 23, 1920, St. Joseph, Missouri. University of Maryland, BS Degree, Military Studies; The Transportation School, Advanced Course; US Army Command and General Staff College; US Armed Forces Staff College; US Industrial College of the Armed Forces. Commissioned Second Lieutenant, US Army Reserve, 1942. WW II; Vietnam War. Director of Transportation, Office, Deputy Chief of Staff for Logistics, US Army, Washington, D.C., 1967-69; Assistant Deputy Chief of Staff for Logistics (Doctrine Systems and Readiness), Office, Assistant Chief of Staff for Logistics, US Army, Washington, D. C., 1969-70; Deputy Chief of Staff for Logistics, US Army, Pacific, Fort Shafter, Hawaii, 1970-72; Assistant Chief of Staff, Logistics, J-4, Director of Logistics, US Military Assistance Command, Vietnam, 1972. Distinguished Service Medal; Legion of Merit with five Oak Leaf Clusters; Bronze Star Medal with two Oak Leaf Clusters; and other medals and awards. Promoted to Brigadier General, August 18, 1967; Major General, September 1, 1969.

G

Gaddis, Walter Donald. Rear Admiral, United States Navy; Assistant Deputy Chief of Naval Operations (Logistics), 1972-   . Born September 8, 1917, in Worland, Wyoming. University of Wyoming, 1936-37; US Naval Academy, 1937-41; Naval Postgraduate School, Ordnance Metallurgical Engineering Course, 1946-47; Carnegie Institute of Technology, MS, 1947-49; Armed Forces Staff College, 1953; Naval War College, Naval Warfare Course, 1958-59. Commissioned Ensign, US Navy, 1941. Served in the Pacific Theater in WW II; Vietnam War. Commanding Officer USS *Yosemite* (AD-19), 1962-63; Assistant Director, Budget and Reports, Office of the Comptroller of the Navy, 1963-65; Commander Destroyer Squadron EIGHT, 1965-66; Director of Programming and Finance, Headquarters Naval Material Command, 1966-68; Director of Budget and Reports, Office of Naval Comptroller, 1968-70; Commander Amphibious Group ONE, 1970-72. Legion of Merit with two Gold Stars; Bronze Star Medal with Combat "V"; Navy Commendation Medal with Gold Star and Combat "V"; and other medals and awards. Promoted to Rear Admiral, January 20, 1968.

Gallardo B., Enrique. Major General, Bolivian Air Force; Deputy Director, Inter-American Defense College; Officer, Inter-American Defense Board. Date of Rank: December 24, 1969.

Galligan, Walter T. Major General, United States Air Force; Commander, US Air Force Security Service, 1973-   . Born March 14, 1925, New York, New York. US Military Academy, 1942-45; US Air Force Institute of Technology, 1951-53, MS, Industrial Administration, 1953; Armed Forces Staff College, 1963; Advanced Management Program, Harvard University, 1965; Industrial College of the Armed Forces, 1966-67. Commissioned Second Lieutenant, US Army Air Corps, 1945. Served in the Vietnam War. Vice Commander, 401st Tactical Fighter Wing, Spain, 1967-68; Director of Operations, US Air Forces, Europe, 1968-69; Commander 35th Tactical Fighter Wing, Vietnam, 1969-70; Director, Tactical Air Control Center, Vietnam, 1970-71; Commandant of Cadets, US Air Force Academy, 1971-73. Meritorious Service Medal; Air Medal; and other medals and awards. Promoted to Brigadier General, May 1, 1970; Major General, 1972.

Galloway, James Vance. Major General, United States Army; Chief, Joint US Military Mission for Aid to Turkey, 1972-   . Born August 10, 1919, Lake Toxaway, North Carolina. Ohio University, BS Degree, Business Administration; The Armored School, Advanced Course; US Army Command and General Staff College; US Army War College; George Washington University, MA Degree, International Affairs. Commissioned Second Lieutenant, US Army Reserve, 1940. WW II; Vietnam War. Secretary, Joint Staff, US Military Assistance Command, Vietnam, 1967-68; Assistant Division Commander, 23d Infantry Division (American), US Army, Pacific-Vietnam, 1968; Assistant Chief of Staff for Military Assistance, US Military Assistance Command, Vietnam, 1968-69; Assistant

Commandant, US Army Armor School, Fort Knox, Kentucky, 1969-71; Commanding General, 1st Armored Division, US Army, Europe, 1971-72. Distinguished Service Medal, Silver Star, Legion of Merit with three Oak Leaf Clusters; Bronze Star Medal; and other medals and awards. Promoted to Brigadier General, August 1, 1968; Major

Galo Soto, Raúl. Colonel, Army of Honduras; Secretary of Defense and Public Security, 1973-   .

Gamassi, Mahammed. Major General, Army of the Arab Republic of Egypt; Cheif of Staff, Egyptian Armed Forces, 1973-   .

Gambetta, Mario. Admiral, Italian Navy; Director General of Naval Personnel.

Gamble, Jack K. Major General, United States Air Force; Commander, 25th North American Air Defense Command/Continental Air Defense Command (NORAD/CONAD) Region, and Commander, 25th Air Division, ADC, 1972-   . Born July 27, 1922, in Belleville, Illinois. University of Utah; University of Maryland; Army Air Corps Flying School, 1942-43; Air Command and Staff College, 1955-56; Industrial College of the Armed Forces, 1963-64. Commissioned Second Lieutenant, US Army Air Corps, 1942. Served in the Mediterranean Theater, WW II. Commander, 52d Fighter Wing, 1967-69; Commander, 35th Air Division, 1969; Commander, 20th NORAD/CONAD Region, and Commander, 20th Air Division, 1969-72. Legion of Merit; Distinguished Flying Cross; and other medals and awards. Promoted to Major General, September 1, 1971.

Ganeyev, K. Lieutenant General, Armor, USSR Army; First Deputy Commander, Central Asian Military District 1972-   . Served on the Soviet-German Front in WW II. Deputy Commander, Central Asian Military District, 1970-72. Member, Communist Party of the Soviet Union.

Garcia Landraeta, Alfredo. Rear Admiral, Venezuelan Navy; Chief of Naval Staff.

Gard, Robert Gibbins, Jr. Major General, United States Army; Commanding General, US Army Training Center (Infantry) and Fort Ord, California, 1973-   . Born January 28, 1928, in West Point, New York. Attended US Military Academy; Artillery School; Command and General Staff College; National War College, 1965-66; Harvard University, MPA and PhD, Politics, Economics, and Government. Commissioned Second Lieutenant in 1950. Served in the Vietnam War. Military Assistant to the Secretary of Defense, 1966-68; Commanding Officer, 9th Infantry Division Artillery, US Army, Pacific-Vietnam, 1968-69; Chief, Program Development Division, later Assistant Director, Manpower and Forces Directorate, Office of the Assistant Chief of Staff for Force Development, 1969-70; Army Fellow, Council on Foreign Relations, New York, NY, 1970-71; Director of Human Resources Development, Office of the Deputy Chief of

Staff for Personnel, 1971-73. Silver Star; Legion of Merit with Oak Leaf Cluster; Distinguished Flying Cross; Bronze Star Medal with V Device and three Oak Leaf Clusters; and other medals and awards. Promoted to Brigadier General August 1, 1971; Major General, August 1, 1973.

Garrett, Francis Leonard. Rear Admiral, Chaplain Corps, United States Navy; Chief of Chaplains, Bureau of Naval Personnel, 1970-   . Born April 7, 1919, in Greenville, South Carolina. Woffard College, Spartanburg, South Carolina, BA, 1940; Chandler School of Theology, Emory University, Atlanta, Georgia, BD, 1943; Naval Training School (Chaplains), 1944; Columbia University Postgraduate Course in Theology, New York, New York, 1954-55; Woffard College, Doctor of Divinity Degree, 1967. Commissioned Lieutenant (j.g.), Chaplain Corps, US Naval Reserve, 1944; transferred to US Navy, 1946. Served at sea in the Pacific Theater, WW II; Vietnam War. Chaplain, Third Marine Division, 1965-66. Assistant Chief of Chaplains for Plans, Bureau of Naval Personnel, 1966-67; Head of Personnel Branch, Chaplains Division, 1967-69; Fleet Chaplain, Staff of Commander in Chief, US Atlantic Fleet, 1969-70. Legion of Merit with Combat "V"; and other medals and awards. Promoted to Rear Admiral, July 1, 1970.

Garriott, Owen K. United States; NASA Scientist-Astronaut, 1965-   . Born November 22, 1930, Enid, Oklahoma. University of Oklahoma, BS, Electrical Engineering, 1953; Stanford University, MS and PhD, Electrical Engineering, 1957, 1960; Flight Training. Taught electronics, electromagnetic theory and ionospheric physics, Department of Electrical Engineering, Stanford University, 1961-65. NASA experience: Science-Pilot, Skylab 3 mission.

Garth, Marshall Bragg. Major General, United States Army; Director of Military Support, Office of Chief of Staff, US Army, 1973-   . Born September 10, 1919, Stony Point, Virginia. The Armored School, Advanced Course; US Army Command and General Staff College; US Armed Forces Staff College; US Army War College. Commissioned Second Lieutenant, US Army Reserve, 1942. Served in WW II and Vietnam War. Assistant Division Commander, 2d Armored Division, Fort Hood, Texas, 1968-69; Chief of Staff, V Corps, US Army, Europe, 1969-70; Commanding General, 1st Infantry Division (Forward), US Army, Europe, 1970-71; Commanding General, 3d Infantry Division, US Army, Europe, 1971-72; Commanding General, Third Regional Assistance Command, and Senior Advisor, Military Region 3, US Military Assistance Command, Vietnam, 1972-73. Silver Star; Legion of Merit with two Oak Leaf Clusters; Bronze Star Medal with V Device and three Oak Leaf Clusters; and other medals and awards. Promoted to Brigadier General, February 1, 1968; Major General, January 1, 1971.

Garton, William Maris. Major-General, Canadian Armed Forces; Commander, Air Defence Command, North Bay, Ontario, 1973-   . Born June 8, 1921, in St. Boniface,

Manitoba. Attended Royal Canadian Air Force Staff College, 1955. Enlisted in the Royal Canadian Air Force in 1940; commissioned Wireless Officer Operator, 1942. Served in the European Theater in WW II. Assistant Chief of the Air Staff, 1962-66; Senior Personnel Staff Officer, CFB St. Hubert, 1966-67; Chief of Staff, Air Defence Command, 1967-69; Deputy Commander, 24 NORAD Region, Great Falls, Montana (USA), 1969-73. Promotions: Brigadier-General, March 15, 1967; Major-General, June 8, 1973.

Gavin, Herbert J. Major General, United States Air Force; Assistant Deputy Chief of Staff, Logistics, Tactical Air Command, Langley Air Force Base, Virginia, 1971- . Born November 15, 1921, in Madison County, Iowa. Aviation Cadet Training Course, 1942-43; Engineering Officers Course, McClellan Field, California, 1943; Northrup Institute of Technology, Aeronautical Engineering, 1949; Air War College, 1965-66; University of Maryland, BS; George Washington University, MS, International Affairs. Commissioned Second Lieutenant, US Army Air Corps, in 1943. Served in the China-Burma-India Theater, WW II, and in Vietnam War. Deputy Commander for Operations, then Vice Commander, 75th Tactical Reconnaissance Wing, Bergstrom Air Force Base, Texas, 1966-68; Deputy Commander for Operations, 460th Tactical Reconnaissance Wing, Pacific Air Forces, Tan Son Nhut Airfield, Vietnam, 1968-69; Assistant Deputy Chief of Staff for Logistics, Headquarters Tactical Air Command, Langley Air Force Base, Virginia, 1969-70; Commander, 474th Tactical Fighter Wing, Tactical Air Command, Nellis Air Force Base, Nevada, 1970-71. Silver Star; Legion of Merit; Distinguished Flying Cross; Bronze Star Medal; Air Medal with seven Oak Leaf Clusters; Meritorious Service Medal; and other medals and awards. Promotions: Brigadier General, September 1, 1971; Major General, 1973.

Gayler, Noel. Admiral, US Navy; Commander in Chief, Pacific, 1972- . Born December 25, 1914, in Birmingham, Alabama. US Naval Academy, 1931-35; Flight Training Course, 1940. Commissioned Ensign, US Navy, 1935; designated Naval Aviator, 1940. Served in the Pacific Theater, WW II. Commander Carrier Division TWENTY, US Atlantic Fleet, 1962-63; Director, Development Programs, Office of the CNO, 1963-65; Assistant Deputy Chief of Naval Operations (Development), 1965-67; Deputy Director, Joint Strategic Target Planning Staff, 1967-69; Director, National Security Agency, and Chief, Central Security Agency, 1969-72. Three Navy Crosses; Bronze Star Medal; Distinguished Service Medal; Legion of Merit with Gold Star; Sperry Award of the Institute of Aeronautical Sciences; and other medals and awards. Promoted to Rear Admiral, 1960.

Geis, Lawrence Raymond. Rear Admiral, United States Navy; Commander Fleet Air, Jacksonville, Florida, 1971- . Born July 14, 1916, in Salina, Kansas. Kansas Wesleyan University, 1934-35; US Naval Academy, 1935-39; Flight Training Course, 1942-43; National War

College, 1958-59; Harvard Business School, Advanced Management Course, 1961. Commissioned Ensign, US Navy, 1939; designated Naval Aviator, 1943. Served in the Pacific Theater, WW II. Commanding Officer USS *Duxbury Bay*, 1961-62; Commanding Officer USS *Forrestal* (CVA-59), 1962-63; Net Evaluation Sub Committee, Office of Secretary of Defense, 1963-65; Chief, US Naval Section, Military Group to Brazil, 1965-67; Commander Carrier Division FOUR, 1967-68; Chief of Information, Navy Department, 1968-71. Legion of Merit with Gold Star; Air Medal; and other US and foreign medals and awards. Promoted to Rear Admiral, July 1, 1965.

Gisel, Orlando. General, Brazilian Army, Retired; Minister of the Army, 1969- . Born September 5, 1905, in Rio Grande do Sul. Attended Brazilian Military Academy, 1925; Army Command and General Staff School; US Army Command and General Staff College, 1946. Assistant Military Attache, Washington, D.C., USA, 1951-52; Commander of 3rd Army; Chief of the Army General Staff, 1967-68; Chief of the Armed Forces General Staff, 1968-69. Orders of Military, Aeronautical and Naval Merit (Brazil). Promoted to General, November 25, 1965.

Gelinet, André. Rear Admiral, French Navy; Naval Attache, Embassy of France, Washington, D.C.

Gerasimov, I. Lieutenant General, USSR Army; Commander, Northern Group of Soviet Forces in Poland, 1972- . Served on the Soviet-German Front in WW II. Member, Communist Party of the Soviet Union.

Gerbe, Kebede. Lieutenant General, Ethiopian Army; Minister of National Defense.

Gestrin, Lars Olof Kristian. Minister of Defense, Finland, 1972- . Born April 10, 1929, Helsinki, Finland. University of Helsinki, LLB, 1952; attended various Officers Training Courses. Member of Helsinki City Council, 1961-64; Member of Diet of Finland since 1962; Vice Chairman of Foreign Affairs Committee of Diet of Finland, 1972- .

Gettys, Charles Martin. Major General, United States Army; Commanding General, US Army, Alaska, 1971- . Born January 1, 1915, Charlotte, North Carolina. Clemson Agricultural College, BS Degree, Chemistry; The Infantry School, Advanced Course; US Army Command and General Staff College; US Army War College. Commissioned Second Lieutenant, US Army Reserve, 1936. Served in WW II and Vietnam War. Deputy Director for Operations (National Military Command Center), J-3, The Joint Staff, Organization, Joint Chiefs of Staff, Washington, D.C., 1966-67; Deputy Special Assistant for Strategic Mobility, Organization, Joint Chiefs of Staff, Washington, D.C., 1967-68; Commanding General, 23d Infantry Division

(Americal), US Army, Vietnam, 1968-69; Director of Individual Training, Office, Deputy Chief of Staff for Personnel, US Army, Washington, D.C., 1969-70; Chief of Staff, US Army, Vietnam, 1970-71. Distinguished Service Medal with Oak Leaf Cluster; Silver Star with Oak Leaf Cluster; Legion of Merit with two Oak Leaf Clusters; Bronze Star Medal with V Device; and other medals and awards. Promoted to Brigadier General, July 1, 1965; Major General, August 1, 1968.

Ghaidan, Saadoun. Major General, Iraqi Army; Minister of the Interior, 1970-   . Born in 1930. Attended Iraqi Military Academy. Commissioned Second Lieutenant in 1953. Member, Revolutionary Command Council, 1968; Commander, Republican Bodyguard Forces, 1968.

Ghazi, Henry. Brigadier General, Lebanese Army; Armed Forces Attache, Embassy of Lebanon, Washington, D.C., 1971-1973.

Ghoerghe, Ion. Colonel General, Army of the Socialist Republic of Romania; First Deputy Minister of National Defense and Chief of the General Staff, 1966-   . Born November 1, 1923, in Cosminele, Prahova County. Attended Romanian Military Academy. Formerly Commander of Division; Commander of Field Army; Chief of Political Department of the Armed Forces; Deputy Minister of National Defense and Chief of General Staff, 1965-66. Member of Romanian Communist Party since 1945; occupied various positions in the political elements of the Youth Communist Union and the Romanian Communist Party; Member, Central Committee of Romanian Communist Party, 1955-60, 1965-   . Member of Grand National Assembly. Decorations include various orders of the Socialist Republic of Romania.

Giai, Do Ke. Brigadier General, Army of the Republic of South Vietnam; Commander Ranger Command.

Giap, Vo Nguyen. Senior General, People's Army of Vietnam; Member, Lao Dong Party Politburo, 1951; Minister of National Defense, 1946, 1948-   ; Deputy Premier, Council of Ministers, 1954; Commander in Chief, People's Army of Vietnam, 1947; Member Lao Dong Party Central Committee, 1951; National Defense Council, 1948; Chairman, Central Military Party Committee, 1959. Born in 1912 in Vo Xa Village, Quang Binh Province. Joined Indochina Communist Party, 1933; Member, Presidium, Vietnam Soviet Friendship Association, 1950-69; Member, Presidium, Vietnam-China Friendship Association, 1950-69; Chairman National Scientific Research Committee, 1962-63; Vice Chairman National Defense Council, 1964-71; elected Deputy to Fourth National Assembly, 1971. Promoted to Senior General, 1948. Publications: *Big Victory, Great Tasks*, 1968; *The Strategic Position of the Local People's War and the Local Armed Forces*, 1970.

Giavedoni, Ruben Paul. Vice Admiral, Argentine Navy; Chief of Naval Operations.

Gibbon, Sir John (Houghton). Lieutenant-General, British Army; Vice-Chief of the Defence Staff, 1972-   . Born September 21, 1917. Attended Trinity College, Cambridge. Commissioned in 1939 in the Royal Artillery. Served in Europe and North Africa in WW II. Brigade Commander, Cyprus, 1962; Director of Defence Plans, Ministry of Defence, 1962-64; Secretary, Chiefs of Staff Committee and Director of Defence Operations Staff, 1966-69; Director, Army Staff Duties, Ministry of Defence, 1969-71. KCB; OBE.

Gibbons, James Joseph. Major General, United States Army; Deputy Commanding General, Sixth US Army, Presidio of San Francisco, California, 1972-   . Born December 14, 1919, Lawrence, Massachusetts. Harvard University, AB Degree, Chemistry and Physics; The Artillery School, Basic and Advanced Courses; US Army Command and General Staff College; Armed Forces Staff College; National War College; George Washington University, MS Degree, International Affairs. Commissioned Second Lieutenant, US Army Reserve, 1941. Served in WW II and Vietnam War. Commanding General, VII Corps Artillery, US Army, Europe, 1966-68; Deputy Director, National Military Command System, J-3, Organization, Joint Chiefs of Staff, Washington, D.C., 1968-70; Deputy Commander, US Military Assistance Command, Thailand, 1970-72. Distinguished Service Medal; Legion of Merit with Oak Leaf Cluster; Bronze Star Medal; and other medals and awards. Promoted to Brigadier General, December 1, 1965; Major General, August 1, 1968.

Gibbs, Sir Roland (Christopher). Lieutenant General, British Army; General Officer Commanding, 1st British Corps, 1972-   . Born June 22, 1921. Attended Royal Military Academy, Sandhurst; Imperial Defence College, 1968. Commissioned in the 60th Rifles, 1940. Served in North Africa, Italy, Northwest Europe, WW II. GSO 1, British Army Staff, Washington, D.C., USA, 1962-63; Commander, 16 Parachute Brigade, 1963-66; Chief of Staff, Headquarters, Middle East, 1966-67; Commander, British Forces, Gulf, 1969-71. KCB; CBE; DSO; MC.

Gibson, Edward G. United States; NASA Scientist-Astronaut, 1965-   . Born November 8, 1936, Buffalo, New York. University of Rochester, BS, Engineering, 1959; California Institute of Technology, MS, Engineering (Jet Propulsion Option), 1960, PhD, Engineering, 1964; Flight Training Course. Senior Research Scientist, Applied Research Laboratories of Philco Corporation, 1964-65. NASA experience: Member, Support Crew, Apollo 12; Science Pilot, Skylab 4 mission.

Gichuru, James S. Minister of Defense, Kenya.

Giddings, Kenneth Charles Michael. Air Marshal, British Royal Air Force; Chief of Staff, No. 18 (M) Group, Strike Command, RAF, 1971-   . Born August 27, 1920. Attended Empire Test Pilots School, 1946; Royal Air Force Staff College, 1953. Joined the RAF in 1940. Combat duty in WW II. Group Captain, Operations, Bomber Command, 1960-62; Superintendent of Flying Aeroplane and

Armament Experimental Establishment, 1962-64; Director, Aircraft Projects, Ministry of Defence, 1964-66; Air Officer Commanding, Central Reconnaissance Establishment, 1967-68; Assistant Chief of the Air Staff, Operational Requirements, 1968-71. OBE; DFC; AFC.

Gideon, Francis C. Lieutenant General, United States Air Force; Vice Commander, Air Force Logistics Command, 1970-   . Born February 18, 1917, in Payne, Ohio. Miami University, Oxford, Ohio, 1934-36; US Military Academy, 1936-40; Flying Schools, 1940-41; Air War College, 1951-52; Air Force Advanced Management Program, Harvard University, 1960. Commissioned Second Lieutenant, US Army, 1940; received pilot wings, 1941. Served in the Southwest Pacific Theater, WW II. Director of Transportation, Air Force Logistics Command, 1959-60; Director, Data Systems, Air Force Logistics Command, 1960-62; Executive Director, Logistics Services, Defense Supply Agency, 1962-64; Deputy Director, Defense Supply Agency, 1964-66; Commander, Warner Robins Air Materiel Area, Air Force Logistics Command, 1966-68; Commander, Thirteenth Air Force, Clark Air Base, Philippines, 1968-70. Distinguished Service Medal (Air Force design); Distinguished Service Medal (Army design); Legion of Merit; Bronze Star Medal; and other medals and awards. Promoted to Brigadier General, October 1, 1957; Major General, June 16, 1961; Lieutenant General, August 1, 1968.

Gilardi Rodriguez, Rolando. Lieutenant General, Peruvian Air Force; Minister of Aeronautics and Commanding General of the Air Force, 1968-   . Born August 31, 1920, in Arequipa. Attended Air Officers School, 1939-42; Air War Academy; Naval Air Training Course (Corpus Christi, Texas, USA); F86F Aircrew Familiarization, Las Palmas; Instrument Flying (USA). Commissioned in 1942; designated Aviator, 1942. Former Air Attache, Embassy of Peru, Washington, D.C.; Office of the Inspector General; Secretary General of Aeronautics; Director, Air Officers School; Director of Instruction, General Staff; Director General of Administration; Minister of Work and Community Affairs, 1968. Cruz Peruana al Mérito Aeronautico; Cruz Peruana al Mérito Militar; Cruz Peruana al Mérito Naval; Orden al Mérito de la Guardia Civil y Policia; Orden Militar de Ayacucho; Orden Gran Almirante Grau; Orden del Sol del Peru; and other medals and awards from many nations. Promoted to Major General, 1965; Lieutenant General, 1968.

Gilbert, Glyn Charles Anglim. Major-General, British Army; Commander, Joint Warfare Establishment, 1972-   . Born August 15, 1920. Attended Eastbourne College; Royal Military Academy, Sandhurst; Staff College, 1952; Imperial Defence College, 1966. Commissioned in 1939. Served in Northwest Europe in WW II; Palestine; Malaya. Staff and Regimental positions, Ministry of Defence, Airborne Forces, Royal Lincolns and Paratroop Regiment, 1952-66; Commandant, School of Infantry, 1967-70; General Officer Commanding, 3d Division, 1970-72. MC.

Gilkeson, Fillmore Bolling. Rear Admiral, United States Navy; US Defense Attache, US Naval Attache and US Naval Attache for Air to the United Kingdom, London, 1970-   . Born October 27, 1915, in Bluefield, West Virginia. US Naval Academy, 1933-37; Flight Training Course, 1940; Naval Postgraduate School, Annapolis, 1946-48; California Institute of Technology, MS, Aeronautical Engineering, 1948-49. Commissioned Ensign, US Navy, 1937; designated Naval Aviator, 1940. Served in the Atlantic and Pacific Theaters, WW II; Vietnam War. Commanding Officer, USS *Shangri-La* (CVA-38), 1960-61; Head, Air Warfare Branch, Office of the CNO, 1961-62; Chief of Staff and Aide to Commander Carrier Division THREE, 1962-64; Project Officer for Nuclear Power Study, Office of the CNO, 1964-65; Commander Antisubmarine Warfare Group THREE, US Pacific Fleet, 1965-66; Commander Naval Base, Subic Bay, Luzon, Philippine Islands, 1966-68; Director, Logistic Plans Division, Office of the CNO, 1968-70. Silver Star Medal; Legion of Merit with Gold Star; Distinguished Flying Cross; Air Medal with Four Stars; and other US and foreign medals and awards. Promoted to Rear Admiral, July 1, 1965.

Gillem, Alvan C., II. Lieutenant General, United States Air Force; Commander, Air University, Maxwell Air Force Base, Alabama, 1970-   . Born April 20, 1917, in Nogales, Arizona. US Military Academy, 1936-40; Pilot Training School, 1940-41; Command and General Staff School, 1943; Air Command and Staff School, Air University, 1947-48; Air War College, 1953-54. Commissioned Second Lieutenant, US Army, 1940; received pilot wings, 1941. Served in the Mediterranean Theater, WW II; Vietnam War. Commander, 57th Air Division, 1961-63; Commander, 823d Air Division, 1963-64; Deputy Director, Operations, Headquarters Strategic Air Command, 1964-65; Director, Operations, Headquarters Strategic Air Command, 1965-66; Deputy Chief of Staff, Operations, Headquarters Strategic Air Command, 1966-68; Commander, 3d Air Division, Guam, 1968-70; Commander Eighth Air Force, Guam, 1970. Distinguished Service Medal with one Oak Leaf Cluster; Legion of Merit; Distinguished Flying Cross with one Oak Leaf Cluster; and other medals and awards. Promoted to Brigadier General, May 1, 1961; Major General, August 1, 1963; Lieutenant General, May 29, 1968.

Gillette, Norman Campbell, Jr. Rear Admiral, United States Navy, Retired; Director, Office of Naval Disability Evaluation, 1970-   . Born November 14, 1915, Newport, Rhode Island. US Naval Academy, 1932-36; Flight Training Course, 1942-43; helicopter pilot training, 1958; Naval War College, 1946-47. Commissioned Ensign, US Navy, 1936; designated Naval Aviator, 1943. Served in North Atlantic and Southwest Pacific Theaters, WW II. Commander Fleet Air Wings, Atlantic Fleet, Commander Fleet Air Wing Five, and Commanding Officer Naval Air Station Norfolk, 1963-64; Director of Aviation Plans Division, Office of the CNO, 1964-66; Chief, Joint US Group/Military Assistance Advisory Group Spain, 1966-68; Commander Antisubmarine Warfare Group THREE and Group FIVE, 1969-70; transferred to retired list, July 1,

1970. Distinguished Service Medal; Legion of Merit; Distinguished Flying Cross with two Gold Stars; and other medals and awards. Promoted to Rear Admiral, June 1, 1964.

Gilmour, Ian. British Secretary of State for Defence until the General Elections in February 1974. Born July 1926. Attended Balliol College, Oxford. Served in Grenadier Guards, 1944-47; commissioned, 1945. Barrister, 1952-54; Editor of *The Spectator*, 1954-59; proprietor, 1954-67; Member of Parliament, 1962- ; Parliamentary Private Secretary to Lord Hailsham, 1963-64; Vice-Chairman, Conservative Parliamentary Committee on the Post Office and Communications, 1966-70; Parliamentary Under-Secretary of State for the Army, 1970-71; Minister of State for Defence Procurement, 1971-72; Minister of State for Defence, 1972-74. Publications: *The Body Politic*, 1969.

Ginsburgh, Robert N. Major General, United States Air Force; Director, Office of Information, Office of the Secretary of the Air Force, 1972- . Born November 19, 1923, Fort Sill, Oklahoma. US Military Academy, 1940-44; Harvard University, Littauer Center, MPA, 1947, MA, 1948, PhD, 1949; Air Command and Staff School, 1953; National War College, 1962-63. Commissioned Second Lieutenant, US Army, 1944; transferred to US Air Force, 1949. Served in the European Theater, WW II. Member, Policy Planning Council, Department of State, 1964-66; Air Force Member, Chairman's Staff Group, Office of the Chairman, Joint Chiefs of Staff, and senior staff member, National Security Council Staff, 1966-68; Armed Forces Aide to the President of the United States, 1968-69; Assistant to Commander, Air University, 1969; Commander, Aerospace Studies Institute, 1969-71; Chief, Office of Air Force History, Headquarters USAF, 1971-72. Silver Star; Legion of Merit with Oak Leaf Cluster; and other medals and awards. Promoted to Major General, April 1, 1971. Publications: *US Military Strategy in the Sixties*, 1965; *US Military Strategy in the Seventies*, 1970 (editor); *US Military Strategy and the Nixon Doctrine*, 1971 (editor); *Economics of National Security*, 1960 (contributor); *Principles of Insurance* (editor), 1949-1950; numerous articles on professional subjects.

Giraudo, John C. Major General, United States Air Force; Commander, Seventeenth Air Force, Sembach Air Base, Germany, 1973- . Born October 2, 1923, in Santa Barbara, California. University of California, Santa Barbara, 1941-42; University of Maryland; Army Air Force Flying School, 1943; Armed Forces Staff College, 1959; National War College, 1963-64. Commissioned Second Lieutenant, US Army Air Corps, 1943. Served in the European Theater, WW II, POW; Korean War, POW; Vietnam War. Vice Commander, Fighter Weapons Center, US Air Forces Europe, Libya, 1964-65; Commander, 49th Tactical Fighter Wing, Germany, 1965-67; Commander, 355th Tactical Fighter Wing, Thailand, 1967-68; Deputy Director, Legislative Liaison, Office of the Secretary of the Air Force, 1968-70; Director, Legislative Liaison, Office of the Secretary of the Air Force, 1970-73. Silver Star; Legion of

Merit with one Oak Leaf Cluster; Distinguished Flying Cross; Bronze Star Medal; Air Medal with 17 Oak Leaf Clusters; and other medals and awards. Promoted to Major General, August 1, 1970.

Gisiger, Louis. Brigadier General, Swiss Army; Chief, Veterinary Service. Born in 1916.

Glasser, Otto John. Lieutenant General, United States Air Force; Deputy Chief of Staff, Research and Development, Headquarters USAF, and Military Director, USAF Scientific Advisory Board, 1970- . Born October 2, 1918, in Wilkes-Barre, Pennsylvania. Cornell University, BS, Electrical Engineering, 1940; Flying Training Course, 1943-44; Ohio State University, MS, Electronic Physics, 1947; Air Command and Staff School, 1951. Commissioned Second Lieutenant, USAR, 1940. Special Assistant to Commander, Air Force Systems Command, 1961-62; Vice Commander, Electronic Systems Division, Air Force Systems Command, 1962-65; Deputy Director for Operational Requirements and Development Plans, Deputy Chief of Staff, Research and Development, Headquarters USAF, 1965-66; Assistant Deputy Chief of Staff, Research and Development, Headquarters USAF, 1966-70. Distinguished Service Medal; Legion of Merit; Air Force Commendation Medal; and other medals and awards. Promoted to Brigadier General, July 1, 1962; Major General, June 1, 1965; Lieutenant General, February 6, 1970.

Glauch, Alden G. Major General, United States Air Force; Deputy Chief of Staff for Operations, Military Airlift Command, Scott Air Force Base, Illinois, 1972- . Born November 14, 1919, in Traverse City, Michigan. Attended Texas Western College, El Paso, Texas, and the University of Maryland. Took Aviation Cadet Pilot Training Course, 1942-43; attended Air Command and Staff School, 1958-59. Commissioned Second Lieutenant, US Army Air Corps, in 1943. Inactive, 1945-49. Fighter pilot in the North African-European and China-Burma-India Theaters, WW II; served in Vietnam War. Director of Current Operations, Twenty-second Air Force, Military Airlift Command, Travis Air Force Base, California, 1965-68; Director of Operations, 834th Air Division, Vietnam, 1968-69; Assistant Deputy Chief of Staff, Operations, and later, Deputy Chief of Staff, Operations, Twenty-first Air Force, McGuire Air Force Base, New Jersey, 1969-70; Commander, 435th Military Airlift Support Wing, Rhein-Main Air Base, Germany, 1970-71; Assistant Deputy Chief of Staff, Operations, Military Airlift Command, Scott Air Force Base, Illinois, 1971-72. Legion of Merit with Oak Leaf Cluster; Distinguished Flying Cross; Meritorious Service Medal; Air Medal with three Oak Leaf Clusters; Armed Forces Honor Medal "First Class Order" (Vietnam); and other medals and awards. Promoted to Brigadier General, August 1, 1971; Major General, 1973.

Gleszer, Roland Merril. Major General, United States Army; Director of Military Support, Office, Chief of Staff, US

Army, Washington, D.C., 1972-   . Born March 18, 1915, Brewer, Maine. US Military Academy; US Army Command and General Staff College; Armed Forces Staff College; US Army War College. Commissioned Second Lieutenant, 1940. Served in WW II. Assistant Division Commander, 2d Infantry Division, US Army, Pacific-Korea, 1965-66; Director of Management, Office, Comptroller of the Army, Washington, D.C., 1966-68; Commanding General, 5th Infantry Division (Mechanized), Fort Carson, Colorado, 1968-69; Commanding General, Military District of Washington, Washington, D.C., 1969-72. Distinguished Service Medal; Legion of Merit; Bronze Star Medal with Oak Leaf Cluster; and other medals and awards. Promoted to Brigadier General, August 1, 1965; Major General, November 1, 1967.

Globa, Ya. N. Rear Admiral, USSR Navy. Served in the Soviet-German War (WW II). First Deputy Commander Baltic Fleet, 1969-71; Member, Communist Party of the Soviet Union.

Glotov, M. Colonel, USSR Army; Chief, Political Branch, Political Directorate, Siberian Military District. Served on the Soviet-German Front in WW II. Member, Communist Party of the Soviet Union.

Gnägi, Rudolf. Federal Councillor; Chief, Federal Military Department, Switzerland. Born on August 3, 1917, Schwadernau. Lawyer. Head, Ministry of Transport, Communication and Power; Member of Swiss Federal Council since 1965.

Godding, George Arthur. Major General, United States Army; Commanding General, US Army Security Agency, Washington, D.C., 1973-   . Born July 12, 1920, Lawrence, Kansas. University of Maryland, BS Degree, Military Science; The Infantry School, Advanced Course; US Army Command and General Staff College; US Army War College; George Washington University, MA Degree, International Affairs. Commissioned Second Lieutenant, US Army, 1942. Served in WW II and Vietnam War. Deputy Assistant Chief of Staff, Intelligence, J-2, US Military Assistance Command, Vietnam, 1967; Chief, US Army Security Agency, Pacific-Hawaii, 1967-69; Assistant Chief of Staff, Intelligence, US Army, Pacific-Hawaii, 1969; Deputy Chief of Staff, Intelligence, US Army, Pacific-Hawaii, 1969-72; Director of Intelligence, US Military Assistance Command, Vietnam, 1972-73. Distinguished Service Medal; Silver Star; Legion of Merit with Oak Leaf Cluster; Bronze Star Medal with Oak Leaf Cluster; and other medals and awards. Promoted to Brigadier General, August 18, 1967; Major General, September 1, 1971.

Goh Keng Swee. Minister of Defense and Deputy Prime Minister, Republic of Singapore.

Golofast, G. Lieutenant General, USSR Army; Assistant to the Commander in Chief, Soviet Ground Forces, for Military Educational Establishments. Served on the Soviet-German Front in WW II. Member, Communist Party of the Soviet Union.

Golovnin, M.I. Lieutenant General, USSR Army; Chief of Staff, Moscow Military District, 1968-   . Served on the Soviet-German Front in WW II. Member, Communist Party of the Soviet Union.

Golushko, I. Lieutenant General, USSR Army; Chief of Staff, Rear Services (Logistics), Ministry of Defense. Served on the Soviet-German Front in WW II. Member, Communist Party of the Soviet Union.

Gomez, Centurion, Luis Carlos. Major General, Argentine Army; Military Attache, Embassy of Argentina, Washington, D.C.; Military Adviser, Argentine Mission to the United Nations, 1973-   .

Gomez Ortega, Miguel A. Rear Admiral, Mexican Navy; Chief of the Naval Staff.

Goncharov, V.A. Lieutenant General, USSR Army; Chief, Political Directorate, Transbaikal Military District, 1967-   . Served on the Soviet-German Front in WW II. Member, Communist Party of the Soviet Union.

Gonen, Shmuel. Major General, Israeli Army; Commander, Southern Front, 1973.

Gonge, John F. Major General, United States Air Force; Commander, Twenty-second Air Force, Military Airlift Command, 1972-   . Born November 5, 1921, in Ansley, Nebraska. US Army Air Corps Flying School, 1942-43; National War College, 1965-66. Commissioned Second Lieutenant, US Army Air Corps, 1943. Served in the China-Burma-India Theater, WW II. Chief, Resources Capability Branch, Office, Special Assistant for Strategic Mobility, and other positions in the Joint Chiefs of Staff Organization, 1966-69; Assistant Deputy Chief of Staff, Operations, Twenty-second Air Force, 1969; Vice Commander, 60th Military Airlift Wing, 1969-70; Commander, 63d Military Airlift Wing, 1970-71; Vice Commander, Twenty-first Air Force, Military Airlift Command, 1971-72. Distinguished Flying Cross; Meritorious Service Medal; and other medals and awards. Promoted to Brigadier General, July 1, 1970; Major General, 1972.

Gonzalez, Hugo. Vice Admiral, Paraguayan Navy; Commandant, Paraguayan Navy, 1966-   . Born June 6, 1920, in Villeta. Attended Paraguayan Military Academy, 1938-42; Advanced War School, Staff Officer Course, 1959; National War College Course. Commissioned Guardiamarina, 1942. Commander of the River Defense Force, 1952-62; Prefect General of Ports, 1954-62; Temporary Commandant of the Navy, 1961, 1963; Interim Professor, Advanced War School, 1962; Professor of Naval Strategy, National War College, 1969. Medalla del

Ministerio de Defensa Nacional; Al Merito (Chile); Medalla Naval de Servicios Distinguidos (Brazil); Gran Cruz del Merito Naval (Spain); Orden de Mayo al Merito Naval; Gran Cruz Almirante Brown (Argentina). Promoted to Vice Admiral, December 31, 1966.

Gonzalez, Victor. Captain, Uruguayan Navy; Commander in Chief, Uruguayan Navy, 1973-   .

Gonzalez Lopez, Excmo. Sr. Don Jose R. Vice Admiral, Spanish Navy; Deputy Chief of the Naval Staff.

Goodpaster, Andrew Jackson. General, United States Army; Supreme Allied Commander, Europe, and Commander in Chief, United States European Command, 1969-   . Born February 12, 1915, Granite City, Illinois. US Military Academy; US Army Command and General Staff College; Princeton University, MSE Degree, Engineering, PhD Degree, International Relations. Commissioned Second Lieutenant, 1939. Served in WW II and Vietnam War. Special Assistant to the Chairman of the Joint Chiefs of Staff, later Assistant to the Chairman of the Joint Chiefs of Staff, Organization, Joint Chiefs of Staff, Washington, D.C., 1962-66; Director of Joint Staff, Organization, Joint Chiefs of Staff, Washington, D.C., 1966-67; Director of Special Studies, Office, Chief of Staff, US Army, Washington, D.C., and Senior Army Member, Military Staff Committee, United Nations, New York, 1967; Commandant, the National War College, Fort Lesley J. McNair, Washington, D.C., 1967-68; Deputy Commander, US Military Assistance Command, Vietnam, 1968-69; Commander in Chief, US European Command, 1969. Distinguished Service Cross; Distinguished Service Medal with two Oak Leaf Clusters; Silver Star; Legion of Merit with Oak Leaf Cluster; and other medals and awards. Promoted to Brigadier General, January 1, 1957; Major General, October 1, 1961; Lieutenant General, January 27, 1964; General, July 3, 1968.

Goranskiy, I. Major General, USSR Army; First Deputy Chief, Political Directorate, Odessa Military District. Served on the Soviet-German Front in WW II. Member, Communist Party of the Soviet Union.

Gorban, V. Lieutenant General, Armor, USSR Army; First Deputy Commander, Kiev Military District. Served on the Soviet-German Front in WW II. Member, Communist Party of the Soviet Union.

Gorbatko, Viktor Vasiliyevich. Colonel, USSR Air Force; Cosmonaut, 1961-   . Born December 3, 1934, in the Krasnodar District. Air Force Pilot School, Bataisk; Zhukovskiy Air Force Engineering War College; Cosmonaut Training Unit, 1961. Commissioned Second Lieutenant, 1956. Air Force Fighter Pilot, 1956-63; Engineer-investigator, Soyuz-7 Spaceship, 1969. Hero of the Soviet Union; Order of Lenin; Order of Red Star; K. Tsiolkovsky Gold Medal of the USSR Academy of Sciences; and other medals and awards. Member, Communist Party of the Soviet Union since 1959.

Gorbovskiy, D.V. Lieutenant General, USSR Army; Commandant, Chemical Defense College. Served on the Soviet-German Front in WW II. Member, Communist Party of the Soviet Union.

Gorchakov, Pyotr Andreyevich. Lieutenant General, USSR Army; Deputy Chief, Main Political Directorate, Soviet Army and Navy, and Chief, Political Directorate, Strategic Missile Forces, 1970-   . Born in 1917. Attended Military-Political College, c. 1952-54. Drafted into Soviet Army, 1938. Served on the Soviet-German Front, 1941-45. Assigned to Army Political Work, 1939; Regimental Political Commissar, and later Deputy Regimental Commander for Political Affairs, 1941-43; Chief, Political Section, 267th Infantry Division, 1944-45; Chief, Political Section of various military formations; 1946-51; assigned to Soviet Forces stationed abroad, 1954-c. 1958; Chief, Political Department of an Army, and member of the Army's Military Council, c. 1958-63; First Deputy Chief, Political Directorate, Moscow Military District, 1963-65; Chief, Political Directorate, Baltic Military District, and member of the District's Military Council, 1965-70. Member, Communist Party of the Soviet Union, 1939-   ; Deputy to Latvian Supreme Soviet, 1967; Deputy to USSR Supreme Soviet, 1970. Hero of the Soviet Union; Order of Lenin; Order of Red Banner; two Orders of Fatherland War; two Orders of Red Star; and other orders and medals.

Gorelov, S. Lieutenant General, USSR Air Force; Commander, Air Force, Carpathian Military District. Served on Soviet-German Front in WW II. Member, Communist Party of the Soviet Union.

Gorshkov, Sergey Georgiyevich. Admiral of the Fleet of the Soviet Union; Commander in Chief, Soviet Navy, 1956-   . Born in 1910. Served in the Soviet-German War (WW II). Formerly First Deputy Commander in Chief, Navy, 1955-56. Member, Communist Party of the Soviet Union; Member, Communist Party Central Committee.

Gossick, Lee V. Major General, United States Air Force; Chief of Staff, Headquarters Air Force Systems Command (AFSC), 1971-   . Born January 23, 1920, in Meadville, Missouri. Army Air Corps Flying School, 1941-42; Ohio State University, BS and MS, Aeronautical Engineering, 1951; Air War College, 1958-59; Advanced Management Program, Harvard University, 1961. Commissioned Second Lieutenant, Army Air Corps, 1942. Served in the Mediterranean Theater, WW II. Commander, Arnold Engineering Development Center, AFSC, 1964-67; Deputy for F-111 Program, Aeronautical Systems Division, AFSC, 1967-68; Vice Commander and later Commander, Aeronautical Systems Division, 1968-70; Deputy Chief of Staff, Systems, AFSC, 1970-71. Distinguished Service Medal; Legion of Merit with one Oak Leaf Cluster; Distinguished Flying Cross; and other medals and awards. Distinguished Alumnus of Ohio State University, 1960; General Hoyt S. Vandenberg Trophy of the Arnold Air Society, 1967; Fellow of the American Institute of Aeronautics and Astronautics, 1970; Ohio State University

Centennial Achievement Award, 1970. Promoted to Major General, April 1, 1968.

Gould, Gordon T., Jr. Lieutenant General, United States Air Force; Director, Defense Communications Agency, 1971-   . Born January 7, 1916, in Mobile, Alabama. US Military Academy, 1937-41; Massachusetts Institute of Technology, MS, Electrical Engineering, 1950; Air War College, 1953-54. Commissioned Second Lieutenant US Army, 1941. Served in the China-Burma-India Theater, WW II. Chief, Communications – Electronics Division, Headquarters Strategic Air Command, 1960-64; Deputy Commander, Headquarters Air Force Communications Service, 1964-65; Director, Command Control and Communications, Headquarters USAF, 1965-71. Distinguished Service Medal; Legion of Merit with two Oak Leaf Clusters; Army Commendation Medal with one Oak Leaf Cluster; and other US and foreign medals and awards. Promoted to Brigadier General, July 15, 1961; Major General, September 24, 1964; Lieutenant General, September 1, 1971.

Gould, John Charles. Major-General, British Army; Paymaster-in-Chief, 1972-   . Born April 17, 1915. Joined Surrey and Sussex Yeomanry (TA) in 1937; transferred to Royal Army Pay Corps in 1941. Served as Deputy Paymaster-in-Chief, 1967-72.

Gourlay, Basil Ian Spencer. Lieutenant-General, British Royal Marines; Commandant-General, Royal Marines, 1971-   . Born November 13, 1920. Attended Eastbourne College; Staff College, 1954. Commissioned in the Royal Marines, 1940. Served at sea and with Commandos in WW II. GSO 1, Headquarters, Plymouth Group, 1961-63; Commanding Officer, 42 Commando, 1963-65; Colonel General Staff, Department of CGRM, Ministry of Defence, 1965-66; Commander, 3d Commando Brigade, 1966-68; Major General, Royal Marines Portsmouth, 1968-71. OBE; KCB; MC.

Govorov, Vladimir L. Colonel General, USSR Army; Commander, Moscow Military District, 1972-   . Born in 1924. Attended General Staff War College. Served on Soviet-German Front in WW II. Formerly First Deputy Commander in Chief, Group of Soviet Forces in Germany; Commander, Baltic Military District, 1971-72. Member, Communist Party of the Soviet Union.

Gowon, Yakubu. Major General, Nigerian Army; Head of Federal Government of Nigeria and Commander in Chief, Nigerian Armed Forces, 1966-   . Born October 19, 1934, in Lur Pankshin, Beneu Plateau State. Attended British Royal Military Academy, Sandhurst, England; Staff College, Camberley, England; Joint Services College, Latimer, England. Commissioned Second Lieutenant, Nigerian Army, 1957. Staff Member, Nigerian Contingent, United Nations Peacekeeping Force, Congo, 1960-61; Command and Staff positions, Nigerian Armed Forces, 1961-66; Adjutant General, Nigerian Army, 1966; Chief of Staff, 1966. Promoted to Major General, 1967.

Graham, Daniel Orrin. Major General, United States Army; Chief of Production Review Group, Office of the Director of Central Intelligence for Intelligence Community, 1973-   . Born April 13, 1925, in Portland, Oregon. Attended US Military Academy; Infantry School, Basic and Advanced Courses; Command and General Staff College; Army War College, 1966-67. Commissioned June 4, 1946. Commanding Officer, 319th Military Intelligence Battalion, US Army, Pacific-Hawaii, 1965-66; Chief of the Current Intelligence, Indications and Estimates Division, Directorate of Intelligence Production, Office of the Assistant Chief of Staff, J-2, US Military Assistance Command, Vietnam, 1967-68; Military Intelligence Officer, Special Activities Group, 1968-70; Assistant Director for Collection, US Defense Intelligence Agency, 1970; Deputy Director for Estimates, Defense Intelligence Agency, US Army, 1970-73. Distinguished Service Medal; Legion of Merit with two Oak Leaf Clusters; and other medals and awards. Promoted to Brigadier General August 1, 1970; Major General March 1, 1973.

Graham, Erwin Montgomery, Jr. Major General, United States Army; Commanding General, US Army Munitions Command, Dover, New Jersey, 1970-   . Born November 18, 1917, Pensacola, Florida. Mississippi State College, BS Degree, Electrical Engineering; The Ordnance School, Advanced Course; US Army Command and General Staff College; US Armed Forces Staff College; US Naval War College; Massachusetts Institute of Technology, MSEE and PhD Degrees, Electical Engineering. Commissioned Second Lieutenant, US Army Reserve, 1938. Served in WW II. Commandant, US Army Ordnance Missile School, later Commanding General and Commandant, US Army Missile and Munitions Center and School, Redstone Arsenal, Alabama, 1965-67; Commanding General, US Army Ordnance Center and Commandant, US Army Ordnance School, Aberdeen Proving Ground, Maryland, 1967-68; Commanding General, US Army Ammunition Procurement and Supply Agency, Joliet, Illinois, 1968-70. Legion of Merit; Bronze Star Medal; and other medals and awards. Promoted to Brigadier General, September 1, 1967; Major General, July 3, 1970.

Graham, Gordon M. Lieutenant General, United States Air Force; Commander, Sixth Allied Tactical Air Force, Supreme Headquarters, Allied Powers Europe (SHAPE), Izmir, Turkey, 1972-   . Born February 16, 1918, in Ouray, Colorado. University of California, Berkeley, California, BS, Petroleum Engineering, 1940; Army Air Corps Flying Schools, 1940-41; University of Pittsburgh, MS, 1948; Air Force Institute of Technology, 1948-49. Commissioned Second Lieutenant, US Army Air Corps, 1941. Served in the European Theater, WW II; Korean War; Vietnam War. Commander, 4th Tactical Fighter Wing, 1962-63; Vice Commander, Nineteenth Air Force, 1963-64; Assistant Deputy for Operations, Headquarters Tactical Air Command Staff, 1964-65; Deputy for Operations, Headquarters Tactical Air Command Staff, 1965-66; Vice Commander, Seventh Air Force, Vietnam, 1966-67; Commander, Ninth Air Force, 1967-68; Vice Commander,

Tactical Air Command, 1968-70; Commander, US Forces Japan, and Commander, Fifth Air Force, Fuchu Air Station, Japan, 1970-72. Distinguished Service Medal; Silver Star; Legion of Merit; Distinguished Flying Cross with one Oak Leaf Cluster; and other US and foreign medals and awards. Promoted to Brigadier General, August 1, 1962; Major General, December 1, 1964; Lieutenant General, August 1, 1968.

Graham, Stuart Clarence. Major General, Royal Australian Army; General Officer Commanding Northern Command, 1971-   . Born October 23, 1920, in Ulmarra. Attended Royal Military College, Duntroon, 1937-40; Imperial Defense College, 1966. Commissioned in 1940. Served in the African-European and Pacific Theaters, WW II; Vietnam War. Director, Military Intelligence, 1960-63; Commandant, Jungle Training Centre, 1964-65; Commandant, 1st Australian Task Force, Vietnam, 1967; Chief of Staff, Northern Command, 1968; Deputy Chief, General Staff, 1969-71. DSO; OBE; MC.

Grandin, Gunnar Emil. Rear Admiral, Swedish Royal Navy; Chief, Naval Material Department, Defense Materiel Administration, 1970-   . Attended Royal Navy Staff College, 1946-49; Royal National Defense College, 1959, 1968; US Naval School of Mine Warfare. Commander, 1st Destroyer/Torpedo Boat Flotilla, 1966-67; Chief, Weapons Directorate, Naval Materiel Department, Defense Materiel Administration, 1969-70. Commander of the Royal Order of the Sword; Order of the Lion (Finland); and other medals and awards. Promoted to Rear Admiral, 1970.

Grantham, Emery Arden. Rear Admiral, United States Navy; Deputy Chief of Staff, Logistics and Management, Commander in Chief, US Naval Forces, Europe, 1972-   . Born December 4, 1914, in Garner, Texas. US Naval Academy, 1933-37; Massachusetts Institute of Technology, MS, Naval Construction, 1939-41. Commissioned Ensign, US Navy, 1937; designated for engineering duty only, 1941. Force Maintenance Officer, Staff of Commander Service Force, US Pacific Fleet, and Fleet Maintenance Officer, Staff of Commander in Chief, US Pacific Fleet, 1962-65; Assistant Chief, Bureau of Ships, for Fleet Maintenance, 1965-66; Deputy Commander for Fleet Maintenance and Logistics Support, Naval Ship Systems Command, 1966-67; Director of Ships Material Readiness Division, Office of the CNO, 1967-72. Distinguished Service Medal; Legion of Merit; Bronze Star Medal; and other medals and awards. Promoted to Rear Admiral, October 1, 1964.

Grasset, Etienne de. Brigadier General, French Army; Member, United Nations Military Staff Committee; Military Attache, Embassy of France, Washington, D.C.

Graves, Ernest, Jr. Major General, United States Army; Division Engineer, US Army Engineer Division, North Central, Chicago, Illinois, 1970-   . Born July 6, 1924, New York, New York. US Military Academy; The Engineer School, Basic and Advanced Courses; US Army Command

and General Staff College; US Army War College, Regular Course; Massachusetts Institute of Technology, PhD Degree, Physics. Commissioned Second Lieutenant, 1944. Served in WW II and Vietnam War. Commanding Officer, 34th Engineer Group (Construction), US Army, Pacific-Vietnam, 1968-69; Assistant for National Aeronautics and Space Administration Support, and Deputy Director of Military Construction, Office, Chief of Engineers, US Army, Washington, D.C., 1969-70; President, Air Defense Evaluation Board, Office, Assistant Chief of Staff for Force Development, US Army, Washington, D.C., 1970. Distinguished Service Medal; Legion of Merit with Oak Leaf Cluster; Bronze Star Medal; and other medals and awards. Promoted to Brigadier General, October 10, 1969; Major General, August 1, 1971.

Gray, (Reginald) John. Major-General, British Army; Director of Medical Services, United Kingdom Land Forces, 1972-   . Born November 26, 1916. College of Medicine, University of Durham, MB and BS Degrees. Commissioned in the Royal Army Medical Corps, 1939. Served in India, Burma, Northwest Europe in WW II. British Military Hospital, Rinteln, 1963-64; The Queen Alexandra Military Hospital, Millbank, 1964-67; Assistant Director-General, Army Medical Service, Ministry of Defense, 1967-69; Deputy Director-General, Army Medical Staff, 1969-71. CB; Queen's Honorary Surgeon, 1970. Fellow of Royal Society of Medicine; Fellow of Medical Society of London; Member of the British Institute of Management; Officer of Order of St. John of Jerusalem; Commander of the Order of St. John of Jerusalem.

Grechko, Andrei Antonovich. Marshal of the Soviet Union; Minister of Defense, USSR, 1967-   . Born October 17, 1903, in Kuybyshevka. Attended Officers School, 1922; Frunze Army War College, 1936; Voroshilov General Staff War College, 1941. Joined the Soviet Armed Forces (Cavalry) in 1919. Served on the Soviet-German front in WW II. Commanding General, Kiev Military District, 1946-53; Commander in Chief, Group of Soviet Forces in Germany, 1953-57; Commander in Chief, Ground Forces, 1957-60; First Deputy Minister of Defense, and Commander in Chief, Warsaw Pact Forces, 1960-67. Member Communist Party of the Soviet Union since 1928; Member of the CPSU Central Committee and Politburo; Deputy to the USSR Supreme Soviet. Hero of the Soviet Union; Five Orders of Lenin; Order of Kutuzov; Order of Suvorov; three orders of Red Banner; and other Soviet and foreign medals and awards.

Grechko, S.N. Colonel General, USSR Army; First Deputy Commander, Moscow Air Defense District, 1966-   . Served on the Soviet-German Front in WW II. Member, Communist Party of the Soviet Union.

Greenlief, Francis Stevens. Major General, United States Army (NGUS); Chief, National Guard Bureau, Washington, D.C., 1971-   . Born July 27, 1921, Hastings, Nebraska. US Army Command and General Staff College. Commissioned Second Lieutenant, Army National Guard,

1942. Served in WW II. Deputy Chief, National Guard Bureau, Washington, D.C., 1964-65; Deputy Chief, National Guard Bureau, and Director, Army National Guard, Washington, D.C., 1965-71. Distinguished Service Medal; Silver Star; Bronze Star; and other medals and awards. Promoted to Brigadier General, October 19, 1962; Major General, October 19, 1964.

Greer, Thomas Upton. Major General, United States Army; Senior Member, United Nations Command, Military Armistice Commission-Korea, 1973-   . Born February 2, 1928, in Colon, Panama. Attended US Military Academy; Infantry School, Basic and Advanced Courses; Command and General Staff College; Armed Forces Staff College, 1963-64; National War College, 1967-68; University of Illinois, MS, Engineering. Commissioned Second Lieutenant in 1950. Served in the Vietnam War. Research and Development Programs Manager, Overseas Defense Research Office, Advanced Research Projects Agency, Office of the Secretary of Defense, 1968-69; Commanding Officer, 2nd Basic Combat Training Brigade, US Army Training Center, Engineer, Fort Leonard Wood, Missouri, 1969-71; Executive, Office of the Deputy Chief of Staff for Personnel, 1971; Executive to the Vice Chief of Staff, US Army, 1971-72; Assistant Division Commander, 2nd Infantry Division, Eighth US Army, Korea, 1972-73. Silver Star; Legion of Merit with Oak Leaf Cluster; Bronze Star Medal with V Device; and other medals and awards. Promoted to Brigadier General July 1, 1972; Major General, 1973.

Grekov, V. Colonel General, USSR Army. Served on the Soviet-German Front in WW II. Chief, Political Directorate, Belorussian Military District, until 1971. Member, Communist Party of the Soviet Union.

Gribble, William Charles, Jr. Lieutenant General, United States Army; Chief of Research and Development, US Army, Washington, D.C., 1971-   . Born May 24, 1917, Ironwood, Michigan. US Military Academy; US Army Command and General Staff College; The National War College; University of Chicago, MS Degree, Physical Science. Commissioned Second Lieutenant, 1941. WW II. Director, Research and Development Division, US Army Materiel Command, Washington, D.C., 1964-66; Deputy Chief, Research and Development, Office, Chief of Research and Development, US Army, Washington, D.C., 1967-69; Commanding General, US Army Engineer Center, Fort Belvoir, Virginia, 1969-70; Deputy Chief, Office, Chief of Research and Development, US Army, Washington, D.C., 1970. Distinguished Service Medal; Legion of Merit with Oak Leaf Cluster; and other medals and awards. Promoted to Brigadier General, April 8, 1963; Major General, April 1, 1966; Lieutenant General, January 1, 1971.

Gribkov, A. Colonel General, USSR Army; Commander, Leningrad Military District, 1973-   . Served on the Soviet-German Front in WW II. First Deputy Commander, Leningrad Military District, 1969-73. Member, Communist Party of the Soviet Union.

Griffin, Sir Anthony Templer Frederick Griffith. Admiral, British Royal Navy; Controller of the Navy, 1971-   . Born November 24, 1920, in Peshawar. Attended Royal Naval College, Dartmouth; Staff College, 1952; Imperial Defence College, 1963. Commissioned c. 1940. Served in the East Indies, Mediterranean, Atlantic and Far East in WW II. Commander, HMS *Ark Royal*, 1964-65; Assistant Chief of Naval Staff (Warfare), 1966-68; Flag Officer, Second-in-Command, Far East Fleet, 1968-69; Flag Officer, Plymouth, Commander Central Sub Area, Eastern Atlantic, and Commander, Plymouth Sub Area, Channel, 1969-71. KCB Promoted to Rear-Admiral, 1966; Vice-Admiral, 1968; Admiral, 1971.

Griffin, Michael Harold. Rear-Admiral, British Royal Navy; Director of Dockyard Production and Support, 1972-   . Born January 28, 1921. Attended Plymouth Junior Technical College. Commissioned in 1941. Served at sea in WW II. Commander, HM Dockyard, Chatham, 1963-65; Commander HMS *St. Vincent*, 1966-69; Commodore Superintendent, Singapore, 1969-71.

Griffiths, Arthur. Air Vice-Marshal, British Royal Air Force; Head of British Defense Liaison Staff, Canberra, 1972-   . Born August 22, 1922. Commissioned in 1940. Served in WW II in fighter reconnaissance. Commander, No. 101 Bomber Squadron, 1962-64; Group Captain Operations, Bomber Command, 1964-67; Commander RAF Waddington, 1967-69; AOA and later Chief of Staff, Far East Air Force, 1969-71. CB; AFC.

Grigaut, Claude. General, French Air Force; Chief of Staff of the Air Force, 1972-   . Born June 24, 1919, Paris. Attended Ecole de l'Air, 1939-40; Ecole du Personnel Navigant de'Essais et de Réception, Brittany, 1945; Centre d'Enseignement Superieur Aérien—Ecole Supérieure de Guerre Aérienne, 1957-58. Commissioned Sub-Lieutenant, 1940. Served as bomber pilot in WW II. Assistant Chief of Staff of the Air Force (Plans), 1965-67; Commandant, Air Academy and Army Air Academy, 1967-69; Commandant, Air Force Schools, 1969-71; Major General of the Air Force, 1971-72. Commandeur de la Légion d'Honneur; Croix de Guerre, 1939-45; Croix de la Valeur Militaire; Médaille de l'Aéronautique. Promoted to Brigadier General, January 1, 1965; Major General, October 1, 1969; Lieutenant General, July 1, 1971; General, December 1, 1972.

Grigorev, M.G. Colonel General, USSR Army; First Deputy Commander, Strategic Rocket Forces, 1968-   . Served on the Soviet-German Front in WW II. Staff member, Odessa Military District. Member, Communist Party of the Soviet Union.

Grishanov, V.M. Admiral, USSR Navy; Deputy Chief, Main Political Directorate, Soviet Army and Navy, and Chief, Naval Political Directorate, 1958-   . Served in the Soviet-Finnish War, 1939-40; and the Soviet-German War, 1941-45. Formerly Chief, Political Directorate, Southern Region, Pacific Fleet; Staff member, Political Directorate,

Baltic Fleet, 1957-58. Member, Communist Party of the Soviet Union.

Grishkov, N. Lieutenant General, USSR Air Force; Deputy Commander, Air Defense Forces. Served on the Soviet-German Front in WW II. Member, Communist Party of the Soviet Union.

Groppi, Silvio E. General, Uruguayan Army; Military Attache, Embassy of Uruguay, Washington, D.C.; Delegate, Inter-American Defense Board. Date of Rank: February 1, 1968.

Gros, Alois. Major General, Army of Czechoslovakia; Chief of Defense and Security Department, Czechoslovak Government Presidium, 1969- . Born c. 1924. Joined Czechoslovak Army, 1949. Deputy Chief, Main Political Directorate, Ministry of National Defense, 1958-68; member of staff of military research institute, 1968-69. Member Czechoslovak Communist Party.

Grossenbacher, Charles. Chief of Armament, Switzerland. Born in 1922.

Grudzien, Mieczyslaw. Lieutenant General, Polish Army; Minister of Veterans Affairs, 1972- . Served on Polish-German Front, WW II. Studied at Military-Political College. Previously Deputy Chief, Military Political Affairs; Internal Service (Military Police), 1964-66; Deputy Commander in Chief, Polish Navy Political Affairs, 1966-68; Deputy Chief, Main Political Directorate, Polish Armed Forces, 1968-71; First Deputy Chief, Main Political Directorate, Polish Armed Forces, 1971-72. Polonia Restituta; Cross of Grunwald; Cross of Valor; Cross of Merit; and other Polish and Soviet orders and awards. Promoted to Rear Admiral, October 10, 1967. In 1968 the Navy rank was changed to Major General in the Army. Member, Polish United Workers Party and Alternate Member of its Central Committee since 1971.

Grushevoy, K. Colonel General, USSR Army; Chief, Political Directorate, Moscow Military District. Served on the Soviet-German Front in WW II. Member, Communist Party of the Soviet Union.

Gubin, I.A. Major General, USSR Army; Chief, Political Directorate, Baltic Military District, 1972- . Served on the Soviet-German Front in WW II. Formerly First Deputy Chief, Political Directorate, Baltic Military District. Member, Communist Party of the Soviet Union.

Guerrero Garcia, Miguel. Lieutenant General, Spanish Air Force; Chief, 1st Air Region (Madrid), 1970- . Formerly Commander, 27th Fighter Group; Chief, 3d Section of Staff, 3d Air Region (Valencia); Secretary, Air Force Staff; Director, Fighter Aircraft School, and Commander, Joint Moron Air Force Base; Commander, 23d Fighter Wing and Tarragona Air Sector; Commander, 1st Fighter Wing and Manises Air Force Base; Air Attache, Embassy of Spain, Washington, D.C., USA; Chief of Staff,

3d Air Region (Valencia); Chief of Staff, 1st Air Region (Madrid); Deputy Chief, 3d Air Region, and Chief of Staff, Valencia Air Sector; Chief, Canary Islands Air Zone. Military Medal (Individual); Air Medal; Great Crosses: Army, Navy and Air Force Merit, and Saint Hermenegild Royal and Military Order; Great Cross of Civil Merit; Military Medal (Collective); two War Crosses; two Red Crosses of Military Merit; War Medal; Order of Crown (Italy); Cross of Merit of Eagle Order (Germany); Cross of War Merit (Italy); Medal of Military Merit (Portugal); Legion of Merit (USA); and other medals and awards. Promoted to Lieutenant General, September 3, 1970.

Guest, William Selman. Rear Admiral, United States Navy; Commander Military Sealift Command, Pacific, 1970- . Born July 3, 1913, in Rome, Georgia. US Naval Academy, 1931-35; Flight Training Course, 1937-39; Air War College, 1949-50; Naval War College, 1954-55. Commissioned Ensign, US Navy, 1935; designated Naval Aviator, 1939. Served in the Pacific and Atlantic Theaters, WW II; Korean War; Vietnam War. Chief of Staff and Aide to Commander Naval Air Force, Pacific, 1960-62; Commander Fleet Air, Whidbey/Commander Naval Air Bases, Thirteenth Naval District, and Commander Fleet Air Wing FOUR, 1962-63; Commander Carrier Division NINE, 1964-65; Deputy Commander Naval Striking and Support Forces, Southern Europe, 1965-67; Chief of Naval Air Reserve Training and Commandant, Ninth Naval District, 1967-69; Navy Deputy to the Department of Defense Manager for Manned Space Flight Support Operations, and Commander Manned Spacecraft Recovery Force, US Atlantic Fleet, 1970. Navy Cross; Distinguished Service Medal; Legion of Merit with Gold Star; Bronze Star Medal; Air Medal with Gold Star; and other US and foreign medals and awards. Promoted to Rear Admiral, August 1, 1963.

Guinn, Dick Henry. Vice Admiral, United States Navy; Deputy and Chief of Staff, Commander in Chief, Atlantic, and Commander in Chief, US Atlantic Fleet, and Chief of Staff to Commander in Chief, Western Atlantic Area, 1972- . Born March 27, 1918, Palestine, Texas. Texas College of Mines, El Paso, 1936-37; US Naval Academy, 1937-41; Flight Training Course, 1943; National War College, 1959-60. Commissioned Ensign, US Navy, 1941; designated Naval Aviator, 1943. Served in the Atlantic and Pacific Theaters, WW II; Korean War. Commanding Officer USS *Forrestal* (CVA-59), 1963-64; Program Appraisal Office, Navy Department, 1964-65; Commander Carrier Division FOUR, 1965-67; Chief of Naval Air Basic Training, 1967-69; Deputy Chief of Naval Personnel, 1969-70; Chief of Naval Personnel and Deputy Chief of Naval Operations (Manpower and Naval Reserve), 1970-72. Navy Cross; Legion of Merit; Air Medal with Gold Star; and other medals and awards. Promoted to Rear Admiral, June 1, 1965; Vice Admiral, August 21, 1970.

Gulyaev, S.A. Colonel General, USSR Naval Air Force; Commander, Baltic Fleet Naval Air Force, 1961- . Born in 1918. Served in the Soviet-German War (WW II).

Promoted to Lieutenant General, 1962; Colonel General, 1970. Member, Communist Party of the Soviet Union.

Gur, Mordechai. Major General Israeli Army; Defense and Armed Forces Attache, Embassy of Israel, Washington, D.C.

Gusakovskiy. General of the Army, USSR Army. Served on the Soviet-German Front in WW II. Chief, Personnel (Cadres) Directorate, Ministry of Defense, 1963-70. Member, Communist Party of the Soviet Union.

Guthrie, John Reiley. Major General, United States Army; Deputy Commanding General for Materiel Acquisition, US Army Materiel Command, Washington, D.C., 1971- . Born December 20, 1921, Phillipsburg, New Jersey. Princeton University, AB Degree, History; The Artillery School, Basic Course; US Army Command and General Staff College; US National War College. Commissioned Second Lieutenant, US Army Reserve, 1942. WW II. Director of Development, Office, Chief of Research and Development, US Army, Washington, D.C., 1966-67; Assistant Division Commander, 2d Infantry Division, US Army, Pacific-Korea, 1967-68; Deputy, later Director of Research, Development and Engineering, US Army Materiel Command, Washington, D.C., 1968-71. Legion of Merit with two Oak Leaf Clusters; Bronze Star Medal with two Oak Leaf Clusters; and other medals and awards. Promoted to Brigadier General, April 1, 1966; Major General, November 1, 1969.

Gutierrez-Rivera, Julio. Brigadier General, Nicaraguan Army; Military and Naval Attache, Embassy of Nicaragua, Washington, D.C.; Chief of Delegation, Inter-American Defense Board. Date of Rank: May 27, 1972.

Guzman, Carlos. General, Army of El Salvador; Armed Forces Attache, Embassy of El Salvador, Washington, D.C., 1971-73.

H

Haaksalo, Magnus. Major General, Army of Finland; Commanding General, Central Finland Military Area, 1971- . Born May 29, 1920, Viipuri (formerly Finland). Attended War College, 1952. Served in Winter War; Continuation War. Liaison Officer, UN Truce Supervision Agency, Egypt, 1956-57; Instructor in Tactics, War College, 1957-63; Commanding Officer, Coastal Jaeger Battalion, 1963-66; Commandant, Military Academy, 1966-71. Medal of Merit of the United Nations; Cross of Freedom, 3d Class with Oak Leaf; Cross of Freedom, 3d and 4th Class with Swords; Commemorative Medals of Winter and Continuation Wars; Order of Finnish White Rose; and other medals and awards. Promoted to Major General, September 4, 1971.

Habyarimana, Juvelnal. Colonel, Army of Rwanda; Minister of National Guard and Police, Rwanda.

Hadden, Mayo Addison, Jr. Rear Admiral, United States Navy; Commander Fleet Air Wings, US Atlantic Fleet, 1970- , and Commandant, First Naval District, and Commander Naval Base, Boston, Massachusetts, 1972- . Born August 14, 1916, in Holland, Michigan. Hope College, Holland, Michigan, BA, 1934-38; Flight Training Course, 1941-42; General Line School, 1945-46; Naval War College, 1953-54; Nuclear Weapons Training Center, 1958; National War College, 1960-61; Harvard University Center for International Affairs, 1965. Commissioned Ensign, US Naval Reserve, 1941; designated Naval Aviator, 1942; transferred to US Navy, 1946. Served in the Atlantic and Pacific Theaters, WW II. Commanding Officer USS *Graffias* (AF-29), 1963-64; Commanding Officer USS *Hornet* (CVS-12), 1964-65; Assistant Director, Political-Military Policy Division, Office of the CNO, 1966-67; Deputy Director, Operations, Office of Politico-Military Affairs, Department of State, 1967-69; Commander Iceland Defense Force and Commander, Fleet Air, Keflavik, 1969-70. Silver Star Medal; Legion of Merit; Distinguished Flying Cross with two Gold Stars; Air Medal with Gold Star; Navy Commendation Medal; and other medals and awards. Promoted to Rear Admiral, April 1, 1969.

Hai, Tran Quy. Major General, People's Army of Vietnam; Vice Minister of National Defense, 1961; Deputy Chief of General Staff, 1963; Alternate Member, Lao Dong Party Central Committee, 1960; Member, Central Military Party Committee. Arrested and imprisoned at Ba To, Quang Ngai Province, 1940-43; Chief, General Directorate of Rear Services, 1961-63; commanded troops in the South, 1967. Promoted to Major General, July 1960.

Hails, Robert E. Major General United States Air Force; Commander, Warner Robins Air Materiel Area, Air Force Logistics Command, 1972- . Born January 20, 1923, in Miami, Florida. Army Air Corps Flying School, 1943-44; Auburn University, Auburn, Alabama, BS, Aeronautical Engineering, 1947; Columbia University, New York, MS, Industrial Management, 1950; Air Command and Staff School, 1956; Advanced Management Program, Harvard School of Business, 1965. Commissioned Second Lieutenant, US Army Air Corps, 1944. Served in the Pacific Theater, WW II. System Program Manager, A-7D Aircraft, Air Force Systems Command, 1966-68; Assistant Deputy Chief of Staff, Maintenance-Engineering, Air Force Logistics Command, 1968-69; Deputy Chief of Staff, Maintenance, Air Force Logistics Command, 1969-71; Commander, Defense Personnel Support Center, Philadelphia, Pennsylvania, 1971-72. Distinguished Service Medal; Legion of Merit with two Oak Leaf Clusters; and other medals and awards. Promoted to Major General, August 1, 1970.

Haise, Fred Wallace, Jr. United States; NASA Astronaut, 1966- . Born Biloxi, Mississippi, November 14, 1933. Perkinston Junior College; University of Oklahoma, BS,

Aeronautical Engineering, 1959; Aerospace Research Pilot School, 1961; Naval Flying School, Pensacola, 1952-54. Commissioned US Marine Corps, Second Lieutenant, 1954. Fighter Pilot, VMF-533 and VMF-114, 1954-56; Instructor, US Navy Advanced Training Command, 1956-57; 185th Fighter Interceptor Squadron, 1957-59; Chief, 164th Standardization-Evaluation Flight, 164th Tactical Fighter Squadron, US Air Force, 1961-62; Research Pilot, NASA Lewis Research Center, 1959-63, NASA Flight Research Center, Houston, 1963-66. NASA experience: Backup Lunar Module Pilot, Apollo 8 and 11; Lunar Module Pilot, Apollo 13, April 11-17, 1970; Backup Spacecraft Commander, Apollo 16. Presidential Medal for Freedom; NASA Distinguished Service Medal; AIAA Haley Astronautics Award, 1971; American Astronautical Society Flight Achievement Award, 1970; City of New York Gold Medal, 1970; City of Houston Medal for Valor, 1970; Jeff Davis Award; Mississippi Distinguished Civilian Service Medal; Society of Experimental Test Pilots Ray E. Tenhoff Award; Honorary ScD, Western Michigan University.

Hall, Charles Maurice. Major General, United States Army; Director of Operations, J-3, US European Command, 1973-   . Born October 5, 1924, in Honolulu, Hawaii. Attended US Military Academy; Artillery School, Basic and Advanced Courses; Command and General Staff College; Armed Forces Staff College; Naval War College, 1964-65; George Washington University, MS, International Affairs. Commissioned Second Lieutenant June 4, 1946. Served in the Vietnam War. Commanding Officer, 2d Battalion, 10th Artillery, 197th Infantry Brigade, Fort Benning, Georgia, 1966-67; Chief of Brigade and Battalion Operations Department, US Army Infantry School, Fort Benning, Georgia, 1967; Commanding Officer, 6th Infantry Division Artillery, Fort Campbell, Kentucky, 1967-68; Commanding Officer, XVIII Airborne Corps Artillery, Fort Bragg, North Carolina, 1968-69; Commanding General I Field Force Artillery, US Army, Pacific-Vietnam, 1969-70. Distinguished Service Medal; Legion of Merit with two Oak Leaf Clusters; Meritorious Service Medal; and other medals and awards. Promoted to Brigadier General August 1, 1970; Major General March 1, 1973.

Hall, Eric G. Air Vice Marshal, Air Force of Pakistan; Air Attache, Embassy of Pakistan, Washington, D.C.

Hall, Geoffrey Penrose Dickinson. Rear-Admiral, British Royal Navy; Hydrographer of the Navy, 1971-   . Born July 19, 1916. Studied at Haileybury. Joined the Royal Navy in 1935. Served at sea in Atlantic and Pacific Theaters and in Southeast Asia Command in WW II. Twice Assistant Hydrographer; surveyed between South Africa and Iceland, 1965-67; Assistant Director (Naval), Hydrographic Department, Taunton. CB; DSC. Fellow of the Royal Geographical Society. Promoted to Captain, 1962; Rear Admiral, 1971.

Hall, Kenneth. Major General, British Army; Director of Army Education, 1972-   . Born July 29, 1916. Attended Worksop College; St. John's College, Cambridge, BA. Commissioned in Royal Tank Regiment, 1940;

transferred to Royal Army Educational Corps in 1949. Served in WW II in northern Europe. Chief Education Officer, General Headquarters, Middle East Land Forces, 1965; Commandant Army School of Education, 1965-66; Commandant Royal Army Education Corps Centre, 1971-72. OBE.

Hallgren, Hal Edward. Major General, United States Army; Commanding General, US Army Concepts Analysis Agency, Bethesda, Maryland, 1973-   . Born May 25, 1925, in Chicago, Illinois. Attended US Military Academy; Artillery School; Artillery and Guided Missile School, Advanced Course; Command and General Staff College; Armed Forces Staff College; Army War College, 1964-65; University of Pennsylvania, MS, Electrical Engineering; George Washington University, MS, International Affairs. Commissioned Second Lieutenant, June 4, 1946. Served in the Vietnam War. Deputy Assistant Chief of Staff, G-2, later Secretary General Staff, II Field Force, then Executive Officer, I Field Force Artillery, US Army Pacific-Vietnam, 1967-68; Chief of Defense Review Division, SENTINEL Systems Office, Alexandria, Virginia, redesignated and relocated to US Army SAFEGUARD Systems Office, Arlington, Virginia, 1968-69; Assistant Comptroller for Cost Analysis, US Army Materiel Command, 1969-70; Comptroller, US Army Materiel Command, 1970-72; Office of the Assistant Chief of Staff for Force Development, 1972-73. Legion of Merit with Oak Leaf Cluster; Air Medal (5 awards); and other medals and awards. Promoted to Brigadier General, April 1, 1971; Major General, August 1, 1973.

Hallila, Allan T. Lieutenant General, Army of Finland; Chief of War Economics, General Headquarters, 1968-   . Born October 16, 1917, Seinäjoki, Finland. War College, 1950; Helsinki Technical University, Graduate Engineer, 1953. Served in Winter War; Continuation War. Chief, Weapon Technical Office, General Headquarters, 1956-62; Chief, Weapon Technical Section, General Headquarters, 1962-63; Chief Engineer, General Headquarters,1963-66. Cross of Freedom, 3d Class with Swords; Cross of Freedom, 4th Class with Sword and with Oak Leaf; Order of Finnish White Rose, 1st Class; Iron Cross, 2d Class (Germany); Commemorative Medals for Winter and Continuation Wars; and other medals and awards. Promoted to Lieutenant General, December 6, 1967.

Halmevaara, Kai Y. Lieutenant General, Army of Finland; Commanding General, South Finland Military Area, 1969-   . Born April 9, 1916, Rauma, Finland. University of Helsinki, MA, Jurisprudence. Served in Winter War; Continuation War. Chief, War Economics Section, General Headquarters, 1966-67; Chief of War Economics, General Headquarters, 1967-68; Chief of Operations, General Headquarters, 1968-69. Cross of Freedom, 3d Class with Sword (awarded twice); Cross of Freedom, 4th Class with Swords; Commemorative Medals of Winter and Continuation Wars; Order of Finnish White Rose, 1st Class; Commander, Order of the Finnish Lion, 1st Class; and other medals and awards. Promoted to Lieutenant General, September 4, 1971.

Halttu, Paavo Oskari. Lieutenant General, Army of Finland; Deputy Chief of Staff for Training, General Headquarters, 1966-   . Born June 4, 1914, Oulu, Finland. Attended War College, 1946-48. Served in Winter War; Continuation War. Chief of Staff, 1st Division, 1958-62; Chief of Ordnance, General Headquarters, 1962-66. Cross of Freedom, 2d Class for Merit; Cross of Freedom, 3d Class with Oak Leaf; Cross of Freedom, 3d Class with Sword; Cross of Freedom, 4th Class with Sword; Commemorative Medals for Winter and Continuation Wars; Order of German Eagle, 2d Class; and other medals and awards. Promoted to Lieutenant General, July 19, 1966.

Hamilton, Colin C., Jr. Major General, United States Air Force; Deputy Director for Command and Control, J-3, US European Command, 1973-   . Born March 6, 1924, in Clayton, North Carolina. Aviation Cadet Training Course, 1942-43; National War College, 1966-67. Commissioned Second Lieutenant, US Army Air Corps, in 1943. Served in the European Theater, WW II and in the Vietnam War. Deputy Chief of Staff for Operations, 3d Air Division, Andersen Air Force Base, Guam, 1967-69; Commander, 379th Bombardment Wing, Wurtsmith Air Force Base, Michigan, 1969-70; Commander, 93d Bombardment Wing, Castle Air Force Base, California, 1970-71; Deputy Director for Operations, National Military Command Center, Organization of the Joint Chiefs of Staff, Washington, D.C., 1971-72; Deputy Director for Operations, US European Command, Germany, 1972-73. Legion of Merit with two Oak Leaf Clusters; Air Medal with six Oak Leaf Clusters; National Order of Vietnam (Vietnam); Gallantry Cross with Palm (Vietnam); and other medals and awards. Promoted to Brigadier General, May 1, 1971; Major General, 1973.

Hamlet, James Frank. Major General, United States Army; Commanding General, 4th Infantry Division (Mechanized), Fort Carson, Colorado, 1972-   . Born December 13, 1921, in Alliance, Ohio. Attended Infantry School, Basic and Advanced Courses; Command and General Staff College; St. Benedict's College, Atchison, Kansas, BS, Business Administration, 1968; Army War College, 1969-70. Commissioned Second Lieutenant July 11, 1944. Served in WW II and the Vietnam War. Operations Officer, 11th Aviation Group, then Commanding Officer, 227th Aviation Battalion, then Executive Officer, 11th Aviation Group, 1st Cavalry Division, US Army, Vietnam, 1966-67; Chief of the Airmobility Branch, Doctrine and Systems Division, US Army Combat Developments Command Combat Arms Group, Fort Leavenworth, Kansas, 1968-69; Commanding Officer, 11th Aviation Group, 1st Cavalry Division (Airmobile), US Army, Vietnam, 1970-71; Assistant Division Commander, 101st Airborne Division (Airmobile), US Army, Vietnam, 1971; Commanding General, 3d Brigade, 1st Cavalry Division, US Army, Vietnam, 1971-72. Distinguished Service Medal; Legion of Merit with two Oak Leaf Clusters; Distinguished Flying Cross; Soldier's Medal; Bronze Star Medal with Oak Leaf Cluster; Air Medal (41 awards). Promoted to Brigadier General September 1, 1971; Major General June 1, 1973.

Hamzah bin Haji Abu Samah, Datu. Prime Minister and Minister of Defense, Malaysia.

Han Hsien-ch'u. General, People's Liberation Army, People's Republic of China; Deputy Chief of Staff, General Staff Department, 1972-   . Born in 1908, in Hunan. Attended Military Academy at K'ang-Ta, Shensi, 1936-37; People's Liberation Army Academy (War College), Peking, 1955-c. 1956. Combat duty in the Sino-Japanese War and the Civil War; took part in the Long March and the Korean War. Regimental Commander and later Deputy Divisional Commander, Fourth Front Army, Szechwan, 1933-35; Divisional Commander, Fourth Front Army, 1935-36; assigned to 129th Division, Eighth Route Army, 1937-c. 1939; Brigade Commander, Po-H'ai Area, Shantung, 1939; Division Commander, Northeast Democratic Allied Army, c. 1946-47; Commander, Third and Fourth Columns (battle groups), Fourth Field Army, 1947-49; Deputy Commander, 12th Corps, 1949-50; Deputy Commander, Hunan Military District, 1949-50; Member, Military and Administrative Committee for Hainan, 1950; Member, Kwantung Provincial People's Government Council, 1950; transferred to the Chinese People's Volunteers Forces, Korea, 1950; Vice-Chairman, Joint Chiefs of Staff, China and North Korea Forces, 1951; Representative of the Chinese People's Volunteers to the Panmunjon Truce Negotiations, 1951-52; Deputy Chief of Staff, Chinese People's Volunteers Forces, Korea, 1952-c. 1954; Member of National Defense Council, 1954; Communist Party Member since c. 1933; Alternate Member of CCP Central Committee, 1958-69; Member of Central Committee, 1969; Commander, Foochow Military Region, 1960; Chief, Communist Army on Fukien Front Line, 1960; Chairman, Fukien Revolutionary Committee, 1968; First Secretary, Provincial Party Committee, 1971.

Han Sin. General, Army of the Republic of Korea; Chairman, Joint Chiefs of Staff, 1972-   . Attended Chu-o Hagaru University, Tokyo, 1943; Korean Military Academy, 1946; Republic of Korea National Defense College, 1961. Commissioned Second Lieutenant, ROK Army, 1946. Combat duty in the Korean War. Vice Chief of Staff, ROK Army, 1968; Commanding General, Second ROK Army, 1968-69; Commanding General, First ROK Army, 1969-72. Decorations: Ulchi with Gold Star; ROK Taeguk with Star; and other medals and awards. Promoted to General, August 6, 1970.

Hansen, Homer K. Major General, United States Air Force; Vice Commander, Aeronautical Systems Division, Air Force Systems Command (AFSC), 1972-   . Born May 6, 1922, St. Ansgar, Iowa. Jackson College, Honolulu, Hawaii, BS, Political Science, 1943; Army Air Corps Flying School, 1943; Armed Forces Staff College, 1958. Commissioned Second Lieutenant, US Army Air Corps, 1943. Served in the European Theater, WW II; Korean War; Vietnam War. Commander, 27th Tactical Fighter Wing, Vietnam, 1968-69; Director, Tactical Air Control Center, Headquarters Seventh Air Force, Vietnam, 1969; Commander, US Air Force Tactical Fighter Weapons Center, 1969-71; Director, Operational Requirements and Development Plans, Deputy Chief of Staff, Research and Development, Headquarters, USAF, 1971-72. Distinguished Service Medal; Legion of Merit; Distinguished Flying Cross with two Oak Leaf Clusters; Bronze Star Medal with

Combat V; Air Medal with 21 Oak Leaf Clusters; and other US and foreign medals and awards. Promoted to Major General, September 1, 1971.

Hao, Song. Lieutenant General, People's Army of Vietnam; Chairman of General Political Directorate of People's Army of Vietnam, 1961; Member, Lao Dong Party Central Committee, 1960; Deputy Secretary, Central Military Party Committee; Vice Minister of National Defense. Deputy Chairman, General Political Directorate, People's Army of Vietnam, 1957; appointed Member of Committee for Cultural Relations with Foreign Countries, 1961; appointed Vice Minister of Defense, 1961; Member, Electoral Board for Fourth National Assembly, 1971; Member, Vietnam Fatherland Front Central Committee, 1971; Deputy to Fourth National Assembly, 1971. Promoted to Major General, September 1959; Lieutenant General, 1961.

Haque, N. Commander, Bangladesh Navy; Chief of Staff, Bangladesh Navy, 1973-   , .

Harbison, William. Air Commodore, British Royal Air Force; Commander, RAF Staff, and Air Attache, Washington, D.C., 1972- . Born April 11, 1922. Attended Joint Services Staff College, 1962; National Defence College, 1965-66. Commissioned in 1941. Served in Fighter Command in WW II; with 4th Fighter Group US Air Force in the Korean War. Commander, RAF Leuchars Fighter Command, 1963-65; Group Captain Operations, Headquarters Fighter Command, 1967-68; No. 11 Group Strike Command, 1968; Director of Control (Operations), National Air Traffic Control Services, 1968-72. CBE; AFC.

Hardin, Ernest C., Jr. Major General, United States Air Force; Commander, Air Force Inspection and Safety Center, and Deputy Inspector General for Inspection and Safety, 1972- . Born December 25, 1916, in Wheatcroft, Kentucky. University of Kentucky; Jefferson School of Law, University of Louisville, LLB, 1942, JD, 1969; Army Air Corps Flying School, 1942-43; Naval War College, 1949-50. Commissioned Second Lieutenant Army Air Corps, 1943. Served in the European Theater, WW II; Vietnam War. Deputy Commander, Ninth Air Force, 1964-65; Commander, 839th Air Division, 1965-66; Deputy Chief of Staff, Plans, Headquarters Tactical Air Command (TAC), 1966-67; Deputy Chief of Staff, Operations, TAC, 1967-68; Deputy Chief of Staff, Operations, Pacific Air Forces, 1968-70; Deputy Chief of Staff, Operations, and later Vice Commander, Seventh Air Force, Vietnam, 1970-71; Chief of Staff, Pacific Air Forces, 1971-72. Distinguished Service Medal; Legion of Merit; Distinguished Flying Cross with three Oak Leaf Clusters; and other US and foreign medals and awards. Promoted to Major General, January 24, 1969.

Harding, Ross Philip. Air Commodore, British Royal Air Force; Defence and Air Attache, Moscow, 1970- . Born January 22, 1921. Attended St. Edmund Hall, Oxford, MA; RAF Staff College, 1951. Commissioned in 1943. Served as fighter pilot in WW II. Deputy Chief, British Military Mission, Berlin, 1963-65; Commanding Officer RAF Valley,

1965-68; Senior Directing Staff (Air), Joint Services Staff College, 1968-69. CBE.

Hargrove, Clifford W. Major General, United States Air Force; Director of Operations, Deputy Chief of Staff, Plans and Operations, Headquarters US Air Force, 1972-   ; with additional duties as US Air Force Member and Steering and Coordinating Member, US Section, Permanent Joint Board of Defense, Canada-United States. Born April 8, 1919, in Dutch Mills, Arkansas. California State Polytechnic College; Army Air Corps Flying School, 1942-43; Industrial College of the Armed Forces, 1963-64. Commissioned Second Lieutenant, US Army Air Corps, 1943. Commander, 19th Bombardment Wing, 1967-68; Commander, 72d Bombardment Wing, Puerto Rico, 1968-69; Commander, 4th Strategic Aerospace Division, 1969-70; Chief of Staff, Second Air Force, 1970-71; Deputy Director of Operations, Deputy Chief of Staff, Plans and Operations, Headquarters USAF, 1971-72. Legion of Merit; and other medals and awards. Promoted to Major General, October 1, 1971.

al Hariri, Abdel Wahab. Brigadier General, Army of the Arab Republic of Egypt; Division Commander, Army of Egypt, Middle East War of 1973.

Harland, Reginald Edward Wynyard. Air Marshal, British Royal Air Force; Air Officer Engineering, Air Support Command, 1972- . Born May 30, 1920. Summer Fields, Oxford; Stowe; Trinity College, Cambridge, MA degree; Royal Air Force College, Cranwell, 1950-52; Royal Air Force Staff College, 1957; Imperial Defence College, 1969. Served in the Mediterranean Theater, WW II. Commanding Officer, Central Development Establishment, Swanton Morley, 1960-62; Senior Technical Staff Officer, Headquarters, No. 3 (Bomber) Group, Mildenhall, 1962-64; Air Officer in Charge of Engineering, Headquarters, Far East Air Force, Singapore, 1964-66; Director, Harrier Project, Headquarters, Ministry of Technology, 1967-68; Air Officer Commanding, No. 24 Group, RAF, Rudloe Manor, 1970-72. CB. Chartered Engineer, 1966; Fellow of the Institution of Electrical Engineers, 1964; Fellow of the Institution of Mechanical Engineers, 1967; Fellow of the Royal Aeronautical Society, 1967; Member of the British Institute of Management, 1968.

Harlfinger, Frederick Joseph, II. Vice Admiral, United States Navy; Director of Command Support Programs, Office of the Chief of Naval Operations, 1971- . Born September 14, 1913, in Albany, New York. US Naval Academy, 1931-35; Submarine Training Course, 1937; Armed Forces Staff College, 1952; Industrial College of the Armed Forces, 1954-55. Commissioned Ensign, US Navy, 1935. Served in submarines in the Pacific Theater, WW II. Commander Submarine Flotilla ONE, 1962-64; Assistant Director for Collection, Defense Intelligence Agency, 1964-67; Commander South Atlantic Force, US Atlantic Fleet, 1967-68; Assistant Chief of Naval Operations (Intelligence) /Commander Naval Intelligence Command, 1968-71. Navy Cross; Silver Star Medal with two Gold Stars; Legion of Merit with Gold Star; Bronze Star Medal with Combat "V"; Navy Commendation Medal with Combat "V"; and other medals and awards. Promoted to Vice Admiral, October 1971.

Harman, Jack Wentworth. Major-General, British Army; Commandant, Military Academy, Sandhurst, 1972-73. Born July 20, 1920. Attended Wellington College; Imperial Defence College, 1967; Royal Military Academy, Sandhurst. Commissioned in The Queen's Bays, 1940. Combat duty in WW II. Commander, 11 Infantry Brigade, 1965-66; Brigadier General Staff, Headquarters, Army Strategic Command, 1968-69; General Officer Commanding, 1st Division, 1970-72. OBE; MC. Promoted to Major General in 1970.

Harnish, William Max. Rear Admiral, United States Navy; Commander, Pacific Missile Range, Point Mugu, California, 1972-   . Born November 1, 1919, in Illinois. University of Illinois, 1937-39; US Naval Academy, 1939-42; Flight Training Course, 1944-45; Naval Postgraduate School, Aeronautical Engineering Course, 1948-49; Massachusetts Institute of Technology, MS, Aeronautical Engineering, 1949-51; Naval War College, 1957-58. Commissioned Ensign, US Navy, 1942; designated Naval Aviator, 1945. Served in the Pacific Theater, WW II; Korean War; Vietnam War. Commanding Officer, USS *Chipola* (AO-63), 1964-65; Assistant to Director of Plans and Programs, Office of the CNO, 1965-66; Commanding Officer, USS *Ranger* (CVA-61), 1966; Deputy Director, Systems Analysis Division, Office of the CNO, 1966-67; Director of Office of Program Appraisal, 1967-69; Commander Carrier Division SIX, 1969-70; Deputy Comptroller of the Navy, 1970-72. Legion of Merit with Gold Star; Distinguished Flying Cross; Air Medal with two Gold Stars; and other US and foreign medals and awards. Promoted to Rear Admiral, August 1, 1968.

Harrell, William S. Major General, United States Air Force; Commander, 24th North American Air Defense Command/Continental Air Defense Command (NORAD/CONAD) Region, and Commander 24th Air Division. Born October 25, 1920, in Pleasant Hill, Alabama. University of Alabama, 1938; Army Air Corps Flying School, 1941; Command and General Staff School, 1945-46; Air Command and Staff College, 1949; Ohio State University, 1950; Air War College, 1958. Commissioned Second Lieutenant, US Army Air Corps, 1941. Served in the China-Burma-India Theater, WW II. Vice Commander Tenth Air Force, 1966-68; Assistant Deputy Chief of Staff, Materiel, Headquarters Aerospace Defense Command (ADC), 1968-69; Deputy Chief of Staff, Materiel, Headquarters ADC, 1969. Silver Star; Legion of Merit; Distinguished Flying Cross with two Oak Leaf Clusters; and other medals and awards. Promoted to Brigadier General, June 1, 1966; Major General, August 1, 1969.

Hartsfield, Henry W., Jr. Lieutenant Colonel, US Air Force; NASA Astronaut, 1969-   . Born November 21, 1933, Birmingham, Alabama. Auburn University, BS, Physics, 1954; graduate work: Duke University, Physics; Air Force Institute of Technology, Astronautics; Aerospace Research Pilot School; University of Tennessee, MSc, Engineering

Science, 1971. Commissioned Second Lieutenant, US Air Force, 1954. 53d Tactical Fighter Squadron; Instructor, Aerospace Research Pilot School; US Air Force Manned Orbiting Laboratory Program. NASA experience: Support Crew Member, Apollo 16.

Hartwig, Paul. Rear Admiral, Navy of the Federal Republic of Germany; Commander in Chief of the Fleet.

Harty, Harry Lafayette, Jr. Vice Admiral, United States Navy; Vice Chairman, the United States Delegation, United Nations Military Staff Committee, New York, and Commander Eastern Sea Frontier, 1971-   . Born July 25, 1917, in Grays Point, Missouri. Virginia Military Institute; US Naval Academy, 1935-39; Flight Training Course, 1942; George Washington University; Industrial College of the Armed Forces, 1957-58. Commissioned Ensign, US Navy, 1939; designated Naval Aviator, 1942. Served in the Atlantic and Pacific Theaters, WW II; Vietnam War. Commanding Officer USS *Randolph* (CVS-15), 1962-63; Assistant Director, Program Appraisal Division, Office of Navy Program Appraisal, 1963-66; Commander Antisubmarine Warfare Group THREE, 1966-67; Deputy Assistant Chief of Staff for Plans and Policy, Supreme Allied Commander, Europe, 1967-70; Assistant Vice Chief of Naval Operations/Director of Naval Administration, 1970-71. Distinguished Service Medal; Legion of Merit; Commendation Ribbon with Combat "V"; and other US and foreign medals and awards. Promoted to Rear Admiral, May 14, 1967; Vice Admiral, September 1, 1971.

Hasani, 'Ali Nasir Muhammad. Minister of Defense, People's Democratic Republic of Yemen.

Hasko, Eris. General, Albanian Air Force; Commander, Albanian Air Command, and Deputy Minister of Defense, 1973-   .

Hassan, Usman Katsina. Brigadier, Nigerian Army; Chief of Staff, Nigerian Armed Forces. Born in 1933, in Katsina, Northern Nigeria. Attended Kaduna College; Nigerian College of Arts, Science and Technology; Officers Training School, Ghana; Royal Military Academy, Sandhurst, England. Commissioned Second Lieutenant in 1958.

Hassett, Francis George. Major General, Royal Australian Army; Vice-Chief, General Staff, 1971-   . Born April 18, 1918, in Sydney. Attended Royal Military College, Duntroon; trained in Darwin Mobile Force, 1939; studied at Imperial Defence College, London, 1963. Commissioned Lieutenant in 1939. Middle East and Southwest Pacific Area, WW II; Korean War; Malaya. Deputy Chief, General Staff, 1963-65; Head, Australian Joint Services Staff, London, 1966-67; General Office, Commanding, Northern Command, 1968-70; Chairman, Army Review Committee, 1970-71. CB; CBE; DSO; MVO.

Hauser, Hans. Major General, Swiss Army; Commander, Engineers and Fortress Troops. Born in 1910.

Hawkins, Desmond Ernest. Air Vice-Marshal, British Royal Air Force; Director General, Personal Services (RAF), Ministry of Defence, 1971-   . Born December 27, 1919.

Attended Royal Air Force Staff College, 1950; Joint Services Staff Course, 1957; Imperial Defence College, 1967. Commissioned in 1938. Served in Coastal Command and Far East in WW II. Senior Air Staff Officer, 19 Group, 1961-63; Commander, Royal Air Force, Tengah, 1963-66; Commander, Royal Air Force, Lyneham, 1968; Senior Air Staff Officer, Headquarters, RAF Strike Command, 1969-71. CB; CBE; DFC and Bar.

Hay, John Hancock, Jr. Lieutenant General, United States Army; Commanding General, XVIII Airborne Corps, Fort Bragg, North Carolina, 1971-   . Born October 2, 1917, Thief River Falls, Minnesota. University of Montana, BS Degree, Forestry and Civil Engineering; The Infantry School, Advanced Course; US Army Command and General Staff College; Canadian National Defense College. Commissioned Second Lieutenant, US Army Reserve, 1939. Served in WW II and Vietnam War. Commanding General, US Army Berlin Brigade, US Army, Europe, 1964-66; Commanding General, 11th Infantry Brigade, US Army, Pacific-Hawaii, 1966-67; Commanding General, 1st Infantry Division, US Army, Pacific-Vietnam, 1967-68; Deputy Commanding General, II Field Force, US Army, Pacific-Vietnam, 1968; Commandant, US Army Command and General Staff College, Commanding General, US Army Combat Developments Command Institute of Combined Arms and Support, and Commanding General, Fort Leavenworth, Kansas, 1968-71. Distinguished Service Cross; Distinguished Service Medal; Silver Star with three Oak Leaf Clusters; Legion of Merit with Oak Leaf Cluster; Distinguished Flying Cross with three Oak Leaf Clusters; Bronze Star Medal with V Device and two Oak Leaf Clusters; and other medals and awards. Promoted to Brigadier General, July 1, 1964; Major General, October 27, 1966; Lieutenant General, April 1, 1971.

Hay, Robert Arthur. Major General, Royal Australian Army; Commandant, Royal Military College, Duntroon, 1972-   . Born April 9, 1920, in Bendigo, Victoria. Studied at Royal Military College, Duntroon; Command and General Staff School, Fort Leavenworth, USA, 1945; Imperial Defence College. Commissioned Lieutenant in 1939. Served in the Pacific Theater, WW II. Director, Military Operations and Plans, 1966; Deputy Chief, General Staff, 1967-69; Commander, 1st Division, Eastern Command, 1970; Chief, SEATO Military Planning Office, 1971. CB; MBE.

Hayes, John Briggs. Rear Admiral, United States Coast Guard; Comptroller, US Coast Guard, 1973-   . Born August 30, 1924, Jamestown, New York. US Coast Guard Academy, 1943-46; Naval War College, 1959-60. Commissioned Ensign, 1946. Served in Vietnam War. Fourth Coastal Zone Advisor and Commander, Division II, Coast Guard Squadron One South Vietnam, 1966-67; Chief, Shore Facilities Branch, Search and Rescue Division, Coast Guard Headquarters, 1967-70; Chief, Planning and Evaluation Staff, Office of Boating Safety, 1970-71; Commandant of the Cadets, US Coast Guard Academy, 1971-73. Bronze Star Medal; and other medals and citations. Promoted to Captain, October 1, 1968; Rear Admiral, August 1, 1973.

Hayes, William R. Major General, United States Air Force, Deputy Director, Logistics (J-4), US European Command, Stuttgart, Germany, 1972-   . Born April 5, 1921, in Yonkers, New York. Studied at University of California; University of Omaha; Aviation Cadet Training Course, 1942-43; National War College, 1969-70. Commissioned Second Lieutenant, US Army Air Corps, in 1943. Served in the European Theater in WW II, and in the Korean War. Deputy Commander for Maintenance, Headquarters 4200th Strategic Reconnaissance Wing, Beale Air Force Base, California, 1965-66; Vice Commander, then Commander, 9th Strategic Reconnaissance Wing, Beale Air Force Base, California, 1966-69; Assistant for Logistics Planning, Deputy Chief of Staff, Systems and Logistics, Headquarters, US Air Force, Washington, D.C., 1970-72. Distinguished Flying Cross; Legion of Merit with Oak Leaf Cluster; Bronze Star Medal; Air Medal with four Oak Leaf Clusters; and other medals and awards. Promoted to Major General, April 2, 1973.

Haynes, Fred E. Major General, United States Marine Corps; Senior Member, Military Armistice Commission, United Nations Command, Korea, 1973-   . Born January 5, 1921, Dallas, Texas. Southern Methodist University, BS, 1941; Reserve Officers Class, Marine Corps School, 1942; Amphibious Warfare School, Junior Course, Quantico, 1953; Foreign Service Institute (Turkish Language), 1957; Air War College, 1961-62; George Washington University, International Affairs, 1963. Commissioned Second Lieutenant, USMC, 1942. Served in Pacific Theater, WW II; Vietnam War. Commander, Fifth Marines, then Chief of Staff, Task Force X-ray, 1st Marine Division, Vietnam, 1966-67; Assistant Chief of Staff, G-3, Headquarters, III Marine Amphibious Force, Vietnam, 1967; Military Secretary, Commandant of the Marine Corps, 1968; Legislative Assistant to Commandant of the Marine Corps, 1968-71; Commanding General, 2d Marine Division, 1971-73. Legion of Merit with Combat "V" and three Gold Stars; Bronze Star Medal with Combat "V"; and other US and foreign medals and awards. Promoted to Brigadier General, September 1, 1968; Major General, September 8, 1971.

Hayward, Harold Ira. Major General, United States Army; Deputy Chief of Staff for Personnel, US Army, Europe and Seventh Army, 1972-   . Born January 21, 1921, St. Charles, Idaho. US Military Academy; The Infantry School, Basic and Advanced Courses; Air Command and Staff College; US Army War College; George Washington University, MA Degree, International Affairs. Commissioned Second Lieutenant, 1944. Served in WW II and Vietnam War. Commanding Officer 2d Brigade, 82d Airborne Division, Fort Bragg, North Carolina, 1966-67; Special Assistant to the Chief of Staff, later Assistant Chief of Staff, G-3, US Army, Vietnam, 1967-68; Commanding Officer, 1st Brigade, 101st Airborne Division (Airmobile), US Army, Pacific-Vietnam, 1968-69; Chief, Plans Division, Office, Deputy Chief of Staff for Operations, US Army, Europe and Seventh Army, 1969; Commanding General, US Army Berlin Brigade, US Army, Europe, 1969-71;

Commanding General, US Army, Europe and Seventh Army Troops, 1971-72. Silver Star; Legion of Merit with Oak Leaf Cluster; Distinguished Flying Cross; Bronze Star Medal; and other medals and awards. Promoted to Brigadier General, January 10, 1970; Major General, December 1, 1971.

Hayward, Thomas Bibb. Vice Admiral, United States Navy; Director of Navy Program Planning, Office of the Chief of Naval Operations, 1973-   . Born May 3, 1924, in Glendale, California. Attended Occidental College; US Naval Academy; flight training, 1948-50; test pilot training, 1954; Naval War College, 1958-59; National War College, 1966-67. Commissioned Ensign June 6, 1947; designated Naval Aviator 1950. Served in the Korean War and the Vietnam War. Commander Attack Carrier Air Wing TEN, 1965-66; Commanding Officer, USS *Graffias* (AF-29), 1967-68; Executive Assistant and Naval Aide to the Under Secretary of the Navy, 1968-69; Commanding Officer, USS *America* (CVA-66), 1969-70; Commander Hawaiian Sea Frontier, Commandant, Fourteenth Naval District, and Commander Fleet Air, Hawaii, and Commander Manned Spacecraft Recovery Forces, Pacific, 1970-71; Director of the Office of Program Appraisal, Navy Department, 1971-73. Legion of Merit with two Gold Stars, Distinguished Flying Cross, Air Medal with ten Gold Stars and Bronze Numeral 3; Navy Commendation Medal with Gold Star and Combat "V"; and other medals and awards. Promoted to Rear Admiral November 1970; Vice Admiral April 1973. Member of the Society of Experimental Test Pilots.

Hazelwood, Frederick Samuel. Air Commodore, British Royal Air Force; Director of Personnel (AIR), 1972-   . Born May 13, 1921. Attended Central Flying School, 1948; Staff College Course, 1955. Joined the Royal Air Force in 1939. Served in the Middle East Air Force and United Kingdom Coastal Command in WW II. Headquarters Staff, Bomber Command, 1961-63; Headquarters Staff, RAF, Germany, 1963-64; Officer Commanding, RAF, Lyneham, 1965-67; Headquarters Staff, RAF, Germany, 1968-69; Air Officer Commanding and Commandant, Central Flying School, 1970-72. CB; CBE; AFC and Bar. Promoted to Group Captain, 1963; Air Commodore, 1968.

Heckman, Albert A. Rear Admiral, United States Coast Guard; Commander, 9th Coast Guard District, Cleveland, Ohio, 1972-   . Born August 29, 1918, Reading, Pennsylvania. Wyomissing Polytechnic Institute, Pennsylvania; US Coast Guard Academy, 1939-42; Service School Command, Great Lakes Naval Training Center, 1950-51; National War College, 1965-66; George Washington University, MA Degree, International Affairs, 1967. Commissioned Ensign, 1942. Served in Atlantic and Pacific Theaters, WW II. Chief Director, National Activities, US Coast Guard Auxiliary, and Chief, Auxiliary Division, Coast Guard Headquarters, 1964-65; Chief, Public Information Division, Headquarters US Coast Guard, 1966-67; Deputy Chief, Office of Public and International Affairs, Headquarters, US Coast Guard, 1967-70; Inspector

General, US Coast Guard, 1970-72. Coast Guard and Army Commendation Medals; and other medals and citations. Promoted to Captain, July 1, 1964; Rear Admiral, July 1, 1970.

Hedlund, Earl C. Lieutenant General, United States Air Force; United States Representative to Permanent Military Deputies Group, Central Treaty Organization (CENTO), and Chief, US Element, CENTO, Ankara, Turkey, 1971-   . Born July 16, 1916, in Valparaiso, Nebraska. University of Nebraska, Lincoln, Nebraska, BS, 1938; University of Illinois, Urbana, Illinois, MS, Agriculture-Economics, 1939, PhD, 1948; Army Air Corps Flying Schools, 1942; Naval War College, 1952-53. Commissioned Second Lieutenant, USAR, 1938; received pilot wings, 1942. Served in the Pacific and European theaters, WW II, POW; Korean War. Director, Transportation, Deputy Chief of Staff, Materiel, Headquarters USAF, 1956-61; Deputy Commander, Ogden Air Materiel Area, Air Force Logistics Command (AFLC), 1961-63; Commander, Warner Robins Air Materiel Area, AFLC, 1963-66; Deputy Director, Defense Supply Agency, Department of Defense, 1966-67; Director, Defense Supply Agency, 1967-71. Distinguished Service Cross; Distinguished Service Medal; Legion of Merit with one Oak Leaf Cluster; Distinguished Flying Cross with one Oak Leaf Cluster; and other US and foreign medals and awards. Promoted to Brigadier General, June 1, 1960; Major General, August 1, 1963; Lieutenant General, July 1, 1967.

Heffner, Grover Chester. Rear Admiral, Supply Corps, United States Navy; Commander, Defense Construction Supply Center, Columbus, Ohio, 1970-   . Born March 25, 1919, Seattle, Washington. University of Washington, Seattle, BS, 1940; Naval Finance Supply School, 1940-41; Stanford University, Graduate School of Business, MBA, 1950; National War College, 1963-64. Commissioned Ensign, US Naval Reserve, 1940; transferred to Supply Corps, US Navy, 1940. Served in the Pacific Theater, WW II. Commander, Naval Supply Center, Long Beach, California, 1964-66; Inspector General, Defense Supply Agency, Cameron Station, Alexandria, Virginia, 1966-67; Commander, Defense Industrial Supply Center, Philadelphia, Pennsylvania, 1967-70. Distinguished Service Medal; and other medals and awards. Promoted to Rear Admiral, August 1, 1967.

Heiser, Rolland Valentine. Major General, United States Army; Director of Plans, Office of the Deputy Chief of Staff for Military Operations, US Army, 1973-   . Born April 25, 1925, in Columbus, Ohio. Attended US Military Academy; Ground General School; Armored School, Basic and Advanced Courses; Command and General Staff College; Naval War College, 1964-65; George Washington University, MS, International Affairs. Commissioned Second Lieutenant, January 1944. Served in WW II; Vietnam War. Senior Advisor, Vietnam National Defense College, Training Directorate, US Military Assistance Command, Vietnam, 1967-68; Commanding Officer, 3d Armored Division Support Command, US Army, Europe,

1968-69; Commanding Officer, 14th Armored Cavalry, US Army, Europe, 1969; Assistant Division Commander, 3d Armored Division, US Army, Europe, 1969-70; Deputy Assistant Chief of Staff for Operations, J-3, US Military Assistance Command, Vietnam, 1970-72; Assistant Division Commander, 9th Infantry Division, Fort Lewis, Washington, 1972-73. Distinguished Service Medal; Legion of Merit with two Oak Leaf Clusters; Distinguished Flying Cross; Bronze Star Medal; and other medals and awards. Promoted to Brigadier General July 3, 1970; Major General July 14, 1973.

Helske, Esko. Rear Admiral, Medical Corps, Navy of Finland; Surgeon General, Finnish Defense Forces, 1967-   . Born March 27, 1914, Turku, Finland. Medical student, Heidelberg University, Germany, 1939; University of Helsinki, MD, 1942; Specialist in Internal Medicine, 1948. Hospital Physician, Deaconess Institute, Helsinki, 1945-47; Assistant Physician, Helsinki General Hospital, 1947-50; Chief, Medical Section, Finnish Defense Forces, 1966-67. Cross of Freedom, 4th Class; Cross of Freedom, 3d Class; Commander's Order of the Finnish Lion, 1st Class; and other medals and awards. Promoted to Rear Admiral, July 9, 1967.

Hendry, Augustus Mallory, Jr. Major General, United States Air Force; Vice Commander, Fifth Air Force, Fuchu Air Station, Japan, 1971-   . Born February 10, 1918, in Atlanta, Georgia. Oglethorpe University, Atlanta, Georgia, 1937-41; US Army Air Corps Flying School, 1941-42; Air Command and Staff School, 1951-52. Commissioned Second Lieutenant, Army Air Corps, 1942. Served in the China-Burma-India Theater, WW II; Vietnam War. Deputy Chief of Staff, Military Assistance Command, Vietnam, 1966-67; Commander, 836th Air Division, 1967-69; Deputy Chief of Staff, Plans, Headquarters Tactical Air Command, 1969-70; Commander, Ninth Air Force, 1970-71. Distinguished Service Medal; Legion of Merit with one Oak Leaf Cluster; Distinguished Flying Cross; and other medals and awards. Promoted to Major General, August 1, 1969.

Henize, Karl G. United States; NASA Scientist-Astronaut. Born October 17, 1926, Cincinnati, Ohio. University of Virginia, BA, Mathematics, 1947; MA, Astronomy, 1948; University of Michigan, PhD, Astronomy, 1954; US Navy V-12, Officer Training Program, 1944-46; NASA Jet Pilot Training Program. Observer for the University of Michigan Observatory, 1948-51, in Union of South Africa; Carnegie Post-doctoral Fellow, Mount Wilson Observatory, 1954-56; Senior Astronomer, Smithsonian Astrophysical Observatory, 1956-59; Associate Professor, Department of Astronomy, Northwestern University, 1959-64; Professor, 1964-67. NASA experience: Member, Support Crew, Apollo 15. NASA Group Achievement Award; Robert Gordon Memorial Award.

Henke, Eugenio. Admiral, Italian Navy; Chief of Defense Staff, 1972-   . Born November 15, 1909, in Genova. Attended Italian Naval Academy. Combat duty in WW II.

Commanding Officer, 4th Naval District, 1965-66; Head, Defense Intelligence, 1966-70; Commander in Chief, Italian Fleet, 1970-72. Two Silver Medals; six Bronze Medals; Cross for Military Gallantry; Cross for War Merit; and other medals and awards. Promoted to Rear Admiral, 1964; Vice Admiral, 1968; Admiral, 1972.

Hennessey, John Joseph. Major General, United States Army; Commandant, US Army Command and General Staff College, and Commanding General, Fort Leavenworth, Kansas, 1971-   . Born August 20, 1921, Chicago, Illinois. US Military Academy; The Infantry School, Basic and Advanced Courses; US Army Command and General Staff College; US Army War College. Commissioned Second Lieutenant, 1944. Served in WW II and Vietnam War. Commanding Officer, 1st Brigade, 1st Cavalry Division, (Airmobile), US Army, Vietnam, 1966; Chief, Troop Operations Division, Operations Directorate, Office, Deputy Chief of Staff for Military Operations, US Army, Washington, D.C. 1966-67; Deputy Director, Operations (readiness), Office, Deputy Chief of Staff for Military Operations, US Army, Washington, D.C., 1967-69; Assistant Division Commander, 82d Airborne Division, Fort Bragg, North Carolina, 1969; Commanding General, 101st Airborne Division (Airmobile), US Army, Vietnam, 1969-71. Distinguished Service Medal; Legion of Merit with Oak Leaf Cluster; Bronze Star Medal with three Oak Leaf Clusters; and other medals and awards. Promoted to Brigadier General, November 1, 1967; Major General, August 1, 1970.

Henning, Geraldo Azevedo. Fleet Admiral, Brazilian Navy; Director General of Naval Personnel. Born December 16, 1917, in Rio de Janeiro. Attended Naval School; Submarine School; Naval War College; Senior War College; Naval Nuclear Propulsion Course, US Navy. Commissioned Guarda-Marinha, December 13, 1934. Combat duty in World War II. Recent duty includes: Commanding Officer, *Laurindo Pitta*, *Aspirante Nascimento*, Submarine Flotilla; Division of Hydrography and Navigation; Inter-American Defense Board; Deputy Chief of the Navy General Staff; Naval Commandant of Brasilia; Commandant, 2d Naval District; Commandant, 1st Naval District. Serviço de Guerra with two stars; Força Naval do Nordeste; Campanha no Atlantico Sul; Medalha de Serviça Militar de Ouro; Ordem do Merito Naval, Grau de Comendador; Medalha do Merito Tamandaré; Medalha do Pacificador; other medals and awards from Brazil and other nations. Promoted to Rear Admiral, September 6, 1966; Vice Admiral, April 29, 1969; Fleet Admiral, March 31, 1973.

Hennock, Keith Selwyn. Air Vice-Marshal, Royal Australian Air Force; Air Member for Personnel, 1972-   . Born February 8, 1918, in Young, NSW. Staff College, 1944; Imperial Defence College, 1963. Commissioned in 1938. Served in the European Theater, WW II. Officer Commanding, 82 Bomber Wing, Amberley, 1960-62; Director General, Plans and Policy, RAAF, 1964-66; Officer Commanding, RAAF Base, Richmond, 1967; Air Officer Commanding, Operational Command, 1967-69;

Chief of Staff, Far East Air Force, 1969-70; Air Officer Commanding, Support Command, 1970-72. CBE; DFC.

Henry, John Bailey, Jr. Major General, United States Air Force; Chief of Staff, United States Southern Command, Canal Zone, 1969-   . Born July 15, 1916, in Christine, Texas. Southwestern University, 1936; Army Air Corps Flying School, 1938-39; Armed Forces Staff College, 1947-48; Air War College, 1954-55. Commissioned Second Lieutenant, Army Air Corps, 1939. Served in the European Theater, WW II. Deputy Inspector General, Headquarters USAF, 1963-66; Director, Secretary of the Air Force Personnel Council, 1966-67; Director, Inter-American Defense College, 1967-69. Legion of Merit with four Oak Leaf Clusters; Distinguished Flying Cross; and other US and foreign medals and awards. Promoted to Major General, August 1, 1963.

Herrera Calderon, Alvaro. General, Colombian Army; Commander of the National Army. Born December 13, 1919, Bogotá. Attended General Staff Course, War College; Advanced Cavalry Course (USA); Military Sanitation Course. Commissioned December 16, 1940. Orden de Boyacá (Gran Oficial); Orden Aeronáutico Antonio Ricaurte (Gran Oficial); Orden Naval Almirante Padilla (Gran Oficial); Orden al Mérito Militar Antonio Nariño (Gran Oficial); Orden al Mérito Militar José Maria Cordoba (Gran Oficial); and other medals and awards, Colombian and from other nations. Promoted to Brigadier General, December 16, 1965; Major General, December 16, 1968; General, December 16, 1971.

Herring, John Henry, Jr. Major General, United States Air Force; Commander, 839th Air Division, 1971-   . Born May 6, 1920, in Trenton, New Jersey. Casey Jones School of Aeronautics; Army Air Corps Flying School, 1941-42; Air Tactical School, 1948; Air Command and Staff School, 1949; Air War College, 1957-58. Commissioned Second Lieutenant, US Army Air Corps, 1942. Served in the Mediterranean Theater, WW II; Korean War; Vietnam War. Deputy Director, General Purpose and Airlift Studies, Directorate of Studies and Analysis, Headquarters USAF, 1965-66; Deputy Assistant Chief of Staff, Studies and Analysis, 1966-68; Commander, 438th Military Airlift Wing, 1968-69; Commander, 834th Air Division, Vietnam, 1969-71. Distinguished Service Medal; Legion of Merit with two Oak Leaf Clusters; Distinguished Flying Cross; and other US and foreign medals and awards. Promoted to Major General, February 26, 1971.

Heward, Sir Anthony (Wilkinson). Air Marshal, British Royal Air Force; Air Officer Commanding in Chief, No. 18 Group (Maritime), 1972-   . Attended Imperial Defence College, 1962. Served in Europe in WW II. Director of Operations (Bomber and Reconnaissance), Ministry of Defence, RAF, 1963-66; Senior Air Staff Officer, RAF, Germany, 1966-68; Air Officer in Charge of Administration, Headquarters, RAF Air Support Command, Upavon, Wiltshire, 1968-70; Chief of Staff, Headquarters, RAF Strike Command, High Wycombe, 1970-72. KCB; OBE; DFC; AFC. Promoted to Group Captain, 1957; Air Commodore, 1963.

Heyworth, Lawrence, Jr. Rear Admiral, United States Navy; Deputy Chief of Staff for Military Assistance, Logistics and Administration, Commander in Chief, Pacific, 1971-   . Born February 10, 1921, in Chicago, Illinois. University of Chicago, 1938-39; US Naval Academy, 1939-42; Submarine School, 1942; Flight Training Course, 1946-47; Naval Air Test Pilot School, 1950; Naval War College, Naval Warfare Course, 1957-58. Commissioned Ensign, US Navy, 1942; designated Naval Aviator, 1947. Served in the Pacific Theater, WW II. Commanding Officer USS *Pawcatuck*, 1963-64; Commanding Officer USS *America*, 1964-66; Executive Assistant and Senior Aide to Vice Chief of Naval Operations, 1966-67; Commandant of Midshipmen, US Naval Academy, 1967-69; Commander of Fleet Air, Jacksonville, Florida, 1969-71. Legion of Merit; Bronze Star Medal with Combat "V" and Gold Star; Navy Commendation Medal with Combat "V"; and other medals and awards. Promoted to Rear Admiral, July 1, 1969.

Hieu, Tran. Senior Colonel, People's Army of Vietnam; Deputy Chief, People's Supreme Procurate, 1960-   . Member of Indochina Communist Party, 1932; Chief of Central Military Intelligence Service, 1953; Member, Hanoi Party Committee, 1968. Promoted to Senior Colonel, 1963.

Higgins, Hugh Richard. Major General, United States Army; Commanding General, US Army Mobility Equipment Command, St. Louis, Missouri, 1972-   . Born February 16, 1919, Columbus, Ohio. Ohio State University, BS Degree, Business Administration; The Artillery School, Basic Course; The Quartermaster School, Advanced Course; US Army Command and General Staff College; Armed Forces Staff College; Industrial College of the Armed Forces; University of Michigan, MBA Degree, Business Administration. Commissioned Second Lieutenant, US Army Reserve, 1942. Served in WW II. Deputy Chief of Staff, Comptroller, Continental Army Command, Fort Monroe, Virginia, 1968-70; Deputy Chief of Staff, Logistics, Continental Army Command, Fort Monroe, Virginia, 1970-71; Director, Distribution and Transportation, later Director of Supply, US Army Materiel Command, Washington, D.C., 1971-72. Silver Star with Oak Leaf Cluster; Legion of Merit with two Oak Leaf Clusters; and other medals and awards. Promoted to Brigadier General, September 1, 1969; Major General, August 1, 1971.

Hightower, John Milton. Major General, United States Army; Commanding General, Fort Hamilton, New York, 1972-   . Born July 29, 1916, Coleman, Texas. New Mexico College of Agriculture and Mechanics, BA Degree, Social Science; The Infantry School, Advanced Course; US Army Command and General Staff College; US Army War College. Commissioned Second Lieutenant, US Army Reserve, 1940. Served in WW II. Deputy Director, Special State-Defense Study Group, Organization, Joint Chiefs of Staff, Washington, D.C., 1965; Commanding General, US Army Training Center, Infantry, and Fort Dix, New Jersey, 1966-67; Deputy Chief, Office of Reserve Components, US Army, Washington, D.C., 1968-69; Chief, Joint US Military

Advisory Group, Greece, 1969-72. Distinguished Service Cross; Silver Star with two Oak Leaf Clusters; Legion of Merit with three Oak Leaf Clusters; Bronze Star Medal with Oak Leaf Cluster; and other medals and awards. Promoted to Brigadier General, October 1, 1963; Major General, May 1, 1966.

Hildreth, James Bertram. Rear Admiral, United States Navy; Deputy Director for Plans, Requirements and Technology, Defense Mapping Agency, 1972-   . Born July 19, 1920, in Ukiah, California. University of California, Berkeley, BS, Commerce, 1936-40; Chemical Warfare School, 1941; General Line School, 1946-47; Armed Forces Staff College, 1956-57; Naval War College, Senior Course, 1960-61. Commissioned Ensign, US Naval Reserve, 1940; transferred to US Navy, 1943. Served in the Pacific Theater, WW II; Korean War. Commander, Destroyer Division SEVENTY-TWO, 1961-62; Naval Aide to the Secretary of the Navy, 1962-64; Commanding Officer USS *Springfield* (CLG-7), 1964-65; Operations and Readiness Officer, 1965-67, and Assistant Chief of Staff, Operations, Commander in Chief, Atlantic Fleet, 1967-68; Commander US Naval Base, Guantanamo Bay, Cuba, 1968-70; Commander Cruiser-Destroyer Flotilla FOUR, 1970-72, and Commander Cruiser-Destroyer Flotilla EIGHT, 1971-72. Legion of Merit with Gold Star; Bronze Star Medal with Gold Star and Combat "V"; and other medals and awards. Promoted to Rear Admiral, March 1, 1969.

Hill, Clarence Arthur, Jr. Rear Admiral, United States Navy; Assistant Deputy Chief of Naval Operations (Manpower), 1972-   . Born October 18, 1920, Short Hills, New Jersey. Stevens Institute of Technology, 1939-40; US Naval Academy, 1940-43; Flight Training Course, 1946-47; Rensselaer Polytechnic Institute, MS, Management Engineering, 1956-57; Naval War College, 1961-62; Defense Language Institute, 1968-69. Commissioned Ensign, US Navy, 1943; designated Naval Aviator, 1947. Served in the Pacific Theater, WW II; Korean War. Commanding Officer USS *Wrangell* (AE-12), 1964-65; Manpower Analyst, Office of the Assistant Secretary of Defense, 1965-67; Commanding Officer USS *Independence* (CVA-62), 1967-68; Chief of Navy Section, US Military Group, Brazil, 1969-72. Two Bronze Star Medals; and other medals and awards. Promoted to Rear Admiral, 1969.

Hill, Homer Spurgeon. Major General, United States Marine Corps; Commanding General, 3d Marine Aircraft Wing, 1972-   . Born July 21, 1919, Winnsboro, Texas. Texas Agricultural and Mechanical College, BA, 1940; Flight Training Course, 1942; Aviation Ground Officers School, 1945; Amphibious Warfare School, Senior Course, Quantico, 1955; National War College, 1964-65. Commissioned Second Lieutenant, USMCR, Naval Aviator, 1942; transferred to USMC, 1946. Served in South Pacific Theater, WW II; Korean War; Vietnam War. Assistant Wing Commander, 2d Marine Aircraft Wing, 1967-68; Assistant Wing Commander, 1st Marine Aircraft Wing, Vietnam, 1968-69; Deputy Chief, then Chief of Staff (Air),

Headquarters, Marine Corps, 1969-72. Legion of Merit with Gold Star; Distinguished Service Medal; two Distinguished Flying Crosses; seven Air Medals; and other medals and awards. Promoted to Brigadier General, July 1, 1967; Major General, August 13, 1970.

Hill, James A. Major General, United States Air Force; Director, Aerospace Programs, Deputy Chief of Staff, Programs and Resources, Headquarters United States Air Force, 1971-   . Born October 22, 1923, in Lancaster, Ohio. Ohio State University, 1942; Army Air Corps Flying School, 1943-44; Air War College, 1960-61. Commissioned Second Lieutenant, US Army Air Corps, 1944. Served in the European Theater, WW II. Deputy Commander, Operations, 61st Military Airlift Wing, Hawaii, 1965-66; Director of Current Operations, and later Assistant Deputy Chief of Staff, Operations, Headquarters Military Airlift Command, 1966-68; Commander, 60th Military Airlift Wing, 1968-70; Deputy Chief of Staff, Operations, Military Airlift Command, 1970-71; Deputy Director, Aerospace Programs, Deputy Chief of Staff, Programs and Resources, Headquarters USAF, 1971. Legion of Merit with one Oak Leaf Cluster; Distinguished Flying Cross with one Oak Leaf Cluster; and other medals and awards. Promoted to Major General, August 1, 1971.

Hill, James E. Major General, United States Air Force; Commander, Third Air Force, United States Air Force, Europe, England, 1972-   . Born October 1, 1921, Stillwater, Oklahoma. Oklahoma State University; University of Oklahoma; Army Air Corps Flying School, 1942-43; Royal Air Force Flying College, England, 1953; Industrial College of the Armed Forces, 1963-64; University of Maryland, BS, Business Administration, 1964. Commissioned Second Lieutenant, US Army Air Corps, 1943. Served in the European Theater, WW II; Korean War. Commander, 3615th Pilot Training Wing, 1966-67; Commander, 40th Air Division, 1967-68; Commander, 825th Strategic Aerospace Division, 1968-70; Commander, 42nd Air Division, 1970-71; Deputy Assistant to the Secretary of Defense (Atomic Energy), Office of the Secretary of Defense, 1971-72. Distinguished Service Cross; Silver Star; Legion of Merit with two Oak Leaf Clusters; Distinguished Flying Cross with three Oak Leaf Clusters; and other medals and awards. Promoted to Major General, February 28, 1972.

Hill, L. Gordon, Jr. Major General, United States Army; Chief of Public Information, Office of the Secretary of the Army, and Chief of Information, Office of the Chief of Staff, US Army, 1973-   . Born September 15, 1922, in Orangeburg, South Carolina. Attended University of Wisconsin, BS, Journalism; Artillery School, Advanced Course; Command and General Staff College; Industrial College of the Armed Forces, 1966-67; George Washington University, MS, Business Administration. Commissioned Second Lieutenant, July 23, 1943. Served in WW II and the Vietnam War. Commanding Officer, 25th Infantry Division Artillery, US Army, Pacific-Vietnam, 1968-69; Chief of Information, US Military Assistance Command, Vietnam,

1969; Special Assistant for Southeast Asia, then Director of Defense Information, Office of the Assistant Secretary of Defense (Public Affairs), 1969-71; Senior Public Affairs Officer, US Military Assistance Command, Vietnam, 1971; Director of Defense Information, Office of the Assistant Secretary of Defense (Public Affairs), 1971-73. Legion of Merit with two Oak Leaf Clusters; Air Medal (5 awards); and other medals and awards.

Hill-Norton, Sir Peter (John). Admiral of the Fleet, British Royal Navy; Chief of the Defence Staff, 1971-   . Born February 8, 1915. Attended Royal Naval College, Dartmouth. Commissioned in 1936. Served in Arctic Convoys and NW Approaches in WW II. Commander, HMS *Ark Royal*, 1959-61; Assistant Chief of Naval Staff, 1962-64; Flag Officer, Second in Command, Far East Fleet, 1964-66; Deputy Chief of the Defence Staff (Personnel and Logistics), 1966; Second Sea Lord and Chief of Naval Personnel, 1967; Vice-Chief of Naval Staff, 1967-68; Commander in Chief, Far East, 1969-70; Chief of the Naval Staff and First Sea Lord, 1970-71. GCB.

Hinh, Nguyen Duy. Brigadier General, Army of the Republic of South Vietnam; Commander 3d Infantry Division.

Hiranyasthiti, Chote. General, Royal Thai Army. Assistant Commander in Chief, Royal Thai Army.

Hirschy, Pierre. Lieutenant General, Swiss Army; Chief of Training and Education. Born in 1913. Promoted to Lieutenant General, 1966.

Hoa, Le Quang. Major General, People's Army of Vietnam; Deputy Chief, General Political Directorate, People's Army of Vietnam, 1963-   . Born in 1918 in Haiphong. Imprisoned by French, 1941; Editor in Chief, *Quan Goi Nhan Dan*, 1961; Member of Committee to Investigate War Crimes of US Imperialists in South, 1966.

Hoad, Norman Edward. Air Commodore, British Royal Air Force; Director, Defence Policy (A), 1972-   . Born July 28, 1923. Brighton Pilot Training Course, South Rhodesia, 1941; Staff College, 1956; Royal Air Force Flying College, 1960; Joint Services Staff College, 1963; Imperial Defence College, 1966. Joined the Royal Air Force in 1941. Served in European Theater in WW II; POW in Germany. Officer Commanding, 216 Squadron, 1960-62; Group Captain, Ministry of Defence, 1963-65; Station Commander, RAF, Lyneham, 1967; Station Commander, RAF Abingdon, 1968. Defence and Air Attache, British Embassy, Paris, France, 1969-72. CVO; CBE; AFC and Bar, and other medals and awards. Group Captain, 1963. Member of British Institute of Management.

Hoban, Richard M. Lieutenant General, United States Air Force; Vice Commander, Air Force Logistics Command, 1972-   . Born March 29, 1922, in St. Louis Missouri. Army Air Force Flying School, 1942-43. Commissioned Second Lieutenant, US Army Air Corps, 1943. Served in

the Korean War; Vietnam War. Inspector General, Fifteenth Air Force, 1965-66; Commander, 5th Bombardment Wing, 1966-67; Commander, 410th Bombardment Wing, 1967-68; Commander, 4258th Stragegit Wing, Thailand, 1968-69; Vice Commander, San Antonio Air Materiel Area, 1969-70; Commander, 4258th Strategic Wing, Thailand, 1968-69; Utah, 1970-72. Distinguished Service Medal; Legion of Merit; Air Medal with six Oak Leaf Clusters; and other medals and awards. Promoted to Major General, August 1, 1970; Lieutenant General, 1973.

Hod, Mordechai. Major General, Israeli Air Force, 1973.

Hodges, Sir Lewis (Macdonald). Air Chief Marshal, British Royal Air Force; Air Member for Personnel, Ministry of Defence, 1970-   . Born March 1, 1918. Attended Royal Air Force College, Cranwell; Imperial Defence College. Commissioned in 1938. Served in Bomber Command and South East Asia in WW II; Palestine, 1945-47. Air Officer in Charge of Administration, Middle East Command, Aden, 1961-63; SHAPE, 1964-65; Assistant Chief of Air Staff (Operations), 1965-68; Air Officer Commanding-in-Chief, RAF Air Support Command, 1968-70. KCB; CBE; DSO and Bar; DFC and Bar; ADC; Légion d'Honneur (France); Croix de Guerre (France); and other medals and awards.

Hodgkinson, Sir (William) Derek. Air Marshal, British Royal Air Force; Air Officer Commanding-in-Chief, Near East Air Force, Commander British Forces Near East, and Administrator of the Sovereign Base Area, Cyprus, 1970-   . Born December 27, 1917. Attended RAF Staff College, 1951; Imperial Defence College, 1964. Commissioned in 1937. Served in WW II; shot down in 1942; POW 1942-45. Staff of Chief of Defence Staff, 1961-63; Commandant, Royal Air Force Staff College, Andover, 1965; Assistant Chief of the Air Staff for Operational Requirements, 1966-68; Senior Air Staff Officer, RAF Training Command, 1969-70. KCB; CEB; DFC; AFC.

Hodson, Kenneth Joe. Major General, United States Army; Chief Judge, US Court of Military Review, US Army Judiciary, Washington, D.C., 1971-   . Born April 27, 1913, Crestline, Kansas. University of Kansas, AB Degree, Political Science; University of Kansas, LLB Degree; Judge Advocate General's School; US Army Command and General Staff College; US Army War College. Commissioned Second Lieutenant, US Army Reserve, 1934. Assistant Judge Advocate General for Military Justice, US Army, Washington, D.C., 1962-67; The Judge Advocate General, Office, The Judge Advocate General, US Army, Washington, D.C., 1967-71. Distinguished Service Medal; Legion of Merit; and other medals and awards. Promoted to Brigadier General, September 1, 1962; Major General, July 1, 1967.

Hoffman, Carl W. Major General, United States Marine Corps; Deputy Director, Personnel, Headquarters, United States Marine Corps, 1972-   . Born December 24, 1919, Omaha, Nebraska. Drake University, BA; George

Washington University, MA, International Affairs; Marine Corps Officers Basic School, 1942; Infantry School, Fort Benning, Georgia; Armed Forces Staff College, 1958; Army War College, 1960-61. Commissioned Second Lieutenant, USMCR, 1942. Served in Pacific Theater, WW II; Vietnam War. Assistant Head, Policy Analysis Division, Headquarters Marine Corps, then Military Secretary to Commandant, Marine Corps, 1965-67; Assistant Chief of Staff, G-2, Headquarters, Marine Corps, 1967-68; Assistant Division Commander, 3d Marine Division, Vietnam, 1968; Assistant Chief of Staff, G-3, III Marine Amphibious Force, Vietnam, 1968-69; Commanding General, Force Troops, Fleet Marine Force, Pacific, and Commanding General, Marine Corps Base, Twentynine Palms, 1969-71; Commanding General, Marine Corps Recruit Depot, Parris Island, South Carolina, 1971-72. Silver Star; Distinguished Service Medal; Legion of Merit with one Gold Star; and other US and foreign medals and awards. Promoted to Brigadier General, August 1967; Major General, April 23, 1971.

Hoffman, Karl Heinz. General, National People's Army, Democratic Republic of Germany; Minister of National Defense, and Deputy to Supreme Commander, Warsaw Pact Forces, 1960-   . Born November 28, 1910, in Mannheim. Attended Frunze Military College, Moscow; Comintern School, USSR; General Staff War College, USSR, 1955-57. Served in the Spanish Civil War with the International Brigade; WW II with the Soviet Armed Forces. Member of German Communist Youth Association, 1926-35; joined German Communist Party, 1930. Left Germany for USSR, 1935; returned to East Germany, 1945; Personal Assistant to First Secretary, United Socialist Party, with various positions in Ministry of the Interior, 1946-49; Deputy Minister of Interior and Chief of People's Police, 1952-56; Deputy Minister of National Defense and Chief of the Main Staff, National People's Army, 1957-60. Member of Socialist Unity Party of Germany since 1946; Candidate Member, Central Committee of Socialist Unity Party, 1950-54, Member, 1954-   ; Member of People's Chamber (Parliament), 1950-   . Author of *The Military Program of the Socialist Revolution* and *The Marxist-Leninist Teaching on War and Armed Forces*. Decorations include Vaterländischer Verdienstorden. Promoted to Lieutenant General, 1956; General, 1961.

Hofi, Yitzhak. Major General, Israeli Army; Commander, Golan Heights area, 1973.

Hökmark, Anders Gösta. Major General, Swedish Royal Army; Chief of Staff, Military Command Upper Norrland, 1972-   . Attended Royal Army Staff College, 1949-51; Royal National Defense College, 1966. Commanding Officer, Armored Regiment, P 7, 1968-72. Commander of the Royal Order of the Sword; and other medals and awards. Promoted to Major General, 1972.

Holland, Ralph T. Major General, United States Air Force; Deputy Chief of Staff, Logistics, Pacific Air Forces (PACAF), Hickam Air Force Base, Hawaii, 1973-   . Born November 16, 1920, Cedartown, George. West

Georgia College, Carrolltown, Georgia, 1939-41; Advanced Flying School, 1941-42; Emory University, Emory, Georgia, BA, Business Administration, 1947; Air War College, 1958-59. Commissioned Second Lieutenant, US Army Air Corps, in March 1942. Flew B-29's in the China-Burma-India and Pacific Theaters, WW II; served in the Korean War, and Vietnam War. Deputy Commander, 3d Air Division, Strategic Air Command, Andersen Air Force Base, Guam, 1965-66; Commander, 7th Bombardment Wing, Carswell Air Force Base, Texas, 1966-67; Commander, 42d Air Division, Blytheville Air Force Base, Arkansas, 1967-68; Commander, 810th Strategic Aerospace Division, Minot Air Force Base, North Dakota, 1968-69; Vice Commander, Warner Robins Air Materiel Area, Robins Air Force Base, Georgia, 1969-71; Deputy Chief of Staff, Logistics, Headquarters Seventh Air Force, Tan Son Nhut Airfield, Vietnam, 1971-72; Deputy Commander, Seventh Air Force, Pacific Air Forces, Tan Son Nhut Airfield, Vietnam, 1972-73. Legion of Merit with two Oak Leaf Clusters; Distinguished Flying Cross with two Oak Leaf Clusters; Air Medal with four Oak Leaf Clusters; and other medals and awards. Promoted to Brigadier General, November 1, 1968; Major General, 1973.

Hollingsworth, James Francis. Major General, United States Army; Deputy Commanding General, Fifth US Army, Fort Sam Houston, Texas, 1973-   . Born March 24, 1918, Sanger, Texas. Texas Agricultural and Mechanical College, BS Degree, General Science; The Armored School, Advanced Course; US Army Command and General Staff College; US Army War College; George Washington University, MA Degree, International Affairs. Commissioned Second Lieutenant, US Army Reserve, 1940. Served in WW II and Vietnam War. Assistant Division Commander, 1st Infantry Division, US Army, Vietnam, 1966-67; Deputy Commanding General, US Army Test and Evaluation Command, Aberdeen Proving Ground, Maryland, 1967-68; Deputy Commanding General, US Army Training Center, Infantry, Fort Jackson, South Carolina, 1958; Commanding General, US Army Training Center, Infantry and Fort Jackson, South Carolina, 1969-70; Commanding General, US Army Alaska, 1970-71; Deputy Commanding General, XXIV Corps, US Army, Vietnam, 1971; Commanding General, Third Regional Assistance Command, and Senior Advisor, Military Region 3, US Military Assistance Command, Vietnam, 1971-72. Distinguished Service Cross with two Oak Leaf Clusters; Distinguished Service Medal with two Oak Leaf Clusters; Silver Star with three Oak Leaf Clusters; Distinguished Flying Cross with two Oak Leaf Clusters; Soldier's Medal; Bronze Star Medal with V Device and three Oak Leaf Clusters; and other medals and awards. Promoted to Brigadier General, December 1, 1965; Major General, October 1, 1969.

Hollins, Hubert Walter Elphinstone. Rear-Admiral, British Royal Navy; Flag Officer Gibraltar, Port Admiral Gibraltar and Commander Gibraltar and Mediterranean, 1972-   . Born June 8, 1923. Attended Royal Naval College, Dartmouth. Commissioned in 1940. Promoted to Rear-Admiral in 1972.

Hollis, Harris Whitton. Lieutenant General, United States Army; Chief, Office of Reserve Components, US Army, Washington, D.C., 1971-   . Born June 25, 1919, Chester, South Carolina. Clemson College, BS Degree, Agronomy; The Infantry School, Basic and Advanced Courses; US Army Command and General Staff College; Armed Forces Staff College; Naval War College. Commissioned Second Lieutenant, US Army Reserve, 1942. Served in WW II and Vietnam War. Director of Operations, Office, Deputy Chief of Staff for Military Operations, US Army, Washington, D.C., 1967-68; Deputy Commanding General, I Field Force, US Army, Pacific-Vietnam, 1968-69; Commanding General, 9th Infantry Division, Pacific-Vietnam, 1969; Commanding General, 25th Infantry Division, US Army, Pacific-Vietnam, 1969-70; Deputy Chief of Staff for Personnel, US Army, Europe and Seventh Army, 1970-71. Distinguished Service Medal with Oak Leaf Cluster; Legion of Merit; Distinguished Flying Cross; Bronze Star Medal; and other medals and awards. Promoted to Brigadier General, April 5, 1966; Major General, August 1, 1969; Lieutenant General, October 1, 1971.

Holloway, James Lemuel, III. Vice Admiral, United States Navy; Commander US Seventh Fleet, 1972-   . Born February 23, 1922, in Charleston, South Carolina. US Naval Academy, 1939-42; Flight Training Course; National War College, 1961-62; Nuclear Reactor Course, 1963-64. Commissioned Ensign, US Navy, 1942; designated Naval Aviator. Served in the Atlantic and Pacific Theaters, WW II; Korean War; Vietnam War. Commanding Officer USS *Salisbury Sound* (AV-13), 1962-63; Assistant to Director of Navy Program Planning, Office of the CNO, 1964-65; Commanding Officer USS *Enterprise* (CVAN-65), 1965-67; Director, Strike Warfare Division, Office of the CNO, 1968-70; Commander Carrier Division SIX, 1970-71; Deputy Commander in Chief, Atlantic, and US Atlantic Fleet, 1971-72. Distinguished Service Medal; two Legions of Merit; Distinguished Flying Cross; Bronze Star Medal with Combat "V"; Air Medal with two Gold Stars; Navy Commendation Medal with Gold Star and Combat "V"; and other US and foreign medals and awards. Promoted to Rear Admiral, 1966; Vice Admiral, February 1, 1971.

Holm, Jeanne M. Major General, United States States Air Force; Director of the Secretary of the Air Force Personnel Council, 1973-   . Born June 23, 1921, in Portland, Oregon. Lewis and Clark College, 1946-48, BA, 1956; Air Command and Staff School, 1952. Commissioned Third Officer, Women's Army Auxiliary Corps, January 1943; Inactive, 1946-48; Transferred to Air Force, 1949. Congressional Staff Officer, Director of Manpower and Organization, Headquarters, US Air Force, 1961-65; Director, Women in the Air Force (WAF), 1965-73. Legion of Merit; Distinguished Alumni Award, Lewis and Clark College, 1968; Citation of Honor, Air Force Association, 1971; Eugene Zuckert Leadership Award, Arnold Air Society, 1972. Promoted to Brigadier General, August 1, 1971; Major General, June 1, 1973.

Holm, Karl Eric. Lieutenant General, Swedish Royal Army; Commander in Chief, Military Command South, 1972-   . Attended Royal Army Staff College, 1949-51; Staff College (England), 1954; Royal National Defense College, 1959; US Air Defense School, Fort Bliss, 1968. Colonel, Defense Staff, 1964-65; Commanding Officer, Infantry Regiment I 19, 1965-66; Chief, Army Staff, 1966-72. Commander of the Royal Order of the Sword; and other medals and awards. Promoted to Lieutenant General, 1972.

Holmquist, Carl Oreal. Rear Admiral, United States Navy; Chief of Naval Research, Office of Naval Research, 1970-   , and Oceanographer of the Navy, 1972-   . Born November 18, 1919, Salt Lake City, Utah. US Naval Academy, 1939-42; Flight Training Course, 1944-46; Naval Postgraduate School, 1948-49; California Institute of Technology, MS, Aeronautical Engineering, 1951, and PhD, Aeronautics, 1953. Commissioned Ensign, US Navy, 1942; designated Naval Aviator, 1945. Served in the Pacific Theater, WW II. Commander, US Naval Missile Center, Point Mugu, California, 1964-67; Executive Director for Research and Technology, Naval Air Systems Command Headquarters, 1967-69; Deputy and Assistant Chief of Naval Research, 1969-70. Navy Commendation Medal with Gold Star; and other medals and awards. Member, Sigma XI. Promoted to Rear Admiral, June 1, 1970.

Holt, William Harvey. Major General, United States Air Force; Chief of Staff, Allied Air Forces Southern Europe (AIRSOUTH), Naples, Italy, 1972-   . Born January 24, 1919, in Raleigh, North Carolina. Army Air Corps Flying School, 1942; Air Command and Staff School, 1955-56. Commissioned in 1942. Served in the Mediterranean Theater, WW II; Korean War; Vietnam War. Commander, 355th Tactical Fighter Wing, 1965-66; Chief, Tactical Division, and other positions in the Directorate of Operations, Headquarters USAF, 1966-69; Assistant Deputy Chief of Staff, Operations, Headquarters US Air Forces, Europe, Germany, 1969-70; Inspector General, US Air Forces, Europe, 1970-72. Legion of Merit; Distinguished Flying Cross with one Oak Leaf Cluster; Meritorious Service Medal; Air Medal with 14 Oak Leaf Clusters; and other medals and awards. Promoted to Major General, September 1, 1971.

Hombs, Roger. Major General, United States Air Force; Assistant Surgeon General, Dental Services, Office of the Surgeon General, Headquarters US Air Force, 1970-   . Born November 29, 1922, Keokuk, Iowa. School of Dentistry, Washington University, DDS, 1945. Commissioned in the US Army Dental Corps, 1946; transferred to US Air Force, 1949. Command Dental Surgeon, Air Force Logistics Command, 1965-66; Command Dental Surgeon, Tactical Air Command, 1966-67; Deputy Assistant Surgeon General, Dental Services, Office of the Surgeon General, Headquarters USAF, 1967-70. Promoted to Major General, August 1, 1972.

Honegger, Ernst. Major General, Swiss Army; Commander of Signal Corps. Born in 1913.

Hongsakula, Marin. Air Chief Marshal, Royal Thai Air Force. Deputy Commander in Chief, Royal Thai Air Force.

Hooper, Edwin Bickford. Vice Admiral, United States Navy, Retired; Director of Naval History, and Curator, Department of the Navy, 1970-   . Born February 16, 1909, in Winthrop, Massachusetts. US Naval Academy, 1927-31; Naval Postgraduate School, 1938-39; Massachusetts Institute of Technology, MS, Electrical Engineering, 1940; National War College, 1952-53. Commissioned Ensign, US Navy, 1931. Served in the Atlantic and Pacific Theaters, WW II, Korean War; Vietnam War; retired, July 1, 1970; returned to active duty, August 1, 1970. Deputy Chief of Naval Operations (Development), 1965; Commander Service Force, US Pacific Fleet, 1965-67; Assistant Deputy Chief of Naval Operations (Logistics), 1967-69; Navy Member, Joint Logistic Review Board, 1969-70. Distinguished Service Medal with Gold Star; Legion of Merit; Bronze Star Medal with Combat "V"; and other medals and awards. Promoted to Vice Admiral March 5, 1969.

Hoover, John Elwood. Major General, United States Army; Deputy Commanding General, US Army Strategic Communications Command, Fort Huachuca, Arizona, 1973-   . Born April 18, 1924, in Timberville, Virginia. Attended US Military Academy; Ground General School; Signal School, Basic and Advanced Courses; Command and General Staff College; Army War College; Georgetown University, MA, International Relations. Commissioned Second Lieutenant, June 3, 2947. Served in the Vietnam War. Chief, Plans and Programs Branch, Communications-Electronics Division, J-6, US Pacific Command, Camp H.M. Smith, Hawaii, 1966-69; Commanding Officer, US Army Strategic Communications Command, Regional Communications Group, Vietnam, US Army, Pacific-Vietnam, 1969-70; Executive Officer, then Special Assistant to the Assistant Chief of Staff for Communications-Electronics, 1970-72; Director of Communications Systems, Office of the Assistant Chief of Staff for Communications-Electronics, 1972; Deputy Assistant Chief of Staff for Communications-Electronics, 1972-73. Legion of Merit with Oak Leaf Cluster; Bronze Star Medal with Oak Leaf Cluster; and other medals and awards. Promoted to Brigadier General, November 1, 1971; Major General, 1973.

Horacek, Vaclav. Lieutenant General, Army of Czechoslovakia; Chief Main Political Directorate.

Horsley, Beresford Peter Torrington. Air Marshal, British Royal Air Force; Air Officer Commanding, No. 1 (Bomber) Group, 1971-   . Born March 26, 1971. Attended Wellington College; Royal Air Force Flying School; Royal Air Force Staff College; Imperial Defence College. Joined the Royal Air Force in 1940. Served in 2d Tactical Air Force and Fighter Command in WW II. Deputy Commandant, Joint Warfare Establishment, RAF, Old Sarum, 1966-68; Assistant Chief of Air Staff (Operations), 1968-70. CBE; MVO; AFC; Croix de Guerre (France); Order of Christ (Portugal); Order of North Star (Sweden); Order of Menelik (Ethiopia).

Hoshino, Seizaburo. Vice Admiral, Japanese Self-Defense Force; Commander in Chief, Japanese Self-Defense Fleet.

Hospelhorn, Cecil Walton. Major General, United States Army; Commander, Army and Air Force Exchange Service, Dallas, Texas, 1973-   . Born January 3, 1921, in Hudson, Illinois. Attended Illinois State Normal University, BS; Quartermaster School, Advanced Course; Command and General Staff College; Army War College, 1964-65. Commissioned November 29, 1944. Served in WW II and the Vietnam War. Commanding Officer, 26th Combat Support Group, Fort Lewis, Washington, later US Army Pacific-Vietnam, 1966-67; Commanding Officer, Tuy Hoa Sub-Area Command and 26th General Support Group, US Army, Pacific-Vietnam, 1967; Director, Materiel Management, SENTINEL Materiel Support Command, US Army Materiel Command, Washington, D.C., 1968; Deputy Commander, then Commanding General, US Army SAFEGUARD Logistics Command, Huntsville, Alabama, 1968-72; Commander, European Exchange System 1972-73. Legion of Merit with three Oak Leaf Clusters; Air Medal; and other medals and awards. Promoted to Brigadier General August 1, 1971; Major General June 1, 1973.

House, David George. Major-General, British Army; Chief of Staff, Headquarters, British Army of the Rhine, 1971-   . Born August 8, 1922. Regents Park School, London. Served in Italy in WW II. Commander, 51 Gurkha Brigade, Borneo, 1965-67. CBE; MC.

Houser, William Douglas. Vice Admiral, United States Navy; Deputy Chief of Naval Operations (Air Warfare), 1972-   . Born November 11, 1921, in Atlanta, Georgia. US Naval Academy, 1938-41; Flight Training Course, 1945-46; Naval War College, Senior Course, 1958-59; Advanced Management Program, Harvard University Graduate School of Business Administration, 1963. Commissioned Ensign, US Navy, 1941; designated Naval Aviator, 1946. Served in the Pacific Theater, WW II; Korean War; Vietnam War. Military Assistant to the Deputy Secretary of Defense, 1962-63; Commanding Officer USS *Mauna Loa* (AE-8), 1964-65; Office of Secretary of Defense, 1965; Commanding Officer USS *Constellation* (CVA-64), 1966-67; Chief of Strategic Plans and Policy Division, J-5, Joint Staff Office, Joint Chiefs of Staff, 1967-68; Director of Aviation Plans and Requirements Division, Office of the CNO, 1968-70; Commander Carrier Division TWO, 1970-72. Distinguished Service Medal; Legion of Merit with three Gold Stars; Bronze Star Medal with Combat "V"; Air Medal with Gold Star; Navy Commendation Medal with Gold Star and Combat "V"; and other US and foreign medals and awards. Promoted to Vice Admiral, August 5, 1972.

Howard-Dobson, Patrick John. Major-General, British Army; Commandant, Staff College, Camberley, 1972-   .

Born August 12, 1921. King's College Choir School, Cambridge; Framlingham College; Staff College, 1950; Joint Services Staff College, 1958; Imperial Defence College, 1968. Commissioned in 1941. Served in North Africa, Burma and Europe, WW II. Commander, the Queen's Own Hussars, 1963-65; Commander, 20 Armoured Brigade, 1965-67; Chief of Staff, Far East Command, 1969-72. CB; Silver Star (USA); Virtuti Militari (Poland); and other medals and awards.

Howman, John Hartley. Minister of Foreign Affairs and Defense, Rhodesia.

Hoxha, Vehbi. Lieutenant General, Albanian Army; Deputy Chief of Staff, Albanian Army, and Deputy Minister of Defense, 1973-   .

Hsiao Chin-kuang. Senior Admiral, Navy of the People's Liberation Army, People's Republic of China; Vice Minister of National Defense, 1954, and Commander, Chinese Naval Forces, 1950-   . Born in 1904, Changsha, Hunan. Attended Communist University of the Toilers of the East, Moscow, USSR, c. 1921 - c. 1924 Whampoa Military Academy, 1924-25; Red Army Military College, Moscow, USSR, c-1928-31. Combat Duty Sino-Japanese War and the Civil War; took part in Long March. Political Commissar, 5th Red Army Corps, Ning-Tu, Kiangsi, 1931-33; Chief of Staff, Cadres Regiment of the Red Army, 1934-35; formed and commanded 29th Independent Army, Shensi, 1936-37; concurrently, Chairman, Kansu Soviet Government's Military Committee, Commander of Rear Echelon, Chief of Staff of Eighth Route Army, and Commander of Yellow River Defense, 1937; Second Deputy Commander, Joint Defense Command, Shansi-Suiyuan and Shensi-Kansu-Ninghsia Border Regions, c. 1940; Deputy Commander, Northeast Democratic Allied Army, 1946-48; Commander, North Manchurian Military Region, 1947-48; Troop Commander, 1948-49; Deputy Commander, 4th Field Army, 1949-50, during advance toward Central and South China; Commander, Hunan Military District, and Chairman, Changsha Military Control Commission, 1949; Member of National Defense Council, 1954; Deputy to National People's Congress, 1954, and Member of Standing Committee, 1965; Communist Party Member, c. 1925-   ; elected Alternate Member of CCP Central Committee, 1945, Member, 1957, 1959; Member of Tenth CCP Central Committee, 1973. Orders of August First, Independence and Freedom, and Liberation, 1st Class.

Hsiao Hua. Colonel General, People's Liberation Army, People's Republic of China. Born in 1915, Hsingkuo Hsien, Kiangsi. Joined the Red Army, 1919. Participated in anti-Japanese guerrilla warfare; took part in the Long March; fought in the Civil War. Director, Youth Section, 1st Army Corps, 1932; Political Commissar, 15th Division, 1934; Political Commissar, 2d Division, 1st Army Corps, 1935-36; Chief, Organization Section, Political Branch, 115th Division, 1937-39; Commander, West Shantung Military District, 1939-42; Director, West Shantung Administrative Office, 1939-42; Commander,

Shantung-Hopei-Honan Military Region, 1942-45; Commander, South Manchuria Field Army, 1945; Political Commissar, Liaotung Military District, 1946; Commander, Jehol-Liaoning Military Region, 1946-48; Political Commissar, 12th Army Group, 1948-49; Member of Central Committee, New Democratic Youth League, and National Committee, All-China Federation of Democratic Youth, 1949-53; Deputy Director, General Political Department, People's Revolutionary Military Council, 1949-64; Member of Board of Directors, Sino-Soviet Frienship Association, 1949-54; Director, General Cadres Department, People's Liberation Army, 1953-54, 1956; Chief, Main Political Administration, People's Liberation Army, 1964. Member of Chinese Communist Party since 1930; Member of Central Committee, CCP; Deputy to National People's Congress; Member of National Defense Council. Order of August 1; Order of Independence and Freedom; Order of Liberation. Promoted to Colonel General, 1955.

Hsieh Fu-chih. Colonel General, People's Liberation Army, People's Republic of China; Minister of Public Security, 1959-   , and Commander and Political Commissar, Public Security Forces, People's Liberation Army, 1963-   . Born 1898, Hupeh. Attended Red Army Academy. Joined the Red Army, c. 1930. Participated in anti-Japanese guerrilla warfare, 1937-45; took part in the Long March; fought in the Civil War. Political Commissar, 386th Brigade, 1938-48; Deputy Commander, Taiyueh Military District, East Shansi, 1940-42; Commandant, Taiyueh Branch, Anti-Japanese Military and Political Academy, 1942; Deputy Commander and Political Commissar, 4th Army Group, 1948; Commander, 10th Army, 3d Army Corps, 2d Field Army, 1949; Member, Chungking Military Control Commission, 1949-52; Political Commissar, East Szechwan Military District, 1949-52; Secretary, East Szechwan Regional Committee, 1949-52; Chairman, Financial and Economic Affairs Committee, East Szechwan Administrative Office, and Member, Administrative Committee, 1949-52; First Party Secretary, Yunnan Provincial Committee, 1953-59; Commander and Pollitical Commissar, Kunming Military Region, 1954-58; Commander, Yunnan Military District, 1957-59; Member National Defence Council, 1965; Chairman, Peking Municipal Revolutionary Committee, 1968; First Secretary, Provincial Party Committee, 1971. Member of Chinese Communist Party, since c. 1930; Member of Central Committee, CCP; Alternate Member of Politburo; Deputy to the National People's Congress. Order of August 1; Order of Independence and Freedom; Order of Liberation. Promoted to Colonel General, 1955.

Hsieh Tang-chung. Major General, People's Liberation Army, People's Republic of China; Chief, Cultural Division, Main Political Administration, People's Liberation Army, 1966-   . Recently Vice-Chairman, Association for Cultural Relations and Friendship with Foreign Countries; Member, Cultural Revolution Group; Member Chinese Communist Party and its Central Committee. Order of August 1 and other medals and awards.

Hsien Heng-han. Lieutenant General, People's Liberation Army, People's Republic of China; Chairman, Provincial Revolutionary Committee, Kansu, 1968-   . Participated in anti-Japanese guerrilla warfare, 1937-45. Fought in the Civil War. Political Commissar, 50th Regiment, 6th Army Group, 1934; Chairman, Sining Municipal Military Control Commission, Tsinghai, 1949; Commander, People's Liberation Army Units, Lanchow, 1957; 1st Political Commissar, Lanchow Military Region, 1958; Chief, Kansu Garrison, 1963; First Secretary, Provincial Party Committee, 1971. Member, Chinese Communist Party; Member of Central Committee, 1969; Deputy to National People's Congress. Member of Tenth CCP Central Committee, 1973; Member of the Presidium, Tenth National Party Congress, 1973. Order of Liberation.

Hsu Hsiang-ch'ien. Marshal, People's Liberation Army, People's Republic of China; Vice Chairman, Military Commission of the Chinese Communist Party Central Committee, 1967-   . Born 1902, Wu-T'ai Hsien, Shansi. Attended Whampoa Military Academy, Canton, 1924-25. Served in the Chinese Nationalist Army, 1925-27; joined the Red Army, 1927; organized and later became Chief of Staff and Commander, 4th Division, 1927-28; Deputy Commander and later Commander, 31st Division, 11th Red Army, Hupeh, 1928-30; Commander, 1st Division, 1st Red Army, 1930-31; Commander, 4th Front Red Army, 1931-37; Deputy Commander, 129th Division, and Commander, 385th Brigade, 8th Route Army, 1937-39; Commander, First Column (a guerrilla force), Shantung, 1939-c. 1941; Deputy Commander, Joint Defense Command, Yenan, 1942-46; Commandant, Anti-Japanese Military and Political Academy, 1940; Vice-Commander, People's Liberation Army Forces in the Shensi-Hopei-Shantung-Honan Border Region, 1947; Deputy Commander, North China Military Region, 1949-54; Commander and Political Commissar, 1st Army Corps, 1948-49; Chief of Staff, then Vice-Chairman, People's Revolutionary Military Council, 1949-54; Chief of Staff, People's Liberation Army, 1949-54; Vice-Chairman, National Defense Council, 1954; Communist Party Member, 1926; Member CCP Central Committee, 1945; Member CCP Politburo, 1967; Deputy to the National People's Congress, 1954; Vice Chairman of the Standing Committee, NPC, 1965; Member of Tenth CCP Central Committee, 1973; Member of the Presidium, Tenth National Party Congress, 1973. Fought in the Sino-Japanese War and the Civil War. Orders of August First, Independence and Freedom, and Liberation 1st Class.

Hsu Kuang-ta (Hsu Hao). General, People's Liberation Army, People's Republic of China. Born in 1902, in Changsha, Hunan. Studied at Whampoa Military Academy, Canton, 1925; Military College, USSR, ca. 1926. Joined the Nationalist Kwangtung Army in 1926; joined the Red Army in 1927. Participated in anti-Japanese guerrilla warfare, 1937-45; took part in the Long March; fought in Civil War. Commander, 2d Independent Brigade, 120th Division, and Commander, 2d Sub-Region, Shensi-Suiyuan Military Region, 1942; Commander, 3d Army Group,

North China, 1948; Commander, Yenmen Military District, 1943-1948; Commander, 2d Army Group, 1st Field Army, and Commander of the Armored Corps, 1st Field Army, 1949-51; Vice Minister of Defense, 1957-67. Member, National Defense Council; Member, Chinese Communist Party since 1927; Member, Central Committee CCP; Deputy of National People's Congress. Order of August 1; Order of Independence and Freedom; Order of Liberation, 1st Class. Promoted to General, 1955.

Hsu Shih-yu. Colonel General, People's Liberation Army, People's Republic of China; Vice Minister, National Defense, 1959-   , and Commander, Nanking Military Region, 1954-   . Born in 1906, Honan. Attended Anti-Japanese Military and Political Academy, c. 1937-38. Served in Sino-Japanese War and the Civil War. Active in Peasant Communist guerrilla armies in late 1920's and early 1930's in the Hupei-Honan-Anhwei Border Area; Commander, 25th Division, Ninth Army, and Deputy Commander, Fourth Area Army, Szechwan-Shensi Border Area, c. 1932-34; Commander, Cavalry Regiment, Western Szechwan and Eastern Sinkiang, c. 1935-36; Brigade Commander, Shantung, 1940; Commander, Ch'ingho Military District, 1942; Commander, Pohai Military District, and Commander, 9th Column, 1944; Commander, Coastal Defense Area, Chefoo and Weihaiwei, Shantung, 1946; Commander, East Front Army Corps, East China Field Army, 1947-48; Commander, Chiao-Tung Military District, Shantung, c. 1948; Commander, 11th Army Corps, 3d Field Army, and Shantung Military District, 1949; Member, East China Military and Administrative Committee, 1950-53; Deputy Commander, Third Field Army, 1954; Member, East China Military Area Committee, 1954; Member, National Defense Council, 1954; Deputy to National People's Congress, 1954-59; Alternate Member of CCP Central Committee, 1956-69, Member, 1969; Chariman, Kiangsu Revolutionary Committee, 1968; First Secretary, Provincial Party Committee, 1970. Member of Politburo, 1969; Member of Tenth CCP Central Committee, 1973. Member of the Presidium, Tenth National Party Congress, 1973.

Hua Shing-chuan. Lieutenant General, Army of Republic of China; Deputy Commander in Chief, Combined Service Forces, 1970-   . Born April 5, 1919, Shensi. Military Academy; Armed Forces Staff College; Command and General Staff College, USA; National War College. Served in Sino-Japanese War; Chinese Civil War. Recent positions: Commander, Matsu Garrison Area, 1957-60; Deputy Commander, 2d Field Army, 1960-64; Deputy Commander in Chief, Taiwan Garrison General Headquarters, 1964-68; Commanding General, Army Special Warfare Command, 1968-70.

Huang Chieh. General, Army of Republic of China, Strategy Adviser to the President, 1972-   . Born November 2, 1903, Hunan Province. Training: Military Academy; Army War College; National Defense College. Served in Sino-Japanese War, Chinese Civil War. Career highlights: Commander in Chief, 11th Army Group,

1943-45; Deputy Commanding General, 1st Theater Army and Garrison Forces of China-India Road, 1945; Commandant, Central Training Corps, 1945-48; Vice Minister of National Defense and Deputy Director, Changsha Pacification, 1948-49; Commanding General, 1st Army Group, and concurrently, Governor of Hunan Province and Commander in Chief, Hunan Pacification, 1949; Commanding General, Chinese Troops, Indochina, 1949-53; Commanding General, Taipei Garrison, 1953-54; Commander in Chief, Chinese Army and Commander in Chief, Taiwan Defense Command, 1954-57; Personal Chief of Staff to the President, 1957-58; Commander in Chief, Taiwan Garrison, General Headquarters, 1958-62; Governor, Taiwan Provincial Government, 1962-69; Minister of National Defense, 1969-72. Author of *Memoirs of War in Yunan*; *The Poetry of Tan Yuan; Memoirs of Indo-China*.

Huang Hsi-lin. Vice Admiral, Navy of the Republic of China; Deputy Commander in Chief, Operations.

Huang Yung-sheng. General, People's Liberation Army, People's Republic of China. Born 1906, Yungfeng, Kiangsi. Attended Red Army Military Academy. Joined the Red Army, 1928. Commander, Guard Regiment, Headquarters Red Army, 1931; Commander, 3d Regiment, 1st Division, 1st Red Army Corps, 1932; Commander, Regiment, 115th Division, 8th Route Army, 1937; Commander, 3d Military Sub-District, Shansi-Hopei-Chahar Military Region, 1937; Commander, Combat Column, People's Liberation Army, Shihchiachuang, 1947; Commander, Jehol-Liaoning Military Region, 1947; 1st Deputy Commander, Kwangsi Military District, 1949; Member, Kwangsi People's Government, 1950-52; Deputy Commander, then Commander, South China Military Region, 1951-54; Chief of Staff, South-Central Military Region, 1954; Commander, Garrison Forces, Canton and Kwangtung, 1953-55; Commander, Canton Military Region, 1955; Chief of General Staff, People's Liberation Army, 1968; Member, National Defense Council, 1954. Whereabouts since September 1971 unknown. Member, Chinese Communist Party; Member, Central Committee, CCP; Chairman, Kwantung Provincial Revolutionary Committee, 1968; Deputy to National Congress. Order of Independence and Freedom, 1st Class; Order of Liberation, and other medals and awards. Promoted to General, 1955.

Hudson, Eugene L. Major General, United States Air Force; Assistant Chief of Staff, J-2, USSAG, 1973-   . Born October 6, 1921, in Los Angeles, California. Los Angeles City College, 1940-42; Army Air Corps Flying School, 1942-43; University of Southern California, BS, Engineering, 1949; George Washington University, MS, 1963; Air War College, 1962-63. Commissioned Second Lieutenant, US Army Air Corps, 1943. Served in the Mediterranean Theater, WW II; Korean War; Vietnam War. Commander, 4000th Combat Support Group, 1963-66; Deputy Commander for Maintenance, Headquarters 68th Bombardment Wing, 1966-67; Commander, 68th Bombardment Wing, 1967-68; Commander, 42d

Bombardment Wing, 1968-70; Commander, 40th Air Division, 1970-72; Deputy Director, Intelligence, Military Assistance Command, Vietnam (MACV), 1972-73. Legion of Merit; Distinguished Flying Crosss; Bronze Star Medal; and other medals and awards. Promoted to Brigadier General, May 7, 1970; Major General, August 1, 1972.

Hudson, John B. Major General, United States Air Force; Deputy Chief of Staff, Systems, Air Force Systems Command, 1972-   . Born May 11, 1922, in Sylvester, Georgia. US Military Academy, 1940-43; Air Command and Staff College, 1954; National War College, 1959-60. Commissioned Second Lieutenant, US Army Air Corps, 1943. Served in the European Theater in WW II. Deputy Chief of Staff, Personnel, Air Force Systems Command, 1966-69; Deputy Chief of Staff, Operations, Air Force Systems Command, 1969-70; Vice Commander, Aeronautical Systems Division, 1970-72. Distinguished Service Medal; Legion of Merit with two Oak Leaf Clusters; Distinguished Flying Cross; 14 Air Medals; and other medals and awards. Promoted to Major General, May 1, 1970.

Huffman, Burnside Elijah, Jr. Major General, United States Army; Senior Army Member, Weapons Systems Evaluation Group, Office of the Secretary of Defense, Washington, D.C., 1971-   . Born January 12, 1920, Columbus, Georgia. US Military Academy; The Artillery School, Basic and Advanced Courses; US Army Command and General Staff College; US Army War College; George Washington University, MA Degree, International Affairs. Commissioned Second Lieutenant, 1941. Served in WW II and Vietnam War. Division Artillery Commander, 2d Infantry Division, Fort Benning, Georgia, 1963-64; Chief of Staff, 2d Infantry Division, Fort Benning, Georgia, 1964-65; Assistant Chief of Staff, G-3, Eighth US Army, Pacific-Korea, 1966-68; Assistant Division Commander, 82d Airborne Division, Fort Bragg, North Carolina; Commanding General, II Field Force Artillery, US Army, Pacific-Vietnam, 1969; Chief of Staff, II Field Force, US Army, Pacific-Vietnam, 1969; Senior Army Member, Military Studies and Liaison Division, Weapons Systems Evaluation Group, Office, Secretary of Defense, Washington, D.C., 1969-71. Legion of Merit with Oak Leaf Cluster; Bronze Star Medal with Oak Leaf Cluster; Air Medal; and other medals and awards. Promoted to Brigadier General, March 1, 1966; Major General, October 1, 1969.

Hughes, Carl Wilson. Major General, United States Army; Commanding General, Tripler Army Medical Center, and Surgeon, US Army, Pacific, 1971-   . Born June 29, 1914, Eminence, Missouri. University of Missouri, AB Degree, Pre-medicine; University of Tennessee, MD Degree; Army Medical Department School, Basic course. Commissioned Second Lieutenant, 1942. Chief, Department of Surgery, Letterman General Hospital, Presidio of San Francisco, California, 1964-65; Chief, Department of Surgery, General Surgeon, Walter Reed General Hospital, Walter Reed Army Medical Center, Washington, D.C., 1965-69; Commanding General, Walter Reed General Hospital, Washington, D.C., 1969-71. Legion of Merit with Oak Leaf Cluster; Bronze Star Medal; and other medals and awards. Promoted to Brigadier General, August 1, 1969; Major General, November 1, 1970.

Hughes, Frederic John. Major General, United States Army; Commanding General, US Army Medical Command, Europe and Surgeon, US Army, Europe and Seventh Army, 1970-   . Born March 21, 1914, Plainfield, New Jersey. Cornell University, BA Degree, Pre-medicine, and MD Degree; Medical Field Service School, Basic Course. Commissioned First Lieutenant, US Army Reserve, 1938. Served in WW II. Commanding General, William Beaumont General Hospital, El Paso, Texas, 1966-67; Commanding General, Walter Reed General Hospital, Washington, D.C., 1967-69; Commanding General, Letterman General Hospital, Presidio of San Francisco, California, 1969-70. Distinguished Service Medal; Legion of Merit with two Oak Leaf Clusters; and other medals and citations. Promoted to Brigadier General, May 1, 1965; Major General, August 1, 1969.

Hughes, Frederick Desmond. Air Vice-Marshal, British Royal Air Force; Senior Air Staff Officer, Near East Air Force, 1972-   . Born June 6, 1919, in Belfast. Campbell College, Belfast; Pembroke College, Cambridge, MA Degree. Joined the Royal Air Force in 1939; received permanent commission, RAF, 1946. Served in Battle of Britain, European and Mediterranean Theaters, WW II. Director of Air Staff Plans, Ministry of Defence, 1962-64; Aide-de-Camp to the Queen, 1963; Air Officer in Charge of Administration, Headquarters, Flying Training Command, RAF, 1966-68; Air Officer Commanding, No. 18 Group, RAF Coastal Command, and Air Officer, Scotland and North Ireland, 1968-70; Commandant, Royal Air Force College, Cranwell, 1970-72. CB; CBE; DSO; DFC and two Bars; AFC.

Hughes, James D. Major General, United States Air Force; Deputy Commander Seventh Air Force/Thirteenth Air Force, Udorn Royal Thai Air Force Base, Thailand, 1972-   . Born July 7, 1922, in Balmville, New York. US Military Academy, 1942-46; George Washington University, MA, International Affairs, 1966; National War College, 1965-66. Commissioned Second Lieutenant, US Army Air Corps, 1946. Served in the Korean War; Vietnam War. Vice Commander, 4525th Fighter Weapons Wing, 1966-68; Director, Safety, Headquarters US Air Force, Europe, 1968; Military Assistant to the President, 1969-72; Vice Commander, Twelfth Air Force, 1972. Distinguished Service Medal; Distinguished Flying Cross with one Oak Leaf Cluster; Bronze Star Medal; and other medals and awards. Promoted to Major General, February 1, 1972.

Hull, A. Chester. Lieutenant-General, Canadian Armed Forces; Vice Chief, Defence Staff, Canadian Armed Forces, 1972-   . Born April 1919 in Edinburgh, Scotland. Attended Royal Military College, Kingston, Ontario, 1936-39; Royal Canadian Air Force Staff College, Toronto, 1946-47. Enlisted in Cameron Highlanders, 1933; commissioned in the Royal Canadian Air Force, 1939.

Combat Duty in bombers in WW II. Chief of Staff, Air Defence Command, Air Defence Command Headquarters, St. Hubert, Quebec, 1962-67; Commander, Air Transport Command, CFB Trenton, 1967-72. Distinguished Flying Cross; Croix de Guerre with Silver Star; and other medals and awards. Promoted to Lieutenant-General, May 1, 1972.

Humphrey, Sir Andrew (Henry). Air Chief Marshal, British Royal Air Force; Air Officer Commanding-in-Chief, RAF Strike Command, and Commander United Kingdom Air Defence Region (NATO), 1971-   . Born January 10, 1921. Attended Bradfield College; Royal Air Force College, Carnwell; Imperial Defence College, 1962. Joined the Royal Air Force in 1940. Served in WW II. Station Commander, Royal Air Force, Akrotiri, Cyprus, 1959-60; Director of Defence Plans, Air Ministry of Defence, 1962-65; Air Officer Commanding, Air Forces Middle East, 1965-68; Air Member for Personnel, 1968-70. KCB; OBE; DFC; AFC and two Bars.

Hung, Le Van. Brigadier General, Army of the Republic of South Vietnam; Commander 21st Infantry Division.

Hunter, D.V. Commodore, Navy of Sri Lanka; Captain of the Navy.

Hunter, John. Surgeon Rear-Admiral (D), British Royal Navy; Director of Naval Dental Services, 1971-   . Born August 21, 1915. Attended Manchester University, LDS, 1939. Commissioned Surgeon Lieutenant (D), RNVR, 1940. Served at sea in WW II. Service ashore in the Admiralty, 1960-63; Surgeon Captain (D), Staff of Commander-in-Chief, Mediterranean, 1965-66; Staff of Commander-in-Chief, Plymouth Command, 1967-68; Fleet Dental Surgeon on Staff of Commander-in-Chief, Western Fleet, 1969-70. OBE; Queen's Honorary Dental Surgeon; Fellow of the Royal Society of Medicine.

Hupalowski, Tadeusz. Lieutenant General, Polish Army; First Deputy Chief of General Staff. Attended General Staff War College, Warsaw. Served in Polish-German War, 1944-45. Formerly First Deputy Inspector General Territorial Defense. Cross of Grunwald; Cross of Valor; Cross of Merit; and other medals and awards. Member, Polish United Workers Party.

Hüssi, Johann. Major General, Swiss Army; Commanding General, 4th Mechanized Division. Born in 1918.

Hutchin, Claire Elwood, Jr. Lieutenant General, United States Army; Commanding General, First US Army, Fort George G. Meade, Maryland, 1971-   . Born January 9, 1916, Decatur, Illinois. US Military Academy; US Army Command and General Staff College; US Army War College. Commissioned Second Lieutenant, 1938. Served in WW II. Commanding General, 4th Infantry Division and Fort Lewis, Washington, 1963-65; Deputy Chief of Staff for Plans and Operations, US Pacific Command, Camp H.M. Smith, Hawaii, 1965-67; Chief of Staff, US Pacific Command, Camp H.M. Smith, Hawaii, 1967-69;

Commanding General, V Corps, US Army, Europe, 1969-71. Distinguished Service Cross with Oak Leaf Cluster; Distinguished Service Medal; Silver Star; Legion of Merit with five Oak Leaf Clusters; Bronze Star Medal; and other medals and awards. Promoted to Brigadier General, June 1, 1960; Major General, April 1, 1962; Lieutenant General, July 1, 1967.

Huu, Chinh. Deputy Chief, Military Training Directorate, General Staff, People's Army of Vietnam, 1972-   .

Huyser, Robert E. Major General, United States Air Force; Assistant Deputy Chief of Staff, Plans and Operations, Headquarters US Air Force, 1973-   . Born June 14, 1924, in Paonia, Colorado. Ouachita College, Arkadelphia, Arkansas; Modesto College, Modesto, California; Army Air Corps Flying School, 1943-44; Air War College, 1962-63. Commissioned Second Lieutenant, US Army Air Corps, 1944. Served in the Southwest Pacific Area, WW II; Korean War. Vice Commander, 454th Bombardment Wing, 1966; Commander, 449th Bombardment Wing, 1966-68; Director, Command Control, Deputy Chief of Staff, Operations, Headquarters Strategic Air Command, 1968-70; Director, Operations Plans, and Chief, Single Integrated Operational Plan Division, Joint Strategic Target Planning Staff, Organization, Joint Chiefs of Staff, 1970-72; Director of Plans, Deputy Chief of Staff, Plans and Operations, Headquarters US Air Force, 1972-73. Distinguished Service Medal; Legion of Merit; Bronze Star Medal; and other medals and awards. Promoted to Major General, October 1, 1971.

Hyatt, Gerhardt Wilfred. Major General, United States Army, Chief of Chaplains, Washington, D.C., 1971-   . Born July 1, 1916, Melfort, Saskatchewan, Canada. Concordia Seminary, AB Degree, Theology; The Chaplain School, Advanced Course; U.S. Army Command and General Staff College; U.S. Army War College; George Washington University, MA Degree, International Affairs. Commissioned First Lieutenant, 1945. Served in Vietnam War. Director, Personnel and Ecclesiastical Relations, Office, Chief of Chaplains, U.S. Army, Washington, D.C., 1967-68; Chaplain, U.S. Military Assistance Command, Vietnam, 1968-69; Deputy Chief of Chaplains, U.S. Army, Washington, D.C., 1970-71. Legion of Merit; Bronze Star Medal; and other medals and awards. Promoted to Brigadier General, January 1, 1970; Major General, August 1, 1971.

I

Ichinomiya, Mayuki. Colonel, Japanese Self Defense Forces; Defense Attache for Air, Embassy of Japan, Washington, D.C., USA, 1972-   . Attended Military Aviation Academy, 1945; JCS College, 1966. Commissioned in 1945. Assigned to Operation Section, Air Staff Office, 1966-67; Assigned to Personnel Section, Air Staff Office, 1967-70; Assigned to Intelligence Section, Air Staff Office. 1970-72. Promoted to Colonel, July 1, 1970.

Ijesselstein, G. Lieutenant General, Royal Netherlands Army; Chief of the General Staff and Commander in Chief, Royal Netherlands Army, 1972-   . Born February 27, 1916, in Leeuwarden. Attended School for Reserve Officers (Infantry); Army Staff College. Commissioned Lieutenant in 1937. Combat duty in WW II, German Prisoner of War, 1942-45. Recent duty: Commander, 102d Quartermaster Battalion, and subsequently Commandant, Quartermaster School; Assistant Chief of Staff, G-4, Army Headquarters; Deputy Chief of Staff (Planning), 1967-69; Vice Chief of The General Staff, 1969-72. Knight in the Order of the Netherlands Lion; Officer in the Order of Orange-Nassau, Military Section; Bronze Cross for Military Valor; War Commemoration Cross; and other medals and awards. Promoted to Brigadier General, March 1, 1968; Major General, November 1, 1969; Lieutenant General, January 1, 1972.

Ileto, Rafael M. Major General, Philippine Army; Vice Chief of Staff, Armed Forces of the Philippines, 1973-   . Born October 24, 1920, at San Isidro, Nueva Ecija. Attended University of the Philippines, Mechanical Engineering, 1937-39; University of Manila, LLB Degree, 1949-53; Philippine Military Academy, Baguio, 1939-40; US Military Academy, West Point, New York, USA, 1940-43; The Infantry School, Fort Benning, Georgia, USA, 1943; US Army Command and General Staff College (USA), Mobilization Course, 1945, Regular Course, 1964-65; Strategic Intelligence Course, Camp Panopio, QC-School; The Armored School (USA), 1965. Commissioned Second Lieutenant in 1943. Served in the Pacific Theater in WW II. Zone Commander, IPC Zone, 1966-67; Deputy Chief of Staff and J-2, GHQ, 1968-69; Commanding General, Philippine Army, 1969-72. Distinguished Service Star with one Anahaw Leaf; Military Merit Medal with one Anahaw Leaf; Bronze Medal for Valor with one Oak Leaf Cluster; and other medals and awards.

Ionita, Ion. General, Army of the Socialist Republic of Romania; Minister of National Defense, 1966-   , and Alternate Member of Executive Committee of the Central Committee of the Romanian Communist Party, 1969- ,   . Born June 14, 1924, in Matasaru, Dimbovita County. Attended Romanian Military Academy; War College. Formerly Deputy Director of the Political Department of the Armed Forces; Commander, Military Air Forces; Commander, Territorial Antiaircraft Defense; Deputy Minister of Armed Forces, 1962-66. Member of Romanian Communist Party since 1945; Alternate Member, Central Committee, Romanian Communist Party, 1955, Member since 1965; Deputy to Grand National Assembly since 1961. Hero of Socialist Labor; Golden Medal "Sickle and Hammer"; and other Romanian and foreign medals and awards.

Ireland, Clare T., Jr. Major General, United States Air Force; Deputy Chief of Staff, Plans, Headquarters, Military Airlift Command (MAC), 1972-   . Born June 8, 1920, in Peoria, Illinois. US Military Academy, 1939-43; Air Command and Staff School, 1950; Army Command and General Staff School; National War College; George

Washington University, MS, 1966. Commissioned Second Lieutenant, US Army Air Corps, 1943. Served in the Mediterranean Theater, WW II. Commander, 62d Military Airlift Wing, 1967-69; Commander, 437th Military Airlift Wing, 1969-70; Vice Commander, Twenty-first Air Force, 1970-71; Deputy Chief of Staff, Operations, Military Airlift Command, 1971-72. Legion of Merit with three Oak Leaf Clusters; Distinguished Flying Cross; and other medals and awards. Promoted to Major General, July 1, 1971.

al Iriani, Muhammad. Commander of Armed Forces, Yemen Arab Republic.

Irvine, John. Major-General, British Army; Deputy Director-General of Army Medical Services, 1971-   . Born May 31, 1914. Attended Glasgow University, MB, ChB, 1940. Commissioned Second Lieutenant, Royal Army Medical Corps, in 1940. Served in Greece, Crete, North Africa, and southern Europe in WW II; Malaya, 1955-58. Deputy Director of Medical Services, Headquarters, British Army of the Rhine, 1964-69; Deputy Director of Medical Services, 1st British Corps, 1969-71. OBE; OStJ; Queen's Honorary Surgeon.

Irwin, Brian St. George. Major-General, British Army; Director General, Ordnance Survey, 1969-   . Born September 16, 1917. Royal Military Academy, Woolwich; Trinity Hall, Cambridge, MA Degree. Commissioned in the Royal Engineers, 1937. Served in Western Desert, Sicily, Italy, Greece, WW II; Cyprus. Director of Military Survey, Ministry of Defence, 1965-69. Fellow of Royal Institution of Chartered Surveyors; Fellow of Royal Geographical Society.

Irwin, James Benson. Colonel, US Air Force; NASA Astronaut, 1966-   . Born March 17, 1930, Pittsburgh, Pennsylvania. US Naval Academy, 1951; US Air Force Flight Training School; University of Michigan, MS degrees, Aeronautical Engineering and Instrumentation Engineering, 1957; Air Force Experimental Test Pilot School, 1961; Aerospace Research Pilot School, 1963. Commissioned Second Lieutenant, US Air Force, 1951. F-12 Test Force, Edwards Air Force Base; AIM-7 Project Office, Wright-Patterson Air Force Base; Chief of the Advanced Requirements Branch, Headquarters, Air Defense Command. Crew Commander, Lunar Module, LTA-8; Member, Support Crew, Apollo 10; Backup Lunar Module Pilot, Apollo 12; Lunar Module Pilot, Apollo 15, July 26-August 7, 1971. NASA Distinguished Service Medal; Air Force Distinguished Service Medal and Command Pilot Astronaut Wings; two Air Force Commendation Medals; Kitty Hawk Memorial Award, 1971; AIAA Haley Astronautics Award for 1972; Arnold Air Society's John F. Kennedy Trophy, 1972; Order of Leopold (Belgium); and other medals and awards.

Isaman, Roy Maurice. Rear Admiral, United States Navy; Commander Naval Air Test Center, Patuxent River, Maryland, 1971-   . Born May 30, 1917, in Lewiston, Idaho. Idaho State Normal School; University of Idaho; Flight Training Course, 1940-41; General Line School,

Newport, Rhode Island, 1946-47; Industrial College of the Armed Forces, 1958-59. Commissioned Ensign, US Naval Reserve, 1941; designated Naval Aviator, 1941; transferred to US Navy, 1944. Served in the Pacific Theater, WW II, Vietnam War. Commanding Officer USS *Midway* (CVA-41), 1962-63; Head, Special Weapons Plans Branch, Office of the CNO, 1963-65; Commander Patrol Force Seventh Fleet/Commander US Taiwan Patrol Force/Commander Fleet Air Wing ONE, 1965-67; Director, Strike Warfare Division, Office of the CNO, 1967-69; Commander Carrier Division SEVEN, 1969-70; Deputy Chief of Staff for Plans and Operations to Commander in Chief, US Pacific Fleet, 1970-71. Navy Cross; Legion of Merit with three Gold Stars; Air Medal; and other US and foreign medals and awards. Promoted to Rear Admiral, 1965.

Ishchenko, F. Major General, USSR Air Force; First Deputy Chief, Political Directorate, Far Eastern Military District. Served on the Soviet-German Front in WW II. Member, Communist Party of the Soviet Union.

Ivanov, B. Colonel General, USSR Army; Commander in Chief, Southern Group of Soviet Forces, Hungary, 1968-   . Served on the Soviet-German Front in WW II. Member, Communist Party of the Soviet Union.

Ivanov, B.A. Lieutenant General, USSR Frontier Troops; Commander, Western Frontier District. Served on the Soviet-German Front in WW II. Member, Communist Party of the Soviet Union.

Ivanov, M.T. Lieutenant General, USSR Army; Chief of Staff, Baltic Military District, 1967-   . Served on the Soviet-German Front in WW II. Member, Communist Party of the Soviet Union.

Ivanov, S.P. General of the Army, USSR Army; Commandant, General Staff War College. Born in 1900. Served on the Soviet-German Front in WW II. First Deputy Chief of the General Staff, until 1965; Commander, Siberian Military District. Member, Communist Party of the Soviet Union. Promoted to General of the Army, February 1968.

Ivanovskiy, Yevgeniy. General of the Army, USSR Army; Commander in Chief, Group of Soviet Forces in Germany, 1972-   . Born in 1918. Served on the Soviet-German Front in WW II. First Deputy Commander, Moscow Military District, 1966-68; Commander, Moscow Military District, 1968-72. Promoted to General of the Army, November 7, 1972. Member, Communist Party of the Soviet Union.

Ivashutin, P.I. Colonel General, USSR Army; Deputy Chief of the General Staff, Intelligence, 1966-   . Served on the Soviet-German Front in WW II. Order of Lenin; Order of Red Banner; Order of Red Star; and other orders and awards. Member, Communist Party of the Soviet Union.

J

Jack, William A. Major General, United States Air Force; Commander, San Antonio Air Materiel Area, Air Force Logistics Command (AFLC), 1972-   . Born April 16, 1921, in Pawtucket, Rhode Island. Bryant College of Business Administration, Providence, Rhode Island; Army Air Corps Flying School, 1942-43; New York University, 1947-49; Air War College, 1958-59. Commissioned in 1943. Served in the European Theater, WW II, POW. Vice Commander, Oklahoma City Air Materiel Area, 1967-68; Assistant Deputy Chief of Staff for Supply, Headquarters AFLC, 1968-69; Assistant Deputy Chief of Staff, Materiel Management, AFLC, 1969-71; Deputy Chief of Staff, Maintenance, 1971-72. Distinguished Service Medal; Legion of Merit; Distinguished Flying Cross; and other medals and awards. Promoted to Major General, March 1, 1972.

Jackson, David Henry. Rear Admiral, United States Navy; Director of Ships Material Readiness Division, Office of the CNO, 1971-   . Born June 5, 1917, in Smackover, Arkansas. Southern State College, Mongolia, Arkansas, 1935-37; US Naval Academy, 1937-41; Naval Postgraduate School, Marine Engineering (Design) Course, 1943-45; Naval War College, Naval Warfare Course, 1957-58. Commissioned Ensign, US Navy, 1941. Served in the Pacific Theater, WW II; Vietnam War. Commander Naval Ship Repair Facility, Subic Bay, Philippine Islands, 1966-68; Fleet Maintenance Officer, Staff of Commander in Chief, US Pacific Fleet, and Commander Service Force, US Pacific Fleet, 1968-71. Legion of Merit; Navy Commendation Medal; and other medals and awards. Promoted to Rear Admiral, March 1, 1969.

Jackson, Ralph Coburn. Air Vice-Marshal, British Royal Air Force; Consultant Adviser in Medicine, 1966-   . Senior Consultant to RAF, Central Medical Establishment, RAF, 1971-   ; Senior Consultant to Medical Department, Civil Aviation Authority. Born June 22, 1914. Trained at Guy's Hospital, London; qualified in medicine in 1937. Commissioned Medical Officer inthe Royal Air Force in 1938. Served in France, Russia, North Africa and Britain In WW II. Consultant in Medicine, Princess Mary's Royal Air Force Hospital, Halton, 1952-63; Royal Air Force Hospital, Wegberg, Germany, 1964-66. CB; Queen's Honorary Physician; City of London Lady Cade Medal, RCS, 1960. Member Royal College of Surgeons; Licentiate of the Royal College of Physicians; Fellow of the Royal College of Physicians; Fellow of the Royal College of Physicians (Edinburgh); Fellow of the Royal Society of Medicine.

Jackson, Sir William Godfrey Fothergill. Lieutenant-General, British Army; General Officer Commanding-in-Chief, Northern Command, 1970-   . Born August 28, 1917. Attended Royal Military Academy, Woolwich; King's College, Cambridge; Imperial Defence College, 1965. Commissioned in the Royal Engineers, 1937. Served in Norway, North Africa, Italy and the Far East in WW II. Colonel, General Staff, Minley Division, Staff College, Camberley, 1961-62; Deputy Director, Staff Duties, War Office, 1962-64; Director, Chief of Defence Staff Unison Planning Staff, 1966-68; Assistant Chief of General Staff (Operational Requirements), Ministry of Defence, 1968-70. KCB; OBE; MC and Bar. Publications; *Attack in the West*, 1953; *Seven Roads to Moscow*, 1957; *The Battle for Italy*, 1967; *Battle for Rome*, 1969; *Alexander of Tunis as a Commander*, 1971.

Jacob, J.F.R. Major General, Army of India; Chief of Staff, Eastern Command, 1972-

Jagas, Waclaw. Major General, Polish Army; commander of infantry units. Formerly Naval, Military and Air Attache, Moscow.

James, Daniel, Jr. Lieutenant General, United States Air Force; Principal Deputy Assistant Secretary of Defense (Public Affairs), 1973-   . Born February 11, 1920, in Pensacola, Florida. Tuskegee Institute, Tuskegee, Alabama, 1937-42, BS, Physical Education; Army Air Force Flying School, 1943; Air Command and Staff School, 1957. Commissioned Second Lieutenant, US Army Air Corps, 1943. Served in the Korean War; Vietnam War. Deputy Commander for Operations, and later Vice Commander, 8th Tactical Fighter Wing, Thailand, 1966-67; Vice Commander, 33d Tactical Fighter Wing, 1967-69; Commander, 7272d Fighter Training Wing, Libyan Arab Republic, 1969-70; Deputy Assistant Secretary of Defense (Public Affairs), 1970-73. Legion of Merit with one Oak Leaf Cluster; Distinguished Flying Cross with two Oak Leaf Clusters; Air Medal with 10 Oak Leaf Clusters; and other medals and awards. Phoenix Urban League Man of the Year Award, 1970; Builders of a Greater Arizona Award, 1969; Distinguished Service Achievement Award from Kappa Alpha Psi Fraternity, 1970; American Legion National Commander's Public Relations Award, 1971; Veterans of Foreign Wars Commander-in-Chief's Gold Medal Award and Citation, 1971; Honorary LLD, University of West Florida, 1971. Promoted to Major General, August 1, 1972; Lieutenant General, 1973.

Janczyszyn, Ludwik. Vice Admiral, Polish Navy; Commander in Chief, Polish Navy, 1969-   . Born in 1923. Attended Infantry Officers School, Ryazan, USSR, 1943; Polish Naval College; Naval War College, USSR. Served on Soviet-German Front, with Polish Army in the USSR, WW II. Chief, Operations, Naval Staff, 1955-61; Chief of Naval Staff, 1962-69. Promoted to Rear Admiral, July 1960; Vice Admiral, 1970. Cross of Grunwald; Cross of Merit; Cross of Valor; Red Star (USSR); and other medals and awards. Member, Polish United Workers Party.

Janes, Mervyn. Major-General, British Army; Director, Royal Artillery, 1971-   . Born October 1, 1920. Attended Staff College, 1951. Commissioned in the Royal Artillery in 1942. Served in the Middle East and Italy in WW II. Assistant Army Instructor (GSO1), Imperial

Defence College, 1961-62; Commander, 1st Regiment Royal Horse Artillery, 1963-65; Commander, Royal Artillery, British Army of the Rhine, 1965-67; DMS2, Ministry of Defence (A), 1967-70; General Officer Commanding, 5th Division, 1970-71. MBE.

Jannuzzi, Arnaldo de Negreiros. Vice Admiral, Brazilian Navy; Director General of Naval Material. Born August 30, 1916, in Rio de Janeiro. Attended Naval School; Naval War College; Special courses, US Navy Schools. Commissioned Guarda-Marinha, January 7, 1937. Combat duty in World War II. Recent duty: Commanding Officer, *Guaiba, Minas Gerais*; Commander Naval Air Force; Commandant, Training Center for Reservists and Volunteers; Commandant of the Center for Instruction of Naval Reserve Officers; Director of the Center for Naval Sports; Head of the Technical Department and later President of the Economic Commission for the Construction of Ships in Europe; Commandant, Recife Naval Base; Director, Naval College; Director of the Naval Information Center; Deputy Chief of the Navy General Staff for Logistics; Director, Marine Arsenal, Rio de Janeiro. Medalha do Serviço de Guerra with two stars; Medalha Militar de Ouro; Medalha Mérito Tamandaré; Ordem de Orange e Nassau, Gráu de Comendador; Ordem Militar de Aviz, Gráu de Official; Ordem do Mérito Naval, Gráu de Comendador; Ordem do Mérito de Aeronautico, Gráu de Comendador. Promoted to Rear Admiral, September 6, 1966; Vice Admiral, September 18, 1969.

Jarry, Pierre. Major General, French Air Force; Defense and Air Attache, Embassy of France, Washington, D.C.

Jaruzelski, Wojciech Witold. General of the Army, Polish Army; Minister of National Defense, 1968-   . Born in 1923 in Kurow, Pulawy District. Attended Officers School, 1943; Senior Infantry School, 1947; General Staff War College, 1948-51. Served in the 1st Polish Army on the Eastern Front, WW II. Commanding General, 12th Motorized Division, 1957-62; Chief, Main Political Directorate, Polish Armed Forces, 1960-62; Deputy Minister of National Defense and Chief of the General Staff, 1962-68. Member of Polish United Workers Party and its Central Committee; Deputy Member, then Member of Political Bureau; Deputy to SEYM. Order of Builders of People's Poland; Banner of Labor, First Class; Order of Polonia Restituta; Commander's Cross (Class III); Order of the Cross of Grunwald in Silver (Class III); Order of Virtuti Militari, Silver Cross (Class V); and other Polish and foreign decorations and awards. Promoted to General October 9, 1968.

Jasinski, Antoni. Major General, Polish Army; Chief of Staff, Pomeranian Military District. Attended Infantry Officers School; General Staff War College, 1949-52. Served in Polish-German War, WW II. Former Deputy Chief of General Staff. Member of Polish United Workers Party. Polonia Restituta; Cross of Grunwald; Cross of Merit; and other orders and medals. Promoted to Major General, 1966.

Jaskilka, Samuel. Major General, United States Marine Corps; Assistant Chief of Staff, G-1, Headquarters, US Marine Corps, 1972-   . Born December 15, 1919, Ansonia, Connecticut. University of Connecticut, BS, 1942; Reserve Officer Class, Marine Corps School, 1942; Sea School, Portsmouth, Virginia, 1943; Amphibious Warfare School, Junior Course, Quantico, 1947-48; Senior Course, 1957. Commissioned Second Lieutenant, USMCR, 1942; Transferred to USMC, 1943. Served Pacific Theater, WW II; Korean War; Vietnam War. Deputy Assistant Chief of Staff, Military Assistance Command, Vietnam, 1969-70; Director, Command and Staff College, Quantico, Then Deputy, Development, and Director, Development Center, Marine Corps Development and Education Command, 1970-72. Distinguished Service Medal; Silver Star Medal with Gold Star; Legion of Merit; Bronze Star Medal with Combat "V"; and other medals and awards. Promoted to Brigadier General, October 18, 1968; Major General, August, 1972.

Jaume, José Pedro. Brigadier, Uruguayan Air Force; National Director General of Airports.

Jeanmaire, Jean-Louis. Brigadier General, Swiss Army; Chief, Air Defense Division. Born in 1910.

Jedidi, Bechir Ben Mohamed Ben Sadok. Captain, Tunisian Navy; Chief of Naval Operations, Tunisian Navy, 1964-   . Attended French Naval Academy; French Naval War College; US Naval Command College. Formerly Commanding Officer, Patrol Craft *Istiqlal* (P-201); Commander, Patrol Boats and Vedettes; Acting Commander of the Navy. Order of the Republic (Officer); Order of the Republic (Commander). Promoted to Captain, April 1, 1972.

Jeffrey, Hugh Crozier. Major-General, British Army; Director of Army Pathology, and Consulting Pathologist to the Army, 1967-   . Born April 19, 1914. Attended University of Edinburgh, ChB. Commissioned in the Royal Army Medical Corps in 1938. Professor of Pathology, Royal Army Medical College, 1960-64; Deputy Director of Pathology, Far East Land Forces, 1964-67. Queen's Honorary Surgeon; Fellow of the Royal College of Physicians of Edinburgh; Fellow of the Royal College of Pathology; Diploma in Tropical Medicine and Hygiene. Joint author of *Atlas of Medical Helminthology and Protozoology*.

Jenkins, William Ambrose. Rear Admiral, United States Coast Guard; Chief, Office of Operations, 1972-   . Born November 2, 1917, Kansas City, Missouri. Kansas City Junior College, 1938; US Coast Guard Academy, 1938-41; Navy Flight Training Course, 1943-44; National War College, 1964-65. Commissioned Ensign, 1941; designated Coast Guard Aviator, 1944. Served in Pacific Theater, WW II. Chief, Law Enforcement Division, and Program Manager, Office of Operations, Headquarters, US Coast Guard, 1965-68; Deputy Chief, Office of Operations, 1968-69; Chief of Staff, 1st Coast Guard District, Boston, Massachusetts, 1969-70; Commander, 9th Coast Guard

District, Cleveland, Ohio, 1970-72. Coast Guard Commendation medal with Gold Star; and other medals and citations. Promoted to Captain, July 1, 1963; Rear Admiral, July 1, 1970.

Jennings, Hal Bruce, Jr. Lieutenant General, United States Army; The Surgeon General, U.S. Army, Washington, D.C., 1969-   . Born August 26, 1915, Seneca, Michigan. University of Toledo, BS Degree, Biology; University of Michigan, MD Degree. Commissioned First Lieutenant, U.S. Army Reserve, 1942. Served in WW II and Vietnam War. Surgeon, U.S. Army Military Assistance Command, Vietnam, 1968-69; Surgeon, U.S. Army, Vietnam, and Commanding General, 44th Medical Brigade, U.S. Army, Pacific, Vietnam, 1969; Deputy Surgeon General, U.S. Army, Washington, D.C., 1969. Distinguished Service Medal; Legion of Merit and other medals and awards. Promoted to Major General, September 1, 1968; Lieutenant General, October 1, 1969.

Jimenez, Ramon Emilio, Jr. Rear Admiral, Navy of the Dominican Republic; Secretary of State of the Dominican Armed Forces, 1971-   . Born December 10, 1926, Santiago de los Caballeros. Attended Naval Academy, 1949-51; Superior Naval Staff College, Peru; Senior Command and Staff Course, Naval War College, Newport, Rhode Island, USA. Commissioned Ensign, Dominican Navy, 1951. Naval Attache, Embassy of the Dominican Republic, London, 1962; Chief, Division of Personnel and Operations, Navy; Assistant Chief of Staff, Navy, 1964-65; Chief of Staff, Navy, 1965-71. Order of Merit of Duarte, Sanchez and Mella, in the grade of Grand Officer; Order of Naval Merit with Medal of Honor; Order of Military Merit with Blue Distinguishing Device; Order of Aerial Merit, second class, with White Distinguishing Device; Order of Police Merit; Great Cross of Peruvian Naval Merit; and other orders and awards. Promoted to Captain, 1963; Commodore, 1965; Rear Admiral, 1971.

Johannessen, Folke Hauger. Vice Admiral, Royal Norwegian Navy; Chief of Defense, 1964-   . Born December 2, 1913, in Gothenburg, Sweden. Commissioned Ensign, Royal Norwegian Navy, 1936. Combat Duty in WW II. Staff Member, NATO Atlantic Forces, 1956-58; Commanding Officer, Sjokrigsskolen, 1958-63; Chief of Staff, Forsvarsstaben, 1963-64. Promoted to Vice Admiral, 1964.

Johansen, Eivind Herbert. Major General, United States Army; Director of Supply, US Army Materiel Command, 1972-   . Born March 7, 1927, in Charleston, South Carolina. Attended Texas A&M University, BS, General Business; Quartermaster School, Basic and Advanced Courses; Command and General Staff College, 1962-63; Naval War College, 1967-68; George Washington University, MS, International Affairs. Commissioned Second Lieutenant, June 1950. Served in the Vietnam War. Member, European, African and Middle East Branch, Operations Division, J-4, Organization, Joint Chiefs of Staff, 1968-69; Commanding Officer, 593d General Support Group, US Army, Pacific-Vietnam, 1969-70; Chief of Supply Division, Office of the Deputy Chief of Staff for Logistics, US Army, Pacific-Vietnam, 1970; Special Assistant to the Assistant Deputy Chief of Staff for Logistics, then Chief of the Supply Distribution Division, the Deputy Director of Supply and Maintenance, Office of the Deputy Chief of Staff for Logistics, US Army, 1970-72. Legion of Merit with Oak Leaf Cluster; Bronze Star Medal; and other medals and awards. Promoted to Brigadier General, July 1, 1972; Major General, 1973.

Johansen, Julian Elliott. Rear Admiral, United States Coast Guard; Chief, Office of Reserve, Headquarters, US Coast Guard, 1973-   . Born March 17, 1923, Charleston, South Carolina. US Coast Guard Academy, 1941-44; Flight Training Courses, 1947-48. Commissioned Ensign, 1944. Served in Pacific Theater, WW II. Group Commander and Commander, Coast Guard Air Station, Port Angeles, Washington, 1965-68; Commander, Coast Guard Air Station, San Diego, California, and Captain of the Port of San Diego, 1968-70; Chief, Coast Guard Auxiliary Division, and Director, National Activities, Coast Guard Auxiliary, Headquarters USCG, 1970-73. Coast Guard Commendation Medal with two Gold Stars; WW II Campaign Medals and Ribbons. Promoted to Captain, November 4, 1966; Rear Admiral, July 1, 1973.

Johnson, F.S.R. Air Vice-Marshal, British Royal Air Force; Director General of Supply, Royal Air Force. 1973.

Johnson, George Marvin, Jr. Major General, United States Air Force; Deputy Chief of Staff for Plans and Operations, Air Force Logistics Command, 1972-   . Born April 1, 1918, in Fort Valley, Georgia. North Georgia College, Dahlonega, Georgia; Army Air Corps Flying School, 1941-42; Air Command and Staff School, 1950; Yale University, Japanese Language Course, 1955; Air War College, 1958-59; University of Maryland, BS; George Washington University, MA. Commissioned Second Lieutenant, US Army Air Corps Reserve, 1942. Served in the European Theater, WW II. Director of Military Assistance, Headquarters US Air Force, 1964-65; Deputy Chief of Staff for Materiel, US Air Forces, Europe, 1965-68; Commander, Oklahoma City Air Materiel Area, 1968-72. Distinguished Service Medal with one Oak Leaf Cluster; Legion of Merit; Distinguished Flying Cross; Croix de Guerre; and other medals and awards.

Johnson, Gerald W. Lieutenant General, United States Air Force; Commander, Eighth Air Force, Strategic Air Command, Andersen Air Force Base, Guam, 1971-   . Born July 10, 1919, in Owenton, Kentucky. Flight Training School, 1941-42; Command and General Staff College, 1946; Boston University, BA, 1950; National War College, 1962-63; George Washington University, 1963. Commissioned Second Lieutenant, US Army Air Corps, 1942. Commander, 95th Bombardment Wing, 1963-65; Commander, 305th Bombardment Wing, 1965-66; Commander, 825th Strategic Aerospace Division, 1966-68; Vice Commander, Second Air Force, 1968-69; Commander, 1st Strategic Aerospace Division, 1969; Deputy Chief of Staff, Operations, Headquarters, Strategic Air Command,

1969-71. Distinguished Service Cross; Distinguished Service Medal; Legion of Merit with two Oak Leaf Clusters; Distinguished Flying Cross with four Oak Leaf Clusters; Bronze Star Medal; and other US and foreign medals and awards. Promoted to Brigadier General, November 1, 1965; Major General, August 1, 1968; Lieutenant General, September 15, 1971.

Johnson, Henry Joseph. Rear Admiral, Civil Engineer Corps, United States Navy; Commanding Officer, Western Division, Naval Facilities Engineering Command, San Bruno, California, 1970-   ; and Civil Engineer, Eleventh Naval District, 1971-   . Born April 10, 1916, New York, New York. Pennsylvania State College; Brooklyn Polytechnic Institute, BCE; Pennsylvania State College, Diesel Engineering Course, 1941; Naval School, Civil Engineer Corps Officers, 1947; Armed Forces Staff College, 1959-60. Commissioned Ensign, US Naval Reserve, 1940; transferred to US Navy, 1946; Transferred to Civil Engineer Corps, US Navy, 1947. Served in the Atlantic and Pacific Theaters, WW II; Vietnam War. Officer in Charge of Construction, Marianas, 1963-64; District Public Works Officer and District Civil Engineer, Fourth Naval District, 1964-66; Deputy Commander, Pacific Division, Naval Facilities Engineering Command, and Deputy Commander, Naval Construction Battalions, Pacific Fleet, Honolulu, Hawaii, 1966-68; Deputy Commander, Pacific Division, Naval Facilities Engineering Command, Southeast Asia, and Officer in Charge of Construction, Vietnam, 1968-70. Distinguished Service Medal; Legion of Merit; and other US and foreign medals and awards. Promoted to Rear Admiral, March 1, 1969.

Johnson, J. Vice Admiral, South African Navy; Commander, Maritime Defence and Chief of the Navy.

Johnson, John Bell. Rear Admiral, United States Naval Reserve; Executive Officer, Reserve Forces Policy Board, Office of the Assistant Secretary of Defense (Manpower and Reserve Affairs), 1972-   . Born March 4, 1915, in Santa Ana, California. Los Angeles (California) City College; Redlands (California) University; Flight Training Course, 1941-42. Commissioned Ensign, US Naval Reserve, 1942; designated Naval Aviator, 1942. Served in The Atlantic and Pacific Theaters, WW II; Korean War; relieved of active duty, 1945; returned to active duty, 1949. Deputy Chief of Staff for Resources Management, Commander Naval Reserve Training Command, Omaha, Nebraska, 1967-69; Director, International Staff, Inter-American Defense Board, 1969-70; Assistant Chief of Naval Personnel for Naval Reserve, 1970-72; Assistant Deputy Chief of Naval Operations (Naval Reserve), 1972. Legion of Merit; Distinguished Flying Cross with Gold Star; Meritorious Service Medal; Air Medal with Gold Star; and other medals and awards. Promoted to Rear Admiral, July 1, 1969.

Johnson, Kenneth Lawson. Major General, United States Army; Deputy Commanding General for Reserve Forces, First US Army, Fort George G. Meade, Maryland, 1972-   . Born September 10, 1919, Portland, Oregon.

University of Maryland, BS Degree, Military Science; The Infantry School, Officers Advanced Course; US Army Command and General Staff College; US Army War College. Commissioned Second Lieutenant, US Army Reserve, 1942. Served in WW II. Assistant Division Commander, 2d Infantry Division, US Army, Pacific-Korea 1966-67; Deputy, later Director for Enlisted Personnel, Office of Personnel Operations, US Army, Washington, D.C., 1967-68; Director of Procurement and Distribution, Office, Deputy Chief of Staff for Personnel, US Army, Washington, D.C., 1968-70; Commanding General, 7th Infantry Division, US Army, Pacific-Korea, 1970; Deputy Chief of Personnel Operations, US Army, Washington, D.C., 1970-71; Chief, Office of Personnel Operations, US Army, Washington, D.C., 1971-72. Distinguished Service Medal; Silver Star; Legion of Merit with three Oak Leaf Clusters; Bronze Star Medal with V Device and Oak Leaf Cluster; and other medals and awards. Promoted to Brigadier General, April 1, 1966; Major General, August 1, 1969.

Johnson, Mobolaji Olufunso. Colonel, Nigerian Army, Military Governor of Lagos, 1967-   . Born February 9, 1936, in Lagos. Attended Hussey College, Warri; Mons Officer Cadet School; Royal Military Academy, Sandhurst, England. Joined the Nigerian Army in 1958. Deputy Adjutant and Quartermaster-General, 2d Brigade, Lagos, 1964; Second in Command 4th Battalion, Ibadan, 1964-66; Station Commander, Mid-West, 1966; Military Administrator for Lagos, 1966.

Johnson, Oris B. Major General, United States Air Force; Deputy Chief of Staff, Logistics, Headquarters Aerospace Defense Command (ADC), 1971-   . Born June 20, 1920, in Ashland, Louisiana. Louisiana State Normal College, 1935-39, BS, 1939; Army Air Corps Flying School, 1940-41; Imperial Defence College, London, England, 1960. Commissioned in the US Army Air Corps, 1941. Served in the European Theater, WW II; Korean War. Assistant Deputy Chief of Staff, United States Air Forces, Europe, 1960-63; Commander, Washington Air Defence Sector, 1963-66; Director of Operations, North American Air Defense/Continental Air Defense Command, and Commander, 9th Aerospace Division, ADC, 1966-69; Commander, 313th Air Division (PACAF), Okinawa, 1969-71. Distinguished Service Medal; Legion of Merit with three Oak Leaf Clusters; Distinguished Flying Cross; and other US and foreign medals and awards. Promoted to Major General, August 1, 1966.

Johnson, Warren D. Major General, United States Air Force; Deputy Director (Operations and Administration), Defense Nuclear Agency, Washington, D.C., 1973-   . Born September 2, 1922, Blackwell, Oklahoma. Oklahoma City University; Officer Candidate School, 1942; Army Air Corps Flying School, 1943-44. Commissioned Second Lieutenant, US Army, 1942. Commander, 380th Strategic Aerospace Wing, SAC, 1966-67; Commander, 57th Air Division, 1967-68; Director, Personnel Resources and Distribution, US Air Force Military Personnel Center, Randolph Air Force Base, Texas, 1968-69; Commander, US Forces, Azores, and Commander, 1605th Air Base Wing,

Lajes Field, Azores, 1969-71; Deputy Chief of Staff, Personnel, then Chief of Staff, Headquarters, Strategic Air Command (SAC), 1972-73; Legion of Merit with two Oak Leaf Clusters; and other medals and awards. Promoted to Major General, March 1, 1972.

Johnson, William Gentry. Major General, United States Marine Corps; Deputy Director, Logistics (Strategic Mobility), J-4, Joint Chiefs of Staff, 1971-   . Born May 29, 1920, Tyler, Texas. Tyler Junior College; Southern Methodist University; George Washington University; Chapman College; Flight Training Course, 1941-42; Amphibious Warfare School, Junior Course, Quantico, 1947; Senior Course, 1954. Commissioned Second Lieutenant, USMCR, Naval Aviator, 1942. Served in Pacific Theater, WW II; Korean War; Vietnam War. Commander, Marine Aircraft Group 36, 1st Marine Aircraft Wing, Vietnam, 1965-66; Assistant Chief of Staff, G-4 (Logistics and supply), Marine Corps Recruit Depot, San Diego, California, 1966-68; Assistant Deputy Chief of Staff (Air), Headquarters, Marine Corps, 1968-69; Commanding General, 1st Marine Aircraft Wing (rear), 1969-70; Vice Director, J-3, Office of the Joint Chiefs of Staff, 1970-71. Legion of Merit with Combat "V"; Distinguished Flying Cross (Army) with two Gold Stars; Bronze Star Medal with Combat "V"; Air Medal with four Gold Stars; and other US and foreign medals and awards. Promoted to Brigadier General, January 2, 1968; Major General, August 31, 1970.

Johnston, Means, Jr. Vice Admiral, United States Navy; Naval Inspector General, 1971-   . US Naval Academy, 1935-39; National War College; Georgetown University Law School. Commissioned Ensign, US Navy, 1939. Served as destroyer escort commander in the Atlantic Theater, WW II; commanded destroyer in Korean War. Formerly Commander Naval Base, Newport, Rhode Island, and Commandant First Naval District; Commander Cruiser-Destroyer Flotilla TEN; Chief of Legislative Affairs, Navy Department; Commander in Chief, Pacific.

Jolly, Robert Malcolm. Air Commodore, British Royal Air Force; Director, Personal Services, Ministry of Defence, 1970-   . Born August 4, 1920. Attended Skerry's College, Newcastle upon Tyne. Commissioned in 1943. CBE. Air Commodore, 1971.

Jones, David C. General, United States Air Force; Commander in Chief, United States Air Force, Europe, Wiesbaden, Germany, 1971-   . Born July 9, 1921, in Aberdeen, South Dakota. University of North Dakota; Minot State College; Flying School, 1942-43; National War College, 1959-60. Commissioned Second Lieutenant, US Army Air Corps, 1943. Served in the Korean War; Vietnam War. Commander, 33d Tactical Fighter Wing, 1965; Inspector General, Headquarters USAF, Europe, Wiesbaden, Germany, 1965-67; Chief of Staff, USAF, Europe, Wiesbaden, Germany, 1967; Deputy Chief of Staff, Plans and Operations, Headquarters USAF, Europe, Wiesbaden, Germany, 1967-69; Deputy Chief of Staff, Operations, Headquarters Seventh Air Force, Vietnam, 1969; Vice Commander, Seventh Air Force, Vietnam,

1969; Commander, Second Air Force, Barksdale Air Force Base, Louisiana, 1969-71; Vice Commander in Chief, Headquarters USAF, Europe, Wiesbaden, Germany, 1971. Distinguished Service Medal; Legion of Merit; Distinguished Flying Cross; Bronze Star Medal; and other US and foreign medals and awards. Promoted to Brigadier General, December 1, 1965; Major General, November 1, 1967; Lieutenant General, August 1, 1969; General, September 1, 1971.

Jones, David M. Major General, United States Air Force; Commander in Chief, US Air Forces, Europe, and Commander, 4th Allied Tactical Air Force, 1972-   . Born December 18, 1913, in Marshfield, Oregon. University of Arizona, 1932-36; Army Air Corps Flying School, 1937; Command and General Staff School, 1946; Armed Forces Staff College, 1948; National War College, 1955-56. Arizona National Guard, 1936-37. Commissioned Second Lieutenant, US Army Air Corps, 1937. Participated in the Doolittle Project and served in the North African Theater, WW II, POW. Vice Commander, Wright Air Development Division, 1960-61; Program Manager, GAM-87 "Skybold" at Aeronautical Systems Division, and later, Vice Commander, Systems Management, Aeronautical Systems Division, 1961-64; Deputy Chief of Staff, Systems, Headquarters Air Force Systems Command, 1964-67; Deputy Associate, Manned Space Flight, National Aeronautics and Space Administration (NASA), 1964-67; Commander, Air Force Eastern Test Range, Cape Kennedy, Florida, and Defense Manager, Manned Space Flight Support Operations, 1967-72. Legion of Merit; Distinguished Flying Cross with Oak Leaf Cluster; Air Medal; and other US and foreign medals and awards.

Jones, Frank Cox. Rear Admiral, United States Navy; Commander, Naval Ship Engineering Center, 1972-   . Born February 9, 1917, in Pittsburgh, Pennsylvania. US Naval Academy, 1934-38; Massachusetts Institute of Technology, MS, Construction and Engineering, 1940-43; George Washington University, MBA, 1955-56. Commissioned Ensign, US Navy, 1938. Served in the Pacific Theater, WW II. Head, Machine Design Branch, Bureau of Ships, 1958-60; Comptroller, Bureau of Ships, 1960-62; Commander Boston Naval Shipyard, 1962-66; Deputy Commander for Plans, Programs and Financial Management, Naval Ship Systems Command Headquarters, 1966-67; Vice Commander, Naval Ship Systems Command, 1967-69; Inspector General, Naval Ship Systems Command, 1969-72. Navy Commendation Medal; and other medals and awards. Promoted to Rear Admiral, July 1, 1965.

Jordão, José de Carvalho. Fleet Admiral, Brazilian Navy, Secretary General of the Navy. Attended Naval School; Naval War College; Submarine Course, Officers School for Improvement and Specialization. Combat duty in WW II. Commandant, 1st Naval District; Commandant, 5th Naval District; Deputy Chief for Communications, Navy General Staff; Deputy Chief for Operations, Navy General Staff; Director, Naval War College; Commander in Chief of the Fleet; Commander, Naval Transport Force; Naval, Military and Air Attache, Embassies of Brazil in Tokyo and Taipei.

Mérito Santos Dumont; Ordem do Mérito Militar; Ordem do Mérito Aeronautico; Ordem do Mérito Naval; Ordem do Mérito Tamandaré; Medalha da Campanha do Atlantico Sul; and other medals and awards from Brazil and other nations. Promoted to Rear Admiral, December 31, 1965; Vice Admiral, August 23, 1968; Fleet Admiral, December 29, 1970.

Joybert, Marc de. Vice Admiral, French Navy; Chief of Staff of the Navy, 1972-   ; Vice President of the Navy Senior Council, 1972-   . Born July 14, 1912, in Vienne (Isere). Attended Naval School, 1932-36; Marine School, 1939; Senior Naval War College, 1948. Commissioned in 1935. Served in WW II; Indochina, 1950-51; Algeria, 1954-57. Commander, Demi-Brigade of Marines, Algeria, 1961; Commander, Destroyer Division, and destroyer, *Jaureguiberry*; Chief of Staff, Mediterranean Squadron; Chief of Staff to the Admiral of the Port, Brest; Commander, Amphibious Landing Force, Lorient, 1966-68; Assistant Chief of Staff for Operations, 1968-70; Major General of the Navy, 1970-72. Grand Officier de la Légion d'Honneur; Croix de Guerre, 1939-45; Croix de Guerre du Théâtre d'Opérations Extérieures; Croix de la Valeur Militaire; and other medals and awards. Promoted to Rear Admiral, 1966; Vice Admiral, 1970; Admiral, 1972.

Judono, Subroto. Rear Admiral, Indonesian Navy; Inspector General of the Navy.

Jumian, Shafik. Major General, Armed Forces of the Hashemite Kingdom of Jordon; Military Attache, Embassy of Jordan, Washington, D.C. 1973-   .

Jumper, Jimmy J. Major General, Unites States Air Force; Senior Air Force Member, Weapons Systems Evaluation Group, 1973-   . Born January 20, 1923, San Antonio, Texas. Army Air Corps Flying School, 1943-44; Air Command and Staff College, 1956-57; Air War College, 1960-61. Enlisted in US Army Air Corps, 1941; commissioned Second Lieutenant, 1944. Combat duty in World War II; Vietnam War. Commander, 27th Tactical Fighter Wing, 1968; Assistant Deputy Chief of Staff, Operations, Headquarters Aerospace Defense Command, 1968-69; Inspector General, Aerospace Defense Command, 1969-70; Deputy Chief of Staff, Plans, Aerospace Defense Command, 1970-71; Assistant Chief of Staff, Plans, US Military Assistance Command, Vietnam, 1971; Deputy Chief of Staff, Intelligence, Seventh Air Force, Vietnam, 1971-72; Chief, Air Force Advisory Group, Military Assistance Command, Vietnam, 1972-73; Special Assistant to Commander, Thirteenth Air Force, 1973. Distinguished Service Medal; Legion of Merit; and other medals and awards. Promoted to Major General, August 1, 1970.

Jungius, James George. Rear-Admiral, British Royal Navy; Assistant Chief of Naval Staff (Operational Requirements), 1972-   . Born November 15, 1923. Attended Royal Naval College, Dartmouth. Commissioned during WW II. Served in Atlantic and Mediterranean and in Commando operations in the Adriatic. Commanding Officer, HMS

Lynx, 1966-67; Assistant Naval Attache, Washington, D.C., 1968-70; Commanding Officer, HMS *Albion*, 1971-72. Member, British Institute of Management. Promoted to Rear-Admiral, 1972.

Junttila, Paavo J. Lieutenant General, Army of Finland; Chief of the General Staff, General Headquarters, 1971-   . Born June 24, 1918, Vuoksela, Finland. Attended War College, 1952. Served in Winter War; Continuation War. Commanding Officer, Pohjanmaa Jaeger Battalion, 1963-65; Chief of Infantry Office, General Headquarters, 1965-67; Director, General Staff Section, War College, 1967-69; Chief of Operations, General Headquarters, 1969-71. Cross of Freedom, 3d Class with Sword; Cross of Freedom, 4th Class with Oak Leaf; Cross of Freedom, 4th Class with Sword; Commemorative Medals of Winter and Continuation Wars; Order of Finnish White Rose, 1st Class; Order of the Finnish Lion, 1st Class. Promoted to Lieutenant General, November 3, 1972.

K

Kabbaj, Muhammad. Colonel, Moroccan Air Force; Commandant, Moroccan Air Force, 1972-   .

Kadir, L.M. Abdul. Rear Admiral, Indonesian Navy; Deputy Chief of Staff (Operations).

Kaech, Arnold. Director, Federal Military Administration, Switzerland. Born in 1914.

Kalashnik, M. Kh. Colonel General, USSR Army; Deputy Chief, Main Political Directorate, Soviet Army and Navy, 1958-   . Served on the Soviet-German Front in WW II. Member, Communist Party of the Soviet Union.

Kalergis, James George. Major General, United States Army; Project Manager for Reorganization, Office, Chief of Staff, US Army, Washington, D.C., 1972-   . Born January 13, 1917, Lowell, Massachusetts. Boston University, BS Degree, Business Administration; The Field Artillery School, Advanced Course; The Artillery School, Advanced Course; US Army Command and General Staff College; US Army War College; George Washington University, MA Degree, International Affairs. Commissioned Second Lieutenant, US Army Reserve, 1942. Served in WW II and Vietnam War. Commanding General, I Field Force Artillery, US Army, Pacific-Vietnam, 1967-68; Chief of Staff, I Field Force, US Army, Pacific-Vietnam, 1968-69; Comptroller, US Army Materiel Command, Washington, D.C., 1969-70; Deputy Commanding General for Logistics Support, US Army Materiel Command, Washington, D.C., 1970-72. Distinguished Service Medal; Legion of Merit with Oak Leaf Cluster; Bronze Star Medal; and other medals and awards. Promoted to Brigadier General, August 18, 1967; Major General, July 1, 1970.

Kaliski, Sylwester. Major General, Polish Army; Commandant, Military Technical College, 1967- . Born December 19, 1925, in Torun. D.Eng., Engineering and Theoretical Physics. Anti-German underground, WW II. Former Instructor and Scientific Worker, Military Technical College; Professor, Military Technical College, 1958-67; corresponding member, Polish Academy of Sciences, 1962-69, Member since 1969, Member of Presidium since 1971; Member, Polish United Workers Party; Deputy to Seym (Parliament), 1972- ; Editor in Chief, "Problems of Vibrations," 1959- . Recipient of State Prize, 1964, 1970.

Kamanin, Nikolai Petrovich. Colonel General, USSR Air Force; Director, Cosmonaut Training Program, 1960- . Born October 18, 1908, in Melinky, Ivanovo District. Attended Air Force Officers School; Zhukovskiy Air Force War College; Voroshilov General Staff War College. Joined the Soviet Armed Forces in 1927. Served on the Soviet-German Front in WW II. Deputy Chief of Staff, Air Force, 1958-66; Deputy Commander in Chief, Air Force, 1966-68. Hero of the Soviet Union; Order of Lenin; Order of Red Banner; Order of Red Star; and other medals and awards.

Kamath, V.A. Rear Admiral, Navy of India; Flag Officer Southern Naval Area.

Kaminski, Josef. Lieutenant General, Polish Army; Commanding General, Silesian Military District. Attended Infantry Officers School; General Staff War College, USSR. Served on Polish-German Front, WW II. Commanding General, Pomeranian Military District, 1964- . Member of Polish United Workers Party. Virtuti Militari; Polonia Restituta; Cross of Grunwald; and other orders and medals. Promoted to Lieutenant General, 1964.

Kamol, Dejatunga. Air Marshal, Royal Thai Air Force; Vice Chief of Air Staff, 1960- . Born June 21, 1917. Attended Chulachomklao Royal Military Academy; Flying Training School, Royal Thai Air Force, 1937; Field Officers Course, United States Air Force, 1952; National War College, 1955. Commissioned Second Lieutenant, Royal Thai Air Force, 1937. Director of Operations, Air Staff, 1955-58; Deputy Chief of Air Staff, Operations, 1958-60.

Kao Kuei-yuan. General, Army of Republic of China; Personal Chief of Staff to the President, 1970- . Born March 26, 1907, Shantung. Attended Military Academy; Armed Forces Staff College; Command and General Staff College, USA. Served in Sino-Japanese War; Chinese Civil War. Earlier career included: Commanding General 295th Brigade, 1938-39; Commanding General, 99th Infantry Division, then 118th Infantry Division, and later 88th Infantry Division, 1940-48; Commanding General, 18th Army Corps, then 96th Army Corps and later, 45th Army Corps, 1950-53; Director, Political Warfare Department, General Headquarters, Chinese Army, 1955-57; Deputy Commander in Chief, Chinese Army, 1957-58; Commanding General, Reserve and Replacement Training Command, 1958; Commanding General, 2d Field Army, 1959-60; Director, General Political Warfare Department, Ministry of National Defense, 1961-65; Commander in Chief, Chinese Army, 1965-67; Chief of the General Staff, Ministry of National Defense, 1967-70.

Karpov, V.N. Lieutenant General, USSR Army; Chief of Staff, Central Asian Military District, 1972- . Served on the Soviet-German Front, WW II. Chief of Staff, The Volga Military District, 1968-72. Member, Communist Party of the Soviet Union.

Kasatonov, Vladimir Afanasievich. Admiral of the Fleet, USSR Navy; First Deputy Commander in Chief, Soviet Navy, 1964- . Born July 21, 1910, in St. Petersburg, Russia. Frunze Naval Academy, Leningrad, 1931; Naval War College, 1941. Commissioned in 1931. Served in the Soviet-German War (WW II). Commander, Submarine Squadron, Pacific Fleet, 1938-40; Command and Staff assignments, 1941-49; Chief of Staff, Pacific Fleet, 1949-54; Commander, Baltic Fleet, 1954-55; Commander, Black Sea Fleet, 1955-62; Commander, Northern Fleet, 1962-64. Member, Communist Party of the Soviet Union since 1939; Deputy to the Supreme Soviet, USSR. Hero of the Soveit Union; two Orders of Lenin; three Orders of the Red Banner; Order of Fatherland War; and other medals and awards.

Käser, Reinhold. Major General, Swiss Army; Surgeon General. Born in 1910.

Katsina, Hassan U. Brigadier General, Nigerian Army; Chief of Staff, Nigerian Army, 1968- . Born March 3, 1937, in Katsina. Attended Government College, Zaria; Institute for administration, Zaria; Nigerian College of Art and Technology. Staff Member, Nigerian Contingent, United Nations Peacekeeping Force, Congo; Commander, Reconnaissance Regiment, 1965; Governor, Northern Region, 1966-67; Chairman, Interim Administration Northern States, 1967-68. UN Congo Medal and other medals and awards. Promoted to Brigadier General, 1968.

Kauffman, Draper Laurence. Rear Admiral, United States Navy; Commandant, Ninth Naval District, and Commander Naval Base, Great Lakes, Illinois, 1970- . Born August 4, 1911, in San Diego, California. US Naval Academy, 1929-33; (forced to resign upon graduation because of poor eyes); Naval Damage Control School, Philadelphia, 1947; Naval War College, Logistics Course, 1950-51. Joined the American Volunteer Ambulance Corps with the French Army, 1940; POW, 1940. Commissioned Sub-Lieutenant, British Royal Navy Volunteer Reserve, 1940; appointed Lieutenant, US Naval Reserve, 1941; transferred to US Navy, 1946. Served in European, Atlantic and Pacific Theaters, WW II. Commanding Officer USS *Helena* (CA-75), 1960-61; Commander, Destroyer Flotilla THREE (later Cruiser-Destroyer Flotilla THREE), 1961-62; Chief, Strategic Plans and Policy Division, Joint Staff, Joint Chiefs of Staff, 1962-63; Director, Office of Program Appraisal, 1963-65; Superintendent US Naval Academy, 1965-68;

Commander US Naval Forces, Philippines, and Commander in Chief Pacific Representative in the Philippines, 1968-70. Navy Cross with Gold Star; Distinguished Service Medal; Legion of Merit; Navy Commendation Medal with two Gold Stars; and other US and foreign medals and awards. Promoted to Captain, January 1, 1954; Rear Admiral, July 1, 1961.

Kay, Patrick Richard. Major-General, British Royal Marines; Chief of Staff to Commandant-General, Royal Marines, 1970-   . Born August 1, 1921. Attended Eastbourne College; Staff College, Camberley, 1951; Imperial Defence College, 1969. Commissioned in the Royal Marines in 1940. Served at sea and with Commandos in WW II. Plans Division, Naval Staff, 1959-62; Commanding Officer, 43 Commando, Royal Marines, 1963-65; Commanding Officer, Amphibious Training Unit Royal Marines, 1965-66; Assistant Director (Joint Warfare), Naval Staff, 1966-67; Assistant Chief of Staff to Commandant-General, Royal Marines, 1968. CB, MBE.

Kayacan, Kemal. Admiral, Turkish Navy; Commander, Turkish Naval Forces Command, 1972-   . Studied at Naval Academy; Naval Training School; Naval War College. Formerly Commander, Mine Warfare Force; Commander, Naval Training Command; Commander, Southern District Command; Chief of Staff, Naval Forces Command; Member, Supreme Military Council; Commander, Turkish Fleet. Distinguished Unit Award; Distinguished Courageous Service; and other medals and awards. Promoted to Admiral, August 30, 1970.

Kazakov, M.I. General of the Army, USSR Army. Born in 1901. Served on the Soviet-German Front in WW II. Formerly Commander, Leningrad Military District; Chief of Staff, Warsaw Pact Forces, 1965-68. Member, Communist Party of the Soviet Union.

Kazalov, L. Lieutenant General, USSR Army; Chief of Staff, Odessa Military District, 1965-   . Served on the Soviet-German Front in WW II. Member, Communist Party of the Soviet Union.

Kaziende, Leopold. Minister of Defense, Niger.

Kearney, Lester T., Jr. Major General, Unites States Air Force; Chief of Staff, Military Airlift Command, Scott Air Force Base, Illinois, 1973-   . Born January 9, 1924, in Sweetwater, Texas. San Angelo College, San Angelo, Texas, 1941-43; Aviation Cadet Training Course, 1943-44; Air Command and Staff College, 1958-59; National War College, 1965-66. Commissioned Second Lieutenant, US Army Air Corps, 1944. Served in the European Theater in WW II. Assistant Executive Officer to the Director of Plans, Deputy Chief of Staff, Plans and Operations, Headquarters US Air Force, 1962-64; Assistant Executive Officer to the Director of Joint Staff, Organization of the Joint Chiefs of Staff, Washington, D.C., 1964-65; Executive Officer to the Deputy Commander in Chief, Headquarters, US European Command, 1967-70; Vice Commander, then Commander,

63rd Military Airlift Wing, Norton Air Force Base, California, 1970-73. Legion of Merit; Air Medal with five Oak Leaf Clusters; Joint Service Commendation Medal; and other medals and awards. Promoted to Brigadier General, August 1, 1971; Major General, June 1, 1973.

Keck, James M. Lieutenant General, Unites States Air Force; Commander, Second Air Force, 1972-   . Born September 4, 1921, in Scranton, Pennsylvania. Brown University, Providence, Rhode Island, 1939-40; US Military Academy, 1940-43; Flight Training Course, 1943; Naval War College, 1951-52; National War College, 1959-60. Commissioned in 1943. Served in the European Theater, WW II; Vietnam War. Commander, 72d Bombardment Wing, 1966-67; Commander, 17th Strategic Aerospace Division, 1967-68; Deputy Chief of Staff, Comptroller, Strategic Air Command, 1968-69; Assistant to Deputy Chief of Staff, Operations, Strategic Air Command, 1969-70; Deputy Director, Operations, Deputy Chief of Staff, Plans and Operations, Headquarters, USAF, 1970-71; Director of Plans, Headquarters, USAF, 1971-72. Legion of Merit with one Oak Leaf Cluster; Distinguished Flying Cross with one Oak Leaf Cluster; and other medals and awards. Promoted to Brigadier General, August 1, 1967; Major General, May 1, 1970; Lieutenant General, May 16, 1972.

Keegan, George J., Jr. Major General, United States Air Force; Commander, Air Force Intelligence Service, 1973-   . Born July 4, 1921, Houlton, Maine. Army Air Corps Flying School, 1943-44; Harvard University, BA, 1947; National War College, 1964-65; George Washington University, MA, International Affairs, 1965. Commissioned Second Lieutenant, Army Air Corps, 1944. Served in South Pacific Area, WW II; Vietnam War. Deputy Assistant for Joint Matters, Assistant for Joint and Naval Security Council Matters, Office of the Deputy Chief of Staff, Headquarters USAF, 1965-66; Special Assistant to the Director, Joint Staff for Joint Matters, Organization, Joint Chiefs of Staff, 1966-67; Deputy Chief of Staff, Intelligence, Seventh Air Force, Vietnam, 1967-69; Deputy Chief of Staff, Intelligence, Headquarters Pacific Command, Hawaii, 1969-70; Deputy Chief of Staff, Plans and Operations, Headquarters Air Force Logistics Command, 1970-72; Assistant Chief of Staff, Intelligence, Headquarters US Air Force, 1972-73. Distinguished Service Medal; Legion of Merit with three Oak Leaf Clusters; and other medals and awards. Promoted to Major General, September 1, 1969.

Keller, Oskar. Brigadier General, Swiss Army; Chief of Administration of War Materiel. Born in 1909.

Keller, Robert Prescott. Lieutenant General, United States Marine Corps; Commanding General, Marine Corps Development and Education Command, 1972-   . Born February 9, 1920, Oakland, California. Flight Training Course; Amphibious Warfare School; Air Command and Staff College, Air University; Armed Forces Staff College; University of Maryland, BS; George Washington University, MA. Served in Pacific Theater, WW II; Korean War; Vietnam War. Assistant Wing Commander, 1st Marine

Aircraft Wing, Vietnam, 1967-68; Commanding General, 4th Marine Aircraft Wing/Marine Air Reserve Training Command, 1968-71; Assistant Chief of Staff, J-3, Pacific Command, 1971-72. Silver Star Medal; Distinguished Flying Cross with two Gold Stars; Legion of Merit with Combat "V" and two Gold Stars; and other medals and awards. Promoted to Brigadier General, August 4, 1966; Major General, August 4, 1969; Lieutenant General, July 1, 1972.

Kendall, Maurice Wesley. Major General, United States Army; Director, Inter-American Region, Office, Assistant Secretary of Defense (International Security Affairs), Washington, D.C., 1971-   . Born October 20, 1921, Lincoln City, Indiana. Indiana University, BS Degree, Public Business Administration; The Infantry School, Advanced Course; U.S. Army Command and General Staff College; Armed Forces Staff College; U.S. Army War College; George Washington University, MA Degree, International Affairs. Commissioned Second Lieutenant, U.S. Army Reserve, 1943. Served in WW II and Vietnam War. Chief of Staff, 9th Infantry Division, U.S. Army, Vietnam, 1967; Deputy Director of Operations, National Military Command Center, Organization, Joint Chiefs of Staff, Washington, D.C., 1968-69; Deputy Director for Command/Areas, J-3, National Military Command Center, Organization, Joint Chiefs of Staff, Washington, D.C., 1969-70; Assistant Division Commander, 4th Infantry Division, U.S. Army, Vietnam, 1970; Deputy Commanding General/Chief of Staff, I Field Force, U.S. Army, Vietnam, 1971. Distinguished Service Medal; Silver Star with Oak Leaf Cluster; Legion of Merit with Three Oak Leaf Clusters; Bronze Star Medal with Three Oak Leaf Clusters, and other medals and awards. Promoted to Brigadier General, August 1, 1969; Major General, September 1, 1971.

Kent, Glenn A. Lieutenant General, United States Air Force; Director, Weapons Systems Evaluation Group, Office, Director, Defense Research and Engineering, Office of the Secretary of Defense, 1972-   . Born June 25, 1915, in Red Cloud, Nebraska. Western State College, Gunnison, Colorado, BA, 1936; California Institute of Technology, MS, 1942; Naval Post Graduate School, 1947-48; University of California, MS, Radiological Engineering, 1950; Air War College, 1956-57; Center for International Affairs, Harvard University, 1962. Commissioned Second Lieutenant, US Army Air Corps, 1942. Served in Labrador and Greenland. Military Assistant to Deputy Director (Strategic and Defensive Systems), Defense Research and Engineering, Office, Secretary of Defense, 1962-65; Deputy Director, Development Plans, Office, Deputy Chief of Staff, Research and Development, Headquarters, USAF, 1965-66; Deputy Director for Research and Development Analysis, Director, Operations Requirements and Development Plans, Headquarters, USAF, 1966; Assistant to Deputy Chief of Staff, Research and Development for Concept Formulation, Headquarters, USAF, 1966; Deputy Chief of Staff, Development Plans, Air Force Systems Command, 1966-68; Assistant Chief of Staff, Studies and Analysis, Headquarters, USAF, 1968-72. Distinguished Service Medal with one Oak Leaf Cluster; Legion of Merit with one Oak Leaf Cluster; and other

medals and awards. Promotions: Brigadier General, February 28, 1963; Major General, July 1, 1966; Lieutenant General, February 1, 1972.

Kerekou, Mathieu. President and Minister of Defense, Dahomey.

Kern, John R., Jr. Major General, United States Air Force; Director of Manpower and Organization, Office of the Deputy Chief of Staff, Programs and Resources, Headquarters US Air Force, Washington, D.C., 1970-   . Born January 20, 1924, in Slatington, Pennsylvania. Muhlenberg College, Allentown, Pennslyvania, BA, 1942; Aviation Cadet Training Course; 1943-44; Air Command and Staff School, 1954-55. Commissioned Second Lieutenant, US Army Air Corps, in 1944. Served in the European Theater in WW II; POW. Director, Manpower and Organization, Headquarters Pacific Air Forces, Hickam Air Force Base, Hawaii, 1966-69; Chief of Command Planning Division, Deputy Chief of Staff, Plans and Operations, Headquarters US Air Force, Washington, D.C., 1969-70; Assistant Deputy Director for Force Development, Headquarters US Air Force, Washington, D.C., 1970. Legion of Merit; Air Medal with three Oak Leaf Clusters; and other medals and awards. Promotions: Brigadier General, March 1, 1971; Major General, 1973.

Kerwin, Joseph P. Commander, US Navy; NASA Scientist-Astronaut, 1965-   . Born February 19, 1932, Oak Park, Illinois. College of the Holy Cross, BA, Philosophy, 1953; Northwestern University Medical School, MD, 1957; Internship, District of Columbia General Hospital; US Naval School of Aviation Medicine, Pensacola; US Navy Flight Training. Commissioned in Navy Medical Corps, 1958; received pilot's wings, 1962. Flight Surgeon, Marine Air Group 14, Cherry Point, North Carolina; Flight Surgeon, Fighter Squadron 101, Oceana NAS, Virginia Beach; Staff Flight Surgeon, Air Wing Four, Cecil Field, Florida. NASA experience: Science-pilot, Skylab 1, May-June 1973. Manned Spacecraft Certificate of Commendation.

Kerwin, Walter Thomas, Jr. General, United States Army; Commanding General, Continental Army Command, Fort Monroe, Virginia, 1973-   . Born June 14, 1917, West Chester, Pennsylvania. US Military Academy; Field Artillery School, Basic Course; US Army Command and General Staff College; Armed Forces Staff College; US Army War College; The National War College. Commissioned Second Lieutenant, 1939. Served in WW II and Vietnam War. Commanding General, 3d Armored Division, US Army, Europe, 1965-66; Assistant Deputy Chief of Staff for Military Operations (Plans and Operations), US Army, Washington, D.C., 1966-67; Chief of Staff, US Military Assistance Command, Vietnam, 1967-68; Commanding General, II Field Force, US Army, Pacific-Vietnam, 1968-69; Director, Civil Disturbance Planning and Operations, Office, Chief of Staff, US Army, and Commanding General, Directorate of Civil Disturbance Planning and Operations, Washington, D.C., 1969; Deputy Chief of Staff for Personnel, US Army, Washington, D.C.,

1969-72; Special Assistant to the Commanding General, Continental Army Command, Washington, D.C., 1972-73. Distinguished Service Medal with two Oak Leaf Clusters; Legion of Merit with Oak Leaf Cluster; Bronze Star Medal; and other medals and awards. Promoted to Brigadier General, July 1, 1961; Major General, June 1, 1964; Lieutenant General, September 1, 1968; General, February 1, 1973.

Khalipov, I.F. Colonel General, USSR Army; Deputy Chief, Main Political Directorate, Soviet Army and Navy, and Chief, Political Directorate, Air Defence Forces, 1958-   . Served on the Soviet-German Front in WW II. Member, Communist Party of the Soviet Union.

Khan Mohammad Khan. Army General, Royal Afghan Army; Minister of National Defense, Afghanistan, 1965-   . Commissioned Second Lieutenant, Afghan Army, ca. 1935. Formerly Commandant, Royal Military Academy. Sardab Ala; Medal-i-Shahwan; and other medals and awards. Member, Afghanistan team, 1936 Olympics.

Khan, Tikka. General, Army of Pakistan; Chief of the Army Staff, 1972-   . Born in 1915, in Jochha Mamdot, Rawalpindi District. Attended Indian Military Academy, Dehra Dun; Command and Staff College, Quetta, 1949. Commissioned Artillery Officer, Royal Indian Army, 1940. Served in the Western Desert and Burma, WW II; Indo-Pakistan War, 1965, 1971. Commander, Divisional Artillery, 1955-58; Director Staff Duties, 1958-60; Commander, Corps Artillery, and Director of Artillery, General Headquarters, 1960; Commander, Infantry Brigade; Commander, Infantry Division, 1962-66; Quartermaster General, General Headquarters, 1966-69; Corps Commander, 1969-71; Martial Law Administrator of West Pakistan; Commander, Eastern Command, and Martial Law Administrator of East Pakistan, 1971; Governor of East Pakistan, 1971; Corps Commander, 1971-72. Decorations; Hilal-i-Jurat; Hilal-i-Quaid-i-Azam; Sitara-i-Pakistan; and other medals and awards. Promotions; Brigadier, 1955; Lieutenant General, 1969; General, 1972.

Khanh, Nguyen Duc. Colonel, Army of the Republic of South Vietnam; Commander 1st Air Division.

Kharchenko, V.K. Colonel General, Engineer, USSR Army; Commander, Engineer Troops. Served in the Soviet-German War (WW II). Member, Communist Party of the Soviet Union.

Khatami, Muhammad. General, Imperial Iranian Air Force; Commander in Chief, Imperial Irania Air Force, 1957-   . Born in 1920 in Rasht. Attended American College, Teheran; Officers College, Air Force Branch; Royal Air Force College, England; Air Force Courses, Federal Republic of Germany. Personal Pilot to His Imperial Majesty the Shah, 1946-58; Commander Iranian Air Force, 1957; Flew Shah and Queen out of the country during Dr. Mossadeg coup d'etat in 1953; member of the Iranian jet aero team. Married to H.R.H. Princess Fatameh Pahlavi.

Khetagurov, Georgiy Ivanovich. General of the Army, USSR Army (Artillery). Born in 1903 in North Caucasus. Attended advanced artillery courses, 1937; Army War College, c. 1946-49. Volunteered for duty in the Army, 1920; commissioned c. 1925. Served in the undeclared Soviet-Japanese War, 1938, and in WW II. Artillery Commander, 21st Mechanized Corps, Northwest Front, 1941; Chief of Staff, 30th Army, Moscow Front, 1941-42; Chief, 3d Guards Army, 1942-43; Chief of Staff, 1st Guards Army, 1944; Commander, Infantry Division, 1945; Commander, Rifle Corps, late forties and early fifties; Commander, Northern Forces Group, Poland, 1956-63; Commander, Baltic Military District, 1963-71. Member, Communist Party of the Soviet Union, 1924-   ; Deputy to the USSR Supreme Soviet, 1958-   . Hero of the Soviet Union; two Orders of Lenin; five Orders of Red Banner; Order of Fatherland War; Order of Red Star; and other USSR and foreign orders and medals. Promoted to General of the Army, February 1968.

Khiem, Tran Thien. General, Army of the Republic of South Vietnam; Prime Minister and Minister of Defense.

Khokhlov, Pyotr Il'ich. Lieutenant General, USSR Naval Air Force; Chief of Staff, Naval Air Force, 1961-   . Born in 1910 in Moscow. Drafted in 1932. Attended Naval Air Force Academy, 1933-36; Naval War College, in the 1940s; General Staff War College, in the 1950s. Commissioned in 1936. Served in the Soviet-German War, 1941-45. Navigator, Air Force Regiment, 1941; Flagship Navigator, Air Force Division, Baltic and later Black Sea Air Fleet, 1941-45; Flagship Navigator, Northern Fleet Air Force, 1945; Chief Navigator, Baltic Fleet Air Force, in the 1950s; Chief of Staff, Baltic Fleet Air Force, late 1950s; Member, Communist Party of the Soviet Union. Hero of the Soviet Union; Order of Lenin; Order of Red Banner; and other USSR and foreign medals and awards.

Khomulo, M.G. Colonel General, USSR Army; Commander, Siberian Military District, 1969-   . Served on the Soviet-German Front in WW II. First Deputy Commander, Group of Soviet Forces in Germany, until 1969. Member, Communist Party of the Soviet Union.

Khondker, A.K. Commodore, Bangladesh Air Force; Chief of Staff, Bangladesh Air Force, 1973-   .

Khoreshko, G. Major General, USSR Army; Deputy Commander, Rear Services, Belorussian Military District. Served on the Soviet-German Front in WW II. Member, Communist Party of the Soveit Union.

Khovrin, Nikolay Ivanovich. Vice Admiral, USSR Navy; First Deputy Commander, Northern Fleet, 1970-   . Born in 1922 in Vladivostok. Attended Makarov Pacific Ocean Naval Academy, 1942-45; Naval College in the 1950s. Drafted into the Navy, 1941. Served in the Soviet-Japanese War, 1945. Cruiser Commander, c. 1955; Commander, Cruiser Brigade, Pacific Fleet, 1968-70; Member, Communist Party of the Soviet Union. Order of the Red Star, and other orders and medals.

Khrenov, V.A. Vice Admiral, USSR Navy; Commandant, Frunze Naval College. Served in the Soviet-German War, 1941-45. Member of Communist Party of the Soviet Union.

Khrunov, Evgeny Vasilievich. Colonel, USSR Air Force; Cosmonaut, 1960-   . Born September 10, 1933. Attended Air Force Pilot School, Bataisk; Zhukovskiy Air Force Engineering College. Commissioned in 1954; joined cosmonaut training unit, 1960. Fighter Pilot, 1956-60; Engineer/Investigator of Soyuz-5 Spacecraft. Hero of the Soviet Union; Gold Star Medal; Order of Lenin; Order of Red Banner; Order of Red Star; K. Tsiolkovskiy Gold Medal of the USSR Academy of Sciences; and other medals and awards. Member, Communist Party of the Soviet Union since 1959.

Kichev, V. Rear Admiral, USSR Navy; Chief of Staff, Northern Fleet, 1971-   . Served in the Soviet-German War, 1941-45. Member, Communist Party of the Soviet Union.

Kidd, Isaac Campbell, Jr. Admiral, United States Navy; Chief of Naval Material, Navy Department, 1971-   . Born August 14, 1919, in Cleveland, Ohio. US Naval Academy, 1938-41; National War College, 1960-61. Commissioned Ensign, US Navy, 1941. Served in the Atlantic and Pacific Theaters, WW II. Commander (Guided Missile) Destroyer Squadron EITHTEEN, 1961-62; Executive Assistant and Senior Aide to the Chief of Naval Operations, Navy Department, 1962-66; Assistant Chief of Staff for Logistics to the Commander in Chief Allied Forces, Southern Europe, 1966-68; Commander Cruiser-Destroyer Flotilla TWELVE and Commander Cruiser-Destroyer Force, US Atlantic Fleet, 1968-69; Commander First Fleet, 1969-70; Commander Sixth Fleet and Commander Naval Striking and Support Forces, Southern Europe, 1970-71. Distinguished Service Medal; Legion of Merit with two Gold Stars; Bronze Star Medal with Combat "V"; and other medals and awards. Promoted to Rear Admiral, July 1, 1965; Admiral, December 1, 1971.

Kidd, John Burns. Major General, United States Air Force; Chief, Military Assistance Advisory Group, Italy, 1972-   . Born April 15, 1919, in Cleveland, Ohio. Oberlin College, 1937-40; Army Air Force Flying School, 1940; United Kingdom Land-Air Warfare School, England; Air War College, 1956-57. Commissioned in the Army Air Corps, 1940. Served in the European Theater, WW II. Deputy Assistant Chief of Staff, Operations, US Pacific Command, 1966-69; Deputy Director and later Director, Personnel Planning, Deputy Chief of Staff, Personnel, Headquarters USAF, 1969-71; Director, Personnel Programs, Deputy Chief of Staff, Personnel, Headquarters USAF, 1971-72. Distinguished Service Medal; Silver Star; Legion of Merit with one Oak Leaf Cluster; Distinguished Flying Cross with one Oak Leaf Cluster; Croix de Guerre with Palm; and other medals and awards. Promoted to Major General, May 1, 1970.

Kidsyzi, Qazim. Deputy Minister of Defense, Albania, 1973-   .

Kierkegaard, Soren Christer Douglas. Rear Admiral, Swedish Royal Navy; Commander, Coastal Fleet, 1970-   . Attended Royal Navy Staff College, 1945-48; US Naval War College, Naval Command Course (USA), 1957-58; Royal National Defense College, 1960, 1966. Commander, 1st Destroyer/Torpedo Boat Flotilla, 1963-65; Deputy Commander in Chief, Military Command South, 1966-69. Commander of the Royal Order of the Sword; Order of the Lion (Finland); and other medals and awards. Promoted to Rear Admiral, 1970. Member of the Royal Society of Naval Sciences.

Kiet, Pham. Major General, People's Army of Vietnam; Vice Minister of Public Security, 1959; Commander, People's Armed Security Forces 1961. Born in 1910 in Son Tinh District, Quang Ngai Province. Imprisoned by French at Ba To, 1945; leader in guerrilla resistance, 1945-54; Chief, Military Intelligence Department, Interregion V Headquarters, 1955; elected Deputy to Third National Assembly, 1964; Chairman, Committee for Brotherly Relations between Quang Ngai and Nghe An Province, 1970. Promotion; Major General, May 1961.

Kim, Kyu Sop. Admiral, Navy of the Republic of Korea; Chief of Naval Operations, 1972-   . Attended IRI Technical School, 1946; Republic of Korea Naval Academy, 1948. Commissioned Ensign, ROK Navy, 1948. Combat duty in the Korean War. Assistant Chief of Naval Operations, Intelligence, 1965-67; Deputy Chief of Naval Operations, 1968-70; Superintendent, Naval Academy, 1970-72. Decorations: Chungmu; Wharang with Gold Star; and other medals and awards. Promoted to Admiral, May 30, 1972.

Kindavong, Prince Sinthanavong. Colonel, Royal Armed Forces of Laos; Commander Royal Lao Navy and Chief of the Naval Staff.

King, Sir Frank (Douglas). Lieutenant-General, British Army; General Officer Commanding and Director of Operations, Northern Ireland, 1973-   . Born March 9, 1919. Attended Royal Military College of Science, 1946; Staff College, Camberley, 1950. Commissioned in the Royal Fusiliers, 1940. Served in Europe in WW II, wounded, POW. Commander, 2d Parachute Battalion, Middle East, 1960-62; Commander, 11th Infantry Brigade Group, Germany, 1963-64; Military Adviser (Overseas Equipment), 1965-66; Director, Land/Air Warfare, Ministry of Defence, 1967-68; Director, Military Assistance Overseas, Ministry of Defence, 1968-69; Commandant, Royal Military College of Science, 1969-71; General Officer Commanding in Chief, Army Strategic Command, 1971-73. KCB; MBE.

King, Jerome H., Jr. Vice Admiral, United States Navy; Director, J-3 (Operations), Joint Staff Office, Joint Chiefs of Staff, 1972-   . Born July 14, 1919, in Youngstown, Ohio. Yale University, BS, Engineering, 1941; Naval Reserve Officers Training Course, Yale University,1937-41; Ordnance Engineering (Special Physics) Course, Postgraduate School, Annapolis, 1948-49; Massachusetts

Institute of Technology, MS, Nuclear Physics, 1949-51; Naval War College, 1957-58. Commissioned Ensign, US Naval Reserve, 1941; transferred to regular Navy, 1943. Served in the Pacific Theater, WW II; Vietnam War. Commanding Officer USS *Yellowstone* (AS-27), 1962-63; Assistant Chief of Staff to Commander Seventh Fleet, 1963-65; Commander Destroyer Squadron ONE, 1965-66; Executive Assistant and Senior Aide to the Chief of Naval Operations, 1966-68; Commander Antisubmarine Warfare Group ONE, 1968-69; Director, Ship Characteristics Division/Chairman, Ship Characteristics Board, Office of the CNO, 1969-70; Director, Strategic Plans Division, Office of the CNO, 1970; Commander US Naval Forces, Vietnam, Chief of the Naval Advisory Group and Naval Component Commander, US Military Assistance Command, Vietnam, 1970-71; Deputy Chief of Naval Operations (Surface Warfare), 1971-72. Distinguished Service Medal; Legion of Merit with Gold Star; Bronze Star Medal; Navy Commendation Medal with Gold Star and Combat "V"; and other US and foreign medals and awards. Promoted to Vice Admiral, May 15, 1970.

Kirkendall, James F. Major General, United States Air Force; Commandant, Armed Forces Staff College, Norfolk, Virginia, 1970-   . Born February 19, 1920, Omaha, Nebraska. University of Nebraska, 1937-41; Army Air Corps Flying School, 1941-42; Command and General Staff School, 1945; Air War College, 1958-59; National War College, 1962-63; George Washington University, MA, 1963. Commisioned Second Lieutenant, US Army Air Corps, 1942. Served in the European and North African Theaters, WW II; Korean War; Vietnam War. Commander, 47th Air Division, 1966; Assistant Deputy Chief of Staff, Operations (Requirements), Headquarters Tactical Air Command, 1966-69; Deputy Chief of Staff, Operations, Headquarters Seventh Air Force, Vietnam, 1969-70; Deputy Commander, Seventh/Thirteenth Air Force, Thailand, 1970. Silver Star; Legion of Merit with three Oak Leaf Clusters; Distinguished Flying Cross with two Oak Leaf Clusters; Bronze Star Medal; Croix de Guerre; and other medals and awards. Promoted to Major General, March 1, 1969.

Kirti Nidhi Bista. Prime Minister and Minister of Defense, Nepal.

Kittikachorn, Thanom. Field Marshal, Royal Thai Army, Admiral of the Fleet, Marshal of the Royal Air Force; Supreme Commander of the Armed Forces, 1964-October 16, 1973. Born August 11, 1911, in the Province of Tak, Thailand. Attended Chulachomklao Royal Military Academy, Royal Thai Army, 1920-29; Military Survey School, Royal Thai Army, 1931-34; Infantry School, Royal Thai Army, 1938-39; National Defense College, Ministry of Defense, 1955. Commissioned Acting Second Lieutenant in 1929. Served in the Military Campaign in the Shan States, WW II, 1941. Commanding General, First Army Area, 1954-57; Assistant Commander in Chief, Royal Thai Army, 1957-59; Deputy Supreme Commander of the Armed Forces, 1959-63; Supreme Commander of the Armed

Forces and Commander in Chief, Royal Thai Army, 1963-64. Deputy Prime Minister and Minister of Defense, 1959; Prime Minister and Minister of Defense, 1963, 1969-73; Chairman, National Executive Council, 1971; Minister of Foreign Affairs, 1972-73; Knight Grand Cross (First Class) of the Most Illustrious Order of Chula Chom Klao; Senangapati (Knight Grand Commander), of the Honorable Order of Rama; Knight Grand Cross (Special Class) of the Most Exalted Order of the White Elephant; Knight Grand Cordon (Special Class) of the Most Noble Order of the Crown of Thailand; Ratanaporn, First Class (Rama 9); Ratanaporn, Third Class (Rama 8); and numerous other medals and decorations, Thai and foreign. Promoted to Major General, 1951; Lieutenant General, 1955; General, 1958; Admiral, Air Chief Marshal, 1959; Field Marshal, Admiral of the Fleet, Marshal of the Royal Air Force, 1964.

Kleppe, Johan. Minister of Defense, Norway, 1972-   . Parliamentary Under Secretary of State, Ministry of Agriculture, 1967-72. Deputy Member of the Storting, 1967-69; Full Member, 1969-   .

Klingenhagen, John Louis. Major General, United States Army; Deputy Chief of Staff for Logistics, US Army, Europe and Seventh Army, 1973-   . Born May 2, 1921, St. Louis, Missouri. University of Maryland, BS Degree, Military Science; The Infantry School, Advanced Course; US Army Command and General Staff College; National War College; George Washington University, MA Degree, Government Administration. Commissioned Second Lieutenant, US Army Reserve, 1942. Served in WW II and Vietnam War. Chief, Operational Readiness, US Army Materiel Command, Washington, D.C., 1966-67; Assistant for Army Aviation Logistics Support, later Assistant Deputy Chief of Staff, Logistics, Office, Deputy Chief of Staff for Logistics, US Army, Washington, D.C., 1967-68; Advanced Aerial Fire Support System Manager, Office, Chief of Staff, US Army, Washington, D.C., 1968-69; Director of Army Aviation, Office, Assistant Chief of Staff for Force Development, US Army, Washington, D.C., 1969; Commanding General, US Army Aviation Systems Command, St. Louis, Missouri, 1969-71; Director, J-4, US European Command, 1971-73. Distinguished Service Medal; Silver Star with Oak Leaf Cluster; Legion of Merit with Oak Leaf Cluster; Soldier's Medal; Bronze Star Medal with V Device and two Oak Leaf Clusters; Distinguished Flying Cross with two Oak Leaf Clusters; and other medals and awards. Promoted to Brigadier General, October 1, 1966; Major General, October 1, 1968.

Klyuev, A. Major General, USSR Army. Served on the Soviet-German Front in WW II. Formerly Deputy Chief, Political Directorate, Soviet Ground Forces. Member, Communist Party of the Soviet Union.

Knight, James A., Jr. Major Genral, United States Air Force; Assistant, Deputy Chief of Staff Operations, for Operations and Training, Tactical Air Command, Langley Air Force Base, Virginia, 1972-   . Born November 26, 1923, in Dallas, Texas. Aviation Cadet Pilot Training

Course, 1943-44; Air Command and Staff College, 1955-56; University of Maryland, BS, Military Science, 1962; National War College, 1963-64. Commissioned Second Lieutenant, US Army Air Corps, March 1944. Served in the China-Burma-India Theater in WW II; Korean War; Vietnam War. Deputy Commander for Operations, 48th Tactical Fighter Wing, Royal Air Force Base Lakenheath, England, 1964-67; Deputy Commander for Operations, 27th Tactical Fighter Wing, Cannon Air Force Base, New Mexico, 1967-68; Vice Commander, 3d Tactical Fighter Wing, Vien Hoa Air Base, Vietnam, 1968; Deputy Director, Tactical Air Control Center, Headquarters, Seventh Air Force, Tan Son Nhut Air Base, Vietnam, 1968-69; Vice Commander, then Commander, 4453d Combat Crew Training Wing, Davis-Monthan Air Force Base, Arizona, 1969-71; Commander, United States Air Force Special Operations Force, Tactical Air Command, Eglin Air Force Base, Florida, 1971-72. Legion of Merit with Oak Leaf Cluster; Distinguished Flying Cross with Oak Leaf Cluster; Bronze Star Medal; Air Medal with seven Oak Leaf Clusters; and other US and foreign medals and awards. Promotions: Brigadier General, July 1, 1971; Major General, May 1, 1973.

Knoop, Joannes Henri. Lieutenant General, Royal Netherlands Air Force; Chief of the Air Staff, 1973- . Born April 18, 1919, in Bandung, Indonesia. Attended Royal Military Academy, 1937-40; Pilot Training Course (USA), 1943; Senior Command and Staff Course, RNLAF, 1952; NATO Defense College, 1967. Commissioned Lieutenant, 1940; received pilot wings, 1943. Flew with the Royal Australian Air Force in the Pacific Theater in WW II. Chief of Air Force Cadets Training, Royal Military Academy, Breda, 1961-63; Commander, Air Force Base Leeuwarden, 1964-67; Staff Appointment SHAPE (Air Defense), 1968-71; Vice Chief of the Air Staff, 1971-73. Cross of Merit; WW II Commemorative Cross with two Clasps; Decoration of Honor for Order and Peace with four Clasps. Promotions: Major General, 1971; Lieutenant General, 1973.

Knowles, Richard Thomas. Lieutenant General, United States Army; Commanding General, I Corps (ROK/US) Group, U.S. Army, Pacific-Korea, 1972- . Born December 20, 1916, Chicago, Illinois. The Artillery School, Basic and Advanced Courses; U.S. Army Command and General Staff College; Armed Forces Staff College; U.S. Army War College. Commissioned Second Lieutenant, U.S. Army Reserve, 1942. Served in WW II and Vietnam War. Chief of Staff, II Field Force, U.S. Army, Pacific-Vietnam, 1966; Commanding General, 196th Infantry Brigade (Light), U.S. Army, Pacific-Vietnam, 1966-67; Deputy, later Commanding General, Task Force OREGON (Provisional) U.S. Army, Pacific-Vietnam, 1967; Assistant Deputy Chief of Staff for Military Operations, U.S. Army, Washington, D.C., 1967-70; Assistant to the Chairman, Joint Chiefs of Staff, Organization, Joint Chiefs of Staff, Washington, D.C., 1970-72. Distinguished Service Medal with two Oak Leaf Clusters; Silver Star; Legion of Merit with Oak Leaf Cluster; Distinguished Flying Cross with Oak Leaf Cluster; Bronze Star Medal with V Device and Oak Leaf Cluster; and other medals and awards. Promoted to Brigadier General, August 1, 1964; Major General, June 1, 1967; Lieutenant General, July 1, 1970.

Knowlton, William Allen. Lieutenant General, United States Army; Superintendent, US Military Academy, West Point, New York, 1970- . Born June 19, 1920, Weston, Massachusetts. US Military Academy; The Armored School, Advanced Course; US Army Command and General Staff College; The National War College; Columbia University, MA Degree, Political Science. Commissioned Second Lieutenant, 1943. Served in WW II and Vietnam War. Secretary, Joint Staff, US Military Assistance Command, Vietnam, 1966; Director, Revolutionary Development Support, US Military Assistance Command, Vietnam 1966-67; Deputy Assistant Chief of Staff, Civil Operations and Revolutionary Development Support, US Military Assistance Command, Vietnam, 1967-68; Assistant Division Commander, 9th Infantry Division, US Army, Pacific-Vietnam, 1968; Secretary of the General Staff, Office, chief of Staff, US Army, Washington, D.C., 1968-70. Distinguished Service Medal; Silver Star with two Oak Leaf Clusters; Legion of Merit with Oak Leaf Cluster; Distinguished Flying Cross; Bronze Star Medal with V Device; and other medals and awards. Promoted to Brigadier General, October 27, 1966; Major General, March 1, 1969; Lieutenant General, November 1, 1971.

Knutton, Harry. Major-General, British Army; Director-General, Weapons (Army), 1970- . Born April 26, 1921, in Rawmarsh, Yorkshire. Attended Royal Military College of Science; Joint Services Staff College, 1958. Commissioned in 1943 in the Royal Artillery. Served in the European Theater in WW II. Commander, Missile Regiment, British Army of the Rhine, 1964-66; Staff Appointments, Ministry of Defence, 1962-64, 1966-67; Commander, Air Defence Brigade, 1967-69; Fellow, Loughborough University of Technology, 1969-70. Chartered Engineer; Fellow of the Institution of Electrical Engineers; Member of the British Institute of Management.

Koczara, Henryk. Major General, Polish Army; Deputy Chief, Main Political Directorate, Polish Armed Forces. Attended Political Officers Military School; Military-Political College. Commissioned Second Lieutenant, Polish Army, 1945. Former Deputy Commanding General for Political Affairs, Warsaw Military District. Member of Polish United Workers Party. Cross of Grunwald; Cross of Merit; and other orders and medals. Promoted to Major General, 1970.

Kohli, S. N. Vice Admiral, Navy of India; Flag Officer Commanding in Chief, West Coast.

Koiner, Gottfried. General of Armored Troops, Austrian Army; Director, Section III, Ministry of Defense, 1972- . Born September 26, 1915. Attended the Austrian War College, 1944; holds a Degree in Engineering. Commissioned Second Lieutenant, Austrian Army, in 1937. Served in the German Army in WW II. Chief of Staff, Armored Brigade, 1956-57; Adjutant to the President of

Austria, 1957-66; Inspector of Armored Troops, 1967-72. Grosses Ehrenzeichen; Silvernes Ehrenzeichen; and other decorations and awards. Promotions: Colonel, 1961; Brigadier, 1965; Major General, 1972.

Koisch, Francis Paul. Major General, United States Army; Engineer, US Army, Europe, 1972-   . Born October 7, 1919, Newburgh, New York. US Military Academy, 1942; University of California, MS Degree, Civil Engineering; The Cavalry School, Basic Course; US Army Command and General Staff College; US Army War College. Commissioned Second Lieutenant, 1942. WW II; Vietnam War. Division Engineer, US Army Engineer Division, North Atlantic, New York, New York, 1966-68; Deputy Director, Civil Works, Office, Chief of Engineers, US Army, 1968-69; Director, Civil Works, Office, Chief of Engineers, US Army, 1969-72. Distinguished Service Medal; Legion of Merit with two Oak Leaf Clusters; Bronze Star Medal with Oak Leaf Cluster; Air Medal; and other medals and awards. Promoted to Brigadier General, July 1, 1966; Major General, August 1, 1969.

Koldunov, A. Colonel General, USSR Air Force; Commander, Moscow Air Defense District, 1970-   . Served on the Soviet-German Front in WW II. Member, Communist Party of the Soviet Union.

Kolesnikov, A. Major General, USSR Army; Chief of Staff, Siberian Military District, 1972-   . Served on the Soviet-German Front in WW II. Member, Communist Party of the Soviet Union.

Kolesnikov, I. S. Lieutenant General, USSR Army; Commandant, Moscow City. Served on the Soviet-German Front in WW II. Member, Communist Party of the Soviet Union.

Komarovskiy, A. N. General of the Army, USSR Army; Deputy Minister of Defense, and Commander in Chief, Construction and Billeting of Troops, 1964-   . Served on the Soviet-German Front in WW II. Member, Communist Party of the Soviet Union. Promoted to General of the Army, November 7, 1972.

Konstantinov, A. Lieutenant General, USSR Air Force; First Deputy Commander, Baku Air Defense District, 1969-   . Served on the Soviet-German Front in WW II. Member, Communist Party of the Soviet Union.

Kopijkowski, Wlodzimierz. Major General, Polish Army; Deputy Commandant, General Staff War College. Attended General Staff War College. Chief, Polish Contingent, Neutral Nations Supervisory Commission, Korea, 1966. Cross of Grunwald; Cross of Merit; and other Polish and foreign medals and awards. Promoted to Major General, 1959. Member, Polish United Workers Party.

Korbela, Martin. General, Army of Czechoslovakia; Chief, Army Personnel Administration.

Kornet, Fred, Jr. Lieutenant General, United States Army; Deputy Chief of Staff for Logistics, US Army, Washington, D.C., 1973-   . Born October 2, 1919, Wortendyke, New Jersey. Lehigh University, BS Degree, Chemical Engineering; US Army Command and General Staff College; US Army War College; University of Chicago, MBA Degree, Industrial Management. Commissioned Second Lieutenant, US Army Reserve, 1940. Served in WW II. Director of Ammunition, Office, Deputy Chief of Staff, Logistics, US Army, Washington, D.C., 1968-69; Assistant Deputy Chief of Staff for Logistics (Programs and Budget), US Army, Washington, D.C., 1969-71; Commanding General, US Army Aviation Systems Command, St. Louis, Missouri, 1971-72; Acting Deputy Chief of Staff for Logistics, US Army, Washington, D.C., 1972. Distinguished Service Medal; Legion of Merit; Bronze Star Medal; and other medals and awards. Promoted to Brigadier General, August 1, 1968; Major General, August 1, 1970; Lieutenant General, January 1, 1973.

Korzeniecki, Konstanty. Major General, Polish Army; Deputy Commanding General for Political Affairs, Silesian Military District. Studied at Military-Political College, Warsaw. Formerly Chief Editor of Na Strazy (weekly); Chief Editor of Zolnierz Polski (weekly). Member Polish United Workers Party. Cross of Grunwald; Cross of Merit; and other orders and medals.

Kosmel, Eduard. Major General, Army of Czechoslovakia; Deputy Chief of General Staff, Ministry of National Defense, 1968-   . Born c. 1923. Slovak. Attended Voroshilov General Staff College, Moscow. Commanded partisan group, WW II, then platoon in 1st Czechoslovak Army Corps. Member of Czechoslovak Communist Party.

Kosov, A. Rear Admiral, USSR Navy; Chief of Staff, Baltic Fleet, 1972-   . Served in the Soviet-German War in 1941-45. Member, Communist Party of the Soviet Union.

Kossler, Herman Joseph. Rear Admiral, United States Navy; Commandant, Sixth Naval District; Commander, Naval Base, Charleston, South Carolina; Commander, Mine Warfare Force, US Navy, 1968-   . Born December 8, 1911, in Portsmouth, Virginia. US Naval Academy, 1930-34; Naval Submarine School, 1936-37; National War College, 1954-55. Commissioned Ensign, US Navy, 1934. Served in the Pacific Theater, WW II; Korean War. Commander Amphibious Squadron TEN, 1960-61; Inspector General and Assistant Chief of Bureau of Naval Weapons for Administration, 1961-62; Assistant Chief of Naval Operations (Personnel), 1962-64; Commander Mine Force, US Atlantic Fleet, 1964-66; Commander Naval Forces, Philippines/Commander in Chief Pacific Representative, Philippines, 1966-68. Navy Cross; Silver Star Medal (three awards); Legion of Merit; and other medals and awards. Promoted to Rear Admiral, July 1, 1961.

Kovalev, I.M. Lieutenant General, USSR Army; Chief of Staff, Northern Group of Soviet Forces, Poland,

1968-   . Served on the Soviet-German Front in WW II. Member, Communist Party of the Soviet Union.

Kozhanov, K. Lieutenant General, USSR Army; Chief Representative, Warsaw Pact High Command in Czechoslovakia. Served on the Soviet-German Front in WW II. Member, Communist Party of the Soviet Union.

Kotov, P.G. Engineer Admiral, USSR Navy; Deputy Commander in Chief of the Soviet Navy. Served in the Soviet-German War, 1941-45. Member, Communist Party of the Soviet Union.

Kozmin, Aleksander. Colonel General, USSR Army; Staff of the Warsaw Pact.

Kraft, William Russell, Jr. Major General, United States Army; Commanding General, 3d Armored Division, US Army, Europe, 1971-   . Born January 22, 1919, Kingston, New York. US Military Academy; The Armored School, Advanced Course; US Naval War College, Naval Warfare I Course; US Army War College; George Washington University, MA Degree, International Affairs. Commissioned Second Lieutenant, 1942. WW II; Vietnam War. Director, Western Hemisphere Region, Office, Assistant Secretary of Defense (International Security Affairs), Washington, D.C., 1967-69; Assistant Division Commander, 9th Infantry Division, US Army, Pacific-Vietnam, 1969; Deputy Assistant Chief of Staff, Operations, J-3, US Military Assistance Command, Vietnam, 1969-70; Commanding General, US Army, Europe and Seventh Army Troops, 1970-71. Distinguished Service Medal; Legion of Merit with two Oak Leaf Clusters; Distinguished Flying Cross; Bronze Star Medal; and other medals and awards. Promoted to Brigadier General, January 1, 1967; Major General, September 1, 1970.

Kremenskiy, S.I. Lieutenant General, USSR Army; First Deputy Chief, Civil Defense, 1972-   . Served on the Soviet-German Front in WW II. Member, Communist Party of the Soviet Union.

Krishnan, N. Vice Admiral, Navy of India; Flag Officer Commanding in Chief, East Coast.

Kroesen, Frederick James, Jr. Major General, United States Army; Commanding General, 82d Airborne Division, Fort Bragg, North Carolina, 1972-   . Born February 11, 1923, Phillipsburg, New Jersey. George Washington University, BA and AM Degrees, International Affairs; The Infantry School, Basic and Advanced Courses; The Armor School, Advanced Course; U.S. Army Command and General Staff College; Armed Forces Staff College; U.S. Army War College. Commissioned Second Lieutenant, U.S. Army Reserve, 1944. Served in WW II and Vietnam War. Director of Manpower and Forces, Office, Assistant Chief of Staff for Force Development, U.S. Army, Washington, D.C. 1969-71; Assistant Chief of Staff for Operations, J-3, U.S. Military Assistance Command, Vietnam, 1971; Commanding General, 23d Infantry Division (Americal), U.S. Army, Pacific-Vietnam, 1971; Deputy Commanding General, XXIV Corps, U.S. Army, Pacific-Vietnam, 1971-72; Commanding General, First Regional Assistance Command, U.S. Military Assistance Command, Vietnam, 1972. Distinguished Service Medal; Silver Star with Oak Leaf Cluster; Legion of Merit with two Oak Leaf Clusters; Distinguished Flying Cross; Bronze Star Medal with V Device and two Oak Leaf Clusters. Promoted to Brigadier General, October 1, 1969; Major General, August 1, 1971.

Krogerus, Holger. Major General, Army of Finland; Commanding General, Pohjanmaa Military Area, 1970-   . Born December 25, 1915, Helsinki, Finland. BA, Forestry, 1941; Technical College, Zurich, Switzerland, 1954. Served in Winter War; Continuation War. Chief of Staff, 4th Infantry Regiment, 1951-52; Commandant, Noncommissioned Officer School, 1952-58; Commanding Officer, Karjala Brigade, 1963-66; Chief, Military Affairs Section, Ministry of Defense, 1966-70. Cross of Freedom, 3d Class with Oak Leaf; Cross of Freedom, 3d Class with Sword; Cross of Freedom, 4th Class (awarded twice); Commemorative Medals of Winter and Continuation Wars; and other medals and awards. Promoted to Major General, September 5, 1970.

Kruimink, F.E. Vice Admiral, Royal Netherlands Navy; Flag Officer Naval Personnel.

Kryukov, A. Lieutenant General, USSR Army; Commander, Railway Troops, Ministry of Defense. Served on the Soviet-German Front in WW II. Member, Communist Party of the Soviet Union.

Kucheman, Henry B., Jr. Major General, United States Air Force; Commander, Armament Development and Test Center, Air Force Systems Command, 1972-   . Born June 8, 1919, in Baltimore, Maryland. Virginia Polytechnic Institute, 1937-38, and 1947-49, BS, Chemical Engineering, 1949; Army Air Corps Flying School, 1941-42; Industrial College of the Armed Forces, 1959-60. Commissioned Second Lieutenant, US Army Air Corps, 1942. Served in the European Theater, WW II. Deputy for Limited War, Aeronautical Systems Division, 1966; Vice Commander, Aeronautical Systems Division, 1966-68; Director, Development, Deputy Chief of Staff, Research and Development, US Air Force, 1968-70; Assistant Deputy Chief of Staff, Research and Development, 1970; Deputy Commandant, Industrial College of the Armed Forces. Distinguished Service Medal; Silver Star; Legion of Merit with two Oak Leaf Clusters; Distinguished Flying Cross with two Oak Leaf Clusters; and other medals and awards. Promoted to Major General, June 24, 1968.

Kuczera, Bohuslaw. Lieutenant General, Army of Czechoslovakia; Deputy Chief of the General Staff.

Kudelkin, Ya. M. Rear Admiral, USSR Navy; Commander, The Caspian Sea Flotilla, 1972-   . Served in the Soviet-German War, 1941-45. Member, Communist Party of the Soviet Union.

Kufel, Teodor. Lieutenant General, Polish Army; Chief, Military Internal Service (Military Police and Counterintelligence).

Kühnle, Heinz. Vice Admiral, Navy of the Federal Republic of Germany; Chief of the Naval Staff, Federal German Navy.

Kulakov, Nikolay Mikhaylovich. Vice Admiral, USSR Navy; Chief, Political Department, and Deputy Commander for Political Affairs, Leningrad Naval Base and Naval Training Facilities, 1962-   . Born in 1908, in Ivanovskoye, Tula Oblast. Naval Faculty, Military-Political College, 1933-36. Commissioned c. 1932. Served in the Soviet-German War, 1941-45. Squadron Commissar and Member of Black Sea Fleet Military Council, 1941; Member, Sevastopol Defense Area Military Council, 1941-42; Staff Position, Main Political Directorate, Soviet Armed Forces, 1943-45; Member, Northern Fleet Military Council, 1945-46; Deputy for Political Affairs to Commander in Chief, Soviet Navy, and Member of the Navy's Military Council, 1946-49; Member, Black Sea Fleet Military Council, 1950-55; Chief of Political Department, Kronstadt Fortress, 1956-60; Chief of Political Department, Leningrad Naval Area, 1960-61; Member, Communist Party of the Soviet Union, 1927-   . Hero of the Soviet Union; Order of Lenin; Order of Red Banner; Order of Red Star; and other USSR and foreign medals and orders.

Kulichev, I. Major General, USSR Air Force; Commander, Air Force, Siberian Military District. Served on the Soviet-German Front in WW II. Member, Communist Party of the Soviet Union.

Kulikov, Victor G. General of the Army, USSR Army; Chief of the General Staff, 1971-   . Born in 1922. Attended General Staff War College, c. 1950. Served on the Soviet-German Front in WW II. Formerly Commander Armored Division; Commander, Kiev Military District, 1967-69; Commander in Chief, Group of Soviet Forces in Germany, 1969-71. Member, Communist Party of the Soviet Union. Order of Lenin; Order of the Red Banner; Order of the Red Star; and other Soviet and foreign orders and medals. Promoted to General of the Army, May 1, 1970.

Kullman, John R. Major General, United States Air Force; Deputy Chief of Staff, Intelligence, North American Air Defense Command/Continental Air Defense Command (NORAD/CONAD), 1970-   . Born June 1, 1922, in San Antonio, Texas. US Military Academy, 1939-43; National War College, 1963-64; George Washington University, MA, 1964. Commissioned Second Lieutenant, US Army Air Corps, 1943. Served in the Italian Theater in WW II. Commander, 4780th Air Defense Wing, 1964-66; Deputy Director, Alaskan Region, Federal Aviation Agency, 1966-68; Director, Plans and Policy, Headquarters NORAD/CONAD, 1968-69; Assistant Deputy Chief of Staff, Plans, Headquarters NORAD/CONAD, 1969-70. Legion of Merit; Distinguished Flying Cross; and other medals and awards. Promoted to Major General, May 1, 1970.

K'ung Shih-ch'uan. Lieutenant General, People's Liberation Army, People's Republic of China; Deputy Political Commissar, Canton Military Region, 1968-   . First Vice Chairman, Kwangtung Provincial Revolutionary Committee, 1968; Secretary, Provincial Party Committee, 1970. Member, Chinese Communist Party; Member Control Commission, Central Committee CCP; Member of Tenth CCP Central Committee, 1973. Order of Independence and Freedom; Order of Independence. Promoted to Major General, 1955; Lieutenant General, 1960.

Kunishima, Kiyonori. Rear Admiral, Japanese Self-Defense Force. Chief of the Administrative Division, Maritime Staff Office.

Kurkotkin, Semyon K. General of the Army, USSR Army; Deputy Minister of Defense and Chief, Rear Services (Logistics), 1972-   . Born in 1917. Served on the Soviet-German Front in WW II. Commander, Tank Brigade, 1945; First Deputy Commander in Chief, Group of Soviet Forces in Germany, 1966-68; Commander, Transcaucasus Military District, 1968-71; Commander in Chief, Group of Soviet Forces in Germany, 1971-72; Member, Communist Party of the Soviet Union. Promoted to General of the Army, November 7, 1972.

Kurochkin, K. Major General, USSR Army; Deputy Commander, Airborne Forces, 1972-   . Served on the Soviet-German Front in WW II. Member, Communist Party of the Soviet Union.

Kuruvila, E.C. Rear Admiral, Navy of India; Flag Officer Commanding Western Fleet.

Kutakhov, Pavel Stepanovich. Chief Marshal of Aviation, USSR Air Force; Commander in Chief, Soviet Air Force, 1969-   . Born in 1917. Attended Air Force Academy, c. 1937-c. 1940; Air Force War College, late 1940s. Commissioned c. 1940. Served in the Soviet-German War, 1941-45. Commander of an Air Force Regiment, c. 1944-45; Command Staff, First Deputy Commander in Chief, Soviet Air Force, 1968-69. Member, Communist Party of the Soviet Union; Deputy to the Ukrainian Supreme Soviet. Hero of the Soviet Union; two Orders of Lenin; three Orders of the Red Banner; Order of the Red Star; and other USSR and foreign orders and medals. Promoted to Marshal of the Air Force, February 1969; Chief Marshal of Aviation, November 1972.

Kuznetsov, G.A. Lieutenant General, USSR Naval Air Force; Commander, Northern Fleet Naval Air Force, 1966-   . Born in 1923. Attended Naval Aviation School, 1943; Air War College. Commissioned in 1943. Flew in Black Sea and Baltic aviation units in WW II. Deputy Commander, Air Force Division, 1959-66. Member, Communist Party of the Soviet Union. Hero of the Soviet Union; Order of Lenin; Order of the Red Banner; and other awards and medals. Promoted to Lieutenant General, 1968.

Kuznetsov, I.M. Vice Admiral, USSR Navy; Chief of Naval Training Establishments. Served in the Soviet-German War, 1941-45. Member, Communist Party of the Soviet Union.

Kuznetsov, Leonid Ivanovich. Major General, USSR Army; Commander, Taman Motorized Rifle Division, Moscow Military District, 1969-   . Born in 1925. Drafted into Soviet Army, 1943. Trained at Vladimir Infantry Academy, 1943-44; Senior Officers Courses; Army War College. Commissioned in 1944. Served on the Soviet-German Front in WW II. Previously Commander of Infantry Battalion and Infantry Regiment; Member, Communist Party of the Soviet Union, 1944-   . Order of Red Star; and other orders and medals.

Kwon, Yu Chan. Rear Admiral, Navy of the Democratic People's Republic of Korea; Commander of the Navy.

Kyari, Abba. Colonel, Nigerian Army; Military Governor, North Central State, 1967-   . Born in 1938, in Dewa, Republic of Niger. Attended Zaria Government College; Mons Officer Cadets School, United Kingdom; Officers Training Courses, United States and Great Britain. Commander, Artillery Battery, 1964-66; Commander, 5th Battalion, 1966-67.

L

Labarthe, Ramon Gomez Leite. Rear Admiral, Brazilian Navy; Naval Attache, Embassy of Brazil, Washington, D.C.; Delegate, Inter-American Defense Board; Member, Brazil-United States Joint Defense Commission. Date of Rank: April 28, 1971.

Lacy, Paul Lindsay, Jr. Rear Admiral, United States Navy; Deputy Chief of Naval Material (Logistic Support), 1972-   . Born August 2, 1920, in Dallas, Texas. Southern Methodist University, Dallas, Texas, 1938-39; US Naval Academy, 1939-42; Submarine School, 1944; Naval Postgraduate School, Annapolis, 1946-47; University of California, Los Angeles, MS, Applied Physics, 1947-49; Naval War College, Naval Warfare Course, 1958-59; Nuclear Propulsion Training Course, 1959-60. Commissioned Ensign, US Navy, 1942. Participated in the North African invasion and operations in the Pacific Theater in WW II; submarine unit commander in the Vietnam War. Commanding Officer, USS *Ethan Allen* (SSBN-608), 1961-64; Head of Plans and Programs Branch, then Deputy Director Special Projects Office, Office of Naval Material, 1964-67; Commander, US Naval Support Activity, Danang, Vietnam, 1967-68; Commander, Amphibious Group THREE and Commander Amphibious Force, Seventh Fleet, 1968; SSN 688 and later Design Attack Submarine Project Manager, Naval Material Command, 1968-70; Commander, Submarine Force, US Pacific Fleet, 1970-72. Distinguished Service Medal; Legion of Merit with Combat "V"; Navy Commendation Medal with Gold Star; and other US and foreign medals and awards. Promoted to Rear Admiral, July 1, 1967.

Lahue, Foster Carr. Lieutenant General, United States Marine Corps; Chief of Staff, Headquarters US Marine Corps, 1972-   . Born September 2, 1917, Corydon, Indiana. DePauw University, BA, 1939; Officers Candidate School, 1940-41; Command and Staff College, Quantico, 1954-55; Industrial College of the Armed Forces, 1964-65; George Washington University, MA, Personnel Management, and MS, Business Administration. Commissioned Second Lieutenant, USMCR, 1941. Served in Pacific Theater, WW II; Korean War; Vietnam War. Military Secretary to Marine Corps Commandant, 1965-67; Assistant Division Commander, then Division Commander, First Marine Division, and Commanding General, Task Force X-ray, Vietnam, 1967-68; Commanding General, Force Troops, Fleet Marine Force, Atlantic, 1968-69; Assistant Deputy Chief of Staff, Plans, Headquarters US Marine Corps, 1969-72. Distinguished Service Medal; Silver Star Medal; Legion of Merit with Combat "V"; Air Medal; and other US and foreign medals and awards. Promoted to Brigadier General, December 1966; Major General, August 1969; Lieutenant General, August 1972.

Lai Ming-tang. General, Air Force of Republic of China; Chief of the General Staff, Ministry of National Defense, 1970-   . Born May 5, 1911, Kiangsi. Military Academy, 1931; Central Aviation School, 1933; Command and General Staff College, USA, 1943. Served in Sino-Japanese War; Chinese Civil War. Chief of Staff, 3d Route Headquarters, Chinese Air Force, 1944-46; Air Attache, Chinese Embassy, London, England, 1946-48; Director, A-2, Headquarters, Chinese Air Force, 1948-50; Director, J-2, Ministry of National Defense, 1950-54; Deputy Chief of General Staff, Chinese Air Force, 1954-59; Vice Chief of General Staff, Ministry of National Defense, 1959-63; Commander in Chief, Combined Service Forces, 1963-67; Commander in Chief, Chinese Air Force, 1967-70; Member, Central Committee, Kuomintang.

Lamb, George Colin. Air Commodore, British Royal Air Force; Director of Control (Operations), National Air Traffic Services, 1972-   . Born July 23, 1923. Attended Flying Training Course; Staff College, 1953. Commissioned in the Royal Air Force in 1942. Served in WW II. Director of Administration Plans, Ministry of Defence, 1961-64; Assistant Commandant, Royal Air Force College, 1964-65; Deputy Commander, Air Forces, Borneo, 1965-66; Fighter Command, 1966; Deputy Command Structure Project Officer, Ministry of Defence, 1967; Headquarters, Strike Command, 1967-69; Officer Commanding, Royal Air Force, Lyneham, 1969-71; Royal College of Defence Studies, 1971-72. CBE; AFC.

Lambert, Valdemar Greene. Rear Admiral, United States Navy; Commander, Naval Base, Los Angeles, Long Beach, California, 1972-   . Born April 5, 1915, in Fullerton, Louisiana. Southwestern Louisiana Institute, Lafayette, Louisiana, BA, 1936; Flight Training Course, Naval Air Station, Pensacola, Florida, 1938-39; General Line School,

Newport, Rhode Island, 1947-48; Naval War College, 1953-54. Commissioned Ensign, US Naval Reserve, 1939; designated Naval Aviator, 1939; transferred to US Navy, 1941. Served in the Pacific Theater, WW II; Korean War. Chief of Staff and Aide to Commander Carrier Division FOUR, 1962-64; Assistant Director, Long Range Objectives Group, Office of CNO, 1964-65; Assistant Chief, Bureau of Naval Weapons, for Field Support, 1965-66; Assistant Commander for Logistics and Fleet Support, Naval Air Systems Command, 1966; Commander Carrier Division SIX, 1966-68; Commander Naval Base, Subic Bay, Luzon, Philippine Islands, 1968-70; Chief of Naval Technical Training, 1970-71; Deputy Director of Naval Education and Training, Office of the CNO, 1971-72. Navy Cross; Silver Star Medal; Legion of Merit with two Gold Stars and Combat "V"; Distinguished Flying Cross with two Gold Stars; Air Medal with seven Gold Stars; Navy Commendation Medal with "V"; and other medals and awards. Promoted to Rear Admiral, July 1, 1965.

Lamizana, Sangoule. Lieutenant Colonel, Army of Upper Volta; President of Upper Volta, and Commander in Chief of the Armed Forces, 1967-   . Born in 1916 in Dianra Tougan, Upper Volta. Served with French Forces in WW II and in Indochina. Chief of Staff of the Army, 1961-66; President, Prime Minister, Minister of Defense, War Veterans, Foreign Affairs, Information, Youth and Sports, 1966-67.

Lan, Bui The. Brigadier General, Army of the Republic of South Vietnam; Commander Marine Division.

Lancucki, Edward. Major General, Polish Army; Commander, Infantry Division. Promoted to Major General, 1970. Member, Polish United Workers Party.

Lang, Clarence Joseph. Major General, United States Army; Commander, Military Traffic Management and Terminal Service, Washington, D.C., 1969-   . Born June 28, 1918, Iowa City, Iowa. University of Iowa, BSC Degree, Commerce; Armed Forces Staff College; Industrial College of the Armed Forces; University of Texas, MBA Degree, Business Administration. Commissioned Second Lieutenant, US Army Reserve, 1940. Served in WW II. Assistant Commandant, US Army Transportation School, and Deputy Commanding General, US Army Transportation Center, Fort Eustis, Virginia, 1963-64; Director of Logistics, J-4, US Strike Command, MacDill Air Force Base, Florida, 1964-67; Chief of Staff, US Army Materiel Command, Washington, D.C., 1967-69. Distinguished Service Medal; Legion of Merit with Oak Leaf Cluster; and other medals and awards. Promoted to Brigadier General, October 1, 1963; Major General, June 1, 1967.

Lascara, Vincent Alfred. Rear Admiral, Supply Corps, United States Navy; Commanding Officer, Naval Supply Center, Norfolk, Virginia, 1973-   . Born December 24, 1919, in Norfolk, Virginia. College of William and Mary, Williamsburg, Virginia, BA, Economics and Accounting, 1942; Mine Warfare School, Yorktown, Virginia, 1943;

Naval Supply Corps School, Bayonne, New Jersey, 1947; Stanford University School of Business, MBA, 1951; Naval War College, Newport, Rhode Island, 1966-67. Commissioned Ensign, US Naval Reserve, 1942; transferred from Naval Reserve to US Navy, 1946; transferred from Line to Supply Corps, 1947. Served in European Theater, WW II. Director, Inventory Control Department, Naval Supply Center, Norfolk, Virginia, 1964-66; Executive Officer, Navy Ships Parts Control Center, Mechanicsburg, Pennsylvania, 1967-68; Commanding Officer, Fleet Material Support Office, Mechanicsburg, Pennsylvania, 1968-69; Assistant Comptroller, Financial Management Systems, Navy Department, and Commanding Officer, Naval Accounting and Financial Center, Washington, D.C., 1969-73. Navy Commendation Medal with Gold Star; American Campaign Medal; National Defense Service Medal with Bronze Star; and other medals and awards. Promoted to Rear Admiral, July 1, 1970.

Lashchenko, Pyotr Nikolayevich. General of the Army, USSR Army; First Deputy Commander in Chief, Soviet Ground Forces, 1968-   . Born in 1910. Drafted into Soviet Army, 1930. Attended Military Academy, 1930-33; Army War College, 1935-39; General Staff War College, 1949-51. Commissioned in 1933. Served on the Soviet-German Front in WW II, as Assistant Chief of Staff, Field Army, 1941-43; Commander, 322d Rifle Division, 1943-45. Superintendent, Military Academy, 1945-49; Commander of large military units and formations in the Baltic, Carpathian and Kiev Military Districts, 1951-60; Commandant, Kiev Garrison, 1960-61; Deputy Commander, Carpathian Military District, 1962-64; Commander, Carpathian Military District, 1964-67; Staff Position, Ministry of Defense, Moscow, 1967-68. Member, Communist Party of the Soviet Union since 1931; Deputy to the USSR Supreme Soviet. Hero of the Soviet Union; Order of Lenin; Order of Red Banner; Order of Kutuzov; Order of Red Star; and other Soviet and foreign orders and medals. Promoted to General of the Army, February 1968.

Lattion, Gérard. Lieutenant General, Swiss Army; Commanding General, 1st Army Corps. Born in 1915. Promoted to Lieutenant General, 1972.

Lavriyenko, N. Colonel General, USSR Frontier Troops; Commander, Transbaikal Frontier District. Served on the Soviet-German Front in WW II. Member, Communist Party of the Soviet Union.

Lawrence, John Thornett. Air Vice-Marshal, British Royal Air Force; Director-General of Personnel Management (RAF), 1971-   . Born April 16, 1920. Attended Imperial Defence College, 1968. Commissioned in 1938. Served in WW II in Coastal Command. Group Captain Operations, Headquarters Air Force Middle East, 1962-64; Commanding Officer, RAF Wittering, 1964-66; Air Officer Commanding, 3 Group, Bomber Command, 1967; Director of Organization and Administration Plans (RAF), 1969-71. CBE; AFC; Order of Leopold II, Belgium; Croix de Guerre, Belgium.

Leabua, Jonathan. Prime Minister and Minister of Defense, Kingdom of Lesotho, 1973-   .

Leach, Henry Conyers. Rear-Admiral, British Royal Navy; Assistant Chief of Naval Staff (Policy), 1971-   . Born November 18, 1923. Attended Royal Naval College, Dartmouth, 1937-40; Staff College, 1952; Joint Services Staff Course, 1961. Commissioned in 1940. Served at sea in the Atlantic, Indian Ocean, and Mediterranean in WW II. Commander, frigate *Galatea*, as Captain (D) 27th Squadron and Mediterranean, 1965-67; Director of Naval Plans, 1968-70; Commander, Commando Ship *Albion*, 1970. Promoted to Captain, 1961; Rear-Admiral, 1971.

Leahy, Osmund Alfred. Major General, United States Army; Commanding General, US Army Physical Disability Agency, Washington, D.C., 1972-   . Born August 31, 1915, Owego, New York. US Military Academy; US Army War College; George Washington University, MA Degree, Public Administration. Commissioned Second Lieutenant, 1940. Served in WW II. Chief of Staff, XVIII Airborne Corps, Fort Bragg, North Carolina, 1966-67; Commanding General, II US Army Corps, Fort Wadsworth, New York, 1967-68; Commanding General, 7th Infantry Division, US Army Pacific-Korea, 1968; Deputy Commanding General, US Army Combat Development Command, Fort Belvoir, Virginia, 1968-69; Commanding General, Institute of Land Combat, US Army Combat Development Command, Fort Belvoir, later Alexandria, Virginia, 1969-70; Chief of Staff, Sixth US Army, Presidio of San Francisco, California, 1970-71; Deputy Commanding General, Sixth US Army, Presidio of San Francisco, California, 1971-72. Distinguished Service Medal; Silver Star with two Oak Leaf Clusters; Legion of Merit with Oak Leaf Cluster; Bronze Star Medal; and other medals and awards. Promoted to Brigadier General, September 1, 1964; Major General, August 1, 1967.

Leal Torres, Homero Ignacio. Major General, Venezuelan Army; Inspector General, Armed Forces, Ministry of Defense, 1973-   . Born February 1, 1923, in Los Teques, Venezuela. Attended Army Military Academy; Advanced Military Course, Venezuela; Advanced Transportation Course, USA; Command and Staff College, Peru; Advanced Management Course, Monterey, California, USA. Commissioned Second Lieutenant, Venezuelan Army, in 1945. Recent Duty: Director, Army Military Academy; Commander, 3d Infantry Division, Barquisimeto; Commander, 4th Infantry Division, Maracay; Commander, Army Organic Elements; Inspector General, Army General Headquarters; Chief of Staff, Venezuelan Army; Commanding General, Venezuelan Army, 1971-73. Promoted to Colonel, July 5, 1963; Brigadier General, July 5, 1967; Major General, July 1972.

LeBailly, Eugene Bernard. Lieutenant General, United States Air Force; Chairman, Inter-American Defense Board, 1970-   . Born January 29, 1915, in Shoshone, Idaho. Idaho State University, 1933-34; University of California, Berkeley, BS, 1939; Army Air Corps Flying School, 1939-40; Air Command and Staff School, 1948; Air War College, 1952. Commissioned Second Lieutenant, US Army Air Corps, 1940. Served in the European Theater, WW II; Korean War. Deputy Director, Office of Information, Office, Secretary of the Air Force, 1958-61; Commander, US Forces Azores, and Commander 1605th Air Base Wing (MATS), Lajes Field, Azores, Portugal, 1961-64; Director of Information, Office, Secretary of Air Force, 1964-67; Commander, Sixteenth Air Force, Torrejon Air Base, Spain, 1967-70. Distinguished Service Medal with one Oak Leaf Cluster; Silver Star; Legion of Merit; Distinguished Flying Cross with two Oak Leaf Clusters; Croix de Guerre with Silver Star; and other US and foreign medals and awards. Promoted to Brigadier General, November 20, 1958; Major General, July 1, 1963; Lieutenant General, August 1, 1970.

Leber, Georg. Federal Minister of Defense, Federal Republic of Germany, 1972-   . Born October 7, 1920, Obertiefenbach, Germany. Attended Business School, Limburg. Served as private, German Air Force, 1939-45. Federal Minister of Transportation, 1966-69; Federal Minister of Transportation, Postal Service, and Telecommunication, 1969-72. Member of Social Democratic Party, 1947-   , and of its Presidium, 1968-   .

Leber, Walter Philip. Lieutenant General, United States Army; SAFEGUARD Systems Manager, US Army SAFEGUARD System Office, Arlington, Virginia, 1971-   . Born September 12, 1918, St. Louis, Missouri. Missouri School of Mines, BS Degree, Petroleum Engineering; US Army Command and General Staff College; Industrial College of the Armed Forces; George Washington University, MBA Degree, Business Administration. Commissioned Second Lieutenant, US Army Reserve, 1940. Served in WW II. Engineer, US Army Engineer Division, Ohio River, Cincinnati, Ohio, 1963-66; Director of Civil Works, Office, Chief of Engineers, US Army, Washington, D.C., 1966-67; Governor of the Canal Zone and President of the Panama Canal Company, Balboa Heights, Canal Zone, 1967-71. Distinguished Service Medal; Legion of Merit with two Oak Leaf Clusters; Bronze Star Medal; and other medals and awards. Promoted to Brigadier General, April 8, 1963; Major General, November 1, 1967; Lieutenant General, April 1, 1971.

LeBourgeois, Julien Johnson. Vice Admiral, United States Navy; Chief of Staff to Supreme Allied Commander, Atlantic, 1972-   . Born November 23, 1923, in Southern Pines, North Carolina. US Naval Academy, 1941-44; Naval Intelligence School, 1949; Naval Language School, 1950; Armed Forces Staff College, 1959; Industrial College of the Armed Forces, 1961-62; George Washington University, MA, International Affairs, 1963. Commissioned Ensign, US Navy, 1944. Served in the Pacific Theater, WW II; Vietnam War. Executive Assistant and Senior Aide to the Deputy CNO (Plans and Policy), 1962-65; Commanding Officer, USS *Halsey* (DLG-23), 1965-67; Systems Analysis Division, Office of CNO, 1967-68; Executive Assistant and Senior Aide to the Chief of Naval Operations, 1968-70; Deputy Assistant Chief of Staff for Plans and Policy to Supreme Allied Commander, Europe, 1970-72.

Distinguished Service Medal; Legion of Merit with Gold Star; Bronze Star Medal with Combat "V"; and other medals and awards. Promoted to Rear Admiral, August 1, 1969; Vice Admiral, May 9, 1972.

Le Cheminant, Sir Peter (de Lacey). Air Vice-Marshal, British Royal Air Force; United Kingdom Member, Permanent Military Deputies Group, Central Treaty Organization, Ankara, 1972-   . Born June 17, 1920. Attended Elizabeth College, Guernsey; Royal Air Force College, Cranwell; Joint Services Staff College, 1958. Commissioned in 1940. Served in the Mediterranean and European Theaters in WW II; Malaya, 1955-57. Commander RAF Geilenkirchen, 1961-63; Director, Air Staff Briefing, 1964-66; Senior Air Staff Officer, Headquarters, Far East Air Force, 1966-67; Chief of Staff, Far East Air Force, 1967-68; Commandant, Joint Warfare Establishment, Ministry of Defence, 1968-70; Assistant Chief of Air Staff (Policy), Ministry of Defence, 1971-72. KCB; DFC and Bar.

Lee, Byong Mun. General, Marine Corps of the Republic of Korea; Commandant, ROK Marine Corps, 1971-   . Attended Korean Military Academy, 1950; Infantry School (USA), 1953; Post Graduate School, Seoul, 1965. Commissioned Second Lieutenant in 1950. Combat duty in the Korean War. Commanding General, 1st Marine Brigade, 1969-70; Assistant Commander, ROK Marine Corps, 1970-71. Decorations: Ulchi; Chungmu; Legion of Merit (USA); and other medals and awards. Promoted to General, July 1, 1971.

Lee, Kent Liston. Vice Admiral, United States Navy; Deputy Director, Joint Strategic Target Planning Staff, 1972-   . Born July 28, 1922, in Florence County, South Carolina. Flight Training Course, Naval Air Station, Corpus Christi, Texas, 1942-43; Undergraduate Course, Naval Reserve Officer Training Corps Unit, Columbia University, New York, 1947-49; General Line School, Newport, Rhode Island, 1949-50; US Naval Postgraduate School, Monterey, California, MS, Physics, 1952-54; Nuclear Propulsion Course, Atomic Energy Commission, 1963-64. Commissioned Ensign, US Naval Reserve, 1943; designated Naval Aviator, 1943; transferred to regular Navy, 1946. Served in the Pacific Theater, WW II; Korean War; Vietnam War. Commander Carrier Air Group SIX, 1962-63; Commanding Officer USS *Alamo* (LSD-33), 1964-65; Executive Assistant and Naval Aide to the Assistant Secretary of the Navy (Research and Development), 1965-67; Commanding Officer USS *Enterprise* (CVA(N)65), 1967-69; Assistant Commander for Logistics and Fleet Support, Naval Air Systems Command, 1969-70; Director, Office of Program Appraisal, 1970-72. Legion of Merit; Air Medal with two Gold Stars; Navy Commendation Medal; and other US and foreign medals and awards. Promoted to Vice Admiral, January 29, 1972.

Lee, Richard McGowan. Major General, United States Army; Deputy Commandant, National War College, Fort Lesley J. McNair, Washington, D.C., 1972-   . Born January 17, 1917, Moscow, Idaho. University of Maryland, BA Degree, Pre-law; Infantry School, Basic Course; US Army Command and General Staff College; US Army War College; Princeton University, MA Degree, Public Affairs. Commissioned Second Lieutenant, US Army Reserve, 1940. Served in WW II and Vietnam War. Deputy Senior Advisor, II Corps Advisory Group, US Military Assistance Command, Vietnam, 1966-67; Director of Programs, Office, Director of Military Assistance, Office, Assistant Secretary of Defense (International Security Affairs), Washington, D.C., 1967-69; Director of Programs and Plans, Office, Deputy Assistant Secretary (Military Assistance and Sales), Office, Assistant Secretary of Defense (International Security Affairs), Washington, D.C., 1969-70; Chief of Staff, US Forces, Japan, 1971-72. Distinguished Service Medal; Legion of Merit with two Oak Leaf Clusters; Bronze Star Medal; and other medals and awards. Promoted to Brigadier General, October 27, 1966; Major General, May 1, 1970.

Lee Tun-chien. Vice Admiral, Navy of the Republic of China; Deputy Commander in Chief, Administration.

Leeb, Anton. General of Infantry, Austrian Army; Inspector General, 1971-   . Born February 2, 1913. Attended the Austrian Military Academy at Enns and Wiener Neustadt, 1933-36. Commissioned Second Lieutenant, Austrian Army, in 1936. Served in the German Army in WW II. Chief of Border Guards, 1959-61; Director, Office of the Minister of Defense, 1961-64; Director, National Defense Policy Office, and Chief, National Defense Policy Group, 1964-66; Deputy Commander, Group I, 1969-71. Grosses Ehrenzeichen; Goldenes Ehrenzeichen; and other medals and awards. Promotions: Colonel, 1960; Brigadier, 1965; Major General, January 1971; General of Infantry, January 1, 1972.

Lees-Spalding, Ian Jaffery. Rear-Admiral, British Royal Navy, Chief Staff Officer (Technical) on the Staff of Commander-in-Chief, Western Fleet, and Inspector General Fleet Maintenance, 1971-   . Born June 16, 1920, in London. Attended Royal Navy Engineering College; Submarine Course. Joined the Royal Navy in 1938. Participated in Sicily, Italy and Normandy Landings, WW II. Commander, HMS *Tiger*, 1960-62; Fleet Engineer Officer on Staff of Commander-in-Chief, Home Fleet, 1962-66; Directorate of Marine Engineering, Ship Department, Ministry of Defence, 1966-69; Chief of Staff to Commander-in-Chief, Naval Home Command, 1969-71. CB. Chartered Engineer; Fellow of the Institution of Mechanical Engineers; Member of the British Institute of Management; Member of the Institute of Marine Engineers. Promotions: Captain, 1962; Rear-Admiral, 1971.

Lehti, Olavi J. Major General, Army of Finland; Commanding General, Southwest Finland Military Area, 1971-   . Born March 2, 1914, Salo, Uusimaa Province, Finland. Technical University, Zurich, Switzerland, 1950s. Served in Winter War; Continuation War. Chief of Staff, 2d Division, 1962-65; Director of National Defense Course, War College, 1965-68; Commandant, War College, 1968-71. Commander's Order of Finnish Lion; Cross of Freedom, 2d Class; Cross of Freedom, 3d Class with Sword; Cross of

Freedom, 4th Class with Oak Leaf; Cross of Freedom, 4th Class with Sword; Commemorative Medals of Winter and Continuation Wars; and other medals and awards. Promoted to Major General, December 31, 1967.

Lei Kai-shuen. General, Army of Republic of China; Vice Minister of National Defense, 1969-   . Born July 15, 1916, Szechwan. Attended Military Academy; Army Artillery College; Army War College; Armed Forces Staff College; Joint Operation Course; Command and General Staff College, USA. Served in Sino-Japanese War; Chinese Civil War. Recent Positions: Commander, 93d Infantry Division, 1954-58; Commander, 8th Army, 1958-62; Executive Officer, Office of Vice Chief of General Staff for Operations, Ministry of National Defense, 1962-65; Commanding General, Matsu Defense Command, Ministry of National Defense, 1965-69.

Leig, Victor Didrich. Brigadier General, Brazilian Air Force; Air Attache, Embassy of Brazil, Washington, D.C., 1971-73.

Leigh Guzman, Gustavo. General, Chilean Air Force; Commander, Chilean Air Force, 1973-   .

Leinonen, Kaarlo O. General, Army of Finland; Commander in Chief, Finnish Defense Forces, 1969-   . Born March 15, 1914, Tervola, Finland. University of Helsinki, LLM, 1955. Served in Winter War; Continuation War. Military Attache, Finnish Embassy, Washington, D.C., USA, 1958-61; Senior Aide de Camp to the President of Finland, 1961-64; Commanding Officer, Armored Brigade, 1965-66; Secretary General to the Minister of Defense, 1966-68; Chief of the General Headquarters, Finnish Defense Forces, 1968-69. Cross of Freedom, 2d Class with Sword; Cross of Freedom, 4th Class with Sword; Cross of Freedom, 3d Class with Oak Leaf; Commemorative Medals of Winter and Continuation Wars; Commander's Order of the Finnish Lion; Legion of Merit (USA); and other medals and awards. Promoted to General, June 4, 1969.

Lekson, John Stephan. Major General, United States Army; Director of Operations, J-3, US Readiness Command, MacDill Air Force Base, Florida, 1972-   . Born April 14, 1917, Fairpoint, Ohio. Western Reserve University, BS Degree, Education; The Infantry School; US Army Command and General Staff College; US Armed Forces Staff College; US Air War College. Commissioned Second Lieutenant, US Army Reserve, 1942. Served in WW II and Vietnam War. Assistant Division Commander, 9th Infantry Division, US Army, Vietnam, 1967; Chief of Staff, II Field Force, US Army, Vietnam, 1967-68; Assistant Division Commander, 101st Airborne Division (Airmobile), US Army, Vietnam, 1968; Commanding General, US Army Training Center, Fort Campbell, Kentucky, 1968-70; Chief, Joint US Military Assistance Group, Korea, 1970-72. Distinguished Service Medal; Silver Star; Legion of Merit with Oak Leaf Cluster; Bronze Star Medal with two Oak Leaf Clusters; and other medals and awards. Promoted to Brigadier General, June 1, 1967; Major General, June 1, 1970.

Lemos, William Edward. Rear Admiral, United States Navy; Deputy Chief of Staff for Personnel, Administration and Logistics to the Commander in Chief, US Atlantic Fleet, 1971-   . Born September 12, 1917, in Riverside, Rhode Island. US Naval Academy, 1937-41; Flight Training Course, 1943; Postgraduate School, Ordnance Engineering Course (Aviation), 1946-47; Massachusetts Institute of Technology, MS, 1947-49; National War College, 1957-58. Commissioned Ensign, US Navy, 1941; designated Naval Aviator, 1943. Served in the Pacific Theater, WW II. Commanding Officer USS *Ranger* (CVA-61), 1963-64; Chief of Staff and Aide to Commander Second Fleet, 1964-65; Deputy Director, National Military Command Center, J-3; Joint Chiefs of Staff, 1965-66; Director, East Asia and Pacific Region, Office of the Assistant Secretary of Defense (International Security Affairs), 1966; Commander Carrier Division FOUR, 1966-69; Director of Plans and National Security Council Affairs, Office of the Assistant Secretary of Defense (International Security Affairs), 1969-71. Distinguished Service Medal; Legion of Merit; Distinguished Flying Cross; Air Medal with Gold Star; Navy Commendation Medal with Combat "V"; and other medals and awards. Promoted to Rear Admiral, December 1, 1965.

Lenoir, William B. United States; NASA Scientist-Astronaut, 1967-   . Born March 14, 1939, Miami, Florida. Massachusetts Institute of Technology, BS, Electrical Engineering, 1961, MS, 1962, PhD, 1965; NASA Flight Training. Instructor, Massachusetts Institute of Technology, 1964-65; Assistant Professor, 1965-67. NASA experience: Backup Pilot, Skylab 3 and 4. Sloan Scholar, Massachusetts Institute of Technology; Carleton E. Tucker Award for Teaching Excellence, Massachusetts Institute of Technology.

Leonenkov, V. M. Vice Admiral, USSR Navy; Commanding Officer, Leningrad Naval Base. Served in the Soviet-German War, 1941-45. Member, Communist Party of the Soviet Union.

Leonov, Alexey Arkhipovich. Colonel, USSR Air Force; Cosmonaut, 1960-   . Born in 1934. Attended Chukuevsky Air Force Pilot School; Zhukovskiy Air Force Engineering War College. Commissioned in 1956; Cosmonaut training, 1960. Air Force Pilot, 1956-59; Crew of Voskhod-2 Spaceship. Member, Communist Party of the Soviet Union since 1957. Hero of the Soviet Union; Pilot-Cosmonaut of the USSR; Order of Lenin; Order of Red Star; and other medals and awards.

Leont'ev, N. Lieutenant General, USSR Army; First Deputy Chief, Political Directorate, Strategic Missile Forces. Served on the Soviet-German Front in WW II. Member, Communist Party of the Soviet Union.

Leslie, Edward Murray Dailzell. Brigadier-General, Royal Canadian Army; Chief of Staff, United Nations Forces, Nicosia, Cyprus, 1968-   . Born October 20, 1915, in Guilford, England. Attended Loyola College, Montreal, Canada, 1934-38. Commissioned Second Lieutenant, Canadian Army, 1938. Distinguished Service Order; Bronze Star (USA); and other medals and awards. Fellow, Royal Canadian Geographical Society; Member, Canadian Institute for Foreign Affairs. Promoted to Brigadier-General, 1966.

LeVan, Cj. Major General, United States Army; Commanding General, US Army Air Defense Center and Commandant US Army Air Defense School, Fort Bliss, 1973-   . Born February 13, 1923, Kansas City, Missouri. University of Omaha; Artillery School, Advanced Course; US Army Command and General Staff College; US Army War College; George Washington University, MS, Political Science. Commissioned Second Lieutenant, US Army, 1942. Served in WW II. Assistant for Anti-Ballistic Missiles, Office of Assistant Secretary of the Army (Research and Development), Washington, D.C., 1968; Director of Air Defense, Office of Assistant Chief of Staff for Force Development, US Army, Washington, D.C., 1968-69; Commanding General, 38th Artillery Brigade (Air Defense), US Army, Pacific-Korea, 1969-70; Commanding General, 1st Region, US Army Air Defense Command, Stewart Field, New York, 1970-71; Commanding General, 32d Army Air Defense Command, US Army, Europe, 1971-73. Legion of Merit with three Oak Leaf Clusters; and other medals and awards. Promoted to Brigadier General, September 18, 1968; Major General, April 1, 1971.

Levchenko, N. Lieutenant General, USSR Army; Deputy Chief, Rear Services (Logistics), Ministry of Defense, 1970-   . Served on the Soviet-German Front in WW II. Member, Communist Party of the Soviet Union.

Levchenko, P. Lieutenant General, USSR Army; Commander, Air Defense, Soviet Ground Forces. Served on the Soviet-German Front in WW II. Member, Communist Party of the Soviet Union.

Lewin, Sir Terence Thornton. Vice-Admiral, British Royal Navy; Vice Chief of Naval Staff, 1971-   . Born November 19, 1920, in Dover. The Judd School, Tonbridge. Joined the Royal Navy in 1939. Served in the Home and Mediterranean Fleets in WW II. Director, Naval Tactical and Weapons Policy Division, Ministry of Defence, 1964-65; Commander, HMS *Hermes*, 1966-67; Assistant Chief of Naval Staff (Policy), 1968-69; Flag Officer, Second in Command, Far East Fleet, 1969-70. KCB; MVO; DSC. Promoted to Rear-Admiral, 1968; Vice-Admiral, 1970.

Lewis, Alfred George. Major-General, British Army; Assistant Chief of Staff (Intelligence) S, 1972-   . Born July 23, 1920. Attended St. Dunstan's College; King's College, London. Served in India and Burma in WW II. Director, Defence Operational Requirements Staff, Ministry of Defence, 1967-68; Deputy Commandant, Royal Military College of Science, 1968-70; Director General, Fighting Vehicles and Engineer Equipment, 1970-72. CBE.

Lewis, Sir Andrew Mackenzie. Admiral, British Royal Navy; Commander-in-Chief, Naval Home Command, and Flag Officer, Portsmouth Area, 1972-   . Born January 24, 1918. Attended Haileybury. Served at sea in WW II. Director of Plans, Admiralty, 1961-63; Commander, HMS *Kent*, 1964-65; Director-General, Weapons (Naval), 1965-68; Flag Officer, Flotillas, Western Fleet, 1968-69; Second Sea Lord and Chief of Naval Personnel, 1970-71. KCB; ADC.

Lewis, Homer I. Major General, United States Air Force; Chief of Air Force Reserve, Headquarters, US Air Force, 1971-   , and Commander, Headquarters Air Force Reserve, 1972-   . Born February 1, 1919, in Asheville, North Carolina. US Naval Academy, 1938-39 (resigned, 1939); University of Texas, 1939-40; Army Air Corps Flying School, 1942-43. Commissioned Second Lieutenant, US Army Reserve, 1940. Served in the European Theater, WW II. Director, Materiel, 433d Wing, 1963-66; Mobilization Assistant, Commander, San Antonio Air Materiel Area, 1966-68; Reserve Deputy to the Commander, Headquarters Command, USAF, 1968-71. Legion of Merit; and other medals and awards. Promoted to Major General, May 12, 1970.

Lewis, John Michael Hardwicke. Major-General, British Army; Assistant Chief of Staff (Intelligence), SHAPE, 1972-   . Born April 5, 1919. Attended Royal Military Academy, Woolwich; Staff College, Camberley, 1949; Imperial Defence College, 1966. Commissioned Second Lieutenant, Royal Engineers, in 1939. Served in India-Burma Theater in WW II. Instructor, Joint Services Staff College, 1961-63; Assistant Chief of Staff (Intelligence), Ministry of Defence, 1970-72. CBE. Author of *Michiel Marieschi: Venetian Artist*, 1967.

Lewis, Leo C. Major General, United States Air Force; Vice Commander, Fifteenth Air Force, Strategic Air Command (SAC), 1972-   . Born April 24, 1921, Pensacola, Florida. Sacramento Junior College, California; Army Air Corps Flying School, 1942-43; Air Tactical School; Air War College, 1958-59. Commissioned Second Lieutenant, US Army Air Corps, 1943. Served in the European and Pacific Theaters; Vietnam War. Director, Operations, Headquarters Fifth Air Force, 1965-67; Director, Command Control, Deputy Chief of Staff, Operations, SAC, 1967-68; Inspector General, SAC, 1968-70; Vice Commander, Eighth Air Force, SAC, Guam, 1970-72. Legion of Merit with two Oak Leaf Clusters; Distinguished Flying Cross with two Oak Leaf Clusters; and other medals and awards. Promoted to Major General, February 26, 1971.

Lewis, Oliver W. Major General, United States Air Force; Director of Personnel Programs, Deputy Chief of Staff, Personnel, Headquarters US Air Force, 1972-   . Born August 12, 1923, in Knoxville, Alabama. University of Alabama, 1941-42; Army Air Corps Flying School, 1943-44; George Washington University, 1957-58, BA, Business Administration, 1958. Commissioned Second Lieutenant, US Army Air Corps, 1944. Served in the Korean War; Vietnam War. Commander, 804th Combat Support Group, 1965-67; Commander, 335th Combat Support Group, Thailand, 1967-68; Commander, Norton Air Force Base, 1968-69; Wing Commander, Scott Air Force Base, Illinois, 1969-70; Deputy Chief of Staff, Personnel, Headquarters Military Airlift Command, 1970-72. Legion of Merit; Air Medal; and other medals and awards. Promoted to Brigadier General, August 1, 1970; Major General, September 20, 1972.

Lewis-Jones, Robert Gwilym. Captain, British Royal Navy; on the Staff of Director, General Ships Directorate (Naval Ship Production), 1970-   . Born February 22, 1922. Attended Gonville and Caius College, Cambridge; Fleet Air Arm Observers Course, 1942-43; Long Air Communications Course, 1945-46; Long Air Electronics/Electrical Course, 1946-47; Long Ships Electrical Course, 1950; Senior Officers War Course, Royal Naval College, Greenwich, 1969-70. Served in the Atlantic and Murmansk convoys in WW II. Executive Officer and Second in Command, HMS *Condor*, 1963-65; General Manager, Royal Navy Aircraft Yard, Belfast, 1965-67; Director of Aircraft Armament, Ministry of Defence (Navy), 1967-68. CBE. Chartered Engineer; Associate Fellow, Royal Aeronautical Society. Promoted to Commander, 1958; Captain, 1967.

Lezhepekov, V. Major General, USSR Frontier Troops; Chief, Political Directorate, Frontier Troops. Served on the Soviet-German Front in WW II. Member, Communist Party of the Soviet Union.

L'Heureux, L.J. Chairman of the Canadian Defence Research Board, 1967-   . Born in 1919, in Gravelbourg, Saskatchewan. University of Ottawa, BA, 1940; University of Saskatchewan, BE (Physics), 1944; Johns Hopkins University, Baltimore, Maryland (USA), MS (Electrical Engineering), 1948, Doctor of Engineering, 1949; Canadian National Defence College, 1960-61. Scientific Advisor to the Chief of the General Staff, Canadian Army, 1961-63; Director General, Defence Research Establishment Valcartier, 1963-67; Vice Chairman, Defence Research Board, 1967.

Li Teh-sheng. Lieutenant General, People's Liberation Army, People's Republic of China; Political Commissar, People's Liberation Army, 1972-   . Attended Red Army Military Academy. Joined the Red Army, 1934. Chairman of Anhwei Military Control Commission and Military District, 1967; Chairman, Anhwei Provincial Revolutionary Committee, 1968; Member, Military Affairs Committee; First Secretary, Anhwei Provincial Party Committee. Member of Chinese Communist Party, since c. 1935;

Member of Central Committee, 1969; Alternate Member, Politburo, 1969; Vice Chairman of Presidium, Tenth National Party Congress, 1973; Vice Chairman, Politburo, 1973-   .

Li T'ien-yu. Colonel General, People's Liberation Army, People's Republic of China; Member, National Defense Council. Born 1905, Honan. Studied at Red Army Academy, Juichin, Kiangsi, 1933; Nanking Military Academy, 1955-58. Joined the Red Army, ca. 1930. Participated in anti-Japanese guerrilla warfare, 1937-45, and the Civil War. Commander, 686th Regiment, 115th Division, 8th Route Army, 1937; Garrison Commander, Harbin, and Commander, Sungkiang Military District, 1946; Commander, 1st Combat Column, Northeast Democratic Allied Army, 1947; Commander, 38th Army, 13th Army Corps, 1948; Commander 13th Army Corps, 1949; Deputy Commander, then Commander, Kwangsi Military District, 1949-51; Member, Kwangsi Provincial People's Government Council, 1949-54; Member, Central-South Military and Administrative Committee, 1951-53; Commander, Canton Military Region, 1958; Deputy Chief of Staff, People's Liberation Army, 1963. Order of August 1; Order of Independence and Freedom; Order of Liberation. Member, Chinese Communist Party since ca. 1930; Member, Central Committee, CCP; Deputy to the 2d and 3d National People's Congresses. Promoted to Colonel General, 1955.

Li Tsai-han. Lieutenant General, People's Liberation Army, People's Republic of China; Political Commissar. Participated in anti-Japanese guerrilla warfare, 1937-45, and the Civil War. Member, Chinese Communist Party. Deputy Political Commissar, Kweichow Military District, 1967; 1st Political Commissar, Kweichow Military District, 1967; Chairman, Kweichow Provincial Revolutionary Committee, 1967; Political Commissar, Kunming Military Region, 1968-71; Alternate Member, Central Committee, 1969. Order of Independence and Freedom; Order of Liberation.

Li Tso-p'eng. Vice Admiral, Navy of the People's Liberation Army, People's Republic of China; 1st Political Commissar, People's Navy. Born in Kiangsi Province. Participated in anti-Japanese guerrilla warfare, 1937-45, and the Civil War. Member, Chinese Communist Party. Possibly Commander, 1st Column, Northeast Democratic Allied Forces, 1946-47; Chief of Staff, Kwangtung Military District; Deputy Commandant, Central-South Military and Political University, 1951; Director, Land Forces Training Department, 1958-64; Deputy Commander of Navy, 1964; Member, National Defense Council, 1965; Member of Politburo, 1972. Order of August 1; Order of Independence and Freedom; Order of Liberation. Promoted to Vice Admiral in 1955.

Li Yuan. Major General, People's Liberation Army, People's Republic of China; Commander, Military Unit, Hunan Military District, 1967-   . Participated in anti-Japanese guerrilla warfare, 1937-45, and the Civil War. With Canton Forces, People's Liberation Army, 1964; Chairman, Hunan Provincial Revolutionary Committee, 1968; Alternate

Member, Central Committee, 1969; Alternate Member, Tenth Central Committee, 1973.

Lich, Tran Quoc. Brigadier General, Army of the Republic of South Vietnam; Commander 5th Infantry Division.

Lier, R.H. Rear Admiral, Canadian Armed Forces; Commander Maritime Forces Pacific.

Lightner, Lawrence Scott. Major General, United States Air Force; Commandant, Air War College, 1971-   , and Vice Commander, Air University, 1972-   . Born October 13, 1918, Painesville, Ohio. Ohio Wesleyan University, BA, 1940; Army Air Corps Flying School, 1941; Army Command and General Staff School, 1946-47; Air Force Manpower Management Course, George Washington University, 1953; Air War College, 1954-55. Commissioned Second Lieutenant, US Army Air Corps, 1941. Served in the European Theater, WW II. Commander 341st Strategic Missile Wing, Strategic Air Command (SAC), 1963-64; Commander, 813th Strategic Aerospace Division, SAC, 1964-65; Deputy Director and later Director, Legislative Liaison, Office of the Secretary of the Air Force, 1965; Commander, Third Air Force, US Air Forces, Europe, United Kingdom; Assistant Chief of Staff, Operations, Supreme Headquarters Allied Powers, Europe, Belgium. Distinguished Service Medal with one Oak Leaf Cluster; Legion of Merit with two Oak Leaf Clusters; Distinguished Flying Cross with one Oak Leaf Cluster; and other US and foreign medals and awards. Promoted to Major General, January 1, 1966.

Likachev, B. Lieutenant General, Armor, USSR Army; First Deputy Commander, Baltic Military District. Served on the Soviet-German Front in WW II. Member, Communist Party of the Soviet Union.

Liljestrand, Bengt. Major General, Swedish Royal Army; Commandant, Royal Staff College of the Armed Forces, 1973-   . Royal Army Staff College, 1947-49; Bachelor of Arts Degree, 1950; Royal National Defense College, 1959, 1970; Institut Universitaire des Hautes Etudes Internationales, Geneva, 1966-68. Commanding Officer, Artillery Regiment A 8, 1968-69; Chief of Staff, Military Command West, 1969-73. Commander of the Royal Order of the Sword; and other medals and awards. Member of the Royal Academy of Military Sciences. Promoted to Major General, 1973.

Lilly, Roger Merrill. Major General, United States Army; Deputy Commanding General, US Army Air Defense Command, Ent Air Force Base, Colorado, 1969-   . Born August 20, 1918, Oil City, Pennsylvania. US Military Academy; The Artillery School, Basic Course; Armed Forces Staff College; The National War College; University of Michigan, MS Degree, Mechanical Engineering. Commissioned Second Lieutenant, 1939. Served in WW II. Artillery Commander, I Corps (Group), Korea, 1964-65; Commanding General, Command and Control Information Systems Group, US Army Combat Developments Command, Fort Belvoir, Virginia, 1965-66; Commanding

General, US Army Combat Developments Command, Automatic Data Field Systems Command, Fort Belvoir, Virginia, 1966-67; Commanding General and Chief of Staff, 2d Region, US Army Air Defense Command, and Deputy Commander, Central North American Air Defense Region, Richards-Gebaur Air Force Base, Missouri, 1967-69. Distinguished Service Medal; Legion of Merit; Bronze Star Medal with V Device; and other medals and awards. Promoted to Brigadier General, July 1, 1964; Major General, June 17, 1968.

Lind, Don Leslie. Commander, US Naval Reserve; NASA Astronaut, 1966-   . Born May 18, 1930, Midvale, Utah. University of Utah, BS, Physics, 1953; University of California, PhD, High Energy Nuclear Physics, 1964; US Navy Officer Candidate School, 1954; US Navy Flight Training Command, 1955. Commissioned Ensign, US Naval Reserve, 1954. Active duty, Navy, 1954-57; research scientist, Lawrence Radiation Laboratory, Berkeley, California; space physicist, NASA Goddard Space Flight Center, 1964-66. NASA experience: Backup Science-Pilot, Skylab 3 and 4.

Lior, Hisrael. Brigadier General, Israel Defense Forces; Chief, Intelligence Service. Born in 1921. Formerly Military Aide to the Prime Minister.

Liskov, V.I. Lieutenant General, USSR Army. Served on the Soviet-German Front in WW II. Deputy Commander, Soviet Air Borne Forces. Member, Communist Party of the Soviet Union.

Litovtsev, D.I. Colonel General, USSR Army; Commander, North Caucasus Military District, 1970-   . Served on the Soviet-German Front in WW II. First Deputy Commander, Central Group of Soviet Forces, Czechoslovakia, 1968-70; Member, Communist Party of the Soviet Union. Promoted to Colonel General, 1971.

Liu An-chi. General of the Army, Army of Republic of China; Advisor, Strategical Council, 1972-   . Born May 15, 1903, Shantung. Attended Military Academy, 1926; Army War College, 1936; National Defense College, 1954. Served in Sino-Japanese War; Chinese Civil War. Commanding General, Infantry Division, 1934-44; Commanding General, Army Corps, 1944-48; Commanding General, Army Group, 1948-50; Commanding General, Central Taiwan Defense, 1950-53; Commanding General, Penghu Defense, 1953-55; Commanding General, Reserve and Replacement Training Command, 1955-57; Commanding General, Field Army, 1957-58; Commanding General, Kinmen Defense Command, 1958-61; Chief of Staff, Chinese Army, 1961-65; Commandant, Armed Forces Staff College, 1965-67; Deputy Commandant, National War College, 1969-72.

Liu Chien-hsun. Major General, People's Liberation Army, People's Republic of China; 1st Political Commissar, Honan Military District, 1967-   . Born in 1907, in Hopei, or Yangch'eng, Shansi. Participated in anti-Japanese guerrilla warfare, 1937-45; took part in Long March; fought in Civil War. Joined Red Army, c. 1932, Chinese Communist Party, 1935. Political Commissar, Hupeh Military District, 1952; 2d Deputy Secretary, Hupeh Provincial Committee, 1950-52; Member, Hupeh Provincial People's Government, 1950-54; Member, Central-South Military and Administrative Committee, 1951-53; Secretary, Hupeh Provincial Committee, 1952-55; Secretary General, Central-South Bureau, CCP, 1953-54; 1st Party Secretary, Kwangsi Provincial Committee, 1957; 1st Party Secretary, Kwangsi-Chuang Autonomous Region, 1958-61; Vice Chairman of Special Committee to Resettle Returned Overseas Chinese, 1960; 1st Party Secretary, Honan Provincial Committee, 1961; Deputy Political Commissar, Wuhan Military Region, 1967; Chairman, Honan Revolutionary Committee, 1968; Member, Peking Municipal Revolutionary Committee, 1967; First Secretary, Provincial Party Committee, 1971; Member, Central Committee, CCP, 1969; Member of Tenth CCP Central Committee, 1973; Member of the Presidium, Tenth National Party Congress, 1973- . Order of Independence and Freedom; Order of Liberation.

Liu Hsien-ch'uan. Major General, People's Liberation Army, People's Republic of China; Deputy Commander, Lanchow Military Region, 1968- . Born in 1914. Attended Red Army Military Academy. Joined the Red Army c. 1930. Member of Chinese Communist Party. Participated in anti-Japanese guerrilla warfare and the Civil War. Commander, Tsinghai Military District, 1965-66; Officer in Charge, Preparatory Group for Inner Mongolia Autonomous Region Revolutionary Committee, 1967; Chairman, Tsinghai Provincial Revolutionary Committee, 1967; First Secretary, Provisional Party Committee, 1971; Member, Executive Group, Military Affairs Committee, 1971; Member of the Tenth CCP Central Committee, 1973. Order of August 1; Order of Independence and Freedom; Order of Liberation.

Liu Hsing-yuan. Lieutenant General, People's Liberation Army, People's Republic of China; First Political Commissar, Chengtu Military Region, 1973- . Born 1914, Hunan. Participated in anti-Japanese guerrilla warfare, 1937-45 and Civil War. Director, Personnel Department, Central-South Military Region, People's Liberation Army, 1952; Director, Personnel Bureau, Political Department, 4th Field Army, 1954; Deputy Political Commissar, then Political Commissar, Canton Military Region, 1955; Second Political Commissar, Canton Forces, People's Liberation Army, 1963; Member, National Defense Council, 1965; Chairman, Revolutionary Committee, Kwangtung; Member, Central Committee, 1969; First Secretary, Kwangtung Provincial Party Committee, 1970; Member, Chinese Communist Party; Deputy to National People's Congress; Member of Tenth CCP Central Committee, 1973; Member of the Presidium, Tenth National Party Congress, 1973. Order of Independence and Freedom; Order of Liberation; and other medals and awards. Promoted to Major General, 1955; Lieutenant General, 1957.

Liu Yu-chang. General, Army of Republic of China; Strategy Adviser to the President, 1970- . Born November 11, 1902, Shensi. Military Academy; Yuanshan Officers Training Institute; Armed Forces Staff College, Joint Operations Course; Command and General Staff College, USA; National War College. Served in Sino-Japanese War and Chinese Civil War. Commanding General, 2d Infantry Division, 1942-48; Commanding General, 52d Army Corps, 1948-53; Commanding General, Taiwan Central Area Garrison Command, 1953-54; Commanding General, Kinmen Defense Command, 1954-57; Commanding General, Reserve Replacement Training Command, 1957-61; Deputy Commander in Chief, Chinese Army, General Headquarters, 1961-64; Deputy Commander in Chief, Taiwan Garrison, General Headquarters and Deputy Commanding General, Taiwan Corps Control Area, 1964-67; Commander in Chief, Taiwan Garrison, General Headquarters, and Commanding General, Taiwan Corps Control Area Command, 1967-70.

Lizychev, A. Major General, USSR Army; First Deputy Chief, Political Directorate, Moscow Military District. Served on the Soviet-German Front in WW II. Member, Communist Party of the Soviet Union. Promoted to Major General, 1971.

Ljubicic, Nikola. General, Yugoslavian Army; Secretary of State for Defense, Yugoslavia, 1967- . Born in 1916 in Karan near Titovo Uzice. Attended Senior Military College; Operational Command School. Served with partisan units and the Yugoslavian National Liberation Army, 1941-45. Recently Commander, Border Troops; Commander, 1st Army District. Member, Federal Executive Council; Member, Communist Party of Yugoslavia since 1941; Member, Presidium of League of Communists of Yugoslavia. Order of the National Hero; Partisan Star with Golden Wreath; Order of Merit for the People with Golden Star; and other medals and awards.

Ljung, Karl Hilmer Lennart. Major General, Swedish Royal Army; Chief of Army Staff, 1972- . Attended Royal Army Staff College, 1952-54; US Army Command and Staff School (USA), 1956-57; Royal National Defense College, 1964, 1971. Commanding Officer, Signal Regiment No. 1, 1968-71; Army Inspector, Military Command East, 1971-72. Commander of the Royal Order of the Sword; and other medals and awards. Promoted to Major General, 1972.

Ljung, Per Ove Poul. Lieutenant General, Swedish Royal Army; Commander in Chief, Military Command East, Commandant General, Stockholm, 1969- . Attended Royal Army Staff College, 1946-48; Royal National Defense College, 1959, 1967; US Air Defense School, Fort Bliss, Modern Weapons and Tactics Course (USA), 1963. Colonel, General Staff, 1963; Commanding Officer, Infantry Regiment No. 13, 1964-66; Chief, Army Staff and General Staff Corps, 1966; Chief, Army Ordnance Corps, 1966-68; Chief, Army Materiel Department, Defense Materiel Administration, 1968-69. Commander of the

Royal Order of the Sword; Knight of the Grand Cross of the Order of the Dannebrog; and other medals and awards. Promoted to Lieutenant General, 1969. Member of the Royal Academy of Military Sciences.

Ljunggren, Lars Rasmus Henning. Director General (equivalent to major general), Sweden; Director General, National Defense Radio Institute, 1972- . Bachelor of Law degree, 1948. Assistant Secretary, Department of Defense, 1965-68; Permanent Secretary, Department of Defense, 1968-72. Commander of the Royal Order of the Northern Star; Knight of the Order of King Charles XIII; and other medals and awards. Promoted to Director General, 1972.

Llewellyn, Jack Rowbottom. Rear-Admiral, British Royal Navy; Assistant Controller of the Navy, 1972- . Born November 14, 1919. Attended Royal Naval Engineering College, Keyham, 1939; Royal Naval College, Greenwich, 1943. Served at sea in WW II. Assistant Director of Marine Engineering, Ministry of Defence (Navy), 1963-66; Commanding Officer, HMS *Fisgard*, 1966-69; Deputy Director of Warship Design, Ministry of Defence (Navy), 1969-72. Promoted to Rear-Admiral in 1972.

Lo Yu-lun. General, Army of Republic of China; Director, General Political Warfare Department, Ministry of Defense, 1969- . Born February 4, 1912, Kwangtung. Attended Whampoa Military Academy; Army War College; Armed Forces Staff College; Command and General Staff College, USA. Served in Sino-Japanese War; Chinese Civil War. Commanding General Army Corps, 1948; Superintendent, Military Academy, 1950-54; Commanding General, Military Police Command, 1954-55; Commandant, Marine Corps, 1957-61; Vice Chief of General Staff, Ministry of National Defense, 1961; Commanding General, 1st Field Army, 1961-64; Vice Commander in Chief, Chinese Army, and Commanding General, Army Combat Development Command, 1964-66; Commanding General, Army Training and Combat Development Command, 1966-68; Vice Commander in Chief, Chinese Army, 1968-69.

Lobov, Semyon Mikhaylovich. Admiral of the Fleet, USSR Navy; Assistant Chief of the General Staff, 1972- . Born in 1913. Attended Frunze Naval School, 1933-37. Volunteered for the Navy, 1932. Commissioned in 1937. Served in the Soviet-Japanese War, 1945. Commander, Destroyer Division; Commander, Cruiser; Commander, Battleship *Sevastopol;* Chief of Staff, Northern Fleet, 1955-61; First Deputy Commander, Northern Fleet, 1961-64; Commander, Northern Fleet, 1964-72. Member, Communist Party of the Soviet Union, 1940- ; Candidate Member, Communist Party Central Committee, 1966- ; Deputy to the USSR Supreme Soviet. Order of Lenin; Two Orders of Red Banner; Order of Red Star; and other orders and medals. Promoted to Admiral of the Fleet, 1965.

Lock, Basil Goodhand. Air Commodore, British Royal Air Force; Director of Operations (AS), Ministry of Defence,

1971- . Born June 25, 1923. Attended Durham University. Commissioned in 1943. Served in WW II in northwest Europe. Officer Commanding Flying, RAF Leeming, 1961-63; Plans (CENTO), 1964-66; Officer Commanding RAF West Raynham, 1967-69; Directing Staff, Joint Services Staff College, 1969-71. CBE; AFC. Promoted to Air Commodore in 1971.

Locke, John Langford. Major General, United States Air Force; Commander, Headquarters Command, United States Air Force, 1972- . Born April 9, 1917, El Paso, Texas. US Military Academy, 1937-41; Army Air Corps Flying School, 1941-42; Stanford University, MBA, 1949; Air War College, 1951-52. Commissioned Second Lieutenant, US Army Air Corps, 1941. Served in the European Theater, WW II. Chief, Air Force Section, Military Assistance Advisory Group, Iran, 1965-67; Deputy Chief of Staff, Technical Training, Air Training Command, 1967-69; Assistant Deputy Chief of Staff, Personnel, Headquarters USAF, 1969-72. Distinguished Service Medal; Silver Star; Legion of Merit with two Oak Leaf Clusters; Distinguished Flying Cross; and other US and foreign medals and awards. Promoted to Major General, July 1, 1967.

Loginov, V. Colonel General, USSR Air Force; Chief, Rear Services (Logistics), Soviet Air Force, 1970- . Served on the Soviet-German Front in WW II. Member, Communist Party of the Soviet Union.

Logofatu, Georghe. Lieutenant General, Romanian Army; Deputy Chief of Staff, Romanian Army.

Logrono Contin, Manuel A. Commodore, Navy of the Dominican Republic; Chief of the Naval Staff.

Lohner, Ernst. Brigadier General, Swiss Army; Auditor in Chief. Born in 1910.

Lomsky, Bohumir. General, Czechoslovak Army; with the Institute of Military History, 1968- . Born April 22, 1914, Ceske Budejovice. Attended War College, Hranice; War College, Moscow. Served as Chief of Staff, First Czechoslovak Brigade and Czechoslovak Corps in the USSR, WW II. First Deputy Minister of National Defense, 1953-56; Minister of National Defense, 1956-68. Member, Central Committee of Communist Party, 1958-68; Deputy, National Assembly, 1960-69; Deputy to People's Chamber Federal Assembly, 1969- . Order of White Lion for Victory; Order of Labor; and other medals and awards.

Long, Robert Lyman John. Vice Admiral, United States Navy; Commander Submarine Force, US Atlantic Fleet; Submarine Operations Advisor for POLARIS/POSEIDON Operations Atlantic Command and Supreme Allied Command, Atlantic, and Commander Submarines, Allied Command, and Commander Submarine Force, Western Atlantic Area, 1972- . Born May 29, 1920, Kansas City, Missouri. Washington University, St. Louis, Missouri, 1939-40; US Naval Academy, 1940-43; Submarine School, 1945-46; Naval War College, 1953-54; Naval Guided

Missiles School, 1959-60, 1963. Commissioned Ensign, US Navy, 1943. Served in the Pacific Theater, WW II; Korean War; Vietnam War. Commander Blue Crew USS *Casimir Pulaski*, 1963-65; Fleet Ballistic Missile Project, Bureau of Naval Weapons, 1965-66; Executive Assistant and Naval Aide to the Under Secretary of the Navy, 1966-68; Commander Service Group THREE, 1968-69; Deputy Commander for Fleet Maintenance and Logistic Support, Naval Ship Systems Command, 1969-72. Legion of Merit with two Gold Stars; Bronze Star Medal with Combat "V"; and other medals and awards. Promoted to Rear Admiral, July 1, 1969; Vice Admiral, June 29, 1972.

Longino, James Charles, Jr. Rear Admiral, United States Navy; Deputy Director for Plans, Defense Intelligence Agency, 1971-   . Born April 23, 1918, in Fairburn, Georgia. US Naval Academy, 1936-40; Columbia University, School of International Affairs, MA, 1955-56; National War College, 1962-63. Commissioned Ensign, US Navy, 1940; designated Naval Aviator, 1943. Served in the Pacific Theater, WW II. Commanding Officer USS *Canisteo*, 1963-64; Commanding Officer USS *Lake Champlain*, 1964-65; Deputy Director for Intelligence, Headquarters, Commander In Chief, US European Command, 1967-69; Commander Fleet Air, San Diego, 1969-71; Commander Antisubmarine Warfare Group THREE, 1970-71. Legion of Merit with Gold Star; Distinguished Flying Cross with two Gold Stars; Bronze Star Medal with Combat "V"; Air Medal with eight Gold Stars; and other US and foreign medals and awards. Promoted to Rear Admiral, November 1, 1967.

Loo Chih-teh. Lieutenant General, Republic of China, Army Medical Corps; Director, National Defense Medical Center, Ministry of National Defense, and Director, Taiwan Veterans General Hospital. Born June 16, 1901, Kwangtung. Educated at New York University, New York, USA; Peking Union Medical College, MD, 1929. Surgeon General, Ministry of War, 1939-43; Commandant, Medical Field Service School, 1944-46.

Lotz, Walter Edward, Jr. Lieutenant General, United States Army; Deputy Director General, North Atlantic Treaty Organization, Integrated Communications Systems Management Agency, 1971-   . Born August 21, 1916, Johnsonburg, Pennsylvania. US Military Academy; Industrial College of the Armed Forces; University of Illinois, MS Degree, Electrical Engineering; University of Virginia, PhD Degree, Physics. Commissioned Second Lieutenant, 1938. Served in WW II and Vietnam War. Director of Army Research, Office, Chief of Research and Development, US Army, Washington, D.C., 1963-65; Assistant Chief of Staff, J-6, Communications-Electronics, US Army Military Assistance Command, Vietnam, 1965-66; Chief of Communications-Electronics, later Assistant Chief of Staff for Communications-Electronics, US Army, Washington, D.C., 1966-68; Commanding General, US Army Strategic Communications Command, Fort Huachuca, Arizona, 1968-69; Commanding General, US Army Electronics Command, Fort Monmouth, New Jersey, 1969-71. Distinguished Service Medal; Legion of Merit with

three Oak Leaf Clusters; Bronze Star Medal; and other medals and awards. Promoted to Brigadier General, January 1, 1963; Major General, July 1, 1966; Lieutenant General, June 4, 1971.

Loudoun, Robert Beverly. Major-General, British Royal Marines; Training Group, Portsmouth, 1971-   . Born July 8, 1922. Attended University College School, Hampstead; Royal Navy Staff College, 1956; US Marine Corps School, Quantico, Virginia, USA, 1959-60. Enlisted in the Royal Marines in 1940; commissioned in 1941. Commando Operations, Central Mediterranean, WW II; Palestine 1948. Second-in-Command, 42 Commando, Singapore and Borneo, 1963-64; Commanding Officer, 40 Commando, Far East, 1967-69; Brigadier, United Kingdom Commandos, Plymouth, 1969-71. CB; OBE. Promoted to Major-General, 1971.

Louie Yen-chun. General, Air Force of Republic of China; Vice Chief of General Staff, Ministry of National Defense, 1967-   . Born December 30, 1914, Kwangtung. Attended Chinese Air Force Academy; US Air Force Command and Staff College, USA. Served in Sino-Japanese War; Chinese Civil War. Chief, Military Section, Chinese Mission in Japan, 1948-51; Chief, Liaison Office, Ministry of National Defense, 1952-54; Deputy Chief of Staff, Operations, Headquarters Chinese Air Force, 1954-59; Vice Chief of Staff, and later Chief of Staff, Headquarters, Chinese Air Force, 1959-63; Commander, Combat Air Command, 1963-64; Deputy Commander in Chief, Chinese Air Force, 1964-67.

Lousma, Jack Robert. Major, US Marine Corps; NASA Astronaut, 1966-   . Born February 29, 1936, Grand Rapids, Michigan. University of Michigan, BS, Aeronautical Engineering, 1959; US Naval Postgraduate School, Aeronautical Engineer, 1965; US Naval Air Training Command, 1959-60. Commissioned June 1959, Second Lieutenant, US Marine Corps; receive pilot's wings, 1960. VMA-224, 2d Marine Air Wing; VMA-224, 1st Marine Air Wing. NASA experience: Support Crew Member, Apollo 9, 10, 13; Pilot, Skylab 2; Backup Docking Module Pilot, Apollo-Soyuz Test Project, July 1975. Manned Spacecraft Center Certificate of Commendation.

Loving, George G., Jr. Major General, United States Air Force; Director of Plans, Deputy Chief of Staff, Plans and Operations, Headquarters US Air Force, 1973-   . Born August 7, 1923, in Roanoke, Virginia. Lynchburg College; Army Air Corps Flying School, 1942-43; Air Command and Staff College, 1955-56; Air War College, 1964-65; University of Alabama; George Washington University, Masters Degree. Commissioned Second Lieutenant, US Army Air Corps, 1943. Served in the European Theater, WW II; Korean War. Branch Chief, Aerospace Doctrine Division, Deputy Chief of Staff, Plans and Operations, Headquarters USAF, 1965-69; Research Associate, Council on Foreign Relations, 1969-70; Commandant, Air Command and Staff College, Maxwell Air Force Base, Alabama, 1970-72. Silver Star; Distinguished Flying Cross with one Oak Leaf Cluster; and other medals and awards. Promoted to Brigadier General, August 1, 1970; Major General, September 1, 1972.

Lowe, Douglas Charles. Air Marshal, British Royal Air Force; Assistant Chief of Air Staff (Operational Requirements), 1971-   . Born March 14, 1922. Attended Bomber Command Instructors School, 1945; Royal Air Force College, Cranwell, 1947; Imperial Defence College, 1966. Commissioned in 1940. Served in bombers in WW II. Exchange Officer, Headquarters, Strategic Air Command, USAF, 1961-63; Station Commander, Cranwell, 1963-66; Director, Operational Requirements 2 (RAF), Ministry of Defence (Air), 1967-69; Senior Air Force Staff Officer, Near East Air Force, 1969-71. CB; DFC; AFC.

Lowe, Jessup D. Major General, United States Air Force; Commander, Space and Missile Test Center (SAMTEC), Air Force Systems Command, 1971-   . Born November 18, 1920, in Ogdensburg, New York. US Military Academy, 1940-43; University of Michigan, Guided Missile Course, MS, Aeronautical Engineering, 1948; Air Tactical School; Air Command and Staff School; National War College, 1964-65. Commissioned Second Lieutenant, US Army Air Corps, 1943. Served with the Eighth Air Force in the ETO in WW II. Assistant Deputy Commander, Space, Headquarters Air Force Systems Command, 1965-67; Director, Space Systems, Headquarters Air Force Systems Command, 1967-69; Commander, Arnold Engineering Development Center, Arnold Air Force Base, 1969-71. Legion of Merit; Distinguished Flying Cross; and other medals and awards. Promoted to Major General, March 1, 1972.

Lowenhielm, Fredrik. Major General, Swedish Royal Army; Chief, National Home Guard, 1971-   . Born June 9, 1916. Attended Royal Army Staff College, 1944-46; Royal National Defense College, 1953, 1968. Commissioned in 1937. Army Inspector, Military Command East, 1966-68; Commander in Chief, Military Command Gotland, 1968-71. Commander of the Royal Order of the Sword; Order of St. John of Malta; Commander of the Order of the Dannebrog; and other medals and awards. Member of the Royal Academy of Military Sciences. Promoted to Major General, October 1, 1971.

Lozowicki, Longin. Major General, Polish Air Force; Chief of Staff, Air Defense Forces, 1968-   . Member, Polish United Workers Party. Promoted to Major General, 1970.

Lucertini, Vincenzo. General, Italian Air Force; Chief of Air Staff, 1971-   . Born January 16, 1914, in Turin. Combat duty in WW II. Brigadier General, assigned to the Supreme Headquarters, Allied Powers Europe; Commanding Officer, 1st Air Brigade, 1960; Deputy Commander, 2d Air Region, 1966; General Officer Commanding, 5th Allied Tactical Air Force, 1969-71. Three Silver Medals for Military Gallantry; and other medals and awards. Promoted to Major General, 1966; Lieutenant General, 1969; General, 1971.

Lucey, Martin Noel. Rear-Admiral, British Royal Navy; Flag Officer Scotland, and Northern Ireland, 1972-   . Joined the Royal Navy in 1938. Served at sea in WW II. Captain "F7" HMS *Puma*, 1964; Commodore, Senior Naval Officer, West Indies, 1968-70; Admiral President, Royal Naval College, Greenwich, 1970-72. CB; DSC. Promoted to Commodore, 1968; Rear-Admiral, 1970.

Lukashin, P.T. Colonel General, USSR Army; First Deputy Chief, Personnel (Cadres) Directorate, Ministry of Defense. Served on the Soviet-German Front in WW II. Member, Communist Party of the Soviet Union.

Lukeman, Robert Patrick. Major General, United States Air Force; Assistant Chief of Staff, Studies and Analysis, Headquarters, US Air Force, Washington, D.C., 1972-   . Born October 15, 1921, in New York, New York. Army Air Corps Flying Schools, 1943; Air Force Bombardment School, 1951; Industrial College of the Armed Forces, 1965-66; George Washington University. Commissioned Second Lieutenant, US Army Air Corps, in 1943. Served in the European Theater in WW II. Chief, Operations Center Division, Directorate of Operations, Headquarters, US European Command, Camp des Loges, Ste. Germaine-en-Laye, France, 1963-65; Staff Member, Objective Plans and Program Division, Directorate for Plans and Policy (J-5), Organization of the Joint Chiefs of Staff, Washington, D.C., 1966-67; Special Assistant for Joint Matters, Office of the Director, Joint Staff, Organization of the Joint Chiefs of Staff, 1967-69; Chief, Strategic Plans and Policy Division, Directorate for Plans and Policy (J-5), Organization of the Joint Chiefs of Staff, 1969-70; Assistant Deputy Chief of Staff, Plans, Strategic Air Command, Offutt Air Force Base, Nebraska, 1970-72. Distinguished Service Medal (Air Force Design); Legion of Merit with two Oak Leaf Clusters; Distinguished Flying Cross with Oak Leaf Cluster; and other medals and awards. Promoted to Brigadier General, August 1, 1969; Major General, 1973.

Lundmark, Karl-Gösta Olof. Brigadier General, Swedish Royal Army; Chief of Staff, Military Command Bergslagen, 1972-   . Attended Artillery and Engineering Staff College, 1949-51; Royal National Defense College, 1966, 1972. Commanding Officer, Artillery Regiment, A 8, 1966-68. Commander of the Royal Order of the Sword; and other medals and awards. Promoted to Brigadier General, 1972.

Lundvall, Bengt Gustav Gottfrid. Vice Admiral, Swedish Royal Navy; Commander in Chief, Swedish Royal Navy, 1970-   . Attended Royal Navy Staff College, 1943-46; Royal National Defense College, 1964. Deputy Chief, Defense Staff, 1964-66; Chief of Staff, Military Command, East, 1966-70. Knight Grand Cross of the Royal Order of the Sword; Legion of Merit (USA); Gran Estrella al Merito Militar (Chile); Cavaliere di Gran Cross al Merito della Republica Italiana; and other medals and awards. Honorary Member of the Royal Society of Naval Sciences; Member of the Royal Academy of Military Sciences. Promoted to Vice Admiral, 1970.

Lung Shu-chin. Major General, People's Liberation Army, People's Republic of China; Commander, Sinkiang Military District, 1968-73. Participated in anti-Japanese guerrilla warfare, 1937-45, and the Civil War. Member, Hunan People's Provincial Council, 1962; Chairman, Sinkiang Autonomous Region Revolutionary Committee, 1968; Member, Central Committee, 1969. Order of Liberation. Member, Chinese Communist Party.

Luong, Le Quang. Brigadier General, Army of the Republic of South Vietnam; Commander Airborne Division.

Luong, Nguyen Van. Brigadier General, Army of the Republic of South Vietnam; Commander 2d Air Division.

Luong, Tran. Major General, People's Army of Vietnam; Member of Central Office for South Vietnam Current Affairs Committee, 1962; Chief of Central Office for South Vietnam Proselyting Office, 1962; Member, Lao Dong Party Central Committee, 1960. Born in 1913, Ha Tinh Province. Organized and led guerrillas in Ba To District, 1945; Member, Lao Dong Party Central Executive Committee and Deputy North Vietnam Politburo Chief, 1950-54; Member, Central Committee for Agrarian Reform, 1955; also known as Tran Nam Trung; went to South in 1961. Promoted to Major General, 1958.

Lütgendorf, Karl Ferdinand. Brigadier, Austrian Army; Minister of Defense, Austria, 1971-   . Born October 15, 1914. Attended the Theresian Military Academy at Wiener Neustadt, 1934-37; War College (General Staff), 1943-44. Commissioned Second Lieutenant, 1937. Served in the German Army in WW II. Chief of Staff, 7th Infantry Brigade, 1956-58; Chief of Military Training, Ministry of Defense, 1959-70. Grosses Ehrenzeichen; Goldenes Ehrenzeichen; Legion of Merit (USA); and other medals and awards. Promoted to Colonel, 1962; Brigadier, January 1, 1966.

Lyall Grant, Ian Hallam. Major-General, British Army, Retired; Director General, Supply Coordination, Ministry of Defence, 1970-   . Born June 4, 1915. Attended Cheltenham College; Royal Military Academy, Woolwich; Cambridge University, MA; Imperial Defence College, 1961. Commissioned in 1935 in the Royal Engineers. Served in India and Burma in WW II. Commandant, Royal School of Military Engineering, 1965-67; Deputy Quartermaster-General, 1967-70. MC. Promoted to Major-General, 1966.

Lyashchenko, Nikolay Grigor'yevich. General of the Army, USSR Army; Commander, Central Asian Military District, 1970-   . Born in 1908. Drafted into Soviet Army in 1929. Attended Joint Services Central Asian Military Academy, 1929-32; Army War College, 1938-41; General Staff War College, 1946-48. Commissioned in 1932. Military Adviser to the Republican Forces, Spanish Civil War, 1936-38; served in the Soviet-German War, 1941-45.

Deputy Commander, Infantry Regiment, 1941; Commander, Infantry Regiment, 1941-42; Commander, 106th Infantry Division, North Caucasus Front, 1942-43; Commander, 90th Infantry Division, Second Assault Army, 1943-45; Commander, Division and later Corps, Moscow Military District, 1948-57; First Deputy Commander, Turkestan Military District, 1957-63; Commander, Volga Military District, 1963-65; Commander, Turkestan Military District, 1965-70. Member, Communist Party of the Soviet Union, 1931-   ; Candidate Member of the Communist Party Central Committee; Deputy to the USSR Supreme Soviet. Order of Lenin; Order of Red Banner; Order of Red Star; and other Soviet and foreign orders and medals. Promoted to General of the Army, February 22, 1968.

Lyashko, N.M. Lieutenant General, USSR Army. Served on the Soviet-German Front in WW II. Chief, Political Directorate, Volga Military District, 1963-71. Member, Communist Party of the Soviet Union.

Lyashko, Veniamin Ivanovich. Major General, USSR Army; Commander, Chapayev Guards Motorized Rifle Division, Kiev Military District, 1970-   . Born in 1925. Drafted into Army, 1942. Attended Military Academy, 1942-43; Senior Officers Training Courses; Army War College. Commissioned in 1943. Served in the Soviet-German War, 1943-45. Commander of company and battalion; Deputy Regimental Commander for Political Affairs; Commander, Infantry Regiment, Kiev Military District. Member, Communist Party of the Soviet Union. Order of Fatherland War, 1st and 2nd class; Order of Red Star; and other orders and medals.

Lygo, Raymond Derek. Rear-Admiral, British Royal Navy; Flag Officer Carriers and Amphibious Ships, 1972-   . Born March 15, 1924. Attended Clarke College, Bromley. Enlisted as Naval Airman in 1942; commissioned Sub-Lieutenant (A), RNVR, in 1943; transferred to Regular Navy, 1945. Served as naval pilot in WW II. Commanding Officer, HMS *Lowestoft*, 1961-63; Deputy Director, Naval Air Warfare, 1964-66; Commanding Officer, HMS *Ark Royal*, 1969-71. Fellow of the Royal Commonwealth Society.

Lykov, I. Major General, USSR Army; First Deputy Chief, Political Directorate, Leningrad Military District. Served on the Soviet-German Front in WW II. Member, Communist Party of the Soviet Union.

Lyness, Douglas Henry. Rear Admiral, Supply Corps, United States Navy; Commanding Officer, Naval Supply Center, San Diego, California, 1971-   . Born July 6, 1919, in Minneapolis, Minnesota. University of Minnesota, BA, Journalism, 1941; Navy Supply Corps School, 1941; Stanford University, MBA, 1949; Industrial College of the Armed Forces, 1963-64. Commissioned Ensign, Supply Corps, US Naval Reserve, 1941; transferred to Supply Corps, US Navy, 1943. Served in Atlantic and Pacific Theaters in WW II; Vietnam War. Commanding Officer, Naval Supply Depot, Seattle, Washington, and Supply

Officer Thirteenth Naval District, 1964-67; Commander Fleet Material Support Office, Mechanicsburg, Pennsylvania, 1967-68; Commander Navy Resale System Office, Brooklyn, New York, 1968-71. Legion of Merit; and other medals and awards. Promoted to Rear Admiral, September 1, 1968.

Lyon, Herbert A. Major General, United States Air Force; Vice Commander, Space and Missile Systems Organization, Air Force Systems Command, Los Angeles, California, 1972- . Born August 20, 1921, in St. Paul, Minnesota. Aviation Cadet Training Course, 1942-43; University of Minnesota, BS, Aeronautical Engineering, 1948; Purdue University, MS, Aeroengineering, 1952; US Army Command and General Staff School, 1957; Industrial College of the Armed Forces, 1964-65; George Washington University, MBA, 1966. Commissioned Second Lieutenant, US Army Air Corps, in 1943. Served in the Southwest Pacific Theater, WW II. Director for Plans and Policy, Office of Deputy Chief of Staff, Science and Technology, Headquarters, Air Force Systems Command, Andrews Air Force Base, Maryland, 1965-67; Commander, Air Force Aero Propulsion Laboratory, Wright-Patterson Air Force Base, Ohio, 1967-69; Deputy for Engineering, Aeronautical Systems Division, Wright-Patterson Air Force Base, Ohio, 1969-70; Assistant Deputy Chief of Staff, Systems, Air Force Systems Command, Andrews Air Force Base, Maryland, 1970-71; Deputy for Re-entry Systems, Space and Missile Systems Organization (SAMSO), Norton Air Force Base, California, 1971-72. Legion of Merit; Air Medal; Fellow, American Institute of Aeronautics and Astronautics; Member, Dayton Laboratories Branch of the Research and Engineering Society of America. Promoted to Major General, April 2, 1973.

Lysenko, V. Major General, USSR Air Force. Served on the Soviet-German Front in WW II. Recently Chief, Political Directorate, Soviet Airborne Forces. Member, Communist Party of the Soviet Union.

M

Mabry, George Lafayette, Jr. Major General, United States Army; Commander, US Army Forces Southern Command, Fort Amador, Canal Zone, 1970- . Born September 14, 1970, Staleburg, South Carolina. Presbyterian College of South Carolina, BA Degree, English Education; The Infantry School, Basic and Advanced Courses; US Army Command and General Staff College; Armed Forces Staff College; The National War College. Commissioned Second Lieutenant, US Army Reserve, 1940. Served in WW II and Vietnam War. Director, J-3, US Southern Command, Quarry Heights, Canal Zone, 1963-65; Assistant Division Commander, 1st Armored Division, Fort Hood, Texas, 1965-66; Commanding General, US Army Combat Developments Command Experimentation Command, Fort Ord, California, 1966-67; Commanding General, 8th Infantry Division, US Army, Europe, 1968-69; Chief of

Staff, US Army, Vietnam, 1969-70. Medal of Honor; Distinguished Service Cross; Distinguished Service Medal; Silver Star; Legion of Merit with two Oak Leaf Clusters; Bronze Star Medal with V Device; and other medals and awards. Promoted to Brigadier General, May 6, 1963; Major General, November 29, 1966.

Macafee, John Leeper Anketell. Colonel, British Royal Marines; Director of Naval Security, 1961- . Born July 24, 1915. Attended Campbell College, Belfast; Staff College, Camberley, 1947. Commissioned in the Royal Marines, 1934. Served at sea and in the Mediterranean Theater, WW II. Commanding Officer, 42 Commando, RM, 1957-59; Headquarters, Royal Marines, Plymouth, 1959; Fleet Royal Marine Officer, Mediterranean Fleet, 1960; Deputy Director, Naval Intelligence, 1961. Aide de Camp to the Queen, 1963-64. CBE.

McAlister, Robert Carter. Major General, United States Army; Commanding General, US Army, Southern European Task Force, 1971- . Born September 15, 1923, Mayfield, Kentucky. US Military Academy; The Field Artillery School, Basic and Advanced Courses; US Army Command and General Staff College; US Army War College; George Washington University, MA Degree, International Affairs. Commissioned Second Lieutenant, 1945. Served in Vietnam War. Contingency Plans Officer, Contingency Plans Branch, Plans Division, Operations and Plans Directorate, J-3, later J-5, US Southern Command, Quarry Heights, Canal Zone, 1964-67; Commanding Officer, 4th Infantry Division Artillery, US Army, Pacific-Vietnam, 1967-68; Assistant Division Commander, 4th Infantry Division, US Army, Pacific-Vietnam, 1968-69; Director, Western Hemisphere Region, Office, Assistant Secretary of Defense (International Security Affairs), Washington, D.C., 1969-71. Distinguished Service Medal; Legion of Merit; Bronze Star Medal with V Device and Oak Leaf Cluster; and other medals and awards. Promoted to Brigadier General, October 1, 1968; Major General, April 1, 1971.

McBride, William P. Major General, United States Air Force; Deputy Chief of Staff Operations, Tactical Air Command, 1970- . Born July 30, 1916, in Corpus Christi, Texas. Attended Army Air Corps Flying School, 1941-42. Commissioned Second Lieutenant, US Army Air Corps, 1942. Served in the Mediterranean and European Theaters, WW II; Korean War. Commander, 401st Tactical Fighter Wing, 1964-65; Commander, 834th Air Division, 1965-66; Deputy for Operations, Ninth Air Force, 1966-67; Commander, Task Force "A", Pacific Air Forces, 1967-69; Vice Commander, Twelfth Air Force, 1969-70; Deputy Chief of Staff, Materiel, Headquarters Tactical Air Command, 1969-70. Distinguished Service Medal; Legion of Merit with two Oak Leaf Clusters; Distinguished Flying Cross with two Oak Leaf Clusters; and other US and foreign medals and awards. Promoted to Major General, March 1, 1969.

McBride, William V. Lieutenant General, United States Air Force; Commander, Air Training Command, 1972-   . Born May 25, 1922, in Wampum, Pennsylvania. Garfield Business Institute, Beaver Falls, Pennsylvania, 1941; Army Air Corps Navigation School, 1942-43; Advance Flying School, 1947-48; New York University, New York City, 1949-50; National War College, 1959-60. Commissioned Second Lieutenant, US Army Air Corps, 1943. Served in the European Theater, WW II; Korean War. Military Assistant to Secretary of the Air Force, 1964-66; Commander, 437th Military Airlift Wing, 1966-69; Deputy Chief of Staff, Materiel, Headquarters, Military Airlift Command (MAC), 1969; Deputy Chief of Staff, Operations, Headquarters, MAC, 1969-70; Chief of Staff, Military Airlift, MAC, 1970-71; Vice Commander in Chief US Air Forces, Europe, Wiesbaden Germany, 1971-72. Distinguished Service Medal; Legion of Merit with two Oak Leaf Clusters; Distinguished Flying Cross; Croix de Guerre; and other US and foreign medals and awards. Promoted to Brigadier General, November 30, 1965; Major General, March 1, 1969; Lieutenant General, September 1, 1971.

McCandless, Bruce, II. Commander, US Navy; NASA Astronaut, 1966-   . US Naval Academy, 1958; Stanford University, MS, Electrical Engineering, 1965; US Naval Aviation Training Command. Commissioned Ensign, US Navy, 1958; designated Naval Aviator, 1960. VF-102 aboard USS *Forrestal* and USS *Enterprise*, 1960-64; Instrument Flight Instructor, VA-43, 1964. NASA experience: Member Support Crew, Apollo 14; Backup Pilot, Skylab 1.

McChrystal, Herbert Joseph, Jr. Major General, United States Army; Deputy Commanding General, MASSTER, Fort Hood, Texas, 1973-   . Born May 30, 1924, Ancon, Canal Zone. US Military Academy; The Infantry School, Basic and Advanced Courses; U.S. Army Command and General Staff College; The National War College; Georgetown University, M.A. Degree, International Relations; Foreign Service Institute. Commissioned Second Lieutenant, 1945. Served in Vietnam War. Commanding Officer, 2d Brigade, 4th Infantry Division, U.S. Army, Vietnam, 1968; Chief of Staff, 4th Infantry Division, U.S. Army, Vietnam, 1968-69; Director, Planning and Programming Analysis, Office, Assistant Vice Chief of Staff, U.S. Army, Washington, D.C., 1970-72. Silver Star with three Oak Leaf Clusters; Legion of Merit with Oak Leaf Cluster; Distinguished Flying Cross; Bronze Star Medal with V Device and Oak Leaf Cluster; and other medals and awards. Promoted to Brigadier General, November 1, 1969; Major General, August 1, 1971.

McClellan, Stan Leon. Major General, United States Army; Director of Logistics, J-4, US Support Activities Group, Thailand, 1973-   . Born August 2, 1924, in Wichita Falls, Texas. Attended University of Omaha, BGE, Military Science, 1964; George Washington University, MS, Business Administration; Transportation School; Infantry School, Advanced Course; Command and General Staff College; Armed Forces Staff College; Industrial College of the Armed Forces, 1967-68. Commissioned Second Lieutenant in April 1947. Served in the Vietnam War. Commanding Officer, 3d Brigade, 4th Infantry Division, then Assistant Chief of Staff, G-3, I Field Force Vietnam, US Army, Pacific-Vietnam, 1968-69; Chief of Army Training Center Division, Office of the Deputy Chief of Staff for Personnel, 1969-70; Executive Officer, Office of the Deputy Chief of Staff for Personnel, 1970; Assistant Division Commander, 3d Infantry Division, US Army, Europe, 1970-71; Director of Training and Special Assistant to the Commander, then Chief and Deputy Chief of the Army Advisory Group, US Military Assistance Command, Vietnam, 1971-72; Chief of Staff, US Army, Vietnam/US Military Assistance Command, Vietnam Support Command, 1972-73. Distinguished Service Medal; Silver Star with Oak Leaf Cluster; Legion of Merit with Oak Leaf Cluster; Bronze Star Medal; and other medals and awards. Promoted to Brigadier General, June 1, 1971; Major General, August 1, 1973.

McClellan, Thomas Rufus. Rear Admiral, United States Navy; Commander Naval Air Systems Command, 1971-   . Born January 1, 1922, Gatesville, Texas. US Naval Academy, 1939-42; Naval Postgraduate School, Ordnance Engineering Course, 1945-46; California Institute of Technology, MS, Aeronautical Engineering, 1946-47; Flight Training Course, 1948-49. Commissioned Ensign, US Navy, 1942; designated Naval Aviator, 1949. Served in the Pacific Theater, WW II. Commanding Officer, USS *Rockbridge* (APA-228), 1964-65; Commander Fleet Air Wing THREE, 1965-66; Assistant Director, Aviation Programs Division, Office of the CNO, 1966-67; Commander Carrier Division FOURTEEN, 1967-69; Deputy Commander for Plans and Programs, and Comptroller, Naval Air Systems Command, 1969-71. Navy Commendation Medal with Combat "V"; and other medals and awards. Promoted to Rear Admiral, August 1, 1968.

McClelland, Joseph James. Rear Admiral, US Coast Guard; Superintendent, US Coast Guard Academy, 1973-   . Born June 19, 1916, Seattle, Washington. University of Washington; US Coast Guard Academy, 1936-40; Stanford University, Palo Alto, California, MA Degree, Education, 1950; National War College, 1963-64; George Washington University, MA Degree, International Affairs. Commissioned Ensign, 1940. Pacific and European Theaters, WW II. Chief, Operations Division, 3d Coast Guard District, 1967-68; Chief of Staff, 3d Coast Guard District, 1968-69; Chief, Office of Boating Safety, Headquarters, US Coast Guard, 1969-70; Commander, 13th Coast Guard District, Seattle, Washington, 1970-73. WW II campaign service medals and ribbons. Promoted to Rear Admiral, January 31, 1969.

McClendon, William Roger. Rear Admiral, United States Navy; Assistant Deputy Chief of Naval Operations (Air Warfare), 1971-   . Born August 21, 1920, in Mabank, Texas. North Texas State University, Denton, 1937-39, 1940-41; Flight Training Course, 1941-42; General Line School, Newport, Rhode Island, 1949-50; Naval War College, Naval Warfare Course, 1958-59; Naval Postgraduate

School, Monterey, California, BS, Political Science, 1962-63. Commissioned Ensign, US Naval Reserve, 1942; designated Naval Aviator, 1942; transferred to US Navy, 1945. Served in Atlantic and Pacific Theaters, WW II; Vietnam War. Commanding Officer USS *Firedrake* (AE-14), 1963-64; Commanding Officer, USS *Bon Homme Richard* (CVA-31), 1964-65; Chief of Staff and Aide to Commander Carrier Division ONE, 1966-67; Deputy Director for Commands/Areas, Operations Directorate, Joint Chiefs of Staff, 1967-69; Commander Carrier Division NINE, 1969-70; Director, Aviation Programs Division, Office of the CNO, 1970-71. Legion of Merit with three Gold Stars; Bronze Star Medal; and other US and foreign medals and awards. Promoted to Rear Admiral, August 1, 1968.

McClintock, Cyril Lawson Tait. Surgeon Rear-Admiral, British Royal Navy; Medical Officer in Charge, Royal Naval Hospital Haslar, and Command Medical Officer, Staff of Commander-in-Chief Naval Home Command, 1972-   . Born August 2, 1916. Trained at Guy's Hospital, 1940. Commissioned in Royal Naval Medical Service in 1940. Served at sea in WW II; Korean War. Medical Officer in Charge of Royal Naval Hospital, Bighi, Malta, 1969-70; Staff of David Bruce Royal Naval Hospital, Mtarfa, Malta, 1970-71; Command Medical Adviser to Commander-in-Chief Naval Forces Southern Europe, 1969-71. OBE; QHS; OStJ. Member of the Royal College of Surgeons; Licentiate of the Royal College of Physicians; DLO; Fellow of the Royal Society of Medicine.

McConnell, Richard Edward. Major General, United States Army; Engineer, North Pacific Division, Portland, Oregon, 1972-   . Born November 19, 1923, in Cliffside Park, New Jersey. Attended US Military Academy; Engineer School, Basic and Advanced Courses; Command and General Staff College; Army War College, 1964-65; New York University, MS, Administrative Engineering; George Washington University, MS, International Relations, 1965. Commissioned Second Lieutenant June 5, 1945. Served in the Vietnam War. Military Engineering and Standardization Loan Representative, US Army Standardization Group, Ottawa, Canada, 1965-66; Commanding Officer, 159th Engineer Group, US Army, Pacific-Vietnam, 1966-67; District Engineer, US Army Engineer Division, North Pacific, 1967-70; Assistant for Construction Operations, Office of the Deputy Assistant Secretary of Defense (Installations and Housing), Office of the Assistant Secretary of Defense (Installations and Logistics), 1970-71; Director of Installations, Office of the Deputy Chief of Staff for Logistics, 1971-72. Legion of Merit with three Oak Leaf Clusters; and other medals and awards. Promoted to Brigadier General December 1, 1970; Major General April 1, 1973.

McCuddin, Leo B. Rear Admiral, United States Navy; Commander, Naval Base, Guantanamo Bay, Cuba, 1972-   . Born February 2, 1917, in Sioux City, Iowa. University of Nevada, BA, 1935-39; University of Arizona Law School, 1940-41; Flight Training Course, 1941-42; Air Command and Staff College, 1951; Naval War College,

1957-58. Commissioned Ensign, US Navy Reserve, 1942; designated Naval Aviator, 1942; transferred to US Navy, 1946. Served in the Pacific Theater, WW II; Korean War; Vietnam War. Commanding Officer, USS *Ranger* (CVA-61), 1965-66; Assistant Director for Aviation, Captain Detailing, Bureau of Naval Personnel, 1966-68; Commandant, Twelfth Naval District, and Commander, Naval Base, San Francisco, California, 1968-70; Commander Carrier Division THREE, 1970-71; Commander United States Naval Support Force, Antarctica, 1971-72. Navy Cross; Silver Star Medal; Legion of Merit with two Gold Stars; Distinguished Flying Cross with Gold Star; Air Medal with Ten Gold Stars; and other US and foreign medals and awards. Promoted to Rear Admiral, August 1, 1968.

McDivitt, James A. Colonel, US Air Force; NASA Astronaut, 1962-   , Manager, Apollo Spacecraft Program, 1969-   . Born June 10, 1929, Chicago, Illinois. University of Michigan, BS, Aeronautical Engineering, 1959. NASA experience: Command Pilot, Gemini 4, June 1965; Commander, Apollo 9, March 1969; Manager for Lunar Landing Operation, Apollo Spacecraft Office, 1969. NASA Distinguished Service Medal; NASA Exceptional Service Medal; Air Force Distinguished Service Medal; Four Distinguished Flying Crosses; Five Air Medals; Air Force Astronaut Wings; Honorary Doctorate in Astronautical Science, University of Michigan; Honorary ScD, Seton Hall University; Honorary ScD, Miami University, Ohio; and other medals and awards.

MacDonald, Arthur Leslie. Major General, Royal Australian Army; Chief, Operations, 1972-   . Born January 30, 1919, in Rockhampton. Attended Royal Military College, Duntroon; Imperial Defence College, London. Commissioned in 1939. Served in the European and Pacific Theaters, WW II; Korean War; Vietnam War. Commander, Papua and New Guinea Command, 1965-66; Deputy Chief, General Staff, 1966-67; Adjutant-General, 1967-68 and 1969-70; Commander, Australian Forces, Vietnam, 1968-69; General Officer Commanding, Northern Command, 1970-72. CB; OBE.

MacDonald, William R. Major General, United States Air Force; Director, Plans, J-5, US Readiness Command, 1972-   . Born November 24, 1919, in Clarkstown, Michigan. Wayne University; Army Air Corps Flying School, 1942-43; Air War College, 1958-59. Commissioned in 1943. Chief, Strategic Offensive/Defensive Division, Directorate of Aerospace Programs, Deputy Chief of Staff, Programs and Requirements, 1965-66; Assistant Deputy Chief of Staff, Operations, Seventeenth Air Force, Germany, 1966; Commander, 26th Tactical Reconnaissance Wing, Germany, 1966-67; Inspector General, United States Air Forces, Europe, 1967-68; Chief of Staff, United States Air Forces, Europe, 1968-69; Chief, National Strategic Target List Division, Joint Strategic Target Planning Staff, 1969-71; Director, Plans, J-5, Headquarters US Strike Command, 1971-72. Legion of Merit with two Oak Leaf Clusters; and other medals and awards. Promoted to Major General, April 1, 1970.

McDonough, Joseph Corbett. Major General, United States Army; Chief of Staff, Combined Military Planning Staff, Central Treaty Organization, 1972- . Born September 30, 1924, in Bronx, New York. Attended US Military Academy; Infantry School; Command and General Staff College; Army War College, 1964-65; Georgetown University, MA, International Relations. Commissioned June 5, 1945. Served in the Korean War and the Vietnam War. Commanding Officer, 2d Battalion, 5th Cavalry, 1st Cavalry Division, US Army, Vietnam, 1967; Commanding Officer, 2d Brigade, 1st Cavalry Division, US Army, Vietnam, 1967-68; Operations Staff Officer, European/Middle East/Africa/ South Asia Division, then Chief of the European Branch of that division, Organization of the Joint Chiefs of Staff, 1968-70; Deputy Director for Operations (National Military Command Center), J-3, Organization of the Joint Chiefs of Staff, 1970-71; Assistant Division Commander, 23d Infantry Division, US Army, Vietnam, 1971; Commanding General, 196th Infantry Brigade (Separate), US Army, Vietnam, 1971-72. Distinguished Service Medal; Silver Star; Legion of Merit with Oak Leaf Cluster; Distinguished Flying Cross; Bronze Star Medal with V Device with Oak Leaf Cluster; Air Medal (33 awards); and other medals and awards. Promoted to Brigadier General April 1, 1971; Major General May 1, 1973.

McEnery, John Winn. Major General, United States Army; Assistant Division Commander, 1st Cavalry Division (TRICAP), Fort Hood, Texas, 1972- . Born December 30, 1925, in San Francisco, California. Attended US Military Academy; Ground General School; Armored School, Basic and Advanced Courses; Command and General Staff College; Spanish Staff College, Madrid, Spain, 1965-66; Air War College, 1967-68; US Army Primary Helicopter Center/School and Army Aviation School, 1970; George Washington University, MS, International Affairs. Commissioned Second Lieutenant in 1948. Served in the Vietnam War. Deputy Chief, later Chief, Materiel and Programming Branch, Army Section, Joint US Military Group-Military Assistance Advisory Group, Spain, 1966-67; Commanding Officer, 3d Squadron, 11th Armored Cavalry Regiment, US Army, Vietnam, 1968-69; Secretary of the General Staff, US Continental Army Command, 1969-70; Commanding Officer, 2d Brigade, 1st Cavalry Division, Fort Hood, Texas, 1970-72. Distinguished Service Cross; Silver Star with Oak Leaf Cluster; Legion of Merit with Oak Leaf Cluster; Bronze Star Medal; Air Medal (26 awards). Promoted to Brigadier General, July 1, 1972; Major General, 1973.

McGarvey, Billie J. Major General, United States Air Force; Deputy Director, Civil Engineering, Headquarters US Air Force, Washington, D.C., 1972- . Born August 11, 1923, in Fort Worth, Texas. Texas Technological University, BS; Flying Training Course, 1943-44; University of Colorado, MS, Civil Engineering; Air Command and Staff School, 1956-57. Commissioned Second Lieutenant, US Army Air Corps, in 1944. Served in the Pacific Theater, WW II, and the Vietnam War. Chief of the Missile Construction Branch, Directorate of Civil Engineering, Headquarters, US Air Force, Washington, D.C., 1965-66; Special Assistant to the Deputy Director for Construction/Air Staff Project Officer for Construction of the Turn Key Air Base, Tuy Hoa, Vietnam, 1966-67; Chief of Construction Division, 1967-68; Deputy Chief of Staff for Civil Engineering, Headquarters Air Force Logistics Command, 1968-71; Deputy Chief of Staff for Civil Engineering, Headquarters Pacific Air Forces, Hickam Air Force Base, Hawaii, 1971-72. Legion of Merit with two Oak Leaf Clusters; Distinguished Flying Cross; Air Medal with six Oak Leaf Clusters; and other medals and awards. Promoted to Brigadier General, December 1, 1969; Major General, 1973.

McGhee, Thomas Kendrick. Lieutenant General, United States Air Force; Commander, Aerospace Defense Command (ADC), 1970- . Born October 8, 1915, in Greenville, Alabama. Alabama Polytechnic Institute, Auburn, Alabama, BS, 1937; Army Air Corps Flying School, 1939-40; Armed Forces Staff College, 1950-51; Air War College, 1954-55. Commissioned Second Lieutenant, US Army Field Artillery Reserve, 1937; received pilot wings, 1940. Served in the European Theater, WW II. Commander, San Francisco Air Defense Sector, 1960-62; Director of Operations, Deputy Chief of Staff, Operations, Headquarters, North America Air Defense Command (NORAD), 1962-63; Deputy Chief of Staff, Operations, Headquarters, Air Defense Command, 1963-65; Commander, 29th NORAD Region/Air Division, 1965-66; Commander, Central NORAD Region/Tenth Air Force, 1966-67; Assistant Deputy Chief of Staff, Programs and Resources, Headquarters, USAF, 1967-68; Commander, US Forces Japan and Fifth Air Force, Fuchu Air Station, Japan, 1968-70. Distinguished Service Medal; Legion of Merit with one Oak Leaf Cluster; Distinguished Flying Cross with one Oak Leaf Cluster; Soldier's Medal; and other US and foreign medals and awards. Promoted to Brigadier General, April 25, 1950; Major General, April 1, 1959; Lieutenant General, May 28, 1968.

McGhie, John. Major-General, British Army; Director of Army Psychiatry, and Consultant in Psychiatry to the Army, 1970- . Born in Larkhall, Scotland. Studied at Hamilton Academy; Glasgow University. Doctor of Medicine; Diploma in Psychological Medicine. Commissioned in the Royal Army Medical Corps in 1938. Served in India in WW II. Officer Commanding, Royal Victoria Hospital, Netley, 1956-61; Director of Army Psychiatry, 1961-67; Deputy Director of Medical Services, Malaya and Western Command, 1967-70. Queen's Honorary Physician.

McGiffert, John Rutherford, II. Major General, United States Army; Deputy Chief of Staff for Reserve Management, US Army Training and Doctrine Command, Fort Monroe, Virginia, 1973- . Born August 5, 1926, Jefferson Barracks, Missouri. Attended University of Maryland, BA, Military Science; Artillery School, Basic and Advanced Courses; Command and General Staff College;

Armed Forces Staff College; National War College; George Washington University, MS, International Affairs; University of Pittsburgh, 1970. Commissioned Second Lieutenant in May 1947. Served in the Vietnam War. Executive Officer, 1st Infantry Division Artillery, US Army, Pacific-Vietnam, 1966-67; Faculty Member, National War College, 1967-69; Commanding Officer, 214th Artillery Group, Fort Sill, Oklahoma, 1969-70; Special Assistant to the Commander, III Corps Artillery, Fort Sill, Oklahoma, 1970; Chief of the Department of the Army Command and Control Division, Operations Directorate, Office of the Deputy Chief of Staff for Military Operations, 1970-71; Deputy Commanding General, TRAC, and Deputy Senior Advisor, MR3, then Chief of Surface Operations, Directorate of Operations, US Military Assistance Command, Vietnam, 1971-73; Distinguished Service Medal; Silver Star; Legion of Merit; Distinguished Flying Cross; Bronze Star Medal; and other medals and awards. Promoted to Brigadier General, October 1, 1971; Major General, 1973.

McGough, Edward A., III. Major General, United States Air Force; Deputy Commander, Industrial College of the Armed Forces, 1972-   . Born October 3, 1918, in Philadelphia, Pennsylvania. US Military Academy, 1940-43; Command and General Staff School, 1945; Stanford University, 1947-49, MBA, 1949; Air Command and Staff School, 1951; Industrial College of the Armed Forces, 1960-61. Enlisted in the US Navy, 1936-69. Commissioned Second Lieutenant, US Army Air Corps, 1943. Served in the European Theater, WW II; Vietnam War. Commander, 355th Tactical Fighter Wing, 1963-65; Commander, 835th Air Division, 1965-66; Deputy Director, Tactical Air Control Center, Headquarters Seventh Air Force, Pacific Air Forces, Vietnam, 1966-67; Deputy Director, Aerospace Programs, Deputy Chief of Staff, Programs and Resources, Headquarters USAF, 1967-69; Director, Personnel Planning, Deputy Chief of Staff, Personnel, Headquarters USAF, 1969-70; Commander, Sixteenth Air Force, Spain, 1970-72. Distinguished Service Medal with one Oak Leaf Cluster; Distinguished Flying Cross; and other US and foreign medals and awards. Promoted to Major General, August 1, 1968.

McGovern, Donald Hugh. Major General, United States Army; US Army Audit Agency, 1973-   . Born November 9, 1917, New York, New York. The Infantry School, Advanced Course; US Army Command and General Staff College; Armed Forces Staff College; US Army War College. Commissioned Second Lieutenant, US Army Reserve, 1942. Served in WW II and Vietnam War. Assistant Chief of Staff for Personnel, J-1, US Military Assistance Command, Vietnam, 1966-67; Assistant Division Commander, 5th Infantry Division (Mechanized), Fort Carson, Colorado, 1967-68; Commanding General, US Army Recruiting Command, Hampton, Virginia, 1968-71; Director, J-7, US European Command, 1971-73. Distinguished Service Medal; Silver Star; Legion of Merit with three Oak Leaf Clusters; Bronze Star Medal; and other medals and awards. Promoted to Brigadier General, February 10, 1966; Major General, August 1, 1969.

McIntosh, Sir Ian Stewart. Vice-Admiral, British Royal Navy; Deputy Chief of Defence Staff (Operational Requirements), 1971-   . Born October 11, 1919. Commissioned in 1938. Submarine duty in WW II. Commander, 2d Submarine Squadron, 1961-63; Commander, HMS *Victorious*, 1966-68; Director General, Weapons (Naval), 1968-70. KBE; CB; DSO; MBE; DSC. Promoted to Captain, 1959; Rear-Admiral, 1968; Vice-Admiral, 1971.

Mack, William Paden. Vice Admiral, United States Navy; Superintendent, US Naval Academy, 1972-   . Born August 6, 1915, in Hillsboro, Illinois. US Naval Academy, 1933-37; National War College, 1955-56. Commissioned Ensign, US Navy, 1937. Served in the Pacific Theater, WW II; Korean War. Commander Destroyer Division, TWENTY-TWO, 1956-57; Assistant Director, Special Projects, General Planning Group, Office of the CNO, 1958-59; Naval Aide to the Secretary of the Navy, 1959-61; Commander Destroyer Squadron TWENTY-EIGHT, 1961-62; Office of Special Assistant for Counterinsurgency, Joint Chiefs of Staff, 1962-63; Chief of Information, Navy Department, 1963-66; Commander Amphibious Group TWO, 1966-67; Chief of Legislative Affairs, Navy Department, 1967-69; Deputy Assistant Secretary of Defense (Manpower and Reserve Affairs), 1969-71; Commander Seventh Fleet, 1971-72. Promoted to Vice Admiral, January 28, 1969.

McKaig, Sir (John) Rae. Vice-Admiral, British Royal Navy; United Kingdom Military Representative to NATO, 1973-   . Born April 24, 1922. Joined the Royal Navy in 1939. Served in cruisers and destroyers, Home Fleet, and Mediterranean, and in amphibious and coastal forces in WW II. Deputy to Chief Polaris Executive, 1963-66; Commandant HM Signal School, 1966-68; Assistant Chief, Naval Staff (Operational Requirements), 1968-70; Flag Officer, Plymouth, Commander, Central Sub Area, Eastern Atlantic, and Commander, Plymouth Sub Area, Channel, 1970-73. KCB; CBE. Promoted to Captain, 1959; Rear-Admiral, 1968; Vice-Admiral, 1970.

McKay, Alexander Matthew. Major-General, British Army; Director of Electrical and Mechanical Engineering (Army), 1972-   . Born February 14, 1921. Attended Royal Navy Dockyard School; Portsmouth Polytechnic; Staff College; Staff College, Quetta, 1954. Commissioned Second Lieutenant, Royal Electrical and Mechanical Engineers, 1943. Served with 6th Airborne Division in WW II. Recent duty includes: Deputy Assistant Adjutant and Quartermaster-General; Deputy Assistant Quartermaster-General; Assistant Quartermaster-General. Chartered Engineer; Fellow of the Institute of Electrical Engineers; Fellow of the Institute of Mechanical Engineers; Member of the British Institute of Management. Promoted to Brigadier in 1968; Major General in 1972.

MacKay, Kenneth. Major General, Royal Australian Army; General Officer Commanding Eastern Command, 1971-   . Born February 17, 1917. Attended Royal

Military College, 1935-38; Royal College of Defence Studies, 1962; Imperial Defence College; Staff College. Commissioned in 1938. Served in the African-European Theaters and in New Guinea in WW II; Vietnam War. Director, Military Operations and Plans, Australian Headquarters, 1963-66; Commander, Australian Forces, Vietnam, 1966-67; Commander, 1st Australian Division, 1967-68; Quartermaster General, Australian Headquarters, 1968-71. CB; MBE.

McKee, George H. Major General, United States Air Force; Deputy Chief of Staff, Logistics, Headquarters Strategic Air Command, 1972-   . Born April 28, 1923, in Pickins, South Carolina. Army Air Corps Flying School, 1942-43; University of Omaha, Nebraska, BA, Education, 1958; Industrial College of the Armed Forces, 1963-64. Commissioned Second Lieutenant, US Army Air Corps Reserve, 1943. Served in the European Theater, WW II. Commander, 319th Bombardment Wing, 1965-66; Commander, 97th Bombardment Wing, 1966-67; Commander, 72d Bombardment Wing, Puerto Rico, 1967-68; Commander, 19th Air Division, 1968-70; Director, Maintenance Engineering, Deputy Chief of Staff, Systems and Logistics, Headquarters USAF, 1970-72. Legion of Merit; Distinguished Flying Cross; and other medals and awards. Promoted to Major General, August 1, 1970.

McKeen, Chester M., Jr. Major General, United States Army; Director of Requirements and Procurement, US Army Materiel Command, 1972-   . Born March 18, 1923, in Shelby, Ohio. Attended University of Maryland, BS, Military Science; Babson Institute, MBA, Business Administration; Ordnance School, Advanced Course; Command and General Staff College; Industrial College of the Armed Forces, 1965-66. Commissioned June 19, 1943. Served in WW II and the Vietnam War. Project Officer, Military Affairs Office, Weapons Evaluation and Control Bureau, US Arms Control and Disarmament Agency, 1966-67; Chief, Procurement of Equipment and Missiles, Army, Execution Division, later Director, Materiel Acquisition, Office of the Deputy Chief of Staff for Logistics, 1967-70; Commanding Officer, US Army Procurement Agency, Vietnam, US Army, Pacific-Vietnam, 1970-71; Director of Procurement and Production, later Deputy Commanding General, US Army Tank Automotive Command, Warren, Michigan, 1971-72. Legion of Merit with Oak Leaf Cluster; Army Commendation Medal with Oak Leaf Cluster; and other medals and awards. Promoted to Brigadier General August 1, 1971; Major General June 1, 1973.

McLaughlin, George W. Major General, United States Air Force; Commander, Sacramento Air Materiel Area, 1972-   . Born December 29, 1919, in Georgetown, Ohio. Ohio State University; Army Air Corps Flying School, 1941-42; Miami University, Ohio, 1946-47, BS, 1947; Air War College, 1958-59; Army Command and General Staff School; Advanced Management Program, Harvard University Business School. Commissioned Second

Lieutenant, US Army Air Corps, 1942. Served in the European Theater, WW II; Vietnam War. Plans Division, US Strike Command, 1962-64; Commander, 50th Tactical Fighter Wing, 1964-66; Deputy Chief of Staff, Operations, Seventeenth Air Force, Germany, 1966-67; Commander, 3d Tactical Fighter Wing, Vietnam, 1967-68; Director, Seventh Air Force Tactical Air Control Center, Vietnam, 1969; Assistant Deputy Chief of Staff, Operations, for Requirements, Tactical Air Command, 1969-70; Deputy Chief of Staff, Materiel, Tactical Air Command, 1970-72. Distinguished Service Medal; Silver Star; Legion of Merit; Distinguished Flying Cross with one Oak Leaf Cluster; and other US and foreign medals and awards. Promoted to Major General, August 1, 1970.

McLaughlin, John Daniel. Major General, United States Army; Commanding General, Theater Army Support Command, Europe, 1973-   . Born December 24, 1917, San Francisco, California. US Armed Forces Staff College; US National War College. Commissioned Second Lieutenant, US Army Reserve, 1942. Served in WW II and Vietnam War. Chief, Supply Management Division, Office, Deputy Chief of Staff for Logistics, US Army, Washington, D.C., 1966-67; Assistant Chief of Staff for Logistics, J-4, US Pacific Command, 1967-69; Commanding General, US Army Quartermaster Center, and Commandant, US Army Quartermaster School, Fort Lee, Virginia, 1969-73. Distinguished Service Medal with Oak Leaf Cluster; Legion of Merit with four Oak Leaf Clusters; Bronze Star Medal with two Oak Leaf Clusters; and other medals and awards. Promoted to Brigadier General, February 1, 1967; Major General, May 22, 1970.

McLaughlin, John N. Major General, United States Marine Corps; Commanding General, 4th Marine Division, 1973-   . Born September 21, 1918, Charleston, South Carolina. Emory University, BA, 1941; Officer Candidates School, 1941; Infantry School, Fort Benning, Georgia, 1948; National War College, 1964-65; George Washington University, MA, International Affairs, 1965. Commissioned Second Lieutenant, USMCR, 1941. Served in Pacific Theater, WW II; Korean War, POW; Vietnam War. Commanding Officer, Sixth Marines, then Chief of Staff, Second Marine Division, 1965-67; Deputy, J-5, Plans, United States Strike Command, 1967-68; Assistant Division Commander, 1st Marine Division, Vietnam, 1968; Director, Combat Operations Center, and Deputy, J-3, Operations, Military Assistance Command, Vietnam, 1968-69; Commanding General, Marine Corps Recruit Depot, San Diego, California, 1969-72. Distinguished Service Medal; Silver Star Medal; Legion of Merit with one Gold Star; Bronze Star with Combat "V"; and other US and foreign medals and awards. Promoted to Brigadier General, January 10, 1967; Major General, September 3, 1969.

McLeod, William Eugene. Major General, United States Army; Chief of Staff, Eighth US Army, US Army Pacific-Korea, 1973-   . Born April 25, 1921, Granite, Oklahoma. The Artillery School, Advanced Course; US Army Command and General Staff College; US Army War

College. Commissioned Second Lieutenant, 1942. Served in WW II. Commanding General, III Corps Artillery, Fort Sill, Oklahoma, 1967-68; Commanding General, VII Corps Artillery, US Army, Europe, 1968, and 1969-70; Chief of Staff, VII Corps, US Army, Europe, 1968-69; Deputy Director, Office, Deputy Assistant Secretary of Defense (Inspection Services), Office, Assistant Secretary of Defense (Administration), Washington, D.C., 1970-71; Director of Organization and Unit Training, Office, Assistant Chief of Staff for Force Development, US Army, Washington, D.C., 1971-72. Legion of Merit with Oak Leaf Cluster; Bronze Star Medal with V Device; and other medals and awards. Promoted to Brigadier General, July 28, 1968; Major General, March 1, 1971.

McLucas, John L. United States Secretary of the Air Force, 1973-   . Born August 22, 1920, in Fayetteville, North Carolina. Davidson College, BS, 1941; Tulane University, MS, physics, 1943; Pennsylvania State University, PhD, physics, 1950. Served as US Naval Reserve officer, 1943-46. President, HRB-Singer, Inc., 1958-62; Deputy Director of Defense Research and Engineering (Tactical Warfare Programs), 1962-64; Assistant Secretary General for Scientific Affairs, NATO Headquarters, Paris, 1964-66; President and Chief Executive Officer, MITRE Corporation, 1966-69; Under Secretary of the Air Force, 1969-73. Department of Defense Distinguished Public Service Award with Bronze Palm; Department of Air Force Exceptional Civilian Service Award.

McManus, Philip Stanley. Rear Admiral, United States Navy; Commander, Amphibious Group TWO, 1972-˙   . Born July 18, 1919, Holyoke, Massachusetts. US Naval Academy, 1939-42; Naval Postgraduate School, 1948-50; Johns Hopkins University, MS, Engineering, 1950-51; Naval War College, 1960-61. Commissioned Ensign, US Navy, 1942. Served in Atlantic and Pacific Theaters, WW II; Korean War; Vietnam War. Director, Missile Ordnance Division, Missile Development Office, Bureau of Naval Weapons, 1962-65; Commander, Landing Ship Flotilla ONE, 1965-66; Commander, Amphibious Squadron FIVE, 1966-67; Navy Deputy to Department of Defense Manager for Manned Space Flight Support Operations, CNO Representative for Manned Space Flight Support Operations, and Commander Manned Spacecraft Recovery Force, Atlantic, 1968-70; Commander, Amphibious Group TWO, 1970; Commander, US Naval Support Activity, Saigon, 1970-71; Commander, Naval Inshore Warfare Command, US Atlantic Fleet, and Commander Amphibious Group TWO, 1972. Legion of Merit with Combat "V"; Navy and Marine Corps Medal; Meritorious Service Medal; Navy Commendation Medal with two Gold Stars and Combat "V"; and other US and foreign medals and awards. Promoted to Rear Admiral, July 1, 1969.

McMeekin, Terence Douglas Herbert. Major-General, British Army; Commandant, National Defence College, 1970-   . Born September 27, 1918. Attended King William's College, Isle of Man; Royal Military Academy, Woolwich; Staff College, Haifa, 1943; Joint Services Staff College,

1955. Commissioned Second Lieutenant, Royal Artillery, in 1938. Served in North Africa and Middle East in WW II. Commander, 29 Field Regiment, Royal Artillery, 1960-62; Chief Instructor (Tactics), School of Artillery, Larkhill, 1962-64; Commander, 28 Commonwealth Infantry Brigade Group, Malaya, 1964-66; Director, Public Relations (Army), 1967-68; General Officer Commanding, 3rd Division, 1968-70. OBE.

McMorries, Edwin Eliot. Rear Admiral, Supply Corps, United States Navy; Commanding Officer, Ships Parts Control Center, Mechanicsburg, Pennsylvania, 1972-   . Born December 15, 1921, at Pensacola, Florida. Duke University, Durham, North Carolina, BA, 1943; Naval Supply Corps School, Wellesley College, Massachusetts, 1943; Stanford University, Palo Alto, California, MBS, 1950; Naval War College, Newport, Rhode Island, 1966-67. Commissioned Ensign, US Naval Reserve, 1942; transferred from Line to Supply Corps, 1943; transferred from Naval Reserve to US Navy, 1946. Served in Pacific Theater in WW II. Field Operations Officer and Director of the Planning Division of the Naval Ships Store Office, Brooklyn, New York, 1961-64; Supply and Fiscal Officer, and Logistics Officer, Headquarters, Naval Activities, Naples, Italy, 1964-66; Director of Procurement, Office of the Assistant Secretary of the Navy (Installations and Logistics), and Director, Office of the Deputy Chief of Naval Material (Procurement and Production), Washington, D.C., 1967-69; Assistant to the Assistant Secretary of the Navy (Installations and Logistics), 1969-70; Assistant Commander, Naval Air Systems Command for Contracts, Washington, D.C., 1970-72. American Campaign Medal; National Defense Service Medal with Bronze Star; and other medals and awards. Promoted to Rear Admiral, July 1, 1970.

McNabb, John M. Major General, United States Air Force; Deputy Chief of Staff, Plans and Operations, Pacific Command, Hawaii, 1973-   . Born November 10, 1917, in Detroit, Michigan. Lehigh University, BS, Electrical Engineering, 1939; Army Air Corps Flying School, 1941; Air Command and Staff School, 1948; National War College, 1956-57. Commissioned Second Lieutenant, USAR, 1939; received pilot wings, 1941. Served in the European Theater, WW II. Deputy Chief of Staff, Plans, Allied Air Forces Southern Europe, 1963-64; Commander, 3524th Pilot Training Wing, Air Training Command, 1964-65; Deputy Chief of Staff, Technical Training, Air Training Command, 1965-67; Chief of Staff, Air Training Command, 1967; Commander, Sheppard Technical Training Center, Sheppard Air Force Base, 1967-69; Director of Plans, Office of Deputy Chief of Staff, Plans and Operations, 1969-70; Assistant Deputy Chief of Staff, Plans and Operations, 1970-71; Deputy Chief of Staff, Plans, Pacific Air Forces, Hawaii, 1971-72; Chief of Staff, Headquarters Pacific Air Forces, Hawaii, 1972-73. Distinguished Service Medal; Legion of Merit with one Oak Leaf Cluster; Distinguished Flying Cross, and other US and foreign medals and awards. Promoted to Major General, March 15, 1968.

McNeff, Edward P. Major General, United States Air Force; Vice Commander, Twelfth Air Force, Bergstrom Air Force Base, Texas, 1972-   . Born March 7, 1924, Camden, New Jersey. Aviation Cadet Training Course, 1942-43; University of Chicago, MBA, 1958. Commissioned Second Lieutenant, US Army Air Corps, 1943. Served in the European Theater, WW II, in the Korean War, and in the Vietnam War. Commander, Combat Crew Training Group, Luke Air Force Base, Arizona, 1965-67; Vice Commander, 35th Tactical Fighter Wing, Phan Rang Air Base, Vietnam, 1967-68; Commander, 405th Fighter Wing, Clark Air Base, The Philippines, 1968-70; Commander, 835th Air Division, McConnell Air Force Base, Kansas, 1970-71; Vice Commander, US Air Force Tactical Air Warfare Center, Eglin Air Force Base, 1971-72. Legion of Merit with Oak Leaf Cluster; Distinguished Flying Cross with two Oak Leaf Clusters; Air Medal with nineteen Oak Leaf Clusters; Vietnam Gallantry Cross with Silver Star; and other medals and awards. Promoted to Brigadier General, May 26, 1971; Major General, 1973.

McNeil, Travis R. Major General, United States Air Force; Commander, Air Force Military Personnel Center, and Assistant Deputy Chief of Staff, Personnel for Military Personnel, Randolph Air Force Base, Texas, 1973-   . Born March 4, 1924, in Malakoff, Texas. Attended University of Alabama, 1941-43; Aviation Cadet Pilot Training, 1943-45; National War College, 1965-66. Commissioned Second Lieutenant, US Army Air Corps, in 1945. Served in the Vietnam War. Deputy Commander of Operations, 12th Tactical Fighter Wing, Cam Rahn Bay, Vietnam, 1966-67; Chief, Programs Status Division, Headquarters Tactical Air Warfare Center, Eglin Air Force Base, Florida, 1967-69; Vice Commander, 33d Tactical Fighter Wing, Eglin Air Force Base, Florida, 1969-70; Commander, 15th Tactical Fighter Wing (redesignated the 1st Tactical Fighter Wing, October 1970), MacDill Air Force Base, Florida, 1970-71; Deputy Director, Operations (J-3), US Readiness Command, MacDill Air Force Base, Florida, 1971-72; Commander, 314th Air Division, PACAF, with additional duty as Chief of Air Force Advisory Group, Military Assistance Advisory Group, Korea; Commander, Korean Aerial Delivery System; Commander, Air Force Korea, and Air Force Advisor to Senior Member, United Nations Military Armistice Commission, Korea, 1972-73. Legion of Merit with Oak Leaf Cluster; Meritorious Service Medal; Distinguished Flying Cross; Bronze Star; Air Medal with nine Oak Leaf Clusters; Republic of Vietnam Medal of Honor; and other medals and awards. Promoted to Brigadier General, November 1, 1971; Major General, 1973.

McNickle, Melvin F. Major General, United States Air Force; Chief of Staff, Air Force Logistics Command, 1968-   . Born January 30, 1914, in Doland, South Dakota. University of South Dakota, 1932-36, BA, 1936; Army Air Corps Flying School, 1937-38; Air War College, 1952-53. Commissioned Second Lieutenant, US Army Reserve, 1936; received Pilot Wings, 1938. Served in the European Theater, WW II, POW. Assistant Deputy Commander, and later Deputy Commander, Aircraft

Weapon Systems, Headquarters Air Force Systems Command, 1956-60; Director, Supply and Services, Deputy Chief of Staff, Systems and Logistics, 1960-64; Commander, Oklahoma City Air Materiel Area, 1964-68. Distinguished Flying Cross; Legion of Merit with two Oak Leaf Clusters; Bronze Star Medal; and other US and foreign medals and awards. Promoted to Major General, April 17, 1962.

McPherson, John B. Lieutenant General, United States Air Force; Commandant, National War College, 1970-   . Born October 4, 1917, in Virginia, Minnesota. University of Arizona, Tucson, Arizona, BS, Civil Engineering, 1940; Army Air Corps Flying School, 1943; Air War College, 1952-53. Commissioned Second Lieutenant, Cavalry, US Army, 1940; received pilot wings, 1943. Served in the Pacific Theater, WW II. Commander, 810th Strategic Aerospace Division, Strategic Air Command, 1962-64; Vice Director, Operations, J-3, Office, Joint Chiefs of Staff, 1964-67; Vice Director, The Joint Staff, Office, Joint Chiefs of Staff, 1967-68; Assistant to the Chairman, Joint Chiefs of Staff, 1968-70. Distinguished Service Medal; Legion of Merit; Bronze Star Medal; and other medals and awards. Promoted to Brigadier General, February 17, 1962; Major General, February 27, 1964; Lieutenant General, August 1, 1968.

Maddox, William Johnston, Jr. Major General, United States Army; Commandant, US Army Aviation Center and Fort Rucker, Alabama, 1973-   . Born May 22, 1921, in Newburgh, New York. Attended Michigan State University, BA, Journalism; George Washington University, BS, International Affairs; Infantry School; Armored School, Advanced Course; Command and General Staff College; National War College, 1964-65. Commissioned Second Lieutenant, USAR, July 25, 1944; regular commission September 1957. Served in WW II, the Korean War and the Vietnam War. Commanding Officer, 13th Aviation Battalion, US Army Pacific-Vietnam, 1965-66; Deputy Plans and Operations Officer, later Senior Division Advisor Detachment Commander, IV Corps Advisory Group, US Military Assistance Command, Vietnam, 1966-67; Chief of Staff, later Assistant Division Commander, 3d Armored Division, US Army, Europe, 1967-69; Commanding Officer, 3d Brigade, 25th Infantry Division, US Army, Pacific-Vietnam, 1969; Commanding Officer, 164th Combat Aviation Group, US Army, Pacific-Vietnam, 1969-70; Director of Army Aviation, Office of the Assistant Chief of Staff for Force Development, 1970-73. Silver Star with three Oak Leaf Clusters; Legion of Merit with four Oak Leaf Clusters; Distinguished Flying Cross with seven Oak Leaf Clusters; Bronze Star Medal with V Device with three Oak Leaf Clusters; Air Medal (128 awards); and other medals and awards. Promoted to Brigadier General August 1, 1970; Major General April 1, 1973.

Madsen, Frank M., Jr. Major General, United States Air Force; Commander, Keesler Technical Training Center, Keesler Air Force Base, Mississippi, 1969-   . Born April

6, 1918, Harvey, Illinois. Illinois Institute of Technology; Army Air Corps Flying School, 1942-44; Air Command and Staff School, 1951; Industrial College of the Armed Forces, 1962-63. Commissioned in 1944. Served in the Pacific Theater in WW II. Deputy Commander, 3510th Flying Training Wing, 1964-65; Commander, 3646th Pilot Training Wing, 1965-67; Commander, 3510th Flying Training Wing, 1967-68; Chief of Staff, Headquarters, Air Training Command, 1968-69; Deputy Chief of Staff, Technical Training, Air Training Command, 1969. Legion of Merit with one Oak Leaf Cluster; and other medals and awards. Promoted to Major General, March 1, 1970.

Magen, Klamam. Major General, Israeli Army; Commander, Tank Forces, Sinai area, 1973.

Maita, Kasim Hassan. Major General, Armed Forces of the Hashemite Kingdom of Jordan; Deputy Commander in Chief, Jordanian Armed Forces, 1970-   . Took various Military Courses. Former Commander, Infantry Brigade; Commander, Infantry Division.

Majali, Habis Rifiafan. Field Marshal, Armed Forces of the Hashemite Kingdom of Jordan; Commander in Chief, Jordanian Armed Forces, 1970-   . College Graduate; Military Courses. Recent assignments: Security Police District Commander; Commander, Western Front; Chief of Staff; Minister of Defense.

Majury, James Herbert Samuel. Major General, British Army; General Officer Commanding, West Midland District, Shrewsbury, 1970-   . Born June 26, 1921. Attended Royal Academical Institution, Belfast; Trinity College, Dublin; Imperial Defence College, 1968. Joined the Royal Ulster Rifles in 1940. Served in WW II and the Korean War; POW in Korea. Commander, Royal Irish Fusiliers, 1961-62; Commander, 2d Infantry Brigade, 1965-67. MBE.

Makarevskiy, B. Major General, USSR Army; Deputy Commandant, Kuybyshev Military Engineering College. Served on the Soviet-German Front in WW II. Member, Communist Party of the Soviet Union.

Makarychev, Mikhail Ivanovich. Major General, USSR Army (Artillery); Commander, Missile Troops and Artillery, Moscow Military District, 1969-   . Born in 1919. Volunteered for the Army in 1936. Attended Sumy Artillery Academy, 1936-39; Army War College, 1951-54; Senior Military Courses, c. 1958. Commissioned in 1939. Served in the Soviet-German War, 1941-45. Commander, Artillery Battery, Southwest Front, 1941; Commander, Artillery Battalion, Stalingrad Front, 1942-43; Commander, Anti-tank Artillery Regiment, Central and Baltic Fronts, 1943-45; Commander, Artillery Regiment, Group of Soviet Forces in Germany, 1945-51; Superintendent, Military Academy, 1954 - c. 1958. Member, Communist Party of the Soviet Union. Hero of the Soviet Union; Order of Lenin; Order of Red Banner; Order of Red Star; Order of Fatherland War; and other orders and medals.

Maksimov, K. Lieutenant General, USSR Army; Chief, Political Directorate, Central Asian Military District. Served on the Soviet-German Front in WW II. Member, Communist Party of the Soviet Union.

Malashenko, E. Lieutenant General, USSR Army; Chief of Staff, Carpathian Military District, 1971-   . Served on the Soviet-German Front in WW II. Member, Communist Party of the Soviet Union.

Maldonado, Marco Aurelio. Rear Admiral, Navy of Ecuador; Military and Naval Attache, Embassy of Ecuador, Washington, D.C.; Chief of Delegation, Inter-American Defense Board. Promoted to Rear Admiral December 31, 1970.

Malloum, Felix. Colonel, Army of Chad; Chief, High Command of the Armed Forces.

Maloy, Robert W. Major General, United States Air Force; Commander, Seventeenth Air Force, Sembach Air Base, Germany, 1972-   . Born February 14, 1924, in Charleston, Illinois. Arizona State University; Army Air Corps Flying School, 1943-44; Air Tactical School, 1949; Royal Air Force Tactical College, Bracknell, England, 1953; National War College, 1961-62. Commissioned in 1944. Served in the China-Burma-India Theater, WW II, Vietnam War. Commander, 33d Tactical Fighter Wing, 1966-67; Commander, 366th Tactical Fighter Wing, Vietnam, 1967; Deputy Assistant, Deputy Chief of Staff, Personnel for Military Personnel, Headquarters USAF, 1968-70; Commander, 314th Air Division, Fifth Air Force, Korea, and Chief, Air Advisory Group, Korea; Commander, Korean Air Defense Sector; Commander, Air Force Korea; Air Force Advisor to the Senior Member, United Nations Military Armistice Commission, 1970-72. Silver Star; Legion of Merit with four Oak Leaf Clusters; Distinguished Flying Cross; Bronze Star; and other US and foreign medals and awards. Promoted to Major General, August 1, 1970.

Maltsev, Y.Y. Colonel General, USSR Army. Served on the Soviet-German Front in WW II. Chief Political Directorate, Group of Soviet Forces in Germany, 1967-71. Member, Communist Party of the Soviet Union.

Mamula, Branko. Vice Admiral, Yugoslavian Navy; Assistant Secretary of State for National Defense for the Navy.

Man, Chu Huy. Major General, People's Army of Vietnam; Commander and Political Officer, Western Highlands Front Area, 1966; Member of Lao Dong Party Central Committee; Deputy Chief, General Political Directorate, People's Army of Vietnam, 1962. Born in 1920 in Nghe An Province. Political Officer, 316th Division, c. 1953; Commander and Political Officer of Tay Bac (Northwest) Military Region, 1960; Deputy to Second National Assembly, 1960; Deputy Commander and Secretary of Lao Dong Party Committee of Fifth (Central Vietnam) Military Region, 1965. Promoted to Major General, 1960.

Mandujano, Galvarino. Major General, Chilean Army; Military Attache, Embassy of Chile, Washington, D.C.

Manley, Michel. Prime Minister and Minister of Defense, Jamaica. Born December 10, 1923, in Kingston. Graduated from the London School of Economics. Served as pilot, Royal Canadian Air Force, in WW II. Formely journalist for British Broadcasting Corporation; co-editor, *Public Opinion;* Vice President, National Workers' Union 1955; President, Caribbean Bauxite and Mine Workers Union. Member of Parliament since 1967.

Mann, Siegfried. Under Secretary, Federal Ministry of Defense, Federal Republic of Germany, 1972-   . Born September 21, 1926, Stuttgart. Studied Law, LLD, 1955. Head, Organization Staff, Federal Ministry of Defense, 1967-71; Head, Financial Division, Federal Defense Ministry, 1971-72.

Manor, Leroy J. Major General, United States Air Force; Deputy Director, Operations/Special Assistant, Counter Insurgency and Special Activities, Organization, Joint Chiefs of Staff, 1971-   . Born February 21, 1921, in Morrisonville, New York. New York State Teachers College; Army Air Corps Flying School, 1942-43; New York University, 1946-47, BS, Education, 1947; Armed Forces Staff College, 1958-59; Industrial College of the Armed Forces, 1963-64. Commissioned in 1943. Served in the European Theater, WW II; Vietnam War. Directorate of Operations, Office of Deputy Chief of Staff, Plans and Operations, 1964-66; Chief, Operations Review Group, Deputy Chief of Staff, Plans and Operations, Headquarters USAF, 1966-68; Commander, 37th Tactical Fighter Wing, Vietnam, 1968-69; Commander, 835th Air Division, 1969-70; Commander, United States Air Force Special Operations Force, 1970-71. Distinguished Service Medal; Legion of Merit with one Oak Leaf Cluster; Distinguished Flying Cross with one Oak Leaf Cluster; and other US and foreign medals and awards. Promoted to Major General, August 1, 1972.

Mansfield, Edward Gerard Napier. Vice-Admiral, British Royal Navy; Deputy Supreme Allied Commander Atlantic, 1972-   . Born July 13, 1921. Attended Royal Naval College, Dartmouth. Entered the Royal Navy in 1935. Served in destroyers and combined operations in WW II. SHAPE, 1960-62; Captain (F), 20th Frigate Squadron, 1963-64; Director of Defence Plans (Navy), 1965-67; Commodore, Amphibious Forces, 1967-68; Senior Naval Member, Directing Staff, Imperial Defence College, 1969-70; Flag Officer, Sea Training, 1971-72. Promoted to Captain, 1959; Vice-Admiral, 1972.

Maples, Herron Nichols. Major General, United States Army; Commanding General, Okinawa Base Command, 1972-   . Born September 7, 1918, Celina, Texas. Texas Agricultural and Mechanical College, BS Degree—Petroleum Engineering; U.S. Army Command and General Staff College; Naval War College, Command and Staff Course; Armed Forces Staff College; U.S. Army War College. Commissioned Second Lieutenant, U.S. Army Reserve, 1940. Served in WW II and Vietnam War. Assistant Division Commander, 24th Infantry Division, U.S. Army, Europe, 1966-67; Deputy Commanding General, Seventh Army

Support Command, U.S. Army, Europe, 1967-68; Deputy Chief of Staff for Logistics, U.S. Army, Europe, 1968-70; Assistant Chief of Staff, J-4, U.S. Military Assistance Command, Vietnam, 1970-72; Deputy Commanding General, U.S. Army, Ryuku Islands/IX Corps, Okinawa, 1972. Distinguished Service Medal with two Oak Leaf Clusters; Bronze Star Medal; and other medals and awards. Promoted to Brigadier General, August 1, 1963; Major General, January 1, 1969.

Marchenko, Y. Lieutenant General, USSR Army; First Deputy Commander, Urals Military District, 1967-   . Served on the Soviet-German Front in WW II. Member, Communist Party of the Soviet Union.

Margelov, Vasiliy Filippovich. General of the Army, USSR Army; Commander, Soviet Airborne Forces, 1962-   . Born in 1909 in the Ukraine. Volunteered for the Army in 1928. Attended Joint Belorussian Military Academy, 1928-31; War College, c. 1947-49. Commissioned in 1931. Served in the Finno-Soviet War, 1939-40; Soviet-German War, 1941-45. Commander Ski-troops Battalion, 1939-40; Commander, Infantry Regiment, 1941; Commander, 1st Volunteer Regiment, Baltic Fleet, Leningrad Front (operated behind German lines), 1941-42; Commander, 1st Guards Rifle Regiment, Stalingrad Front, 1942-43; Commander, Guards Rifle Division, Ukrainian Front, 1943-45; Commander, large units and formations, 1946-62. Member, Communist Party of the Soviet Union. Hero of the Soviet Union; two Orders of Lenin; two Orders of Red Banner, Order of Suvorov; Order of Red Star; and other Soviet and foreign medals and orders. Promoted to General of the Army, October 28, 1967.

Marks, Sidney Michael. Major General, United States Army; Chief of Staff, First US Army, Fort George G. Meade, Maryland, 1971-   . Born January 8, 1919, Keota, Oklahoma. Oklahoma State University, BS Degree, Military Science; The Infantry School, Advanced Course; US Army Command and General Staff College; Armed Forces Staff College; US Army War College. Commissioned Second Lieutenant, US Army Reserve, 1942. Served in WW II and Vietnam War. Deputy Assistant Commandant, US Army Infantry School, Fort Benning, Georgia, 1968; Director, J-3, US Southern Command, Quarry Heights, Canal Zone, 1968-69; Assistant Division Commander, 7th Infantry Division, Eighth US Army, US Army, Pacific-Korea, 1969-71. Silver Star with Oak Leaf Cluster; Legion of Merit with four Oak Leaf Clusters; Distinguished Flying Cross; Soldier's Medal; Bronze Star Medal with V Device and five Oak Leaf Clusters; and other medals and awards. Promoted to Brigadier General, August 1, 1969; Major General, June 1, 1971.

Marques, Roberval Pizarro. Vice Admiral (FN), Brazilian Navy; Commanding General of the Marine Corps, 1972-   . Army Paratrooper Course; Command and Staff School of the Armed Forces and Senior War College of ESG; Bachelor of Education; Naval War College; Amphibious Operations (Quantico, Virginia, USA); Infantry Officers School for Improvement; CIC, Naval School (Marine). Combat duty in WW II. Squadron Marine

Force; Staff, 1st Division of Marines, FFE; Marine Corps Instruction Center; 1st Battalion of Infantry, Staff of the 1st Marine Division; Naval Representative on the Frontier Demarkation Service of the Ministry of Foreign Relations. Medalha de Prata; Medalha do Merito Tamandare; Medalha do Pacificador; Medalha de Servicos de Guerra, Medalho do Merito Naval. Promoted to Vice Admiral, 28 November 1972.

Marschall, Albert Rhoades. Rear Admiral, Civil Engineer Corps, United States Navy; Commander, Naval Facilities Engineering Command, and Chief of Civil Engineers of the Navy, 1973- . Born May 5, 1921, in New Orleans, Louisiana. Tulane University, New Orleans, Louisiana, 1937-40; US Naval Academy, 1941-44; Rensselaer Polytechnic Institute, Troy, New York, MS, Civil Engineering, 1948; Junior Course, Amphibious Warfare School, Marine Corps School, Quantico, Virginia, 1950; Armed Forces Staff College, Norfolk, Virginia, 1960-61. Commissioned Ensign, US Navy, 1944; transferred from Line to Civil Engineer Corps, 1948. Served in Pacific Theater, WW II, and in the Vietnam War. Director, Weapons and Other Support Divisions, Bureau of Yards and Docks, Navy Department, Washington, D.C., 1962-64; Public Works Officer, US Naval Academy, Annapolis, Maryland, 1964-66; Commander, 30th Naval Construction Regiment, 1966-67; Commanding Officer, South East Division, Naval Facilities Engineering Command, and District Civil Engineer on Staff of Commandant of Sixth Naval District, Charleston, South Carolina, 1967-70; Deputy Commander, Pacific Division, Naval Facilities Engineering Command, Southeast Asia, Saigon, Vietnam, with additional duty as Officer in Charge of Construction, Naval Facilities Engineering Command Contracts, Vietnam, and Commander, Third Naval Construction Brigade, 1970-71; Director, Shore Installations Division, Office of Chief of Naval Operations, Navy Department, Washington, D.C., 1971-72; Vice Commander, Naval Facilities Engineering Command, and Deputy Civil Engineer of the Navy, Navy Department, Washington, D.C., 1972-73. Distinguished Service Medal; Legion of Merit with Combat Device; Order of Military Merit, Chung Mu (Korea); National Order of Vietnam; George Goethals Medal, of Society of American Military Engineers; and other medals and awards. Promoted to Rear Admiral, July 1, 1970.

Marshall, Robert Creel. Major General, United States Army; Commanding General, US Army SAFEGUARD Systems Command, Redstone Arsenal, Alabama, 1969- . Born November 10, 1921, Washington, D.C. Attended US Military Academy; Engineer School, Basic and Advanced Courses; US Army Command and General Staff College; Industrial College of the Armed Forces; Cornell University, BCE Degree, Civil Engineering. Commissioned Second Lieutenant, 1943. Served in WW II and Vietnam War. Engineer, US Military Assistance Command, Vietnam, 1968; Engineer, Provisional Corps, Vietnam, US Army, Pacific-Vietnam, 1968; Director, Site Activation Directorate, US Army SENTINEL Systems Command, Later SAFEGUARD Systems Command, Redstone Arsenal, Alabama, 1968-69. Silver Star; Legion of Merit with Oak

Leaf Cluster; Bronze Star Medal with V Device and two Oak Leaf Clusters; and other medals and awards. Promoted to Brigadier General, February 1, 1969; Major General, April 1, 1971.

Marshall, Roger Sydenham. Major-General, British Army; Director, Army Legal Services, Ministry of Defence, 1971- . Born July 15, 1913. Commissioned in the Territorial Army, 1933; transferred to Army Legal Services in 1948. Active duty, 1939; served with the Royal Artillery in WW II. Headquarters, East Africa Command, 1961-62; Deputy Director, Army Legal Services, General Headquarters, Far East Land Forces, 1962-63; Legal Staff, Ministry of Defense (Colonel), 1964-69; Legal Staff, Ministry of Defense (Brigadier), 1969-71.TD. Promoted to Major-General, 1971.

Marshall, Winton W. Major General, United States Air Force; Deputy Chief of Staff, Plans, Pacific Air Forces, Hawaii, 1972- . Born July 6, 1919, in Detroit, Michigan. Army Air Corps Flying School, 1942-43; Tactical Air School, 1948; Air War College, 1958-59. Commissioned in 1943. Served in the Vietnam War. Deputy Chief, then Chief, Air Defense Division, then Deputy Director for Forces, Directorate of Operations, Air Force Headquarters, 1964-66; Deputy Director, Operations, J-3, National Military Command Center, Joint Chiefs of Staff, 1966-67; Chief, European Division, J-5, Joint Chiefs of Staff, 1967-68; Chief of Staff, Allied Air Forces Southern Europe, Italy, 1968-69; Director, J-5, US European Command, Germany, 1969-71; Vice Commander, Seventh Air Force, Vietnam, 1971-72. Distinguished Service Medal; Silver Star; Legion of Merit with two Oak Leaf Clusters; Bronze Medal; and other medals and awards. Promoted to Major General, August 1, 1968.

Martes, Grigore. Vice Admiral, Romanian Navy. Commander in chief of the Navy.

Martin, Glen Webster. Lieutenant General, United States Air Force; Vice Commander in Chief, Strategic Air Command, 1969- . Born May 23, 1916, in Chicago, Illinois. Purdue University, BS, 1937; Army Air Corps Flying School, 1939-40. Commissioned Second Lieutenant in 1937; received Pilot Wings, 1939. Served in the Pacific and European Theaters, WW II; Vietnam War. Commander, 47th Air Division, 1956-57; Director of Plans, Deputy Chief of Staff, Plans and Programs, Headquarters, US Air Force, 1957-61; Military Assistant to the Secretary of the Air Force, 1961-62; Deputy Chief of Staff, Plans and Operations, Headquarters Pacific Air Forces, Hawaii, 1962-65; Inspector General, United States Air Force, Headquarters, US Air Force, 1965-67; Deputy Chief of Staff, Plans and Operations, Headquarters, US Air Force, 1967-69. Distinguished Service Medal (Air Force); Distinguished Service Medal (Army); Legion of Merit with Oak Leaf Cluster; and other medals and awards. Promoted to Brigadier General, December 1, 1956; Major General, August 15, 1959; Lieutenant General, September 1, 1965.

Martin, Sir Harold Brownlow (Morgan). Air Marshal, British Royal Air Force; Commander-in-Chief, RAF, Germany, and

Commander, NATO 2nd Tactical Air Force, 1970-   .
Born February 27, 1918, in Edgecliffe, NSW, Australia.
Attended Bloomfields; Sydney; Handwick; Joint Services
Staff College, 1958; Imperial Defence College, 1965. Joined
Royal Air Force in 1939. Served in Bomber Command in
WW II. Senior Air Staff Officer, Near East Air Force, and
Joint Services Chief of Staff, 1966-67; Air Officer
Commanding, No. 38 Group, Air Support Command,
1967-70; Aide de Camp to the Queen, 1963. KCB; DSO
and two Bars; AFC. Promoted to Air Vice-Marshal, 1967;
Air Marshal, 1970.

Martin, Peter Lawrence de Carteret. Major-General, British
Army; Director of Personal Services (Army), 1971-   .
Born February 15, 1920. Attended Wellington College;
Royal Military Academy, Sandhurst; Staff College, 1951.
Commissioned in the Cheshire Regiment in 1939. Served in
the Middle East, North Africa, Sicily and France in WW II;
Palestine, 1945-47; Malaya, 1957-58. Commanding Officer,
1st Cheshire, North Ireland and British Army of the Rhine,
1961-63; Assistant Adjutant and Quartermaster-General,
Cyprus District, 1963-65; Commander, 48 Gurkha Infantry
Brigade, Hong Kong, 1966-68; Brigadier Assistant
Quartermaster, Headquarters, Army Strategic Command,
1968-71. CBE.

Martini, Hugo. Captain, Uruguayan Navy; Chief of Staff,
Uruguayan Navy.

Marushchak, F. Lieutenant General, USSR Army; Chief of
Staff, Southern Group of Soviet Forces, Hungary,
1966-   . Served on the Soviet-German Front in WW II.
Member, Communist Party of the Soviet Union.

Martynov, I. Major General, USSR Army; First Deputy
Chief, Political Directorate, Central Group of Soviet Forces,
Czechoslovakia, 1970-   . Served on the Soviet-German
Front in WW II. Member, Communist Party of the Soviet
Union.

Maslov, V. Vice Admiral, USSR Navy; First Deputy
Commander in Chief, Pacific Fleet, 1972-   . Served in
the Soviet-German War WW II. Member, Communist Party
of the Soviet Union.

Mason, Roy. British Secretary of State for Defence,
1974-   . Born April 1924. Attended Royston Senior
School; London School of Economics (TUC course). First
worked as a miner. Branch official, National Union of
Mineworkers, 1947-53; Member, Yorkshire Miners' Council,
1949-53. Member of Parliament since 1953, dealing with
Post Office affairs, broadcasting and television, 1959-64.
Minister of State (shipping, Board of Trade, 1964-67;
Minister of Defence (Equipment), 1967; Postmaster
General, 1968; Minister of Power, 1968; President, Board
of Trade, 1969-70. Consultant to Amalgamated Distilled
Products and H. P. Bulmer. Appointed Secretary of State
for Defence following the General Elections of February
1974.

Mastrantonis, Michael. Lieutenant General, Hellenic Army;
Commanding General, First Hellenic Army, 1972-   .
Born March 19, 1919, Thessaloniki. Army Cadet School;

Infantry School, Basic Course; Military Topography School;
Armored School, Basic and Advanced Courses; Armored
School, Fort Knox, Kentucky, USA; Higher War School.
Commissioned Second Lieutenant, July 28, 1939. Served in
Albanian Campaign, 1940-41; National Resistance in
Greece, POW; Antiguerrilla Campaigns, 1946-49. Chief of
Staff and Commander Combat Command, Armored
Division, 1966-67; Deputy Commander, then Commander,
Armored Division, 1967-70; Commander, Higher Military
Command, Interior and Islands, 1970-72. Golden Order of
Merit for Gallant Actions; War Cross, "C" Class; Medal for
Military Valor, "A" Class; Medal for Distinguished Services;
Medal of Helleno-Italo-German War, 1940-41; Medal of
National Resistance during the Helleno-Italo-German War,
1941-44; Silver Cross of the Royal Order of King George I,
with Swords; Golden Cross of the Royal Order of King
George I, with Swords; Higher Knight Commander, Cross of
the Royal Order of King George I; Higher Knight
Commander, Cross of the Royal Order of the Phoenix; and
other medals and awards. Promoted to Colonel, December
7, 1965; Brigadier General, February 3, 1968; Major
General, February 5, 1969; Lieutenant General, June 25,
1970.

Mastrigt, Harry van. Rear Admiral, Royal Netherlands
Navy; Defense and Naval Attache, Royal Netherlands
Embassy, Washington, D.C., USA, 1972-   . Born April
29, 1921, in The Hague. Attended Naval College at Den
Helder; Communications Course; Naval Staff Course,
Greenwich, UK. Commissioned Ensign, 1942. Served at sea
in WW II; and in the Korean War. Commanding Officer
HNLMS Holland, 1964-65; Chief of Staff, NLTG 5, 1965;
Director, Plans and Organization MOD, Navy, 1965-68;
Commanding Officer, HNLMS De Ruyter, 1968-69; Deputy
Flag Officer, Materiel, 1969-72. Officer in the Order of
Orange-Nassau; War Commemoration Cross; Knight 1st
Class, Order of St. Olav; United Nations Service Medal.
Promoted to Commodore, December 24, 1969; Rear
Admiral, July 1, 1972.

Matheson, Salve Hugo. Major General, United States Army;
Deputy Commanding General for Reserve Forces, Third US
Army, Fort McPherson, Georgia, 1972-   . Born August
11, 1920, Seattle, Washington. University of California, BA
Degree, Liberal Arts; The Infantry School, Advanced
Course; US Army Command and General Staff College;
Armed Forces Staff College; Naval War College.
Commissioned Second Lieutenant, US Army Reserve,
1942. Served in WW II and Vietnam War. Commanding
General, 1st Brigade (Separate), 101st Airborne Division,
US Army, Pacific-Vietnam, 1967-68; Army Deputy to the
Commanding General, III Marine Amphibious Force, and
Deputy Senior Advisor, I Corps Tactical Zone, US Military
Assistance Command, Vietnam, 1968; Director, Reserve
Officers Training Corps/National Defense Cadet Corps,
Office, Deputy Chief of Staff for Individual Training,
Continental Army Command, Fort Monroe, Virginia, 1968;
Commanding General, US Army Training Center, Infantry,
and Fort Campbell, Kentucky, 1968-69; Commanding
General, 2d Infantry Division, US Army, Pacific-Korea,
1969-70; Director of Staff, Inter-American Defense Board,

Washington, D.C., 1970-71; Chief of Staff, Third US Army, Fort McPherson, Georgia, 1971-72. Distinguished Service Medal with Oak Leaf Cluster; Silver Star; Legion of Merit; Distinguished Flying Cross; Bronze Star Medal with three Oak Leaf Clusters; and other medals and awards. Promoted to Brigadier General, April 1, 1966; Major General, September 1, 1968.

Mati, Abdi. Admiral, Albanian Navy; Commander, Albanian Naval Command, and Deputy Minister of Defense, 1973- .

Mattingly, Thomas K. Commander, US Navy; NASA Astronaut, 1966- . Born March 17, 1936, Chicago, Illinois. Auburn University, BS, Aeronautical Engineering, 1958; Air Force Aerospace Research Pilot School, 1955-56. Commissioned Ensign, US Navy, 1958; received pilots wings, 1960. VA-35, aboard USS Saratoga, 1960-63; VAH-11, aboard USS Franklin D. Roosevelt, 1963-65. NASA experience: Member Support Crew, Apollo 8 and 11; Command Module Pilot, Apollo 16, April 16-27, 1972. NASA Distinguished Service Medal; Manned Spacecraft Center Certificate of Commendation; Navy Distinguished Service Medal; Navy Astronaut Wings; SETP Ivan C. Kinchloe Award; Delta Tau Delta Achievement Award; Auburn Alumni Engineers Council Outstanding Achievement Award.

Mau, Phan Ngoc. Major General, People's Army of Vietnam; Deputy Chief, General Political Directorate, People's Army of Vietnam, 1961; Member of Central Military Party Committee. Chief of Cadres Bureau, 1961; elected Deputy to Third National Assembly, 1964. Promoted to Major General, May 1961.

Maurer, Fritz. Major General, Swiss Army; Commanding General, 8th Division. Born in 1917.

Maurer, John Howard. Rear Admiral, United States Navy; Commander Key West Force and Commander Navl Base, Key West, Florida, 1971- . Born April 28, 1912, Washington, D.C. US Naval Academy, 1931-35; Naval Submarine School, 1939; National War College, 1953-55. Commissioned Ensign, US Navy, 1935. Served in the Pacific Theater, WW II; Korean War. Commanding Officer, USS *Saint Paul* (CA-73), 1959-60; Chief of Staff and Aide to Commander Submarine Force, Atlantic, 1960-62; Director Submarine Warfare Division, Office of the CNO, 1962-63; Office of the Director Navy Program Planning, 1963-64; Commander Middle East Force, 1964-66; Commander Submarine Force, US Pacific Fleet, 1966-68; Special Assistant for Strategic Mobility, Joint Chiefs of Staff, 1968-70; Chief of Staff to Commander in Chief, United States Strike Command, 1970-71. Navy Cross; Silver Star Medal with Gold Star; Legion of Merit with three Gold Stars; and other medals and awards. Promoted to Rear Admiral, December 1, 1962.

Maurin, Francois. General, French Air Force; Chief of Staff of the Armed Forces, France, 1971- . Born March 9, 1918, Paris. Attended Lycee Concorcet; Lycee Saint-Louis; Ecole de l'Air, 1938-39; Ecole Superieure de Guerre

Aerienne, 1957. Commissioned as pilot, 1939. Served in WW II; Algeria; Indochina. Assistant Chief for Plans, Air Force General Staff, 1963-66; Commander, II Air Region, Bordeaux, 1966-67; Commander, Air Defense, 1967-70; Major General of the Air Force, 1970-71. Croix de Guerre, 1939-45; Croix de Guerre des Theatre d'Operations Exterieures; Medaille de l'Aeronautique. Promoted to Brigadier General, July 1, 1963; Major General, January 1, 1966; Lieutenant General, September 1, 1967; General, April 1, 1971.

Mayalarp, Surakij. General, Royal Thai Army. Chief of Staff, Supreme Command of the Armed Forces.

Maynard, Sir Nigel Martin. Air Marshal, British Royal Air Force; Deputy Commander-in-Chief, Strike Command, 1972- . Born August 28, 1921. Attended Royal Air Force College, Cranwell; Royal Air Force Staff College, 1952; Joint Services Staff College, 1957; Imperial Defence College, 1967. Served in Europe, the Mediterranean and the Middle East in WW II. Commanding Officer, Royal Air Force, Changi, 1960-62; Group Captain, Operations, Transport Command, 1963-64; Director, Defence Plans (Air), 1965; Director of Defence Plans and Chairman Defence Planning Staff, 1966; Commandant, Royal Air Force Staff College, Bracknell, 1968-70; Commander, Far East Air Force, 1970-72. KCB; CBE; DFC; AFC. Air Commodore, 1965.

Mayo, George, Jr. Major General, United States Army; Deputy SAFEGUARD System Manager, US Army SAFEGUARD System Office, Arlington, Virginia, 1969- . Born November 29, 1918, San Francisco, California. US Military Academy; The Field Artillery School, Basic and Advanced Courses; US Army Command and General Staff College; US National War College; George Washington University, MA Degree, International Affairs. Commissioned Second Lieutenant, 1940. Served in WW II. Member, North Atlantic Treaty Organization Policy Branch, European Division, J-5, Joint Staff, Organization, Joint Chiefs of Staff, Washington, D.C. 1966; Deputy NIKE X Systems Manager for Plans, US Army NIKE X Systems Office, Office, Chief of Research and Development, US Army, Alexandria, Virginia, 1966-67; Deputy SENTINEL System Manager for Plans, US Army, SENTINEL System Office, Arlington, Virginia, 1967-69. Legion of Merit; Bronze Star Medal with Oak Leaf Cluster; and other medals and awards. Promoted to Brigadier General, March 1, 1967; Major General, June 1, 1970.

Mayorov, A.M. Colonel General, USSR Army; Commander, Baltic Military District, 1972- . Served on the Soviet-German Front (company commander), WW II. Commander, Central Group of Soviet Forces in Czechoslovakia, 1969-72. Member, Communist Party of the Soviet Union. Promoted to Major General, 1960; Colonel General, 1969.

Mayorov, Ya. Lieutenant General, USSR Army; Chief, Political Branch, Railway Troops. Served on the Soviet-German Front in WW II. Member, Communist Party of the Soviet Union.

Mazhayev, F.A. Colonel General, USSR Army. Served on the Soviet-German Front in WW II. Chief, Political Directorate Leningrad Military District, 1963-70. Member, Communist Party of the Soviet Union.

Mazhorov, G.I. Lieutenant General, USSR Army; Chief, Political Branch, Frunze Army War College. Served on the Soviet-German Front in WW II. Member, Communist Party of the Soviet Union.

M'bahia Ble, Kouadio. Minister of the Armed Force, Ivory Coast.

Mednikov, I. Lieutenant General, USSR Army; Chief Political Directorate, Group of Soviet Forces in Germany, 1971-   . Served on the Soviet-German Front in WW II. Member, Communist Party of the Soviet Union.

Melekhin, B. Lieutenant General, USSR Air Force; Commander, Air Force, Northern Group of Soviet Forces, Poland, 1969-   . Served on the Soviet-German Front in WW II. Member, Communist Party of the Soviet Union.

Mellen, Thomas Wright. Major General, United States Army; Deputy Commander, US Military Assistance Command, Thailand, 1972-   . Born July 26, 1918, San Francisco, California. US Army Command and General Staff College; US Army War College. Commissioned Second Lieutenant, 1942. Served in WW II and Vietnam War. Deputy, later Director of Developments, Office, Chief of Research and Development, US Army, Washington, D.C., 1967-68; Deputy Chief of Research and Development for Southeast Asia, and Director of Developments, Office, Chief of Research and Development, US Army, Washington, D.C., 1968-69; Director of Logistics, J-4, US Strike Command, MacDill Air Force Base, Florida, 1969-71. Distinguished Service Medal with Oak Leaf Cluster; Silver Star with two Oak Leaf Clusters; Legion of Merit with Oak Leaf Cluster; Bronze Star Medal with Oak Leaf Cluster; and other medals and awards. Promoted to Brigadier General, July 1, 1968; Major General, April 1, 1971.

Mellersh, Francis Richard Lee. Air Vice-Marshal, British Royal Air Force; Assistant Chief of Defence Staff (Operations), 1972-   . Born July 30, 1922. Attended Imperial Service College; Royal College of Defence Studies, 1969. Commissioned in the RAF Volunteer Reserve in 1941. Served in WW II. Deputy Director of Operations (Flying), 1961-63; Officer in Command RAF West Raynham, 1965-67; Chief of Current Plans, SHAPE, 1967-68; Senior Air Staff Officer, RAF Germany, 1970-72. DFC and Bar.

Mello de Almeida, Reynaldo. Major General, Brazilian Army; Vice Chief, Army Services Department, 1973-   . Attended Brazilian Military Academy, 1934; Command and General Staff School; Superior War School. Commandant, Army Command and General Staff School, 1967-70; Vice Chief of Staff of the Army, 1970-72; Commanding General,

9th Military Region, 1972-73. Decorations from Brazil, Paraguay, Portugal and Venezuela.

Mel'nikov, P. Major General, Armor, USSR Army; Assistant Commander, Siberian Military District for Military Educational Establishments. Served on the Soviet-German Front in WW II. Member, Communist Party of the Soviet Union.

Meltz, Andre. General of the Armies, French Army; Military Governor of Paris, and Commander 1st Military Region, 1968-   , and Member Higher War Council. Born May 24, 1910, Vagney, France. Attended Ecole Polytechnique; War College, 1949. Commissioned Second Lieutenant, French Army, 1930. Served in France and North Africa in WW II. Member, French Military Mission, Washington, D.C., 1952-55; Staff Posts, Germany and Algeria, 1956-58; Staff, General Staff, 1959; Commander 14th Infantry Division and North Constantinois, 1960; Commander 9th Military Region, 1965-68. Grand Officier, Legion d'Honneur; Croix de Guerre; and other medals and awards. Promoted to General, 1963; General of the Armies, 1968.

Mendieta, Jaime Florentino. General, Bolivian Army; Minister of National Defense, Bolivia, 1973-   .

Mendoza, Cesar. General, Chilean Army; National Police Chief, 1973-   .

Mercado Jarrin, Edgardo. Peruvian Prime Minister and Minister of War, 1973-   .Foreign Minister, 1968-72; Chief of Staff, Peruvian Army, 1972-73.

Merimskiy, V. Lieutenant General, USSR Army; First Deputy Commander, Far Eastern Military District, 1969-   . Served on the Soviet-German Front in WW II. Member, Communist Party of the Soviet Union.

Merino Castro, Jose Toribio. Admiral, Chilean Navy; Acting Navy Commander in Chief, 1973-   .

Messmer, Hans. Brigadier General, Swiss Army; Head of the General Provisioning and Accounting Division. Born in 1913.

Metzger, Louis. Lieutenant General, United States Marine Corps; Commanding General, III Marine Amphibious Force, 1972-   . Born November 18, 1916, San Francisco, California. Stanford University, BA, 1939; Armored School, Fort Knox, Kentucky; Army Command and Staff College; National War College, 1959-60. Commissioned Second Lieutenant, USMCR, 1939. Served in Pacific Theater, WW II; Korean War; Vietnam War. Assistant Deputy Chief of Staff (Programs), Headquarters, US Marine Corps, 1964-66; Commanding General, 9th Marine Amphibious Brigade/Commanding General, Fleet Marine Force, 7th Fleet, 1966-67; Assistant Division Commander, 3d Marine Division, Vietnam, 1967-68; Deputy Chief of Staff (Research, Development, Studies) Headquarters, US

Marine Corps, 1968-71; Commanding General, I Marine Amphibious Force/Third Marine Division, 1971. Distinguished Service Medal; Bronze Star with Combat "V" and Gold Star; Navy Commendation with Gold Star; and other medals and awards. Promoted to Brigadier General, July 1965; Major General, January 1, 1968; Lieutenant General, December 28, 1971.

Meyer, Edward Charles. Major General, United States Army; Deputy Chief of Staff for Operations, US Army Europe/Seventh Army, 1973-   . Born December 1928, at St. Marys, Pennsylvania. Attended US Military Academy; Infantry School, Advanced Course; Command and General Staff College; Armed Forces Staff College; National War College, 1966-67; George Washington University, MS, International Affairs. Commissioned Second Lieutenant, June 1951. Served in the Vietnam War. Member, Long Range Branch, Strategic Division, J-5, then Member, Analysis Branch, Objectives Plans and Programs Division, Joint Chiefs of Staff Organization, 1967-69; Chief of Staff, 1st Cavalry Division, US Army, Pacific-Vietnam, 1969-71; Assistant Division Commander, 82d Airborne Division, Fort Bragg, North Carolina, 1971-72; Deputy Commandant, US Army War College, 1972-73. Silver Star with Oak Leaf Cluster; Legion of Merit with two Oak Leaf Clusters; Bronze Star Medal with V Device and two Oak Leaf Clusters; Air Medal (35 awards); and other medals and awards. Promoted to Brigadier General August 1, 1971; Major General, August 1, 1973.

Meyer, John C. General, United States Air Force; Commander in Chief, Strategic Air Command, and Director, Joint Strategic Target Planning Staff, 1972-   . Born April 3, 1919, in Brooklyn, New York. Primary, Basic and Advanced Flying School, 1939-40; Dartmouth College, BA, 1948; Air War College, 1956. Commissioned Second Lieutenant, US Army Air Corps, 1940. Combat duty in the European Theater, WW II; Korean War. Commander, 57th Air Division, 1959-61; Commander, 45th Air Division, 1961-62; Deputy Director, Plans, Directorate of Plans, Strategic Air Command, 1962-63; Commander, Twelfth Air Force, 1963-66; Deputy Director, Joint Staff, Office, Joint Chiefs of Staff, 1966; Vice Director, Joint Staff, Office, Joint Chiefs of Staff, 1967; Director for Operations, J-3, Joint Staff, Office, Joint Chiefs of Staff, 1967-69; Vice Chief of Staff, US Air Force, 1969-72. Distinguished Service Cross with two Oak Leaf Clusters; Distinguished Service Medal with one Oak Leaf Cluster; Silver Star with one Oak Leaf Cluster; Legion of Merit; Distinguished Flying Cross with six Oak Leaf Clusters; Air Medal with 14 Oak Leaf Clusters; and other US and foreign medals and awards. Promoted to Brigadier General, August 1, 1959; Major General, April 1, 1963; Lieutenant General, June 12, 1967; General, August 1, 1969.

Meyer, Stewart Canfield. Major General, United States Army; Director, Research, Development and Engineering, US Army Materiel Command, Washington, D.C., 1971-   . Born April 14, 1921, El Paso, Texas. US Military Academy; The Field Artillery School, Basic Course; The Artillery School, Advanced Course; US Army Command and General Staff College; US Army War College; University of Michigan, MSE Degree, Mechanical Engineering. Commissioned Second Lieutenant, 1943. Served in WW II and Vietnam War. Commanding Officer, 9th Infantry Division Artillery, US Army, Pacific-Vietnam, 1967-68; Deputy Director, Missiles and Space, later Executive Officer, Office, Chief of Research and Development, US Army, Washington, D.C., 1968; Military Assistant to Deputy Director (Tactical Warfare Programs), Directorate of Defense Research and Engineering, Office, Secretary of Defense, Washington, D.C. 1968-70; Commanding General, XXIV Corps Artillery, US Army, Pacific-Vietnam, 1970-71. Distinguished Service Medal; Silver Star; Legion of Merit; Bronze Star Medal with V Device and five Oak Leaf Clusters; and other medals and awards. Promoted to Brigadier General, August 1, 1969; Major General, August 1, 1971.

Meza-Cuadra, Anibal. Major General, Peruvian Army; Delegate, Inter-American Defense Board. Date of Rank: January 1, 1973.

Michaelis, Frederick Hayes. Vice Admiral, United States Navy; Commander Naval Air Force, US Atlantic Fleet, and Commander Fleet Air, Norfolk, Virginia, 1972-   . Born March 4, 1917, in Kansas City, Missouri. Kansas City Junior College, 1934-36; US Naval Academy, 1936-40; Flight Training Course, 1942-43; Postgraduate School, Annapolis, and Massachusetts Institute of Technology, MS, Aeronautical Engineering, 1946-49; Naval War College, 1958-59. Commissioned Ensign, US Navy, 1940; designated Naval Aviator, 1943. Served in Pacific Theater, WW II; Vietnam War. Commanding Officer USS *Enterprise* (CVA (N) 65), 1963-65; Director of Development Programs, Office of the CNO, 1965-67; Commander Carrier Division NINE, 1967-68; Assistant Chief of Naval Operations (Air), Navy Department, 1968-69; Deputy Director of Joint Strategic Target Planning, 1969-72. Navy Cross; Silver Star Medal; Legion of Merit; Distinguished Flying Cross; Air Medal with three Gold Stars; and other US and foreign medals and awards. Promoted to Vice Admiral, September 1, 1969.

Michalowski, Henryk. Major General Pilot, Polish Army; Commander of the Air Force.

Michta, Norbert. Major General, Polish Army; Deputy Chief, Main Political Directorate, Polish Armed Forces. Deputy Commandant, Political Affairs, Military Technical College, Warsaw; Staff, Polish Contingent, International Control Commission, Laos, 1966; Deputy Chief, Office of Military History, 1970. Cross of Grunwald; Cross of Merit; and other medals and awards. Member, Polish United Workers Party.

Miehlke, Erich. Colonel General, National People's Army, Democratic Republic of Germany; Minister for State Security, 1957-   . Born December 28, 1907, Berlin. Captain in the International Brigade, Spanish Civil War;

served in Soviet Armed Forces, 1940-45. Formerly State Secretary, Ministry for State Security, 1950-57. Member, Communist Youth Association; joined Communist Party, 1925; Member of Socialist Unity Party and its Central Committee; Member of People's Chamber, 1958- . Member, National Executive of the German Gymnastics and Sports Federation, 1957- . Promoted to Colonel General, 1959.

Mielonen, Unto Oskar. Major General, Army of Finland; Commanding General, Savo-Karjala Military Area, 1971- . Born January 5, 1915, Viipuri (formerly Finland). Cadet School, 1935-37; War College, 1949-50. Served in Winter War; Continuation War. Chief, Artillery Office, General Headquarters, 1955-57; Aide to the Minister of Defense, 1957-58; Military, Naval and Air Attache, Finnish Embassies, Washington, D.C., USA, and Ottawa, Canada, 1961-65; Commanding Officer, Pohjanmaa Artillery Regiment, 1965-70. Cross of Freedom, 3d Class with Oak Leaf; Cross of Freedom, 3d Class with Sword; Cross of Freedom, 4th Class with Sword; Commander, Order of the Finnish Lion; Commemorative Medals of Winter and Continuation Wars; Legion of Merit (USA); and other medals and awards. Promoted to Major General, January 9, 1971.

Mikhailin, V.V. Admiral, USSR Navy; Commander in Chief, Baltic Fleet, 1967- . Born in 1915. Attended Naval War College, 1953; General Staff War College, 1962. Served on minesweepers with the Northern Fleet in WW II. Former Commander, Cruiser *Kuibyshev*; Squadron Commander, 1962-63; First Deputy Commander, Baltic Fleet, 1963-67. Member, Communist Party of the Soviet Union.

Mildren, Frank Thomas. General, United States Army; Commanding General, Allied Land Forces, Southeastern Europe, 1971- . Born July 8, 1913, Pima, Arizona. US Military Academy; US Army Command and General Staff College; Armed Forces Staff College; The National War College. Commissioned Second Lieutenant, 1939. Served in WW II and Vietnam War. Director, Materiel Requirements, later Director for Doctrine and Systems, Office, Assistant Chief of Staff for Force Development, US Army, Washington, D.C., 1964-65; Deputy Assistant Chief of Staff for Force Development, later Acting Assistant Chief of Staff for Force Development, US Army, Washington, D.C., 1965; Commanding General, VII Corps, US Army, Europe, 1965-68; Deputy Commanding General, US Army, Vietnam, US Army, Pacific-Vietnam, 1968-70; Deputy Commanding General, Continental Army Command, Fort Monroe, Virginia, 1970-71. Distinguished Service Medal with Oak Leaf Cluster; Silver Star with four Oak Leaf Clusters; Legion of Merit with Oak Leaf Cluster; Bronze Star Medal with V Device and two Oak Leaf Clusters; and other medals and awards. Promoted to Brigadier General, August 1, 1960; Major General, July 1, 1962; Lieutenant General, July 1, 1965; General, April 1, 1971.

Miley, Henry Augustine, Jr. General, United States Army; Commanding General, US Army Materiel Command, Washington, D.C., 1970- .Born February 14, 1915, Boston, Massachusetts. US Military Academy; The Coast Artillery School; The Antiaircraft Artillery School; US Army War College; Northwestern University, MBA Degree, Industrial Management. Commissioned Second Lieutenant, 1940. Served in WW II. Deputy Director, later Director, Procurement and Production, US Army Materiel Command, Washington, D.C., 1964-66; Assistant Deputy Chief of Staff for Logistics (Programs and Budget), US Army, Washington, D.C., 1966-69; Deputy Commanding General, US Army Materiel Command, Washington, D.C., 1969-70. Distinguished Service Medal; and other medals and awards. Promoted to Brigadier General, August 1, 1963; Major General, April 1, 1966; Lieutenant General, June 23, 1969; General, November 1, 1970.

Miliani Aranguren, Francisco. Brigadier General, Venezuelan Army; Minister-Military Adviser, Venezuelan Mission to the United Nations.

Miller, Andrew John. Rear-Admiral, British Royal Navy; Flag Officer, Second Flotilla, 1972- . Born December 12, 1926. Attended Royal Naval College, Dartmouth. Commissioned Sub-Lieutenant, Royal Navy, 1946. Commanded HMS *ML 3513*, *Asheldham*, *Grafton*, *Scorpion*, and *Nubian*; Director of Public Relations (Navy), 1970-71. Promoted to Captain, 1965; Rear-Admiral, 1972.

Miller, George Harold. Rear Admiral, United States Navy, Retired; Special Assistant to the Administrator, Maritime Administration, 1970- . Born June 30, 1911, Chicago, Illinois. US Naval Academy, 1929-33; Naval War College, Strategy and Tactics Course, 1946-47. Commissioned Ensign, US Navy, 1933. Served in the Pacific Theater, WW II; Korean War. Commander Cruiser Division FIVE, 1959-60; Navy Member, Joint Strategic Survey Council, Joint Chiefs of Staff, 1960-62; Chief of Staff, Headquarters, US Forces, Japan, 1962-64; Director, Long Range Objectives Group, Office of the CNO, 1964-67; Director, Navy Strategic Offensive and Defensive Systems, Office of the CNO, 1967-70; transferred to the retired list, July 1, 1972, but continues to serve in the Maritime Administration. Navy Cross; Distinguished Service Medal; Legion of Merit with Combat "V"; and other US and foreign medals and awards. Promoted to Rear Admiral, July 1, 1959.

Miller, Gerald E. Vice Admiral, United States Navy; Commander Sixth Fleet and Commander Naval Striking and Support Forces, Southern Europe, 1972- . Born in 1919. US Naval Academy, 1938-41; Stanford University, MA, Personnel Administration, 1950. Commissioned Ensign, US Navy, 1941. Served in the Pacific Theater, WW II; Korean War. Commanding Officer USS *Franklin D. Roosevelt*; Commander Carrier Division THREE; Assistant Deputy Chief of Naval Operations (Air); Commander Second Fleet and Commander Striking Fleet, Atlantic, 1970-72. Distinguished Service Medal; Legion of Merit with three Gold Stars; Distinguished Flying Cross; Bronze Star; Air Medal with one Silver and two Gold Stars; and other medals and awards.

Miller, Thomas H., Jr. Major General, United States Marine Corps; Commanding General, 2d Marine Aircraft Wing, 1972-   . Born June 3, 1923, San Antonio, Texas. University of Texas; Flight Training Course, 1942-43; Air Technical School, Quantico, 1947; Naval War College, 1957-58; Amphibious Warfare School, Senior Course, Quantico, 1962; Army War College, 1965-66. Enlisted in US Naval Reserve, 1942. Commissioned Second Lieutenant, USMCR, Naval Aviator, 1943; transferred to USMC, 1946. Served in South Pacific Theater, WW II; Korean War; Vietnam War. Head, Air Weapons Systems Branch, Office of Deputy Chief of Staff (Air), Headquarters, Marine Corps, 1966-69; Deputy Assistant Chief of Staff, G-3, Headquarters, Marine Corps, 1969; Chief of Staff, III Marine Amphibious Force, Vietnam, 1970; Assistant Wing Commander, 2d Marine Aircraft Wing, 1971-72. Set 500 kilometer closed course world speed record on September 5, 1960. Legion of Merit; Distinguished Flying Cross with three Gold Stars; 16 Air Medals; and other US and foreign medals and awards. Promoted to Brigadier General, August 15, 1969; Major General, August 1, 1972.

Milloy, Albert Ernest. Major General, United States Army; Chief of Staff, Sixth US Army, Presidio of San Francisco, California, 1971-   . Born November 25, 1921, Hattiesburg, Mississippi. The Armored School, Advanced Course; Command and General Staff College; Army War College. Commissioned Second Lieutenant, US Army Reserve, 1941. Served in WW II and Vietnam War. Chief of Staff, 82d Airborne Division, Fort Bragg, North Carolina, 1964-65; Senior Division Advisor, III Corps, US Military Assistance Command, Vietnam, 1965; Commanding Officer, 2d Brigade, 1st Infantry Division, US Army Vietnam, 1965-66; Deputy Commanding Officer, US Army John F. Kennedy Center for Special Warfare, Fort Bragg, North Carolina, 1966; Commanding General, US Army John F. Kennedy Center for Special Warfare, and Commandant, US Army Special Warfare School, Fort Bragg, North Carolina, 1966-68; Director, International and Civil Affairs, Office, Deputy Chief of Staff for Military Operations, Department of the Army, Washington, D.C., 1968-69; Commanding General, 1st Infantry Division, US Army, Vietnam, 1969-70; Commanding General, 23d Infantry Division (Americal), US Army, Vietnam, 1970; Deputy Commanding General, XXIV Corps Vietnam, US Army, Vietnam, 1970-71. Distinguished Service Medal; Silver Star with two Oak Leaf Clusters; Legion of Merit with Oak Leaf Cluster; Distinguished Flying Cross; Bronze Star Medal with two Oak Leaf Clusters; and other medals and awards. Promoted to Brigadier General, October 27, 1966; Major General, August 1, 1969.

Milton, Theodore R. General, United States Air Force; United States Representative, NATO Military Committee, 1971-   . Born December 29, 1915, at Schofield Barracks, Hawaii. US Military Academy, 1936-40; Army Air Corps Flying Training School, 1940-41; Air War College, 1952. Enlisted in the US Army, 1934; commissioned Second Lieutenant, US Army, 1940; received pilot wings, 1941. Combat duty in the European

Theater, WW II. Executive Assistant to the Secretary of the Air Force, 1957; Commander, 41st Air Division, Johnson Air Base, Japan, 1958-61; Commander, Thirteenth Air Force, Clark Air Base, Philippine Islands, 1961-63; Deputy Chief of Staff, Plans and Operations, Commander in Chief Pacific, 1963-65; Chief of Staff, Headquarters, Tactical Air Command, 1965-67; Inspector General, Headquarters, USAF, 1967; Comptroller of the Air Force, Headquarters, USAF, 1967-69; Vice Director, International Military Staff, NATO Military Committee, Brussels, Belgium, 1969-70; Deputy Chairman, NATO Military Committee, 1970. Distinguished Service Cross; Distinguished Service Medal; Silver Star; Legion of Merit with two Oak Leaf Clusters; Bronze Star Medal; Air Medal with four Oak Leaf Clusters; British Distinguished Flying Cross; and other US and foreign medals and awards. Promoted to Brigadier General, October 1, 1957; Major General, July 1, 1961; Lieutenant General, February 17, 1967; General, August 1, 1971.

Minh, Nguyen Van. Lieutenant General, Army of the Republic of South Vietnam; Commander III Corps/MR 3.

Minh, Tran Van. Lieutenant General, Army of the Republic of South Vietnam; Commander Air Force (VNAF).

Minter, Charles F., Sr. Major General, United States Air Force; Deputy Chief of Staff for Maintenance, Headquarters Air Force Logistics Command, Wright-Patterson Air Force Base, Ohio, 1972-   . Born August 20, 1925, in Columbus, Georgia. Texas Christian University, Fort Worth, Texas; Centenary College, Shreveport, Louisiana; Aviation Cadet Flight Course, 1943-45; Navigator-Bombardier School, 1956-57; University of Omaha, BS, Political Science, 1966; National War College, 1970-71. Commissioned Second Lieutenant, US Army Air Corps, 1945. Served in the Korean War. Executive Officer to the Director of Operations, Headquarters Strategic Air Command, Offutt Air Force Base, 1966-67; Vice Commander, then Commander, 9th Strategic Reconnaissance Wing, Strategic Air Command, Beale Air Force Base, California, 1967-70; Vice Commander, Ogden Air Material Area, Hill Air Force Base, Utah, 1971-72. Legion of Merit; Distinguished Flying Cross; Air Medal with three Oak Leaf Clusters; and other medals and awards. Promoted to Brigadier General, September 1, 1971; Major General, 1973.

Minter, Charles Stamps, Jr. Vice Admiral, United States Navy; Deputy Chief of Naval Operations (Logistics), 1971-   . Born January 23, 1915, Pocahontas, Virginia. Bluefield (West Virginia) Junior College, 1932-33; US Naval Academy, 1933-37; Flight Training Courses, 1940-41; National War College, 1955-56. Commissioned Ensign, US Navy, 1937; designated Naval Aviator, 1941. Served in the Atlantic and Pacific Theaters, WW II; Korean War; Vietnam War. Commanding Officer USS *Intrepid*, 1960-61; Commandant of Midshipmen, US Naval Academy, 1961-64; Superintendent, Naval Academy, and Commandant Severn River Naval Command, 1964-65; Deputy Assistant Chief of Staff for Plans and Policy to the Supreme Allied

Commander, Europe, 1965-67; Commander Carrier Division SIXTEEN, 1967-69; Commander Fleet Air Wings, Pacific/Commander Fleet Air Moffett, 1969-71. Distinguished Service Medal, Legion of Merit with two Gold Stars; Bronze Star Medal with Gold Star and Combat "V"; Air Medal with Gold Star; and other medals and awards. Promoted to Vice Admiral, March 1, 1971.

Mironenko, Aleksandr Alekseyevich. Colonel General, USSR Naval Air Force; Commander, Naval Air Force, Black Sea Fleet, 1961-   . Born in 1918 in Yakhniky, Poltava Oblast. Volunteered for the Navy in 1937. Attended Naval Air Force Academy, 1937-40; Naval War College, c. 1946-48; holder of degree, Doctor of Naval Sciences. Commissioned in 1940. Served in the Soviet-German War, 1941-45. Squadron Commander, 5th Air Force Regiment, Baltic Fleet, 1942-43; Commander, Air Force Regiment, Baltic Fleet, 1943-45; Commander, various Air Force units, 1948-54; Assistant Commander, Air Force, Pacific Fleet, c. 1954-56; Member, Military Council, Black Sea Fleet, 1956-   ; Member, Communist Party of the Soviet Union, 1941-   ; Deputy to the Ukrainian Supreme Soviet. Hero of the Soviet Union; two Orders of Lenin; three Orders of Red Banner; Order of Red Star; and other medals and orders. Promoted to Colonel General, 1965.

Mironov, N.A. Major General, USSR Air Force; Chief, Political Branch, Air Force, Group of Soviet Forces in Germany. Served on the Soviet-German Front in WW II. Member, Communist Party of the Soviet Union.

Mishchenko, A. Major General, USSR Army; Chief, Political Branch, Kuybyshev Military Engineering College. Served on the Soviet-German Front in WW II. Member, Communist Party of the Soviet Union.

Mitchell, Edgar Dean. Captain, US Navy; NASA Astronaut, 1966-   . Born September 17, 1930, Hereford, Texas. Carnegie Institute of Technology, BS, Industrial Management, 1952; US Naval Postgraduate School, BS, Aeronautical Engineering, 1961; Massachusetts Institute of Technology, ScD, Aeronautics/Astronautics, 1964; US Navy Officers Candidate School; Air Force Aerospace Research Pilot School. Commissioned Ensign, US Navy, 1953. Patrol Squadron 29, Okinawa; Heavy Attack Squadron Two, aboard USS *Bon Homme Richard* and USS *Ticonderoga*, 1957-58; Research Project Pilot, Air Development Squadron Five, 1958-59; Chief, Project Management Division, Navy Field Office for Manned Orbiting Laboratory, 1964-65. NASA experience: Member, Support Crew, Apollo 9; Backup Lunar Module Pilot, Apollo 10; Lunar Module Pilot, Apollo 14; Backup Lunar Module Pilot, Apollo 16. Presidential Medal of Freedom; NASA Distinguished Service Medal; Manned Spacecraft Center Superior Achievement Award; Navy Astronaut Wings; Navy Distinguished Service Medal; City of New York Gold Medal; Arnold Air Society's John F. Kennedy Award.

Mitchell, Newell Dwight. Colonel, United States Air Force; Defense Attache and Air Attache, Caracas, Venezuela,

1971-   . Born January 18, 1924, in Seattle, Washington. Squadron Officers School, 1954; Air Command and Staff College, 1962; University of Alabama, BA, History, 1967; Defense Intelligence School, 1970. Commissioned Second Lieutenant, Army Air Corps, 1946. Combat duty in the Korean War; Vietnam War. Operations Officer and Commander RF4C, 16th Tactical Reconnaissance Squadron, Vietnam, 1967-68; International Political-Military Affairs Officer, Pacific-Southeast Asia Branch, Directorate of Plans, Deputy Chief of Staff, Plans and Operations, Headquarters USAF, 1968-69; Assistant for Joint Chiefs of Staff Matters, Eastern Region Division, Directorate of Plans, Deputy Chief of Staff, Plans and Operations, Headquarters USAF, 1969-70. Promoted to Colonel, June 19, 1968.

Mitchell, Robert Imrie. Major-General, British Army; Director of Medical Services, British Army of the Rhine, 1971-   . Born January 25, 1916. Glasgow University, BSc, 1936; MB; ChB, 1939. Commissioned Second Lieutenant, Territorial Army, 1937. Lieutenant, Royal Army Medical Corps, 1939. Deputy Director I (British) Corps, British Army of the Rhine, 1968-69; Deputy Director, Medical Services, Army Strategic Command, 1969-71. OBE; Queen's Honorary Physician, 1970. Promoted to Colonel, 1962; Brigadier, 1968; Major-General, 1969.

Mitsanas, Thomas B. Lieutenant General, Hellenic Air Force; Chief, Hellenic Air Force, 1972-   . Born November 17, 1926, Orestias, Department of Evros, Greece. Hellenic Air Force, Air Academy, 1946-48; Hellenic Army, Air Photography School; Air Gunnery School; Instrument Flying School; Jet Aircraft Transition Course, USA, 1951; Instrument Flying Instructors School, USA, 1952; NATO Special Weapons School, Federal Republic of Germany, 1958; US Air Force Command and Staff College, USA, 1961; US Air Force Command and Staff College Instructors Course, 1962. Commissioned Second Lieutenant, Hellenic Air Force, 1948. Served in WW II; Antiguerrilla War, 1946-48. Director of Air Defense Operations, Headquarters, 28th Tactical Air Force, 1962-64; Chief, Air Defense Operations Branch, Headquarters, Air South, Naples, Italy, 1964-67; Commander, 110th Hellenic Air Force Combat Wing, 1967; Director, Division "A", Headquarters 28th Tactical Air Force, 1967-68; Chief of Staff, 31st Air Training Command, and Commander Hellenic Air Force War College, 1968-69; Director, Division "C", Hellenic Air Force Command, 1969-70; Vice Chief, Hellenic Air Force, 1970-72. Golden Medal for Valor; Commander of the Royal Order of George I; Golden Cross of the Royal Order of George I; Knight Commander of the Royal Order of Phoenix; Commander of the Royal Order of Phoenix; Distinguished Flying Cross; War Cross, 2d Class (twice); War Cross, 3d Class; Medal for Military Valor, 1st Class; Legion of Merit (USA); and other medals and awards. Promoted to Colonel, June 30, 1965; Brigadier General, March 22, 1968; Major General, June 22, 1970; Lieutenant General, June 22, 1972.

Mizin, L.V. Vice Admiral, USSR Navy; First Deputy Commander, Baltic Fleet, 1971-   . Served in the Soviet-German War, 1941-45. Chief of Staff, Black Sea Fleet, 1969-71. Member, Communist Party of the Soviet Union.

Moats, Sanford K. Major General, United States Air Force; Commander, Sixth Allied Tactical Air Force, Izmir, Turkey, 1973-   . Born December 4, 1921, in Kansas City, Missouri. Kansas State University; Army Air Corps Flying School, 1943; Military Assistance Institute, 1963. Commissioned Second Lieutenant, US Army Air Corps, 1943. Combat duty in the European and Pacific Theaters, WW II; Vietnam War. Director, Operations and Training, 26th Air Division, 1962-63; Military Assistance Advisory Group, Taiwan, 1963-65; Vice Commander, then Commander, 401st Tactical Fighter Wing, 1965-68; Vice Commander, Sixteenth Air Force, Spain, 1968-69; Vice Commander, Tenth Air Force, 1969; Commander, 26th Air Division and 26th North American Air Defense Command (NORAD) Region, 1969-70; Chief, Joint US Military Group, Military Assistance Advisory Group, Spain, 1970-72; Commander, Sixteenth Air Force, Spain, 1972-73. Distinguished Service Cross; Distinguished Service Medal; Legion of Merit; Distinguished Flying Cross with one Oak Leaf Cluster; and other US and foreign medals and awards. Promoted to Major General, August 1, 1970.

Mobasser, Mohsen. General, Imperial Iranian Army; Official, Ministry of the Interior, 1971-   . Born in 1910, in Tabriz. Attended Officers College, Teheran; War College, Teheran. Recent Positions: Chief of Staff to Teheran Military Commandant, 1953-56; Military Attache, Baghdad; Deputy Chief, General Police Administration; Chief, General Police Administration, 1965-70; Chief, Civil Defense Organization, 1970-71.

Mobutu, Sese Seko Kuku Ngbendo Wa Za Banga (Joseph Désiré). President of Zaire and Minister of Defense. Born October 14, 1930, in Lisala. Attended Ecole des Cadres, Luluabourg; Institut des Etudes Sociales, Brussels. Joined Force Publique, 1950; rose to highest rank, sergeant major; Colonel, Chief of Staff, Congolese Army, 1960; Major-General, Commander in Chief, Congolese Army, 1961; Lieutenant-General, 1965; President of the Republic, November 24, 1965. Grand Officier de l'Ordre de la Couronne (Belgium); Legion of Merit (USA); Honorary LLD, Duquesne University (USA).

Moench, John O. Major General, United States Air Force; Director, Security Assistance Plans, Policy, and Programs Formulation, Deputy Assistant Secretary of Defence (Security Assistance), Office of the Assistant Secretary of Defense (International Affairs), 1973-   . Born August 4, 1921, Chicago, Illinois. Army Air Corps Flying School, 1942-43; Air Command and Staff School, 1954; Air War College, 1958-59; Maryland University, BS and MS, Political Science. Commissioned Second Lieutenant, US Army Air Corps, 1943. Combat duty in the European Theater, WW II. Strategic Plans and Policy Division, Joint Staff, Joint Chiefs of Staff Organization, 1964-66; Chief, Plans and Policy Branch, Staff, Commander in Chief, United States Command Pacific, Hawaii, 1966-68; Deputy Chief of Staff, Plans, Headquarters Pacific Air Forces, Hawaii, 1968-71; Director, Programs and Plans, Office of the Assistant Secretary of Defense (International Security Affairs), 1971-73. Legion of Merit; Distinguished Flying Cross; and other medals and awards. Promoted to Major General, 1969.

Moezzi, Muhammad. General, Imperial Iranian Gendarmerie; Supreme Head of State, Gendarmerie. Born in 1910. Attended Advanced School of Gendarmerie, Paris, France. Commander, Advanced School of Gendarmerie; Head, Personnel Department of Gendarmerie; Commander of Gendarmerie, Teheran No. 1; Deputy Director, Department of Security; Commander of the Fars.

Mogg, Sir John. General, British Army; Adjutant-General, Ministry of Defence (Army), 1970-   . Born February 17, 1913. Malvern College; Royal Military Academy, Sandhurst, Coldstream Guards, 1933-35; Royal Military Academy, Sandhurst (Sword of Honor), 1935-37. Commissioned in the Oxfordshire and Buckinghamshire Light Infantry, 1937. Served in Northwest Europe in WW II; Malaya, 1958-60. Commandant, Royal Military Academy, Sandhurst, 1963-66; Commander, 1st (British) Corps, 1966-68; General Officer Commanding-in-Chief, Southern Command, 1968; General Officer Commanding-in-Chief, Army Strategic Command, 1968-70; Aide de Camp General to the Queen, 1971-   . KCB, CBE, DSO. Meritorious Medal (Malaya).

Mohr, Wilhelm. Lieutenant General, Norwegian Royal Air Force; Deputy Commander in Chief, Allied Forces, Northern Europe, 1969-   . Born June 27, 1917, in Fana, near Bergen, Norway. Attended Army Flying School, 1937; Norwegian War College, 1939; NATO Defense College, Paris, 1954. Commissioned Second Lieutenant, Norwegian Royal Air Force, 1939. Combat duty in WW II. Member, Standing Group, Washington, D.C., 1957-60; Commander in Chief, Royal Norwegian Air Force, 1964-69. War Cross with Swords; Distinguished Flying Cross (Great Britain); Legion of Merit (USA); and other medals and awards. Promoted to Lieutenant General, 1964.

Molczyk, Eugeniusz. Lieutenant General, Polish Army; Deputy Minister of National Defense, 1971-   ; Chief Inspector for Training, 1971-   . Attended General Staff War College; War College, USSR. Commander, Silesian Military District, 1964-68; First Deputy Chief of General Staff, 1968-71. Cross of Grunwald; Polonia Restituta; Cross of Merit; and other medals and awards. Promoted to Major General, July 1960; Lieutenant General, October 1966. Member, Polish United Workers Party.

Mommersteeg, J.A. State Secretary of Defense (Personnel), The Netherlands, 1973-   . Born March 6, 1917, in 'sHertogenbosch (Bois le Duc). Studied law at Utrecht University. Assistant Director and Editor, Keesings

International Publishing Company. Member, Netherlands Parliament (Catholic Peoples Party), 1963- . Member, Council of Europe, Western European Union, North Atlantic Parliamentary Council, National Advisory Council for Development Cooperation, and Defense Advisory Committee. Chairman, Parliamentary Defense Committee. Vice Chairman, Parliamentary Development Cooperation Committee.

Momyer, William Wallace. General, United States Air Force; Commander, US Air Force Tactical Air Command, 1968- . Born September 23, 1916, in Muskogee, Oklahoma. University of Washington, Seattle, Washington, BA, 1937; Primary-Basic Pilot Training Course, 1938-39; Air War College, 1949-50; National War College, 1953-54. Commissioned Second Lieutenant, US Army Air Corps, 1939. Combat duty in the North African Theater, WW II; Vietnam War. Commander, 314th Air Division, Far East Air Force, 1955; Commander, 312th Fighter-Bomber Wing, 1955-57; Commander, 832d Air Division, 1957-58; Director of Plans, Headquarters Tactical Air Command, 1958-61; Director of Operational Requirements, Deputy Chief of Staff, Programs and Requirements, Headquarters, US Air Force, 1961-64; Assistant Deputy Chief of Staff, Programs and Requirements, Headquarters, US Air Force, 1964; Commander, Air Training Command, 1964-66; Deputy Commander for Air Operations, Military Assistance Command, Vietnam, and Commander Seventh Air Force, Vietnam, 1966-68. Distinguished Service Cross; Distinguished Service Medal with two Oak Leaf Clusters; Silver Star with two Oak Leaf Clusters; Legion of Merit with two Oak Leaf Clusters; Distinguished Flying Cross; Air Medal with 16 Oak Leaf Clusters; and other US and foreign medals and awards. Promoted to Brigadier General, December 13, 1955; Major General, September 1, 1959; Lieutenant General, August 1, 1964; General, December 13, 1967.

Moncrief, William Henry, Jr. Major General, United States Army; Commanding General, Walter Reed Army Medical Center, and Walter Reed General Hospital, Washington, D.C., 1972- . Born August 16, 1921, Denver, Colorado. Medical Field Service School, Basic Course; The National War College. Commissioned Second Lieutenant, US Army, 1942. Served in WW II. Commanding General, Brooke General Hospital, Brooke Army Medical Center, Fort Sam Houston, Texas, 1968-70; Commanding General, Letterman General Hospital, Presidio of San Francisco, California, 1970-72. Legion of Merit with two Oak Leaf Clusters; and other medals and awards. Promoted to Brigadier General, April 1, 1969; Major General, February 1, 1970.

Montel Touzet, Arturo. Lieutenant General, Spanish Air Force; Chief, Materiel Command, 1970- . Diplomate of Air Force Staff; Diplomate in Army Communication Systems. Formerly Air Attache, Embassy of Spain, London; Director of Air Force Joint Operations School; Chief, Albacete Air Sector, and Commander, 26th Bomber Wing; General Secretary, Military Joint Staff Board, and Assistant to the Vice President of the Government; Chief of Staff, Materiel Command; Chief of Air Defense Command; Counselor of Nuclear Energy Board. Military Medal (Individual); Great Crosses: Navy and Air Force Merit and Saint Hermenegild Royal and Military Order; three War Crosses; two Red Crosses of Military Merit; Medal of Endurance for the Fatherland with Red Cross; Campaign Medal; King Alphonse XIII Medal; Legion of Merit (USA); and other medals and awards. Promoted to Lieutenant General, April 2, 1972.

Moore, George Everett. Vice Admiral, Supply Corps, United States Navy; Vice Chief, Naval Material, 1970- . Born January 6, 1918, Westbrook, Maine. US Naval Academy, 1935-39; Navy Supply Corps School, Harvard University, 1941-42; Naval War College, 1960-61. Commissioned Ensign, US Navy, 1939; transferred to Supply Corps, 1941. Served in the Pacific Theater, WW II; Korean War. Deputy Commander for Supply Operations, Naval Supply Systems Command, 1966-67; Vice Commander, Naval Supply Systems Command, 1967-69; Deputy Chief of Naval Material for Logistic Support, Naval Material Command Headquarters, 1969-70. Legion of Merit; and other medals and awards. Promoted to Vice Admiral, November 20, 1970.

Moore, Harley Lester, Jr. Major General, United States Army; Commanding General, US Army Training Center and Fort Gordon, Georgia, 1971- . Born December 25, 1918, Carthage, Illinois. Coe College, BA Degree, Education; The Infantry School, Basic Course; The Provost Marshal General's School, Advanced Course; US Army Command and General Staff College; Industrial College of the Armed Forces. Commissioned Second Lieutenant, US Army Reserve, 1940. Served in WW II and Vietnam War. Provost Marshal, US Army, Europe, 1964-66; Provost Marshal, US Army, Vietnam, 1966-67; Provost Marshal, US Army, Europe and Seventh Army, 1967-71. Distinguished Service Medal; Legion of Merit with two Oak Leaf Clusters; Bronze Star Medal; and other medals and awards. Promoted to Brigadier General, August 1, 1964; Major General, September 1, 1971.

Moore, Harold Gregory. Major General, United States Army; Commanding General, US Army Training Center (Infantry) and Fort Ord, California, 1971- . Born February 13, 1922, Bardstown, Kentucky. US Military Academy; Infantry School, Basic and Advanced Courses; US Army Command and General Staff College; US Armed Forces Staff College; US Naval War College; George Washington University, MA Degree, International Affairs. Commissioned Second Lieutenant, 1945. Served in Vietnam War. Deputy Director of Plans, Office, Deputy Chief of Staff for Military Operations, US Army, Washington, D.C., 1968-69; Assistant Chief of Staff, G-3, Eighth US Army, US Army, Pacific-Korea, 1969-70; Commanding General, 7th Infantry Division, Eighth US Army, US Army, Pacific-Korea, 1970-71. Distinguished Service Cross; Legion of Merit with two Oak Leaf Clusters; Bronze Star Medal with V Device and three Oak Leaf

Clusters; and other medals and awards. Promoted to Brigadier General, September 1, 1968; Major General, August 1, 1970.

Moore, Howard Shackleford. Rear Admiral, United States Navy; Commander, Fleet Air, Western Pacific, 1972-   . Born October 24, 1920, in Washington, D.C. US Naval Academy, 1939-42; Electronics School, 1949; Naval War College, Command and Staff Course, 1952-53; University of Oklahoma, MA, 1967. Commissioned Ensign, US Navy, 1942; designated Naval Aviator, 1946. Served in the Pacific Theater, WW II. Commanding Officer USS *Platte* (AO-24), 1964-65; Commanding Officer USS *Forrestal* (CVA-59), 1965-66; Commander in Chief, Pacific, Representative to Joint Strategic Target Planning Staff, 1966-68; Deputy Director, National Military Command Center, J-3, Joint Chiefs of Staff, 1968-69; Commander, Pacific Missile Range, Point Mugu, California, 1969-72. Legion of Merit; Meritorious Service Medal; and other medals and awards. Promoted to Rear Admiral, July 1, 1969.

Moore, Otis C. Major General, United States Air Force; Commander, Fourteenth Aerospace Force, Aerospace Defense Command, 1972-   . Born September 20, 1926, in Charlotte, North Carolina. Clemson College, South Carolina; US Military Academy, 1944-48; National War College, 1966-67; University of Omaha, MS. Commissioned in 1948. Combat duty in the Vietnam War. Staff, Directorate of Plans, Headquarters Strategic Air Command, 1962-65; Chief, Space Branch, Future Systems Division, 1965-66; Staff, Directorate of Doctrine, Concepts and Objectives, Deputy Chief of Staff, Plans and Operations, Headquarters USAF, 1967-69; Executive Officer to the Chief of Staff, USAF, 1969-71; Chief of Staff, Seventh Air Force, Vietnam, 1971-72. Distinguished Service Medal; Legion of Merit; and other medals and awards. Promoted to Brigadier General, August 1, 1970; Major General, November 1, 1972.

Moore, Sam Howard. Rear Admiral, United States Navy; Deputy Comptroller of the Navy, 1972-   . Born April 11, 1918, Rugby, Texas. East Texas State University, 1937-41; Cornell University, Diesel Engineering Course; General Line School, Monterey California, 1950; Marine Corps School, Senior Course, 1957-58; National War College, 1966-67. Commissioned Ensign, 1942. Served in the Atlantic and Pacific Theaters, WW II; Vietnam War. Director, Plans and Programs, Surface Missiles Systems Project, 1963-65; Commanding Officer, USS *Chicago* (CG 11), 1965-66; Commander Cruiser-Destroyer Flotilla SEVEN, 1967-68; Commander Military Sea Transportation Service, Far East, 1968-70; Director of Budget and Reports, Office of the Comptroller of the Navy, 1970-72. Legion of Merit with two Gold Stars; Navy Commendation Medal with two Gold Stars; and other US and foreign medals and awards. Promoted to Rear Admiral, 1967.

Moore, William Grover, Jr. Lieutenant General, United States Air Force; Commander, Thirteenth Air Force, Clark Air Base, Philippines, 1972-   . Born May 18, 1920, in

Waco, Texas. Kilgore College, Kilgore, Texas, 1937-39; Army Air Corps Flying School, 1940-41; Air Command and Staff School, 1950; Air War College, 1957; George Washington University, 1961-62; National War College, 1961-62. Commissioned Second Lieutenant, US Army Air Corps, 1941. Combat duty in the European Theater, WW II; Korean War; Vietnam War. Commander, 839th Air Division, 1963-65; Deputy Director, Operations, J-3, US Strike Command, 1965-66; Commander, 834th Air Division, Vietnam, 1966-67; Director, Operational Requirements and Development Plans, Headquarters, USAF, 1967-70; Commander, Twenty-second Air Force, Military Airlift Command, 1970-72. Distinguished Service Medal; Silver Star; Legion of Merit with four Oak Leaf Clusters; Distinguished Flying Cross with one Oak Leaf Cluster; and other US and foreign medals and awards. Promoted to Brigadier General, July 1, 1965; Major General, December 8, 1967; Lieutenant General, September 1, 1972.

Moorer, Joe Park. Vice Admiral, United States Navy; Senior Navy Member, US Delegation to the United Nations Military Staff Committee, and Commander, Eastern Sea Frontier, 1973-   . Born October 18, 1922, in Mount Willing, Alabama. Attended US Naval Academy, 1941-44; Armed Forces Staff College, 1957-58. Commissioned June 7, 1944; designated Naval Aviator July 1, 1948. Served in the Pacific Theater in WW II, and in the Vietnam War. Assistant Chief of Staff to Commander SEVENTH Fleet, 1966-67; Commanding Officer, USS *Camden* (ACE-2), 1968-69; Commanding Officer, USS *Ranger* (CVA-61), 1969-70; Chief, Current Plans Branch, Office of Chief of Naval Operations, Deputy Director, then Director, Strategic Plans and Policy Division, 1970-72; Commander Carrier Division SIX, 1972-73. Legion of Merit, Bronze Star Medal, and other medals and awards. Promoted to Vice Admiral, 1973.

Moorer, Thomas Hinman. Admiral, United States Navy; Chairman, The Joint Chiefs of Staff, 1970-   . Born February 9, 1912, in Mount Willing, Alabama. US Naval Academy, 1929-33; Flight Training Course, 1935-36; Naval War College, 1952-53. Commissioned Ensign, US Navy, 1933; designated Naval Aviator, 1936. Served in the Pacific and Atlantic Theaters, WW II. Aide to the Assistant Secretary of the Navy (Air), 1955-56; Commanding Officer, USS *Salisbury Sound* (AV-13), 1956-57; Special Assistant, Strategic Plans Division, Office of the CNO, 1957-58; Assistant Chief of Naval Operations (War Gaming Matters), 1958-59; Commander Carrier Division SIX, 1959-60; Director, Long Range Objectives Group, Office of CNO, 1960-62; Commander Seventh Fleet, 1962-64; Commander in Chief, Pacific Fleet, 1964-65; Commander, NATO's Allied Command, Atlantic, US Unified Atlantic Command, and US Atlantic Fleet, 1965-67; Chief of Naval Operations, 1967-70. Distinguished Service Medal with three Gold Stars; Silver Star Medal; Legion of Merit; Distinguished Flying Cross; Honorary LLD, Auburn University (Alabama), 1968; Honorary Doctor of Humanities, Sanford University (Alabama), 1970; Stephen Decatur Award for

Operational Competence; General William Mitchell Award; Frank M. Hawks Award; Gray Eagle of the United States Navy Award; and other US and foreign medals and awards. Promoted to Rear Admiral, August 1, 1958; Vice Admiral, October 5, 1962; Admiral, June 26, 1964.

Moran, William Joseph. Vice Admiral, United States Navy; Director of Research, Development, Test and Evaluation, Office of the Chief of Naval Operations, 1972-   . Born July 20, 1919. Santa Rosa Junior College; University of Nevada, BA; Flight Training Course, Naval Air Station, Corpus Christi, Texas, 1941; General Line School, Monterey, California, 1949; Naval War College, 1954-55; National War College, 1964-65. Commissioned Ensign, US Naval Reserve, 1941; designated Naval Aviator, 1941; transferred to US Navy, 1946. Served in the Pacific Theater, WW II; Korean War; Vietnam War. Commanding Officer USS *Rainier* (AE-5), 1965-67; Commander Antisubmarine Warfare Group THREE, 1967-68; Director, Navy Space Program Division, Office of the CNO, 1968-70; Commander Naval Weapons Center, China Lake, California, 1970-72. Legion of Merit with Gold Star; Distinguished Flying Cross with two Gold Stars; Air Medal with three Gold Stars; and other US and foreign medals and awards. Promoted to Vice Admiral, December 1, 1972.

Moreau, James Walter. Rear Admiral, United States Coast Guard; Chief, Office of Engineering, US Coast Guard, 1973-   . Born February 5, 1921, Glenwood, Minnesota. US Coast Guard Academy, 1939-42; Rensselaer Polytechnic Institute, Troy, New York, 1952-53, BS Degree, Civil Engineering, 1953; Washington University, St. Louis, Missouri, MS, Engineering Administration, 1959. Commissioned Ensign, 1942. Served in Pacific and European Theaters, WW II. Assistant Chief and later Chief, Civil Engineering Division, US Coast Guard, 1965-68; Assistant Project Manager, Polar Transportation Requirements, 1968; Assistant Chief of Staff for Ocean Sciences, Headquarters, US Coast Guard, 1968-69; Chief, Engineering Division, 14th Coast Guard District, Honolulu, Hawaii, 1969-70; Chief, Operations, 14th Coast Guard District, 1970-71; Chief, Office of Reserve, Headquarters, US Coast Guard, 1971-73. Legion of Merit; and other medals and citations. Promoted to Captain, July 1, 1964; Rear Admiral, April 26, 1971.

Morgan, Brinley John. Instructor Rear-Admiral, British Royal Navy; Director, Naval Education Service, 1970-   . Born April 3, 1916. Attended University College, Cardiff, BS, 1937; Senior Officers' War Course, 1961. Commissioned in the Royal Navy as Instructor Lieutenant, 1939. Served at sea and in Naval Weather Service in WW II. Staff of Director Naval Education Service, 1959-61, 1963-64; HMS *Ganges*, 1961-63; Dean, Royal Navy Engineering College, Manadon, 1964-69. Promoted to Instructor Captain, 1960; Instructor Rear-Admiral, 1970.

Morgan, David Archibald Stevenson. Air Vice Marshal, Royal Australian Air Force; Director-General, Medical Services, 1971-   . Educated at the University of Adelaide. Served with the RAAF in WW II; and with the British Commonwealth Forces Korea in the Korean War. OBE; MB.

Morgan, Thomas W. Major General, United States Air Force; Commander, Air Force Special Weapons Center, Air Force Systems Command, Kirtland Air Force Base, New Mexico, 1972-   . Born January 11, 1922, in DeRidder, Louisiana. Alabama Polytechnical Institute, BS, Aeronautical Engineering, 1942; Aviation Cadet Training Course, Yale University, 1942-43; Pilot and Advanced Pilot Training Course, 1948-49; University of Michigan, MS, Aerospace Engineering, 1952; Air War College. Commissioned Second Lieutenant, US Army Air Corps, in 1943. Director of Engineering, Space Systems Division, and Director of Operations, Manned Orbiting Laboratory Program, Los Angeles, California, 1963-67; Manager, Apollo Applications Program Office (redesignated Apollo/Skylab Programs Office, May 1970), NASA John F. Kennedy Space Center, Florida, 1967-71; Vice Commander, Space and Missile Systems Organization, Air Force Systems Command, Los Angeles, California, 1971-72. Promoted to Major General, April 2, 1973.

Moroz, I.M. Colonel General, USSR Air Force; Deputy Chief, Main Political Directorate, Soviet Army and Navy, 1967-   , and Chief, Political Directorate, Soviet Air Forces, 1957-   . Served on the Soviet-German Front in WW II. Member, Communist Party of the Soviet Union.

Morris, John Woodland. Major General, United States Army; Director of Civil Works, Office, Chief of Engineers, US Army, Washington, D.C., 1972-   . Born September 10, 1921, Princess Anne, Maryland. US Military Academy; Engineer School, Advanced Course; US Army Command and General Staff College; US Army War College; University of Iowa, MS Degree, Civil Engineering. Commissioned Second Lieutenant, 1943. Served in WW II and Vietnam War. Deputy Chief of Legislative Liaison, Office, Secretary of the Army, Washington, D.C., 1967-69; Commanding Officer, 18th Engineer Brigade, US Army, Pacific-Vietnam, 1969-70; Division Engineer, US Army Engineer Division, Missouri River, Omaha, 1970-72. Distinguished Service Medal; Legion of Merit with two Oak Leaf Clusters; Bronze Star Medal; and other medals and awards. Promoted to Brigadier General, August 1, 1969; Major General, July 1, 1971.

Morris, Ronald James Arthur. Air Vice-Marshal, British Royal Air Force; Deputy Director General, Medical Services (RAF), 1971-   . Born November 27, 1915. Madras College, St. Andrews; St. Andrews University, Bachelor of Medicine and of Surgery, 1939; School of Aviation Medicine, US Air Force, 1955-56. Commissioned in 1939. Served in Burma and India in WW II. Principal Medical Officer, Signals Command, 1963-65; Deputy Principal Medical Officer, Far East Air Forces, 1965-69; Principal Medical Officer, Maintenance Command, 1969-70. DPH; MFCM. Queen's Honorary Surgeon, 1971-   .

Morrison, George Stephen. Rear Admiral, United States Navy; Commander, United States Naval Forces, Marianas, 1972-   . Born January 7, 1919, Rome, Georgia. US Naval Academy, 1937-41; Canadian Defense College, 1960-61. Commissioned Ensign, US Navy, 1941; designated Naval Aviator, 1944. Served in the Pacific Theater, WW II; Korean War; Vietnam War. Commanding Officer USS *Bon Homme Richard* (CVA-39), 1963-64; Assistant Chief of Staff for Strategic Naval Plans, Commander in Chief, US Naval Forces, Europe, 1965-67; Assistant Commander for Logistics and Fleet Support, Naval Air Systems Command Headquarters, 1967-68; Commander, Carrier Division NINE, 1968-69; Director, Electronic Warfare and Tactical Command Systems Division, Office of the CNO, 1969-71; Assistant Deputy Chief of Naval Operations (Surface Warfare), 1971-72. Legion of Merit with Gold Star; Bronze Star Medal with Combat "V"; Air Medal with two Gold Stars; and other medals and awards. Promoted to Rear Admiral, July 1, 1967.

Morrison, William L. Rear Admiral, United States Coast Guard; Commander, 14th Coast Guard District, Honolulu, Hawaii, 1973-   . Born November 21, 1914, North Smithfield, Rhode Island. US Coast Guard Academy, 1935-39; George Washington University Law School, 1947-49, LLB. Commissioned Ensign, 1939. Served in Atlantic Theater WW II. Deputy Chief of Staff, US Coast Guard, 1966-67; Assistant to the General Counsel, Office of the Secretary of Transportation, 1967-68; Chief, Office of Boating Safety, 1968-69; Chief Counsel, US Coast Guard, 1969-73. Legion of Merit; Navy Commendation Ribbon with Bronze Star; World War II medals and ribbons. Promoted to Captain, July 1, 1960; Rear Admiral, January 1, 1968.

Moskalenko, Kiril Semyonovich. Marshal of the Soviet Union; Deputy Minister of Defense, and Chief Inspector of the Ministry of Defense, 1962-   . Born in 1902 in Grishino, Donetsk Oblast. Volunteered for military service, c. 1919. Training: Cossack Officers courses, 1921-22; Advanced Officers Training courses, 1926-28; Dzherzhinskiy Artillery College, 1939. Commissioned c. 1922. Served in the Finno-Soviet War, 1939-40; Soviet-German War, 1941-45. Commander Artillery Division, Finnish Front, 1939-40; Commander, 1st Antitank Brigade, Southwest Front, 1941; Commander, 15th Rifle Corps, Kiev Front, 1941 (July-September); Commander, 6th Army, 1941-42 (December-January); Commander, 6th Cavalry Corps, 1942 (January-February); Commander, 38th Army, Kharkov Front, 1942 (February-July); Commander, 1st Tank Army, 1942 (July-August); Commander, 1st Guards Army, Stalingrad Front, 1942 (August); Commander, 40th Army, Voronezh and Kharkov Fronts, 1942-43; Commander, 38th Army, Ukrainian Front, 1943-45; Commander, Antiaircraft Defense System, Moscow Military District, 1948-53; Commander, Moscow Military District, 1953-60; Commander, Strategic Missile Forces, 1960-62. Member, Communist Party of the Soviet Union, 1926-   ; Member, Communist Party Central Committee; Deputy to the USSR Supreme Soviet. Hero of the Soviet-Union; three Orders of Lenin; five Orders of Red Banner; Order of Suvorov; Order of Kutuzov; Order of Fatherland War; and other Soviet and foreign orders and medals. Promoted to Marshal of the Soviet Union, 1955.

Morton, Anthony Storrs. Rear-Admiral, British Royal Navy; Assistant Chief of Defence Staff (Policy), 1973-   . Born November 6, 1923. Joined the Royal Navy in 1941. Served in Atlantic, Mediterranean and Far East Theaters in WW II. Commander, HMS *Rocket*, 1960-62; Captain (F), 20th Frigate Squadron, 1964-66; Chief Staff Officer, Plans and Policy, to Commander, Far East Fleet, 1966-68; Senior Naval Officer, Northern Ireland, 1968-70; Senior Naval Member, Directing Staff, Royal College of Defence Studies, 1971-73. Promoted to Captain, 1964; Rear Admiral, 1971.

Mosyaikin, V. Colonel, USSR Army; First Deputy Chief, Political Directorate, Turkestan Military District. Member, Communist Party of the Soviet Union.

Mounir, A. Major General, Army of the Arab Republic of Egypt; Defence Attache, Embassy of Egypt, London.

Muangmanee, Siri. Air Chief Marshal, Royal Thai Air Force; Vice Commander in Chief, Royal Thai Air Force. Born April 3, 1914. Attended Military Academy, Royal Thai Army; US Air Force Senior Officers Military Management Course, 1949; National War College, 1960. Commandant Flying Training School, 1948; Deputy Chief of Air Staff, Logistics; Acting Director of Civil Engineers, 1957; Chief of Air Staff, 1961.

Mujibur Rahman, Sheikh. Prime Minister and Minister of Defense, Bangladesh, 1972-   . Born March 17, 1920, in Tungipara. Attended Islamia College, Calcutta, 1947; Dacca University. General Secretary, Awami League, 1953; Member, East Bengal Provincial Assembly, 1954; Minister for Co-operatives and Agricultural Credit, 1954; Member, Constituent Assembly of Pakistan, 1955; Minister for Commerce, Labour and Industries and Anti-corruption, 1956-57; Chairman, Pakistan Tea Board, 1957-58. Named "Bangabandhu" (Friend of Bengal) by the Students Action Committee, 1969; Joliot Curie Peace Medal of the World Peace Council.

Murcia Rubio, Javier. Lieutenant General, Spanish Air Force; Chief of 3d Air Region (Valencia), 1970-   . Formerly Chief of Flight Research Group, Air Force Staff; Commander, Torrejon Joint Air Force Base; Commander, Tajima Air Force Base, and Chief of Melilla (Africa) Air Sector; Commander, 3d Fighter Wing; Commander, 1st Fighter Wing; Chief of 3d Section, Air Force Staff; Chief of Search and Rescue Service; Air Attache, Embassy of Spain in Paris, Brussels and The Hague; Chief of Staff, Air Defense Command; Chief of Air Branch, Peninsular Joint Staff Committee; Chief of Valencia Air Sector; Chief of Canary Islands Air Zone. Air Medal; Great Cross of Air Force Merit, and Saint Hermenegild Royal and Military Order; two War Crosses; three Red Crosses of Military

Merit; Medal of Endurance for the Fatherland; and other medals and awards. Promoted to Lieutenant General, November 4, 1970.

Murphy, John R. Major General, United States Air Force; Vice Commander, Fifth Air Force, Pacific Air Forces, Japan, 1972-   . Born September 19, 1918, in Minot, North Dakota. North Dakota State University; Notre Dame University; US Military Academy, 1938-42; Army Air Corps Flying School, 1942; Air Command and Staff School, 1947-48; National War College, 1962-63. Commissioned in 1942. Combat duty in the European Theater, WW II; Korean War; Vietnam War. Commander, 4th Tactical Fighter Wing, 1962-64; Commander 833d Air Division, 1964-65; Deputy Commander, 2d Air Division, Thirteenth Air Force, Thailand, 1965-66; Assistant Deputy Commander, Seventh/Thirteenth Air Force, Thailand, 1966; Deputy Director, and later Director, Legislative Liaison, Office of the Secretary of the Air Force, 1966-70; Vice Commander, Air Training Command, 1970-72. Distinguished Service Medal; Silver Star; Legion of Merit with two Oak Leaf Clusters; Distinguished Flying Cross with three Oak Leaf Clusters; and other US and foreign medals and awards. Promoted to Major General, July 23, 1968.

Murphy, Raymond Patrick. Major General, United States Army; Commanding General, 1st Region, US Army Air Defense Command, Stewart Field, New York, 1972-   . Born December 11, 1917, Anaconda, Montana. US Military Academy; The Artillery School, Basic and Advanced Courses; US Army Command and General Staff College; US Army War College; Springfield College, MS Degree, Physical Education. Commissioned Second Lieutenant, 1942. Served in WW II and Vietnam War. Commanding General, II Field Force Artillery, US Army, Pacific-Vietnam, 1967-68; Assistant Deputy Chief of Staff for Operations, US Army, Europe and Seventh Army, 1968-70; Director, Joint Continental Defense Systems Integrated Planning Staff, Washington, D.C. 1970-72; Senior Member, United Nations Command Military Armistice Commission, Korea, 1972. Distinguished Service Medal; Legion of Merit with Oak Leaf Cluster; Bronze Star Medal; and other medals and awards. Promoted to Brigadier General, June 1, 1967; Major General, November 1, 1970.

Musgrave, Story. United States; NASA Scientist-Astronaut, 1967-   . Born August 19, 1935, Boston, Massachusetts. Syracuse University, BS, Statistics, 1958; University of California at Los Angeles, MBA, 1959; Marietta College, BA, Chemistry, 1960; Columbia University, MD, 1964; University of Kentucky, MS, Biophysics, 1966, PhD, Physiology, 1972. Enlisted in US Marine Corps, 1953; duty as electrician, instrument technician and aircraft crew chief; holds ratings as instructor, instrument instructor, and airline transport pilot as well as pilot; parachutist. Surgical intern, University of Kentucky Medical Center, 1964-65; US Air Force Post-doctoral Fellow in Aerospace Physiology and Medicine; National Heart Institute Post-doctoral Fellow. NASA experience: Backup Science-Pilot, Skylab 2.

International Jumpmaster Class C. License; President and Jumpmaster, Bluegrass Sport Parachuting Association, Lexington, Kentucky, 1964-67.

Mussared, Brynmor Wheatley. Rear Admiral, Royal Australian Navy; Chief, Naval Technical Services, 1972-   . Born January 22, 1917, in Semaphore. Attended Royal Australian Naval College; Royal Australian Naval Engineer College. Commissioned Lieutenant (Engineer) in 1940. Chief Staff Officer (Technical) to Australian Naval Representative, London, 1962-64; Chief Staff Officer (Technical) to Flag Officer Commanding HMA Fleet, 1965-67; Assistant Chief, Technical Planning, 1967; General Manager, HM Naval Dockyard, Garden Island, 1968-71; Light Destroyer Project Director, 1971-72. Promoted to Commodore, 1968; Rear Admiral, 1971.

Myer, Charles Robert. Major General, United States Army; Commanding General, US Army School/Training Center and Fort Gordon, Georgia, 1973-   . Born March 12, 1924, in Wellsburg, West Virginia. Attended US Military Academy; Infantry School; Signal School, Basic and Advanced Courses; Command and General Staff College; Armed Forces Staff College, 1963-64; Army War College, 1967-68; University of Illinois, MS, Electrical Engineering. Commanding Officer, 11th Signal Group, US Army Strategic Communications Command, Fort Huachuca, Arizona, 1968-69; Director of Plans, later Special Assistant to the Commanding General, US Army Strategic Communications Command, Fort Huachuca, Arizona, 1969; Commanding General, US Army Strategic Communications Command, Europe, and Deputy Chief of Staff, Communications-Electronics, US Army, Europe, and Seventh Army, 1969-71; Commanding General, 1st Signal Brigade, US Army Strategic Communications Command-Southeast Asia, and Assistant Chief of Staff, Communications-Electronics, US Army, Vietnam, 1972; Deputy Commanding General, US Army School/Training Center and Fort Gordon, Georgia, 1973. Legion of Merit with two Oak Leaf Clusters and other medals and awards. Promoted to Brigadier General January 1, 1970; Major General October 1, 1972.

N

Nachinkin, N.A. Colonel General, USSR Army; Deputy Chief, Main Political Directorate, Soviet Army and Navy, 1962-   . Served on the Soviet-German Front in WW II. Member, Communist Party of the Soviet Union.

Nagibin, N. Colonel, USSR Frontier Troops; Chief, Political Branch, Transbaikal Frontier District. Member, Communist Party of the Soviet Union.

Nam, Nguyen Khoa. Brigadier General, Army of the Republic of South Vietnam; Commander 7th Infantry Division.

Nam, Nguyen Van. Senior Colonel, People's Army of Vietnam; Deputy Chief, General Directorate of Rear Services, 1960-64; Deputy Chief, People's Supreme Procurate, 1967; Chief, Central Military Procurate, 1967-69; Charge d'Affaires, Sofia, Bulgaria, 1970. Promoted to Senior Colonel, 1961.

Nanda, S.M. Admiral, Navy of India; Chief of the Naval Staff. PVSM.

Nash, Slade. Major General, United States Air Force; Deputy Director of Information, Office of the Secretary of the Air Force, 1972-   . Born June 26, 1921, in Moville, Iowa. Attended Iowa State College; US Military Academy, 1942-45; Tactical Fighter Pilot Training Course, 1945-46; Air Command and Staff College, 1959-60; Army War College, 1964-65; George Washington University, MA, International Affairs, 1965. Commissioned Second Lieutenant, US Army Air Corps, in 1945. Served in the Vietnam War. Commander 92d Tactical Fighter Squadron, and later Assistant Deputy Wing Commander for Operations, 81st Tactical Fighter Wing, Royal Air Force Station, Bentwaters, England, 1965-67; Chief, Tactical Fighter and Reconnaissance Division, Office of the Deputy Chief of Staff, Operations, Headquarters US Air Force Europe, 1967-68; Deputy Commander, Operations, and later Vice Commander, 8th Tactical Fighter Wing, Ubon Airfield, Thailand, 1968-69; Vice Commander, Air Defense Weapons Center, Tyndall Air Force Base, Florida, 1969-71; Vice Director, Defense Special Projects Group, Department of Defense, Naval Observatory, Washington, D.C., 1971-72. Legion of Merit; Henri de la Vaulx International Aviation award for 1952; Distinguished Flying Cross with Oak Leaf Cluster; Meritorious Service Medal; Air Medal with seven Oak Leaf Clusters; and other US and foreign medals and awards. Promoted to Brigadier General, November 1, 1971; Major General, 1973.

Nassiri, Ne'motollah. General, Imperial Iranian Army; Head, State Security and Intelligence Organization (SAVAK), and Assistant to the Prime Minister, 1965-   . Born in 1907. Attended Teheran Military Academy. Commander, Imperial Guard, 1950; Deputy Adjutant to His Imperial Majesty the Shah, 1958; Military Governor, Teheran and Suburbs, 1963; Chief of Police. Promoted to Major General, 1958.

Naumenko, Yu. Colonel General, USSR Army; Commander, Volga Military District, 1971-   . Served on the Soviet-German Front in WW II. Member, Communist Party of the Soviet Union.

Nazaire, Breton. Secretary of State for the Interior and National Defense, Haiti, 1973-   .

Neel, Spurgeon Hart, Jr. Major General, United States Army; Deputy Surgeon General, Office of the Surgeon General, US Army, Washington, D.C. 1969-   . Born September 24, 1919, Memphis, Tennessee. University of Tennessee, MD Degree; Medical Field Service School, Basic Course; US Air Force School of Air Medicine, Advanced Course; US Army Command and General Staff College; US Industrial College of the Armed Forces; Harvard University, MPH Degree; George Washington University, MBA Degree. Commissioned Second Lieutenant, 1942. Served in WW II and Vietnam War. Surgeon, US Army, Vietnam, and Commanding General, 44th Medical Brigade, US Army, Pacific-Vietnam, 1968-69; Surgeon, US Military Assistance Command, Vietnam, 1969; Special Assistant to the Surgeon General, US Army, Washington, D.C., 1969. Distinguished Service Medal; Legion of Merit with three Oak Leaf Clusters; Bronze Star Medal with Oak Leaf Cluster; and other medals and awards. Promoted to Brigadier General, August 1, 1968; Major General, June 1, 1970.

Neij, Arvid Hans Magnus. Major General, Swedish Royal Air Force; Chief of Staff, Military Command East, 1970-   . Attended Royal Air Force Academy, 1947-49; Air Intelligence Course (RAF), England, 1950; Royal National Defense College, 1956, 1968. Wing Commander, 1964-66; Chief of Department, Air Staff, 1966-70. Commander of the Royal Order of the Sword; Commander of the Order of the Dannebrog; and other medals and awards. Member of the Royal Academy of Military Services. Promoted to Major General, 1970.

Nelson, Douglas T. Major General, United States Air Force; System Program Director, Deputy for B-1, Aeronautical Systems Division, Air Force Systems Command (AFSC), 1970-   . Born January 9, 1921, in Astoria, Oregon. Oregon State College, 1940; Army Air Corps Flying School, 1941-42; Air Tactical School, 1948. Commissioned Second Lieutenant, US Army Air Corps, 1942. Combat duty in China-Burma-India Theater, WW II. Director of Plans, 14th Strategic Aerospace Division, and Vice Commander, then Commander, 9th Strategic Reconnaissance Wing, 1964-66; Commander, 14th Strategic Aerospace Division, 1966-68; Assistant Deputy Chief of Staff, Plans, Headquarters Strategic Air Command, 1968-70; Deputy Director, B-1 Program, Aeronautical Systems Division, Air Force Systems Command, 1970. Legion of Merit; Distinguished Flying Cross; and other medals and awards. Promoted to Major General, February 26, 1971.

Nghi, Nguyen Vinh. Major General, Army of the Republic of South Vietnam; Commander IV Corps/MR 4.

Nghia, Tran Dai. Major General, People's Army of Vietnam; Chairman, State Science and Technical Committee, 1965; Deputy Chief, General Directorate of Rear Services, 1967. Born in 1915 in South Vietnam. Director, Arms Supply Department, People's Army of Vietnam, 1950; Founding Member, Vietnam-Soviet Friendship Association, 1950; Vice Minister for Economic Affairs, 1950-54; Vice Minister of Industry, 1954-60; Member of National Scientific Research Board, 1958; Vice Minister of Heavy Industry, 1960-63; Deputy to Second National Assembly, 1960; Deputy Director, State Capital Reconstruction Committee, 1963; Deputy to Third National Assembly, 1964; Chairman of State Basic Construction Committee, 1964. Promoted to Major General, 1950.

Nhan, Luong. Senior Colonel, People's Army of Vietnam; Deputy Chief, General Directorate of Rear Services, 1964. Promoted to Senior Colonel, 1964.

Nhut, Tran Van. Brigadier General, Army of the Republic of South Vietnam; Commander 2d Infantry Division.

Nicolescu, Mariu. Colonel General, Romanian Army; Deputy Minister of National Defense.

Nieh Jung-chen. Marshal, People's Liberation Army, People's Republic of China; Chairman, Scientific and Technological Commission, 1958- . Born in 1899, in Chiangtsin, Szechwan. Studied at universities in France and Belgium, 1920-24; University of the Toilers of the East, Moscow, USSR, 1924; Red Army Military College, Moscow, USSR, 1924-25. Served in Sino-Japanese War and the Civil War; took part in Long March. Secretary General, Political Department, Whampoa Military Academy, Canton, 1925-26; organizer of Nanchang Military Uprising, 1927; Chief Political Officer, Eleventh Army, 1927; Communist Party Political Organizer, 1928-31; Deputy Chief, Political Department, Red Army Headquarters, 1931-32; Political Commissar, First Army Corps, First Front Army, Kiangsi, 1932 - c. 1936; Deputy Commander and Political Commissar, 115th Division, Eighth Route Army, 1937; Commander, Shansi-Chahar-Hopei Field Army, c. 1937-48; Commander, North-China Military Region, and Commander of all Communist Forces (armies) Operating in North China Area, 1948-49; Commander, Peking-Tientsin Garrison, 1949-55; Mayor of Peking, 1949-51; Acting Chief of Staff, PLA, 1949-54; Member, Central People's Government, 1949-54; Vice-Chairman National Defense Council, 1954; Communist Party Member since 1923; Council Member, Sino-Soviet Friendship Association, 1949-54; Member CCP, Central Committee, 1945; Member CCP Politburo, 1967; Deputy to National People's Congress, 1954; Member Standing Committee, 1954-57; Vice Premier, State Council, 1956; Vice Chairman, Military Commission of the CCP Central Committee, 1967; Member of Presidium, Ninth National Party Congress, 1969; Member of Tenth CCP Central Committee, 1973; Member of the Presidium, Tenth National Party Congress, 1973. Order of August First; Order of Independence and Freedom; Order of Liberation.

Niem, Phan Dinh. Brigadier General, Army of the Republic of South Vietnam; Commander 22d Infantry Division.

Nikitin, M. Colonel General, USSR Army; Chief of Staff, Ground Forces, 1968- . Served on the Soviet-German Front in WW II. Member, Communist Party of the Soviet Union.

Nikitin, Vasiliy Vasil'evich. Lieutenant General, USSR Army; Engineering and Technical Service, Chief, Pipeline Laying Branch of the Soviet Armed Forces. Born c. 1915. During and after WW II held various positions in the Supply Service (fuel, lubricants and special liquids). Member, Communist Party of the Soviet Union. Order of Red Banner; Order of Fatherland War; Order of Red Star; and other orders and medals. Promoted to Lieutenant General, 1960.

Nikolayev, Andrian Grigorievich. Major General, USSR Air Force; Cosmonaut, 1960- ; Commander, Cosmonaut Detachment, 1964- . Born September 5, 1929. Attended Forestry College; Air Force Officers School; Zhukovskiy Air Force Engineering War College. Joined the Soviet Air Force in 1950. Air Force Fighter Pilot; Air Force Test Pilot; Space Flight (66 orbits), 1964; Pilot, Soyuz-9 Spaceship, 1970. Member, Communist Party of the Soviet Union since 1957; Deputy, Supreme Soviet of the Russian Soviet Federal Socialist Republic; husband of Cosmonaut Valentina Tereshkova. Twice Hero of the Soviet Union; Gold Star Medal; two Orders of Lenin; Order of Red Banner; Order of Red Star; Daniel and Florence Guggenheim International Astronautics Award, 1970; and other medals and awards.

el Nimeiry, Gaafar Mohamed. President of Sudan and Minister of Defense, 1972- . Born January 1, 1930, in Omdurman. Attended Sudan Military College. Formerly Commander Khartoum Garrison; Chairman Revolutionary Command Council, 1969- ; Commander in Chief, Sudanese Armed Forces, 1969- ; Prime Minister, 1969-72; Minister of Foreign Affairs, 1970-71.

Nixon, Harry Desmond. Rear-Admiral, British Royal Navy; Vice-President (Naval), Ordnance Board, 1971- . Born May 6, 1920. Attended Royal Naval Engineering College, 1939-42; Imperial Defence College, 1967. Commissioned in 1942. Served at sea in WW II. Naval District Engineer Overseer Midlands, 1962-64; Commanding Officer, HMS *Sultan*, 1964-66; Director of Fleet Maintenance, 1968-71. Chartered Engineer; Fellow of the Institution of Mechanical Engineers; Member of the Institute of Marine Engineers; Fellow of the Institute of Petroleum. MVO. Promoted to Captain, 1962; Rear-Admiral, 1971.

Noble, Charles Carmin. Major General, United States Army; Division Engineer, US Army Engineer Division, Lower Mississippi Valley, and President, Mississippi River Commission, Vicksburg, Mississippi, 1971- . Born May 18, 1916, Syracuse, New York. US Military Academy; US Army Command and General Staff College; US Army War College; The National War College; Massachusetts Institute of Technology, MS Degree, Civil Engineering; George Washington University, MS Degree, International Affairs. Commissioned Second Lieutenant, 1940. Served in WW II and Vietnam War. Director, Southeast Asia Construction Group, Office, Assistant Secretary of Defense, Washington, D.C., 1966-67; Deputy Director of Civil Works for Comprehensive Basic Planning, Office, Chief of Engineers, US Army, Washington, D.C., 1967-68; Director, Civil Works, Office, Chief of Engineers, US Army, Washington, D.C., 1968-69; Engineer, US Army, Europe and Seventh Army, 1969-70; Commanding General, US Army Engineer Command, Vietnam, and Engineer United States Army, Vietnam, United States Army, Pacific-Vietnam, 1970-71.

Distinguished Service Medal with Oak Leaf Cluster; Legion of Merit with two Oak Leaf Clusters; Bronze Star Medal with Oak Leaf Cluster; and other medals and awards. Promoted to Brigadier General, October 1, 1964; Major General, October 1, 1969.

Nol, Lon. Marshal, Cambodian Khmer Army; President and Commander in Chief, Armed Forces, 1972- , . Born November 13, 1913. Attended Khmer Royal Military Academy. Minister of National Defense and Chief of General Staff, 1955-60; Commander in Chief, Khmer Royal Armed Forces, 1960-63; Deputy Prime Minister, 1963-66; Prime Minister, 1966-67; First Vice President in Charge of National Defense, 1967-69; Chief of General Staff, 1970; Prime Minister and Minister of National Defense, 1970-71.

Nolan, Eileen Joan. Brigadier, British Army; Director, Women's Royal Army Corps, 1973- . Born June 19, 1920. Enlisted in the Army Territorial Service, 1942; commissioned in 1945. Staff Captain, War Office, 1954-57; Staff Captain, Headquarters Tripolitania District, 1958-61; Deputy Assistant Adjutant General, War Office, 1963-64; Deputy Assistant Adjutant General, Ministry of Defence, 1965-66; Assistant Director, Headquarters Scottish Command, 1967-68; Assistant Director, Headquarters Far East Land Forces, 1968-70; Assistant Adjutant General of AG 16, Ministry of Defense, 1970-73. Promoted to Colonel, June 30, 1970; Brigadier, 1973.

Nordlöf, Gunnar. Major General, Swedish Royal Army; Chief, Stores and Workshop Directorate, Defense Materiel Administration, 1972- . Attended Artillery and Engineering Staff College, 1947-49; Royal National Defense College, 1961, 1967. Commanding Officer, Engineering Regiment Ing 2, 1964-66; Chief of Staff, Military Command, Bergslagen. Commander of the Royal Order of the Sword; and other medals and awards. Promoted to Major General, 1972.

Nordström, Kjell Alarik. Major General, Swedish Royal Army; Commander in Chief, Military Command Gotland, 1971- . Attended Royal Army Staff College, 1948-50; Royal National Defense College, 1960, 1970. Commanding Officer, Army Service Regiment T-2, 1967-68; Army Inspector, Military Command East, 1968-71. Commander of the Royal Order of the Sword; and other medals and awards. Member of the Royal Academy of Military Sciences. Promoted to Major General, 1971.

Norton, John. Lieutenant General, United States Army; Commanding General, US Army Combat Developments Command, Fort Belvoir, Virginia, 1970- . Born April 14, 1918, Fort Monroe, Virginia. US Military Academy; Armed Forces Staff College; The National War College. Commissioned Second Lieutenant, 1941. Served in WW II and Vietnam War. Deputy Commanding General, US Army Vietnam, and Commanding General, Support Troops, US Army, Vietnam, US Army, Pacific-Vietnam, 1965-66; Assistant Deputy Commanding General, US Army, Vietnam, 1966; Commanding General, 1st Cavalry Division

(Airmobile), US Army, Pacific-Vietnam, 1966-67; Commanding General, US Army Aviation Systems Command, St. Louis, Missouri, 1967-69; Deputy Director, Project MASSTER, Fort Hood, Texas, 1969-70. Distinguished Service Medal with Oak Leaf Cluster; Silver Star; Legion of Merit with two Oak Leaf Clusters; Bronze Star Medal with two Oak Leaf Clusters; and other medals and awards. Promoted to Brigadier General, April 8, 1963; Major General, April 1, 1966; Lieutenant General, October 22, 1970.

Novikov, V.G. Engineer Vice Admiral, USSR Navy; Deputy Commander in Chief, Soviet Navy. Served in the Soviet-German War, 1941-45. Member, Communist Party of the Soviet Union.

Nunes, Adalberto de Barros. Fleet Admiral, Brazilian Navy; Minister of the Navy, 1969- . Attended Military College; Naval College; Armament Course, Officers School for Improvement and Specialization; Naval War College; Basic Course, Command and Staff School. Commissioned Guarda-Marinha, December 14, 1925. Combat Duty in World War II. Chief of Navy General Staff; Navy Secretary-General; Director of Ports and Shores; Squadron Commander-in-Chief; Navy Director of Communications and Electronics; Director of Hydrography and Navigation; Director of the Naval School; Chief of Staff to the Minister of the Navy; Chief of Naval Information Service; Captain of the Ports of the State of Bahia; Military Director of the Marine Arsenal of Rio de Janeiro; Vice Director of Naval Personnel; Chief of Staff of the Antisubmarine Force. Medalha do Mérito Santos Dumont; Medalha do Mérito Tamandaré; Medalha Naval de Serviços Distintos; Medalha Militar de Platina; Ordem do Rio Branco; Ordem do Mérito Aeronautico; Ordem do Mérito Militar; Ordem do Mérito Naval; Medalha da Força Naval do Sul (com palma); Medalha de Serviços de Guerra (com duas estrelas); and other medals and awards from Brazil and other nations. Promoted to Rear Admiral, June 20, 1958; Vice Admiral, November 17, 1959; Fleet Admiral, August 29, 1966.

Nunn, Donald G. Major General, United States Air Force; Commander, Air Force Contract Management Division, Air Force Systems Command, Kirtland Air Force Base, New Mexico, 1972- . Born June 28, 1918, in St. Paul, Minnesota. Hamline University, BA, 1940; Officer Candidate School, 1942; Air Command and Staff School, 1951; Armed Forces Staff College, 1960. Commissioned Second Lieutenant, US Army Air Corps, 1942. Served in the European Theater, WW II, and in the Korean War. Comptroller, Headquarters Electronic Systems Division, L.G. Hanscom Field, Massachusetts, 1965-67; Assistant for Management, then Chief of Staff, Air Force Space and Missile Systems Organization, Los Angeles Air Force Station, California, 1967-70; Commander, Air Force Contract Management Division, Air Force Systems Command, Los Angeles Air Force Station, California, 1970-72. Legion of Merit; Bronze Star Medal; Air Force Commendation Medal with three Oak Leaf Clusters; and other medals and awards. Promoted to Brigadier General, August 1, 1971; Major General, May 16, 1973.

Nura'i, Abdollah. General, Imperial Iranian Air Force; Deputy Chief, Iranian Air Force, 1969-   . Born in 1921, in Teheran. Attended Officers College, Teheran; Pilot Training School, Teheran, 1947; Aviation Teaching School, Teheran, 1950; Jet Aircraft Flying Course, 1951; Squadron Leadership Course, Air University, Maxwell Air Force Base, USA, 1953; Air Force Staff and Command Course, Air University, USA, 1961; Air Transport Course, USA, 1962. Commissioned in the Imperial Iranian Air Force, 1947. Commander, Air Transport Squadron, 1956-61; Deputy Commander, Mixed Squadrons, 1962; Commander, Air Transport Brigade, 1963; Commander, Air Base, 1964. Merit and Efficiency Medals.

O

Obaturov, G.I. Colonel General, Armor, USSR Army; Commander, Carpathian Military District, 1969-   . Served on the Soviet-German Front in WW II. Member, Communist Party of the Soviet Union.

Obermair, Hubert. Major General, Austrian Army; Commanding General, Group III, 1969-   . Born November 1, 1911. Attended Military Academy, Enns and Wiener Neustadt, 1931-34. Commissioned Second Lieutenant, Austrian Army, in 1934. Served in the German Army in WW II. Chief of Staff, Group III, 1960; Commander, 4th Infantry Brigade, 1960-62; Military Commander, Upper Austria (Oberösterreich), 1962-66; Deputy Commander, Group III, 1966-68. Grosses Ehrenzeichen; Goldenes Ehrenzeichen; and other medals and awards. Promoted to Colonel, 1959; Brigadier, 1965; Major General, January 1, 1969.

Obiedzinski, Mieczyslaw. Lieutenant General, Polish Army; Quartermaster General, Polish Armed Forces, 1970-   . Attended General Staff War College. Served on Soviet-German Front, 1943-45, with the Polish 1st Army in the USSR. Formerly Chief, Food Supply Service, Office of Rear Services, Polish Armed Forces; Chief of Staff, Rear Services, Polish Armed Forces, 1964-66; Deputy Quartermaster General, 1966-70. Cross of Grunwald; Polonia Restituta; Cross of Valor; and other Polish and foreign medals and awards. Promoted to Major General, October 1965; Lieutenant General, 1970. Member, Polish United Workers Party.

Obroniecki, Tadeusz. Major General, Polish Air Force; Commander, Anti-Aircraft Forces, 1968-   . Promoted to Major General, 1970. Member, Polish United Workers Party.

Ochs, Elmer Raymond. Major General, United States Army; Commanding General, US Army Operational Test and Evaluation Agency, Fort Belvoir, Virginia, 1973-   . Born April 11, 1925, in Newton, Illinois. Attended US Military Academy; Infantry School, Basic and Advanced Courses; Command and General Staff College; Army War College, 1965-66; George Washington University, MS, International Affairs. Commissioned Second Lieutenant June 4, 1946. Served in the Vietnam War. Chief of Policy and Plans Branch, Directorate of Instruction, later Secretary, US Army Infantry School, Fort Benning, Georgia, 1966-68; Chief of the Doctrine, Systems and Training Division, G-3, US Army, Pacific-Vietnam, 1968; Military Senior Advisor, Civil Operations and Revolutionary Development Support, III Corps Tactical Zone, US Military Assistance Command, Vietnam, 1968-69; Deputy Commander, then Commanding Officer, 173d Airborne Brigade, US Army, Pacific-Vietnam, 1969-71; Commanding General, Combat Development Experimentation Command, Fort Ord, California, 1971-73. Distinguished Service Medal; Legion of Merit with Oak Leaf Cluster; Bronze Star Medal with V Device; Air Medal (10 awards) and other medals and awards. Promoted to Brigadier General, April 1, 1971; Major General, August 1, 1973.

Ochsner, Richard. Major General, Swiss Army; Commanding General, 11th Mechanized Division. Born in 1922.

O'Connor, Anthony. Surgeon Rear-Admiral, British Royal Navy; Medical Officer in Charge, Institute of Naval Medicine, and Dean of Naval Medicine, 1972-   . Born November 8, 1917. Attended Kings College, Strand, London; Westminster Hospital Medical School, BS, MB. Commissioned RNVR in 1942; permanent commission, 1945. Served in WW II. Deputy Medical Director General (Naval), 1969-72. MVO; QHP. Member, Royal College of Surgeons; Licentiate of the Royal College of Physicians; Diploma in Anaesthesia; Fellow of Faculty of Anaesthetists, Royal College of Surgeons.

O'Connor, Edmund F. Lieutenant General, United States Air Force; Vice Commander, Air Force Systems Command (AFSC), 1972-   . Born March 31, 1922, in Fitchburg, Massachusetts. US Military Academy, 1940-43; Flying School, 1942-43; Command and General Staff School, 1944-45; Air Force Institute of Technology, 1946-48; BS, Aeronautical Engineering, 1948; Air War College, 1958-59. Commissioned in 1943; received pilot wings, 1943. Combat duty in the European Theater, WW II; Korean War. Deputy Director, Ballistic Systems Division, Air Force Systems Command, 1962-64; Director of Program Management, George C. Marshall Space Flight Center (NASA), 1964-69; Vice Commander, Aeronautical Systems Division, AFSC, 1969-70; Deputy Chief of Staff, Procurement and Production, Headquarters, AFSC, 1970-72. Distinguished Service Medal; Distinguished Flying Cross; and other medals and awards. Promoted to Brigadier General, June 1, 1965; Major General, August 1, 1968; Lieutenant General, September 1, 1972.

Ogarkov, Nikolay Vasilyevich. Colonel General, USSR Army; First Deputy Chief of the General Staff, Research and Development, 1968-   . Born in 1917. Military Engineering Academy, c. 1938-41; Voroshilov General Staff War College, 1959. Commissioned in 1939. Served on the

Soviet-German Front in WW II. Headquarters Staff Member, Far Eastern Military District, 1949-53; Commander, Rifle Division, 1959-61; Chief of Staff, Belorussian Military District, 1961-65; Commander, Volga Military District, 1965-68. Member of Communist Party of the Soviet Union; Candidate Member of Central Committee, CPSU. Order of Lenin; Order of Red Banner; Order of Red Star; and other orders and medals. Promoted to Colonel General, 1968.

Ogbemudia, Samuel Osaigbovo. Colonel, Nigerian Army; Military Governor, Mid-western State, 1967-   . Born September 17, 1932, in Benin. Attended Government School, Victoria; Officer Cadet School, Aldershot, England, 1960-62; US Army Special Warfare School, Fort Bragg, North Carolina, 1962-63. Member, Nigerian Contingent, United Nations Peacekeeping Force, Congo; Instructor, Nigerian Military Training College, 1964-65; Chief Instructor, Nigerian Military Training College, 1965; Brigade Major, 1966-67; Military Administration of Mid-west, 1967. Promoted to Lieutenant Colonel, 1967; Colonel, August 1969.

Oh, Yun-Kyong. Commodore, Navy of the Republic of Korea; Commander in Chief of the Fleet.

Ok, Man Ho. General, Air Force of the Republic of Korea; Chief of Staff, ROK Air Force, 1971-   . Attended Republic of Korea Air Force Academy, 1950; Air University, US Air Force, USA, 1958; Kyonghui University, Seoul, 1961. Commissioned Second Lieutenant, ROK Air Force, 1950. Combat duty in the Korean War. Military Attache, Republic of China, 1960-63; Commanding General, 10th Fighter Wing, 1963-64; Superintendent, ROK Air Force Academy, 1968-70; Vice Chief of Staff, ROK Air Force, 1970-71. Ulchi; Chungmu with Gold Star; Legion of Merit (USA); Distinguished Flying Cross (USA); Air Medal (USA); and other medals and awards. Promoted to General, August 25, 1971.

O'Keefe, Timothy Francis. Lieutenant General, United States Air Force; Vice Commander in Chief, Pacific Air Forces (PACAF), 1971-   . Born January 18, 1919, in Brooklyn, New York. St. Francis College, Brooklyn, New York, 1937-38; Army Air Corps Flying School, 1940; Advanced Flying School, 1952-53; Command and General Staff School, 1944; Air Command and Staff School, 1947-48; National War College, 1959-60. Commissioned Second Lieutenant, US Army Air Corps Reserve, 1940. Combat duty in the Southwest Pacific Theater, WW II; Korean War. Deputy Chief of Staff, Operations, Seventeenth Air Force, Germany, 1960-63; Deputy Director, Operational Requirements, Deputy Chief of Staff, Programs and Requirements, Headquarters, USAF, 1963-64; Assistant for Logistics Planning, Deputy Chief of Staff, Systems and Logistics, Headquarters, USAF, 1964-67; Vice Commander, Fifth Air Force, Pacific Air Forces (PACAF), Fuchu Air Base, Japan, 1967-68; Commander, Ninth Air Force, 1968-69; Director for Logistics, The Joint Staff, Organization of the Joint Chiefs

of Staff, 1969-71. Distinguished Service Medal; Legion of Merit with two Oak Leaf Clusters; Distinguished Flying Cross; Bronze Star Medal; and other US and foreign medals and awards. Promoted to Brigadier General, July 1, 1963; Major General, November 1, 1965; Lieutenant General, October 1, 1969.

Okunev, V.V. Colonel General, USSR Army. Served on the Soviet-German Front in WW II. Commander, Moscow Air Defense District, 1965-70; Detached to Soviet Air Defense Forces, United Arab Republic, 1970-72. Member, Communist Party of the Soviet Union.

Olazabal, Conrado. Captain, Uruguayan Navy; Uruguayan Member, Inter-American Defense Board, 1973-   .

Olenchuk, Peter George. Major General, United States Army; Director of Materiel Acquisition, Office of the Deputy Chief of Staff for Logistics, 1973-   . Born July 14, 1922, in Bayonne, New Jersey. Attended Lebanon Valley College, BS, Chemistry and Biology; University of Wisconsin, MS, Bacteriology; George Washington University, MBA, Business Administration; Command and General Staff College; Industrial College of the Armed Forces, 1962-63. Commissioned Second Lieutenant June 9, 1945. Served in WW II. Staff Officer, Special Warfare Branch, later Chief of the Chemical Operations Branch, J-3, US Military Assistance Command, Vietnam, 1963-64; Member, Special Projects Branch, J-5, Joint Staff, Joint Chiefs of Staff Organization, 1964-66; Commanding Officer, US Army Biological Center and Fort Detrick, Maryland, 1966-68; Chief of Staff, US Army Munitions Command, Dover, New Jersey, 1968-70; Commanding General, US Army Ammunition Procurement and Supply Agency, Joliet, Illinois, 1970-72; Director of Plans, Doctrine and Systems, Office of the Deputy Chief of Staff for Logistics, 1972. Legion of Merit with three Oak Leaf Clusters; Air Medal with Oak Leaf Cluster; and other medals and awards. Promoted to Brigadier General August 1, 1970; Major General March 1, 1973.

Oleynik, G.G. Admiral, USSR Navy; Chief, Naval Logistics Service, 1967-   . Served in the Soviet-German War in 1941-45. Commander, Caspian Flotilla, 1955-56, and 1960-67. Member, Communist Party of the Soviet Union.

Olifirov, F.A. Colonel General, USSR Army; Commander, Baku Air Defense District, 1966-   . Served on the Soviet-German Front in WW II. Member, Communist Party of the Soviet Union.

Olin, Sven-Olof. Major General, Swedish Royal Air Force; Chief, Air Materiel Department, Defense Materiel Administration. Attended Royal Air Force Academy, 1947-48, 1949-50; Royal National Defense College, General Studies, 1965; Royal National Defense College, Staff Course, 1969. Chief, Air Force Test Center, 1959-66. Commander of the Royal Order of Sword; and other medals and awards. Promoted to Major General, 1968.

Oliwa, Wlodzimierz. Lieutenant General, Polish Army; Commanding General, Warsaw Military District. Attended Infantry Officers School; General Staff War College. Served on the Polish German Front, WW II. Formerly on the Staff, Silesian Military District; Chief, Intelligence Directorate General Staff. Member of Polish United Workers Party. Polonia Restituta; Cross of Grunwald; Cross of Merit; and other orders and medals.

Olnev, E. Major General, USSR Army; Deputy Commander, Northern Group of Soviet Forces, Poland. Served on the Soviet-German Front in WW II. Member, Communist Party of the Soviet Union.

Olson, Harry C. Major General, United States Marine Corps; Quartermaster General, US Marine Corps, 1972- , . Born January 27, 1918, Des Moines, Iowa. Drake University, BA, 1941; Reserve Officers Class, Marine Corps Schools, 1942; Industrial College of the Armed Forces, 1963-64; Navy Comptroller Course; Army Command Management School; George Washington University, MA, Business Administration. Commissioned Second Lieutenant, USMCR, 1941. Served in South Pacific, WW II; Korean War; Vietnam War. Force Supply Officer, Staff of the Commander in Chief, Fleet Marine Force, Pacific, 1964-67; Commanding General, Force Logistic Command, Vietnam, 1967-68; Commanding General, Marine Corps Supply Activity, Philadelphia, Pennsylvania, 1969-70; Commanding General, Marine Corps Supply Center Barstow, California, 1971-72. Legion of Merit with Combat "V" and Gold Star; Bronze Star Medal with Combat "V"; and other medals and awards. Promoted to Brigadier General, October 1, 1967; Major General, August 12, 1971.

Olson, Sven-Olof. Major General, Swedish Royal Air Force; Deputy Chief, Defense Staff, 1973-   . Attended Royal Air Force Academy, 1953-54; 1956-57; Royal National Defense College, 1969. Wing Commander F-16, 1971-73. Commander of the Royal Order of the Sword; and other medals and awards. Member of the Royal Academy of Military Sciences. Promoted to Major General, 1973.

Oprita, Constantin. Major General, Romanian Army; Deputy Secretary, Political Council of Armed Forces.

Ordoñez, Luis Arturo. Major General, Venezuelan Air Force; Commanding General, Venezuelan Air Force, 1971-   . Born April 23, 1922, in Ejido, Merida State. Attended Officer Candidate Training, Flight Instruction, 1944; Flying Training Course, Corpus Christi Naval Air Station, Texas, USA, 1945; General Staff Course, Superior War College, Peru, 1950-51; Superior Air Forces College, Spain, 1957-58. Commissioned Second Lieutenant, Venezuelan Air Force, in 1945. Director of Civil Aviation, Ministry of Communication, 1962-65; Chief, J-2, Joint General Staff, Armed Forces, 1965-67; Chief, J-4, Joint General Staff, Armed Forces, 1967-69; Chief of Air Staff, Venezuelan Air Force, 1969-71. Order of Liberator, Caballero grade; Cross of the Venezuelan Air Forces,

second class; Military Order General Rafael Urdaneta, third Class; Order of the Liberator, officer grade; Order of Aviation Merit, Antonio Ricaurte; Order of Naval Merit, second class; and other medals and awards. Promoted to Colonel, July 1962; Brigadier General, July 1967; Major General, July 1972.

Orël, E.A. Admiral, USSR Navy; Commandant, Naval War College, 1967-   . Born August 25, 1908, in St. Petersburg, Russia. Attended Voroshilov General Staff War College. Commissioned in 1929. Served in the Soviet-German War, 1941-45. Commander Baltic Fleet, 1959-67. Member, Communist Party of the Soviet Union since 1937; Deputy to USSR Supreme Soviet. Order of Lenin; Order of Red Banner; and other orders and awards.

Ornelas e Vasconcelow, Fernando. Admiral, Portuguese Navy; Chief of the Naval Staff.

Orr, Kenneth Dew. Major General, United States Army; Commanding General, Brooke Army Medical Center, and Commandant, US Army Medical Field Service School, Fort Sam Houston, Texas, 1970-   . Born November 1, 1913, Moscow, Idaho. University of Idaho, BS Degree, Zoology; MS Degree, Zoology; University of Chicago, MD Degree; Medical Field Service School, Basic Course. Commissioned Second Lieutenant, US Army Reserve, 1934. Served in WW II. Surgeon, US Army, Japan, and Commanding General, US Army Medical Command, Japan, 1966-68; Commanding General, William Beaumont General Hospital, El Paso, Texas, 1968-70. Distinguished Service Medal; Legion of Merit with two Oak Leaf Clusters; Bronze Star Medal with V Device; and other medals and awards. Promoted to Brigadier General, June 1, 1967; Major General, August 1, 1969.

Ortega Ortega, Jorge. Rear Admiral, Ecuadorean Navy; Delegate, Inter-American Defense Board. Promoted to Rear Admiral December 20, 1972.

Osborn, James Butler. Rear Admiral, United States Navy; Director, Strategic Offensive and Defensive Systems, Office of the Chief of Naval Operations, 1970-   . Born May 5, 1918, Stockton, Missouri. University of Missouri, Columbia, 1936-38; US Naval Academy, 1938-41; Submarine School, New London, Connecticut, 1944; Naval Postgraduate School, Annapolis, 1946-47; Rensselaer Polytechnic Institute, MS, Mechanical Engineering, 1947-48; Naval War College, 1957-58. Commissioned Ensign, US Navy, 1941. Served in the Pacific Theater, WW II; Vietnam War. Commanding Officer, USS *Simon Lake* (AS-33), 1964-66; Chief of Staff and Aide to Commander Submarine Force US Atlantic Fleet, 1966-67; Ad Hoc Vice Chairman, Joint Chiefs of Staff Special Studies Group, 1967-68; Commander, Naval Support Activity, Danang, Vietnam, 1968-69; Commander Submarine Flotilla SIX, 1969-70; Assistant Chief of Naval Operations (Safety), 1970. Distinguished Service Medal; Legion of Merit with Gold Star; and other US and foreign medals and awards. Promoted to Rear Admiral, August 1, 1968.

Osman bin Tunku Mohd, Jewa. General, Malaysian Army; Chief of Staff, Malaysian Armed Forces and Chairman, Joint National Operations Command. Born November 24, 1919. Attended Sultan Abdul Hamid College. Commissioned in 1945. Commander, 2d Battalion, Royal Malay Regiment, 1958; Commander, 2d Federal Infantry Brigade, 1960; Chief of Staff, Malaysian Armed Forces, 1964. Johan Mangku Negara; Panglima Mangku Negara; National Order, 2d Class, Vietnam; and other medals and awards from Malaya and other nations. Promoted to Brigadier, 1961; Major General, 1964; General, 1966.

Ott, David Ewing. Major General, United States Army, Commanding General, US Army Field Artillery Center, and Commandant, US Army Field Artillery School, Fort Sill, 1973- . Born July 31, 1922, Schofield Barracks, Hawaii. US Military Academy; The Field Artillery School, Basic Course; The Artillery School, Advanced Course; US Army Command and General Staff College; US Army War College; George Washington University, MA, International Affairs. Commissioned Second Lieutenant, US Army, 1944. Served in WW II and Vietnam War. Commanding Officer, 25th Infantry Division Artillery, US Army, Pacific-Vietnam, 1967; Chief, Artillery Branch, Officer Personnel Directorate, Office of Personnel Operations, US Army, Washington, D.C., 1967-68; Commanding General, US Army Support, Thailand, US Army, Pacific-Thailand, 1968-70; Deputy for Intelligence, Office of Assistant Chief of Staff, Intelligence, US Army, Washington, D.C., 1970-72; Director, Vietnam Task Force, Office of the Assistant Secretary of Defense (International Security Affairs), Washington, D.C., 1972-73. Distinguished Service Medal with Oak Leaf Cluster; Legion of Merit with three Oak Leaf Clusters; Distinguished Flying Cross; Bronze Star Medal with Oak Leaf Cluster; and other medals and awards. Promoted to Brigadier General, August 1, 1969; Major General, October 1, 1971.

Ovcharenko, I. Lieutenant General, USSR Army; Chief, Political Directorate, Volga Military District, 1971- . Served on the Soviet-German Front in WW II. Member, Communist Party of the Soviet Union.

Ovcharov, A. Major General, Armor, USSR Army; Military Commissar, Volgograd Region (Oblast). Served on the Soviet-German Front in WW II. Member, Communist Party of the Soviet Union.

Oveisi, Gholam Ali. General, Imperial Iranian Army; Commanding General, Ground Forces. Born in 1918, in Teheran. Attended Military Officers College, Teheran, 1938; War College, Teheran. Commissioned in the Imperial Iranian Army, 1938. Commander, Home Guard; Commander, Central (Teheran) Forces; Commander in Chief, Gendarmerie; Member of His Imperial Majesty's Entourage. Promoted to General, 1969.

Overmyer, Robert F. Major, US Marine Corps; NASA Astronaut, 1969- . Born July 14, 1936, Lorain, Ohio. Baldwin-Wallace College, BS, Physics, 1958; US Naval Postgraduate School, MS, Aeronautics, 1964; US Air Force Aerospace Research Pilot School, 1965-66. Commissioned Second Lieutenant, US Marine Corps, December 1957. VMA-214; Marine Aircraft Maintenance Squadron-17, Iwakuni, Japan; Member, US Air Force Manned Orbiting Laboratory Program. NASA experience: Member, Support Crew, Apollo 17; Member, Apollo-Soyuz Test Project Mission, July 1975. Baldwin-Wallace College Alumni Merit Award.

Owen, John Ivor Headon. Major-General, British Royal Marines; Major-General, Commando Forces Royal Marines, Plymouth, 1972- . Born October 22, 1922. Attended Marine Staff College; Joint Services Staff College; Imperial Defence College, 1971-72. Commissioned Second Lieutenant (temporary) in 1942; inactive, 1946-47; rejoined in 1947. Served in Far East in WW II. Naval Plans Staff, Admiralty, Ministry of Defence, 1962-64; 42 Commando, Royal Marines, 1964-66; Instructor, Joint Services Staff College, 1966-67; Commanding Officer, 45 Commando, Royal Marines, 1967-68; Staff of Commanding General, Royal Marines, 1969-70. OBE. Promoted to Major-General in 1972.

P

Page, Charles Edward. Major-General, British Army; Director, Combat Development (Army), 1971- . Born August 23, 1920. Attended Marlborough College; Trinity College, Cambridge; BS (English), London, 1949; Royal Military College of Science, 1947-49; Staff College, 1951; NATO Defence College, 1965-66. Commissioned in the Royal Signals in 1941. Served in the Guards Armoured Divisional Signals in WW II. Commanding Officer, 1st Division Signal Regiment, 1963-65; Commander Corps Royal Signals, 1st (British) Corps, 1966-68; Secretary, NATO Military Committee, Brussels, 1968-70. MBE. Chartered Engineer; Fellow of the Institution of Electrical Engineers.

Pain, Horace Rollo Squarey. Major General, British Army; Director, Army Training, 1972- . Born May 11, 1921. Attended Staff College, Camberley, 1951; Imperial Defence College, 1968. Commissioned in Reconnaissance Corps. Served in Europe in WW II. Commander, Regiment of Royal Dragoons, British Army of the Rhine, 1962-64; Commander, Division, Staff College, Camberley, 1964; Commander, 5 Infantry Brigade, Borneo, 1965-68; Aide-de-Camp to the Queen, 1969; Brigadier, General Staff, Headquarters, British Army of the Rhine, 1969-70; General Officer Commanding, 2d Division, 1970-72. MC. Promoted to Brigadier, 1965; Major General, 1970.

Paladini, Dante. Brigadier, Uruguayan Air Force; Chief of Staff, Uruguayan Air Force.

Palmer, Bruce, Jr. General, United States Army; Commander in Chief, US Readiness Command, MacDill Air

Force Base, Florida, 1973-   . Born April 13, 1913, Austin, Texas. US Military Academy; The Cavalry School, Advanced Course; US Army War College. Commissioned Second Lieutenant, 1936. Served in WW II and Vietnam War. Deputy Chief of Staff for Military Operations, US Army, Washington, D.C., 1964-65; Deputy Chief of Staff for Military Operations, US Army, and Commanding General, US Forces, Dominican Republic, 1965; Commanding General, XVIII Airborne Corps, Dominican Republic, later Fort Bragg, North Carolina, 1965-67; Commanding General, II Field Force, US Army, Pacific-Vietnam, 1967; Deputy Commanding General, US Army, Vietnam, US Army, Pacific-Vietnam, 1967-68; Vice Chief of Staff, US Army, Washington, D.C., 1968-73. Distinguished Service Medal with three Oak Leaf Clusters; Silver Star; Legion of Merit; Bronze Star; and other medals and awards. Promoted to Brigadier General, August 1, 1959; Major General, May 1, 1962; Lieutenant General, August 1, 1964; General, August 1, 1968.

Palmer, James Alexander. Rear Admiral, United States Coast Guard; Chief, Office of Public and International Affairs, 1973-   . Born January 23, 1917, Climax Springs, Missouri. US Coast Guard Academy, 1937-41; Flight Training Courses, 1942-43; Naval Academy Post-Graduate School, Applied Communications Course, 1949-50. Commissioned Ensign, 1941; designated Coast Guard Aviator, 1943. Served in Atlantic and Pacific Theaters, WW II. Commander, Coast Guard Base, Charleston, South Carolina, 1966-67; Assistant Superintendent and Chief of Staff, US Coast Guard Academy, 1967-70; Commander, 17th Coast Guard District, Juneau, Alaska, 1970-73. Coast Guard Commendation Medal; WW II service medals and ribbons. Promoted to Captain, July 1, 1962; Rear Admiral, June 1, 1970.

Palmstierna, Nils-Fredrik. Major General, Swedish Royal Air Force; Chief of Staff, Military Command East, 1973-   . Attended Royal Air Force Academy, 1947-49; Royal National Defense College, 1959, 1970. Wing Commander, 1963-67. Commander of the Royal Order of the Sword; Knight of the Royal Order of Wasa; Knight of the Order of Orange-Nassau. Member of the Royal Academy of Military Sciences. Promoted to Major General, 1970.

Panggabean Maradem. General, Indonesian Army; Minister of State for Defense and Security Affairs; Indonesia.

Papadopoulos, George. Brigadier General, Hellenic Army, Retired; President of Greece and Commander in Chief Hellenic Armed Forces, 1973. Born in 1919, Eleochorion, Achaia, Greece. Attended Military Academy; Army Engineer School, 1950; Army Senior War College, Thessaloniki, 1955; Navy Senior War College, Athens, 1956; Armed Forces Special Weapons School, 1958. Commissioned Second Lieutenant, Hellenic Army, 1940. Served in the Albanian Campaign, 1940-41; Member, Resistance Organization during German occupation of

Greece, 1941-44; fought against Communist guerrillas, 1948-49. Intelligence Division, Army General Staff, 1955-57; Chief of Staff, Artillery Command, VI Infantry Division; General Intelligence Service, 1959-64; Commander, 117th Field Artillery Battalion, 1964-65; Staff, 1st Field Army, 1965-67; Operations Division, Army General Staff, 1967; Minister to the Prime Minister, 1967; Prime Minister and Minister of National Defense, 1967-73. Gold Medal of Gallantry; Silver Cross of the Royal Order of King George I, with Swords; Gold Cross of the Royal Order of King George I, with Swords; Commander of the Royal Order of the Phoenix; War Cross (awarded four times); Medal for Distinguished Acts; Medal of Military Merit; and other medals and awards. Promoted to Lieutenant Colonel, June 13, 1957; Colonel, August 7, 1966; Brigadier General, December 20, 1967; Retired from the Army, December 20, 1967.

Papanikolau, Alexander. Major General, Hellenic Air Force; Commander 28th Tactical Air Force, 1971-   ,   . Born September 16, 1927, Kastelia, Department of Phokis, Greece. Hellenic Air Force Air Academy, 1947-49; Flying Instructors School; Instrument Flying School; Jet Aircraft Transition Course, USA, 1951; Air Gunnery Instructors Course, USA, 1952; F-84G Transition Course; F-84F Transition Course; Programming, Planning and Budgeting System Center, USA; Hellenic National Defense College, 1966-67; NATO Special Weapons School; F-5 Transition Course. Commissioned Second Lieutenant, Hellenic Air Force, January 15, 1949. Section Head, Directorate of Training, and Chairman, Hellenic Air Force Standardization and Evaluation Committee, Directorate of Operations, 1962-64; Commander 115th Combat Wing, 1964-66; Director of Operations, Hellenic Air Force Command, 1967-68; Director, Division "A" (Operations), Hellenic Air Force Command, 1968-69; Assistant Chief of Staff, Plans and Operations, NATO Headquarters, Naples, Italy, 1969-71. Golden Cross of the Royal Order of George I; Knight Commander of the Royal Order of Phoenix; Commander of the Royal Order of Phoenix; Golden Cross of the Royal Order of Phoenix; War Cross, 1st and 3d Class; Medal for Military Value, 1st Class; and other medals and awards. Colonel, June 20, 1966; Brigadier General, March 22, 1968; Major General, June 10, 1971.

Pardi Davila, Gustavo. Major General, Venezuelan Army; Minister of Defense, Venezuela, 1973-   . Born November 19, 1923, in Merida, State of Merida. Attended Venezuelan Military Academy; Advanced Infantry Course, Senior Officers School, Rio de Janeiro, Brazil, 1953-54; Superior War School, Chorrillos, Peru, 1956-58. Commissioned Second Lieutenant, Venezuelan Army, in 1944. Chief, Section 4 (logistics), Army General Staff, 1963-64; Commander, 1st Division, San Cristobal, 1964-67; Commander, 5th Division, Maturin, 1967-68; Commander, 3d Division, Barquisimeto, 1968-69; Chief, Joint Operations Center, Ministry of Defense, 1969-70; Chief, Armed Forces Intelligence Service, 1970-72; Chief of Staff, Joint General Staff, 1972-73. Military Order of General Rafael Urdaneta (bronze); Cross of the Venezuelan Ground

Forces, second and third class; Order of the Liberator; and other orders and awards. Promoted to Colonel, January 1963; Brigadier General, July 1967; Major General, July 5, 1972.

Paredes, A. Isaias. Rear Admiral, Peruvian Navy; Delegate, Inter-American Defense Board. Date of Rank: January 1, 1972.

Parfitt, Harold Robert. Major General, United States Army; Division Engineer, US Army Engineer Division, Southwest, Dallas, Texas, 1969-   . Born August 6, 1921, Coaldale, Pennsylvania. US Military Academy; Engineer School, Basic Course; US Army Command and General Staff College; Canadian National Defense College; Massachusetts Institute of Technology, MS Degree, Civil Engineering. Commissioned Second Lieutenant, 1943. Served in WW II and Vietnam War. Lieutenant Governor of the Canal Zone and Vice President of the Panama Canal Company, Balboa Heights, Canal Zone, 1965-68; Commanding Officer, 20th Engineer Brigade, US Army, Pacific-Vietnam, 1968-69. Distinguished Service Medal; Legion of Merit with Oak Leaf Cluster; Bronze Star Medal; and other medals and awards. Promoted to Brigadier General, August 1, 1969; Major General, July 1, 1971.

Parker, David Stuart. Major General, United States Army; Governor of the Canal Zone, and President, Panama Canal Company, Balboa Heights, Canal Zone, 1971-   . Born March 22, 1919, Fort Huachuca, Arizona. US Military Academy; US Army War College; University of California, MS Degree, Civil Engineering. Commissioned Second Lieutenant, 1940. Served in WW II and Vietnam War. Division Engineer, US Army Engineer Division, North Atlantic, New York, New York, 1965-66; Director, Force Planning and Analysis, Office, Assistant Vice Chief of Staff, US Army, Washington, D.C., 1966-68; Engineer, US Army, Vietnam, and Commanding General, Engineer Troops, Vietnam, US Army, Pacific-Vietnam, 1968-69; Chairman, Special Review Panel, Office, Chief of Staff, US Army, Washington, D.C., 1969-71. Distinguished Service Medal with Oak Leaf Cluster; Legion of Merit; and other medals and awards. Promoted to Brigadier General, August 1, 1965; Major General, September 1, 1967.

Parker, Harold Edward. Major General, United States Army; Assistant Judge Advocate General, US Army, Washington, D.C., 1971-   . Born March 25, 1918, Canton, New York. Cornell University, BA Degree, Economics; The Field Artillery School, Basic and Advanced Courses; US Army Command and General Staff College; US Army War College; Stanford University, JD Degree. Commissioned Second Lieutenant, US Army Reserve, 1939. Served in WW II. Staff Judge Advocate, Office, US Commander, Berlin/Commanding General, US Army, Berlin, 1964-67; Assistant Judge Advocate General for Military Law, Office, The Judge Advocate General, Washington, D.C., 1967-71. Legion of Merit; and other medals and awards. Promoted to Brigadier General, August 1, 1968; Major General, July 1, 1971.

Parker, Robert Allan Ridley. United States; NASA Scientist-Astronaut, 1967-   . Born December 14, 1936, New York, New York. Amherst College, BA, Astronomy and Physics, 1958; California Institute of Technology, PhD, Astronomy, 1962; NASA Flight Training Course. Associate Professor of Astronomy, University of Wisconsin. NASA experience: Member, Support Crew, Apollo 15 and 17. NASA Group Achievement Award.

Parra Ramirez, Jaime. Admiral, Colombian Navy; Commander of the National Fleet, 1967-   . Born August 20, 1921, Pamplona (Santander del Norte). Naval Command Course, War College; General Line Officers Course (Newport, Rhode Island, USA); Naval War College (USA); Advanced Military Studies, War College. Commissioned November 11, 1943. Participated in Korean War. Orden de Boyacá (Gran Oficial); Medalla Militar Antonio Nariño (Comendador); Medalla Militar Francisco José de Caldas (Al Mérito); Orden Naval Almirante Padilla (Comendador); Orden del Mérito Militar José Maria Cordoba (Comendador); Medalla Militar José Antonio Ricaurte (Gran Oficial); and other medals and awards, Colombian and from other nations. Promoted to Rear Admiral, 30 June 1966; Vice Admiral, 30 June 1969; Admiral, 30 June 1972.

Parshikov, A. Colonel General, USSR Army; Chief Representative, Warsaw Pact High Command, Bulgaria, 1972-   . Served on the Soviet-German Front in WW II. Chief of Staff, Leningrad Military District until 1968; Commander, Volga Military District, 1968-71. Member, Communist Party of the Soviet Union.

Paschall, James E. Major General, United States Air Force; Deputy Chief of Staff, Plans and Programs (J-5), North American Air Defense Command/Continental Air Defense Command (NORAD/CONAD), Ent Air Force Base, Colorado, 1973-   . Born March 31, 1923, in LaGrange, North Carolina. US Military Academy, 1942-46; Advanced Pilot Training Course, 1946; Air Force Institute of Technology, Wright-Patterson Air Force Base, Ohio, BS, Aeronautical Engineering, 1951; George Washington University, Washington, D.C., MBS, 1961; Industrial College of the Armed Forces, 1964-65. Commissioned Second Lieutenant, US Army Air Corps, in 1946. Chief of Special Projects, Directorate of Science and Technology, later Executive Officer, Directorate of Development, Deputy Chief of Staff, Research and Development, Headquarters US Air Force, 1965-68; Vice Commander, then Commander, Air Force Special Weapons Center, Kirtland Air Force Base, New Mexico, 1968-70; Deputy Commander, 22d North American Air Defense Command, North Bay, Ontario, Canada, 1970-73. Legion of Merit and Air Force Commendation Medal. Promoted to Brigadier General, August 1, 1970; Major General, February 1, 1972.

Paschall, Lee M. Major General, United States Air Force; Director of Command Control and Communications, Headquarters US Air Force, 1971-   . Born January 21, 1922, in Sterling, Colorado. University of Colorado; Air

Command and Staff School, Communications-Electronics Officers Course, 1951; University of Alabama, BA, History, 1957; Air War College, 1963-64; George Washington University, MA, International Affairs, 1964. Commissioned Second Lieutenant, Infantry, 1942. Combat duty in the European Theater, WW II. Assistant Director, Defense Communications System Programs and Requirements, 1964-65; Executive Officer to the Deputy Director, Defense Communications System, 1966-67; Commander, United Kingdom Communications Region (AFCS), 1967-68; Deputy Director, Command Control and Communications, Headquarters USAF, 1968-71. Promoted to Major General, August 1, 1971.

Pascual Sanz, Ramiro. Lieutenant General, Spanish Air Force; Chief, Air Defense Command, 1973- . Diplomate of Air Force Staff. Formerly Chief 2d and 3d Sections, Air Force Staff; Chief, University Air Militia; Commander 3d Wing and Villanubla (Valladolid) Air Force Base; Chief of Staff, 2d Air Region (Seville) and Commander Tactical Air Force; Undersecretary of the Air Force. Great Crosses: Army, Navy and Air Force Merit and Saint Hermenegild Royal and Military Order; Cross of Merit of Eagle Order (Germany); Military Medal (Portugal); and other medals and awards. Promoted to Lieutenant General, April 10, 1973. Vice President of "Esteban Terradas" National Institute of Aerospace Technology; Vice President of National Committee for Space Research.

Pashchuk, K. Major General, USSR Army. Served on the Soviet-German Front in WW II. Chief of Staff, Siberian Military District, 1969-72; Member, Communist Party of the Soviet Union.

Paszkowski, Roman. Lieutenant General, Polish Air Force; Commanding General, Air Defense Forces, 1967- . Attended Air Force Officers School; General Staff War College. Formerly member of the Staff, Air Defense Forces. Member of Polish United Workers Party. Polonia Restituta; Cross of Grunwald; Cross of Merit; and other orders and medals. Promoted to Major General, 1961; Lieutenant General, 1970.

Patayakul, Samran. General, Royal Thai Army. Assistant Commander in Chief, Royal Thai Army.

Patch, Paul F. Brigadier General, US Air Force; Deputy Chief of Staff for Logistics, Headquarters Military Airlift Command, 1972- . Born May 28, 1920, in Denver, Colorado. University of Denver, 1939-41; University of Maryland, 1961; George Washington University, MA. Commissioned Second Lieutenant, US Army Air Corps, 1942. Combat duty in the Vietnam War. Successively Director of Transportation, Chief, Transportation Division, and Chief, Logistics Plans Division, Directorate of Materiel, Headquarters Pacific Air Forces, 1964-67; Chief, Plans Division, Office of Special Assistant for Strategic Mobility, Joint Chiefs of Staff Organization, 1967-69; Deputy Chief of Staff for Materiel, Headquarters Seventh Air Force, Vietnam, 1969-70; Deputy Chief of Staff for Logistics,

Headquarters Military Airlift Command, 1970-72. Legion of Merit with two Oak Leaf Clusters; Air Force Commendation Medal; and other medals and awards. Promoted to Brigadier General, October 1, 1969.

Patou, André. Admiral, French Navy; Chief of Naval Staff, 1968- . Born July 5, 1910, Parthenay, France. Attended Naval Academy. Commissioned Lieutenant Commander, French Navy, 1939. Served in Free French Naval Forces, WW II. Commander 1st Flotilla of Squadron Escort Vessels, 1958; Squadron Commander; Maritime Prefect, 2d Naval District, 1965; Member, Superior Naval Council, 1963-70. Grand Officier Légion d'Honneur; Compagnon de la Libération; Croix de Guerre; Distinguished Service Order (GB); Distinguished Service Cross (USA); and other medals and awards. Promoted to Vice Admiral, 1959; Admiral, 1965.

Patterson, Robert A. Lieutenant General, United States Air Force; Surgeon General, United States Air Force, 1972- . Born September 3, 1915, in Palestine, Illinois. University of Illinois, Urbana, 1935; School of Medicine, University of Louisville, Kentucky, MD, 1939. Commissioned First Lieutenant, US National Guard, 1940; transferred to US Army Medical Corps, 1946; transferred to US Air Force Medical Service, 1949. Served in the European Theater, WW II. Director, Plans Hospitalization, Office, Surgeon General, Headquarters USAF, 1965-68; Surgeon, Headquarters, US Air Forces, Europe (USAFE), Germany, 1968-71; Surgeon, Headquarters, Strategic Air Command, 1971-72. Distinguished Service Medal; Legion of Merit with one Oak Leaf Cluster; and other medals and awards. Promoted to Brigadier General, April 21, 1966; Major General, February 24, 1970; Lieutenant General, August 1, 1972.

Pattillo, Charles C. Major General, United States Air Force; Deputy Director, Logistics (J-4), the Joint Staff, Joint Chiefs of Staff Organization, 1971- . Born June 3, 1924, in Atlanta, Georgia. Army Air Corps Flying School, 1942-44; Georgia School of Technology, 1946-47; University of Colorado, BA, Mathematics, 1962; US Army War College, 1964-65; George Washington University, MA, International Affairs, 1965. Commissioned in 1944. Combat duty in the European Theater, WW II; Vietnam War. Director, Operations and Training, Headquarters Seventeenth Air Force, Germany, 1965-67; Commander, 36th Tactical Fighter Wing, Germany, 1967-68; Vice Commander and later Commander, 8th Tactical Fighter Wing, Thailand, 1968-69; Vice Commander, Oklahoma City Air Materiel Area, 1969-71. Legion of Merit with three Oak Leaf Clusters; Distinguished Flying Cross with one Oak Leaf Cluster; and other US and foreign medals and awards. Promoted to Major General, May 1, 1972.

Pattillo, Cuthbert A. Major General, United States Air Force; Director of Operations, US Air Force Deputy Chief of Staff, Plans and Operations, 1973- . Born June 3, 1924, in Atlanta, Georgia. Army Air Corps Flying School, 1942-44; Georgia Institute of Technology, 1946-47;

University of Colorado, 1959-62, BA, Mathematics, 1962; Army War College, 1964-65; George Washington University, MA, International Affairs, 1965. Commissioned in 1944. Combat duty in the European Theater, WW II, POW; Vietnam War. Operations Staff Officer, Executive Office, Policy and Plans Branch Chief, and Operations Division Chief, 4450th Standardization and Evaluation Group, 1962-64; Deputy Commander, Operations, 50th Tactical Fighter Wing, 1965-67; Director, Safety, United States Air Forces, Europe, Germany, 1967-68; Vice Commander, 3d Tactical Fighter Wing, Vietnam, 1968; Vice Commander and later Commander, 31st Tactical Fighter Wing, Vietnam, 1968-69; Assistant Deputy Chief of Staff, Plans, Headquarters Tactical Air Command, 1969-70; Assistant Deputy Chief of Staff, Operations, for Operations and Training, Tactical Air Command, 1970-72; Deputy Director of Operations, US Air Force Deputy Chief of Staff, Plans and Operations, 1972-73. Silver Star; Legion of Merit with one Oak Leaf Cluster; Distinguished Flying Cross with one Oak Leaf Cluster; and other US and foreign medals and awards. Promoted to Brigadier General, August 1, 1970; Major General, September 1, 1972.

Patton, George Smith. Major General, United States Army; Director, J-7, US European Command, 1973-   . Born December 24, 1923, Boston, Massachusetts. US Military Academy; The Infantry School; The Armored School; Army Command and General Staff College; Armed Forces Staff College; Army War College; George Washington University, MS, International Affairs; Army Primary Helicopter School; Army Aviation School. Commissioned June 4, 1946. Served in the Vietnam War. Chief, Operations Branch, Far East and Pacific Division, Office of Deputy Chief of Staff for Military Operations, 1967; Chief, Force Developments Branch, Office of Assistant Chief of Staff, G-3, US Army, Vietnam, 1968; Acting Deputy Assistant Chief of Staff, G-3, US Army, Vietnam, 1968; Commanding Officer, 11th Armored Cavalry Regiment, US Army, Vietnam, 1968-69; Assistant Division Commander, 4th Armored Division, US Army, Europe, 1970-71; Assistant Commandant, US Army Armor School, Fort Knox, Kentucky, 1971-73. Distinguished Service Cross with Oak Leaf Cluster; Silver Star with Oak Leaf Cluster; Legion of Merit with two Oak Leaf Clusters; Distinguished Flying Cross; Bronze Star Medal with V Device and Oak Leaf Cluster; and other medals and awards. Promoted to Brigadier General, June 1, 1970; Major General, July 14, 1973.

Patton, John S. Major General, United States Air Force; Military Advisor to the Chairman, and Executive Officer, Reserve Forces Policy Board, Office of the Secretary of Defense, 1969-   . Born January 18, 1918, in Carthage, Missouri. University of Southern California, BS, Marketing; National War College, 1955-56; American University, PhD, International Relations, 1963. Commissioned Ensign, US Naval Reserve, 1942; Transferred to Air Force Reserve, 1949. Combat duty in the Pacific and European Theaters, WW II. Consultant to the Assistant Chief of Staff, Studies and Analysis, Headquarters USAF, 1964-67; Special

Advisor to the Assistant Administrator, Policy, National Aeronautics and Space Administration, 1967-68; Assistant to the Director of Doctrine, Concepts and Objectives, Deputy Chief of Staff, Plans and Operations, Headquarters USAF, 1968-69. Legion of Merit; and other medals and awards. Promoted to Major General, May 19, 1967.

Pauly, John W. Major General, United States Air Force; Commander, 1st Strategic Aerospace Division, Vandenberg Air Force Base, 1973-   . Born March 12, 1923, in Albany, New York. Rensselaer Polytechnic Institute, Troy, New York; US Military Academy, 1942-45; National War College, 1964-65; George Washington University, MS, International Relations, 1965. Commissioned in 1945. Combat duty in the Korean War; Vietnam War. Assistant Executive Officer to Chief of Staff, US Air Force, 1962-64; Deputy Commander, Operations, 317th Troop Carrier Wing (TAC), 1965-66; Assistant Deputy Chief of Staff, Operations, and later Deputy Chief of Staff, Operations, 315th Air Division, Japan, 1966-68; Commander, 315th Air Commando Wing, and later Commander, 315th Special Operations Wing, Vietnam, 1968-69; Air Force Member of the Chairman's Staff Group, Office of the Chairman, Joint Chiefs of Staff Organization, 1969-71; Deputy Director, Operations, J-3, the Joint Staff, Joint Chiefs of Staff Organization, 1971-72; Vice Director, Operations, J-3, Joint Staff, Organization of Joint Chiefs of Staff, 1972-73. Legion of Merit with two Oak Leaf Clusters; Distinguished Flying Cross with one Oak Leaf Cluster; and other medals and awards. Promoted to Brigadier General, August 1, 1970; Major General, August 1, 1972.

Pavlovskiy, Ivan Grigoryevich. General of the Army, USSR Army; Deputy Minister of Defense, and Commander in Chief, Ground Forces, 1967-   . Born in 1909 in Ternovka, Kamenets-Podolsk Oblast. Attended Agricultural Technical School; Voroshilov General Staff War College. Joined the Soviet Army, 1931. Served on the Soviet-German Front in WW II. Commander, Platoon, Company, Battalion, 1932-41; Commander, Infantry Regiment; Commander, Infantry Brigade and later Division, 1943-52; Commander, Corps, 1952-55; First Deputy Commander, Transcaucasian Military District, 1958-61; Commander, Volga Military District, 1961-64; Commander, Far Eastern Military District, 1964-67. Hero of the Soviet Union; two Orders of Lenin; five Orders of Red Banner; Order of Suvorov; Order of Kutuzov; and other orders and awards. Promoted to General of the Army, 1967.

Pearce, Leslie Arthur. Major General, Royal New Zealand Army; Chief of Army General Staff, 1971-   . Born in 1918, in Auckland. Attended Staff College, Camberley, 1947-49; Imperial Defence College, 1966-67. Commissioned in 1941. Served in the Middle East and Italy in WW II and in Malaysia, 1961-63; Instructor, Australian Staff College, Queenscliff, 1957-60; Commandant, The Army Schools, 1960-61; Commanding Officer, 1st Royal New Zealand Infantry Regiment, Malaysia, 1961-63; Quartermaster General, 1968-69; Project Leader for Reorganization, Defence Headquarters, 1969-70; Deputy

Chief, Defence Staff, Defence Headquarters, 1970-71. Commander of the British Empire, and other honors and awards. Promoted to Brigadier, 1968; Major General, October 1, 1971.

Pearson, Cedric Maudsley Ingram. Major General, Royal Australian Army; Chief of Personnel, 1972- . Born August 24, 1918, Kurri Kurri, NSW. Newington College, Sydney; Royal Military College, Duntroon, 1937-40. Commissioned in 1940. Served in WW II; Vietnam War. Director, Military Intelligence, 1964-65; Commander, Australian Army Force Far East Land Forces, Singapore, 1966-68; with Australian Task Force, Vietnam, 1968-69; Commander, 1st Division, 1969; Commandant, Royal Military College, Duntroon, 1970-72. OBE; DSO; MC.

Pearson, Helmer Sheppard. Rear Admiral, United States Coast Guard; Commander, 1st Coast Guard District, Boston, Massachusetts, 1973- . Born November 20, 1916, Fairfield, Alabama. Marion Military Institute, Marion, Alabama; US Coast Guard Academy, 1937-41; Massachusetts Institute of Technology, Radar Course, 1943, MS Degree, Electronics Engineering, 1949. Commissioned Ensign, 1941. Served in Atlantic and Pacific Theaters, WW II. Chief, Engineering Division, 5th Coast Guard District, Portsmouth, Virginia, 1965-67; Chief, Operations Division, 5th Coast Guard District, 1967-68; Deputy Chief, Office of Engineering, Headquarters, US Coast Guard, 1968-69; Chief, Office of Engineering, 1969-72. WW II campaign service medals and ribbons. Promoted to Captain, February 1, 1962; Rear Admiral, January 31, 1969.

Pearson, Rufus Judson, Jr. Rear Admiral, Medical Corps, United States Navy; Attending Physician, the US Capitol, 1966- . Born October 8, 1915, Atlanta, Georgia. Emory University School of Medicine, Atlanta, Georgia, MD. Commissioned Lieutenant (j.g.), Medical Corps, US Naval Reserve, 1942; transferred to US Navy, 1951. Served in the European Theater, WW II. Chief of Medicine, Naval Hospital, Charleston, South Carolina, 1961-63; Chief of Naval Hospital, Portsmouth, Virginia, 1963-65; Professional Assistant to the Commanding Officer, Naval Hospital, Bethesda, Maryland, 1965-66. Various medals and awards. Promoted to Rear Admiral, Medical Corps, March 20, 1967.

Pearson, Sir Thomas (Cecil Hook). General, British Army; Commander-in-Chief, Allied Forces, Northern Europe, 1972- . Born July 1, 1914. Royal Military Academy, Sandhurst; Staff College, 1952; Joint Services Staff College, 1950; National Defence College, Canada, 1956-57. Commissioned Second Lieutenant, Rifle Brigade, 1934. Served in the Middle East and Europe in WW II. Major-General Commanding, 1st Division, British Army of the Rhine, 1961-63; Chief of Staff, Northern Army Group, 1963-67; Commander, Far East Land Forces, 1967-68; Military Secretary, Ministry of Defence, 1968-72. KCB; CBE; DSO and Bar.

Pearson, Willard. Lieutenant General, United States Army; Commanding General, V Corps, US Army, Europe, 1971- . Born July 4, 1915, West Elizabeth, Pennsylvania. Columbia University, MS Degree, Personnel Administration; The Infantry School, Advanced Course; US Army Command and General Staff College; US Army War College; George Washington University, MA Degree, International Affairs. Commissioned Second Lieutenant, US Army Reserve, 1936. Served in WW II and Vietnam War. Assistant Division Commander, 101st Airborne Division, Fort Campbell, Kentucky, 1965-66; Commanding General, 1st Brigade, 101st Airborne Division, US Army, Pacific-Vietnam, 1966-67; Assistant Chief of Staff, Operations, J-3, US Military Assistance Command, Vietnam, 1967-68; Director of Individual Training, Office, Deputy Chief of Staff for Personnel, US Army, Washington, D.C., 1968-69; Commanding General, US Army Training Center (Infantry) and Fort Lewis, Washington, 1969-71. Distinguished Service Medal with Oak Leaf Cluster; Silver Star with two Oak Leaf Clusters; Legion of Merit with three Oak Leaf Clusters; Bronze Star Medal with two Oak Leaf Clusters; and other medals and awards. Promoted to Brigadier General, July 1, 1963; Major General, April 1, 1967; Lieutenant General, March 1, 1971.

Peek, Richard Innes. Rear Admiral, Royal Australian Navy; Chief, Naval Staff, 1970- . Born July 30, 1914, in Tamworth, NSW. Attended Penrith, and Royal Australian Naval College. Served in the Pacific Theater in WW II; Korean War. Commander, HMAS *Melbourne*, 1962; Fourth Naval Member, Australian Naval Board, 1964; Deputy Chief, Naval Staff, 1965-66; Flag Officer Commanding HMA Fleet, 1967; Second Naval Member, Australian Naval Board, 1968-70. CB; OBE; DSC; Legion of Merit (USA).

Peers, William Raymond. Lieutenant General, United States Army; Deputy Commanding General, Eighth US Army, US Army, Pacific-Korea, 1971- . Born June 14, 1914, Stuart, Iowa. The Infantry School, Battalion Command Course; US Army War College. Commissioned Second Lieutenant, US Army Reserve, 1937. Served in WW II and Vietnam War. Assistant Deputy Chief of Staff for Military Operations (Special Operations), US Army, Washington, D.C., 1964-65; Special Assistant for Counterinsurgency and Special Activities, Organization, Joint Chiefs of Staff, Washington, D.C., 1965-66; Commanding General, 4th Infantry Division, US Army, Pacific-Vietnam, 1966-68; Deputy, later Commanding General, I Field Force, Vietnam, US Army, Pacific-Vietnam, 1968-69; Chief, Office of Reserve Components, US Army, Washington, D.C., 1969-71. Distinguished Service Medal with two Oak Leaf Clusters; Silver Star; Legion of Merit with three Oak Leaf Clusters; Distinguished Flying Cross; Bronze Star Medal with Oak Leaf Cluster; and other medals and awards. Promoted to Brigadier General, April 1, 1962; Major General, October 1, 1964; Lieutenant General, June 26, 1968.

Peet, Raymond Edward. Vice Admiral, United States Navy; Deputy Assistant Secretary of Defense (Security

Assistance) and Director of the Defense Security Assistance Agency, 1972- . Born January 27, 1921, Oneonta, New York. US Naval Academy, 1939-42; Gunnery Officers Ordnance School, 1944-45; Naval Postgraduate School (Ordnance Engineering) and Massachusetts Institute of Technology, MS, Electrical Engineering, 1945-48; Advanced Underseas Weapons School, 1948; Fleet Sonar School, 1956; National War College, 1964-65. Commissioned Ensign, US Navy, 1942. Served in the Pacific Theater, WW II. Commanding Officer USS *Bainbridge* (DLG(N)25), 1962-64; Military Assistant to the Principal Deputy Secretary of Defense (International Security Affairs), 1964-66; Director, Naval Ship Acquisition and Support Study Group, Naval Material Command, 1966-67; Commander Amphibious Group Two, 1967-68; Commander Amphibious Training Command, US Atlantic Fleet, 1968-69; Director, Office of Program Appraisal, 1969-70; Commander First Fleet, 1970-72. Legion of Merit; Bronze Star Medal with Combat "V"; Navy Commendation Medal with Gold Star and Combat "V"; and other medals and awards. Promoted to Vice Admiral, August 1, 1970.

Peijnenburg, Gerard Henri Joan Marie. Secretary-General, The Netherlands Ministry of Defense, 1969- . Born June 12, 1919, Asten. Attended Rotterdam School of Economics; College for Reserve Officers. Served in WW II, with American 82d Airborne Division in the Nijmegen area. Deputy Secretary General for Defense (Land Forces), Ministry of Defense, 1963-65; State Secretary for Defense, 1965-67. Knight in the Order of the Netherlands Lion; Officer in the Order of Orange Nassau; Bronze Cross; and other orders and medals.

P'eng Shao-hui. Colonel-General, People's Liberation Army, People's Republic of China; Deputy Chief of General Staff, People's Liberation Army, 1955- . Born in 1910 in Hunan. Served in Sino-Japanese War and the Civil War; took part in the Long March. Commander, 1st Division, 3d Army Corps, 1933; Commander, 358th Brigade, Northwest Shansi, 1938-40; Guerrilla Commander, Anti-Japanese Operations in Shansi-Suiyuan Area, 1940-43; Department Head, Anti-Japanese Military and Political Academy, Yenan Region, North Shensi, c. 1943 - c. 1945; Unit Commander, Shansi-Hopeh-Shantung-Honan Military Region, c. 1946-1948; Commander of 7th Column Forces (combat group), Shansi, 1948; Chief of Staff, Northwest Military Region, and 1st Field Army, Lanchow, Kansu, c. 1950-54; Deputy Commander, Northwest Military Region, 1954-55; Member, National Defense Council, 1954; Deputy Chief, General Training Department, and Director, Military Science and Regulations Division, 1955; Deputy to National People's Congress, and Member, Standing Committee, 1959; Member Chinese Communist Party; Member, CCP Ninth Central Committee, 1969; Member of Tenth CCP Central Committee, 1973. Red Star Medal; Orders of August First, Independence and Freedom, and Liberation.

Penney, Howard Wilson. Lieutenant General, US Army; Director, Defense Mapping Agency, Washington, D.C., 1972- . Born December 5, 1918, Royal Oak, Michigan. US Military Academy; The Engineer School, Field Grade Officer Course; US Army Command and General Staff College; The National War College; Agricultural and Mechanical College of Texas, MS Degree, Civil Engineering. Commissioned Second Lieutenant, 1940. Served in WW II and Vietnam War. Deputy Director of Civil Works for Comprehensive Basin Planning, Office, Chief of Engineers, US Army, Washington, D.C., 1963-64; Deputy Chief of Legislative Liaison, Office, Secretary of the Army, Washington, D.C., 1964-66; Chief of Legislative Liaison, Office, Secretary of the Army, Washington, D.C., 1966-68; Commanding General, US Army, Europe and Seventh Army Troops, 1968-70; Engineer, US Army, Europe, 1970-72. Distinguished Service Medal; Legion of Merit with Oak Leaf Cluster; Bronze Star Medal with Oak Leaf Cluster; and other medals and awards. Promoted to Brigadier General, April 8, 1963; Major General, June 1, 1967; Lieutenant General, February 28, 1972.

Pepke, Donn Royce. Major General, United States Army; Chief of Staff, United States Continental Army Command, Fort Monroe, Virginia, 1971- . Born September 7, 1916, Minot, North Dakota. University of North Dakota, BS Degree, History and Sociology; U.S. Army War College. Commissioned Second Lieutenant, U.S. Army Reserve, 1939. Served in WW II and Vietnam War. Deputy Commanding General, U.S. Army Training Center, Infantry, Fort Gordon, Georgia, 1964-65; Deputy Director of Strategic Plans and Policy, Office, Deputy Chief of Staff for Military Operations, U.S. Army, Washington, D.C., 1965-67; Director of Plans, Office, Deputy Chief of Staff for Military Operations, U.S. Army, Washington, D.C., 1967-68; Commanding General, 4th Infantry Division, U.S. Army, Pacific-Vietnam, 1968-69; Deputy Chief of Staff for Individual Training, U.S. Continental Army Command, Fort Monroe, Virginia, 1969-71. Distinguished Service Medal with Oak Leaf Cluster; Silver Star; Legion of Merit; Bronze Star Medal; and other medals and awards. Promoted to Brigadier General, October 1, 1964; Major General, August 1, 1969.

Peredelskiy, G. Colonel General, Artillery, USSR Army; Commander, Missiles and Artillery Forces. Served on the Soviet-German Front in WW II. Member, Communist Party of the Soviet Union.

Pereira Crespo, Manuel. Rear Admiral, Portuguese Navy; Minister of Navy.

Pereira do Nascimento, Jose. Brigadier, Portuguese Air Force; Secretary of State for Air.

Perez Caldes, José. Brigadier, Uruguayan Air Force; Commander in Chief, Uruguayan Air Force.

Perez de Eulate y Vida, Teodoro. Major General, Spanish Air Force; Under Secretary of Air Force, 1973- .

Diplomate in Communication Systems. Formerly Commander, 26th Fighter Group, 22d Regiment; Chief of Communications and Flight Navigation Aids, 2d Air Region (Sevilla); Commander, 25th Wing and Tablada (Sevilla) Air Force Base; Chief of Communications and Flight Navigation Aids, 1st Air Region (Madrid); Chief of Automobile Park Service; Chief of Communications Branch. Great Crosses: Air Force Merit and Saint Hermenegild Royal and Military Order; Red Cross Military Merit; War Cross; and other medals and awards. Promoted to Major General, September 3, 1970.

Perez Leffmans, Armando José. Rear Admiral, Venezuelan Navy; Chief of Naval Operations, 1973-   . Born January 1, 1924, in Caracas, Venezuela. Attended Metallurgy and Inspection of Materials Course, Philadelphia Naval Shipyard, USA, 1950-51; Submarine Basic Course and Submarine Command Course, New London, Connecticut, USA, 1959-60; US Naval War College, USA, 1965; Inter-American Defense College, Washington, D.C., USA, 1966. Commissioned Ensign, Venezuelan Navy, in 1945. Member, Board of Directors, Yards and Docks, 1964-65; Commandant, Contralmirante Agustin Armario Naval Base, 1969-70; Director, National Drydocks and Shipyards, 1970-73. Military Order General Rafael Urdaneta, second and third class; Order of Naval Merit, second and third class; Order of Liberator; and other medals and awards. Promoted to Captain, July 5, 1961; Rear Admiral, July 5, 1968.

Perry, Ellis Lee. Rear Admiral, United States Coast Guard; Commander, 8th Coast Guard District, New Orleans, Louisiana, 1973-   . Born September 29, 1919, Lawrenceburg, Tennessee. US Coast Guard Academy, 1938-41; Massachusetts Institute of Technology, MS Degree, Naval Construction and Engineering, 1946. Commissioned Ensign, 1941. Served in Atlantic Theater WW II. Head, Department of Applied Science and Engineering, US Coast Guard Academy, 1965-68; Chief, Planning and Evaluation Staff, Headquarters, US Coast Guard, 1968; Assistant Chief, Office of Research and Development, Headquarters, US Coast Guard, 1968-69; Commander, US Coast Guard Yard, Curtis Bay, 1969-70; Chief, Office of Personnel, Headquarters, 1970-71; Chief of Staff, US Coast Guard, 1971-73. Coast Guard Commendation Medal, National Defense Service Medal; and other medals and citations. Promoted to Captain, March 1, 1963; Rear Admiral, June 5, 1970.

Personne, Nils Birger Valdemar. Lieutenant General, Swedish Royal Air Force; Commander in Chief, Military Command, Upper Norrland, 1972-   . Attended Royal Air Force Academy, 1944-47; Royal National Defense College, 1955. Wing Commander F 11, 1959-61; Deputy Chief, Air Force Staff, 1961-66; Chief of Staff, Military Command, Upper Norrland. Commander of the Royal Order of the Sword; and other medals and awards. Promoted to Lieutenant General, 1972.

Petelin, Aleksandr Ivanovich. Vice Admiral, USSR Navy. Born in 1913 in Shurala, Sverdlovsk Oblast. Drafted into Navy in 1932. Attended Frunze Naval Academy, 1932-37; Submarine Officers courses, 1940; Naval War College, 1952-55. Commissioned in 1937. Served in the Soviet-Japanese War, 1945. Submarine Commander, Baltic Fleet, 1946-51; Chief of Staff and subsequently Commander, Submarine Formation, Northern Fleet, 1955-60; Commander, Submarine Flotilla, Northern Fleet, 1960-64; First Deputy Commander, Northern Fleet, 1964-70. Member, Communist Party of the Soviet Union, 1940-   . Hero of the Soviet Union; two Orders of Lenin; Order of Red Banner; two Orders of Red Star; and other orders and medals.

Peterson, Donald H. Lieutenant Colonel, US Air Force; NASA Astronaut, 1969-   . Born October 2, 1933, Winona, Mississippi. US Military Academy, 1951-55; Air Force Institute of Technology, MS, Nuclear Engineering, 1962; Aerospace Research Pilot School. Commissioned Second Lieutenant, US Air Force, 1955. Flight Instructor and Military Training Officer, Air Training Command; Nuclear Systems Analyst, Air Force Systems Command; US Air Force Manned Orbiting Laboratory Program. NASA experience: Member, Support Crew, Apollo 16. Air Force Commendation Medal; Meritorious Service Medal.

Petersen, Thorleif. Rear Admiral, Royal Norwegian Navy; Commander Naval Logistics Services.

Petit, Robert Lindsay. Major General, United States Air Force; Commander, Sheppard Technical Training Center, Sheppard Air Force Base, 1972-   . Born July 10, 1918, in Oxnard, California. University of Redlands, California, BA, 1939; Army Air Corps Flying School, 1941; Air War College, 1958-59. Commissioned in 1941. Combat duty in the Southwest Pacific Area and China-Burma-India Theater in WW II; Vietnam War. Deputy Commander, Third Air Force, England, 1964-65; Deputy Director of Operational Requirements, Weapons Effect Testing, Deputy Chief of Staff, Research and Development, 1965-66; Deputy Director, Forces, Directorate of Operations, Deputy Chief of Staff, Plans and Operations, 1966-68; Chief of Staff, Seventh Air Force, Vietnam, 1968-69; Deputy Commander, Seventh Air Force/Thirteenth Air Force, Thailand, 1969-70; Deputy Chief of Staff, Operations, Headquarters Pacific Air Force, Hawaii, 1970-72. Distinguished Service Medal; Silver Star with one Oak Leaf Cluster; Legion of Merit with one Oak Leaf Cluster; Distinguished Flying Cross with one Oak Leaf Cluster; and other US and foreign medals and awards. Promoted to Major General, January 24, 1969.

Petmezas, G. Rear Admiral, Hellenic Navy; Deputy Commander in Chief, Hellenic Navy.

Petrenko, P. Lieutenant General, USSR Army; Chief, Political Directorate, Southern Group of Soviet Forces, Hungary, 1968-   . Served on the Soviet-German Front in WW II. Member, Communist Party of the Soviet Union.

Petronis, P. Major General, Artillery, USSR Army; Military Commissar, Lithuania. Served on the Soviet-German Front in WW II. Member, Communist Party of the Soviet Union.

Petrov, I.V. General of the Army, USSR Army; Commander, Far Eastern Military District, 1972-   . Served on the Soviet-German Front in WW II. Chief of Staff, Far Eastern Military District, 1968-72. Promoted to Colonel General, April 1972; General of the Army, December 1972.

Petukhov, N.V. Colonel General, USSR Air Force; Chief, Political Directorate, Moscow Air Defense District, 1962-   . Served on the Soviet-German Front in WW II. Member, Communist Party of the Soviet Union.

Peyron, Gustaf Fredrik Carl. Brigadier General, Swedish Royal Army; Chief of Staff, Military Command Lower Norrland, 1972-   . Attended Royal Army Staff College, 1952-54; Staff College, England, 1960; Royal National Defense College, 1964, 1971. Commandant, Armor School, 1966; Commanding Officer, Armored Regiment, P 4, 1967. Commander of the Royal Order of the Sword; and other medals and awards. Member of the Royal Academy of Military Sciences. Promoted to Brigadier General, 1972.

Pezdirtz, Joseph Warren. Major General, United States Army; Commanding General, Korea Support Command, US Army, Pacific-Korea, 1971-   . Born October 14, 1920, Omaha, Nebraska. University of Michigan, AB Degree, History; The Infantry School, Basic Course; The Armored School, Advanced Course; US Army Command and General Staff College; US Armed Forces Staff College; US Naval War College. Commissioned Second Lieutenant, US Army Reserve, 1972. Served in WW II. Assistant Division Commander, 4th Armored Division, US Army, Europe, 1967-68; Deputy Commanding General for Area Support, US Army Communications Zone, Europe, 1968-69; Deputy Commanding General, US Army Theater Army Support Command, Europe, 1969; Commanding General, First Republic of Korea Army Advisory Detachment, US Army Advisory Group, Korea, 1969-70; Chief, Korea Military Advisory Group, 1970-71; Special Assistant to Commander, US Forces, Korea, 1971. Silver Star; Legion of Merit with Oak Leaf Cluster; Bronze Star Medal with three Oak Leaf Clusters; and other medals and awards. Promoted to Brigadier General, August 18, 1967; Major General, November 1, 1970.

Phelps, L.T.H. Major General, British Army; Director of Ordnance Services, 1973.

Philipchenko, Anatoly Vasilievich. Colonel, USSR Air Force; Cosmonaut, 1963-   . Born February 26, 1928, in Davydkovo, Voronezh Oblast. Attended Air Force Pilot School, Chuguev; Air Force War College; Cosmonaut Training Unit, 1963. Commissioned Second Lieutenant, Soviet Air Force, 1950. Commander, Soyuz-7 Spaceship, October, 1969. Hero of the Soviet Union; Order of Lenin; Order of Red Banner; Order of Red Star; Pilot-Cosmonaut

of USSR; K. Tsiolkovskiy Gold Medal of the USSR Academy of Sciences; and other medals and awards. Member, Communist Party of the Soviet Union since 1952.

Phillips, Samuel C. Lieutenant General, United States Air Force; Commander, Air Force Systems Command, 1973-   . Born February 19, 1921, Springerville, Arizona. University of Wyoming, BS, Electrical Engineering, 1942; Army Air Corps Flying School, 1942-43; University of Michigan, MS, Electrical Engineering, 1950; Air Command and Staff School, 1951. Commissioned Second Lieutenant, US Army Reserve, 1942; received pilot wings in 1943. Combat duty in the European Theater, WW II. Director, Minuteman Intercontinental Ballistic Missile Program, Headquarters, Ballistic Systems Division, 1963-64; Deputy Program Director Apollo Program, National Aeronautics and Space Administration (NASA), 1964; Director, Apollo Program, NASA, 1964-69; Commander, Space and Missile Systems Organization, Air Force Systems Command, 1969-72. Distinguished Service Medal; Legion of Merit; Distinguished Flying Cross with one Oak Leaf Cluster; and other medals and awards. Promoted to Brigadier General, September 1, 1961; Major General, May 1, 1964; Lieutenant General, May 29, 1968; General, 1973.

Philpott, Jammie M. Lieutenant General, United States Air Force; Vice Commander in Chief, United States Air Forces Europe (USAFE), Germany, 1972-   . Born September 28, 1919, in Ashland, Oklahoma. Oklahoma State University, 1937-40; US Military Academy, 1940-43; Flying School, US Military Academy, 1943; Air Tactical School, 1947; Atomic Special Weapons School, 1948. Commissioned Second Lieutenant, US Army Air Corps, 1943. Combat duty in the European Theater, WW II; Korean War; Vietnam War. Director of Intelligence, Headquarters Strategic Air Command, 1965-66; Deputy Chief of Staff, Intelligence, Seventh Air Force, Vietnam, 1966-67; Deputy Assistant Chief of Staff, Intelligence, Headquarters USAF, 1968-69; Assistant Chief of Staff, Intelligence, Headquarters, USAF, 1969; Deputy Director, Defense Intelligence Agency, 1969-72. Distinguished Service Medal with one Oak Leaf Cluster; Legion of Merit with one Oak Leaf Cluster; Distinguished Flying Cross with one Oak Leaf Cluster; and other medals and awards. Promoted to Brigadier General, August 1, 1964; Major General, August 1, 1968; Lieutenant General, November 11, 1969.

Pickett, George Edward. Lieutenant General, United States Army; Deputy Assistant Secretary of Defense (Management), Office, Assistant Secretary of Defense (Telecommunications), Washington, D.C., 1972-   . Born May 26, 1918, Palestine, Texas. US Military Academy; Armed Forces Staff College; The National War College. Commissioned Second Lieutenant, 1939. Served in WW II. Chief, Combat Support Division, Officer Personnel Directorate, Office of Personnel Operations, US Army, Washington, D.C., 1963-64; Director, Officer Personnel Directorate, Office of Personnel Operations, US Army,

Washington, D.C., 1964-65; Deputy Director, Defense Communications Systems, Defense Communications Agency, Washington, D.C., 1965-67; Vice Director, Defense Communications Agency, Washington, D.C., 1967-68; Assistant Chief of Staff for Communications-Electronics, US Army, Washington, D.C., 1968-72. Silver Star; Legion of Merit with two Oak Leaf Clusters; Bronze Star Medal with V Device; and other medals and awards. Promoted to Brigadier General, August 1, 1962; Major General, August 1, 1964; Lieutenant General, April 10, 1972.

Pickford, R. John. Commodore, Canadian Armed Forces; Canadian Forces Attache (Navy), Embassy of Canada, Washington, D.C., 1971-73.

Pieklik, Joseph Edward. Major General, United States Army; Commanding General, US Army Tank-Automotive Command, Warren, Michagan, 1971-   . Born September 24, 1918, Clinton, Massachusetts. University of Maryland, BS Degree, Military Science; US Army Command and General Staff College; US Armed Forces Staff College; US Army War College; Indiana University, MBA Degree, Business Administration; George Washington University, MA Degree, International Affairs. Commissioned Second Lieutenant, US Army Reserve, 1942. Served in WW II and Vietnam War. Commanding Officer, Combat Service Support Agency, Automatic Data Field Systems Command, US Army Combat Developments Command, Fort Lee, Virginia, 1967-68; Deputy Assistant Chief of Staff for Logistics (Supply and Maintenance), US Army, Washington, D.C., 1968-69; Commanding General, US Army Materiel Command, Europe, US Army, Europe, 1969-71. Legion of Merit with three Oak Leaf Clusters; and other medals and awards. Promoted to Brigadier General, August 1, 1969; General, August 1, 1970.

Pietraszkiewicz, Henryk. Rear Admiral, Polish Navy; Chief of Naval Staff, 1969-   . Attended Senior Naval School; Naval War College, USSR. Commander, Submarine, 1957; Commander, Naval Base, Gdynia, 1966. Cross of Grunwald; Cross of Merit; and other medals and awards. Promoted to Rear Admiral, 1969. Member, Polish United Workers Party.

Pikalov, V.K. Lieutenant General, USSR Army; Commander, Chemical Warfare Troops. Served on the Soviet-German Front in WW II. Member, Communist Party of the Soviet Union.

Pinochet Ugarte, Augusto. General, Chilean Army; Commander in Chief, Chilean Army and President, governing junta, 1973-   .

Pinto Telleria, Xavier. Vice Admiral, Bolivian Navy; Commander of the Bolivian Navy, 1971-   . Attended Military Academy, 1944; School of Application, 1951; Command and General Staff College, 1957; Naval War College, Peru, 1961; School of Advanced Military Studies, 1969. Commissioned in 1944. Chief of Naval Operations, 1963; Commander, Naval District No. 1, 1964; Navy Chief of Staff of River Forces, 1965; Navy Chief of Staff, 1966;

Naval Attache, Bolivian Embassy, Buenos Aires, Argentina, 1967-69; Supreme Counsel of National Defense, 1969-70; Sub-Secretary of the Navy, 1970-71. Army Medal "Guerrillero Lanza" (officer); Air Force Medal "Merito Aeronautico"; Navy Medal "Merito Naval"; Air Force Medal "Medalla de la Amistad" (Argentina); Navy Medal "Merito Naval" (Argentina); and other medals and awards.

Pirhonen, Jouko K.E. Vice Admiral, Navy of Finland; Commander, Finnish Naval Forces, 1966-   . Born December 13, 1915, Sortavala, Finland. Naval Academy, 1935-37; War College, 1946-48. Served in Soviet-Finnish War, WW II. Operations Officer, Finnish Navy, 1949-52; Instructor, War College, 1953-58; Chief of Supply, Finnish Navy, 1958-61; Assistant to the Minister of Defense, 1961-66. Mannerheim Cross; Cross of Freedom, 2d, 3d, and 4th Class; Cross of Freedom, 3d Class with Oak Leaf Cluster; Finland's Order of White Rose, 1st Class; German Iron Cross, 1st and 2d Class; and other medals and awards. Promoted to Vice Admiral, August 7, 1966.

Pirog, Jan. Major General, Polish Army; Chief, Military Staff, Lublin Voivodship Territorial Forces, 1966-   . Member, Polish United Workers Party.

Pita de Veiga y Sanz, Excmo. Sr. Don Gabriel. Vice Admiral, Spanish Navy; Commander in Chief of the Fleet.

Pitt, Basil M.P. Minister of National Security, Trinidad and Tobago, 1973-   .

Pittet, Oliver. Major General, Swiss Army; Commanding General, 1st Mechanized Division. Born in 1916.

Pitts, William Frederick. Lieutenant General, United States Air Force; Commander, Fifteenth Air Force, Strategic Air Command, 1972-   . Born November 27, 1919, in March Field, California. US Military Academy, 1939-43; Flying School, 1942; Army Language School, 1948-49; Strategic Intelligence School, 1949; National War College, 1961-62; Advanced Management Program Course, Harvard Business School, 1964. Commissioned Second Lieutenant, US Army Air Corps, 1943. Combat duty in the Pacific Theater, WW II. Commander, 327th Air Division, and Chief, Air Force Section, Military Assistance Advisory Group, Republic of China, 1966-67; Deputy Director of Budget, Headquarters, USAF, 1967-69; Director of Budget, Headquarters, USAF, 1969-71; Commander, Third Air Force, United States Air Forces, Europe, England, 1971-72; Commander Sixth Allied Tactical Air Force, 1972. Distinguished Service Medal; Legion of Merit with one Oak Leaf Cluster; Distinguished Flying Cross with one Oak Leaf Cluster; and other medals and awards. Promoted to Brigadier General, September 1, 1966; Major General, August 1, 1969; Lieutenant General, July 1, 1972.

Plate, Douglas Caulfield. Vice Admiral, United States Navy; Commander Second Fleet, 1972-   . Born July 20, 1920, in New York, New York. US Naval Academy, 1938-41; Naval War College, Command and Staff Course, 1952-53;

Industrial College of the Armed Forces, 1959-60. Commissioned Ensign, US Navy, 1941. Served in the Atlantic and Pacific Theaters, WW II; Vietnam War. Commanding Officer USS *Richmond K. Turner* (DLG20), 1964-65; Commanding Officer, US Naval Destroyer School, 1965-67; Commander Cruiser-Destroyer Flotilla TWO and Flotilla TEN, 1967-68; Commander Atlantic Fleet Mine Force, 1968-70; Commander Pacific Fleet Cruiser-Destroyer Force, 1970-71; Deputy Chief of Naval Personnel, 1971-72. Distinguished Service Medal; Legion of Merit; and other medals and awards. Promoted to Rear Admiral, 1967; Vice Admiral, 1972.

Plekhanov, A.A. Rear Admiral, Engineer, USSR Navy; First Deputy Chief, Political Directorate, Baltic Fleet. Formerly Chief of Political Directorate, Leningrad Naval Base. Served in the Soviet-German War (WW II). Member of Communist Party of the Soviet Union.

Ploger, Robert Riis. Major General, United States Army; Commanding General, US Army Engineer Center and Fort Belvoir, and Commandant, US Army Engineer School, Fort Belvoir, Virginia, 1970-   . Born August 15, 1915, Makay, Idaho. US Military Academy; US Army War College; Industrial College of the Armed Forces; Cornell University, MSE Degree, Civil Engineering; George Washington University, MBA Degree, Business Administration. Commissioned Second Lieutenant, 1939. Served in WW II and Vietnam War. Commanding General, 18th Engineer Brigade, and Engineer Officer, US Army, Vietnam, US Army, Pacific-Vietnam, 1965; Commanding General, US Army Engineer Command, Vietnam (Provisional), and Engineer, US Army, Vietnam, US Army, Pacific-Vietnam, 1966-67; Director of Topography and Military Engineering, later Director of Military Engineering, Office, Chief of Engineers, US Army, Washington, D.C., 1967-70. Distinguished Service Medal; Silver Star with Oak Leaf Cluster; Legion of Merit; Bronze Star Medal with Oak Leaf Cluster; and other medals and awards. Promoted to Brigadier General, June 1, 1965; Major General, November 1, 1966.

Plumtree, Eric. Air Vice-Marshal, British Royal Air Force; Commander, Southern Maritime Air Region, 1971-   . Born March 9, 1919. Attended Staff College, Haifa, 1946; Joint Services Staff College, 1959; Imperial Defence College, 1964. Served in fighter squadrons in WW II. Officer Commanding, Royal Air Force, Leuchars, 1959-61; Deputy Director, Joint Planning Staff, 1962-63; Air Adviser to United Kingdom High Commissioner, and Head, British Defence Liaison Staff (Air), Ottawa, Canada, 1965-67; Director of Air Plans, Ministry of Defence (Air), 1968-69; Air Officer Commanding, No. 22 Group, Royal Air Force, 1970-71. OBE; DFC. Promoted to Air Commodore, 1966; Air Vice-Marshal, 1971.

Pochupaylo, Y.G. Vice Admiral, USSR Navy; Chief, Political Directorate, Baltic Fleet, 1958-   . Served in the Soviet-German War, 1941-45. Member, Communist Party of the Soviet Union.

Poe, Bryce, II. Major General, United States Air Force; Commander, Ogden Air Materiel Area, Hill Air Force Base, Utah, 1972-   . Born October 10, 1924, Wichita, Kansas. Kansas University; Colorado School of Mines; US Military Academy, 1943-46; Armed Forces Staff College, 1959-60; University of Omaha, Nebraska, MA, History, 1964; National War College, 1964-65; George Washington University, MS, International Affairs, 1965. Commissioned in 1946. Combat duty in the Korean War; Vietnam War. Missile Plans Officer, Headquarters Strategic Air Command, then Chief, Missile Plans Section, Operations and Training Division, 1962-64; Chief, Plans Group, Office of Legislative Liaison, Office of the Secretary of the Air Force, 1965-67; Vice Commander, 75th Tactical Reconnaissance Wing, 1967-68; Vice Commander, 460th Tactical Reconnaissance Wing, Vietnam, 1968-69; Commander, 26th Tactical Reconnaissance Wing, Germany, 1969-70; Deputy Chief of Staff, Materiel, Headquarters US Air Force, Europe, Germany, 1970-72. Legion of Merit; Distinguished Flying Cross with three Oak Leaf Clusters; Bronze Star Medal; and other medals and awards. Promoted to Brigadier General, August 1, 1970; Major General, September 1, 1972.

Poggemeyer, Herman, Jr. Major General, United States Marine Corps; Commanding General, Marine Corps Base, Camp Pendleton, California, 1972-   . Born April 22, 1919, Leavenworth, Kansas. Baker University, 1938-39; US Naval Academy, 1939-42; Advanced Artillery Officers Course, Fort Sill, 1948; Amphibious Warfare School, Senior Course, Quantico, 1957; Air War College, 1960-61; George Washington University, MA, Engineering Administration, 1960. Commissioned in 1942. Served in South Pacific, WW II; Korean War; Vietnam War. Assistant Chief of Staff, G-3, Headquarters, Fleet Marine Force, Pacific, 1967-68; Assistant Chief of Staff, G-3, 1st Marine Division, Fleet Marine Force, Vietnam, 1966-67; Deputy Assistant Chief of Staff, G-4, Headquarters Marine Corps, 1968-70; Assistant Chief of Staff, G-4, Headquarters Marine Corps, 1970-71; Assistant Base Commander, Camp Pendleton, California, 1971-72. Legion of Merit with Combat "V" and two Gold Stars; Navy Commendation Medal with Combat "V" and Gold Star; and other US and foreign medals and awards. Promoted to Brigadier General, March 1, 1968; Major General, September 1, 1970.

Pogue, William Reid. Colonel, US Air Force; NASA Astronaut, 1966-   . Born January 23, 1930, Okemah, Oklahoma. Oklahoma Baptist University, BS, Education, 1951; Oklahoma State University, MS, Mathematics, 1960; Empire Test Pilots' School, Farnborough, England. Commissioned Second Lieutenant, US Air Force, 1952. Served in Korean War. Member US Air Force Thunderbirds, 1955-57; Instructor in Mathematics, US Air Force Academy, 1960-63; Test Pilot with British Ministry of Aviation, 1963-65. NASA experience: Member, Support Crew, Apollo 7, 11, and 14; Pilot, Skylab 4 mission. Manned Spacecraft Center Superior Achievement Award; Air Medal; Air Force Commendation; and other medals and awards.

Pokryshkin, Alexandr Ivanovich. Colonel General, USSR Army; Chairman, Central Committee, Association for Promotion of Army, Navy and Air Force, 1972- . Born in 1913. Attended Officers Training School; Frunze Army War College; Voroshilov General Staff War College. Joined the Soviet Army in 1932. Served on the Soviet-German Front in WW II. Deputy Commander, Air Defense Forces, 1968-71. Member, Communist Party of the Soviet Union; Deputy to the USSR Supreme Soviet. Hero of the Soviet Union; three Orders of Lenin; Order of Suvorov; Order of Kutuzov; Order of Red Banner; and other orders and awards.

Polanski, Wladyslaw. Lieutenant General, Polish Army; Commandant of Politico-Military College. Director, Military Publishing House, Ministry of Defense, 1957-60; Chief, Propaganda Branch, Main Political Directorate; Deputy Chief, Propaganda, Main Political Directorate, Polish Armed Forces, 1968- . Cross of Grunwald, Cross of Merit; and other Polish and foreign orders and medals. Member, Polish United Workers Party.

Polekhin, B. Vice Admiral, USSR Navy; Assistant Commander in Chief, Pacific Fleet. Served in the Soviet-German War (WW II). Member, Communist Party of the Soviet Union.

Pollock, Sir Michael (Patrick). Admiral, British Royal Navy; Chief of the Naval Staff and First Sea Lord, 1971- . Born October 19, 1916. Royal Naval College, Dartmouth. Entered Navy, 1930. Served in North Atlantic, Mediterranean and Indian Ocean in WW II. Commander, HMS *Ark Royal*, 1963-64; Assistant Chief of Naval Staff, 1964-66; Flag Officer Second in Command Home Fleet, 1966-67; Flag Officer Submarines, and NATO Commander Submarines, Eastern Atlantic, 1967-69; Controller of the Navy, 1970-71. GCB, MVO, DSC. Promoted to Captain, 1955; Rear Admiral, 1964; Vice-Admiral, 1968; Admiral, 1970.

Polynin, F. Colonel General, USSR Air Force. Served on the Soviet-German Front, in WW II. Chief, Rear Services (Logistics), Soviet Air Force until 1970. Member, Communist Party of the Soviet Union.

Ponomarev, M. Lieutenant General, USSR Army; Deputy Chief, Rear Services (Logistics), Ministry of Defense, 1970- . Served on the Soviet-German Front in WW II. Member, Communist Party of the Soviet Union.

Pope, John Ernle. Vice-Admiral, British Royal Navy; Chief of Staff to Commander-in-Chief, Western Fleet, 1971- . Born May 22, 1921. Attended Royal Naval College, Dartmouth. Served on destroyers in WW II. Commanding Officer, HMS *Decoy*, 1962-64; Director, Naval Equipment, 1964-66; Commanding Officer, HMS *Eagle*, 1966-68; Flag Officer, Western Fleet Flotillas, 1969-71. Promoted to Rear-Admiral, 1969; Vice-Admiral, 1972.

Popov, G. Major General, USSR Army; Chief, Political Directorate, Far Eastern Military District, 1969- . Served on the Soviet-German Front in WW II. Member, Communist Party of the Soviet Union.

Popovich, Pavel Romanovich. Colonel, USSR Air Force; Cosmonaut, 1960- . Born October 5, 1930. Studied at Industrial Technical School, Magnitogorsk; Air Force Pilot School; Zhukovskiy Air Force Engineering War College; Cosmonaut Training Unit. Joined the Soviet Army in 1951; transferred to the Air Force. Fighter Pilot; space flight (48 orbits) in Vostok-4 Spaceship, August 12, 1962. Order of Red Banner; Order of Red Star; and other medals and awards. Member, Communist Party of the Soviet Union; Deputy to the Supreme Soviet Ukrainian Soviet Socialist Republic.

Poppe, Helmut. Lieutenant General, National People's Army, Democratic Republic of Germany; Vice Minister of National Defense.

Post, Alton Gustav. Major General, United States Army; Deputy Chief of Staff for Logistics, US Army, Pacific-Hawaii, 1973- . Born December 26, 1920, in Zumbrota, Minnesota. Attended University of Omaha, BGE, Economics; US Army Transportation School, Basic and Advanced Courses; Command and General Staff College; National War College, 1967-68; George Washington University, MS, International Affairs. Commissioned Second Lieutenant, November 13, 1942. Served in the Vietnam War. Commanding Officer, US Army Aviation Materiel Maintenance Command, US Army, Pacific-Vietnam, 1968-69; Commanding Officer, 34th General Support Group, US Army, Pacific-Vietnam, 1969; Deputy Assistant Commandant, then Assistant Commandant, US Army Transportation School, Fort Eustis, Virginia, 1969-70; Deputy Chief of Staff, then Assistant Deputy Chief of Staff, Logistics, US Army, Vietnam, 1970-71; Director, Military Assistance Program, Pacific Command, Camp H.M. Smith, Hawaii, 1972-73. Distinguished Service Medal with Oak Leaf Cluster; Legion of Merit with Oak Leaf Cluster; Distinguished Flying Cross; Bronze Star Medal with V Device with Oak Leaf Cluster; and other medals and awards. Promoted to Brigadier General February 1, 1971; Major General July 14, 1973.

Potts, William Edward. Major General, United States Army; Assistant Chief of Staff, Intelligence, US Army, Washington, D.C. 1972- . Born November 9, 1921, Oklahoma City, Oklahoma. Oklahoma Military Academy, AA Degree, Engineering; University of Maryland, BS Degree, Political and Military Science; The Cavalry School, Basic Course; The Armor School, Advanced Course; US Army Command and General Staff College; US Armed Forces Staff College; US National War College; George Washington University, MA Degree, Personnel Administration, International Affairs. Commissioned Second Lieutenant, US Army Reserve, 1942. Served in WW II and Vietnam War. Chief of Staff, US Army Security Agency, Arlington Hall Station, Arlington, Virginia,

1966-67; Assistant Chief of Staff, G-2, US Army, Pacific, Fort Shafter, Hawaii, 1967-69; Assistant Chief of Staff, Intelligence, J-2, US Military Assistance Command, Vietnam, 1969-72. Distinguished Service Medal; Silver Star; Legion of Merit with two Oak Leaf Clusters; Bronze Star Medal with V Device and four Oak Leaf Clusters; and other medals and awards. Promoted to Brigadier General, November 1, 1967; Major General, January 1, 1971.

Povaly, M.I. Colonel General, USSR Army; Staff, General Staff War College. Served on the Soviet-German Front in WW II. Chief, Operations, General Staff. Member, Communist Party of the Soviet Union.

Power, Arthur Mackenzie. Vice-Admiral, British Royal Navy; Flag Officer Plymouth and Port Admiral Devonport, 1973- . Born June 18, 1921. Joined the Royal Navy in 1938; specialized in gunnery. Served at sea in WW II and the Korean War. Admiral Superintendent, Portsmouth, 1968; Flag Officer, Spithead, 1969; Aide-de-Camp to the Queen, 1968; Flag Officer Flotillas, Western Fleet, 1971-73. MBE. Promoted to Captain, 1959; Rear-Admiral, 1968; Vice-Admiral, 1971.

Powers, Patrick William. Major General, United States Army; Commanding General, US Army Readiness Region II, Fort Dix, New Jersey, 1973- . Born March 21, 1924, in Honolulu, Hawaii. Attended US Military Academy; Field Artillery School, Basic and Advanced Courses; Command and Staff College; Naval War College, 1964-65; University of Southern California, MS, Guided Missiles. Commissioned Second Lieutenant June 5, 1945. Served in the Vietnam War. Ballistic Missile Staff Officer, Operations Division, Supreme Headquarters, Allied Powers, Europe, 1965-67; Commanding Officer, 56th Artillery Group, US Army, Europe, 1967-68; Joint Secretary, US Military Assistance Command, Vietnam, 1968-69; Commanding Officer, 1st Infantry Division Artillery, US Army, Pacific-Vietnam, 1970; Deputy Assistant Chief of Staff, G-3, US Army, Vietnam, 1970; Chief of Staff, I Field Force, Vietnam, 1970; Commanding General, 56th Artillery Brigade, US Army, Europe, 1970-72; Director, Task Force Pershing II, Office of the Assistant Chief of Staff for Force Development, US Army, 1973. Legion of Merit with three Oak Leaf Clusters; Distinguished Flying Cross; Bronze Star Medal; and other medals and awards. Promoted to Brigadier General January 1, 1971; Major General May 1, 1973.

Price, Frank Hoblitzell, Jr. Vice Admiral, United States Navy; Director of Ship Acquisition and Improvement Division, Chairman of Ship Acquisition and Improvement Council, 1970- . Born June 11, 1919, in Van Lear, Kentucky. US Naval Academy, 1937-41; Ordnance Engineering Course, Postgraduate School, Annapolis, 1944-46; National War College, 1956-57; Nuclear Reactor Course, Atomic Energy Commission, 1962-63. Commissioned Ensign, US Navy, in 1941. Served on destroyers in the Atlantic and Pacific Theaters, WW II. Head, Underseas Warfare Division, Staff, Commander Operational Test and Evaluation Force, 1961-62;

Commanding Officer USS *Long Beach* (CGN9), 1963-66; Deputy Project Manager, Surface Missile Systems, Naval Material Command, and Executive Director, Anti-Air Warfare Systems Directorate, Naval Ordnance Systems Command, 1966-68; Commander Cruiser Destroyer Flotilla Eight, 1968-69; Vice Commander, Naval Ordnance Systems Command, 1969-70. Legion of Merit; Air Force Commendation Medal; and other medals and awards. Promoted to Vice Admiral, November 1, 1972.

Price, Harold L. Major General, United States Air Force; Director of Military Assistance and Sales, Deputy Chief of Staff, Systems and Logistics, Headquarters US Air Force, Washington, D.C., 1972- . Born July 2, 1918, in Potter, New York. Pennsylvania State College, BA, 1941; Aviation Training Course, 1941-42; Air Command and Staff School, 1953; National War College, 1962-63; George Washington University, MA, 1963. Commissioned Second Lieutenant, US Army Air Corps, 1942. Served in the European Theater, WW II, the Korean War, and the Vietnam War. Assistant Deputy for Operations, Ninth Air Force, Shaw Air Force Base, South Carolina, 1963-64; Director for Operations, 2d Air Division, Vietnam, 1964-65; Commander, 354th Tactical Fighter Wing, Myrtle Beach, South Carolina, 1965-66; Operations and Staff Officer, Directorate of Inspection, Office of the Assistant Secretary of Defense, Washington, D.C., 1966-69; Chief, Air Force Section, Military Assistance Advisory Group, Iran, 1969-72. Legion of Merit with Oak Leaf Cluster; Distinguished Flying Cross with two Oak Leaf Clusters; Soldiers Medal; Bronze Star; Air Medal with eleven Oak Leaf Clusters; Republic of Vietnam Air Force Distinguished Flying Cross; and other US and foreign medals and awards. Promoted to Brigadier General, March 1, 1969; Major General, 1973.

Price, James L. Major General, United States Air Force; Commander, 21st NORAD/CONAD Region, and Commander 21st Air Division, 1972- . Born November 23, 1921, in Hornersville, Missouri. Army Air Corps Flying School, 1942-43; University of Maryland, BS, Military Science, 1952; Syracuse University, 1956-57, MBA, 1957; National War College, 1963-64; George Washington University, MA, International Affairs, 1964. Commissioned in 1943. Combat duty in the European Theater, WW II; Vietnam War. Chief, Weapons Division, Deputy Chief of Staff, Operations, Headquarters Air Defense Command, 1964-66; Commander, 505th Tactical Control Group, Vietnam, 1966-67; Vice Commander, and later Commander, 57th Fighter Group, Aerospace Defense Command, 1967-68; Vice Commander and later Commander, Air Defense Weapons Center, 1968-71; Deputy Chief of Staff, Operations, Headquarters Aerospace Defense Command, 1971-72. Silver Star; Legion of Merit with two Oak Leaf Clusters; Distinguished Flying Cross; and other medals and awards. Promoted to Major General, November 1, 1971.

Pringle, Sir Charles (Norman Seaton). Air Marshal, British Royal Air Force; Air Officer Engineering, Strike Command, 1970- . Born June 6, 1919. St. John's College,

Cambridge, MA; Imperial Defence College, 1968. Commissioned in the Royal Air Force, 1941. Served in the India-Burma Theater in WW II. Senior Technical Staff Officer No. 3 Group, Bomber Command, 1960-62; Senior Technical Staff Officer, Air Forces Middle East, 1962-64; Commandant, Royal Air Force, St. Athan, and Air Officer Wales, 1964-66; Staff, Ministry of Defence, 1967; Director-General of Engineering, Royal Air Force, Ministry of Defence, 1969-70. KBE. Chartered Engineer; Fellow of the Royal Aeronautical Society.

Proudfoot, Robert James. Major General, United States Army; Deputy for Material Acquisition, Office of the Assistant Secretary of the Army (Installations and Logistics), 1973-   . Born January 30, 1922, in Philippi, West Virginia. Attended University of Maryland, BS, Military Science; US Army Command and General Staff College; Industrial College of the Armed Forces, 1967-68; Babson Institute, MBS, Business Administration. Commissioned Second Lieutenant, December 31, 1943. Served in WW II and the Vietnam War. Commanding Officer, 725th Maintenance Battalion, US Army Pacific-Hawaii, later US Army Pacific-Vietnam, 1965-67; Deputy Project Manager, Practice 9, US Army Materiel Command, 1967; Project Manager, SHILLELAGH, US Army National Guard, Redstone Arsenal, Alabama, 1968-71; Project Manager, LANCE, US Army Materiel Command, Redstone Arsenal, Alabama, 1971-73. Legion of Merit; Bronze Star Medal; Air Medal (2 awards), and other medals and awards. Promoted to Brigadier General January 1, 1972; Major General 1973.

Prugh, George Shipley. Major General, United States Army; The Judge Advocate General, US Army, Washington, D.C., 1971-   . Born June 1, 1920, Norfolk, Virginia. San Francisco Junior College, AA Degree, Arts and Sciences; University of California, AB Degree, Political Science; The Artillery School Basic Course; US Army Command and General Staff College; US Army War College; Hastings College of Law, JD Degree; George Washington University, MA Degree, International Affairs. Commissioned Second Lieutenant, US Army Reserve, 1942. Served in WW II and Vietnam War. Staff Judge Advocate, US Military Assistance Command, Vietnam, 1964-66; Legal Advisor, US European Command, 1966-69; Judge Advocate, US Army, Europe and Seventh Army, 1969-71. Distinguished Service Medal; Legion of Merit with Oak Leaf Cluster; and other medals and awards. Promoted to Brigadier General, November 1, 1969; Major General, July 1, 1971.

Purdon, Corran William Brooke. Major-General, British Army; General Officer Commanding North West District, 1972-   . Born May 4, 1921. Attended Campbell College, Belfast; Royal Military College Sandhurst; Staff College, 1955. Commissioned in the Royal Ulster Rifles in 1939. Served with Commandos in WW II in northwest Europe; in Palestine, 1945-46; Malaya, 1956-58. Commanding Officer, 1st Battalion Royal Ulster Rifles, British Army of the Rhine and Borneo War, 1962-64; General Staff Officer 1 and Chief Instructor, School of Infantry, Warminster,

1965-67; Commander, Sultan's Armed Forces, Oman, and Director of Operations, Dhofar War, 1967-70; Commandant, School of Infantry, Warminster, 1970-72. CBE; MC; OStJ: Sultan's Bravery Medal (Oman); Distinguished Service Medal for Gallantry (Oman).

Purisic, Ivo. Vice Admiral, Yugoslavian Navy; Commander in Chief of the Fleet.

Pursley, Robert E. Lieutenant General, United States Air Force; Commander, Fifth Air Force, Pacific Air Forces (PACAF), and Commander United States Air Forces, Japan, 1972-   . Born November 23, 1927, in Muncie, Indiana. Ball State University; US Military Academy, 1945-49; Air Tactical School, 1949; Pilot Training Courses, 1950-51; Harvard University, School of Business, 1955-58, BA, 1957; Air War College, 1965-66. Commissioned in 1949. Combat duty in the Korean War. Staff Analyst, Systems Analysis Office, Office of Secretary of Defense, 1963-65; Military Assistant to the Secretary of Defense, 1966-72; Vice-Commander, Fifth Air Force, Fuchu Air Station, Japan, 1972. Distinguished Service Medal (Department of Defense and Air Force Designs); Legion of Merit; Distinguished Flying Cross; and other medals and awards. Promoted to Major General, February 1, 1972; Lieutenant General, November 19, 1972.

Putnam, George Washington, Jr. Major General, United States Army; Director of Military Personnel Policies, Office, Deputy Chief of Staff for Personnel, US Army, Washington, D.C., 1971-   . Born May 5, 1920, Fort Fairfield, Maine. The Artillery School, Advanced Course; US Army Command and General Staff College; US Army War College. Commissioned Second Lieutenant, 1942. Served in WW II and Vietnam War. Chief of Staff, 1st Cavalry Division (Airmobile), US Army, Pacific-Vietnam, 1967-68; Deputy Director, later Director, Officer Personnel Directorate, Office of Personnel Operations, US Army, Washington, D.C., 1968-70; Commanding General, 1st Aviation Brigade, and Aviation Officer, US Army Vietnam, US Army, Pacific-Vietnam, 1970; Commanding General, 1st Cavalry Division (Airmobile), US Army, Pacific-Vietnam, 1970-71. Distinguished Service Medal; Legion of Merit with three Oak Leaf Clusters; Distinguished Flying Cross; Soldier's Medal; Bronze Star Medal with Oak Leaf Cluster; and other medals and awards. Promoted to General, June 1, 1969; Major General, May 1, 1971.

Q

Qaddafi, Muammar el. Colonel, Libyan Army; Head of State, Chairman of Revolutionary Council, and Commander in Chief, Armed Forces, 1969-   . Born in 1938 in Misurata. Attended University of Libya, Benghazi; course at Sandhurst Military College, Britain.

Quang, Tran Van. Major General, People's Army of Vietnam; Member of Central Military Party Committee;

Deputy Commander, 304th Division, 1958; Deputy Chief, General Staff, 1958. Promoted to Major General, 1961.

Quaye, P.F. Commodore, Navy of Ghana; Commander of the Navy.

Quiñónez, Vicente F. Brigadier General, Paraguayan Air Force; Commander of the Paraguayan Air Force, 1969- . Born October 27, 1922, in Paraguari. Attended Paraguayan Military Academy, 1947-48; Pilots Course, Brazil, 1948; Advanced War School, Staff Officer Course, 1959; US Air Command and Staff College, and other specialized air training, USA; National War College Course, 1970. Enlisted in the Navy in 1940; transferred to the Army, 1945. Commissioned Sub-Lieutenant in the Air Force, 1948. Air Attache, Embassy of Paraguay in Brazil, 1960-64; Chief of Staff of the Air Force, 1964-66; Administrator General of Civil Airports, 1966-69; Acting Commander of the Paraguayan Air Force, 1969-71, Permanent, 1971; President, Paraguayan Air Lines, 1969-70; Professor of Spatial Air Strategy and Air-Ground Cooperation at the National War College, 1969; President of the Board of Directors, Paraguayan Air Lines, 1970- . Medalla del Pacificador (Brazil); Medalla Cultural y Civica José Bonifacio de Andra e Silva el Patriarca (Brazil); Diploma et Brevet de Piloto Aviador "H.C." (Nationalist China Air Force); and other medals and awards.

R

Radziyevskiy, Aleksey Ivanovich. General of the Army, USSR Army; Commandant, Frunze Army War College, 1969- . Born August 13, 1911, in Uman, Cherkassy Oblast. Drafted into Soviet Army, 1931. Attended Cavalry Academy, 1929-31; Army War College, 1935-38; General Staff War College, c. 1940-41. Commissioned in 1931. Served on the Soviet-German Front in WW II. Chief of Staff, 53d Cavalry Division, Smolensk Front, 1941; Chief of Staff, 2d Guard Cavalry Corps, Moscow Front, 1941-42; Chief of Staff, 1st Cavalry Corps, 1942-43; Chief of Staff, 2d Tank Army, Ukrainian and Belorussian Fronts, 1944-45; Commander in Chief, Northern Group of Forces, Poland; Commander, Turkestan Military District; Commander, Armored Troops; Commander, Odessa Military District; First Deputy Commandant, General Staff War College, 1959-c. 1965; Chief, Main Directorate, Military Educational Establishments, Ministry of Defense, c. 1965-69. Member, Communist Party of the Soviet Union, 1931- ; Deputy to the USSR Supreme Soviet. Order of Lenin; four orders of Red Banner; two Orders of Suvorov; Order of Kutuzov; Order of Red Star; and other Soviet and foreign orders and medals. Promoted to General of the Army, November 7, 1972.

Radziyevskiy, S.I. Major General, USSR Army; Chief of Staff, Central Group of Soviet Forces, Czechoslovakia, 1969- . Served on the Soviet-German Front in WW II. Member, Communist Party of the Soviet Union.

Rafalko, Edmund A. Major General, United States Air Force; Deputy Chief of Staff, Plans and Operations, Air Force Logistics Command, Wright-Patterson Air Force Base, Ohio, 1973- . Born August 6, 1924, in Stoughton, Massachusetts. US Military Academy, 1942-45; Air War College, 1960-61; George Washington University, MA, 1962. Commissioned Second Lieutenant, US Army Air Corps, in 1945. Served in the Pacific Theater in WW II. Director of Athletics, US Air Force Academy, Colorado, 1964-67; Vice Commander, then Commander, 2d Bombardment Wing, Barksdale Air Force Base, Louisiana, 1967-69; Vice Commander, 4258th Strategic Wing, U-Tapao Airfield, Thailand, 1968-70; Deputy Inspector General, Headquarters, Strategic Air Command, Offut Air Force Base, Nebraska, 1970; Commander, 2750th Air Base Wing, Wright-Patterson Air Force Base, Ohio, 1970-72; Vice Commander, Ogden Air Materiel Area, Hill Air Force Base, Utah, 1972-73. Legion of Merit with two Oak Leaf Clusters, Air Medal with Five Oak Leaf Clusters, and other medals and awards. Promoted to Brigadier General, February 1, 1971; Major General, August 1, 1972.

Rahim Kahn, A. Air Marshal, Air Force of Pakistan; Commander in Chief, Pakistani Air Force. Served in India-Pakistan War, 1972.

Rahman, Unku Ahmed bin Abdul. Brigadier General, Army of Malaysia. Military Advisor in London.

Rahman, Ziaur. Brigadier, Bangladesh Army; Deputy Chief of Staff, Bangladesh Army, 1973- .

Raikes, Iwan Geoffrey. Rear-Admiral, British Royal Navy; Flag Officer First Flotilla, 1973- . Born April 21, 1921. Attended Royal Naval College, Dartmouth; Submarine Course, 1941. Commissioned c. 1940. Duty in submarines in WW II. Naval Secretary, 1970-73. CBE; DSC. Promoted to Captain, 1960; Rear Admiral, 1970.

Ram, Jagjivan. Defence Minister of India, 1972- .

Ramage, James David. Rear Admiral, United States Navy; Commander Naval Air Reserve, headquartered at Naval Air Station, Glenview, Illinois, and Commander Naval Air Reserve Force, 1972- . Born July 19, 1916, Waterloo, Iowa. Iowa State Teachers College, Cedar Falls, 1934-35; US Naval Academy, 1935-39; Flight Training Course, 1941-42; Naval War College, 1946-47; National War College, 1957-58; George Washington University, MA, International Affairs, 1963. Commissioned Ensign, US Navy, 1939; designated Naval Aviator, 1942. Served in the Pacific Theater, WW II; Korean War; Vietnam War. Commanding Officer USS *Independence* (CVA-62), 1963-64; Staff of Commander Joint Task Force TWO, 1964-66; Chief of Staff and Aide to Commander Carrier Division FIVE, 1966-67; Commander Fleet Air, Whidbey, Whidbey Island, Washington, 1967; Deputy Chief of Staff for Plans and Operations to Commander in Chief, US Pacific Fleet, 1967-70; Commander Carrier Division SEVEN, 1970-72. Navy Cross; Distinguished Service Medal;

Legion of Merit with Gold Star; Distinguished Flying Cross with Gold Star; Air Medal with five Gold Stars; and other US and foreign medals and awards. Promoted to Rear Admiral, July 1, 1967.

Ramarolahy, Philibert. General of Brigade, Army of Malagasy; Minister of National Defense, Malagasy.

Ramgoolam, Sir Seewoosagur. Prime Minister, Minister of Defense and Internal Security, and Minister of Information and Broadcasting, Mauritius, 1969-   . Born in 1900, in Belle Rive. Attended Royal College, Curepipe; University College, London, Doctor of Medicine degree. Ministerial Secretary of Treasury, 1958; Leader of the House, 1960; Chief Minister and Minister of Finance, 1961; Minister of External and Internal Affairs, 1960-69; Premier, 1965. Knight of the Order of the Thistle; Grand Croix de L'Ordre National de la Republique Malagasy; Honorary LLD, University of New Delhi; Honorary Citizen of City of Port Louis; First Honorary Member, African Psychiatric Association; Médaille de l'Assemblée Nationale, Française; Member of Royal College of Surgeons of England; and other medals and awards. Knighted, June 1965.

Ramos, Fidel V. Brigadier General, Philippine Army; Chief, Philippine Constabulary, 1971-   . Born March 18, 1928, in Lingayen, Pangasinan. Attended National University, Manila, 1946; US Military Academy, West Point, New York, USA, 1950; University of Illinois, USA, MS Degree, Civil Engineering, 1951; Basic Air Force Course and Psychological Operations Course, Fort Bragg, North Carolina, USA, 1960; University of The Philippines, MS Degree, Business Administration, 1962; Army Command and General Staff College, PA, 1966; National Defense College of The Philippines, 1969; and other special schools and courses. Commissioned Second Lieutenant, 1950. Served in the Korean War and the Vietnam War. G3, PHILCAG, Vietnam, 1965-67; Presidential Assistant on Military Affairs, 1968-69; Assistant Chief of Staff, J-2, 1969-70. Three Distinguished Service Star Medals; Military Merit Medal for Gallantry in Action, Korea; Four Military Merit Medals for Outstanding Staff Performance; and other medals and awards.

Ramos Ramirez, Angel. Vice Admiral, Mexican Navy; Naval Attache, Embassy of Mexico, Washington, D.C., 1973-   ; Delegate, Inter-American Defense Board, 1973-   . Date of Rank: April 21, 1971.

Ramsey, Lloyd Brinkley. Major General, United States Army; The Provost Marshal General, US Army, Washington, D.C., 1970-   . Born May 29, 1918, Somerset, Kentucky. University of Kentucky, BA Degree, Physical Education; US Army War College, US Army Command and Staff College. Commissioned Second Lieutenant, US Army Reserve, 1940. Served in WW II and Vietnam War. Deputy Commanding General, US Army Training Center, Engineer, Fort Leonard Wood, Missouri, 1964-66; Deputy Chief of Public Information, Office, Secretary of the Army, and Deputy Chief of Information, Office, Chief of Staff, US

Army, Washington, D.C., 1966-67; Chief of Staff, Third US Army, Fort McPherson, Georgia, 1967-68; Deputy Commanding General, 1st Logistical Command, US Army, Pacific-Vietnam, 1968-69; Commanding General, 23d Infantry Division (Americal), US Army, Pacific-Vietnam, 1969-70. Distinguished Service Medal; Silver Star with two Oak Leaf Clusters; Legion of Merit with Oak Leaf Cluster; Distinguished Flying Cross; Bronze Star Medal with V Device and three Oak Leaf Clusters; and other medals and awards. Promoted to Brigadier General, August 1, 1964; Major General, July 1, 1968.

Rancudo, José L. Brigadier General, Armed Forces of the Philippines; Commanding General, Philippine Air Force, 1972-   . Born January 16, 1920, in Alaminos, Pangasinan. Attended Philippine Nautical School, 1941; Philippine Army Air Corps Flying School, 1941; US Army Air Force Flying School, 1945-46; Staff Officer Course, Air Officer School, Nichols Air Force Base, 1950; Staff Officers School, Maxwell Air Force Base, USA, 1953; Air Command and General Staff College, Maxwell Air Force Base, USA, 1965; various specialized air force courses, Philippines, USA, Japan and Okinawa. Commissioned Second Lieutenant in 1941. Served in WW II; survivor of Bataan and Corregidor; fought as guerrilla with the Allied Intelligence Bureau; combat duty in Hukbalahap and Muslim uprisings. Commander, 6th Fighter Squadron, 1951-57; Commander, Philippine Air Force Jet Training, 1957-58; Chief, Tactical Education Branch, A-3, 1960-62; Commander, 9th Tactical Fighter Squadron "Limbas" and Wing Commander, United Nations Fighter Wing, Congo, Africa, 1963; Director, Operational Readiness Evaluation and Flight Safety, Headquarters Philippine Air Force, 1964-66; Chief of the Anti-Smuggling Office, Headquarters Philippine Air Force, 1966-68; Vice Commander, 1st Air Division, Headquarters Philippine Air Force, 1968; Commander, 5th Fighter Wing, 1968-72; Outstanding Achievement Medal; Military Merit Medal with Bronze Anahaw Leaf; Philippine Defense Medal; Philippine Liberation Medal; Silver Wing Medal with two Bronze Anahaw Leaves; and other medals and awards.

Raper, Sir (Robert) George. Vice-Admiral, British Royal Navy; Director-General, Ships, Chief Naval Engineer Officer, and Senior Naval Representative, Bath, 1968-   . Born August 27, 1915. Attended Royal Naval College, Dartmouth; Royal Naval Engineering College, Keyham; Advanced Engineering Course, Royal Naval College, Greenwich; Imperial Defence College, 1958. Served at sea and in the Admiralty in WW II. Commander HMS *Caledonia*, 1959-61; Deputy Director, Marine Engineering, Admiralty, 1961-63; Chief Scientific Officer (T) to Flag Officer, Sea Training, 1963-65; Director, Marine Engineering, Ministry of Defense (Navy Department), 1966-67. KCB. Promoted to Captain, 1957; Vice-Admiral, 1968.

Raphael, Antoine. Brigadier General, Army of Lebanon; Naval, Military and Air Attache, Embassy of Lebanon, London.

Rapold, Hans. Major General, Swiss Army; Deputy Chief of General Staff, Planning. Born in 1920.

Rapp, William Theodore. Vice Admiral, United States Navy; Commander Antisubmarine Warfare Force, US Pacific Fleet, 1972-   . Born March 31, 1920, Newark, New Jersey. US Naval Academy, 1939-42; Flight Training Course, 1944-45; Guided Missile School, 1951-52; Naval War College, 1961-62; George Washington University, MA, International Affairs, 1962-63. Commissioned Ensign, US Navy, 1942; designated Naval Aviator, 1945. Served in the Atlantic and Pacific Theaters, WW II. Director of Programs and Budget Division, Office of the CNO, 1963-64; Commanding Officer USS *Rankin* (AKA103), 1964-65; Faculty Advisor, Armed Forces Staff College, 1965-66; Commander Fleet Air Wing THREE, 1966-67; Director, Fleet Resources Office, Naval Material Command, 1967-68; Commander, Patrol Force, Seventh Fleet/Commander US Taiwan Patrol Force/Commander Fleet Air Wing ONE, 1968-70; Deputy Commander for Plans, Programs, and Financial Management/Comptroller, Naval Ship Systems Command, 1970-72. Legion of Merit; Navy Commendation Medal; and other medals and awards. Promoted to Vice Admiral, October 1, 1972.

Rasin, Bengt Göran. Commodore, Swedish Royal Navy; Chief of Staff, Military Command West, 1972-   . Attended Royal Navy Staff College, 1961. Commander, 1st Submarine Squadron, 1971-72. Knight of the Royal Order of Sword; and other medals and awards. Member of the Royal Society of Naval Sciences.

Rassai, Farajolla. Admiral, Imperial Iranian Navy; Commander in Chief, Imperial Iranian Navy.

Rassokho, A.I. Vice Admiral, USSR Navy; Chief of the Hydrographic Service. Served in the Soviet-German War, 1941-45. Member, Communist Party of the Soviet Union.

Ratkovich, Edward. Major General, United States Air Force; Director of Intelligence, J-2, Headquarters, US European Command, Germany, 1972-   . Born August 11, 1924, in Detroit, Michigan. Western Reserve University, Ohio; Texas Christian University; Army Air Corps Flying School, 1942-44; Industrial College of the Armed Forces, 1964-65. Commissioned Second Lieutenant, US Army Air Corps, 1944. Combat duty in the European Theater, WW II; Vietnam War. Director, Plans and Programs, Deputy Chief of Staff, Intelligence, Headquarters Tactical Air Command, 1962-64; Director, Targets, Assistant Chief of Staff, Intelligence, US Military Assistance Command, Vietnam, 1965-66; Chief, Combat Applications Group, Assistant Chief of Staff, Intelligence, Headquarters, USAF, 1966-69; Deputy Assistant Chief of Staff, Intelligence, Headquarters USAF, 1969-72. Distinguished Service Medal; Legion of Merit; and other medals and awards. Promoted to Major General, August 1, 1972.

Rattan, Donald Volney. Major General, United States Army; Deputy Chief, Office of Reserve Components, US Army, Washington, D.C., 1972-   . Born September 12, 1924, Fort Benning, Georgia. US Military Academy; The Infantry School, Basic and Advanced Courses; US Army Command and General Staff College; Armed Forces Staff College; NATO Defense College; US Army War College; George Washington University, MA Degree, International Affairs. Commissioned Second Lieutenant, 1945. Served in Vietnam War. Executive Officer, US Army Special Warfare School, Fort Bragg, North Carolina, 1968; Chief of Staff, XVIII Airborne Corps, Fort Bragg, North Carolina, 1968-70; Assistant Division Commander, 82d Airborne Division, Fort Bragg, North Carolina, 1970; Commanding General, 8th Infantry Division, US Army, Europe, 1970-72. Silver Star with two Oak Leaf Clusters; Legion of Merit with two Oak Leaf Clusters; Distinguished Flying Cross; Bronze Star Medal with V Device and two Oak Leaf Clusters; and other medals and awards. Promoted to Brigadier General, March 8, 1969; Major General, April 1, 1971.

Ratti, Ricardo Allen. Rear Admiral, United States Coast Guard; Chief Counsel, US Coast Gaurd, 1973-   . Born September 3, 1922, Humacao, Puerto Rico. US Coast Guard Academy, 1941-44; University of California; George Washington University Law School, JD Degree, 1956. Commissioned Ensign, 1944. Served in Pacific Theater, WW II. Legal Officer, 12th Coast Guard District, San Francisco, California, 1967-69; Chief, Claims and Litigation Division, Office Chief Council and Judge, US Court of Military Review, 1969-72; Inspector General, Coast Guard, 1972-73. WW II campaign medals and ribbons. Promoted to Captain, April 1, 1967; Rear Admiral, May 25, 1972.

Ravenna, Walter. General, Army of Uruguay; Minister of Defense, 1973-   .

Raymond, Daniel Arthur. Major General, United States Army; Division Engineer, US Army Engineer Division, South Atlantic, Atlanta, Georgia, 1972-   . Born December 1, 1917, Jacksonville, Florida. US Military Academy; The Engineer School, Basic Course; US Army Command and General Staff College; US Army War College; Harvard University, MS Degree, Civil Engineering. Commissioned Second Lieutenant, 1942. Served in WW II and Vietnam War. Special Assistant to Assistant Chief of Staff, J-4, later Chief Engineer Division, J-4, later Deputy for Engineering, J-4, US Military Assistance Command, Vietnam, 1965-66; Deputy, later Director, Construction Directorate, US Military Assistance Command, Vietnam, 1966-67; Staff Director of Southeast Asia Construction Division, Office, Assistant Secretary of Defense (Installations and Logistics), Washington, D.C., 1967-69; Director of Military Construction, Office, Chief of Engineers, US Army, Washington, D.C., 1969-72. Distinguished Service Medal with Oak Leaf Cluster; Legion of Merit with Oak Leaf Cluster; Bronze Star Medal with V Device and Oak Leaf Cluster; and other medals and awards. Promoted to Brigadier General, July 1, 1966; Major General, August 1, 1970.

Rea, William Freeland, III. Rear Admiral, United States Coast Guard; Chief, Office of Merchant Marine Safety, 1970-   . Born October 8, 1918, Philadelphia, Pennsylvania. Mississippi State College, 1936-38; US Coast Guard Academy, 1938-41; Merchant Marine Industrial Training, 1948-49. Commissioned Ensign, 1941. Served in North Atlantic Theater, WW II. Assistant Chief, Merchant Vessel Inspection Division, 1962-64; Officer in Charge, Marine Inspection Office, New York, 1964-67; Deputy Chief, Office of Merchant Marine Safety, 1967-68; Commander, 9th Coast Guard District, Cleveland, Ohio, 1968-70. WW II service medals and ribbons; and other medals and citations. Promoted to Captain, July 1, 1963; Rear Admiral, July 1, 1968.

Read, Charles Frederick. Air Vice-Marshal, Royal Australian Air Force; Chief of Air Staff, RAAF, 1970-   . Born October 9, 1918, in Sydney. Commander, RAAF Base, Point Cook, Victoria, 1965-68; Commander, RAAF Base, Richmond, NSW, 1968-70; Deputy Chief, Air Staff, 1970. CBE; DFC; AFC.

Read, Sir (John) Antony (Jervis). General, British Army; Commandant, Royal College of Defence Studies, 1973-   . Born September 10, 1913. Attended Winchester College; Royal Military Academy, Sandhurst. Commissioned in the Oxford and Bucks Light Infantry in 1934. Served in Kenya, Abyssinia, Somaliland and Burma in WW II. Commandant, School of Infantry, 1959-62; General Officer Commanding, Northumbrian Area and 50 (Northumbrian) Division (Territorial Army), 1962-64; Vice-Quarter-Master-General, Ministry of Defence, 1964-66; General Officer Commanding-in-Chief, Western Command, 1966-69; Quartermaster-General, 1969-73. KCB; CBE; DSO; MC.

Read, John Hugh Sherlock. Lieutenant-General, British Army; Director, International Military Staff, Headquarters, NATO, Brussels, 1971-   . Born September 6, 1917. Attended Royal Military Academy, Woolwich; Magdalene College, Cambridge University, BA, 1939, MA, 1944; Imperial Defence College, 1962. Commissioned Second Lieutenant, Royal Engineers, 1937. Served in Europe and the Middle East in WW II. Commander, Training Brigade, Royal Engineers, 1963; Assistant Commandant, Royal Military Academy, 1966-68; Director of Military Operations, Ministry of Defence, 1968-70; Assistant Chief of Defense Staff (Policy), Ministry of Defence, 1970-71. OBE.

Rebh, George Anthony. Major General, United States Army; Director of Postal Construction and Director of Military Construction, Office of the Chief of Engineers, 1970-   . Born September 14, 1921, in Detroit, Michigan. Attended US Military Academy; Engineer School; Command and General Staff College; Industrial College of the Armed Forces; Oxford University, BA, MA, Politics, Psychology and Economics. Commissioned Second Lieutenant February 6, 1943. Served in WW II and the Vietnam War. Chief of Staff, Seventh Army Support Command, later Deputy Chief of Staff, Seventh Army, US Army, Europe, 1963-65; District Engineer, US Army Engineer Division, Southwest, Tulsa District, Tulsa, Oklahoma, 1965-67; Deputy Division Engineer, US Engineer Division, Huntsville, Alabama, 1967-69; Deputy Commander, 18th Engineer Brigade, US Army, Pacific-Vietnam, 1969; Chief of Force Development Plans Division, Office of the Assistant Chief of Staff for Force Development, 1970. Legion of Merit with Oak Leaf Cluster; Bronze Star Medal; and other medals and awards. Promoted to Brigadier General August 1, 1970; Major General April 1, 1973.

Reich, Eli Thomas. Vice Admiral, United States Navy; Deputy Assistant Secretary of Defense (Production Engineering and Material Acquisition), 1970-   . Born March 20, 1913, in New York, New York. US Naval Academy, 1931-35; Submarine School, 1939; Armed Forces Staff College, 1949-50; Industrial College of the Armed Forces, 1955-56. Commissioned Ensign, US Navy, 1935. Served in submarines in the Philippines and the Pacific Theater in WW II; antisubmarine command in the Vietnam War. Assistant Chief, Bureau of Naval Weapons, for Surface Missile Systems, 1961-63; Director, Surface Missile System Project, Office of Naval Material, 1963-65; Commander Anti-Submarine Warfare Group FIVE, 1965-67; Assistant Deputy Chief of Naval Operations (Logistics), 1967; Deputy Comptroller of the Navy, 1967-70. Navy Cross with two Gold Stars; Distinguished Service Medal with Gold Star; Legion of Merit; Bronze Star Medal; and other US and foreign medals and awards. Promoted to Vice Admiral, June 1, 1970.

Reichel, Ignaz. General of Artillery, Austrian Army; Commanding General, Group I, 1968-   . Born May 3, 1908. Attended the Austrian Military Academy, 1929-32; Higher Officer Courses, 1936-38. Commissioned Second Lieutenant, Austrian Army, in 1932. Served in the German Army in WW II. Brigade Commander, 1957; Military Commander of Lower Austria (Niederösterreich), 1962-64; Deputy Commander, Group I, 1964-68. Grosses Ehrenzeichen; Goldenes Ehrenzeichen; and other medals and awards. Promoted to Colonel, 1957; Brigadier, 1963; Major General, 1968; General of Artillery, 1970.

Reichlin, Georg. Major General, Swiss Army; Commanding General, 9th Mountain Division. Born in 1917.

Reilly, M.R. Major General, United States Air Force; Director of Civil Engineering, Headquarters US Air Force, 1972-   . Born August 27, 1921, in Great Falls, Montana. University of Colorado, 1940-43, 1946-47, BS, Civil Engineering, 1947; Army Air Corps Flying School, 1943-44; Purdue University, 1951-52, MS, Civil Engineering, 1952; Air Command and Staff School; Air War College. Commissioned in 1944. Combat duty in the Pacific Theater, WW II. Chief, Strategic Missile Construction Branch, Assistant Chief of Construction Division, and Deputy Chief of Programs Division, US Air Force Directorate of Civil Engineering, 1961-66; Director, Civil

Engineering, Air Force Systems Command, 1966-68; Deputy Director, Civil Engineering, Air Force Deputy Chief of Staff, Programs and Resources, 1968-72. Legion of Merit; Bronze Star Medal; and other medals and awards. Promoted to Brigadier General, 1968; Major General, August 1, 1971.

Reindl, Jiri. Major General, Army of Czechoslovakia; Commanding General, Military Political Academy.

Repin, I.P. Major General, USSR Army; First Deputy Chief, Political Directorate, Soviet Ground Forces. Served on the Soviet-German Front in WW II. Member, Communist Party of the Soviet Union.

Rey, Carlos Alberto. Brigadier General, Argentina; Commander in Chief of the Argentine Air Force, 1970-73. Attended Colegio Militar, 1941-44. Commissioned in 1944. Member, Interamerican Defense Board, 1961-63; Chief of the Staff of the Commander of Air Operations, 1963-66; Chief, VII Air Brigade of Fighter-bombers, 1966-67; Assistant Chief of the Joint General Staff, 1967-68; Chief of General Staff of the Air Force, 1968-69; Commander of Air Operations, 1969-70. Caballero de la Orden del Condor de los Andes (Oficial), Bolivia; Gran Cruz Peruana al Merito Aeronautico; Gran Medalla al Merito Militar de Chile; Légion d'Honneur, France. Promoted to Brigadier General, March 12, 1970.

Rheborg, Rolf. Rear Admiral, Swedish Royal Navy; Chief of Staff, Military Command South, 1973- . Born March 7, 1922. Commissioned in 1943. Attended Royal Naval Staff College, 1950-52; Royal National Defense College, 1966, 1972. Commandant, Royal Navy Staff College, 1969-71. Commander of the Royal Order of the Sword; and other medals and awards. Member of the Royal Academy of Military Sciences; Member of the Royal Society of Naval Sciences. Promoted to Rear Admiral, 1973.

Rhodarmer, Roger K. Major General, United States Air Force; Commander, Ninth Air Force, Tactical Air Command, 1971- . Born February 18, 1922, in Canton, North Carolina. North Carolina State College, 1940-42; Army Air Corps Flying School, 1942-43; Armed Forces Staff College, 1956-58; Army War College, 1960-61. Commissioned in 1943. Combat duty in the European and Pacific Theaters, WW II. Chief of Reconnaissance Laboratory and Assistant Deputy for Reconnaissance, Wright-Patterson Air Force Base, 1961-66; Deputy Assistant, Reconnaissance, Deputy Chief of Staff, Research and Development, Headquarters, USAF, 1966-68; Deputy Director, Operational Requirements and Development Plans, Headquarters USAF, 1968-69; Assistant Deputy Chief of Staff, Research and Development, 1969; Director, Reconnaissance and Electronic Warfare, Headquarters USAF, 1969-70; Commander, US Air Force Tactical Air Reconnaissance Center, 1970-71. Distinguished Service Medal; Legion of Merit; Distinguished Flying Cross with

one Oak Leaf Cluster; and other US and foreign medals and awards. Promoted to Major General, August 1, 1970.

Rhodes, George. Major General, United States Air Force; Deputy Chief of Staff, Materiel, Air Force Logistics Command, Wright-Patterson Air Force Base, Ohio, 1971- . Born February 15, 1923, in Corrine, West Virginia. US Army Air Corps Officer Candidate School, 1943; Air Command and Staff College, 1956-57; Armed Forces Staff College, 1959-60; Industrial College of the Armed Forces, 1965-66. Commissioned Second Lieutenant, US Army Air Corps, 1943. Served in the China-Burma-India Theater, WW II. Deputy Commander, Materiel, and Commander, 7101st Materiel Squadron, Wiesbaden Air Base, Germany, 1966-67; Director of Maintenance Engineering, Deputy Chief of Staff, Materiel, United States Air Forces, Europe, Lindsey Air Station, Germany, 1967-69; Director of Materiel Management then Vice Commander, San Antonio Air Materiel Area, Kelly Air Force Base, Texas, 1969-71; Assistant Deputy Chief of Staff, Materiel, Air Force Logistics Command, Wright-Patterson Air Force Base, Ohio, 1971. Meritorious Service Medal; Air Force Commendation Medal; and other US and foreign medals and awards. Promoted to Brigadier General, August 1, 1970; Major General, 1973.

Rice, Joseph Enoch. Rear Admiral, United States Navy; Director, Tactical Digital Systems Office, 1971- . Born April 22, 1914, Anderson, South Carolina. US Naval Academy, 1932-36; Naval Postgraduate School, Radio Engineering Course, Annapolis, 1944. Commissioned Ensign, US Navy, 1936. Served in the Pacific Theater in WW II. Director, Electronics Division, Bureau of Ships, 1959-61; Commander Philadelphia (Pennsylvania) Naval Shipyard and Industrial Manager of Fourth Naval District, 1961-64; Industrial Manager, Potomac River Naval Command (later Naval District, Washington, D.C.), 1964-65; Commander Naval Shore Electronics Engineering Center, 1965-66; Commander Naval Electronics Systems Command, 1966-72. Bronze Star Medal with Combat "V"; and other medals and awards. Promoted to Rear Admiral, May 1, 1964.

Richards, Darrie Hewitt. Major General, United States Army; Deputy Director, Defense Supply Agency, Cameron Station, Alexandria, Virginia, 1973- . Born May 31, 1921, Washington, D.C. US Military Academy; The Engineer School, Basic and Advanced Courses; US Army Command and General Staff College; US Armed Forces Staff College; US Industrial College of the Armed Forces; Princeton University, MSE Degree, Civil Engineering. Commissioned Second Lieutenant, 1943. Served in WW II and Vietnam War; Commanding General, US Army Support Command, Qui Nhon, US Army, Pacific-Vietnam, 1968-69; Commander, Western Area Military Traffic Management and Terminal Service, Oakland Army Base, California, 1969-70; Assistant Deputy Chief of Staff for Logistics (Supply and Maintenance), US Army, Washington, D.C., 1970-72; Assistant Deputy Chief of Staff for Logistics, US Army, Washington, D.C., 1972-73. Distinguished Service

Medal; Legion of Merit with two Oak Leaf Clusters; Bronze Star Medal with V Device, and other medals and awards. Promoted to Brigadier General, February 1, 1968; Major General, August 1, 1970.

Richards, Ralph Julian, Jr. Major General, United States Army; Assistant Comptroller of the Army for Information Systems and Commanding General, Financial Information Systems Command, Washington, D.C., 1970-   . Born September 1, 1921, Sapulpa, Oklahoma. George Washington University, AB Degree, Accounting; Harvard University, MBA and DBA Degrees, Business Administration; US Army War College; George Washington University, MSIA Degree, International Affairs. Commissioned Second Lieutenant, US Army, 1942. Served in WW II. Special Assistant to Commanding General for Stock Fund, US Army Materiel Command, Washington, D.C., 1967; Commanding General, Finance Center, US Army, Fort Benjamin Harrison, Indiana, 1967-70; Chief of Finance and Accounting, and Assistant Comptroller of the Army, Information Systems, Office, Comptroller of the Army, Washington, D.C., 1970. Legion of Merit with three Oak Leaf Clusters; Bronze Star Medal; and other medals and awards. Promoted to Brigadier General, February 1, 1968; Major General, October 1, 1971.

Richardson, James. Minister of National Defence, Canada, 1972-   . Born March 28, 1922, Winnipeg, Manitoba. Attended Queen's University, Kingston, Ontario, BA, 1943. Served in the Royal Canadian Air Force as First Pilot in WW II. Minister without Portfolio, with special responsibilities in the Department of Transport, 1968-69; Minister, Department of Supply and Services, 1969-72; Member of Parliament (Liberal Party), 1968-   .

Richardson, Thomas Anthony. Major-General, British Army; Director, Army Aviation, 1971-   . Born August 9, 1922. Attended Wellington College, Berkshire; Royal Military College of Science; Staff College. Commissioned in the Royal Artillery in 1942. Served in France and Germany in WW II. Commanding Officer, 7th Paratroop Regiment, 1965-67; Commander, Royal Artillery 2 Division, 1967-69; Director, Operational Requirements (Army), 1969-71. MBE.

Richmond, Chester Arthur, Jr. Rear Admiral, United States Coast Guard; Commander, 13th Coast Guard District, Seattle, Washington, 1973-   . Born February 22, 1917, San Francisco, California. US Coast Guard Academy, New London, Connecticut, 1937-41; Navy Flight Training Courses, 1942-43; Aircraft Maintenance Course, 1947; Navy Test Pilot School, 1953. Commissioned Ensign, 1941; designated Coast Guard Aviator, 1943. Served in Atlantic Theater, WW II. Chief, Search and Rescue Division, Headquarters, US Coast Guard, 1965-68; Chief of Staff, 13th Coast Guard District, Seattle, Washington, 1968-69; Chief, Office of Research and Development, Headquarters, US Coast Guard, 1969-73. Distinguished Flying Cross; and other medals and citations. Promoted to Captain, February 1, 1962; Rear Admiral, August 1, 1969.

Rickenmann, Kurt. Major General, Swiss Army; Chief of the Adjutant General's Division. Born in 1914.

Rickover, Hyman George. Vice Admiral, United States Navy, Retired; Director, Division of Naval Reactors, Atomic Energy Commission, and Deputy Commander for Nuclear Propulsion, Naval Ship Systems Command, 1966-   . Born January 27, 1900. US Naval Academy, 1918-22; Naval Postgraduate School, Electrical Engineering Course, 1927-28; Columbia University, New York, 1928-29, MS, Electrical Engineering, 1929; Submarine School, 1930. Commissioned Ensign, US Navy, in 1922; transferred to retired list in 1964. Assistant Director of Operations, Manhattan District, 1946; Bureau of Ships, 1947-49; various positions in the Division of Reactor Development, US Atomic Energy Commission, since 1949, with related positions in the Bureau of Ships. Distinguished Service Medal; Legion of Merit with Gold Star; and other US and foreign medals and awards. Promoted to Vice Admiral, October 24, 1958.

Rienzi, Thomas Matthew. Major General, United States Army; Assistant Chief of Staff for Communications-Electronics, US Army, Washington, D.C., 1972-   . Born February 5, 1919, Philadelphia, Pennsylvania. US Military Academy; US Army Signal School, Basic and Advanced Courses; US Army Command and General Staff College; US Army War College; University of Illinois, MS, Electrical Engineering; George Washington University, MA, International Affairs. Commissioned Second Lieutenant, 1942. Served in WW II and Vietnam War. Commanding General, US Army Signal Center, and Commandant, US Army Signal School, Fort Monmouth, New Jersey, 1966-68; Deputy Commanding General, 1st Signal Brigade, US Army Strategic Communications Command, US Army, Pacific-Vietnam, 1968-69; Commanding General, 1st Signal Brigade, US Army Strategic Communications Command, and Assistant Chief of Staff, Communications-Electronics, US Army, Vietnam, US Army, Pacific-Vietnam, 1969-70; Commanding General, US Strategic Communications Command, Pacific, and Deputy Chief of Staff, Communications and Electronics, US Army, Pacific, Schofield Barracks, Hawaii, 1970-72. Distinguished Service Medal; Legion of Merit with Oak Leaf Cluster; Bronze Star Medal with Oak Leaf Cluster; and other medals and awards. Promoted to Brigadier General, May 1, 1966; Major General, December 1, 1969.

Riera, Robert Emmett. Rear Admiral, United States Navy; Commandant, Eighth Naval District, 1972-   . Born November 30, 1912, in Pensacola, Florida. US Naval Academy, 1931-35; Flight Training Course, 1938-39; Naval Postgraduate School, 1941-42; Naval War College, 1950-51. Commissioned Ensign, US Navy, in 1935; designated Naval Aviator in 1939. Pacific Theater, WW II. Assistant Chief of Naval Operations (Fleet Operations), 1961-63; Commander Carrier Division FOURTEEN, 1963-64; Commander Alaskan Sea Frontier and Commandant, Seventeenth Naval District, Commander Fleet Air Alaska/Commander Naval

Air Bases, Seventeenth Naval District, 1964-66; Commander Fleet Air, Mediterranean and Commander Naval Activities, Mediterranean/Commander Antisubmarine Warfare, Sixth Fleet, 1966-68; Assistant Deputy Chief of Naval Operations (Fleet Operations and Readiness), 1968-70; Commander Fleet Air, Western Pacific, 1970-72. Navy Cross; Legion of Merit with three Gold Stars and Combat "V"; Distinguished Flying Cross with two Gold Stars; Air Medal with seven Gold Stars; and other medals and awards. Promoted to Rear Admiral, April 1, 1963.

Rieve, Roland. Rear Admiral, Supply Corps, United States Navy; Force Supply Officer, Staff of Commander Service Force, US Pacific Fleet, 1972-   . Born March 29, 1919, in Baltimore, Maryland. US Naval Academy, 1937-41; Radar School, Bowdoin College, and Naval Research Laboratory, 1941-42; Navy Supply Corps School, 1947; Armed Forces Staff College, 1952; Harvard University, Graduate School of Business Administration, 1953-55; Industrial College of the Armed Forces, 1961-62. Commissioned Ensign, US Navy, in 1941; transferred to Supply Corps, US Navy, in 1946. Served in the Pacific Theater in WW II; at sea in the Korean War. Executive Officer, Naval Aviation Supply Office, Philadelphia, Pennsylvania, 1964-66; Commander Naval Supply Depot, Subic Bay, Philippines, 1966-67; Deputy Commander for Plans and Policy, Naval Supply Systems Command, 1967-69; Auditor General of the Navy, Office of the Naval Comptroller, 1969-72. Legion of Merit; and other medals and awards. Promoted to Rear Admiral, December 15, 1967.

Rios-Montt, José Efraim. Brigadier General, Guatemalan Army; Chief of Studies, Inter-American Defense College, Washington, D.C.

Ro, Jae Hyun. General, Army of the Republic of Korea; Chief of Staff, ROK Army, 1972-   . Attended Korean Military Academy, 1947; Artillery School, Fort Sill, Oklahoma, USA, 1953; Republic of Korea Army Command and General Staff College, 1955; Republic of Korea National War College, 1966. Commissioned Second Lieutenant, ROK Army, 1947. Combat duty in the Korean War. TIG, ROK Army, 1960-64; Commanding General, II Corps, 1966-69; Vice Chief of Staff, ROK Army, 1969-72. Chungmu; Wharang with Gold Star, three awards; Legion of Merit (USA); and other medals and citations. Promoted to General, May 30, 1972.

Robbins, Jack Bonds. Major General, United States Air Force; Director of Data Automation, Comptroller of the Air Force, Headquarters US Air Force, Washington, D.C., and Commander, Air Force Data Automation Agency, Gunter Air Force Base, Alabama, 1971-   . Born May 21, 1923, in New Albany, Mississippi. Mississippi State University; Aviation Cadet Training Course, 1944-45; Pilot Training Course, 1947-48; Air Command and Staff School, 1956-57; University of Alabama, BA, 1960; Oklahoma State University, MA, Mathematics, 1962; Air War College, 1965-66. Commissioned Second Lieutenant, US Army Air

Corps, 1945. Combat duty in the Pacific Theater, WW II, and in the Korean War. Branch and Division Chief, Directorate of Data Automation, Office of the Comptroller of the Air Force, Headquarters US Air Force, Washington, D.C., 1966-69; Deputy Director, Directorate of Data Automation, Office of the Comptroller of the Air Force, Headquarters US Air Force, Washington, D.C., 1969-70; Chief of Staff, Air Force Communications Service, Richards-Gebaur Air Force Base, 1970-71. Decorations include Bronze Star Medal, Meritorious Service Medal, Air Medal. Promoted to Major General, April 2, 1973.

Robbins, Jay T. Lieutenant General, United States Air Force; Vice Commander Military Airlift Command, 1972-   . Born September 16, 1919, in Coolidge, Texas. Texas Agricultural and Mechanical University, BS, 1940; Advanced Flying School, 1941-42; Air Command and Staff School, 1950; National War College, 1961-62. Commissioned Second Lieutenant, US Army Air Corps Reserve, 1941; received pilot wings, 1943. Combat duty in the Southwest Pacific Area, WW II; Vietnam War. Director, Aerospace Safety, Office of the Inspector General, 1963-65; Commander, 313th Air Division, Pacific Air Force, Kadena Air Base, Okinawa, 1965-67; Chief of Staff, Headquarters, Pacific Air Forces, 1967-68; Commander, Twelfth Air Force, 1968-70; Vice Commander, Tactical Air Command, 1970-72. Distinguished Service Cross with one Oak Leaf Cluster; Distinguished Service Medal; Silver Star with one Oak Leaf Cluster; Legion of Merit with one Oak Leaf Cluster; Distinguished Flying Cross with three Oak Leaf Clusters; and other medals and awards. Promoted to Brigadier General, August 1, 1962; Major General, June 1, 1965; Lieutenant General, March 1, 1970.

Roberts, Elvy Benton. Major General, United States Army; Special Assistant to the Chairman, Joint Chiefs of Staff (MBFR), Washington, D.C., 1972-   . Born August 21, 1917, Manchester, Kentucky. Eastern Kentucky State College, BS Degree in Chemistry and Biology; US Military Academy; The Infantry School, Basic and Advanced Courses; US Armed Forces Staff College; US Army Command and General Staff College; US Army War College. Commissioned Second Lieutenant, 1943. Served in WW II and Vietnam War. Deputy Commanding General, US Army Training Center (Infantry) and Fort Jackson, South Carolina, 1966-68; Assistant Division Commander, 9th Infantry Division, US Army, Pacific-Vietnam, 1969-70; Director of Plans, Office, Deputy Chief of Staff for Military Operations, US Army, Washington, D.C., 1970-71; Assistant Deputy Chief of Staff for Military Operations, US Army, Washington, D.C., 1971-72. Distinguished Service Medal; Silver Star with Oak Leaf Cluster; Legion of Merit with Oak Leaf Cluster; Distinguished Flying Cross; Bronze Star Medal with V Device and two Oak Leaf Clusters; and other medals and awards. Promoted to Brigadier General, October 1, 1966; Major General, September 8, 1969.

Roberts, J. Milnor, Jr. Major General, United States Army; Chief, Army Reserve, US Army, Washington, D.C., 1971-   . Born September 16, 1918, Pittsburgh,

Pennsylvania. The Infantry School, Advanced Course; US Army Command and General Staff College. Commissioned Second Lieutenant, US Army Reserve, 1940. Served in WW II. Commanding General, 99th US Army Reserve Command, Leetsdale and Pittsburgh, Pennsylvania, 1967-70; Deputy Chief, Army Reserve, US Army, Washington, D.C., 1970-71. Legion of Merit; Bronze Star Medal; and other medals and awards. Promoted to Brigadier General (ORC), May 9, 1968; Major General (ORC), April 5, 1971.

Roberts, John W. Major General, United States Air Force; Assistant Deputy Chief of Staff for Personnel, Headquarters, US Air Force, 1973-   . Born January 1, 1921, in Mankato, Minnesota. Mankato State Teachers College, BS, Industrial Education, 1942; Army Air Corps Flying School, 1943-44; Air Command and Staff College, 1956-57; George Washington University, 1960-61, MS, Business Administration, 1961; National War College, 1964-65. Commissioned in 1944. Combat duty in the Korean War; Vietnam War. Assistant Chief, Special Warfare Division, Directorate of Plans, Deputy Chief of Staff, Plans and Operations, 1965-66; Chief, Systems Division, Defense Communications Planning Group, Naval Observatory, Washington, D.C., 1966-67; Vice Commander, 4453d Combat Crew Training Wing, 1967-68; Commander, 366th Tactical Fighter Wing, Vietnam, 1968-69; Director, Tactical Air Control Center, Headquarters Seventh Air Force, Vietnam, 1969-70; Deputy Director, Personnel Planning, Deputy Chief of Staff, Personnel, Headquarters USAF, 1970-71; Director, Personnel Plans, Deputy Chief of Staff for Personnel, Headquarters US Air Force, 1971-73. Distinguished Service Medal (Air Force Design); Legion of Merit with one Oak Leaf Cluster; Distinguished Flying Cross; and other US and foreign medals and awards. Promoted to Major General, December 1, 1971.

Robertson, Horace Bascomb, Jr. Rear Admiral, Judge Advocate General Corps, United States Navy; Deputy Judge Advocate General, Navy Department, 1972-   . Born November 13, 1923, Charlotte, North Carolina. Davidson (North Carolina) College; US Naval Academy, 1942-45; Fleet Sonar School, 1948; George Washington University, Law School, JD, 1953; Armed Forces Staff College, 1961; Naval War College, Senior Naval Warfare Course, 1967-68; George Washington University, MS, International Affairs, 1968. Commissioned Ensign, US Navy, in 1941. Special Counsel to the Secretary of the Navy, 1964-67; Assistant Chief of Staff for Legal Affairs to Commander US Naval Forces, Philippines, 1968-70; Special Counsel to the Chief of Naval Operations, 1970-72. Legion of Merit with Gold Star; and other medals and awards. Promoted to Rear Admiral, April 1, 1972. Publication: *International Law for Seagoing Officers* (with Commander Burdick H. Brittin).

Robertson, Ian George William. Rear-Admiral, British Royal Navy; Admiral Commanding Reserves, 1972-   . Born October 21, 1922. Attended Radley College; Imperial Defence College, 1968. Enlisted in Royal Naval Volunteer Reserve, 1941; commissioned Sub-Lieutenant, 1943;

qualified as pilot. Served in WW II. Commanding Officer, HMS *Mohawk*, 1963-65; Royal Naval Air Services, Culdrose, 1965-68; HMS *Eagle*, 1970-72. DSC. Promoted to Rear-Admiral in 1972.

Robertson, James Howden. Major-General, British Army; Director, Army Dental Service, 1970-   . Born October 16, 1915. Glasgow Dental Hospital, Licentiate in Dental Surgery, 1939. Commissioned in the Army Dental Corps, 1939. Served in the European Theater in WW II. Consultant, CMH Aldershot, 1962-67; Consulting Dental Surgeon to the Army, 1967-70. Officer of the Order of St. John of Jerusalem, 1969; Queen's Honorary Dental Surgeon, 1967. Promoted to Brigadier, 1967; Major-General, 1970.

Robertson, John Fraser. Secretary of Defence, New Zealand, 1969-   . Associate Chartered Accountants, 1951; Victoria University, Diploma in Public Administration, 1956; Harkness Commonwealth Fund Fellow, 1960-61; attended Imperial Defence College, 1968. Served in WW II, with the Royal New Zealand Air Force. Assistant Commissioner, State Services Commission, 1964-67; Deputy Secretary of Defense, 1967-69.

Robertson, William Duncan. Air Commodore, British Royal Air Force. Born June 24, 1922. Attended Robert Gordon's College, Aberdeen; Royal College of Defence Studies, 1971. Group Director, Royal Air Force Staff College, 1962-65; Station Commander, RAF Wildenrath, 1965-67; Deputy Director, Administrative Plans, 1967; Director of Operations (Plans), 1968; Director of Operations, Air Defence and Overseas, 1969-71. CBE.

Robinson, Ray A., Jr. Major General, United States Air Force; Deputy Chief of Staff, Operations, Headquarters Aerospace Defense Command, Ent Air Force Base, Colorado, 1972-   . Born June 30, 1921, in Little Rock, Arkansas. Arkansas Polytechnic College, 1939-40; Aviation Cadet Training Course, 1941-42; Air Command and Staff College, 1958-59; Air War College, 1965-66. Commissioned Second Lieutenant, US Army Air Corps, in 1942. Served in the European Theater, WW II; and the Vietnam War. Deputy for Operations, 328th Fighter Wing, Aerospace Defense Command, Richards-Gebaur Air Force Base, Missouri, 1966-67; Director of Operations, 30th Air Division, Aerospace Defense Command, Sioux City Air Base, Iowa, 1967-68; Director of Operations, 35th Air Division, Hancock Field, New York, 1968-69; Commander, 33d Air Division, Fort Lee Air Force Station, Virginia, 1969-70; Assistant Deputy Chief of Staff, Plans, Headquarters Aerospace Defense Command, Ent Air Force Base, Colorado, 1970; Inspector General, Headquarters Aerospace Defense Command, Ent Air Force Base, Colorado, 1970-72. Distinguished Flying Cross with Oak Leaf Cluster; Bronze Star; Air Medal with sixteen Oak Leaf Clusters; Croix de Guerre (France); Meritorious Service Medal; and other US and foreign medals and awards. Promoted to Brigadier General, August 1, 1970; Major General, 1973.

Robinson, Wallace Hamilton, Jr. Lieutenant General, United States Marine Corps; Director, Defense Supply Agency, 1971-   . Born February 11, 1920, Washington, D.C. Virginia Polytechnic Institute, BS, Civil Engineering, 1940; Marine Corps Officers Basic School, 1940-41; Industrial College of the Armed Forces, 1958-59; George Washington University, MA, Business Administration, 1961. Commissioned in 1940. Served in Pacific Theater, WW II; Korean War. Commanding Officer, 3d Force Service Regiment, 3d Marine Division, 1963-64; Chief of Staff, Marine Corps Supply Activity, Philadelphia, Pennsylvania, 1964-66; Commander, Marine Corps Supply Activity, 1966-69; Quartermaster General, US Marine Corps, 1969-71. Legion of Merit with Gold Star; Navy Commendation Medal; and other medals and awards. Promoted to Brigadier General, March 14, 1966; Major General, August 1, 1967; Lieutenant General, March 12, 1971.

Rodriguez Theodor, Ervaldo. Brigadier General, Chilean Army; Military Attache, Embassy of Chile, Washington, D.C., and Delegate, Inter-American Defense Board, 1973-   .

Roest, Eric. Vice Admiral, Royal Netherlands Navy; Commander in Chief, Royal Netherlands Navy, and Chief of Netherlands Naval Staff, 1972-   . Born November 1, 1921, in Blerick. Attended Royal Navy College; various naval courses. Commissioned Sub-Lieutenant, RNN, 1945. Political prisoner in German concentration camps, 1941-45. Director of Personnel Department (Officers), Ministry of Defense, Naval Staff, 1961-64; Aide de Camp to HM The Queen of the Netherlands, 1964-67; Commanding Officer, HNLMS *Poolster*, 1967-68; Chief of Staff to the Admiral, Netherlands Home Command, 1968-70; Deputy Chief, Netherlands Naval Staff, 1970-71; Commander, Netherlands Task Group, 1971-72. Officer in the Order of Orange-Nassau; Netherlands War Commemorative Cross with one bar; Officer in the Home-Order of Orange; and other orders and medals. Promoted to Rear Admiral, February 5, 1971; Vice Admiral, April 12, 1972.

Rogers, Bernard William. Lieutenant General, United States Army. Deputy Chief of Staff for Personnel, US Army, Washington, D.C., 1972-   . Born July 16, 1921, Fairview, Kansas. US Military Academy; The Infantry School, Basic and Advanced Courses; US Army Command and General Staff College; US Army War College; Oxford University, England, BA and MA Degrees, Philosophy, Politics, and Economics. Commissioned Second Lieutenant, 1943. Served in WW II and Vietnam War. Assistant Division Commander, 1st Infantry Division, US Army, Pacific-Vietnam, 1966-67; Commandant of Cadets, US Military Academy, West Point, New York, 1967-69; Commanding General, 5th Infantry Division (Mechanized), and Fort Carson, Colorado, 1969-70; Chief of Legislative Liaison, Office, Secretary of the Army, Washington, D.C. 1971-72. Distinguished Service Cross; Silver Star; Legion of Merit with three Oak Leaf Clusters; Distinguished Flying Cross with two Oak Leaf Clusters; Bronze Star Medal with

V Device and Oak Leaf Cluster; and other medals and awards. Promoted to Brigadier General, October 27, 1966; Major General, February 1, 1970; Lieutenant General, November 1, 1972.

Rogers, Felix M. Major General, United States Air Force; Vice Commander, Air Training Command, 1972-   . Born July 6, 1921, in Somerville, Massachusetts. Army Air Corps Flying School, 1942-43; University of Virginia, 1947-49; University of Maryland, BS, Military Science, 1952; National War College, 1960-61. Commissioned in 1943. Combat duty in the European Theater, WW II. Secretary, Air Force Council, Office Vice Chief of Staff, 1962-63; Director of Secretariat, Air Force Council, 1963-66; Assistant Deputy, then Deputy Chief of Staff, Development Plans, Air Force Systems Command, 1966-70; Senior Member, United Nations Command, Military Armistice Commission, Korea, 1970-71; Deputy Chief of Staff, Technical Training, Air Training Command Headquarters, 1971-72. Distinguished Service Medal with one Oak Leaf Cluster; Silver Star; Legion of Merit with one Oak Leaf Cluster; Bronze Star Medal; and other US and foreign medals and awards. Promoted to Major General, February 28, 1972.

Rogers, Norman Charles. Major-General, British Army; Director of Army Surgery, 1969-   . Born October 14, 1916. Attended Imperial Service College; St. Bartholomew's Hospital, Bachelor of Medicine and Surgery, London; Licentiate of the Royal College of Physicians, London, 1939. Commissioned in the Royal Army Medical Corps, 1939; permanent commission, 1956. Served in North African and European Theaters, WW II; POW in Italy, 1942-43. Surgical appointments in various military hospitals, 1956-67; Command Consultant Surgeon, British Army of the Rhine, 1967-69; Surgeon to the Queen, 1969-   . Fellow of the Royal College of Surgeons.

Rollins, Andrew Peach, Jr. Major General, United States Army; Deputy Chief of Engineers, US Army, Washington, D.C., 1971-   . Born August 2, 1918, Gettysburg, Pennsylvania. Agricultural and Mechanical College of Texas, BS Degree, Civil Engineering; California Institute of Technology, MS Degree, Civil Engineering; US Army Command and General Staff College; US Army War College. Commissioned Second Lieutenant, US Army Reserve, 1939. Served in WW II and Vietnam War. Director of Military Construction, Office, Chief of Engineers, US Army, Washington, D.C., 1966-67; Commanding General, 18th Engineer Brigade, US Army, Pacific-Vietnam, 1967; Director of Construction, US Military Assistance Command, Vietnam, 1967-68; Commanding General, US Army Training Center, Engineer, and Fort Leonard Wood, Missouri, 1968-69; Division Engineer, US Army Engineer Division, Lower Mississippi Valley, and President, Mississippi River Commission, Vicksburg, Mississippi, 1969-71. Distinguished Service Medal with Oak Leaf Cluster; Silver Star; Legion of Merit with Oak Leaf Cluster; Bronze Star Medal; and other medals and awards. Promoted to Brigadier General, October 1, 1965; Major General, August 1, 1968.

Roman, Pierre. Lieutenant General, Belgian Army; Chief of the Army General Staff, 1972-   . Born in 1918, in Paris, France. Attended Ecole Royale Militaire, 1936-38; Ecole d'Application de l'Artillerie et du Génie, 1940, 1945-46. Commissioned Sub-lieutenant, 1940. Served in a Commando unit in Italy, Yugoslavia, Walcheren, and Germany during WW II; Congo, 1960. Military Attache, Staff of the Minister of National Defense, 1961-65; Commander, Para-Commando Regiment, 1965-68; First Deputy Chief of Staff, Army General Staff, 1968-69; Commander, 1st Infantry Division, 1970-72. Ordre de Léopold avec Palme; Croix de Guerre; British Military Cross. Promoted to Major General, December 26, 1969; Lieutenant General, December 26, 1971.

Romero, Carlos Humberto. Colonel, Army of El Salvador; Minister of Defense, 1973-   .

Roosa, Stuart Allen. Lieutenant Colonel, US Air Force; NASA Astronaut, 1966-   . Born August 16, 1933, Durango, Colorado. Oklahoma State University; University of Arizona; University of Colorado, BS, Aeronautical Engineering; Aerospace Research Pilots School, 1965. Commissioned Second Lieutenant, US Air Force, 1953. Fighter Pilot, Langley Air Force Base, Virginia; Chief of Service Engineering (AFLC), Tachikawa Air Base; Maintenance Flight Test Pilot, Olmsted Air Force Base, Pennsylvania, 1962-64; Experimental Test Pilot, Edwards Air Force Base, California, 1965-66. NASA experience: Member, Support Crew, Apollo 9; Command Module Pilot, Apollo 14, January 31-February 9, 1971; Backup Command Module Pilot, Apollo 16 and 17. NASA Distinguished Service Medal; Manned Spacecraft Center Superior Achievement Award; Air Force Command Pilot Astronaut Wings; Air Force Distinguished Service Medal; Arnold Air Society's John F. Kennedy Award; City of New York Gold Medal; American Astronautical Society's Flight Achievement Award; Honorary LLD, University of St. Thomas, Houston, Texas.

Roost, Hans. Major General, Swiss Army; Deputy Chief, Training and Education. Born in 1913.

Rosales, Francisco. Brigadier General, Venezuelan Army; Chief of Delegation, Inter-American Defense Board. January 1, 1966.

Roseborough, Morgan Garrott. Major General, United States Army; Commanding General, Fort Devens, Massachusetts, 1973-   . Born June 14, 1918, Memphis, Tennessee. University of Mississippi, BA, Economics; The Infantry School, Advanced Course; US Army Command and General Staff College; US Army War College. Commissioned Second Lieutenant, US Army Reserve, 1939. Served in WW II and Vietnam War. Assistant Division Commander, 9th Infantry Division, Fort Riley, Kansas, later, US Army Pacific-Vietnam, 1966-68; Director of Plans, Programs and Budget, Office, Deputy Chief of Staff for Personnel, US Army, Washington, D.C., 1968-69; Commanding General, 3d Armored Division, US Army,

Europe, 1969-71; Deputy Chief, Office of Reserve Components, US Army, Washington, D.C., 1971-72; Chief of Staff, later Acting Deputy Commanding General, US Army Vietnam, and Commanding General, The Support Troops, US Army Vietnam, US Army Pacific-Vietnam, 1972; Commanding General, US Army Vietnam/Military Assistance Command, Vietnam Support Command, US Army Pacific-Vietnam, 1972-73. Distinguished Service Medal; Silver Star with Oak Leaf Cluster; Legion of Merit with three Oak Leaf Clusters; Distinguished Flying Cross; Bronze Star Medal; and other medals and awards. Promoted to Brigadier General, August 1, 1966; Major General, September 1, 1969.

Rosenberg, Edwin Miller. Rear Admiral, United States Navy; Deputy Commander in Chief, US Naval Forces, Europe, and Chief of Staff, Commander in Chief, US Naval Forces, Europe, 1971-   . Born February 24, 1919, Moscow, Idaho. US Naval Academy, 1938-41; Flight Training Course, 1944-45; Johns Hopkins University, 1947; Industrial College of the Armed Forces, 1960-61. Commissioned Ensign, US Navy, in 1941; designated Naval Aviator in 1945. Served in the Atlantic Theater in WW II; Korean War; Vietnam War. Commander Destroyer Division TWO HUNDRED THIRTY-TWO, 1963-64; Assistant Chief of Staff for Operations and Readiness, Staff of Commander First Fleet, 1964-66; Commanding Officer USS *Canberra* (CAG-2), 1966-67; Fleet Plans Officer, Staff of Commander in Chief, Pacific Fleet, 1967-68; Deputy Chief of Staff for Logistics, Personnel and Administration, US Pacific Fleet, 1968; Commander Amphibious Group THREE, 1968-70, and Commander Amphibious Group Eastern Pacific, 1969-70; Commander Naval Reserve Training Command, Omaha, Nebraska, 1970-71. Legion of Merit with two Gold Stars and Combat "V"; Meritorious Service Medal; Navy Commendation Medal; and other US and foreign medals and awards. Promoted to Rear Admiral, July 1, 1969.

Rosencrans, Evan W. Major General, United States Air Force; Deputy Chief of Staff, Plans, US Air Forces in Europe, Germany, 1973-   . Born May 31, 1926, in Sayre, Pennsylvania. US Military Academy, 1944-48; Basic and Advanced Pilot Training Course, 1948-49; Air Command and Staff College, 1959-60; Industrial College of the Armed Forces, 1967-68; George Washington University, MBA, 1968. Commissioned Second Lieutenant, US Air Force, 1948. Served in the Korean War and the Vietnam War. Assistant Deputy Commander for Operations, 37th Tactical Fighter Wing, Phu Cat Air Base, Vietnam, 1968-69; Chief, Current Operations Division, and later, Chief, Current Plans Division, Headquarters Seventh Air Force, Tan Son Nhut Air Base, Vietnam, 1969; Vice Commander, 4531st Tactical Fighter Wing, Homestead Air Force Base, Florida, 1969-70; Commander, 4554th Tactical Fighter Wing, Myrtle Beach Air Force Base, South Carolina, 1970-71; Deputy Director of Inspection, 1002d Inspector General Group, Norton Air Force Base, California, 1971; Director of Inspection, US Air Force Inspection and Safety Center, Norton Air Force Base, California, 1971-73. Legion of Merit with Oak Leaf Cluster; Distinguished Flying Cross with three Oak Leaf Clusters; Air Medal with sixteen Oak Leaf Clusters; Republic of Vietnam Medal of Honor, First Class; and other US and foreign medals and awards. Promoted to Brigadier General, February 1, 1972; Major General, 1973.

Rosenius, Bengt. Major General, Swedish Royal Air Force; Commanding General, 1st Air Command, 1973-   . Attended Royal National Defense College, 1957, 1966. Wing Commander F 3, 1962-65; Inspector General, Flight Safety, 1965-73. Commander of the Royal Order of the Sword; and other medals and awards. Promoted to Major General, 1973.

Ross, Donald Henry. Major General, United States Air Force; Assistant Director, Plans, Programs, and Systems, DSA, 1973-   . Born October 14, 1923, Modesto, California. Civilian Flying School, 1940; Royal Air Force Flying Courses, 1941-42; Air Tactical School, 1947; University of Southern California, 1947-49, BS, Industrial Management, 1953; National War College, 1964-65; George Washington University, MS, International Affairs, 1965. Enlisted in Royal Air Force, 1941; transferred to US Army Air Force, 1942; commissioned Second Lieutenant by direct appointment, US Army Air Corps, 1942. Combat duty in the European Theater in WW II, POW, 1943-45. Deputy Chief, Air Force Section, Joint US Military Advisory Group, Thailand, 1962-63; Director of Operations, Headquarters 2d Air Division, Vietnam, 1962-64; Vice Commander, then Commander, 479th Tactical Fighter Wing, 1966-67; Chief, Tactical and Airlift Division, Directorate of Aerospace Programs, Headquarters USAF, 1967-68; Director, Special Projects, Directorate of Aerospace Programs, 1968-70; Commander, 347th Tactical Fighter Wing, Japan, 1970-71; Commander, 327th Air Division, Taipei Air Station, Taiwan, and Chief of Air Force Section, Military Advisory Assistance Group, Republic of China, 1971-73. Legion of Merit with Oak Leaf Cluster; Distinguished Flying Cross; Bronze Star Medal; and other medals and awards.

Ross, Marion Collier. Major General, United States Army; Director, Human Resources Development, Office of the Deputy Chief of Staff for Personnel, 1973-   . Born January 24, 1927, in Moberly, Missouri. Attended US Military Academy; Ground General School; Infantry School, Basic and Advanced Courses; Command and General Staff College; Armed Forces Staff College; Army War College, 1966-67; George Washington University, MS, International Affairs. Commissioned Second Lieutenant June 3, 1949. Served in the Vietnam War. Commanding Officer, 2d Batallion, 12th Cavalry, then Assistant Chief of Staff, G-3, Operations, 1st Cavalry Division (Airmobile), US Army, Pacific-Vietnam, 1967-68; Commanding Officer, 3d Regiment, US Corps of Cadets, US Military Academy, West Point, New York, 1968-70; Commanding Officer, 3d Brigade, 4th Infantry Division (Mechanized), Fort Carson, Colorado, 1970-71; Commanding General, 173d Airborne Brigade, Fort Campbell, Kentucky, 1971-72; Deputy Commanding General, US Army Training Center, and Fort

Campbell, Kentucky, 1972; Assistant Division Commander, 101st Airborne Division (Airmobile), Fort Campbell, Kentucky, 1972-73; Deputy Director of Operations, Office of the Deputy Chief of Staff for Military Operations, 1973. Silver Star; Legion of Merit with two Oak Leaf Clusters; Distinguished Flying Cross; Bronze Star Medal with V Device with two Oak Leaf Clusters; Air Medal with V Device (13 awards); and other medals and awards. Promoted to Brigadier General February 1, 1972; Major General 1973.

Rosseykin, I. Major General, USSR Army; Deputy Chief, Political Directorate, Group of Soviet Forces in Germany. Served on the Soviet-German Front in WW II. Member, Communist Party of the Soviet Union.

Rosson, William Bradford. General, United States Army; Commander in Chief, US Southern Command, Quarry Heights, Canal Zone, 1973-   . Born August 25, 1918, Des Moines, Iowa. University of Oregon, BS Degree, Business Administration; US Army Command and General Staff College; US Army War College; The National War College. Commissioned Second Lieutenant, US Army Reserve, 1940. Served in WW II and Vietnam War. Commanding General, I Field Force, Vietnam, US Army, Pacific-Vietnam, 1967-68; Commanding General, Provisional Corps, Vietnam, US Army, Pacific-Vietnam, 1968; Director, Plans and Policy Directorate, J-5, Organization, Joint Chiefs of Staff, Washington, D.C., 1968-69; Deputy Commander, US Military Assistance Command, Vietnam, 1969-70; Commander in Chief, US Army, Pacific, Fort Shafter, Hawaii, 1970-73. Distinguished Service Cross; Distinguished Service Medal with four Oak Leaf Clusters; Legion of Merit with Oak Leaf Cluster; Bronze Star Medal with two Oak Leaf Clusters; and other medals and awards. Promoted to Brigadier General, April 1, 1961; Major General, May 1, 1962; Lieutenant General, August 1, 1967; General, May 15, 1969.

Rousselot. Admiral, French Navy; Commander in Chief Atlantic Theater and Prefet Maritime of the Second Region.

Rowland, James Anthony. Air Vice Marshal, Royal Australian Air Force; Air Member for Technical Services, 1972-   . Born November 1, 1922. Attended St. Paul's College, Sydney University; Empire Test Pilots' Course, 1949; Royal Australian Air Force Staff College, 1956; Royal College of Defence Science, London, 1971. Commissioned in 1943. Served with the RAF Bomber Command in WW II. Commanding Officer, 3rd Aircraft Depot, Amberley, Queensland, 1967-69; Senior Engineer Staff Officer, Operational Command, 1969. DFC; AFC; BE (Aero). Fellow of the Royal Aeronautical Society.

Rowny, Edward Leon. Lieutenant General, United States Army; Deputy Chairman, North Atlantic Treaty Organization Military Committee, 1971-   . Born April 3, 1917, Baltimore, Maryland. US Military Academy; US Command and General Staff College; Armed Forces Staff College; The National War College; Johns Hopkins

University, BS Degree, Civil Engineering; Yale University, MS Degree, Civil Engineering, and MA Degree, International Relations. Commissioned Second Lieutenant, 1941. Served in WW II. Commanding General, 24th Infantry Division, US Army, Europe, 1965-66; Deputy Chief of Staff for Logistics, US Army, Europe and Seventh Army, 1966-68; Deputy Chief of Staff, US European Command, 1968-69; Deputy Chief of Research and Development, US Army, Washington, D.C., 1969-70; Commanding General, I Corps (Group), US Army, Pacific-Korea, 1970-71. Distinguished Service Medal; Silver Star with two Oak Leaf Clusters; Legion of Merit with four Oak Leaf Clusters; Bronze Star Medal with V Device; and other medals and awards. Promoted to Brigadier General, August 1, 1961; Major General, December 1, 1962; Lieutenant General, August 1, 1970.

Rozlubirski, Edwin. Lieutenant General, Polish Army; Deputy Inspector General of Training (Airborne Troops) 1968-   . Born 1926. General Staff War College, 1956. Commissioned Captain in the Polish Army, 1945. Participated in Anti-German guerrilla warfare in Poland, WW II. Commander, 6th Airborne Division, 1963-68. Polonia Restituta, III and V Class; Cross of Grunwald, III Class; Virtuti Militari, V Class; Order of Valor (twice); and other orders and awards. Member, Polish United Workers Party. Promoted to Major General, October 1965.

Rubio, Fausto David. General, Guatemalan Army; Minister of National Defense, 1973-   .

Ruchibhan, Chanien. Admiral, Royal Thai Navy. Assistant Commander in Chief, Royal Thai Navy.

Rudberg, Per Y. Rear Admiral, Swedish Royal Navy; Commander in Chief, Military Command, Lower Norrland, 1973-   . Born August 29, 1922. Attended Royal Naval Staff College, 1950-53; Ecole Superieure Interarmées, 1960. Commissioned in the Royal Navy, 1944. Commander, 1st Destroyer/Torpedo Boat Flotilla, 1967-70. Commander of the Royal Order of the Sword; and other medals and awards. Member, Royal Academy of Military Sciences; Member, Royal Society of Naval Sciences. Promoted to Rear Admiral, October 1, 1973.

Rudnev, I.S. Vice Admiral, USSR Navy; Chief, Political Directorate, Black Sea Fleet, 1966-   . Served in the Soviet-German War, 1941-45. Member, Communist Party of the Soviet Union.

Ruiz, Hilario M. Commodore, Philippine Navy; Flag Officer in Command, Philippine Navy. Born January 14, 1915, in Bustos, Bulacan. Attended Philippine Nautical School, Pasay, 1938; General Line Officers Course, OSP School, Port Area Manila, 1941; Ship Damage Control and Fire, US Service School, Treasure Island, USA, 1951; MLQ University (Pre-Law), 1957; Command and General Staff Course, Command and General Staff School, Fort McKinley, Rizal, 1959; Advanced Management Program, Baguio City, 1968. Commissioned Ensign in 1941. Served in the Philippines in WW II. Recent duty includes Commander, Naval Training Command; Acting Commander, Cavite Naval Base; Acting Commander, Patrol Force; Assistant Chief for Logistics, J-4; Vice Commander, Philippine Navy; Deputy Chief of Staff, GHQ. Philippine Defense Medal with one Bronze Star; Philippine Liberation Medal; Distinguished Service Star; and other medals and awards.

Ruiz Velarde, Cesar. General, Bolivian Army; Director of National Intelligence Service, 1973-   .

Russell, Austin J. Lieutenant General, United States Air Force; Assistant Vice Chief of Staff, US Air Force, and Senior Air Force Member, Military Staff Committee, United Nations, 1970-   . Born June 4, 1915, in Monett, Missouri. Monett Junior College, Monett, Missouri, 1936; US Military Academy, 1936-40; Flying School, 1942; Armed Forces Staff College, 1948-49; National War College, 1955-56. Commissioned in 1940; received pilot wings, 1942. Combat duty in the China-Burma-India Theater, WW II; Korean War. Commander, 822d Air Division, 1959-61; Director of Personnel, Headquarters, Strategic Air Command, 1961; Deputy Director, Operations, Headquarters, Strategic Air Command, 1961-63; Director, Operations, Headquarters, Strategic Air Command, 1963-64; Deputy Commander, Eighth Air Force, 1964-65; Deputy Commander, Fifteenth Air Force, 1965-66; Commander, Second Air Force, 1966-69; Deputy Chief of Staff, Personnel, Headquarters, USAF, 1969-70. Distinguished Service Medal, Legion of Merit with four Oak Leaf Clusters; Distinguished Flying Cross; and other medals and awards. Promoted to Brigadier General, September 1, 1957; Major General, June 1, 1961; Lieutenant General, August 1, 1966.

Russell, Kendall. Major General, United States Air Force; Director of Development and Acquisition, Deputy Chief of Staff, Research and Development, Headquarters USAF, 1973-   . Born January 25, 1925, Fort Leavenworth, Kansas. US Military Academy, 1942-45; Purdue University, MS, Nuclear Physics, 1950; Air Command and Staff College, 1960-61; Industrial College of the Armed Forces, 1965-66; George Washington University, MBA, 1966. Commissioned Second Lieutenant, US Army Air Corps, 1945. Space Development Plans Officer, Directorate of Development, Headquarters US Air Force, Washington, D.C., 1963-65; Director, General Purpose and Airlift Systems Planning, Office of Deputy Chief of Staff, Development Plans, Headquarters Air Force Systems Command, Andrews Air Force Base, Maryland, 1966-68; Director, Airborne Warning and Control Systems, Headquarters Electronic Systems Division, L.G. Hanscom Field, Massachusetts, 1968-71; Deputy for Airborne Warning and Control Systems, Headquarters Electronic Systems Division, Air Force Systems Command, 1971-73. Legion of Merit; and other medals and awards. Promoted to Brigadier General, August 1, 1971; Major General, 1973.

Ryabov, Yu. Lieutenant General, USSR Army; Deputy Commander, Armored Forces, 1972- . Degree in Mechanical Engineering. Served on the Soviet-German Front in WW II. Formerly Commander, Armored Division. Member, Communist Party of the Soviet Union.

Ryan, Michael Patrick. Major General, United States Marine Corps; Commanding General, III Marine Amphibious Force, and Commanding General, 3d Marine Division, 1973- . Born January 31, 1916, Osage City, Kansas. Rockhurst College; Amphibious Warfare School, Junior Course, Quantico, 1946; Command and General Staff College, 1953-54; National War College, 1963-64; George Washington University, BA, Political Science, 1966. Enlisted in Marine Corps Reserve, 1933; Commissioned Second Lieutenant, USMCR, 1940. Served in Iceland and South Pacific Area, WW II; Korean War; Vietnam War. Assistant Director, Joint Planning Group, Office of Deputy Chief of Staff (Plans and Programs), Headquarters Marine Corps, 1964; Assistant Chief of Staff, G-2, Headquarters Marine Corps, 1966; Commanding General, 9th Marine Amphibious Brigade and Commanding General, Fleet Marine Force, Seventh Fleet, 1966; Assistant Division Commander, 3d Marine Division, Vietnam, 1967; Director, Command and Staff College, and Deputy for Education Director, Education Center, Quantico, 1967-69; Commanding General, 2d Marine Division, Fleet Marine Force, 1969-71; Deputy Commander, Fleet Marine Force, Atlantic, 1971-72. Navy Cross; Legion of Merit with Combat "V"; and other US and foreign medals and awards. Promoted to Brigadier General, January 1966; Major General, September 1, 1968.

Ryder, Charles Wolcott, Jr. Major General, United States Army; Chief, Joint US Military Aid Group to Greece, 1972- . Born November 24, 1920, Trenton, New Jersey. US Military Academy; The Infantry School, Basic Course; US Army Command and General Staff College; US Army War College. Commissioned Second Lieutenant, 1942. Served in WW II and Vietnam War. Commanding General, 199th Infantry Brigade, Fort Benning, Georgia, later US Army, Pacific-Vietnam, 1966-67; Assistant Division Commander, 4th Infantry Division, US Army, Pacific-Vietnam, 1967; Assistant Division Commander, 23d Infantry Division (Americal), US Army, Pacific-Vietnam, 1967-68; Assistant Chief of Staff, G-1, later Deputy Chief of Staff for Personnel, US Army, Pacific, Fort Shafter, Hawaii, 1968-70; Chief of Staff, Fourth, later Fifth US Army, Fort Sam Houston, Texas, 1970-72. Distinguished Service Medal; Silver Star with two Oak Leaf Clusters; Legion of Merit with three Oak Leaf Clusters; Distinguished Flying Cross; Bronze Star Medal with V Device and three Oak Leaf Clusters; and other medals and awards. Promoted to Brigadier General, October 27, 1966; Major General, September 1, 1970.

Rytir, Otakar. General, Army of Czechoslovakia; Chairman, Czechoslovak Union for Cooperation with the Army, 1970- . Born June 23, 1913. Attended Voroshilov General Staff College, Moscow, 1947-48. Joined Czechoslovak Army, 1935. Served in Czechoslovak units in USSR in WW II. Assigned to General Staff Headquarters, Ministry of National Defense, 1945-47; First Deputy Minister of National Defense and Chief of Army General Staff, 1957-68; staff of Military History Museum, 1968-69; Government Liaison Representative to Soviet forces in Czechoslovakia, 1969-70. Member of Czechoslovak Communist Party.

S

Sa'adatmand, Abol-Hassan. General, Imperial Iranian Army; Director, Public Relations, Supreme General Staff. Born in 1923. Attended Military College, Teheran; War College; degree of Doctor, of the Faculty of Law, Teheran, 1962. Deputy Director, State Intelligence and Security Organization (SAVAK), 1964; General Under-Secretary, Ministry of Information. Promoted to Brigadier, 1964; Major General, 1968.

al Sabah, al Salem. Minister of Defense, Kuwait.

Sadek, Frantisek. Colonel General, Army of Czechoslovakia; Commander of the Border Guard, Ministry of the Interior, 1970- . Born December 24, 1921, in Zilina, Slovakia. Attended Reserve Officers' School, 1945; Career Branch School, 1947; Field Grade Officers' Advanced Course, 1954; Voroshilov General Staff College, Moscow, 1956-58. Served in Slovak Army, then Sklabina Partisan Battalion, then 1st Czechoslovak Army Corps, in WW II. Deputy Minister of National Defense, 1964-66; Head of Department, Ministry of National Defense 1966-68; Commander, Western Military District, 1968-69. Member of Czechoslovak Communist Party.

Sadri, Ja'afar-Qoli. Lieutenant General, Imperial Iranian Army; Chief of Police, 1970- . Born in 1917, in Isfahan. Attended Military Academy, Teheran; Command and Staff College, Teheran. Deputy Division Commander, "Khanah" (Kurdistan); Deputy Adjutant, later Chief Adjutant to the Acting Adjutant General of His Imperial Majesty the Shahanshah Aryamehr.

Safiullah, K.M. Brigadier, Bangladesh Army; Chief of Staff, Bangladesh Army, 1973- .

St. George, Douglas Fitzclarence. Air Vice Marshal, Royal New Zealand Air Force; Chief of Staff, RNZAF, 1971- . Born in Nelson, c. 1922. Attended Seddon Memorial Technical College; Imperial Defence College, 1968. Commissioned Lieutenant in 1940. Served in the Pacific Theater in WW II. Commanding Officer, 14th Squadron, Japan, 1947-48; Commanding Officer, RNZAF Station Ohakea, New Zealand, 1958-60; New Zealand Military Advisers Representative, SEATO, Bangkok, 1963-66; Air Officer Commanding RNZAF Training Group, 1966-68; Air Member for Personnel, 1969-70; Deputy Chief, Air Staff, 1970-71. Commander of the British

Empire; Distinguished Flying Cross; Air Force Cross; Legion of Merit (USA). Promoted to Air Vice Marshal, July 23, 1971.

St. John, Adrian, II. Major General, United States Army; Commanding General, 1st Armored Division, US Army, Europe, 1972- . Born November 16, 1921, Fort Leavenworth, Kansas. US Military Academy; The Cavalry School, Basic Course; The Army Armored School, Advanced Course; US Army Command and General Staff College; US Army War College; University of Virginia, MA Degree, International Relations. Commissioned Second Lieutenant, 1943. Served in WW II and Vietnam War. Commanding Officer, 14th Armored Cavalry Regiment, US Army, Europe, 1967-69; Executive Officer to the Commander in Chief, US Army, Europe, and Seventh Army, 1969; Assistant Division Commander, 4th Armored Division, US Army, Europe, 1969-70; Chief, Strategic Plans and Policy Division, J-5, Joint Staff, Organization, Joint Chiefs of Staff, Washington, D.C., 1970-71; Director of Plans, Office, Deputy Chief of Staff for Military Operations, US Army, Washington, D.C., 1971-72. Distinguished Service Medal; Silver Star; Legion of Merit with two Oak Leaf Clusters; Bronze Star Medal; and other medals and awards. Promoted to Brigadier General, December 1, 1969; Major General, September 1, 1971.

Salisbury, Arthur G. Major General, United States Air Force; Commander, US Air Forces Southern Command, 1972- . Born September 13, 1916, in Sedalia, Missouri. University of Arkansas, Law School, 1939; Army Air Corps Flying School, 1939-40; Air War College, 1949-50. Commissioned Second Lieutenant, US Army Air Corps, 1940. Combat duty in the Mediterranean and European Theaters, WW II. Commander, New York Air Defense Sector and New York NORAD Sector, 1962-63; Director of Operations, J-3, North American Air Defense Command/Continental Air Defense Command (NORAD/CONAD), 1963-64; Chief, Joint Command and Control Requirements Group, Joint Chiefs of Staff Organization, 1964-66; Deputy Chief of Staff, Plans, Headquarters Air Defense Command, 1966-67; Director, Joint Continental Defense Systems Integration Planning Staff, Joint Chiefs of Staff Organization, 1967-70; Chief of Staff, Headquarters Aerospace Defense Command (ADC), 1970-72. Distinguished Service Medal; Legion of Merit with three Oak Leaf Clusters; and other US and foreign medals and awards. Promoted to Major General, November 1, 1964.

Salleh, Mohn Zain bin Mohd. Captain, Malaysian Navy; Deputy to Chief of the Naval Staff.

Salmela, Eero J.V. Major General, Air Force of Finland; Commanding General, Finnish Air Forces, 1969- . Born April 22, 1920, Pori (Turku and Pori Province), Finland. Attended War College, 1953-55. Served in Winter War; Continuation War. Chief of Air Defense Headquarters Finnish Air Force, 1962-65; Chief of Staff, Headquarters, Finnish Air Force, 1965-68; Commanding Officer,

Satakunta Air Wing, 1968-69. Cross of Freedom, 4th Class with Sword; Order of Finnish Lion, 1st Class; Commemorative Medals of Winter and Continuation Wars; and other medals and awards. Promoted to Major General, February 7, 1969.

Salmanov, G. Colonel General, USSR Army; Commander, Kiev Military District, 1969- . Served on the Soviet-German Front in WW II. Member, Communist Party of the Soviet Union.

Salter, Sylvan Edwin. Major General, United States Army; Director of Air Defense, Office of the Assistant Chief of Staff for Force Development, 1972- . Born November 9, 1924, in Shreveport, Louisiana. Attended US Military Academy; Artillery School; Command and General Staff College; Industrial College of the Armed Forces, 1967-68; University of Southern California, MS, Guided Missiles. Commissioned June 5, 1945. Commanding Officer, 4th Missile Battalion, 57th Artillery, US Army, Europe, 1965-67; Member, Strategic Defense Branch, later Development Branch, Requirements and Development Division, J-5, Joint Chiefs of Staff Organization, 1968-70; Commanding Officer, 31st Artillery Brigade (Air Defense), Homestead Air Force Base, Florida, 1970-71; Director of Missiles and Space, Office of the Chief of Research and Development, 1971-72; Director of Developments, Office of the Chief of Research and Development, 1972. Legion of Merit with two Oak Leaf Clusters and other medals and awards. Promoted to Brigadier General August 1, 1971; Major General June 1, 1973.

Salvador Diaz-Benjumea, Julio. Lieutenant General, Spanish Air Force; Air Minister (Secretary of the Air Force), 1969- . Formerly Commander, 23d Fighter Group; Director, Fighter Aircraft School; Air Attache, Spanish Embassy, Washington, D.C., USA; Director of Air Force Military Academy, and Chief of Murcia Air Sector; Commander, 5th Fighter Wing and Joint Base Moron de la Frontera; Chief of Staff, 2d Air Region (Seville); Chief, Air Defense Command; Deputy Chief, Joint Staff. Military Medal (Individual); Air Medal; Great Crosses: Army, Navy and Air Force Merit and Saint Hermenegild Royal and Military Order; Great Crosses: Civil Merit, King Alphonse X and Queen Isabela the Catholic; War Cross with Palms; two War Crosses; two Red Crosses of Military Merit; Red Arrows Imperial Order; Legion of Honor (Great Official Rank), France; US Legion of Merit (Official and Commander Ranks), USA; Great Cross of Aviz Military Order, Portugal; and other medals and awards. Promoted to Lieutenant General, March 25, 1970.

Salzer, Robert Samuel. Vice Admiral, United States Navy; Commander Amphibious Force, US Pacific Fleet, 1972- . Born July 29, 1919, New York, New York. Yale University, New Haven, Connecticut, BA, Economics, 1937-40; Naval Intelligence School, 1948-49; Industrial College of the Armed Forces, 1959-60. Commissioned Ensign, US Naval Reserve, in 1940; transferred to US Navy in 1946. Served in the Atlantic Theater in WW II; Vietnam

War. Commanding Officer USS *Bryce Canyon*, 1961-63; Commander Destroyer Division ONE HUNDRED THIRTY TWO and later ONE HUNDRED NINETY TWO, 1963-64; Head of Analytical Support Group, Office of CNO, 1964-65; Deputy Program Director, Fast Deployment Logistic Ship Project, and Deputy Project Manager, Fast Deployment Logistic Ship Project, Office of the Chief of Naval Operations/Office of the Chief of Naval Material, 1965-66; Commander Amphibious Squadron FOUR, 1966-67; Commander River Assault Flotilla ONE/Commander River Support Squadron SEVEN/Commander Riverine Assault Force, 1967-68; Project Officer, Future Professional Manpower Requirements Study, Office of CNO, 1968-69; Commander Cruiser-Destroyer Flotilla THREE, 1969-70; Commander Cruiser-Destroyer Flotilla SEVEN, 1970-71; Commander United States Naval Forces, Vietnam, and Chief of Naval Advisory Group, Military Assistance Command, Vietnam, 1971-72. Distinguished Service Medal with Gold Star; Air Medal; Navy Commendation Medal; and other US and foreign medals and awards. Promoted to Rear Admiral, August 1, 1969; Vice Admiral, September 1, 1972.

Sam, Tran. Major General, People's Army of Vietnam; Vice Minister of National Defense, 1962; Deputy Chief, General Staff, 1965; Member, Central Military Party Committee. Chief, General Directorate of Rear Services, 1963-64; Deputy to Third National Assembly, 1964. Promoted to Major General, 1961.

Samater, Mohamed Ali. Brigadier General, Somali Army; Minister of Defense.

Sammet, George, Jr. Major General, United States Army; Deputy Chief of Research and Development, US Army, Washington, D.C., 1971- . Born September 18, 1919, Chicago, Illinois. University of Illinois, BS Degree, Agronomy; The Artillery School, Basic and Advanced Courses; US Army Command and General Staff College; US Armed Forces Staff College; US National War College. Commissioned Second Lieutenant, US Army Reserve, 1940. Served in WW II. Executive Officer, Office, Chief of Research and Development, US Army, Washington, D.C., 1966-67; Deputy Director of Development, US Army Materiel Command, Washington, D.C., 1967-68; Senior Advisor, First Republic of Korea Army, and Commander, Detachment "L" (Provisional), US Army Advisory Group Korea, 1968-69; Director, Plans and Programs, and Deputy Chief of Research and Development for International Programs, Office, Chief of Research and Development, US Army, Washington, D.C., 1969-71. Legion of Merit with two Oak Leaf Clusters; Bronze Star Medal with V Device and other medals and awards. Promoted to Brigadier General, August 18, 1967; Major General, November 1, 1970.

Samokhodskiy, P. Ya. Major General, USSR Army; Chief of Staff, Urals Military District, 1969- . Served on the Soviet-German Front in WW II. Member, Communist Party of the Soviet Union.

Sampaio Fernandes, Octavio José. Fleet Admiral, Brazilian Navy; Director-General of Naval Material, 1972- . Attended Brazilian Naval School; Naval War College; Senior War College; Submarine Course, Officers School for Improvement and Specialization. Combat duty in World War II. Commandant, 1st Naval District; Commandant, 4th Naval District; Deputy Chief for Operations, Navy General Staff; Commander in Chief of the Fleet, Naval Transport Force, Submarine Flotilla, submarine *Riachuelo* and tug *Triunfo*. Instructor, Air Command and General Staff School; Naval Attache, Embassies of Brazil in Buenos Aires and Montevideo. Medalha do Pacificador (Army); Ordem do Mérito Militar; Ordem do Mérito Aeronáutico; Ordem do Mérito Naval; Medalha do Mérito Tamandaré; Medalha da Força Naval do Sul; Medalha da Força Naval do Nordeste; and other medals and awards of Brazil and other nations. Promoted to Rear Admiral, December 31, 1965; Vice Admiral, October 11, 1968; Fleet Admiral, December 31, 1971.

Sancar, M. Semih. General, Turkish Army; Chief of Turkish General Staff, 1973- . Studied at Military Academy; Artillery School; War College. Formerly Division Commander; Assistant Chief of Staff for Operations to Chief of General Staff; Commander, War College; Commander, Army Corps; Assistant Chief of Staff to Commander Land Forces; Commander, Gendarmerie Forces; Army Commander; Commander, Land Forces. Distinguished Courageous Service Award; Distinguished Unit; Distinguished Homeland Service; and other medals and awards. Promoted to General, August 30, 1969.

Sanches, Eliado. General, Bolivian Army; Chief of Staff, Armed Forces of Bolivia, 1973- . Formerly Commander of the Army.

Sanchez, Heberto. Colonel, Army of Nicaragua; Minister of Defense, Nicaragua, 1973- .

Sanders, Frank. United States Under Secretary of the Navy, 1972- . Born July 30, 1919, Tarboro, North Carolina. Armstrong Junior College, Savannah, Georgia; George Washington Law School. US Army, private to captain, 1941-45; Army Officer Reserve Corps, 1945- ; combat duty, World War II. Staff Member, Committee on Appropriations, House of Representatives, 1950-69; Assistant Secretary of the Navy (Installations and Logistics), 1969-70; Assistant Secretary of the Navy (Financial Management), 1971-72. Bronze Star Medal.

Sanguinetti, A.M.F. Rear Admiral, French Navy; Assistant Chief, French Naval Staff.

Sarendy, Vong. Commodore, Cambodian Navy; Chief of Staff of Khmer National Navy.

Sargent, Thomas Reece, III. Vice Admiral, United States Coast Guard; Vice Commandant, US Coast Guard, 1970- . Born December 20, 1914, London, England; naturalized US Citizen, 1930. US Coast Guard Academy,

1934-38; Rensselaer Polytechnic Institute, Troy, New York, BS Degree, Civil Engineering, 1952. Commissioned Ensign, 1938. Served in Atlantic and Pacific Theaters WW II; Vietnam War. Chief, Operations Division, 11th Coast Guard District, Long Beach, California, 1966-67; Commander, 11th Coast Guard District, 1967-68; Chief of Staff, Headquarters, US Coast Guard, 1968-70. Legion of Merit, Bronze Star Medal, Coast Guard Commendation Medal; and other medals and citations. Promoted to Rear Admiral, July, 1967; Vice Admiral, July 1, 1970.

Sarma, S.H. Rear Admiral, Navy of India; Flag Officer Commanding Eastern Fleet.

Sarmanne, Kai B. Lieutenant General, Army of Finland; Secretary General to the Minister of Defense, 1970- . Born April 18, 1919, Ollila, Finland. Military Academy, 1941; War College, 1951-53. Served in Winter War; Continuation War. Staff Officer, Supply Section, General Headquarters, 1953-61; Chief of Transportation Section, General Headquarters, 1963-64; Chief of Planning Office, General Headquarters, 1965-66; Chief of Staff, Secretariat, Defense Council, 1966-70. Cross of Freedom, 3d and 4th Class; Cross of Freedom, 3d Class for Merit; Commander, Order of Finnish Lion; Commemorative Medals for Winter and Continuation Wars; and other medals and awards. Promoted to Lieutenant General, December 6, 1972.

Sartorio, Jorge José. Brigadier General, Argentine Air Force; Air Attache, Embassy of Argentina, Washington, D.C., c. 1971-73.

Saud, His Royal Highness Prince Sultan ibn 'Abd al-'Aziz al. Minister of Defense and Aviation, Saudi, Arabia.

Savelev, F.I. Vice Admiral, USSR Navy. Served in the Soviet-German War (WW II). Chief of Staff, Baltic Fleet, 1967-72. Member, Communist Party of the Soviet Union.

Savitskiy, V. Marshal of Aviation, USSR Air Force; Deputy Commander, Air Defense Forces. Served on the Soviet-German Front in WW II. Member, Communist Party of the Soviet Union.

Sawczuk, Wlodzimierz. Lieutenant General, Polish Army; Chief, Main Political Directorate, and Vice Minister of National Defense, Polish Armed Forces, 1972- . Born in 1925 in Bialystok. Officers School; General Staff War College, USSR, 1961-64. Served in Polish-German War, 1944-45, with the 1st Polish Army in the USSR. Recent positions: Deputy Commander, Political Affairs, Silesian Military District, 1965-70; Deputy Chief, Main Political Directorate, Polish Armed Forces, 1970-72. Polonia Restituta; Cross of Grunwald; Cross of Valor; and other medals and awards. Member Polish United Workers Party; Member of PUWP Control Commission since 1971.

Sawers, James Maxwell. Major-General, British Army; Signal Officer in Chief (Army), 1971- . Born May 14, 1920. Attended Royal Military Academy, Woolwich; Staff College; Joint Services Staff College; Imperial Defence College, 1970. Served in North Africa and Burma in WW II. Brigadier General Staff, Ministry of Defence, 1966-68; Commander of Corps Royal Signals, 1st British Corps, 1968-69. MBE. Member, British Institute of Management.

Sawicki, Florian. Lieutenant General, Polish Army; Chief of General Staff; Vice Minister of National Defense.

Scarborough, Robert Henry, Jr. Rear Admiral, United States Coast Guard; Deputy Chief, Office of Operations, 1973- . Born March 12, 1923, Hawkinsville, Georgia. United States Merchant Marine Academy, 1942-44; Armed Forces Staff College, 1962-63; National War College, 1970-71; Old Dominion University; University of Hawaii, MBA; George Washington University, MS, International Affairs. Commissioned Ensign, USMS, and Ensign, USNR, 1944; Lieutenant (jg), USCG, 1949. Served in WW II. Staff of Commander, Antisubmarine Warfare Force Pacific (US Navy), 1966-69; Chief of Personnel Division, 14th Coast Guard District, Honolulu, Hawaii, 1969-70; Chief, Enlisted Personnel Division, Headquarters US Coast Guard, 1971-73. WW II Campaign Service Medals and Ribbons; and other medals and awards. Promoted to Captain, July 1, 1969; Rear Admiral, 1973.

Schaus, Eugene. Minister of Justice, Interior and Armed Forces, Grand Duchy of Luxembourg.

Scheiderer, Edward Donald. Rear Admiral, United States Coast Guard; Chief of Staff, US Coast Guard, 1973- . Born June 25, 1917, Detroit, Michigan. US Coast Guard Academy, 1939-42; University of Pennsylvania, Philadelphia, Pennsylvania, MA Degree, Business Administration, 1953; Commissioned Ensign, 1942. Served in Atlantic Theater WW II. Chief, Program Analysis Division, Headquarters, US Coast Guard, 1964-68; Chief, Operations Division, 9th Coast Guard District, Cleveland, Ohio, 1969-70; Comptroller, US Coast Guard, 1970-73. Legion of Merit; and other medals and citations. Promoted to Captain, July 1, 1964; Rear Admiral, July 1, 1970.

Schlesinger, James R. United States Secretary of Defense, 1973- . Born February 15, 1929, New York, New York. Harvard University, BA, 1950, MA, 1952, PhD, 1956, Economics. Associate Professor of Economics, University of Virginia, 1955-63; Academic Consultant, US Naval War College, 1957; Director of Strategic Studies, Rand Corporation, Santa Monica, California, 1963-69; Assistant Director, Bureau of the Budget; Assistant Director, Office of Management and Budget; Chairman, US Atomic Energy Commission; Director, Central Intelligence Agency, February-July, 1973. Publication: *The Political Economy of National Security*, 1960.

Schmitt, Harrison H. United States; NASA Scientist-Astronaut, 1965- . Born July 3, 1935, Santa Rita, New Mexico. California Institute of Technology, BS, Science, 1957; University of Oslo, Norway, 1957-58; Harvard University, PhD, Geology, 1964; NASA Flight

Training Course. Geologist with Norwegian Geological Survey and US Geological Survey; Teaching Fellow at Harvard, 1961; Geologist at US Geological Survey's Astrogeology Center, Flagstaff, Arizona. NASA experience: Backup Lunar Module Pilot, Apollo 15; Lunar Module Pilot, Apollo 17. Fellowships: Fulbright (1957-58), Kennecott (1958-59), Harvard (1959-60), Harvard Traveling (1960), Parker Traveling (1961-62), National Science Foundation Post-Doctoral (1963-64); Manned Spacecraft Center Superior Achievement Award.

Schneider, Raymond John. Rear Admiral, United States Navy; Commander, Naval Electronic Systems Command (NAVELEX), 1972- . Born October 20, 1917, Cleveland, Ohio. John Carroll University, Ohio, 1934-36; US Naval Academy, 1936-40; Flight Training Course, 1942-43; Naval Postgraduate School, Aeronautical Engineering Course, 1944-45; Massachusetts Institute of Technology, MS, Aeronautical Engineering; Industrial College of Armed Forces, 1959-60. Commissioned Ensign, US Navy, in 1940; designated Naval Aviator in 1943. Served in the Pacific Theater in WW II. Director, Aeronautical Electronic and Electrical Laboratory, Naval Air Development Center, 1960-64; Bureau of Naval Weapons Representative, Westinghouse Electric Corporation, Baltimore, 1964-65; Missile Development Officer, Bureau of Naval Weapons, 1965-66; Executive Director and Acting Assistant Commander for Research and Technology, Naval Air Systems Command Headquarters, 1966-67; Assistant Deputy Commander for Plans, Programs, and Comptroller, Naval Air Systems Command Headquarters, 1967-68; Assistant Commander for Research and Technology, 1968-71; Vice Commander, Naval Electronic Systems Command, 1971-72. Legion of Merit with Gold Star; and other medals and awards. Promoted to Rear Admiral, August 1, 1968.

Schoning, William M. Major General, United States Air Force; Director, Policy Plans and National Security Council Affairs, Office of the Secretary of Defense (ISA), 1973- . Born February 22, 1922, in Seattle, Washington. Aviation Cadet Training Course, 1943-44; University of Washington, BA, Accounting, 1948, MA, Business Administration, 1950; National War College, 1967-68; George Washington University, MA, International Affairs, 1968. Commissioned Second Lieutenant, US Army Air Corps, 1944. Combat duty in the European Theater, WW II, and the Korean War. Deputy Chief, Control Division, Headquarters Strategic Air Command, Offutt Air Force Base, Nebraska, 1964-66; Chief, Strategic Plans Branch, Directorate of Plans, Deputy Chief of Staff, Plans and Operations, Headquarters US Air Force, Washington, D.C., 1966-67; Deputy Assistant for Joint Matters, Directorate of Plans, Deputy Chief of Staff, Plans and Operations, Headquarters US Air Force, Washington, D.C., 1968-69; Assistant Director, Joint and National Security Council Matters, Headquarters US Air Force, Washington, D.C., 1969-71; Deputy Director for Plans and Policy, Directorate of Plans, Deputy Chief of Staff, Plans and Operations, Headquarters US Air Force, Washington, D.C.,

with additional duties as Air Force Delegate to the United States Delegation, Inter-American Defense Board, Air Force Member, United States Delegation, Joint Brazil-United States Defense Commission, and Air Force Member, United States Section, Joint Mexican-United States Defense Commission, 1971-73. Air Medal with two Oak Leaf Clusters; Air Force Commendation Medal with two Oak Leaf Clusters; Army Commendation Medal; and other medals and awards. Promoted to Brigadier General, June 1, 1970; Major General, 1973.

Schrader, Henry Carl. Major General, United States Army; Commanding General, US Army Computer Systems Command, Fort Belvoir, Virginia, 1971- . Born January 5, 1918, Chicago, Illinois. University of Illinois, BS Degree, Civil Engineering; US Army Command and General Staff College; Industrial College of the Armed Forces; University of Illinois, MS Degree, Civil Engineering. Commissioned Second Lieutenant, US Army Reserve, 1939. Served in WW II and Vietnam War. Chief, Systems Analysis Group, later Studies and Models Group, Force Planning and Analysis Office, Office, Chief of Staff, US Army, Washington, D.C., 1966-67; Director, Management Information Systems, Office, Assistant Vice Chief of Staff, US Army, Washington, D.C., 1967-70; Commanding General, 18th Engineer Brigade, US Army, Pacific-Vietnam, 1970-71. Distinguished Service Medal; Legion of Merit with three Oak Leaf Clusters; and other medals and awards. Promoted to Brigadier General, August 1, 1968; Major General, April 1, 1971.

Schroth, Enrique. Major General, Peruvian Air Force; Air Attache, Embassy of Peru, Washington, D.C.

Schuler, Ernst. Brigadier General, Swiss Army; Director of Military Science, Federal Institute of Technology. Born in 1915.

Schulke, Herbert Ardis, Jr. Major General, United States Army; Director, J-6, Office of the Joint Chiefs of Staff, 1973- . Born November 12, 1923, in New Ulm, Minnesota. Attended US Military Academy; Infantry School; Signal School, Basic and Advanced Courses, Command and General Staff College; Armed Forces Staff College, 1963-64; Industrial College of the Armed Forces, 1965-66; University of Illinois, MS, Communications Engineering, and PhD, Electrical Engineering. Commissioned Second Lieutenant, June 4, 1946. Communications-Electronics Staff Advisor to the Chief, later Project Officer, Office of the Secretary of Defense/Advanced Research Projects Agency, Research and Development Field Unit, Washington, DC, with station Saigon, Vietnam, 1964-65; Staff Officer, Office of Director of Defense Research and Engineering, Office of the Secretary of Defense, 1965; Principal Military Assistant to Director, Tactical Systems Review and Analysis, Tactical Warfare Programs, later Military Assistant to Deputy Director (Tactical Warfare Programs), Office of the Director of Defense Research and Engineering, Office of the Secretary of Defense, 1966-69; Commanding Officer, 29th

Signal Group, US Army Strategic Communications Command, Thailand, 1969-70; Deputy Director for Operations, then Deputy Director for Plans, Defense Communications Agency, 1970-73. Legion of Merit with Oak Leaf Cluster; Bronze Star Medal; and other medals and awards. Promoted to Brigadier General January 1, 1970; Major General December 1, 1972.

Schultz, Kenneth W. Lieutenant General, United States Air Force; Commander, Space and Missile Systems Organization (SAMSO), Air Force Systems Command (AFSC), 1972-   . Born April 1, 1920, in Buffalo, New York. Army Air Corps Flying School, 1941-42; New York University, BS, Aeronautical Engineering, 1951; Ohio State University, Columbus, Ohio, 1952; Industrial College of the Armed Forces, 1960; George Washington University, MBA, 1962. Commissioned Second Lieutenant, US Army Air Corps, 1942. Combat duty in the Mediterranean Theater, WW II. Deputy, Ballistic Missile Re-entry Systems, Ballistic Systems Division, AFSC, 1965-67; Deputy for Minuteman, SAMSO, 1967-71; Deputy Chief of Staff, Systems, AFSC, 1971-72. Distinguished Service Medal; Legion of Merit; Distinguished Flying Cross; and other medals and awards. Promoted to Brigadier General, September 1, 1966; Major General, August 1, 1969; Lieutenant General, August 25, 1972.

Schweickart, Russell L. United States; NASA Astronaut, 1963-   . Born October 25, 1935, Neptune, New Jersey. Massachusetts Institute of Technology, BA, Aeronautical Engineering, MS, Aeronautics and Astronautics. Pilot in US Air Force and Air National Guard, 1956-63. NASA experience: Lunar Module Pilot, Apollo 9, March 3-12, 1969; Backup Commander, Skylab 2. NASA Distinguished Service Medal; FAI De La Vaulx Medal; National Academy of Television Arts and Sciences Special Trustees Award.

Scott, David R. Colonel, US Air Force; NASA Astronaut, 1963-   . Born June 6, 1932, San Antonio, Texas. US Military Academy; Massachusetts Institute of Technology, MS, Aeronautics and Astronautics; Air Force Experimental Test Pilot School; Aerospace Research Pilot School. Commissioned Second Lieutenant, US Army; transferred to Air Force. 32d Tactical Fighter Squadron, 1956-60, Soesterberg Air Base (RNAF), Netherlands. NASA experience: Pilot, Gemini 8; Command Module Pilot, Apollo 9; Backup Spacecraft Commander, Apollo 12; Spacecraft Commander, Apollo 15. Two NASA Distinguished Service Medals; NASA Exceptional Service Medal; Manned Spacecraft Center Superior Achievement Award; two Air Force Distinguished Service Medals; Air Force Command Pilot Astronaut Wings; Air Force Distinguished Flying Cross; AIAA Haley Astronautics Awards, 1966 and 1972; National Academy of Television Arts and Sciences Special Trustees Award; City of New York Gold Medal; United Nations Peace Medal; City of Chicago Gold Medal; Air Force Association's David C. Schilling Trophy; Kitty Hawk Memorial Award; Arnold Air Society's John F. Kennedy Trophy; Robert J. Collier Trophy; Order of Leopold (Belgium); New York Police

Department St. George Association's Golden Rule Award; Honorary Doctorate of Astronautical Science, University of Michigan.

Scott, John Alexander. Rear Admiral, Supply Corps, United States Navy; Commander, Defense Electronics Supply Center, Dayton, Ohio, 1972-   . Born February 7, 1920, in Belfast, Northern Ireland. Whittier College, California, BA, History and Economics; Navy Supply Corps School, Harvard University, 1942-43; Graduate School of Business, Stanford University, MBA, 1952; Industrial College of the Armed Forces, Washington, D.C., 1963-64. Commissioned Ensign, Supply Corps, US Naval Reserve, 1942; transferred from Naval Reserve to US Navy, 1944. Served in the Aleutian Islands Area, WW II. Recently Aide and Special Assistant to Chief of Naval Material, Navy Department, 1960-63; Executive Officer, Naval Supply Center, San Diego, California, 1964-66; Director, Supply Corps Personnel, Naval Supply Systems Command Headquarters, Washington, D.C., and Supply Corps Plans Assistant, Bureau of Naval Personnel, 1966-69; Commander, Ships Parts Control Center, Mechanicsburg, Pennsylvania, 1969-72. Decorations include National Defense Service Medal with Bronze Star; American Campaign Medal. Promoted to Rear Admiral, July 1, 1970.

Scott, William David Stewart. Rear Admiral, British Royal Navy; Naval Attache, Embassy of Great Britain, Washington, D.C., Chief of British Naval Staff, and UK Representative to Supreme Allied Commander Atlantic, 1971-   . Born April 5, 1921. Joined Royal Navy as Naval Cadet in 1938. Commanding Officer, HMS *Adamant*, 1963; *Fife*, 1969. Promoted to Rear-Admiral in 1971.

Scott-Barrett, David William. Major-General, British Army; General Officer Commanding Eastern District, 1971-   . Born December 16, 1922. Attended Imperial Defence College in 1970. Commissioned in the Scots Guards in 1942. Served in northwest Europe in WW II; Malaya, 1951. Commandant Guards Depot, 1963-65; General Staff Officer 1, 4th Division, British Army of the Rhine, 1965-67; Commander 6th Infantry Brigade, British Army of the Rhine, 1967-70. MBE; MC.

Scott-Bowden, Logan. Major-General, British Army; Head of British Defence Liaison Staff, India, 1971-   . Born February 21, 1920. Attended Malvern College; Royal Military Academy, Woolwich; Staff College, 1945; Joint Services Staff College, 1956; National Defence College (India), 1969. Commissioned in the Royal Engineers in 1939. Served in Northwest Europe and North America in WW II. Head, UK Land Forces Planning Staff, 1963-64; Assistant Director of Defence Plans, Ministry of Defence, 1964-66; Commander Training Brigade, Royal Engineers, 1966-69. Commander, Ulster Defence Regiment, 1970-73. CBE; DSO; MC and Bar.

Scotter, William Norman Roy. Major-General, British Army; Director of Military Operations, Ministry of Defence, 1972-   . Born February 9, 1922. Attended

Royal Military Academy, Dehra Dun; Staff College, 1951; Joint Services Staff College, 1959; National Defence College, Canada, 1969-70. Commissioned in the 7th Gurkha Rifles, 1942. Served in India and Burma in WW II; Malaya, 1948-51. Instructor, Army Staff College, Camberley, 1960-63; Member of Staff, Ministry of Defence, 1963-65; Commanding Officer, I King's Own Royal Border Regiment, 1965-67; Commander, 19 Infantry Brigade, 1967-69; Chief of Staff, Southern Command, 1970-72. OBE, MC. Member of the British Institute of Management.

Scowcroft, Brent. Major General, United States Air Force; Military Assistant to the President, 1972-   . Born March 19, 1925, in Ogden, Utah. US Military Academy, 1943-47; Pilot Training Course, 1948; Columbia University, MA, 1953, PhD, 1967, International Relations; attended Lafayette College; Georgetown University School of Language and Linguistics; Strategic Intelligence School, 1957; Armed Forces Staff College, 1961-62; National War College, 1966-67. Commissioned Second Lieutenant, US Army, in 1947. Professor and Acting Head of Political Science Department, US Air Force Academy, Colorado, 1962-64; Staff member, Long Range Planning Division, Directorate of Doctrine, Concepts, and Objectives, Office of the Deputy Chief of Staff, Plans and Operations, Headquarters US Air Force, Washington, D.C., 1964-66; Staff member, Western Hemisphere Region, Office of the Assistant Secretary of Defense, International Security Affairs, 1968-69; Deputy Assistant for National Security Council Matters, Directorate of Plans, Headquarters US Air Force, Washington, D.C., 1969-70; Special Assistant to the Director of the Joint Staff, Organization of the Joint Chiefs of Staff, Washington, D.C., 1970-72. Legion of Merit with Oak Leaf Cluster; Distinguished Service Medal (Air Force design); and other medals and awards. Promoted to Brigadier General, March 1, 1972; Major General, 1973.

Searles, Dewit R. Major General, United States Air Force; Deputy Inspector General, Headquarters, United States Air Force, 1972-   . Born August 7, 1920, in Birmingham, Alabama. Army Air Forces Flying School, 1942-43; Army Command and General Staff School, 1945; University of Maryland, 1947-49, BA, English, 1949; Air Command and Staff School, 1955-56; National War College, 1963-64; George Washington University, MA, International Affairs, 1964. Commissioned Second Lieutenant, US Army Air Corps, 1943. Combat duty in the Pacific Theater, WW II; Vietnam War. Vice Commander, later Commander, 81st Tactical Fighter Wing, England, 1965-67; Inspector General, Tactical Air Command, 1967-69; Commander, 327th Air Division, Pacific Air Forces, and Chief, Air Section, Military Assistance Advisory Group, Taiwan, 1969-71; Deputy Commander, Seventh Air Force/Thirteenth Air Force, Thailand, 1971-72. Legion of Merit with one Oak Leaf Cluster; Distinguished Flying Cross; and other medals and awards. Promoted to Major General, February 26, 1971.

Seignious, George Marion, II. Lieutenant General, United States Army; Director, Joint Staff, Organization, Joint Chiefs of Staff, Washington, D.C., 1972-   . Born June 21, 1921, Orangeburg, South Carolina. The Citadel, BS Degree, Business Administration; The Armored School, Advanced Course; US Army Command and General Staff College; Joint Service Staff College, England; The National War College. Commissioned Second Lieutenant, US Army Reserve, 1942. Served in WW II. Deputy Director, Plans and Policy, J-5, Organization, Joint Chiefs of Staff, Washington, D.C., 1967-68; Special Assistant to the Director of the Joint Staff, Organization, Joint Chiefs of Staff, Washington, D.C., 1968; Senior US Representative, United States Vietnam Peace Delegation, Paris, France, 1968-69; Commanding General, 3d Infantry Division, US Army, Europe, 1969-70; United States Commander, Berlin, US Army, Europe, 1970-71; Deputy Assistant Secretary of Defense (Security Assistance), and Director, Defense Security Assistance Agency, Washington, D.C., 1971-72. Distinguished Service Medal with Oak Leaf Cluster; Silver Star; Legion of Merit with four Oak Leaf Clusters; Bronze Star Medal with two Oak Leaf Clusters; and other medals and awards. Promoted to Brigadier General, June 30, 1965; Major General, January 1, 1968; Lieutenant General, August 1, 1971.

Seijas Villalobos, José Constantino. Vice Admiral, Venezuelan Navy; Chief of Staff, Joint General Staff, Venezuelan Armed Forces, 1973-   . Born May 19, 1923. Attended Naval School, Venezuela, 1941-43; United States Naval Academy, 1943-46; Metallurgical Course, Philadelphia Navy Yard, 1950-51; Naval War College, Spain, 1956-58. Commissioned Ensign, Venezuelan Navy, in 1946. Commanding Officer, First Division of Destroyers and Destroyer *Nueva Esparta*, 1963; Commanding Officer, Second Division of Destroyers and Destroyer *Zulia*, 1963-64; Director, Naval Academy, 1964-68; Director, Naval War College, 1968-69; Chief of Naval Operations, 1969-73. Military Order General Rafael Urdaneta, second and third class; Order of Naval Merit, second and third class; Cross of the Armed Forces of Cooperation, second class; Order of Liberator, officer grade; Order of Liberator, commander grade; Cross of Naval Merit, second class (Spain); Military Order of Ayacucho, grade of Caballero (Peru); Great Star of Military Merit (Chile); and other Venezuelan and foreign medals and awards. Promoted to Captain, June 2, 1961; Rear Admiral, July 5, 1964; Vice Admiral, July 5, 1972.

Seith, Louis Theodore. Lieutenant General, United States Air Force; Director, Plans and Policy, J-5, Organization of the Joint Chiefs of Staff, 1972-   . Born January 17, 1921, in Quincy, Massachusetts. United States Military Academy, 1939-43; Army Air Corps Flying School, 1943; Air Command and Staff School, 1953; National War College, 1960-61. Commissioned Second Lieutenant, US Army Air Corps, 1943. Combat duty in the Mediterranean Theater, WW II; Korean War; Vietnam War. Deputy Director, Personnel Training and Education, Deputy Chief of Staff, Personnel, 1963-65; Commandant of Cadets, US Air Force Academy, 1965-67; Chief of Staff, Headquarters Seventh Air Force, Vietnam, 1967-68; Deputy Commander,

Seventh Air Force and Thirteenth Air Force, Thailand, 1968-69; Commander, US Military Assistance Group, Thailand, and Chief Joint Military Advisory Group, Thailand, 1969-71; Vice J-3 (Operations), Organization of Joint Chiefs of Staff, 1971-72. Distinguished Service Cross; Distinguished Service Medal (Air Force design) with one Oak Leaf Cluster; Legion of Merit with one Oak Leaf Cluster; Distinguished Flying Cross; and other US and foreign medals and awards. Promoted to Brigadier General, November 1, 1965; Major General, August 1, 1968; Lieutenant General, August 1, 1972.

Seitz, Richard Joe. Major General, United States Army; Assistant Deputy Chief of Staff for Personnel, US Army, Washington, D.C., 1970-   . Born February 18, 1918, Leavenworth, Kansas. University of Omaha, BGE Degree, Military Science; US Army Command and General Staff College; Armed Forces Staff College; US Army War College. Commissioned Second Lieutenant, US Army Reserve, 1939. Served in WW II and Vietnam War. Deputy Commanding General, US Army Support Command, Vietnam, 1965; Assistant Deputy Commanding General for Operations, and Deputy Commanding General, Support Troops, US Army, Vietnam, 1965-66; Chief of Staff and Assistant Deputy Commanding General, and Commanding General, Support Troops, US Army, Vietnam, 1966-67; Commanding General, 82d Airborne Division, Fort Bragg, North Carolina, 1967-68; Commander, US Military Group, Brazil, 1968-70. Distinguished Service Medal with Oak Leaf Cluster; Silver Star; Legion of Merit with Oak Leaf Cluster; Bronze Star Medal with Oak Leaf Cluster; and other medals and awards. Promoted to Brigadier General, August 1, 1963; Major General, March 1, 1967.

Sell, Leslie Hale. Rear Admiral, United States Navy; Deputy Chief of Staff for Plans and Operations, Commander in Chief, US Atlantic Fleet, 1971-   . Born May 20, 1921, Johnson City, Tennessee. US Naval Academy, 1939-42; Naval Postgraduate School, Annapolis, Maryland, 1946-47; University of Pennsylvania, MS, Electrical Engineering, 1949; Industrial College of the Armed Forces, 1962-63. Commissioned Ensign, US Navy, in 1942. Served in the Atlantic and European Theaters in WW II; Vietnam War. Commander, Destroyer Division THREE HUNDRED TWENTY-TWO, and Destroyer Squadron THIRTY-TWO, 1963-64; Readiness Training Officer and Assistant Operations Officer, Second Fleet, 1964-65; Commanding Officer, USS *England* (DLG-220), 1965-66; Chief of Staff and Aide to Commander, Seventh Fleet, 1966-68; Assistant for War Gaming Matters, Office of CNO, 1968; Chief of Joint Command and Control Requirements Group, Joint Chiefs of Staff, 1968-70; Vice Commander, Naval Ordnance Systems Command, 1970; Commander Cruiser-Destroyer Flotilla TEN, 1970-71. Legion of Merit with Gold Star; Navy Commendation Medal with Gold Star; and other US and foreign medals and awards. Promoted to Rear Admiral, August 1, 1968.

Semengue, Pierre. Lieutenant Colonel, Cameroon Army; Commander, Cameroon Army. Born in 1935 in Cameroon.

Attended French Military Academy, St. Cyr; General Staff College, Paris, France.

Semenov, I. Lieutenant General, USSR Army; Chief, Political Directorate, Odessa Military District. Served on the Soviet-German Front in WW II. Promoted to Lieutenant General in 1971. Member, Communist Party of the Soviet Union.

Semerdzhiev, Atanas. Colonel General, Bulgarian Army; First Deputy Minister of National Defense, 1966-   , and Chief of the General Staff, 1962-   . Born in 1924, in Pazardzhik, Bulgaria. Attended General Staff College, USSR, 1958-60. Started military career as member of Chavdar Partisan Brigade, fighting German Forces in Bulgaria, WW II; after war held variety of command and staff positions. Member of Bulgarian Communist Party. Author of several books. Twenty Years of the Bulgarian People's Army; Twenty-five Years of the Bulgarian People's Army; Order of the Red Banner (USSR); and other orders and awards. Promoted to Major General, 1957.

Seneff, George Phillip, Jr. Lieutenant General, United States Army; Commanding General, III Corps and Fort Hood, and Commanding General, MASSTER, Fort Hood, Texas, 1971-   . Born August 27, 1916, Chicago, Illinois. US Military Academy. The Field Artillery School, Basic Course; The Armored School, Advanced Course; US Army Command and General Staff College; The National War College. Commissioned Second Lieutenant, 1941. Served in WW II and Vietnam War. Director of Army Aviation, Office, Assistant Chief of Staff for Force Development, US Army, Washington, D.C., 1965-66; Commanding General, 1st Aviation Brigade, and Aviation Officer, US Army, Pacific-Vietnam, 1966-67; Commanding General, 3d Infantry Division, US Army, Europe, 1967-69; Director of Operations, J-3, US Strike Command, MacDill Air Force Base, Tampa, Florida, 1969-70; Deputy Project Director, MASSTER, Later Project Director, MASSTER, Fort Hood, Texas, 1970-71. Distinguished Service Medal with Oak Leaf Cluster; Silver Star; Legion of Merit with three Oak Leaf Clusters; Distinguished Flying Cross with Oak Leaf Cluster; Bronze Star Medal with two Oak Leaf Clusters; and other medals and awards. Promoted to Brigadier General, August 1, 1965; Major General, June 1, 1967; Lieutenant General, August 1, 1971.

Seniwong Na Ayudhya, Tawit. General, Royal Thai Army. Deputy Commander in Chief, Royal Thai Army.

Senn, Hans. Lieutenant General, Swiss Army; Commanding General, 4th Army Corps. Born in 1918. Promoted to Lieutenant General, 1972.

Sergeyev, Nikolay Dmitriyevich. Admiral of the Fleet, USSR Navy; Chief of the Main Naval Staff, Soviet Navy, 1964-   . Born in 1909. Drafted into the Navy, c. 1929. Attended Frunze Naval Academy, c. 1929-c. 1932; General Staff War College, c. 1946-48; Commissioned c. 1932. Served in the Soviet-German War, 1941-45. Chief of Staff,

Volga Naval Flotilla, 1943-45; held various command and staff positions in the Soviet Navy. Member, Communist Party of the Soviet Union. Order of Lenin; two Orders of Red Banner; Order of Hakhimov; Order of the Fatherland War; four Orders of Red Star; and other Soviet and foreign orders and medals. Promoted to Admiral of the Fleet, April 30, 1970.

Serrano de Pablo Jimenez, Luis. Lieutenant General, Spanish Air Force; Chief of 2d Air Region (Sevilla), and Commander, Tactical Air Force, 1973- . Civil Engineer, Masters Degree; Montefiore Institute (Italy), Electrical Engineer Degree; Ordinance Doctor of Engineering; Diplomate of Air Force Staff; Diplomate in Communication Systems. Formerly Commander, 11th Bomber and Reconnaissance Group; Chief of Staff, Canary Islands Air Zone; Chief of Search and Rescue Service; Commander, 3d Air Transport Wing and Los Llanos (Albacete) Air Force Base; Chief, Albacete Air Sector; Deputy Chief, Materiel Command; Deputy Chief, 2d Air Region (Sevilla) and Chief, Sevilla Air Sector; Commander, Tactical Air Force. Great Crosses: Army, Navy and Air Force Merit, and Saint Hermenegild Royal and Military Order; two War Crosses; two Red Crosses for Military Merit; Medal of Endurance for the Fatherland; Medal for Military Merit (Portugal); and other medals and awards. Promoted to Lieutenant General, October 1, 1972. Paul Tissandier Diploma of FAI; Former Vice President of FAI; Vice President, General and Technical Secretary, Royal Aero Club of Spain; Member of Spanish Olympic Committee.

Setälä, Erkki V. Major General, Army of Finland; Commanding General, Southeast Finland Military Area, 1971- . Born April 4, 1917, Helsinki, Finland. Military Academy, 1938-39; War College, 1955-57. Served in Winter War; Continuation War. Chief of Training Office, General Headquarters, 1963-65; Commandant, Reserve Officer School, 1965-68; Commanding Officer, Pori Brigade, 1968-70; Inspector of Infantry, General Headquarters, 1970-71. Cross of Freedom, 3d Class with Oak Leaf; Cross of Freedom, 3d Class with Sword; Cross of Freedom, 4th Class with Sword; Order of Finnish Lion; Commemorative Medals for Winter and Continuation Wars; German Iron Cross, 2d Class; and other medals and awards. Promoted to Major General, April 1, 1970.

Shabalin, A.O. Rear Admiral, USSR Navy; Deputy Commandant, Naval War College. Served in the Soviet-German War, 1941-45. Member, Communist Party of the Soviet Union.

Shablikov, N.I. Rear Admiral, USSR Navy; First Deputy Chief, Naval Political Directorate, 1970- . Served in the Soviet-German War, 1941-45. Promoted to Rear-Admiral, 1970. Member, Communist Party of the Soviet Union.

Shaefer, Richard F. Major General, United States Air Force; Assistant Chief of Staff, Operations, Supreme Headquarters Allied Powers Europe, 1971- . Born December 30, 1919, Lansing, Michigan. University of New Mexico, BS,

Engineering, 1940; US Military Academy, 1940-43; UK Joint Services Staff College, 1953; National War College, 1961-62. Commissioned Second Lieutenant, US Army Air Corps, 1943. Combat duty with the Ninth Air Force in the European Theater, WW II; Vietnam War. US Delegation, NATO Military Committee and Standing Group, 1962-64; Deputy Director, Plans, NATO Military Committee's International Military Staff, 1964-65; Vice Commander, Third Air Force, England, 1965-67; Chief of Staff, Headquarters, United States Air Forces, Europe, 1967-68; Assistant Chief of Staff, Plans, J-5, US Military Assistance Command, Vietnam, 1968-70; Deputy Director, Plans and Policy, J-5, Joint Staff, Joint Chiefs of Staff Organization, 1970-71. Distinguished Service Medal; Legion of Merit; Distinguished Flying Cross; and other US and foreign medals and awards. Promoted to Major General, May 1, 1968.

Shaker, Zaid Ben. Major General, Armed Forces of the Hashemite Kingdom of Jordan; Chief of Staff, Jordanian Army, 1972- . College Graduate; Military Courses; Command and Staff College, USA. Commander, Armored Brigade; Commander, Armor Corps; Commander, Armor Division; Assistant Chief of Staff.

Shanshal, Abdul-Jabbar. Lieutenant General, Iraqi Army; Chief of Staff, Army of Iraq.

Shaposhnikov, P. Major General, USSR Army; Military Commissar, Bashkiria. Served on the Soviet-German Front in WW II. Member, Communist Party of the Soviet Union.

Sharif, Bashir. Brigadier General, Army of the Arab Republic of Egypt; Liaison Officer with the United Nations Force, Egypt, 1973. Unit commander, in 1973 War.

Sharp, Sir John (Aubrey Taylor). Lieutenant-General, British Army; Military Secretary, Ministry of Defence (Army), 1972- . Born September 6, 1917. Attended Jesus College, Cambridge, MA, 1939; Staff College, Quetta, 1944; Imperial Defence College, 1963. Served with Royal Artillery units and as Personal Liaison Officer to Field-Marshal Montgomery in WW II. Commander, 11th Infantry Brigade Group, 1961-62; Commandant, School of Artillery, Larkhill, 1964-66; General Officer Commanding, 2d Division, 1966-67; Commandant, Staff College, Camberley, 1967-69; General Officer Commanding, 1st Corps, 1970-71. KCB; MC and Bar.

Shavrov, I.E. Colonel General, USSR Army. Served on the Soviet-German Front in WW II. Commander, Leningrad Military District, 1967-73. Member, Communist Party of the Soviet Union.

al-Shazili, Sa'd al-Din Muhammad al-Husayni. General, Army of the Arab Republic of Egypt; Chief of Staff, Egyptian Armed Forces, 1971-73. Born April 1, 1922. Attended Royal Military Academy; Military Staff College; Fuad I University, MA, 1952; Paratroop Course, Fort Benning, Georgia, USA, 1953; Air Transport Course, Fort

Lee, Virginia, USA, 1953; military school in USSR, 1958. Commissioned Second Lieutenant, Army Service Corps, 1940; transferred to royal bodyguard unit, 1943; transferred to Paratroop Corps, 1953. Served in the Arab-Israeli War, 1948; Instructor, Army Service School, Abbasiya, 1949-50; Commander, Ranger School, 1955; Commander of paratroop division in 1956 Suez crisis; Commander of Egyptian contingent of UN forces in the Congo, 1960-61; Military Attache, Egyptian Embassy, London, 1961-65; Commander of paratroop division in Yemen Civil War, 1965; distinguished action in Arab-Israeli War of 1967; Commander of Special Forces, 1967-70. Arab League Assistant Secretary General for Military Affairs, 1971-73. Promoted to Brigadier General, 1961; Major General, 1967; Lieutenant General, January 5, 1972.

Shcheglov, Afanasiy Fyodorovich. General of the Army, USSR Army (Artillery); First Deputy Commander in Chief, Soviet Air Defense Forces, 1966- . Born in 1912. Volunteered for Soviet Army in 1929. Attended Artillery Academy, 1929-33; Army War College, 1936-39; General Staff War College, c. 1950. Commissioned in 1933. Served in the Soviet-Finnish War, 1939-40; Soviet-German War, 1941-45. Commander, Antitank Artillery Regiment, Leningrad Front, 1941; Commander, Ski Regiment, Leningrad Front, 1941-42; Commander, 63d Guards Infantry Division, 67th Army, Leningrad Front, 1942-44; Commander, Infantry Corps, Baltic Front, 1945- ; Commander, various Antiaircraft Defense Units, c. 1950-59; Commander, Baku Air Defense District, 1959-66. Member, Communist Party of the Soviet Union, 1939- ; Deputy to the USSR Supreme Soviet. Hero of the Soviet Union; two Orders of Lenin; three Orders of Red Banner; Order of Fatherland War; Order of Red Star; and other Soviet and foreign orders and medals. Promoted to General of the Army, May 1, 1970.

Shchukin, N. Major General, USSR Army; Chief, Political Directorate, Turkestan Military District, 1971- . Served on the Soviet-German Front in WW II. Chief, Political Directorate, Odessa Military District until 1971. Member, Communist Party of the Soviet Union.

Shear, Harold Edson. Vice Admiral, United States Navy; Director of Antisubmarine Warfare and Tactical Electromagnetic Programs, 1973- . Born December 6, 1918, New York, New York. US Naval Academy, 1938-41; Naval Submarine School, 1944; Armed Forces Staff College, 1954-55; National War College, 1964-65; Defense Language Institute, 1966-67. Served in the Atlantic and Pacific Theaters, WW II; Vietnam War. Commissioned Ensign, US Navy, in 1941. Director of Polaris Operations, Joint Staff of Commander in Chief Atlantic, 1962-64; Commanding Officer USS *Sacramento* (AOE-1), 1965-66; Chief, US Naval Mission, Brazil, 1967-69; Director, Submarine Warfare Division, Office of the CNO, 1969-71; Director of Antisubmarine Warfare Programs, Office of the Chief of Naval Operations, 1971-73. Silver Star Medal; Commendation Ribbon with Combat "V"; and other US

and foreign medals and awards. Promoted to Rear Admiral, July 1, 1967; Vice Admiral, May 1, 1971.

Shebab, Hammad. Lieutenant General, Iraqi Army; Minister of Defense, 1970- . Born in 1922. Attended Military Secondary School; Military Academy. Member Revolutionary Command Council and Commander Baghdad Area Forces; Chief of Staff, 1968.

Shedd, William Edgar, III. Major General, United States Army; Deputy Chief of Staff, Operations, US Army, Europe and Seventh Army, 1971- . Born January 20, 1920, Washington, D.C. US Military Academy; The Armored School, Basic and Advanced Courses; US Army Command and General Staff College; US Army War College. Commissioned Second Lieutenant, 1942. Served in WW II and Vietnam War. Deputy Commanding General, US Army Training Center, Infantry, Fort Ord, California, 1966-67; Deputy Director, Operations, National Military Command Center, J-3, Organization, Joint Chiefs of Staff, Washington, D.C. 1967-68; Assistant Division Commander, 1st Cavalry Division (Airmobile), Vietnam, 1968-69; Chief of Staff, XXIV Corps, US Army, Vietnam, 1969-70; Deputy Director (Operations and Administration) Defense Atomic Support Agency, Washington, D.C. 1970-71. Distinguished Service Medal; Legion of Merit with Oak Leaf Cluster; Distinguished Flying Cross; Bronze Star Medal; and other medals and awards. Promoted to Brigadier General, September 1, 1966; Major General, August 7, 1970.

Shelepin, A. Lieutenant General, USSR Army; Chief, Political Directorate, Transcaucasus Military District, 1971- . Served on the Soviet-German Front in WW II. Member, Communist Party of the Soviet Union.

Shepard, Alan B., Jr. Rear Admiral, US Navy; NASA Astronaut, 1959- . Chief of the Astronaut Office, 1971- . Born November 18, 1923, East Derry, New Hampshire. US Naval Academy, 1940-44; US Navy Test Pilot School, Patuxent River, Maryland; US Naval War College. Commissioned Ensign, US Navy, 1944; designated Naval Aviator, 1947. Fighter Squadron 42; two tours as Test Pilot at Patuxent River; Fighter Squadron 193, Moffett Field, California; Aircraft Readiness Officer, Staff of Commander-in-Chief, Atlantic Fleet, 1957-59. NASA experience: Flight in Freedom 7 Spacecraft, May 5, 1961; Chief of the Astronaut Office, 1963-69, 1971- ; Spacecraft Commander, Apollo 14, January 31-February 9, 1971. Two NASA Distinguished Service Medals; NASA Exceptional Service Medal; Navy Astronaut Wings; Navy Distinguished Service Medal; Navy Distinguished Flying Cross; Langley Medal; Lambert Trophy; Kinchloe Trophy; Cabot Award; Collier Trophy; City of New York Gold Medal; American Astronautical Society's Flight Achievement Award; Honorary MS, Dartmouth College, 1962; Honorary ScD, Miami University, Oxford, Ohio, 1971; Honorary Doctorate of Humanities, Franklin Pierce College, 1972.

Shepard, Tazewell Taylor, Jr. Rear Admiral, United States Navy; Director, Joint Continental Defense Systems Integration Planning Staff, 1971- . Born January 22, 1921, Mobile, Alabama. US Naval Academy, 1939-42; Flight Training Course, 1946-47; Naval Postgraduate School, BS, Electrical Engineering, 1949-50; University of California at Los Angeles, MS, 1950-51; Naval War College, 1959-60. Commissioned Ensign, US Navy, in 1942; designated Naval Aviator in 1947. Served in the Pacific Theater in WW II; Vietnam War. Naval Aide to the President, 1961-64; Commanding Officer, USS *Aucilla* (AO-56), 1964-65; Member, Secretary of the Navy's Retention Board, 1965-66; Commanding Officer, USS *Princeton* (LPH-5), 1966-67; Study Director for Navy Requirements, Western Pacific and Indian Ocean to 1980, 1967-68; Director East Asia and Pacific Region, Office of the Assistant Secretary of Defense (International Security Affairs), 1968-70; Commander, Antisubmarine Warfare Group TWO, 1970-71. Navy Cross; Legion of Merit; Navy Commendation Medal with Combat "V"; and other US and foreign medals and awards. Promoted to Rear Admiral, August 1, 1968.

Shepherd, Charles William Haimes. Rear-Admiral, British Royal Navy; Assistant Controller (Polaris), Ministry of Defence, 1971- . Born December 10, 1917. Attended Royal Naval College, Greenwich; Senior Officers War Course, 1961-62. Joined the Royal Navy in 1933, as Artificer Apprentice; commissioned in 1940. Served at sea in the Pacific in WW II. Technical Director, United Kingdom Polaris Weapon System, 1962-68; Director, Project Teams (Submarines), and Deputy Assistant Controller (Polaris), Ministry of Defence (Navy), 1968-71. CBE. Promoted to Captain, 1960; Rear-Admiral, 1970.

Sherrill, James C. Lieutenant General, United States Air Force; Commander in Chief, Alaskan Command, and Commander, Alaskan North American Air Defense Command/Continental Air Defense Command (NORAD/CONAD) Region, 1972- . Born February 18, 1920, in San Marcos, Texas. Southwest Texas State College, San Marcos, Texas, 1937-40; Army Air Corps Flying Schools, 1940-41; Southern Methodist University, Dallas, Texas, BS, Education, 1947; Air Command and Staff School, 1948. Commissioned in 1941. Combat duty in the Pacific Theater, WW II; Vietnam War. Chief of Staff, Headquarters Military Air Transport Service (MATS), 1960-61; Commander, 1608th Air Transport Wing, MATS, 1961-64; Deputy Chief of Staff, Plans, Headquarters, MATS, 1964-65; Director of Logistics (Transportation), J-4, Organization, Joint Chiefs of Staff, 1965-66; Special Assistant, Strategic Mobility (SASM), Organization Joint Chiefs of Staff, 1966-68; Commander, Twenty-second Air Force, 1968-70; Vice Commander, Military Airlift Command, 1970-72. Distinguished Service Medal with one Oak Leaf Cluster; Legion of Merit with one Oak Leaf Cluster; and other medals and awards. Promoted to Brigadier General, July 1, 1960; Major General, May 1, 1964; Lieutenant General, February 6, 1970.

Shevchenko, A.I. Lieutenant General, USSR Army. Served on the Soviet-German Front in WW II. First Deputy Commander, Volga Military District; Member, Communist Party of the Soviet Union.

Shevchuk, V. Lieutenant General, USSR Air Force; Chief, Rear Services (Logistics), Air Defense Forces. Served on the Soviet-German Front in WW II. Member, Communist Party of the Soviet Union.

Shiely, Albert R., Jr. Major General, United States Air Force; Commander, Air Force Electronic Systems Division, Air Force Systems Command (AFSC), 1971- . Born July 14, 1920, in St. Paul, Minnesota. US Military Academy, 1940-43; University of Illinois, MS, Electrical Engineering, 1947; Industrial College of the Armed Forces, 1961-62. Commissioned Second Lieutenant, Army Air Corps, 1943. Combat duty in the European Theater, WW II. Program Director, and Deputy Commander for Surveillance and Control Systems, Electronic Systems Division, AFSC, 1962-65; Vice Commander, Electronic Systems Division, AFSC, and Deputy Chief of Staff, Communications-Electronics, to Commander in Chief, US Air Forces, Europe, 1965-67; Commander, European Communications Area, Air Force Communications Service (AFCS), 1967-69; Vice Commander, AFCS, 1969-71. Legion of Merit with three Oak Leaf Clusters; Air Medal; and other medals and awards. Promoted to Major General, April 1, 1970.

Shirogov, K. Major General, USSR Army; First Deputy Chief, Political Directorate, Northern Group of Soviet Forces, Poland. Served on the Soviet-German Front in WW II. Member, Communist Party of the Soviet Union.

Shoemaker, Raymond Leroy. Major General, United States Army; Commanding General, US Army Air Defense Center, and Commandant, US Army Air Defense School, Fort Bliss, Texas, 1971- . Born May 4, 1919, Washington, D.C. US Military Academy; The Field Artillery School, Basic and Field Officer Courses; US Army Command and General Staff College; Armed Forces Staff College; The National War College; Stanford University, MA Degree, Communication and Journalism; George Washington University, MA Degree, International Affairs. Commissioned Second Lieutenant, 1940. Served in WW II. Commanding General, 38th Artillery Brigade (Air Defense), US Army, Pacific-Korea, 1964-65; Assistant Chief of Staff, G-3, US Army Air Defense Command, Ent Air Force Base, Colorado, 1965-66; Deputy Chief of Staff, Operations, US Army Air Defense Command, Ent Air Force Base, Colorado, 1966; Chief of Staff, later Deputy Commanding General and Chief of Staff, US Army Air Defense Command, Ent Air Force Base, Colorado, 1966-69; Commanding General, 32d Air Defense Command, US Army, Europe, 1969-71. Distinguished Service Medal; Silver Star; Legion of Merit with three Oak Leaf Clusters; Bronze Star Medal with Oak Leaf Cluster; and other medals and awards. Promoted to Brigadier General, July 1, 1963; Major General, July 27, 1967.

Shoemaker, Robert Morin. Major General, United States Army; Commanding General, 1st Cavalry Division (TRICAP), Fort Hood, Texas, 1973-   . Born February 18, 1924, Almont, Michigan. US Military Academy; The Infantry School, Basic and Advanced Courses; US Army Command and General Staff College; US Army War College. Commissioned Second Lieutenant, 1946. Served in Vietnam War. Assistant, later Chief, Plans and Programs Division, Office of the Director of Army Aviation, Office, Assistant Chief of Staff for Force Development, US Army, Washington, D.C., 1967-69; Chief of Staff, 1st Cavalry Division (Airmobile), US Army, Pacific-Vietnam, 1969; Assistant Division Commander, 1st Cavalry Division (Airmobile) US Army, Pacific-Vietnam, 1969-70; Deputy Commanding General and Chief of Staff, III Corps and Fort Hood, Texas, 1970-71; Deputy Commanding General, MASSTER, Fort Hood, Texas, 1971-73. Distinguished Service Medal; Silver Star with Oak Leaf Cluster; Legion of Merit with three Oak Leaf Clusters; Distinguished Flying Cross; Bronze Star Medal; and other medals and awards. Promoted to Brigadier General, December 1, 1969; Major General, December 1, 1971.

Shonin, Georgy Stepanovich. Colonel, USSR, Naval Air Force; Cosmonaut, 1963-   . Born August 2, 1935, in Rovenki, Ukraine. Attended Naval Pilots School; Zhukovskiy Air Force Engineering War College; Cosmonaut Training Unit, 1963. Commissioned in 1956. Air Force Pilot, Baltic and North Fleets, 1957-63; Commander, Soyuz-6 Spaceship, October 1969. Member Communist Party of the Soviet Union since 1957. Hero of Soviet Union; Order of Lenin; Order of Red Star; Pilot-Cosmonaut of the USSR; K. Tsiolkovskiy Gold Medal of the USSR Academy of Sciences; and other medals and awards.

Shotts, Bryan M. Major General, United States Air Force; Commander, United States Logistics Group (TUSLOG), Ankara, Turkey, 1971-   . Born October 29, 1922, in Laurel, Mississippi. University of Omaha; Army Air Corps Flying School, 1942; Air Command and Staff School, 1953-54; Industrial College of the Armed Forces, 1964-65. Commissioned Second Lieutenant, US Army Air Corps, 1942. Combat duty in the European Theater, WW II; Korea. Vice Commander, 93d Bombardment Wing, 1962-64; Chief Strategic Division, and later Assistant Director, Operations for Joint Matters, Directorate of Operations, Headquarters USAF, 1965-69; Commander, 93d Bombardment Wing, 1969-70; Chief of Staff, Fifteenth Air Force, 1970-71. Legion of Merit with one Oak Leaf Cluster; Distinguished Flying Cross; Bronze Star Medal; and other medals and awards. Promoted to Brigadier General, February 6, 1970; Major General, August 1, 1972.

Shurupov, A.G. Colonel General, USSR Army; Commander, Odessa Military District, 1968-   . Served on the Soviet-German Front in WW II. Member, Communist Party of the Soviet Union.

Shydi, Tanush. Deputy Minister of Defense, Albania, 1973-   .

Sianis, Pete C. Major General, United States Air Force; Deputy Chief of Staff, Operations, Headquarters Strategic Air Command (SAC), 1971-   . Born January 22, 1920, in Kansas City, Missouri. Army Air Corps Flying School, 1940-41; Air Command and Staff School, 1949. Commissioned Second Lieutenant, US Army Air Corps, 1941. Combat duty in the European Theater, WW II; Korean War. Chief, Weapons Maintenance Division, SAC, 1961-63; Commander, 319th Bombardment Wing, 1963-64; Commander, 410th Bombardment Wing, 1964-66; Deputy Director for Logistics, Joint Chiefs of Staff Organization, 1966-68; Deputy Director of the Joint Staff, Joint Chiefs of Staff Organization, 1968-69; Deputy Chief of Staff, Materiel, SAC, 1969-71. Distinguished Service Medal; Legion of Merit; Distinguished Flying Cross; Bronze Star Medal; and other medals and awards. Promoted to Major General, August 1, 1968.

Sidey, Sir Ernest (Shaw). Air Marshal, British Royal Air Force; Director-General, RAF Medical Services, 1971-   . Born January 2, 1913. St. Andrews University, MD, ChB and DPH Degrees. Commissioned in 1937. Served in Burma in WW II. Principal Medical Officer, Flying Training Command, 1961-63; Principal Medical Officer, Middle East Command, 1963-65; Principal Medical Officer, Transport Command, 1965-66; Deputy Director General Medical Services, RAF, 1966-68; Principal Medical Officer, Strike Command, 1968-70. KBE; CB; MFCM. Queen's Honorary Surgeon, 1966-   .

Sidle, Winant. Major General, United States Army; Chief of Public Information, Office, Secretary of the Army, and Chief of Information, Office, Chief of Staff, US Army, Washington, D.C. 1969-   . Born September 7, 1916, Springfield, Ohio. Hamilton College, AB Degree, History; University of Wisconsin, MA Degree, Journalism; The Artillery School, Basic and Advanced Courses; US Army Command and General Staff College; US Army War College. Commissioned Second Lieutenant, Army National Guard, 1941. Served in WW II and Vietnam War. Special Assistant for Vietnam, later Director for Defense Information, Office, Secretary of Defense (Public Affairs), Washington, D.C., 1966-67; Chief of Information, US Military Assistance Command, Vietnam, 1967-69; Commanding General, I Field Force Artillery, US Army, Pacific-Vietnam, 1969. Distinguished Service Medal; Legion of Merit with two Oak Leaf Clusters; Bronze Star Medal with Oak Leaf Cluster; and other medals and awards. Promoted to Brigadier General, November 29, 1966; Major General, September 1, 1970.

Sidney-Wilmot, Aubrey. Air Vice-Marshal, British Royal Air Force; Director, Legal Services (RAF), 1970-   . Born January 4, 1915. Attended Framlingham College; admitted Solicitor, 1938. Commissioned in the Administrative Branch, RAF, 1940; transferred to Office of Judge Advocate General, 1942. Deputy Director of Legal Services (RAF), 1969-70. OBE.

Sidorov, M.D. Lieutenant General, Artillery, USSR Army; Chief of Staff, Missiles and Artillery Forces. Served on the Soviet-German Front in WW II. Member, Communist Party of the Soviet Union.

Siemens, Abe Harold. Rear Admiral, United States Coast Guard; Chief, Office of Research and Development, Headquarters, US Coast Guard, 1973- . Born March 9, 1924, Chicago, Illinois. US Coast Guard Academy, 1942-45; Flight Training Course, 1949-51; Aircraft Maintenance Officer School, 1955-56; Purdue University, Industrial Management Graduate School, MS Degree, 1961. Commissioned Ensign, 1945; designated Coast Guard Aviator, 1951. Chief, Testing and Development Division, Office of Research and Development, Chief, Applied Technology Division, and Chief, Plans and Evaluation Staff, 1965-70; Commander, Coast Guard Air Station, San Diego, California, and Group Commander and Captain of the Port of San Diego, 1970-72; Commanding Officer, Coast Guard Base, New York, 1972-73. Coast Guard Commendation Medal; World War II campaign medals and ribbons; China and Korea occupation. Promoted to Captain, August 1, 1967; Rear Admiral, July 1, 1973.

Siilasvuo, Ensio. Major General, Army of Finland; Chief of Staff, United Nations Truce Supervision Organization, Palestine, 1970- . Born January 1, 1922, Helsinki. Attended Military Academy; Command and Staff College, 1951-52. Commissioned Second Lieutenant, 1941. Served in Finnish-Soviet War, WW II. Military Observer, United Nations Observation Group, Lebanon, 1958; Defense Attache, Finnish Embassy, Warsaw, Poland, 1959-61; Staff Officer, 3d Division, 1962-64; Commander, Finnish Contingent, United Nations Force, Cyprus, 1964-65; Instructor, National Defense College, 1965-67; Chief, Foreign Department, General Headquarters, 1967; Senior Staff Officer, United Nations Truce Supervision Organization, Palestine, 1967-70. Cross of Freedom, 3d and 4th Class; Knight of the Order of the White Rose of Finland, 1st Class; and other medals and awards.

Silantyev, A. Colonel General, USSR Air Force; Chief of Staff, Soviet Air Force, 1970- . Served on the Soviet-German Front in WW II. Member, Communist Party of the Soviet Union.

Sil'chenko, N.K. Colonel General, USSR Army; Commander, Urals Military District, 1970- . Served on the Soviet-German Front in WW II. Promoted to Colonel General in 1971. Member, Communist Party of the Soviet Union.

Siler, Owen Wesley. Rear Admiral, United States Coast Guard; Commander, 2d Coast Guard District, St. Louis, Missouri, 1971- . Born January 10, 1922, Seattle, Washington. Santa Maria Junior College, California, AA, 1940; US Coast Guard Academy, 1940-43; Navy Flight Training Courses, 1947-48 and 1952; National War College, 1966-67. Commissioned Ensign, 1943; designated Coast Guard Aviator, 1948. Served in Pacific Theater, WW II.

Commanding Officer, Coast Guard Air Station, Miami, Florida, 1965-66; Chief, Administrative Management Division, Headquarters, US Coast Guard, 1967-68; Assistant Chief of Staff for Management, 1968-69; Deputy Chief of Staff, Headquarters, US Coast Guard, 1969-71. WW II campaign service medals and ribbons; and other medals and citations. Promoted to Captain, July 1, 1965; Rear Admiral, July 1, 1971.

Simmons, Charles James. Major General, United States Army; Director of International and Civil Affairs, Office of the Deputy Chief of Staff for Military Operations, 1972- . Born September 1, 1925, in Bellevue, Texas. Attended US Military Academy; Armored School, Basic and Advanced Courses; Command and General Staff College; Air War College, 1965-66; Columbia University, AM, International Relations. Commissioned Second Lieutenant June 4, 1946. Plans and Operations Officer, G-3, I Field Force, Vietnam, then Executive Officer, 1st Brigade, 4th Infantry Division, US Army, Pacific-Vietnam, 1966-67; Assistant Chief of the Political-Military Division, Office of the Deputy Chief of Staff for Military Operations, 1967-68; Chief of the Operations Division, Directorate for Concepts and Operations Readiness, Defense Communications Planning Group, Defense Communications Agency, 1968-69; Commanding Officer, 1st Brigade, 3d Infantry Division, 1969; Assistant Division Commander, 3d Infantry Division, US Army, Europe, 1969-71; Commanding General, 1st Infantry Division (Forward), US Army, Europe, 1971-72. Legion of Merit with Oak Leaf Cluster; Air Medal; and other medals and awards. Promoted to Brigadier General January 1, 1970; Major General February 1, 1973.

Simokaitis, Frank J. Major General, United States Air Force; Commandant, Air Force Institute of Technology, Air University, Wright-Patterson Air Force Base, Ohio, 1973- . Born December 12, 1922, in St. Louis, Missouri. Took aviation cadet training course, 1942-43; attended Washington University, St. Louis, Missouri; St. Louis University, School of Law, LLD, 1950; Air Command and Staff School, 1953-54. Commissioned Second Lieutenant, US Army Air Corps, 1943. Served in the European Theater, WW II. Plans and Program Officer, and Chief of Contingency Plans Division, Directorate of Plans, Headquarters Pacific Air Forces, Hickam Air Force Base, Hawaii, 1960-63; Executive Officer to the Administrative Assistant, Office of the Secretary of the Air Force, Washington, D.C., 1963-69; Executive Assistant to the Secretary of the Air Force, Washington, D.C., 1969-73. Legion of Merit; Air Medal with three Oak Leaf Clusters; and other medals and awards. Promoted to Brigadier General, July 1, 1971; Major General, 1973.

Simon, Henry. Major General, United States Air Force; The Auditor General, Air Force Comptroller, and Commander of Air Force Audit Agency, Norton Air Force Base, California, 1973- . Born February 12, 1921, in Rosemont, West Virginia. Pilot Training Course, 1943-44; Rutgers University, BS, 1948, MS, 1962, Industrial

Management; Air Command and Staff College, 1958-59; Industrial College of the Armed Forces, 1963-64; George Washington University, MBA, 1964; Advanced Management Program, Harvard Graduate School of Business Administration, 1968. Commissioned Second Lieutenant, US Army Air Corps, 1945; commissioned in U.S. Air Force, 1947. Served in the China-Burma-India Theater, WW II. Chief, Management Review Division, Office of the Deputy Director for Contract Administration Services, Defense Supply Agency, Cameron Station, Virginia, 1965-67; Chief, Weapons Systems and Major Equipment Procurement Division, 1967-69, then Director of Production and Procurement, 1969-70, and later, Director of Materiel Management, San Antonio Air Materiel Area, Air Force Logistics Command, Kelly Air Force Base, Texas, 1967-71; Inspector General, Air Force Logistics Command, Wright-Patterson Air Force Base, Ohio, 1971; Assistant Deputy Chief of Staff for Materiel Management, Air Force Logistics Command, Wright-Patterson Air Force Base, Ohio, 1971-73. Distinguished Flying Cross with three Oak Leaf Clusters; Air Medal with three Oak Leaf Clusters; and other medals and awards. Promoted to Brigadier General, October 1, 1971; Major General, 1973.

Simonsson, Nils Victor. Director General (equivalent to major general), Sweden; Director General of the Civil Administration of Swedish Armed Forces, 1968- . Masters Degree in Political Science, 1943; attended Royal National Defense College, 1960. Permanent Secretary, Department of Defense, 1965-68. Commander of the Royal Order of the Northern Star; and other medals and awards. Member of the Royal Academy of Military Sciences; Member of the Board of the National Institute of Defense Organization and Management. Promoted to Director General, 1968.

Simpson, Ormond Ralph. Lieutenant General, United States Marine Corps; Director of Personnel, Deputy Chief of Staff (Manpower), Headquarters, US Marine Corps, 1971- . Born March 16, 1915, Corpus Christi, Texas. Texas Agricultural and Mechanical College, BS, Mechanical Engineering, 1936; Marine Corps Officers Basic School, 1937; Army War College, 1954-55. Commissioned Second Lieutenant, USMC, 1936. Served in Pacific Theater, WW II; Korean War; Vietnam War. Assistant Division Commander, 3d Marine Division, 1961-62; Assistant Director, Personnel, HQMC, 1962-63; Assistant Chief of Staff, G-1, HQMC, 1963-65; Commanding General, 2d Marine Division, Fleet Marine Force, 1965-67; Commanding General, Marine Corps Recruit Depot, Parris Island, South Carolina, 1967-68; Commanding General, 1st Marine Division, Vietnam, 1968-69; Commanding General, Marine Corps Supply Center, Albany, Georgia, 1969-71. Distinguished Service Medal; Legion of Merit with three Gold Stars; Bronze Star Medal; and other medals and awards. Promoted to Brigadier General, August 1961; Major General, January 1966; Lieutenant General, July 1971.

Singlaub, John Kirk. Major General, United States Army; Commanding General, US Army Readiness Region VIII,

Rocky Mountain Arsenal, Denver, Colorado, 1973- . Born July 10, 1921, in Independence, California. Attended University of California at Los Angeles, BA, Political Science; Infantry School, Advanced Course; Command and General Staff College; Air War College. Commissioned Second Lieutenant (ORC) January 14, 1943. Served in WW II. Chief, Studies and Observations Group, US Military Assistance Command, Vietnam, 1966-68; Assistant Division Commander, 8th Infantry Division, US Army, Europe, 1968-69; Deputy Project Director for Planning and Evaluation, later Chief of Staff, Project MASSTER, Fort Hood, Texas, 1969-71; Director of Plans, Studies and Budget, Office of the Deputy Chief of Staff for Personnel, 1971; Deputy Assistant Secretary of Defense (Drug and Alcohol Abuse), Office of the Assistant Secretary of Defense (Health and Environment), 1971-73. Distinguished Service Medal with Oak Leaf Cluster; Silver Star; Legion of Merit with two Oak Leaf Clusters; Soldier's Medal; Bronze Star Medal with Oak Leaf Cluster; and other medals and awards. Promoted to Brigadier General August 1, 1969; Major General October 1, 1972.

Sinzogan, Benoit. Lieutenant Colonel, Dahomeyan Army; Chief of Staff, National Gendarmerie, 1970- . Minister of Foreign Affairs, 1967-68; Director, National Police Force, 1968-69; Co-Head of State and Member of the Ruling Triumvirate, 1969-70; Minister of Foreign Affairs, Justice and National Education, 1969-70. Promoted to Lieutenant Colonel, 1969.

Sirigaya, Amorn. Admiral, Royal Thai Navy. Chief of Staff, Royal Thai Navy.

Sisouk Na Champassak. Delegate of the Prime Minister for Defense, Laos.

Sisto, Mikko J. Lieutenant General, Army of Finland; Commanding General North Finland Military Area, 1971- . Born March 22, 1915, Ähtäri, Finland. Attended Cadet School, 1940-41. Served in Winter War; Continuation War. Commanding Officer, Pori Brigade, 1958; Commandant, Cadet School, 1958-61; Commandant, War College, 1964-67; Commanding General, Savo-Karjala Military Area, 1968-70. Cross of Freedom, 2d Class for Merit; Cross of Freedom, 3d Class with Oak Leaf; Cross of Freedom, 3d Class with Sword; Cross of Freedom, 4th Class with Sword; Commander, Order of Finnish Lion, 1st Class; Commemorative Medals for Winter and Continuation Wars; German Iron Cross, 2d Class; and other medals and awards. Promoted to Lieutenant General, 1971.

Sitton, Ray B. Major General, United States Air Force; Deputy Chief of Staff for Plans, Strategic Air Command, Offutt Air Force Base, Nebraska, and Commander in Chief, SAC, Representative to Joint Strategic Target Planning Staff, 1973- . Born November 6, 1923, in Calhoun, Georgia. Aviation Cadet Training Course, 1943; University of Maryland, BS, Military Science, 1953; Air Command and Staff School, 1954; National War College, 1966-67; George Washington University, MA, International Affairs, 1967.

Commissioned Second Lieutenant, US Army Air Corps, in 1943. Served in the Southwest Pacific in WW II and in Korean War. Assistant Deputy Director of Operations, National Military Command Center, then Chief, Current Operations Branch, and later Chief, Strategic Operations Division, Joint Chiefs of Staff, 1967-70; Commander, 17th Bombardment Wing, Strategic Air Command, Wright-Patterson Air Force Base, Ohio, 1970-71; Commander, 19th Air Division, Strategic Air Command, Carswell Air Force Base, Texas, 1971-72; Assistant Deputy Chief of Staff for Plans, Strategic Air Command, Offutt Air Force Base, Nebraska, 1972-73. Decorations include Legion of Merit with Oak Leaf Cluster, Air Force Commendation Medal with Oak Leaf Cluster. Promoted to Major General, April 2, 1973.

Sivara, Kris. General, Royal Thai Army. Commander in Chief, Royal Thai Army.

Siyad Barre, Muhammad. Major General, Somali Army; Commander in Chief, Armed Forces, and President of the Supreme Revolutionary Council, 1969-   .

Sizov, F. Ya. Vice Admiral, USSR Navy; Chief, Political Directorate, Northern Fleet, 1961-   . Served in the Soviet-German War, 1941-45. Member, Communist Party of the Soviet Union.

Skalski, Jerzy. Major General, Polish Army; Deputy Chief of General Staff.

Skjong, Hans Sigurd. Rear Admiral, Royal Norwegian Navy; Commander in Chief (Inspector General).

Skoglund, Claes Gösta. Major General, Swedish Royal Army; Commander in Chief, Military Command West, 1972-   . Attended Royal Army Staff College, 1944-46; School of Land/Air Warfare (England), 1954; Royal National Defense College, 1958, 1966; US Army Air Defense School, Fort Bliss (USA), 1969. Commanding Officer, Infantry Regiment I 18, 1963-66; Chief of Staff, Military Command West, 1966-68; Commander in Chief, Military Command, Gotland, 1968; Commandant, Royal National Defense College, 1968-72. Commander of the Royal Order of the Sword; Knight of the Royal Order of Wasa; and other medals and awards. Promoted to Major General, 1968.

Sköld, Nils Gunnar. Major General, Swedish Royal Army; Chief, Army Materiel Department, Defense Materiel Administration, 1969-   . Attended Royal Army Staff College. Commanding Officer Infantry Regiment, No. 14, 1967-68; Chief of Staff, Military Command West, 1968-69. Commander of the Royal Order of the Sword; and other medals and awards. Member of the Royal Academy of Military Sciences. Promoted to Major General, 1969.

Skubilin, V. Lieutenant General, Engineer, USSR Air Force; Chief Engineer, Long Range Aviation, 1970-   .

Served on the Soviet-German Front in WW II. Member, Communist Party of the Soviet Union.

Slay, Alton D. Major General, United States Air Force; Commander, Lowry Technical Training Center, Lowry Air Force Base, Colorado. Born November 11, 1924, Crystal Springs, Mississippi. Army Air Force Flying School, 1943-44; George Washington University, BS, Mathematics; Harvard University, Advanced Management Program; Canadian National Defence College. Commissioned Second Lieutenant, US Army Air Corps, 1944. Combat duty in the Korean War; Vietnam War. Assistant Deputy Chief of Staff, Plans and Operations, US Air Forces, Europe; Commander, Air Force Flight Test Center; Deputy Chief of Staff, Operations, Air Force Systems Command; Deputy Chief of Staff, Operations, Seventh Air Force, and Director, Operations, Military Assistance Command, Vietnam. Distinguished Service Medal; Legion of Merit with four Oak Leaf Clusters; and other US and foreign medals and awards. Promoted to Major General, August 1, 1971.

Slayton, Donald K. United States; Director, Flight Crew Operations, Manned Spacecraft Center, Houston, Texas, 1963-   . Born March 1, 1924, Sparta, Wisconsin. University of Minnesota, BS, Aeronautical Engineering, 1949; US Air Force Test Pilot School, 1955-56. Commissioned Second Lieutenant, US Army Air Corps, 1943. Served in European and Pacific Theaters, WW II. Test Pilot, Edwards Air Force Base, California, 1956-59. NASA experience: Named Mercury Astronaut, April 1959; Coordinator of Astronaut Activities, 1962-63; Flight Crew Member, Apollo-Soyuz Test Project Mission, July 1975. Two NASA Distinguished Service Medals; NASA Exceptional Service Medal; Collier Trophy; SETP Kinchloe Award; General Billy Mitchell Award; SETP J.H. Doolittle Award; Honorary ScD, Carthage College, Carthage, Illinois, 1961; Honorary Doctorate in Engineering, Michigan Technological Institute, Houghton, Michigan, 1965.

Slipchenko, P.F. Lieutenant General, Artillery, USSR Army; Commandant, Artillery College. Served on the Soviet-German Front in WW II. Member, Communist Party of the Soviet Union.

Small, Walter Lowry. Rear Admiral, United States Navy; Assistant Deputy Chief of Naval Operations (Plans and Policy), 1972-   . Born October 31, 1916, Elizabeth City, North Carolina. US Naval Academy, 1934-38; Submarine School, New London, Connecticut, 1940; Armed Forces Staff College, 1952-53; Naval War College, 1957-58. Commissioned Ensign, US Navy in 1938. Duty in the Pacific Theater in submarines in WW II. Commander Submarine Squadron TEN, 1962-63; Chief of Staff and Aide to Commander Submarine Force, Pacific Fleet, 1963-64; Head, Navy Plans Branch, Strategic Plans Division, Office of the CNO, 1964-65; Assistant for War Gaming Matters, Office of the CNO, 1965-67; Commander Middle East Force, 1967-68; Commander Submarine Force, US Pacific Fleet, 1968-70; Director, Politico-Military Policy Division, Office of the CNO, 1970-72. Distinguished Service

Medal; Silver Star Medal with Gold Star; Legion of Merit with Gold Star; Commendation Medal with Star and Combat "V"; and other medals and awards. Promoted to Rear Admiral, August 10, 1965.

Smallwood, Sir Denis (Graham). Air Chief Marshal, British Royal Air Force; Vice-Chief of the Air Staff, 1970- . Born August 13, 1918. Attended Royal Air Force Staff College; Joint Services Staff College; Joint Warfare Staff School; Imperial Defence College. Joined the Royal Air Force in 1938. Served in Fighter Command in WW II. Air Officer Commanding, and Commandant, Royal Air Force College of Air Warfare, Manby, 1961-62; Assistant Chief, Air Staff (Operations), 1962-65; Air Officer Commanding, No. 3 Group, RAF Bomber Command, 1965-67; Senior Air Staff Officer, Bomber Command, 1967-68; Senior Air Staff Officer, Strike Command, 1968-69; Air Officer Commanding-in-Chief, Near East Air Forces, Commander, British Forces, Near East, and Administrator, Sovereign Base Area, Cyprus, 1969-70. KCB; CBE; DSO; DFC. Aide-de-Camp to the Queen, 1959-64.

Smirnov, N.I. Admiral, USSR Navy; Commander in Chief, Pacific Fleet, 1969- . Born in 1920. Served in the Soviet-German War, 1941-45. Chief, Operations Section, Main Naval Staff, c. 1965-69. Member, Communist Party of the Soviet Union.

Smith, Albert Hamman, Jr. Major General, United States Army; Deputy Chief of Staff for Personnel, Continental Army Command, Fort Monroe, Virginia, 1972- . Born April 29, 1919, Baltimore, Maryland. Johns Hopkins University, BA Degree, Chemistry and Economics; The Infantry School, Basic and Advanced Courses; US Marine Corps School, Senior Course; US Army War College; Harvard University, MBA Degree. Commissioned Second Lieutenant, US Army Reserve, 1940. Served in WW II and Vietnam War. Director, J-3, US Southern Command, Quarry Heights, Canal Zone, 1967-68; Assistant Division Commander, 1st Infantry Division, US Army, Pacific-Vietnam, 1968-69; Assistant Chief of Staff for Personnel, J-1, US Military Assistance Command, Vietnam, 1969-70; Director Procurement and Distribution, Office, Deputy Chief of Staff for Personnel, Department of the Army, Washington, D.C., 1970-72. Distinguished Service Medal; Silver Star with Oak Leaf Cluster; Legion of Merit with three Oak Leaf Clusters; Distinguished Flying Cross, with Oak Leaf Cluster; Bronze Star Medal with Oak Leaf Cluster; and other medals and awards. Promoted to Brigadier General, March 27, 1967; Major General, June 1, 1970.

Smith, DeWitt Clinton, Jr. Major General, United States Army; Assistant Deputy Chief of Staff for Personnel, 1973- . Born March 31, 1920, in Baltimore, Maryland. Attended University of Maryland, BA, Government and Politics; Infantry School, Basic and Advanced Courses; Command and General Staff College; Armed Forces Staff College; Army War College, 1965-66. Commissioned Second Lieutenant (ORC) July 12, 1943; transferred to

USAR 1946; regular Army commission 1950. Served in WW II, the Korean War, and the Vietnam War. Military Assistant to the Chairman, Joint Chiefs of Staff (Public Affairs), Organization of the Joint Chiefs of Staff, 1966-67; Commanding Officer, 2d Brigade, 3d Armored Division, US Army, Europe, 1967-68; Assistant Chief of Staff, G-3, Central Army Group, Europe, 1968-69; Member, Chairman's Staff Group, Joint Chiefs of Staff Organization, 1969; Assistant Division Commander, 5th Infantry Division (Mechanized), later Assistant Division Commander, 4th Infantry Division, Fort Carson, Colorado, 1969-71; Deputy Chief of Public Information, Office of the Secretary of the Army, and Deputy Chief of Information, Office of the Chief of Staff, US Army, 1971-73. Silver Star; Legion of Merit with three Oak Leaf Clusters; Bronze Star Medal with Oak Leaf Cluster; and other medals and awards. Promoted to Brigadier General April 14, 1970; Major General February 1, 1973.

Smith, Donavon F. Major General, United States Air Force; Commander, Alaskan Air Command, and Vice Commander, Alaskan North American Air Defense Command/Continental Air Defense Command (NORAD/CONAD) Region, 1972- . Born October 2, 1922, Dowagiac, Michigan. Army Air Corps Flying School, 1942; National War College, 1962-63; Harvard University, Advanced Management Course, 1966. Commissioned Second Lieutenant, US Army Air Corps, 1942. Combat duty with fighters in the European Theater, WW II; Vietnam War. Chief, Air Defense Division, Directorate of Operations Requirements, Deputy Chief of Staff for Programs and Requirements, 1963-66; Deputy Director of Strategic and Defense Forces for Operational Requirements and Development Plans, 1966; Chief, Air Force Advisory Group, Military Assistance Command, Vietnam, 1966-68; Vice Commander, Ninth Air Force, 1968-69; Commander, Nineteenth "Suitcase" Air Force, 1969-70; Director, Operational Requirements and Development Plans, Headquarters USAF, 1970-71; Assistant Deputy Chief of Staff, Plans and Operations, Headquarters USAF, 1971-72. Distinguished Service Cross; Distinguished Service Medal; Legion of Merit; Distinguished Flying Cross with three Oak Leaf Clusters; and other US and foreign medals and awards. Promoted to Major General, August 1, 1969.

Smith, Edwin Howell, Jr. Major General, United States Army; Assistant Surgeon General (Dental), US Army, Washington, D.C. 1971- . Born May 3, 1916, Philadelphia, Pennsylvania. University of Pennsylvania, DDS Degree; Northwestern Dental School, MSD Degree, Prosthetics; University of Maryland, BS Degree, Military Science. Commissioned First Lieutenant, US Army Reserve, 1941. Chief, Dental Service, Fitzsimons General Hospital, Denver, Colorado, 1963-65; Dental Surgeon and Director of Dental Education, US Army Infantry Center, Fort Benning, Georgia, 1965-67; Chief, Department of Dentistry, Walter Reed General Hospital, Walter Reed Army Medical Center, Washington, D.C., 1967-71. Legion of Merit; Meritorious Service Medal; and other medals and awards. Promoted to Major General, December 1, 1971.

Smith, Foster L. Major General, United States Air Force; Director, Plans and Policy, J-5, Headquarters, United States European Command, Germany, 1971-   . Born September 6, 1922, in Bryan County, Oklahoma. Southeastern State College, Oklahoma, 1939-41; US Military Academy, 1941-44; Harvard University, Littauer Center, 1961-62, MA, Public Administration, 1962; National War College, 1965-66. Commissioned Second Lieutenant, US Army Air Corps, 1944. Combat duty in WW II; Korean War; Vietnam War. Chief, War Plans Division, Office of Deputy Chief of Staff, Operations, US Air Forces in Europe (USAFE), 1962-65; Vice Commander, then Commander 4453d Combat Crew Training Wing, 1966-67; Vice Commander, 3d Tactical Fighter Wing, Vietnam, 1967; Deputy Director, Seventh Air Force Tactical Air Control Center, Vietnam, 1967-68; Air Force Member, Personal Staff Group, for the Chairman, Joint Chiefs of Staff, 1968-69; Deputy Director, Operations, National Military Command Center, 1969-70; Chief, Far East Division, Plans and Policy Directorate, 1970-71. Distinguished Service Medal; Silver Star; Legion of Merit; Distinguished Flying Cross with three Oak Leaf Clusters; and other US and foreign medals and awards. Promoted to Major General, September 1, 1971.

Smith, Homer Duggins, Jr. Major General, United States Army; Director of Supply and Maintenance, Office of the Deputy Chief of Staff for Logistics, 1972-   . Born February 16, 1922, in Brackenridge, Texas. Attended Texas A & M College, BS, Chemical Engineering; Purdue University, MS, Industrial Economics; Artillery School; Ordnance School, Advanced Course; Command and General Staff College; Industrial College of the Armed Forces, 1966-67. Commissioned Second Lieutenant May 15, 1943. Served in WW II and the Vietnam War. Commanding Officer, 8th Logistical Command, US Army, Europe, 1967-68; Assistant Chief of Staff, Comptroller, later Chief of Staff, 1st Logistical Command, US Army, Pacific-Vietnam, 1969; Commanding Officer, US Army Support Command, Da Nang, US Army, Pacific-Vietnam, 1969-70; Deputy Assistant Chief of Staff for Logistics (Supply and Maintenance), US Army, with additional duty as Chairman of the XM705/M715E1 Review Committee, US Materiel Command, 1970-71; Director of Plans, Office of the Deputy Chief of Staff for Logistics, 1971-72. Distinguished Service Medal; Legion of Merit; and other medals and awards. Promoted to Brigadier General November 1, 1970; Major General April 1, 1973.

Smith, Howard P. Major General, United States Air Force; Deputy Director for Intelligence, Defense Intelligence Agency, Washington, D.C., 1973-   . Born November 30, 1924, in West Palm Beach, Florida. Aviation Cadet Training Course, 1943-44; University of Georgia, 1946-47; University of Omaha, BA, 1962; Industrial College of the Armed Forces, 1963-64; George Washington University, MBA, 1964. Commissioned Second Lieutenant, US Army Air Corps, in August 1944. Served in the Vietnam War. Single Integrated Operational Plan Officer, Strategic Operations Division, Directorate of Operations, The Joint Staff, Organization of the Joint Chiefs of Staff, 1964-67; Director of Targets, Deputy Chief of Staff, Intelligence, Headquarters Seventh Air Force, Tan Son Nhut Air Field, Vietnam, 1967-68; Director of Targets, Headquarters Pacific Air Force, Hickam Air Force Base, Hawaii, 1968-70; Deputy Chief of Staff for Intelligence, Headquarters Pacific Air Force, Hickam Air Force Base, Hawaii, 1970-71; Director of Intelligence Applications, Headquarters US Air Force, Washington, D.C., 1971-72; Deputy Assistant Chief of Staff, Intelligence, Headquarters, US Air Force, Washington, D.C., 1972-73. Decorations include Legion of Merit with three Oak Leaf Clusters, and other medals and awards. Promoted to Brigadier General, July 1, 1971; Major General, April 2, 1973.

Smith, James Clifton. Major General, United States Army; Deputy Commanding General for Reserve Forces, Northern Area, Fifth US Army, Fort Sheridan, Illinois, 1973-   . Born September 5, 1923, Fort Oglethorpe, Georgia. University of Omaha, BGE Degree, Military Science; The Cavalry School, Basic and Advanced Courses; The Armored School, Advanced Course; US Army Command and General Staff College; US Army War College. Commissioned Second Lieutenant, 1943. Served in WW II and Vietnam War. Deputy Brigade Commander, 1st Aviation Brigade, US Army, Pacific-Vietnam, 1968-69; Assistant Division Commander, 101st Airborne Division (Airmobile), US Army, Pacific-Vietnam, 1969-70; Deputy Commandant, US Army Aviation School, and Commanding General, US Army Flight Training Center, Fort Stewart, Georgia, 1970-71; Commanding General, 1st Cavalry Division (TRICAP) (Redesignated from 1st Armored Division in May 1971), Fort Hood, Texas, 1971-72. Distinguished Service Medal; Silver Star with Oak Leaf Cluster; Legion of Merit with Oak Leaf Cluster; Distinguished Flying Cross with three Oak Leaf Clusters; Bronze Star Medal with Oak Leaf Cluster; and other medals and awards. Promoted to Brigadier General, August 1, 1966; Major General, July 1, 1971.

Smith, John Victor. Vice Admiral, United States Navy; Commandant, Industrial College of the Armed Forces, 1970-   . Born May 24, 1912, Seattle, Washington. US Naval Academy, 1930-34; Ordnance Engineering Course, Postgraduate School, 1940-42; Armed Forces Staff College, 1949-50; National War College, 1953-54. Commissioned Ensign, US Navy, 1934. Served in the Atlantic and Pacific Theaters in WW II; Korean War. Commander Cruiser-Destroyer Flotilla EIGHT, 1963-64; Director of Naval Warfare Analyses, Office of the CNO, 1964-65; Director, Strategic Plans Division, 1965-66; Assistant Chief of Naval Operations (Plans and Policy), 1966-67; Senior Member, United Nations Command, Military Armistice Commission, Korea, 1967-68; Commander Amphibious Force, US Pacific Fleet, 1968-70. Distinguished Service Medal; Legion of Merit; Bronze Star with Combat "V"; Commendation Ribbon with Combat "V"; and other medals and awards. Promoted to Rear Admiral, July 1, 1962.

Smith, Larry Allen. Major General, United States Air Force; Command Surgeon, Air University, Maxwell Air Force Base, Alabama, 1972-   . Born August 28, 1913, in Noonan, North Dakota. University of North Dakota, BA, 1935, BS, 1936; Northwestern University Medical School, MB, 1938, MD, 1939; Medical Field Service School, 1941; School of Aviation Medicine, 1946. Commissioned First Lieutenant, US Army Medical Corps, 1939; transferred to US Army Air Force, 1946. Wartime duty in Iceland and the China-Burma-India Theater, WW II. Director, Medical Staffing and Education, Office of the Surgeon General, 1959-63; Command Surgeon, Air Training Command, 1963-69; Command Surgeon, Headquarters Pacific Air Forces, Hawaii, 1969-72. Legion of Merit; and other medals and awards. Promoted to Brigadier General, September 21, 1961; Major General, March 20, 1967.

Smith, Levering. Rear Admiral, United States Navy, Retired; Director, Strategic Systems Projects, Department of the Navy, 1965-   . Born March 5, 1910, in Joplin, Missouri. US Naval Academy, 1928-32; Naval Postgraduate School, Ordnance Course, 1938-40. Commissioned Ensign, US Navy, in 1932. Served in the Pacific Theater in WW II. Commander Naval Ordnance Missile Test Facility, White Sands Proving Ground, New Mexico, 1954-56; Deputy Director, Technical Division, Special Projects Office, 1956-57; Technical Director (1957-65) and Director, Strategic Systems Project Office, 1965-72; transferred to retired list, April 1, 1972, but continued active duty. Two Distinguished Service Medals; Captain Robert Dexter Conrad award; L.T.E. Thompson Award; C.N. Hickman Award; Honorary LLD, New Mexico State University; and other US and foreign medals and awards. Promoted to Rear Admiral, April 1, 1963.

Smith, Robert Bruce. Major General, United States Army; Deputy Commanding General for Reserve Forces, Sixth US Army, Presidio of San Francisco, 1972-   . Born April 22, 1920, De Quincy, Louisiana. Louisiana State University, BA Degree in Journalism; The Artillery School, Basic Course; US Army Command and General Staff College; US Army War College. Commissioned Second Lieutenant, US Army Reserve, 1941. Served in WW II. Deputy Director, Operations, National Military Command Center, J-3, Joint Staff, Organization, Joint Chiefs of Staff, Washington, D.C., 1964-65; Assistant Division Commander, 7th Infantry Division, US Army, Pacific-Korea, 1965-66; Deputy Commandant, US Army War College, and Deputy Commanding General, Carlisle Barracks, Pennsylvania, 1966-67; Deputy Chief of Public Information, Office, Secretary of the Army, and Deputy Chief of Information, Office, Chief of Staff, US Army, Washington, D.C., 1968-69; Deputy Commanding General, US Army, Ryukyu Islands and IX Corps, Okinawa, 1969-72. Distinguished Service Medal; Legion of Merit with two Oak Leaf Clusters; Bronze Star medal with Oak Leaf Cluster; and other medals and awards. Promoted to Brigadier General, August 1, 1963; Major General, August 1, 1969.

Smith, Robert Nelson. Lieutenant General, United States Air Force; Chief of Staff, United Nations Command, Korea, and Chief of Staff, United States Forces, Korea, 1969. Born September 12, 1915, in Burlington, Massachusetts. Bowdoin College, Brunswick, Maine, BS, 1938; Army Air Corps Flying School, 1941. Commissioned Second Lieutenant, US Army Air Corps, 1941. Combat duty in the Southwest Pacific Area, WW II. Director of Intelligence, Headquarters, Strategic Air Command, 1955-65; Director of Plans, Deputy Chief of Staff, Plans and Operations, Headquarters, US Air Force, 1966-68; Vice Commander in Chief, Headquarters, US Air Force, Europe, Germany, 1968-69. Distinguished Service Medal (Air Force Design); Distinguished Service Medal (Army Design); Distinguished Flying Cross; Soldier's Medal; and other US and foreign medals and awards. Promoted to Brigadier General, May 4, 1960; Major General, April 1, 1963; Lieutenant General, May 29, 1968.

Smith, Sir Victor (Alfred Trumper). Admiral, Royal Australian Navy; Chairman, Australian Chiefs of Staff Committee, and Military Adviser to SEATO, 1970-   . Born May 9, 1913. Attended Royal Australian Naval College. Commissioned Sub-Lieutenant in 1935. Chief of Naval Staff and First Naval Member, Australian Commonwealth Naval Board, 1968-70. Promoted to Rear-Admiral, 1963; Vice-Admiral, 1968; Admiral, 1970.

Smith, William Y. Major General, United States Air Force; Commander, Oklahoma City Air Materiel Area, Tinker Air Force Base, Oklahoma, 1972-   . Born August 13, 1925, in Hot Springs, Arkansas. Washington and Lee University, Virginia, 1943-44; US Military Academy, 1944-48; Harvard University, MA, 1954, Public Administration, PhD, Political Economy, 1961; Air Command and Staff School, 1958-59; National War College, 1964-65. Commissioned Second Lieutenant, US Air Force, 1948. Served in the Korean War. Assistant to the Chairman, Joint Chiefs of Staff, and Staff Member, National Security Council, 1962-64; Staff Member, Policy and Negotiations Division, then Chief, War Plans Division, Deputy Chief of Staff, Operations, Headquarters US Air Forces Europe, Lindsey Air Station, Wiesbaden, Germany, 1965-67; Commander, 603d Air Base Wing, Sembach, Germany, 1967-68; Military Assistant to the Secretary of the Air Force, Washington, D.C., 1968-71; Vice Commander, Oklahoma City Materiel Area, Tinker Air Force Base, Oklahoma, 1971-72. Distinguished Service Medal; Silver Star; Legion of Merit; Air Medal with three Oak Leaf Clusters; and other medals and awards. Promoted to Brigadier General, September 1, 1970; Major General, 1973.

Snavely, William W. Major General, United States Air Force; Assistant Deputy Chief of Staff, Systems and Logistics, Headquarters, US Air Force, 1971-   . Born April 6, 1920, in Los Angeles, California. US Military Academy, 1940-43; Air Force Institute of Technology; University of Southern California, Los Angeles, 1948-50, MA, 1950; Industrial College of the Armed Forces, 1962-63; Harvard University, Advanced Management

Program. Commissioned Second Lieutenant, US Army Air Corps, 1943. Combat duty in the European Theater, Eighth Air Force, WW II. Deputy Director of Production, Office of Deputy Chief of Staff, Systems and Logistics, 1963-65; Director, Procurement Policy, Assistant Secretary of Defense (Procurement), 1965-68; Vice Commander, Oklahoma City Air Materiel Area, 1968-69; Deputy Chief of Staff Plans, later Materiel Management, Headquarters, Air Force Logistics Command, 1969-71. Distinguished Service Medal; Legion of Merit with two Oak Leaf Clusters; Distinguished Flying Cross with one Oak Leaf Cluster; and other medals and awards. Promoted to Major General, August 1, 1969.

Snowden, Lawrence Fontaine. Major General, United States Marine Corps; Chief of Staff, US Forces, Japan, 1972-   . Born April 14, 1921, Charlottesville, Virginia. University of Virginia, BS, Commerce, 1942; Officers Candidate School, Quantico, 1942; Administrative School, Quantico, 1946-47; Northwestern University, 1949-50, MA, Personnel Administration, 1950; Senior School, Quantico, 1958-59; Industrial College of the Armed Forces, 1967-68; Advanced Management Course, Graduate School of Business, Harvard University, 1968. Commissioned Second Lieutenant, USMCR, 1942. Served in Pacific Theater, WW II; Korean War; Vietnam War. Commander, 7th Marine Regiment, 1st Marine Division, Vietnam, 1966-67; Assistant G-3, Operations Officer, III Marine Amphibious Force, 1967; Assistant Director of Personnel, Marine Corps Headquarters, 1968; Director, Management Analysis Group, Office of the Chief of Staff, and Inspector General, Headquarters Marine Corps, 1969-70; Director, Systems Support Group, Marine Corps, 1970; Director, Marine Corps Development Center, Marine Corps Development and Education Command, 1970-72. Legion of Merit with Combat "V" and three Gold Stars; and other US and foreign medals and awards. Promoted to Brigadier General, August 20, 1968; Major General, April 1, 1970.

Soedardjo, Nichlany. Brigadier General, Indonesian Army; Defense and Military Attache, Embassy of the Republic of Indonesia, Washington, D.C., 1973-   .

Soedarman, Soesilo. Brigadier General, Indonesian Army; Defense and Military Attache, Embassy of the Republic of Indonesia, Washington, D.C., 1971-73.

Sokolov, I. Major General, USSR Army; Deputy Chief, Political Directorate, Soviet Ground Forces. Served on the Soviet-German Front in WW II. Member, Communist Party of the Soviet Union.

Sokolov, S.I. General of the Army, USSR Army; First Deputy Minister of Defense, Administration, Ministry of Defense, 1967-   . Born in 1911. Served on the Soviet-German Front in WW II. Commander Leningrad Military District, 1965-67. Member, Communist Party of the Soviet Union. Order of Lenin; Order of Red Banner; Order of Red Star; and other orders and awards. Promoted to Colonel General, 1965; General of the Army, 1967.

Somerville, Ronald Macaulay. Major-General, British Army; Vice Quartermaster-General, 1972-   . Born July 2, 1919. Attended George Watson's College, Edinburgh; Staff College, 1944; Joint Services Staff College, 1956; Imperial Defence College, 1967. Commissioned in the Royal Artillery in 1940. Served in Northwest Europe and the Far East in WW II; Cyprus Emergency, 1957-59; Borneo Emergency, 1965. Commanding Officer, 4th Light Regiment, Royal Artillery, 1963-65; Commander, Royal Artillery, 51st Heavy Division, 1965-66; Deputy Quartermaster-General, British Army of the Rhine, 1968-70; General Officer Commanding, Yorkshire District, 1970-72. OBE; Knight Officer, Order of Orange Nassau with Swords.

Somoza Debayle, Anastasio. General, Army of Nicaragua; Commander, Nicaraguan National Guard, 1972-   ; President, National Emergency Committee, 1972-   . Born December 5, 1925. Formerly President of Nicaragua.

Sonenshein, Nathan. Rear Admiral, United States Navy; Head of the Shipbuilding Council, Naval Material Command, 1972-   . Born August 2, 1915, in Lodi, New Jersey. US Naval Academy, 1934-38; Massachusetts Institute of Technology, MS, Naval Construction and Marine Engineering, 1941-44; Advanced Management Program, Harvard Graduate School of Business, 1964. Commissioned Ensign, US Navy, in 1938. Served at sea in the Korean War. Director, Ship Design Division, Bureau of Ships, 1962-64; Assistant Chief of Bureau of Ships for Design, Shipbuilding and Fleet Maintenance, 1965; Project Officer, Fast Deployment Logistics Ship Project, 1965-67; Deputy Chief of Naval Material (Logistic Support), 1967-69; Commander Naval Ship Systems Command, 1969-72. Legion of Merit; Navy Commendation Medal with Combat "V"; and other medals and awards. Promoted to Rear Admiral, May 1, 1965.

Sorokin. Lieutenant General, USSR Army; First Deputy Commander in Chief, Southern Group of Soviet Forces, Hungary. Served on the Soviet-German Front in WW II. Member, Communist Party of the Soviet Union.

Souvanna Phouma, His Highness Prince. Prime Minister and Minister of Defense, Laos, 1962-   . Born October 7, 1901. Attended University of Paris, France; Electrotechnical Institute, Grenoble, France. Minister of Public Works, 1950-51; Minister of National Defense and Veterans, 1954-56; Prime Minister, Minister of Defense and Veterans, and Minister of Foreign Affairs and Information, 1956-57; Prime Minister, 1957-58; Ambassador to France, 1958-60; President, National Assembly, 1960; Head, Neutralist Government, 1960-62. Grand Cross Order of Million Elephants; Commander Légion d'Honneur (France); and other awards and medals.

Sowrey, Frederick Beresford. Air Vice-Marshal, British Royal Air Force; Commandant, National Defence College, Latimer, 1972-   . Born September 14, 1922. Flying Training Course, Canada, 1941; Flying Instructors School,

1944; Royal Air Force Staff College, 1954; Imperial Defence College, 1965. Joined the Royal Air Force in 1940. Flew Fighter-Reconnaissance in Europe in WW II. Personal Staff Officer to Chief of Air Staff, 1960-62; Commanding Officer, Royal Air Force, Abingdon, 1962-64; Senior Air Staff Officer, Middle East Command (Aden), 1966-67; Director of Defence Policy, Ministry of Defence, 1968-70; Senior Air Staff Officer, RAF Training Command, 1970-72. CB; CBE; AFC.

Sozinov, V. Lieutenant General, USSR Air Force; Chief of Staff, The Main Staff, Soviet Air Defense Forces, 1968-   . Served on the Soviet-German Front in WW II. Staff, Moscow District Air Defense Forces; Member, Communist Party of the Soviet Union.

Spanjer, Ralph H. Major General, United States Marine Corps; Assistant Chief of Staff, J-3, Pacific Command, 1972-   . Born September 20, 1920, Hillside, New Jersey. New York University; Flight Training Course, 1942; Amphibious Warfare School, 1946; US Air Force Command and Staff College, 1950-51; Armed Forces Staff College, 1963; National War College, 1966-67; George Washington University, BA, 1962, MA, International Affairs, 1967. Commissioned Second Lieutenant, USMCR, Naval Aviator, 1942; USMC, 1946. Served in Central Pacific Theater, WW II; Korean War; Vietnam War. Commanding Officer, 1st Marine Brigade, FMF, 1965-66; Deputy Assistant Director, Plans, Programs and Systems, Headquarters, Defense Supply Agency, 1967-69; Assistant Wing Commander, 1st Marine Aircraft Wing, Fleet Marine Force, Vietnam, 1969-70; Director, Systems Support Group, Headquarters Marine Corps, 1970-71; Deputy Director, Personnel, 1971-72. Legion of Merit with two Gold Stars; Distinguished Flying Cross with Gold Star; and other medals and awards. Promoted to Brigadier General, September 1967; Major General, August 26, 1971.

Sparrow, Herbert George. Major General, United States Army; Director, Army Council of Review Boards, Washington, D.C., 1970-   . Born November 24, 1910, Boston, Massachusetts. US Military Academy; The Artillery School, Advanced Course; US Army Command and General Staff College; US Army War College. Commissioned Second Lieutenant, 1933. Served in WW II. Commanding General, XX US Army Corps, Fort Hayes, Ohio, 1964-65; Director of Programs, later Director of Plans, Programs, and Budget, Office, Deputy Chief of Staff for Personnel, US Army, Washington, D.C., 1965-66; Assistant Deputy Chief of Staff for Personnel, US Army, Washington, D.C., 1966-67; Chief, US Army Audit Agency, Washington, D.C., 1967-70. Distinguished Service Medal with Oak Leaf Cluster; Bronze Star Medal; and other medals and awards. Promoted to Brigadier General, January 26, 1960; Major General, April 17, 1962.

Speigl, Matthaus. Brigadier General, Army of the Federal Republic of Germany; Defense Attache, Embassy of the Federal Republic of Germany, Washington, D.C.

Spickernell, Derek Garland. Rear-Admiral, British Royal Navy; Director-General, Quality Assurance, Ministry of Defence (PE), 1972-   . Born June 1, 1921. Attended Royal Naval Engineering College, Keyham. Commissioned in 1943. Served at sea in WW II. Deputy Manager, Engineering Department, HM Dockyard, Portsmouth, 1962-64; Commanding Officer, HMS *Fisgard*, 1965-66; Deputy Director of Naval Ship Production, 1967-70; Deputy Chief Executive, Defence Quality Assurance Board, 1970-71. Chartered Engineer; Fellow of the Institute of Mechanical Engineering; Member of the Institute of Production Engineering; Member of the British Institute of Management; Member of the Institute of Marine Engineering; Member of the Institute of Personnel Management.

Spotswood, Sir Denis (Frank). Air Chief Marshal, British Royal Air Force; Chief of the Air Staff, 1971-   . Born September 26, 1916. Commissioned in the Royal Air Force in 1936. Served in Britain and Southeast Asia in WW II. Assistant Chief of Staff (Air Defence), SHAPE, 1961-63; Air Officer Commanding, No. 3 Group, Royal Air Force Bomber Command, 1964-65; Commander-in-Chief, Royal Air Force, Germany, 1965-68; Commander, Second Allied Tactical Air Force, 1966-68; Air Officer Commanding-in-Chief, Royal Air Force Strike Command, and Commander, United Kingdom Air Defence Region, 1968-71. GCB; CBE; DSO; DFC; Legion of Merit (USA). Aide-de-Camp to the Queen, 1957-61; Air Aide-de-Camp to the Queen, 1970. Promoted to Air Commodore, 1958; Air Vice-Marshal, 1961; Air Marshal, 1965; Air Chief Marshal, 1968.

Spragins, Charles Echols. Major General, United States Army; Commanding General, US Army Training Center (Infantry) and Fort Polk, Louisiana, 1973-   . Born April 11, 1923, in Colon, Panama. Attended US Military Academy; Infantry School; Command and General Staff College; Armed Forces Staff College; Army War College, 1963-64; New York University, MA, Government and International Relations. Commissioned June 5, 1945. Served in the Korean War, and the Vietnam War. Deputy Commander, 5th Special Forces Group, 1st Special Forces, US Army, Vietnam; Staff Officer, Operations Division, Special Operations, later Chief of the Policy Planning Branch, and then Assistant Chief, International Policy Division, Strategic Plans and Policy Directorate, Office of the Deputy Chief of Staff for Military Operations, 1965-66; Deputy Chief of the General Staff, Office of the Chief of Staff, US Army, 1966-68; Commanding Officer, 2d Brigade, 82d Airborne Division, Fort Bragg, North Carolina, 1968-69; Commanding General, 4th Brigade, 25th Infantry Division, US Army, Pacific-Hawaii, 1969-71; Deputy Chief of Staff, Operations, US Army, Pacific-Hawaii, 1971-73. Legion of Merit with two Oak Leaf Clusters; Bronze Star Medal with Oak Leaf Cluster; Meritorious Service Medal; and other medals and awards. Promoted to Brigadier General February 1, 1970; Major General February 1, 1973.

Sredin, G.R. Lieutenant General, USSR Army; Deputy Chief, Main Political Directorate of the Soviet Army and Navy, 1972-   . Served on the Soviet-German Front in WW II. Deputy Chief, Political Directorate, Southern Group of Forces in Hungary; Deputy Chief, Political Directorate, and Member, Military Council, Carpathian Military District, 1967-72. Member, Communist Party of the Soviet Union.

Stack, Sir (Thomas) Neville. Air Marshal, British Royal Air Force; Air Officer Commanding-Chief, RAF Training Command, 1972-   . Born October 19, 1919. St. Edmund's College, Ware; Royal Air Force College, Cranwell; Staff College, 1950; Royal Air Force Flying College, 1953. Flew Flying Boats in Coastal Command in WW II. Deputy Captain, The Queen's Flight, 1960-62; Transport Support Duties, Far East, 1963-64; Headquarters, Flying Training Command, 1965-67; Commandant, Royal Air Force College, 1967-70. United Kingdom Permanent Military Deputy, Central Treaty Organization, Ankara, Turkey, 1970-72. KCB; CVO; CBE; AFC; Order of Leopold (Belgium); Croix de Guerre (Belgium). Fellow, Royal Meteorological Society.

Stafford, Thomas P. Brigadier General, US Air Force; Deputy Director, Flight Crew Operations, Manned Spacecraft Center, Houston, Texas, 1971-   . Born September 17, 1930, Weatherford, Oklahoma. US Naval Academy, 1948-52; US Air Force Experimental Flight Test School. Commissioned Second Lieutenant, US Air Force, 1952. Chief, Performance Branch, US Air Force Aerospace Research Pilot School. NASA experience: Selected as Astronaut, September 1962; Backup Pilot, Gemini 3; Pilot, Gemini 6, December 15-16, 1965; Command Pilot, Gemini 9, June 3-6, 1966; Backup Commander, Apollo 7; Spacecraft Commander, Apollo 10, May 18-26, 1969; Chief of the Astronaut Office, 1969-71; Commander, Apollo-Soyuz Test Project, July 1975. NASA Distinguished Service Medal; two NASA Exceptional Service Medals; Manned Spacecraft Center Certificate of Commendation; Air Force Command Pilot Astronaut Wings; Air Force Distinguished Flying Cross; AIAA Astronautics Award; Harmon International Aviation Trophy; National Academy of Television Arts and Scientists Special Trustees Award; Honorary ScD, Oklahoma City University, 1967; Honorary LLB, Western State University College of Law, 1969; Honorary Doctorate of Communications, Emerson College, 1969; Honorary Doctorate of Aeronautical Engineering, Embry-Riddle Aeronautical University, 1970.

Stahl, Carl-Gustaf. Major General, Swedish Royal Army; Chief, Central Planning Directorate, Defense Materiel Administration, 1972-   . Attended Artillery and Engineering Staff College, 1947-49; Royal National Defense College, 1962, 1972. Commanding Officer, Engineering Regiment Ing 2, 1963-64; Defense and Army Attache, Washington, D.C., USA, 1966-72. Commander of the Royal Order of the Sword; Legion of Merit (USA); United Nations Medal (Cyprus); and other medals and awards. Promoted to Major General, 1972.

Stapleton, Carl W. Major General, United States Air Force; Commander, United States Air Force Security Service (USAFSS), 1969-   . Born November 13, 1917, in Knoxville, Tennessee. US Military Academy, 1938-42; Army Air Corps Flying School, 1942; Columbia University, New York, MS, Business Administration, 1948; American University, 1961. Commissioned Second Lieutenant, US Army, 1942; received Pilot Wings, 1942. Combat duty in the European-African Theater, WW II. Commander, 6940 Technical Training Wing, US Air Force Security Service, 1961-63; Deputy Commander, and later Commander, Pacific Security Region, USAFSS, Hawaii, 1963-66; Vice Commander, US Air Force Security Service, 1966-69. Legion of Merit, Distinguished Flying Cross with one Oak Leaf Cluster; and other medals and awards. Promoted to Brigadier General, October 1, 1966; Major General, August 1, 1969.

Staring, Merlin Howard. Rear Admiral, Judge Advocate General's Corps, United States Navy; Judge Advocate General, Navy Department, 1972-   . Born March 20, 1919, in Frankfort, New York. Louisiana State University, Baton Rouge, BA, 1941; George Washington University, LLB, 1947, LLM, 1952; Naval Justice School, 1951. Commissioned in the US Naval Reserve in 1941; transferred to US Navy in 1947. Force and Staff Legal Officer, Staff of Commander in Chief, US Naval Forces, Europe, 1967-68; Special Counsel to the Secretary of the Navy, 1968-71; Deputy Judge Advocate General, Navy, 1971-72. Legion of Merit; Navy Commendation Medal; and other medals and awards. Promoted to Rear Admiral, February 1, 1971.

Starnes, William Love. Major General, United States Army; Division Engineer, US Army Engineer Division, Ohio River, Cincinnati, Ohio, 1970-   . Born March 23, 1919, Columbus, Ohio. US Military Academy; US Army Command and General Staff College; US Industrial College of the Armed Forces; Massachusetts Institute of Technology, MS Degree, Civil Engineering; The George Washington University, MBA Degree, Business Administration. Commissioned Second Lieutenant, 1943. Served in WW II and Vietnam War. Deputy Director of Military Construction, and Assistant Chief of Engineers for National Aeronautics and Space Administration Support, Office, Chief of Engineers, US Army, Washington, D.C., 1969; Staff Director, Southeast Asia Construction Division, Office, Assistant Secretary of Defense (Installations and Logistics), Washington, D.C., 1969-70; Assistant for Construction Operations, Office, Deputy Assistant Secretary of Defense (Installations and Housing), Office, Assistant Secretary of Defense (Installations and Logistics), Washington, D.C. 1970. Legion of Merit with three Oak Leaf Clusters; Bronze Star Medal with V Device; and other medals and awards. Promoted to Brigadier General, October 2, 1968; Major General, August 1, 1970.

Starry, Donn Albert. Major General, United States Army; Commanding General, US Army Armor Center, Commandant, Armor School, and Commanding General, US Army Training Center (Armor), Fort Knox, Kentucky,

1973-   . Born May 31, 1925, in New York, NY. Attended US Military Academy; Ground General School; Armored School, Basic and Advanced Courses; Command and General Staff College; Armed Forces Staff College; 1964-65; Army War College, 1965-66; George Washington University, MS, International Affairs. Commissioned Second Lieutenant June 8, 1948. Served in the Korean War and the Vietnam War. Chief, Plans Branch, later Operations Branch, Operations Division, G-3 (Mechanized and Armor Combat Operations in Vietnam Study Group, January-April 1967), US Army, Pacific-Vietnam, 1966-67; Operations Research Analyst, Weapons Systems Methodology, Office of the Assistant Vice Chief of Staff, 1967-68; Staff Officer, later Military Staff Assistant, Directorate of Organization and Management Planning, Office of the Assistant Secretary of Defense (Administration), 1968-69; Chief of the Combat Studies Operations Branch, Research and Analysis Division, Office of the Assistant Chief of Staff, J-3, US Military Assistance Command, Vietnam, 1969; Commanding Officer, 11th Armored Cavalry Regiment, US Army, Pacific-Vietnam, 1969-70; Deputy Director, Operations Directorate, Office of the Deputy Chief of Staff for Military Operations, 1970-71; Director of Manpower and Forces, Office of the Assistant Chief of Staff for Force Development, 1971-73. Silver Star; Legion of Merit with two Oak Leaf Clusters; Distinguished Flying Cross; Soldier's Medal; Bronze Star Medal with V Device with Oak Leaf Cluster; and other medals and awards. Promoted to Brigadier General April 1, 1971; Major General May 1, 1973.

Stebelski, Josef. Lieutenant General, Polish Army; First Deputy Inspector General of Training, Main Inspectorate of Training. Born in 1921. Political Officers School; General Staff War College, Warsaw, 1947-50. Served in Polish-German War, 1943-45. Recent positions: Commander, 12th Motorized Division, 1960-64; Chief of Staff, Pomeranian Military District, 1964-68; Deputy Inspector General of Training and Chief of the Inspectorate of Training, 1968. Cross of Grunwald; Cross of Valor; Cross of Merit; and other Polish and foreign orders and medals. Member of Polish United Workers Party.

Steedman, Alexander McKay Sinclair. Air Vice-Marshal, British Royal Air Force; Commandant, Royal Air Force Staff College, 1972-   . Born January 29, 1922. Attended Central Flying School, 1951; Royal Air Force Staff College, 1955; Joint Services Staff College, 1959-60. Joined the Royal Air Force in 1941. Served in European Theater in WW II. Commander, Royal Air Force, Lyneham, 1962-65; Group Captain (Operations), Headquarters, Transport Command, 1965; Chief of Air Staff, Royal Malaysian Air Force, 1965-67; Director, Defence Plans (Air), Ministry of Defence, 1967-68; Director, Defence Operations Staff, Ministry of Defence, 1968-69; Assistant Chief of Air Staff (Policy), Ministry of Defence, 1969-71; Senior Air Staff Officer, Strike Command, 1971-72. CB; CBE; DFC. Associate of the Royal Aeronautical Society; Member of the British Institute of Management.

Steinhoff, Johannes. General, Air Force of the Federal Republic of Germany; Chairman, NATO Military Committee, 1971-   . Born September 15, 1913, Bottendorf, Thuringia. Attended University of Jena; Officers School. Drafted into German Navy, 1934; transferred to Air Force, 1936. Served in WW II as Fighter Pilot. Joined Armed Forces (Bundeswehr), 1955, with rank of Colonel; Division Commander, 1963-65; Inspector of the Air Force, 1966-70. Promoted to Lieutenant General, 1965; General, January 1971.

Steel, Maxwell W., Jr. Major General, United States Air Force; Deputy Surgeon General, United States Air Force, 1972-   . Born November 3, 1918, in Huntingdon, Pennsylvania. Haverford College, Philadelphia, Pennsylvania, BS, 1940; Jefferson Medical College, Philadelphia, Pennsylvania, MD, 1944; Graduate School of Medicine, University of Pennsylvania, Internal Medicine Training, 1947. Commissioned First Lieutenant, US Army Medical Corps Reserve, 1944; received Regular Commission, 1947; transferred to US Air Force, 1949. Commander, Malcolm Grow US Air Force Medical Center and Surgeon, Headquarters Command, US Air Force, 1969-70; Command Surgeon, Military Airlift Command, 1970-72. Distinguished Service Medal; and other US and foreign medals and awards. Promoted to Major General, September 1, 1971.

Steele, Joseph Rodgers. Rear Admiral, United States Coast Guard; Chief, Office of Personnel, US Coast Guard, 1971-   . Born January 20, 1920, Birmingham, Alabama. Birmingham Southern College, 1936-39; University of Alabama, 1939-40, BA Degree; US Coast Guard Academy, 1940-43; Navy Flight Training Courses, 1945-47; US Air Force Institute of Technology, MS Degree, Aeronautical Engineering, 1952. Commissioned Ensign, 1943; designated Coast Guard Aviator, 1947. Served in Atlantic and Pacific Theaters, WW II. Chief, Aeronautical Engineering Division, Headquarters, US Coast Guard, 1964-67; Chief of Engineering, 17th Coast Guard District, Juneau, Alaska, 1967-69; Commander, Coast Guard Air Station, Kodiak, 1969-70; Chief of Operations, 2d Coast Guard District, St. Louis, Missouri, 1970-71. WW II campaign service medals and ribbons. Promoted to Captain, July 1, 1965; Rear Admiral, June 11, 1971.

Steffes, Eugene Q., Jr. Major General, United States Air Force; Director of Operations Plans, Deputy Chief of Staff for Operations, Headquarters Strategic Air Command, and Chief, Single Integrated Operational Plans Division, Joint Strategic Target Planning Staff, Organization of the Joint Chiefs of Staff, Offutt Air Force Base, Nebraska, 1972-   . Born September 6, 1921, in Gary, Indiana. Attended University of Notre Dame; US Military Academy, 1941-44; Primary and Advanced Flying Schools, 1944; Air War College, 1959-60. Commissioned Second Lieutenant, US Army Air Corps, 1944. Commander, 416th Bombardment Wing, Strategic Air Command, Griffiss Air Force Base, New York, 1966-67; Director of Strategic Offensive and Defensive Studies, Headquarters, US Air

Force, Washington, D.C., 1967-69; Deputy Assistant Chief of Staff, Studies and Analysis, Headquarters US Air Force, Washington, D.C., 1969-70; Commander, 817th Air Division, Strategic Air Command, Pease Air Force Base, New Hampshire, 1970-71; Commander, 45th Air Division, Strategic Air Command, Pease Air Force Base, New Hampshire, 1971-72. Legion of Merit with Oak Leaf Cluster; Joint Service Commendation Medal; and other medals and awards. Promoted to Brigadier General, February 6, 1970; Major General, 1973.

Steinkraus, Lawrence W. Major General, US Air Force; Deputy Director for Operations, J-3 (Command and Control), The Joint Staff, Organization of the Joint Chiefs of Staff, 1972-   . Born November 29, 1922, in Cambridge, Massachusetts. Florida State University, BS, Industrial Management; University of Colorado, Advanced Management School. Commissioned in February 1943 in US Army Air Corps Reserve; received regular commission in 1946. Served as B-29 pilot in WW II. Chief, Operations and Training Division, Eighth Air Force, 1963-66; Assistant Deputy Director for Operations, Directorate of Operations, Joint Chiefs of Staff Organization, 1966-68; successively Commander, 319th Bombardment Wing, 379th Bombardment Wing, and 22d Bombardment Wing, 1968-70; Director of Command Control, Deputy Chief of Staff, Operations, Headquarters Strategic Air Command, 1970-72; Deputy Chief of Staff for Logistics, Headquarters Strategic Air Command, 1972. Distinguished Service Medal; Legion of Merit; Joint Service Commendation Medal; Air Force Commendation Medal with two Oak Leaf Clusters. Promoted to Major General, August 1, 1972.

Stemerdink, A. State Secretary of Defense (Materiel), The Netherlands, 1973-   . Born March 6, 1936, in Winterswijk. Attended Royal Netherlands Military Academy, Breda. Took degree in law, 1969. Commissioned Second Lieutenant, 1958. Member, Permanent Army Court Martial at 'sHertogenbosch (Bois le Duc). Member Netherlands Parliament (Labor Party). Member, North Atlantic Parliamentary Council, Defense Advisory Committee, and 'sHertogenbosch City Council.

Stenberg, Dick. Lieutenant General, Swedish Royal Air Force; Commander in Chief, Swedish Air Force, 1973-   . Attended Royal Air Force Academy, 1948-49; Royal National Defense College, 1959, 1969. Wing Commander, 1963-66; Chief, Air Force Staff, 1966-68; Deputy Chief, Defense Staff, 1968-70. Commander of the Royal Order of the Sword; Order of the Icelandic Falcon; and other medals and awards. Member of the Royal Academy of Military Sciences. Promoted to Lieutenant General, 1973.

Stepanov, V. Colonel, USSR Army; Deputy Chief, Political Directorate, Far Eastern Military District. Served on the Soviet-German Front in WW II. Member, Communist Party of the Soviet Union.

Stepchenko, F.P. Colonel General, USSR Army. Served on the Soviet-German Front in WW II. Chief, Political Directorate, Transcaucasus Military District, 1961-71. Member, Communist Party of the Soviet Union.

Stevens, Siaka Probyn. President and Minister of Defense, Sierra Leone.

Stevenson, Hugh David. Rear Admiral, Royal Australian Navy; Chief, Naval Personnel, and Second Naval Member, 1971-   . Born August 24, 1918, in Brisbane. Attended Royal Australian Naval College; Imperial Defence College, London, 1965. Commissioned Sub-Lieutenant in 1938. Served in the Pacific Theater in WW II. Commanding Officer, HMAS *Melbourne*, 1964-65; Deputy Chief, Naval Staff, 1968-69; Flag Officer Commanding, HMA Fleet, 1970-71. CBE.

Stewart, James T. Lieutenant General, United States Air Force; Commander, Aeronautical Systems Division, Air Force Systems Command (AFSC), 1970-   . Born April 2, 1921, in St. Louis, Missouri. Army Air Corps Flying School, 1941-42; University of Michigan, Ann Arbor, Michigan, BS, Aeronautical Engineering, 1948; Industrial College of the Armed Forces, 1960; George Washington University, MBA, 1963. Commissioned Second Lieutenant, US Army Air Corps Reserve, 1942. Combat duty in the European-African Theater, WW II; Korean War. Director, Office of Space Systems, Office, Secretary of the Air Force, 1964-67; Vice Director, Manned Orbiting Laboratory, Office, Secretary of the Air Force, 1967-69; Deputy Chief of Staff, Systems, AFSC, 1969-70. Distinguished Service Medal; Legion of Merit with one Oak Leaf Cluster; Distinguished Flying Cross with one Oak Leaf Cluster; Bronze Star Medal; and other US and foreign medals and awards. Promoted to Brigadier General, January 1, 1964; Major General, October 1, 1966; Lieutenant General, June 1, 1970.

Stewart, Richard R. Major General, United States Air Force; Deputy Director, Intelligence; Defense Intelligence Agency, 1970-   . Born August 16, 1917, Seymour, Indiana. Wabash College, Indiana, BA, 1939; Army Air Corps Flying School, 1940-41; Air War College, 1954-55. Commissioned Second Lieutenant, US Army Air Corps, 1941. Combat duty in the European Theater, WW II. Commander, 820th Strategic Aerospace Division, 1963-65; Director of Operations, Eighth Air Force, 1965-66; Deputy Chief of Staff, Intelligence, Headquarters, Strategic Air Command, 1966-70. Distinguished Service Medal, Legion of Merit with one Oak Leaf Cluster, Distinguished Flying Cross; and other US and foreign medals and awards. Promoted to Major General, February 24, 1970.

Stilwell, Richard Giles. Lieutenant General, United States Army; Commanding General, Sixth US Army, Presidio of San Francisco, California, 1972-   . Born February 24, 1917, Buffalo, New York. US Military Academy; US Army Command and General Staff College; US Army War College. Commissioned Second Lieutenant, 1938. Served in

WW II and Vietnam War. Commander, US Military Assistance Command, Thailand, and Chief, Joint US Military Advisory Group, Thailand, 1965-67; Commanding General, 1st Armored Division, Fort Hood, Texas, 1967-68; Army Deputy to Commanding General, III Marine Amphibious Force, US Military Assistance Command, Vietnam, 1968; Commanding General, Provisional Corps, Vietnam, later XXIV Corps, US Army, Pacific-Vietnam, 1968-69; Deputy Chief of Staff for Military Operations, US Army, Washington, D.C., and Senior US Army Representative, Military Staff Committee of the United Nations, 1969-72. Distinguished Service Medal with three Oak Leaf Clusters; Silver Star with Oak Leaf Cluster; Legion of Merit with two Oak Leaf Clusters; Distinguished Flying Cross; Bronze Star Medal with two Oak Leaf Clusters; and other medals and awards. Promoted to Brigadier General, June 1, 1961; Major General, August 1, 1963; Lieutenant General, August 1, 1968.

Stoney, Roberts Paul. Major General, United States Air Force; Commander, Air Force Communications Service (AFCS), 1969- . Born March 24, 1919, in Nashville, Tennessee. Emory University, Atlanta, Georgia, BA, Psychology, 1941; Army Air Corps Flying School, 1941-42; Communications Officer School, 1944-45; Air Command and Staff School, 1953-54; US Army War College, 1959-60. Commissioned Second Lieutenant, US Army Air Corps, in 1942. Office of Director of Defense Research and Engineering, Office of the Secretary of Defense, 1963-64; Chief, Communications-Electronics, Headquarters, Strategic Air Command, 1964-66; Vice Commander, Air Force Communications Service, 1966-69. Legion of Merit with one Oak Leaf Cluster; and other. medals and awards. Promoted to Major General, August 1, 1969.

Storheill, Skule Valentin. Vice Admiral, Royal Norwegian Navy; Commandant, National Defense College, 1967- . Born August 17, 1907, in Bronnysund, Norway. Attended Norwegian Naval College; British Royal Naval Staff College, Greenwich. Commissioned Sub-Lieutenant, Royal Norwegian Navy, 1928. Combat duty in WW II. Commander in Chief, Royal Norwegian Navy, 1951-54; Member Military Representative Committee, NATO, 1954-58; Commander, Allied Task Force Northern Norway, 1958-67. War Cross with Swords; Commander Royal Order of St. Olav with Star; St. Olav Medal with Oak Leaf; War Medal; Distinguished Service Cross with two bars (Great Britain); Legion of Honor (France); Croix de Guerre (France); Grand Cross Order of Nassau (Netherlands); Legion of Merit (USA); Order of Dannebrog (Denmark); and other medals and awards. Promoted to Vice Admiral, 1951.

Stovel, Richard Carlton. Major-General, Canadian Armed Forces; Commander, Canadian Defence Liaison Staff, Washington, D.C. (USA), 1971- . Born March 31, 1921, in Winnipeg. Attended University of Manitoba; Central Flying School, Trenton, 1940; Royal Air Force Empire Central Flying School, 1943; US Army Adjutant General's Staff School, 1948; National Defence College, Kingston,

Ontario, 1962-63. Commissioned in the Royal Canadian Air Force in 1940. Instructional duty in WW II. Chief of Staff, 1st Air Division, Metz, France, 1963-65; Director General, Organization and Manpower Control, Canadian Forces Headquarters, Ottawa, 1965-66; Commander, Training Command, Winnipeg, 1966-68; Deputy Chief of Personnel Support Services, Canadian Forces Headquarters, Ottawa, 1968-69; Deputy Chief of Operations and Reserves, Canadian Forces Headquarters, Ottawa, 1969-71. Air Force Cross and other medals and awards. Promoted to Air Commodore, July 1963; Air Vice Marshal, July 1966; upon reorganization of the Canadian Forces, assumed the rank of Major-General, February 1, 1968.

Strawson, John Michael. Major-General, British Army; Chief of Staff, Headquarters, United Kingdom Land Forces, 1972- . Born January 1, 1921. Attended Christ's College, Finchley; Staff College, Camberley, 1950; Joint Services Staff College; Imperial Defence College, 1969. Commissioned in 1942. Served in the Middle East and Europe, WW II. Commander, Queen's Royal Irish Hussars, Malaysia and British Army of the Rhine, 1963-65; Colonel, General Staff, Ministry of Defence, 1965-66; Commander, 39 Infantry Brigade, 1967-68; Chief of Staff, Live Oak, SHAPE, 1970-72. OBE; Bronze Star (USA). Publications: *The Battle for North Africa*, 1969; *Hitler as Military Commander*, 1971.

Street, Oliver Day, III. Major General, United States Army; Commanding General, 1st Region, US Army Air Defense Command, Stewart Field, New York, 1973- . Born August 25, 1925, in Guntersville, Alabama. Attended US Military Academy; Artillery School; Artillery and Guided Missile School, Advanced Course; Command and General Staff College; Armed Forces Staff College, 1963-64; Army War College, 1967-68; George Washington University, MS, Personnel Management. Commissioned August 13, 1946. Member, Gaming Branch, General War Division, Joint War Games Agency, Joint Chiefs of Staff Organization, 1965-67; Commanding Officer, 101st, later 18th Artillery Group (Air Defense), Lockport, New York; Assistant Chief, later Chief, Strategic Forces Division, Plans Directorate, Office of the Deputy Chief of Staff for Military Operations, 1969-71; Acting Deputy Director of Plans, Office of the Deputy Chief of Staff for Military Operations, 1971; Assistant Chief of Staff for Land Operations, and Commanding General, US Army Element, Allied Forces, Central Europe, 1971-73. Legion of Merit with Oak Leaf Cluster; Army Commendation Medal with three Oak Leaf Clusters; and other medals and awards.

Streletz, Fritz. Lieutenant General, National People's Army, Democratic Republic of Germany; Deputy Chief, Main Staff of the People's Army.

Streubel, Johannes. Rear Admiral, People's Navy, Democratic Republic of Germany; Chief of the Naval Staff.

Stroessner, Alfredo. General, Paraguayan Army; President of the Republic, 1954- , and Commander in Chief of the Armed Forces, 1951-   . Born November 3, 1912, in Encarnacion. Attended Paraguayan Military Academy, 1929-32. Commissioned Second Lieutenant, Artillery, 1932. Served in the Chaco War, 1932-35. Acting Commander, then Commander, 1st Infantry Regiment, "General Bruguez," 1945-50; Commander of Artillery, Paraguayan Army, 1950-51; Acting Commander of the 1st Military Region, 1951; Commander, 1st Cavalry Division, "General Bernadino Caballero," 1954. Cruz del Chaco; Cruz del Defensor; Medalla Conmemorativa de la Victoria de Boqueron; Pergamino y Medalla de Oro de la Comuna de Asunción; Medalla de la Aeronáutica; Medalla de Ingenieria; El Collar Mariscal Francisco Solano Lopez de la Orden Nacional del Mérito; Medalla al Mérito de la Asociación de Mutilados y Lisiados de la Guerra del Chaco; Medalla de Oro Conmemorativa del Dia del Camino; numerous foreign medals and awards.

Stryga, Michal. Lieutenant General, Polish Army; Chief of Staff, Rear Services. Born in 1920. Officers School, 1943; General Staff War College, 1948-51. Served in Polish-German War, 1943-45, with the 1st Polish Army in the USSR. Was previously Commander, Infantry Division, Chief of Staff, Warsaw Military District; Commander, Military District. Cross of Grunwald; Polonia Restituta; Cross of Valor; Cross of Merit; and other orders and awards. Promoted to Brigadier General, October 12, 1961. Member of Polish United Workers Party.

Stucki, Robert. Major General, Swiss Army; Deputy Chief of General Staff. Born in 1914.

Studzinski, Zozislaw. Vice Admiral, Polish Navy; Staff, Warsaw Pact Forces, 1969-   . Born in 1923 in Lodz. Political Officers School, 1945; Naval College, 1946-49; Naval War College, Leningrad, USSR. Commissioned Second Lieutenant, Polish Army, 1945; transferred to Navy, 1946. Commanded many naval units from 1949 to 1955; Commander in Chief of Polish Navy, 1958-69. Order of Sztandar Pracy, 1st Class; Polonia Restituta; Cross of Grunwald; Cross of Merit; Order of Lenin (USSR); and other Polish and foreign orders and awards. Promoted to Rear Admiral, 1955; Vice Admiral, July 1960. Member of Polish United Workers Party and Alternate Member of its Central Committee since 1968.

Su Chen-hua. People's Liberation Army Navy, People's Republic of China; First Political Commissar, People's Liberation Army Navy, 1973. Member of Tenth CCP Central Committee, 1973.

Su Yü. Senior General, People's Liberation Army, People's Republic of China; Vice Minister of National Defense, 1959-   . Born in 1909, Fukien. Served in Sino-Japanese War and the Civil War. Joined Army of Mao Tse-Tung and Chu Teh at Chingkangshan (Kiangsi-Hunan Border Area), c. 1928; Commander, 64th Red Division, 1929; Chief of Staff, 10th Army, Kiangsi-Anhwei Border Area, 1932-35; Commander, Combat Group, Kiangsi-Fukien-Chekiang Border Area, 1935-37; Commander, Vanguards Section,

New Fourth Army, Kiangnan, 1938-39; Vice-Commander, North Kiangsu Command, New Fourth Army, 1939-41; Commander, 1st Division, and Commander and Political Commissar, Central China Military Region, 1941-1946; Commander, Kiangsi-Chekiang Military District, 1944-46; Political Commissar, 1st Division, c. 1943; Deputy Commander, New Fourth Army, 1945-47; Commander, Central China Field Army, New Fourth Army, and Deputy Commander, Central China Military Region, c. 1945; Vice-Commander, East China Military Region, and Member, East China Sub-Bureau, 1946; Vice Chairman, Shanghai Military Control Commission, 1949; Chairman, Nanking Military Control Commission, 1949-51; Member, People's Revolutionary Military Council, 1949-54; Vice Chairman, East China Military and Administrative Committee, 1949-54; Council Member, Sino-Soviet Friendship Association, 1950-54; Deputy Chief of Staff, People's Revolutionary Military Council, 1952-54; Chief of Staff, People's Liberation Army, 1954-58; Member, National Defense Council, 1954-58; Deputy, National People's Congress, 1954, Member of Standing Committee, 1965; Communist Party Member, c. 1927; Elected Alternate Member CCP Central Committee, 1945; Member Eighth Central Committee, 1956-69, Ninth, 1969-   ; Member of Presidium of Ninth National Party Congress, 1969; Member of Tenth CCP Central Committee, 1973; Member of the Presidium, Tenth National Party Congress, 1973. Order of August First; Order of Independence and Freedom; Order of Liberation, 1st Class.

Sucre Figarella, Juan Manuel. Major General, Venezuelan Army; Commanding General, Venezuelan Army, 1973-   . Born September 12, 1925, in Tumeremo, Bolivar State. Attended Venezuelan Military Academy, 1945; US Army Artillery and Missile School, Advanced Course, USA, 1956-57; Command and General Staff Course, Brazil, 1959-61; Inter-American Defense College, USA, 1967-68. Commissioned Second Lieutenant, Venezuelan Army, 1945. Staff Member, Counterinsurgency Section, Ministry of Defense, 1964-65; Staff Member, UN Peacekeeping Force, Pakistan, 1965; Director, Artillery and Armor School, 1966-67; Deputy, J-3, Joint General Staff, 1968-69; Chief, Military Household of the President, 1969-73. Promoted to Colonel, January, 1966; Brigadier General, July 5, 1970; Major General, July 5, 1973.

Sudiono. Rear Admiral, Indonesian Navy; Chief for Naval Material.

Sudomo, R. Vice Admiral, Indonesian Navy; Commander in Chief of the Navy and Chief of the Naval Staff.

Suerstedt, Henry, Jr. Rear Admiral, United States Navy; Commander, Naval Weapons Center, China Lake, California, 1972-   . Born October 14, 1920, in Berkeley, California. San Francisco College, 1937-40; Flight Training Course, 1941; General Line School, 1949-50; Armed Forces Staff College, 1954-55; University of Maryland, BS, Military Science, 1957. Commissioned Ensign, US Naval Reserve, 1941; designated Naval Aviator, 1941; transferred to US Navy, 1946. Combat duty in the Pacific Theater in WW II; Korean War; Vietnam War. Commanding Officer USS *Union* (AKA-106), 1964-65; Commanding Officer USS *Tripoli* (LPH-10), 1965-67; Executive Director for Logistics and Fleet Support, Naval Air Systems Command Headquarters, 1967-68; Assistant Commander for Logistics/Fleet Support, 1968-70; Deputy Commander of US Naval Forces, Vietnam, 1970; Commander Joint Task Force EIGHT, Defense Atomic Support Agency Field Command, Sandia Base, 1970-71; Deputy Commander for Plans and Programs, and Comptroller of Naval Air Systems Command, 1971-72. Silver Star Medal; Legion of Merit with three Gold Stars and Combat "V"; Distinguished Flying Cross with Gold Star; Bronze Star Medal with Combat "V"; Air Medal with nine Gold Stars; Navy Commendation Medal with Gold Star and Combat "V"; and other US and foreign medals and awards. Promoted to Captain, April 1, 1961; Rear Admiral, May 1, 1969.

Suharto, T.N.J. Lieutenant General, Indonesian Army; President of Indonesia, Supreme Commander, and First Minister for Defense and Security, 1967-   . Born June 8, 1921. Commissioned in Japanese-sponsored Indonesian Army, 1943. Deputy Chief of Army Staff, 1960-65; Chief of Army Staff, 1965-68; Minister of Army, 1965, 1966; Deputy Prime Minister for Defense and Security, 1966; Chairman of the Presidium of Cabinet, 1966. Promoted to Brigadier General, 1960; General, 1966.

Sulatskov, S. Major General, USSR Army; Chief, Rear Services (Logistics), Siberian Military District. Served on the Soviet-German Front in WW II. Member, Communist Party of the Soviet Union.

Sumner, Gordon, Jr. Major General, United States Army; Director, Near East and South Asia Region, Office of the Assistant Secretary of Defense (International Security Affairs), 1973-   . Born July 23, 1924, in Albuquerque, New Mexico. Attended Louisiana State University, BA, Political Science; Artillery School, Basic and Advanced Courses; Command and General Staff College; Armed Forces Staff College, 1963-64; National War College, 1964-65; University of Maryland, MS, Political Science; US Army Primary Helicopter Center/School, Fort Wolters, Texas. Commissioned Second Lieutenant (ORC), June 30, 1944; permanent commission July 5, 1946. Served in WW II and the Vietnam War. Operations Staff Officer, Strategic Operations Division, J-3, Joint Staff, Joint Chiefs of Staff Organization, 1966-68; Commanding Officer, 25th Infantry Division Artillery, then Chief of Staff, 25th Infantry Division, US Army, Pacific-Vietnam, 1968-69; Chief of the Field Artillery Branch, Officer Personnel Directorate, Office of Personnel Operations, US Army, 1969-70; Senior Military Assistant, Office of the Assistant to the Secretary and Deputy Secretary of Defense, 1970-72; Chief, Western Hemisphere Division, J-5, Organization of the Joint Chiefs of Staff, 1972-73. Silver Star; Legion of Merit with three Oak Leaf Clusters; Distinguished Flying Cross; Bronze Star Medal with V Device and Oak Leaf Cluster; Air Medal with V Device (14 awards); and other medals and awards.

Promoted to Brigadier General August 1, 1971; Major General September 1, 1973.

Sun Chien-lin. Major General, Army of the Republic of China; Defense and Military Attache, Chinese Embassy, Washington, D.C.

Sung Chang-chih. Admiral, Navy of Republic of China; Commander in Chief, Chinese Navy, 1970-   . Born June 10, 1916, Liaoning. Trained at Chinese Naval Academy, 1937; Royal Naval College, Greenwich, England; National War College; Armed Forces War University. Served in Sino-Japanese War and Chinese Civil War. Commanding Officer, Rating Training School, 1949-52; Commander, Landing Ship Squadron, 1954-55; Superintendent, Chinese Naval Academy, 1955-62; Commandant, 1st Naval District, 1962-65; Chief of Staff, Headquarters, Chinese Navy, 1965-67; Deputy Commander in Chief, Chinese Navy, 1967-70.

Suprapto. Rear Admiral, Indonesian Navy; Chief for Naval Personnel.

Suromihardjo, Suadi. Major General, Indonesian Army; Governor, National Defense Council, Indonesia, 1968-   . Born in 1921. Attended Staff College, Quetta, Pakistan; Staff College, USA. Commissioned Second Lieutenant in 1941. Commanding Officer, 23d Regiment, 7th Division, South Sulawesi, 1954-57; Commanding Officer, Indonesian Contingent, United Nations Emergency Force, Egypt, 1957; Commandant, Command and General Staff College, Bandung, 1959; Ambassador to Australia, 1961-64; Ambassador to Ethiopia, 1964-69.

Susans, Ronald Thomas. Air Vice Marshal, Royal Australian Air Force; Commander, Integrated Air Defense System, Butterworth, 1971-   . Born February 15, 1917, in Manly, NSW. RAAF College, Point Cook, 1940. Commissioned in 1940. Served in the Pacific Theater, WW II; Korean War. Commander, RAAF Base, Williamtown, 1963-66; Director-General, Operational Requirements, Department of Air, 1966-69; Commander, RAAF Base, Butterworth, Malaysia, 1969-70; Director,, Malaysia-Singapore Air Defense Planning, 1970-71. DSO; DFC; Distinguished Flying Cross (USA); Air Medal (USA).

Sutela, Lauri J. Lieutenant General, Army of Finland; Chief of the General Headquarters, 1971-   . Born October 11, 1918, Äänekoski, Finland. Attended Cadet School, 1938-39; War College, 1947-48. Served in Winter War; Continuation War. Chief, Military Affairs Section, Ministry of Defense, 1964-66; Chief of Operations, 1966-67; Secretary General of the Defense Council, 1966-68; Chief of the General Staff, General Headquarters, 1968-71. Cross of Freedom, 2d Class for Merit; Cross of Freedom, 3d Class with Oak Leaf; Cross of Freedom, 3d Class with Sword; Cross of Freedom, 4th Class with Sword; Commander, Order of Finland's White Rose, 1st Class; Commemorative Medals for Winter and Continuation Wars; and other medals and awards. Promoted to Lieutenant General, June 4, 1968.

Sutherland, James William, Jr. Lieutenant General, United States Army; Chief of Staff, U.S. European Command, 1971-   . Born February 8, 1918, Bentonville, Arkansas. The Infantry School, Basic Course; U.S. Army Command and General Staff College; The National War College. Commissioned Second Lieutenant, U.S. Army Reserve, 1940. Served in WW II and Vietnam War. Commanding General, 4th Armored Division, U.S. Army, Europe, 1965-67; Deputy Chief of Staff for Military Operations, U.S. Army, Europe and Seventh Army, 1967-68; Commanding General, U.S. Army Armor Center, and Commandant, U.S. Army Armor School, Fort Knox, Kentucky, 1968-70; Deputy Commanding General, II Field Force, U.S. Army, Pacific-Vietnam, 1970; Commanding General, XXIV Corps, U.S. Army, Pacific-Vietnam, 1970-71. Distinguished Service Medal with Oak Leaf Cluster; Silver Star with Oak Leaf Cluster; Legion of Merit with Oak Leaf Cluster; Bronze Star Medal, and other medals and awards. Promoted to Brigadier General, July 1, 1962; Major General, August 1, 1963; Lieutenant General, August 1, 1970.

Sutherling, Elton Woodrow. Rear Admiral, Supply Corps, United States Navy; Commander, Naval Supply Center, Norfolk, Virginia, 1970-   . Born June 12, 1914, in Seattle, Washington. University of Washington, BBA, 1935; Naval Finance and Supply School, 1936-37; Harvard University, Cambridge, Massachusetts, 1944; Armed Forces Staff College, 1948-49; Stanford University, MBS, 1951-53. Commissioned Ensign, US Naval Reserve, 1936; transferred to Supply Corps, US Navy, 1936. Served in the Pacific Theater, WW II. Commander Naval Supply Center, Bayonne, New Jersey, 1963-65; Deputy Commander, Military Traffic Management and Terminal Service, 1965-67; Force Supply Officer, Staff of Commander in Chief, Pacific Fleet, and Fleet Supply Officer, 1967-70. Legion of Merit with Gold Star; and other medals and awards. Promoted to Captain, 1955; Rear Admiral, November 1, 1963.

Svoboda, Ludvik. General, Czechoslovak Army; President of Czechoslovakia and Commander in Chief, Armed Forces, 1968-   . Born November 25, 1895, in Kroznatin. Attended Military Academy; War College. Served with Czechoslovak Legions, WW I, 1915-20; organized and commanded Czechoslovak Army in the USSR, WW II. Minister of National Defense, 1945-50; organized Czechoslovak People's Army; Deputy Prime Minister, 1950-51; Chief of Military Academy, 1955-59. Member of Communist Party of Czechoslovakia; Member of Executive Committee and of the Central Committee of the Presidium of the Communist Party of Czechoslovakia; Member, National Assembly; retired from active military service in 1959. Published *From Buzuluk to Prague*, 1960. Awarded Czechoslovak Peace Prize, 1968; Lenin Prize, 1970; and numerous other medals and awards.

Swanson, Leroy Vincent. Rear Admiral, United States Navy; Commander, Field Command, Defense Nuclear Agency, 1972-   . Born November 11, 1915, in Oneida,

Illinois. Bradley Polytechnic Institute, Peoria, Illinois, BS, 1933-37; Flight Training Course, Pensacola, Florida, 1937-38; General Line School, Newport, Rhode Island, 1947-48; National War College, 1961-62. Commissioned Ensign, US Naval Reserve, 1939; designated Naval Aviator, 1938; transferred to US Navy, 1941. Served in the Atlantic and Pacific Theaters in WW II; Vietnam War. Commanding Officer, USS *Haleakala* (AE-25), 1960-61; Commanding Officer USS *Independence* (CVA-62), 1962-63; Chief of Staff and Aide to Commander, Carrier Division ONE, 1963-65; Director, Fleet Operations Division, Office of the CNO, 1965-68; Commander Carrier Division TWO, 1968-69; Deputy Commander in Chief, US Naval Forces, Europe, and Chief of Staff and Aide to Commander in Chief, US Naval Forces, Europe, 1969-72. Distinguished Service Medal; Legion of Merit; Air Medal with three Gold Stars; Navy Commendation Medal with Gold Star and Combat "V"; and other US and foreign medals and awards. Promoted to Rear Admiral, August 10, 1965.

Swanstein, Stig Nils Sigvard. Director General (equivalent to major general), Sweden; Director General, Royal Fortifications Administration, 1971-   . Bachelor of Laws Degree, 1941; attended Royal National Defense College. Assistant Secretary, Department of Defense, 1962-65; Deputy Provincial Governor, 1965-71. Promoted to Director General, 1971.

Sweat, Dale S. Lieutenant General, United States Air Force; Vice Commander, Tactical Air Command (TAC), 1972-   . Born March 11, 1921, in Lafayette, Illinois. University of Illinois, 1939-40; US Military Academy, 1940-43; National War College, 1960-61. Commissioned in 1943. Combat duty in the European Theater, WW II; Vietnam War. Commander, 832d Air Division, 1965-67; Director, Combat Operations, Headquarters Seventh Air Force, Vietnam, 1967-68; Deputy Chief of Staff for Plans, Headquarters, US Air Force, Europe, Germany, 1968-71; Commander, Seventeenth Air Force, Germany, 1971-72. Distinguished Service Medal with one Oak Leaf Cluster, Distinguished Flying Cross; and other medals and awards. Promoted to Brigadier General, August 1, 1967; Major General, August 1, 1969; Lieutenant General, August 1, 1972.

Sweeney, Arthur Hamilton, Jr. Major General, United States Army; Commanding General, White Sands Missile Range, White Sands, New Mexico, 1972-   . Born November 9, 1920, Charleston, West Virginia. Massachusetts Institute of Technology, BS Degree, Chemical Engineering; Ordnance School, Advanced Course; US Army Command and General Staff College; Industrial College of the Armed Forces; Harvard University, MBA Degree, Business Administration. Commissioned Second Lieutenant, US Army Reserve, 1942. Served in WW II and Vietnam War. Commanding Officer, Springfield Armory, US Army Materiel Command, Springfield, Massachusetts, 1965-67; Commanding Officer, Watervliet Arsenal, US Army Materiel Command, Watervliet, New York, 1967-68; Deputy Commanding General, US Army, Weapons

Command, Rock Island, Illinois, 1968-70; Commanding General, Danang Support Command, US Army, Pacific-Vietnam, 1970-72. Distinguished Service Medal; Legion of Merit; and other medals and awards. Promoted to Brigadier General, August 1, 1969; Major General, June 1, 1971.

Swigert, John Leonard, Jr. United States NASA Astronaut, 1966-   . Born August 30, 1931, Denver, Colorado. University of Colorado, BS, Mechanical Engineering, 1953; Rensselaer Polytechnic Institute, MS, Aerospace Science, 1965; University of Hartford, MBA, 1967. Engineering Test Pilot, Pratt and Whitney, 1957-64; North American Aviation, 1964-66. Air Force, 1953-56, fighter pilot; Massachusetts Air National Guard, 1957-60; Connecticut Air National Guard, 1960-65. NASA experience: Member, Support Crew, Apollo 7; Command Module Pilot, Apollo 13, April 11-17, 1970. Presidential Medal for Freedom; NASA Distinguished Service Medal; American Astronautical Society Flight Achievement Award; AIAA Haley Astronautics Award and Octave Chanute Award; Colorado University's Distinguished Alumnus Award; City of New York Gold Medal; City of Houston Medal for Valor; City of Chicago Gold Medal; Honorary ScD, American International College, 1970; Honorary LLD, Western State University, 1970; Honorary ScD, Western Michigan University, 1970.

Sykes, William. Air Vice-Marshal, British Royal Air Force; Vice-President, Ordnance Board, Ministry of Defence, 1972-   . Born March 14, 1920. Attended Technical College, Barnsley, Yorkshire; Mechanical and Aeronautical Engineering; Electrical Specialist Course, 1948; Staff College, 1953-54; Joint Services Staff College, 1959-60; Imperial Defence College, 1967. Enlisted in Royal Air Force in 1936; commissioned in 1942. Served in WW II in Bomber Command, Coastal Command. Formerly Officer Commanding Engineering Wing, Wyton; Station Commander, Weeton; Command Engineering Officer, Far East Air Force; Director of Mechanical Engineering (RAF), Ministry of Defence (AFD); Air Officer Engineering, Near East Air Force. OBE. Chartered Engineer; Associate Fellow of the Royal Aeronautical Society.

Synnergren, Stig Gustaf Eugen. General, Swedish Royal Army; Supreme Commander of the Armed Forces, 1970-   . Attended Royal Army Staff College, 1946-48; Royal National Defense College, 1960, 1965. Commanding Officer, Infantry Regiment I 21, 1962-63; Chief, Army Staff, 1963-65; Commander in Chief, Military Command Bergslagen, 1966-67; Chief, Defense Staff, 1967-70. Knight Grand Cross of the Royal Order of the Sword; The Order of St. Olav (Norway); The Order of the White Rose (Finland); and other medals and awards. Member of the Royal Academy of Military Sciences; Member of the Royal Society of Naval Sciences. Promoted to General, 1970.

Synnot, Anthony Monckton. Rear Admiral, Royal Australian Navy; Flag Officer Commanding HMA Fleet, 1972-   . Born January 5, 1922, in Corowa, NSW.

Attended Imperial Defence College, London, in 1968. Enlisted in 1939; commissioned, c. 1942. Served in the Pacific in WW II. Commanding Officer, HMAS *Sydney*, 1966; Commanding Officer, HMAS *Melbourne*, 1967; Director General, Fighting Equipment, 1969-70; Chief, Personnel, and Second Naval Member, 1970-71; Deputy Chief, Naval Staff, 1971-72.

Sysoyev, P. Lieutenant General, USSR Army; First Deputy Chief, Rear Services (Logistics), Ministry of Defense, 1970-   . Served on the Soviet-German Front in WW II. Member, Communist Party of the Soviet Union.

Sysoyev, V.S. Admiral, USSR Navy; Commander in Chief, Black Sea Fleet, 1968-   . Served in the Soviet-German War, 1941-45. Commander, Destroyer Division, Black Sea Fleet; Instructor, Naval Staff College; First Deputy Commander in Chief, Black Sea Fleet, 1966-68. Member, Communist Party of the Soviet Union.

Szpitel, Edward. Major General, Polish Army; Deputy Chief, Main Political Directorate, Polish Armed Forces, 1970-   . Born 1921 in Stanislawow. Military-political College. Served on Soviet-German Front in WW II with the 1st Polish Army in the USSR. Held position of Director, Military Publishing House, Ministry of Defense, 1966-70. Cross of Grunwald; Cross of Valor; Cross of Merit; and other orders and awards. Promoted to Major General, 1970. Member of Polish United Workers Party.

Szydlowski, Zbigniew. Major General, Polish Army; Chairman of Main Administration of the League for the Defense of the Country.

T

Taber, Robert Clinton. Lieutenant General, United States Army; Deputy Assistant Secretary of Defense (Manpower and Reserve Affairs), Washington, D.C., 1971-   . Born October 11, 1917, Ithaca, New York. Cornell University, BS Degree, Engineering; The Field Artillery School, Advanced Course; U.S. Army Command and General Staff College; Armed Forces Staff College; U.S. Army War College. Commissioned Second Lieutenant, U.S. Army Reserve, 1941. Served in WW II and Vietnam War. Deputy Director of Strategic Plans and Policy, Office, Deputy Chief of Staff for Military Operations, U.S. Army, Washington, D.C., 1965-66; Assistant Commandant, U.S. Army Command and General Staff College, and Deputy Commanding General, Institute of Combined Arms and Support, U.S. Army Combat Developments Command, Fort Leavenworth, Kansas, 1966-67; Chief of Staff, U.S. Army, Vietnam, U.S. Army, Pacific-Vietnam, 1967-68; Director of Doctrine and Systems, Office, Assistant Chief of Staff for Force Development, U.S. Army, Washington, D.C., 1968-70; Commanding General, 3d Infantry Division, U.S. Army, Europe, 1970-71. Distinguished Service Medal with Oak Leaf Cluster; Legion of Merit with three Oak Leaf

Clusters; Soldier's Medal; Bronze Star Medal; and other medals and awards. Promoted to Brigadier General, April 8, 1963; Major General, October 1, 1969; Lieutenant General, May 1, 1971.

Tackaberry, Thomas Howard. Major General, United States Army; Chief of Legislative Liaison, Office of the Secretary of the Army, 1972-   . Born September 6, 1923, in Los Angeles, California. Attended Gonzaga University, BA; Tulane University, MS, Psychology; George Washington University, MS, International Affairs; Infantry School, Advanced Course, Command and General Staff College; Army Language School, 1963; Italian Army War College, 1963-64; US Army War College, 1965-66. Commissioned Second Lieutenant August 30, 1945. Served in the Korean War and the Vietnam War. Commanding Officer, 2d Battalion, 8th Cavalry, 1st Cavalry Division (Airmobile), US Army, Pacific-Vietnam, 1966-67; Assistant Chief of Staff, G-5, 1st Cavalry Division (Airmobile), US Army, Pacific-Vietnam, 1967; Deputy Director of Legislative Liaison, Office of the Assistant to the Secretary of Defense (Legislative Affairs), 1967-68; Military Assistant, Office of the Under Secretary of the Army, 1968-69; Commanding Officer, 196th Infantry Brigade, then Chief of Staff, Americal Division, US Army, Pacific-Vietnam, 1969-70; Deputy Director for Reserve Officers Training Corps Affairs, Directorate of Individual Training, then Acting Director of Procurement, Training, and Distribution, Office of the Deputy Chief of Staff for Personnel, 1970-72. Distinguished Service Cross with two Oak Leaf Clusters; Silver Star with four Oak Leaf Clusters; Legion of Merit with two Oak Leaf Clusters; Distinguished Flying Cross; Soldier's Medal; and other medals and awards. Promoted to Brigadier General August 1, 1970; Major General April 1, 1973.

Tai, Phung The. Senior Colonel, People's Army of Vietnam; Deputy Chief, General Staff, 1969; Commander, Air Defense Force and People's Air Force, 1965-67. Promoted to Senior Colonel, c. 1965.

Tait, Allan Gordon. Rear-Admiral, British Royal Navy; Naval Secretary, 1972-   . Born October 30, 1921. Attended Royal Naval College, Dartmouth. Served in WW II. Commanding Officer, HMS *Ajax*, and 24th Escort Squadron, 1965-66; Commanding Officer, HMS *Maidstone*, 1967; Commanding Officer, 3d Submarine Squadron, 1967-69; Commandant, Britannia Royal Naval College, 1970-72. DSC. ADC to Governor-General of New Zealand, 1949-51; Naval Aide to the Queen, 1972.

Takenaka, Yoshio. Major General, Japanese Self Defense Force; Defense Attache and Defense Attache for Army, Embassy of Japan, Washington, D.C.

Talbi, Azzeddine Bel El Abed Ben Abderrahman. Lieutenant Colonel, Tunisian Air Force; Acting Chief of Staff, Tunisian Air Force, 1972-   . French Baccalaureate in Mathematics; Advanced Studies in Mathematics, two years; attended French Air School, Salon de Provence.

Formerly member of the Bureau of Liaison; Engineer in Telecommunications; Director of Technical Services, Tunisian Air Force. Order of the Republic (Chevalier). Promoted to Lieutenant Colonel, December 15,1972.

Talbot, Sir Norman (Graham Guy). Lieutenant-General, British Army; Director-General of Army Medical Services, 1969-   . Born February 16, 1914, at Hastings. King's College, London; King's College Hospital; Licentiate of the Royal College of Physicians, London, 1937; Bachelor of Medicine and Bachelor of Surgery, London, 1938; Diploma of Anesthesia, 1939; Doctor of Medicine, London, 1953. Commissioned in the Royal Army Medical Corps, 1939. Served in the European Theater and Middle East in WW II. Adviser in Obstetrics and Gynaecology to the Army, 1963-66; Deputy Director of Medical Services 1st (British) Corps, 1967-68; Commandant and Director of Studies, Royal Army Medical College, 1968-69. KBE; TD; Queen's Honorary Surgeon, 1968. Examiner, Royal College of Gynaecology; Central Midwives Board; Fellow, Medical Society of London; Member, Anglo-German Medical Society. Promoted to Brigadier, 1967; Major-General, 1968; Lieutenant-General, 1969.

Talbott, Carlos M. Major General, United States Air Force; Chief of Staff, US SAG, 1973-   . Born January 28, 1920, in Charleston, Illinois. Eastern Illinois University, 1936-39; US Military Academy, 1940-42; Army Command and General Staff School, 1945-46; Air War College, 1957-58; George Washington University, MA, International Affairs, 1964. Commissioned Second Lieutenant, US Army Air Corps, 1943. Served in the European Theater, WW II; Vietnam War. Deputy Director, Tactical Air Control Center (In-country), Headquarters Seventh Air Force, 1966-67; Chief of Staff, United States Taiwan Defense Command, Republic of China, 1967-68; Vice Commander, Tenth Air Force, 1968-69; Vice Commander, Ninth Air Force, 1969-70; Director of Operations, Deputy Chief of Staff, Plans and Operations, Headquarters, US Air Force, 1970-72; Director of Operations, United States Military Assistance Command, Vietnam (MACV), and Deputy Chief of Staff, Operations, Headquarters, Seventh Air Force, Vietnam, 1972-73. Distinguished Service Cross; Distinguished Service Medal; Legion of Merit with Oak Leaf Cluster; Air Medal with 15 Oak Leaf Clusters; and other US and foreign medals and awards. Promoted to Major General, August 1, 1969.

Talbott, Orwin Clark. Major General, United States Army; Commanding General, US Army Infantry Center, and Commandant, US Army Infantry School, Fort Benning, Georgia, 1969-   . Born June 18, 1918, San Jose, California. The Infantry School, Advanced Course; US Army Command and General Staff College; The National War College. Commissioned Second Lieutenant, Army National Guard, 1941. Served in WW II and Vietnam War. Assistant Chief of Staff, G-3, Central Army Group, US Army, Europe, 1964-66; Assistant Division Commander, 5th Infantry Division, Fort Carson, Colorado, 1966-67; Assistant Deputy Chief of Staff for Individual Training, US Continental Army Command, Fort Monroe, Virginia, 1967;

Deputy Chief of Staff for Individual Training, US Continental Army Command, Fort Monroe, Virginia, 1967-68; Assistant Division Commander, later Commanding General, 1st Infantry Division, US Army, Pacific-Vietnam, 1968-69. Distinguished Service Medal; Silver Star with two Oak Leaf Clusters; Legion of Merit; Distinguished Flying Cross with Three Oak Leaf Clusters; Bronze Star Medal with V Device and Oak Leaf Cluster; and other medals and awards. Promoted to Brigadier General, March 1, 1966; Major General, August 1, 1969.

Talley, George Clyde, Jr. Vice Admiral, United States Navy; Deputy Commander in Chief, US Pacific Fleet and Chief of Staff to the Commander in Chief, US Pacific Fleet, 1972-   . Born March 28, 1922, Eastland, Texas. University of Oklahoma, 1939-40; US Naval Academy, 1940-43; Flight Training Course, 1944-45; Naval War College, Command and Staff Course, 1953-54; Naval War College, Naval Warfare Course, 1960. Commissioned Ensign, US Navy, in 1943; designated Naval Aviator in 1945. Served in the European Theater, WW II; Korean War; Vietnam War. Commander Carrier Air Group ONE, 1961-63; Deputy Chief of Staff for Operations to Commander Operational Test and Evaluation Force, 1963-65; Commanding Officer USS *Chilton* (APA-38), 1965-66; Commanding Officer USS *Franklin D. Roosevelt* (CVA-42), 1966-67; Head, Aviation Plans Branch, Office of DCNO (Air), 1967-68; Deputy Director, Strategic Plans and Policy Division, Office of the CNO, 1968-70; Commander Carrier Division FOUR, 1970-71; Assistant Deputy Chief of Naval Operations (Plans and Policy), 1971-72. Legion of Merit with three Gold Stars; Air Medal with two Gold Stars; and other US and foreign medals and awards. Promoted to Vice Admiral, June 7, 1972.

Tallman, Kenneth L. Major General, United States Air Force; Director of Personnel Plans, Deputy Chief of Staff, Personnel, Headquarters US Air Force, 1973-   . Born March 22, 1925, Omaha, Nebraska. US Military Academy, 1942-46; National War College, 1966-67. Commissioned Second Lieutenant, US Army Air Corps, 1946. Combat duty in the Vietnam War. Executive Assistant to the Commander, US Military Assistance Command, Vietnam, 1965-66; Assistant for Colonel Assignments, Deputy Chief of Staff, Personnel, Headquarters, US Air Force, 1967-70; Commander, 836th Air Division, 1970-71; Deputy Assistant Deputy Chief of Staff, Personnel for Military Personnel, and Deputy Commander, Air Force Military Personnel Center, 1971-72; Assistant Deputy Chief of Staff, Personnel, Headquarters US Air Force, and Commander, Air Force Military Personnel Center, Randolph Air Force Base, Texas, 1972-73. Legion of Merit with Oak Leaf Cluster; and other medals and awards. Promoted to Major General, November 1, 1972.

Tan, Chu Van. Lieutenant General, People's Army Vietnam; Commander and Political Officer, Viet Bac (Northwest) Military Zone; Chairman of Viet Bac Autonomous Region Administrative Committee; Vice Chairman of National Assembly Standing Committee;

Member, Presidium Vietnam Fatherland Front; Member of Executive Committee, Viet-China Friendship Committee; Member of Central Military Party Committee, 1960. Joined Indochina Communist Party, 1935; Minister of Defense, Provisional Government, 1945-46; appointed Deputy to Second, Third, and Fourth National Assembly. Promoted to Colonel General, 1959.

Tan, Le Trong. Major General, People's Army of Vietnam; Deputy Chief General Staff, 1961; Deputy Commander, Central Office for South Vietnam, 1963. Born in 1917 in North Vietnam. Commander, 312th Division, 1949-53; Commander, 320th Division, 1953; Commandant Ground Forces Officer School, 1957; Chief of Staff, Central Office for South Vietnam, 1968. Promoted to Major General, May 1961.

Tan, Nguyen Huu. Colonel, Army of the Republic of South Vietnam; Commander 4th Air Division.

T'an Fu-jen. Lieutenant General, People's Liberation Army, People's Republic of China; Political Commissar, People's Liberation Army Kunming Units, and Chairman, Yunnan Provincial Revolutionary Committee, 1968-   . Born in Kwangtung. Participated in Anti-Japanese guerrilla warfare, 1937-45 and the Civil War. Deputy Political Commissar, 7th Column, Northeast Field Army, 1948; Political Department, Headquarters, Canton Garrison, 1949-50; Deputy Political Commissar, then Commissar, Kwangsi Military District, 1953-54; Council Member, Kwangsi Provincial People's Government, 1954-55; Headquarters, Wuhan Military Region, 1955; Deputy Political Commissar, Wuhan Military Units, 1957, Political Commissar, 1963; Chief Judge, Military Judicial Committee, Supreme People's Court, 1964-65; Political Commissar, Engineering Corps, People's Liberation Army, 1965; Member of Presidium, Ninth National Party Congress, 1969; Member, Central Committee, 1969. Order of August First; Order of Independence and Freedom; Order of Liberation; and other medals and awards. Promoted to Lieutenant General, 1955.

Tanassi, Mario. Italy; Deputy Prime Minister and Minister of Defense, 1972-   . Born March 17, 1916, in Ururi, Campobasso, Italy. Attended University of Political Sciences, Rome. Minister of Industry and Commerce, 1968; Minister of Defense, 1970-72. Deputy Secretary, Italian Socialist Democratic Party (PSDI), 1950; Co-Secretary, Unified Italian Socialist Democratic Party, 1956; President and then Secretary of the Reconstituted PSDI, 1969; President, PSDI, since 1972. Member, Chamber of Deputies, 1963.

Tanberg, Lawrence F. Major General, United States Air Force; Inspector General, Pacific Command, Hawaii, 1973-   . Born January 29, 1919, in Dickinson, North Dakota. North Dakota University, BS, Pharmacy, 1941; Army Air Corps Flying School, 1941-42; George Washington University, Advanced Management Course; Industrial College of the Armed Forces, 1959-60; Basic Airborne Course. Commissioned Second Lieutenant, US

Army Air Corps, 1942. Combat duty in the Southwest Pacific Area WW II. Commander, 839th Air Division, 1962-63; Deputy, Operations, Ninth Air Force, 1963-64; Headquarters, Tactical Air Command, 1964-65; Deputy, Materiel, Headquarters Tactical Air Command, 1965-66; Vice Commander, Ninth Air Force, 1966-67; Director, Maintenance Engineering, Deputy Chief of Staff (Systems and Logistics), Headquarters US Air Force, 1967-70; Vice Commander, Thirteenth Air Force, Philippines, 1970-71; Commander, 313th Air Division, Pacific Air Forces (PACAF), 1971-73. Distinguished Service Medal; Silver Star; Legion of Merit; Distinguished Flying Cross; and other medals and awards. Promoted to Major General, August 1, 1966.

Tanh, Lam Nquon. Commodore, Navy of the Republic of South Vietnam; Vice Chief of Naval Operations.

Tankayev, Magomed Tankayevich. Colonel General, USSR Army. Born in 1919 in Urada, Daghestan. Drafted into the Army, 1939. Attended Infantry Academy, 1939-41; Army War College, 1945-48. Commissioned in 1941. Served in the Soviet-German War, 1941-45. Commander, Infantry Division, and later Commander, Paratroop Forces, 1948-64; Deputy Commander, Belorussian Military District, 1965-67; First Deputy Commander, Odessa Military District, 1967-69; Commander, Northern Group of Forces in Poland, 1969-72. Member, Communist Party of the Soviet Union, 1944- ; Deputy to the USSR Supreme Soviet. Order of Lenin; four Orders of Red Banner; Order of Fatherland War; Order of Red Star; and other Soviet and foreign orders and medals. Promoted to Colonel General, 1969.

Tarpley, Thomas McKee. Major General, United States Army; Commanding General, US Army Infantry Center and Fort Benning, and Commandant, US Army Infantry School, Fort Benning, Georgia, 1973- . Born July 4, 1922, Quincy, Illinois. US Military Academy; US Army Command and General Staff College; The Infantry School, Basic and Advanced Courses; US Army War College; University of Maryland, MA Degree, Russian History; George Washington University, MA Degree, International Affairs. Commissioned Second Lieutenant, US Army, 1944. Served in WW II and Vietnam War. Chief, Individual Training Division, Office, Deputy Chief of Staff for Personnel, US Army, Washington, D.C., 1967-68; Chief, Office, Deputy Chief of Staff for Personnel Study Group, and Executive Officer, Office, Deputy Chief of Staff for Personnel, US Army, Washington, D.C., 1968-69; Deputy Secretary, General Staff (Coordination and Reports), Office, Chief of Staff, US Army, Washington, D.C., 1969; Deputy Commanding General, US Army Training Center (Infantry) and Fort Lewis, Washington, 1969-71; Commanding General, 101st Airborne Division (Airmobile), US Army, Pacific-Vietnam, 1971-72; Commanding General, Delta Regional Assistance Command, US Military Assistance Command, Vietnam, 1972-73. Distinguished Service Medal; Legion of Merit with three Oak Leaf Clusters; Bronze Star Medal with V Device and Oak Leaf

Cluster; and other medals and awards. Promoted to Brigadier General, October 1, 1969; Major General, August 1, 1971.

Taylor, Sir Allan (Macnab). Lieutenant-General, British Army; Deputy Commander-in-Chief, United Kingdom Land Forces, 1973- . Born March 26, 1919. Studied at Staff College, 1948; Imperial Defence College, 1967. Served in armored units in WW II. Assistant Adjutant and Quartermaster-General, 1st Division, 1962; Commandant, Royal Army Corps Gunnery School, 1963; Commander, Berlin Brigade, 1964-66; Commander, 1st Division, 1968; Commandant, Staff College, Camberley, 1969-72; General Officer Commanding South East District, 1972. KBE; MC.

Taylor, Leonard Burbank. Major General, United States Army; Commanding General, US Army Administrative Schools Center and Fort Benjamin Harrison, Indiana, 1971- . Born January 15, 1917, Chinock, Montana. Washington University, BS Degree, Business Administration; US Army Command and General Staff College; US Army War College; University of Maryland, MBA Degree, Business Administration. Commissioned Second Lieutenant, US Army Reserve, 1938. Served in WW II. Comptroller, US Army, Pacific, Fort Shafter, Hawaii, 1963-66; Assistant Director of Army Budget, Office, Comptroller of the Army, Washington, D.C., 1966-67; Director of Army Budget, Office, Comptroller of the Army, Washington, D.C., 1967-71. Distinguished Service Medal; Legion of Merit; and other medals and awards. Promoted to Brigadier General, October 1, 1964; Major General, August 1, 1968.

Teller, Gunther. Major General, National People's Army; Democratic Republic of Germany; Chairman, Society for Sport and Technology.

Templeton-Cotill, John Atrill. Rear-Admiral, British Royal Navy; Flag Officer, Malta, and NATO Commander, Southeast Area, Mediterranean, 1971- . Born June 4, 1920. New College, Oxford; Joint Services Staff College, 1956. Joined the Royal Navy Volunteer Reserve in 1939. Various assignments ashore and afloat in WW II. Commander, HMS *Tiger*, 1959-61; Naval Attache, British Embassy, Moscow, USSR, 1962-64; Commander, HMS *Rhyl*, and Captain (D), 23d Escort Squadron, 1964-66; Senior Naval Member, Defence Operational Analysis Establishment, 1966-68; Commander, HMS *Bulwark*, 1968-69; Chief of Staff to Commander Far East Fleet, 1970-71. CB. Promoted to Captain, 1961; Rear-Admiral, 1970.

T'eng Hai-ch'ing. Lieutenant General, People's Liberation Army, People's Republic of China; Commander Inner Mongolian Military Region and Vice Commander of Peking Units, 1967-c. 71; Chairman, Inner Mongolian Autonomous Republic Revolutionary Committee, 1967- . Anti-Japanese Guerrilla Warfare, 1937-45; Civil War. Head of People's Liberation Army Peking Units, 1963; Member of Presidium, CCP, Ninth National Party Congress, 1969; Member, CCP Central Committee, 1969.

Tenishchev, I. Colonel General, USSR Army; Commander, Central Group of Soviet Forces in Czechoslovakia, 1972-   . Served on the Soviet-German Front in WW II. Promoted to Colonel General, 1972. Member, Communist Party of the Soviet Union.

Tereshkova-Nikolayeva, Valentina Vladimirovna. Captain, USSR Air Force; Cosmonaut, 1962-   . Born March 6, 1937. Attended Textile College, Yaroslavl; Zhukovskiy Air Force Engineering College. Textile worker, Krasny Perekop Textile Mill; volunteered service as Cosmonaut, 1961; started Cosmonaut training, 1962; first woman to participate in space flight, three days (48 orbits) flight in Vostok-6, 1963. Member of Communist Party of the Soviet Union since 1962. Wife of Cosmonaut Major General Andrian Grigorievich Nikolayev. Hero of the Soviet Union; Order of Lenin; Order of Red Star; Order of the Nile (Egypt); and other medals and awards. Promoted to Captain, 1963.

Terry Lloyd, M.R. Rear Admiral, South African Navy; Armed Forces Attache in London. SM.

Terry, Robert Davis. Major General, United States Army; Vice Director, Defense Communications Agency, Washington, D.C., 1971-   . Born September 4, 1920, Indianapolis, Indiana. US Military Academy; The Signal School, Basic Course; US Army Command and General Staff College; US Naval War College; University of Illinois, MS Degree, Electrical Engineering. Commissioned Second Lieutenant, 1942. Served in WW II and Vietnam War. Commanding General, 1st Signal Brigade, US Army Strategic Communications Command, and Assistant Chief of Staff Communications-Electronics, US Army, Vietnam, US Army, Pacific-Vietnam, 1966-67; Commanding General, US Army Strategic Communications Command, Pacific, and Assistant Chief of Staff Communications-Electronics, US Army, Pacific, Fort Shafter, Hawaii, 1967-69; Deputy Director, National Military Command Systems Technical Support, Defense Communications Agency, Washington, D.C., 1969-71. Distinguished Service Medal; Legion of Merit with Oak Leaf Cluster; Bronze Star Medal; and other medals and awards. Promoted to Brigadier General, July 1, 1966; Major General, August 3, 1970.

Terry, Roy M. Chaplain, Major General, United States Air Force; Chief of Chaplains, United States Air Force, 1970-   . Born in Brooklyn, New York. Syracuse University, BS, 1937; Yale University Divinity School, BD, 1942; Chaplain School, 1942; Atlanta Law School, Honorary LLD, 1963. Commissioned in 1942. Served in North Africa and Italy, WW II. Staff Chaplain, Headquarters, Fifth Air Force, Japan, 1962-65; Command Chaplain, Headquarters, Aerospace Defense Command, 1965-67; Command and Protestant Cadet Chaplain, US Air Force Academy, 1967-68; Deputy Chief of Chaplains, United States Air Force, 1968-70. Legion of Merit with one

Oak Leaf Cluster; Bronze Star Medal; and other medals and awards. Promoted to Major General, August 10, 1970.

Teubner, Harold C. Major General, United States Air Force; Auditor General of the Air Force, 1970-   . Born March 11, 1919, in Dallas, Texas. North Texas Agriculture College; Army Air Corps Flying School, 1941; Army Command and General Staff School, 1946; Texas Agricultural and Mechanical University, 1946-48, BS, Aeronautical Engineering, 1948; Massachusetts Institute of Technology, MS, 1951; Air War College, 1957-58; Industrial College of the Armed Forces, 1961-62; George Washington University, MBA, 1962. Commissioned Second Lieutenant, US Army Air Corps, 1941. Combat Duty in the China-Burma-India Theater in WW II. Chief of Electronics Division, Deputy Director of Science and Technology, Assistant for Research and Development Programming, Office of Deputy Chief of Staff (Research and Development), 1962-66; Deputy Director, Budget, US Air Force Comptroller, 1966-67; Deputy Chief of Staff, Comptroller, Air Force Systems Command, 1967-70. Distinguished Service Medal; Legion of Merit with one Oak Leaf Cluster; Distinguished Flying Cross with two Oak Leaf Clusters; and other medals and awards. Promoted to Major General, February 24, 1970.

Thai, Hoang Van. Lieutenant General, People's Army of Vietnam; Deputy Chief of General Staff, People's Army of Vietnam, 1953; Member, Lao Dong Party Central Committee, 1960; Chairman of Physical Culture and Sports Committees; Vice Minister of National Defense, 1961; Member, Central Military Party Committee. Born in 1906 in Thai Binh Province. Studied at Hanoi Faculty of Pedagogy; Hoang Pho Military Academy. Joined Indochina Communist Party, 1930; assisted in organization of Viet Minh, 1945; Founding Member, Viet-Chinese Friendship Association, 1950; Deputy Chief of Staff, Armed Forces, 1946-54; Member of State Science Committee, 1958; Director General of Training in Ministry of Defense; Deputy to Third National Assembly; Member, National Defense Council; Chairman, Viet GANEFO Committee, 1965; Commander of Military Region Five (northern region of South Vietnam), 1965-68. Promoted to Brigadier General, 1946; Major General, 1959; Lieutenant General, 1962.

Than, Le Van. Brigadier General, Army of the Republic of South Vietnam; Commander 1st Infantry Division.

Thanabalasingan, Dato K. Commodore, Malaysian Navy; Chief of Naval Staff.

Thao, Hoang Minh. Major General, People's Army of Vietnam; Deputy Chief, General Political Directorate, People's Army of Vietnam; Commander, B-3 Front (Western Highlands and Lower Laos). Born in 1919, Thai Binh Province. Attended Hoang Pho Military Academy; also had University education. Participated in Chinese Long March; Member of Committee of National Defense, 1946;

Commander, 304th Division, 1949-54; Deputy Director Middle and High-Class Military School, 1963; Director, Military and Political Institution, 1964-65; Director, Vietnam Military College, 1964-65. Promoted to Major General, 1950.

Thejatunka, Kamol. Air Chief Marshal, Royal Thai Air Force. Chief of Staff, Royal Thai Air Force.

Thiébaud, Jämes. Major General, Swiss Army; Commander, Mechanized and Motorized Troops. Born in 1913.

Tho, Tran. Senior Colonel, People's Army of Vietnam; Deputy Chief, General Directorate of Rear Services, 1963. Promoted to Senior Colonel, 1963.

Thomas, Sir (John) Noel. General, British Army; Master-General of the Ordnance, 1971- . Born February 28, 1915. Attended Liverpool University; Imperial Defence College, 1963. Commissioned in the Royal Engineers, 1936. Served in the European Theater in WW II. General Officer Commanding, 42 (Lancashire and Cheshire) Division (Territorial Army), Northwest District, 1963-65; Director of Combat Development (Army), Ministry of Defence, 1965-68; Deputy Chief of Defence Staff (Operational Requirements), Ministry of Defence, 1968-70. KCB; DSO; MC. Fellow of Royal Society of Arts. Promoted to Lieutenant-General, 1968; General, 1971.

Thompson, Glen Owen. Rear Admiral, United States Coast Guard; Commander, 17th Coast Guard District, Juneau, Alaska, 1973- . Born July 31, 1920, Deming, New Mexico. Whittier College, Whittier, California, BA Degree, 1942; US Coast Guard Reserve Officers Training School, 1942-43; Flight Training Courses, 1947-48. Commissioned Ensign, USCGR, 1943; Lieutenant, USCG, 1948; designated Coast Guard Aviator, 1948. Served in Pacific Theater, WW II. Chief, Aviation Units Division, Headquarters, Coast Guard, 1964-66; Chief of Operations, Office, Coast Guard Commander, Western Area, 1966-69; Commanding Officer, Coast Guard Section, Marianas Islands, and Commander, Coast Guard Activities, Marianas Islands Area, 1969-71; Chief, Operations Division, 3rd Coast Guard District, Governors Island, New York, 1971-72; Chief of Staff, 3rd Coast Guard District, 1972-73. WW II Campaign Service Medals and Ribbons. Promoted to Captain, July 1, 1965; Rear Admiral, July 1, 1973.

Thompson, John Fawdrey, Jr. Rear Admiral, United States Coast Guard; Chief, Office of Boating Safety, 1973- . Born May 30, 1919, Franklin, New York. Syracuse University, 1937-38; US Coast Guard Academy, 1938-41. Commissioned Ensign, 1941. Served in Atlantic and Pacific Theaters, WW II. Officer in Charge, Marine Inspection Office, Philadelphia, Pennsylvania, 1965-67; Chief, Operations Division, and later Chief of Staff, 7th Coast Guard District, Miami, Florida, 1967-70; Superintendent, US Coast Guard Academy, 1970-73. Navy Commendation Medal; WW II campaign service medals and ribbons. Promoted to Captain, June 23, 1963; Rear Admiral, July 1, 1970.

Thomya, Cherdchai. Admiral, Royal Thai Navy. Commander in Chief, Royal Thai Navy.

Thorne, Edward Courtenay. Rear Admiral, Royal New Zealand Navy; Chief of Naval Staff, RNZN, 1972- . Born in 1923 in Wellington. Attended Nelson College, Nelson, New Zealand, 1938-41; Royal Navy College, Dartmouth, United Kingdom, 1942; Royal Navy Staff Course, Greenwich, 1956; Imperial Defence College, United Kingdom, 1966. Commissioned Sub-Lieutenant, 1943. Served with the British Royal Navy in the Indian Ocean, Mediterranean, and northern European waters in WW II. Captain, 11th Frigate Squadron, 1967-68; Head, New Zealand Defence Liaison Staff, London, 1969-72. Commander of the British Empire, and other honors and awards. Promoted to Rear Admiral, July 1, 1972.

Thornton, William Edgar. United States; NASA Scientist-Astronaut, 1967- . Born April 14, 1929, Faison, North Carolina. University of North Carolina, BS, Physics, 1952, MD, 1963; NASA Flight Training Course. Commissioned Second Lieutenant, US Air Force, 1952. Officer-in-Charge, Instrumentation Lab, Flight Test Air Proving Ground, and Consultant to Air Proving Ground Command, 1952-55; US Air Force Aerospace Medical Division, Brooks Air Force Base, 1965-67. Chief Engineer, Electronics Division, Del Mar Engineering Labs, Los Angeles. NASA experience: Training. Legion of Merit.

Thostrup, Sven. Vice Admiral, Royal Danish Navy; Commander in Chief, Royal Danish Navy and Chief of Naval Staff, 1966- . Born January 28, 1915, Aalborg, Denmark. Attended Naval Academy, Copenhagen, 1933-38; Swedish Naval Staff College, 1947-48. Commissioned Lieutenant, Royal Danish Navy, 1938. Commanding Officer, Frigate, 1956-57; Commander, Frigate Division, 1957-58; Staff Officer, Danish Defense Staff, 1958-60; Commander, Submarine Squadron, 1960-61; Chief of Staff, Allied Command, Baltic Approaches, 1962-65. Commander, Order of Dannebrog; and other medals and awards. Promoted to Vice Admiral, 1965.

Thunborg, Anders I. Deputy Secretary of Defense, Sweden, 1969- .

Thurman, John Royster. Major General, United States Army; Director of Planning and Programming Analysis, Office of the Assistant Vice Chief of Staff, 1972- . Born April 11, 1924, in Lexington, Kentucky. Attended US Military Academy; Artillery School; Artillery and Guided Missile School; Command and General Staff College; Armed Forces Staff College; Naval War College, 1964-65; George Washington University, MS, International Affairs. Commissioned Second Lieutenant June 4, 1946. Served in the Vietnam War. Chief, Schools and Doctrine Division, later Sector Advisor and Mission Coordinator, US Military Assistance Command, Vietnam, 1965-66; Commanding Officer, 1st Battalion, 8th Artillery, 25th Infantry Division, US Army, Pacific-Vietnam, 1967-68; Military Assistant, Office of the Special Assistant to the Secretary and Deputy

Secretary of Defense, 1968-69; Deputy Chief of Staff, Plans, III Marine Amphibious Force, US Military Assistance Command, Vietnam, 1970; Assistant Division Commander, 25th Infantry Division, US Army, Pacific-Vietnam, 1970-71; Assistant Division Commander, 8th Infantry Division, US Army, Europe, 1971-72. Legion of Merit with five Oak Leaf Clusters; Distinguished Flying Cross with Oak Leaf Cluster; Bronze Star Medal with V Device with four Oak Leaf Clusters; Air Medal (35 awards); and other medals and awards. Promoted to Brigadier General, June 1, 1970; Major General, March 1, 1973.

Tibbets, Joseph Bonafield. Rear Admiral, United States Navy; Senior Member Navy Department Board of Decorations and Medals, 1972-   . Born February 20, 1911, in Phillippi, West Virginia. US Naval Academy, 1930-34; Flight Training Course, 1936-37; Naval War College, Strategy and Tactics Course, 1951-52. Commissioned Ensign, US Navy, in 1934; designated Naval Aviator in 1937. Served in the Atlantic and Pacific Theaters, WW II. Commander Carrier Division FIFTEEN, 1962-63; Chief, Military Assistance Advisory Group, Portugal, 1963-66; Deputy Director of Antisubmarine Warfare Programs, Office of the CNO, 1966-67; Deputy Commander in Chief, US Naval Forces, Europe, and Chief of Staff to the Commander in Chief, US Naval Forces, Europe, 1967-69; Commander Fleet Air, Quonset, Commander Carrier Division TWENTY, and Commander Hunter-Killer Force, US Atlantic Fleet, 1969-72. Legion of Merit with Gold Star; and other US medals and awards. Promoted to Rear Admiral, July 1, 1962.

Tien, Phan Phung. Brigadier General, Army of the Republic of South Vietnam; Commander 5th Air Division.

Tighe, Eugene Francis, Jr. Major General, United States Air Force; Assistant Chief of Staff for Intelligence, Pacific Command, Camp Smith, Hawaii, 1972-   . Born June 19, 1921, in New Raymer, Colorado. Artillery Officer Candidate School, Camp Columbia, Australia, 1944; Loyola University, Los Angeles, California, BA, History, 1949; Air War College, 1965-66. Commissioned Second Lieutenant, US Army Reserve, 1944; released from active duty and became member of Air Force Reserve, 1946; entered active duty with Air Force as intelligence officer, July 1950. Served in the Pacific Theater, WW II, Korean War, and Vietnam War. Director of Targets, Headquarters Seventh Air Force, Tan Son Nhut Airfield, Vietnam, 1966-67; Special Assistant, Reconnaissance Division, then Chief, Operations Review Group, Directorate of Operations, Deputy Chief of Staff, Plans and Operations, Headquarters US Air Force, Washington, D.C., 1967-69; Director of Estimates (later renamed Directorate of Intelligence Applications), Office of the Assistant Chief of Staff, Intelligence, Headquarters US Air Force, Washington, D.C., 1970-71; Deputy Chief of Staff, Intelligence, Pacific Air Forces, Hickam Air Force Base, Hawaii, 1971-72. Legion of Merit with three Oak Leaf Clusters; Bronze Star; Air Force Commendation Medal; and other medals and awards. Promoted to Brigadier General, September 1, 1971; Major General, 1973.

Tin, Thaung. Commodore, Burmese Navy; Chief of Burmese Navy, 1964-   ; Minister of Mines and Fisheries, 1973-   . Born c. 1920. Attended Rangoon University. Served in the Burma Independence Army in WW II. Held various staff and command positions. Member of Secretariat of the Central Committee of the Burma Socialist Program Party.

Ting Sheng. General, People's Liberation Army, People's Republic of China; Commander, Canton Military Region, 1972-   . Born 1912, Kiangsi. Attended Red Army School; Military College. Joined Red 1st Front Army, 1930. Served in Sino-Japanese War; Chinese Civil War; Korean War. Took part in Long March. Battalion Commander, Division 115, 8th Route Army, 1937; Brigade Major, 3d Column, Northeast Democratic Allied Army, 1945; Divisional Commander, 4th Field Army, 1949; Commander, 54th Army, 1954; 1st Vice Commander, Sinkiang Production and Construction Corps, 1965; Vice Commander, Sinkiang Military Region, 1967; Member Central Commitee, 1969; Member of Tenth CCP Central Committee, 1973; Member of the Presidium, Tenth National Party Congress, 1973.

Tinh, Huynh Ba. Brigadier General, Army of the Republic of South Vietnam; Commander 3d Air Division.

Tirca, Sterian. Deputy Minister of Defense, Romania.

Titov, Herman Stepanovich. Colonel, USSR Air Force; Cosmonaut, 1958-   . Born September 11, 1935, in the Altay Region. Attended Air Force Pilots School, Volgograd; Zhukovskiy Air Force Engineering War College, 1968. Commissioned Second Lieutenant, Soviet Air Force in 1957. Space Flight, Vostok-2, August 6-7, 1961. Member, Communist Party of the Soviet Union, since 1961; Deputy, Supreme Soviet, USSR. Hero of the Soviet Union; Order of Lenin; Order of Red Banner; and other orders and medals.

Tkach, Walter Robert. Major General, United States Air Force; Physician to the President of the United States, 1969-   . Born February 9, 1917, in LaBelle, Pennsylvania. Pennsylvania State College, BS, Chemistry, 1941; University of Pittsburgh Medical School, MD, 1945; Basic Doctor of Medicine Course, Army Medical Corps, 1946; School of Aviation Medicine, 1949-50; Courses in Strategic Intelligence and Medical Aspects of Nuclear Energy. Commissioned in 1945. Served in the Vietnam War. Chief, Professional Division, and Deputy Surgeon, Strategic Air Command, 1962-65; Director, Professional Services, and Deputy Surgeon, Pacific Air Forces, Hawaii, 1965-68; Command Surgeon, Headquarters, Seventh Air Force, Vietnam, 1968-69. Legion of Merit; Bronze Star Medal; and other medals and awards. Promoted to Brigadier General, January 6, 1970; Major General, July 1, 1972; Chief Flight Surgeon.

Tkachev, F. Major General, USSR Army; Deputy Chief, Political Directorate, Air Defence Forces. Served on the

Soviet-German Front in WW II. Member, Communist Party of the Soviet Union.

Tlas, Mustafa. General, Syrian Army; Minister of Defense and Deputy Commander in Chief, Syrian Army. Born in 1928. Attended Syrian Military Academy. Member, Syrian Baath Party.

Toan, Nguyen Van. Major General, Army of the Republic of South Vietnam; Commander II Corps/MR 2.

Tobiason, Orville Leroy. Major General, United States Army; Headquarters, Allied Land Forces, Southeastern Europe, 1973-   . Attended the Artillery School, Advanced Course; Armed Forces Staff College; Command and General Staff College; National War College, 1964-65. Commissioned Second Lieutenant, October 29, 1942; US Army Reserve, 1946-47; transferred to National Guard, 1947; returned to active duty with commission in regular Army, 1950. Served in WW II and the Vietnam War. Commanding Officer, 52d Artillery Group, Fort Sill, Oklahoma, later US Army, Pacific-Vietnam, 1965-67; Director, Field Artillery Materiel Test Directorate, US Army Test and Evaluation Command, Aberdeen Proving Ground, Maryland, 1967-69; Director of Tactics and Combined Army, US Army Field Artillery School, Fort Sill, Oklahoma, 1969; Deputy Director, later Director, of Training and Testing, then Assistant Chief of Staff for Operations and Training, finally Chief of Staff, Project Mobile Army Sensor Systems Test and Evaluation Review, Fort Hood, Texas, 1969-71; Assistant Chief of Staff, G-3, Eighth US Army, US Army, Pacific-Korea, 1971-73. Legion of Merit with two Oak Leaf Clusters; Bronze Star Medal; and other medals and awards. Promoted to Brigadier General, August 1, 1971; Major General, 1973.

Tolstikov, O.V. Colonel General, USSR Army; Deputy Chief, Civil Defense, Ministry of Defense. Served on the Soviet-German Front in WW II. Member, Communist Party of the Soviet Union.

Tolubko, Vladimir Fyodorovich. General of the Army, USSR Army; Deputy Minister of Defense and Commander in Chief, Strategic Missile Forces, 1972-   . Born in 1914. Drafted into Soviet Army, c. 1935. Attended Army War College; General Staff War College; Military College of Armored and Mechanized Troops. Commissioned in the late 1930s. Served in the Soviet-German War, 1941-45. Held command and staff positions in various military districts and with the Soviet Forces in Germany; First Deputy Commander in Chief, Strategic Missile Forces, 1960-68; Commander, Siberian Military District, 1968-69; Commander, Far Eastern Military District, 1969-72; Member, Communist Party of the Soviet Union; Deputy to the USSR Supreme Soviet. Two Orders of Lenin; three Orders of Red Banner; Order of the Fatherland War; Order of Red Star; and other Soviet and foreign orders and medals. Promoted to Colonel General, May 7, 1960; General of the Army, May 1, 1970.

Tomashevskiy, A. Colonel General, USSR Naval Air Force; Deputy Commander in Chief, Naval Air Force, 1972-   . Served in the Soviet-German War, 1941-45. Commander, Pacific Fleet Naval Air Force, c. 1969-72. Member, Communist Party of the Soviet Union.

Tombalbaye, François. President of the Republic of Chad, Chief of State, President of the Council of Ministers, Minister of Defense and of Veterans Affairs, 1960-   . Born June 15, 1918. Grand Croix de la Légion d'Honneur; Grand Croix de l'Ordre National Gabonais; and other honors and awards.

Torres Negreira, Pedro. Rear Admiral, Uruguayan Navy; Inspector General of the Navy.

Tovma, Vsevolod S. Major General, USSR Army; Military Attache, Embassy of the Union of Soviet Socialist Republics, Washington, D.C.

Tra, Tran Van. Lieutenant General, People's Army of Vietnam; Deputy Chief of General Staff, 1959; Deputy Commander of People's Liberation Armed Forces; Deputy Commander, Central Office for South Vietnam, 1964; Alternate Member of Lao Dong Party Central Committee, 1960; Member, Central Military Party Committee. Joined Indochina Communist Party, 1940; imprisoned at Ba To, 1940-43; held high military and political posts in the south, 1945-54; Commander and Secretary of Interzone 8, 1946; Commander and Political Officer of Saigon-Cholon Special Zone, 1949; Commander of Interzone 7, 1950; Deputy Commander of Nam Bo Region, 1951; studied guerrilla warfare in China and Russia, 1954; Commander, 330th Division, 1958; Director of Institute of Military Administration, 1961; Deputy Chief of Military Training, 1961; Judge of Central Military Court, 1961; Chairman, Central Military Committee, Central Office of South Vietnam. Promoted to Major General, 1958; Lieutenant General, 1961.

Transki, Stavcho. Deputy Minister of National Defense, Bulgaria.

Traore, Daouda. Minister of National Defense, Upper Volta.

Trautweiler, Hans. Major General, Swiss Army; Commanding General, 5th Border Division. Born in 1920.

Treacher, John Devereux. Vice-Admiral, British Royal Navy; Flag Officer, Naval Air Command, 1972-   . Born September 23, 1924, in Chile. Joined the Royal Navy, 1942; qualified as Fleet Air Arm Pilot, 1947. Served in the Mediterranean, Russian Convoys, Second Front in WW II; flew in the Korean War. Naval Assistant to the Controller of the Navy; Commanding Officer, HMS *Lowestoft*, 1964-66; Director, Naval Air Warfare (Naval Staff), 1966-68; Commanding Officer, HMS *Eagle*, 1968-70; Flag Officer, Carriers and Amphibious Ships, and Commander, Carrier Striking Group Two, 1970-72. Promoted to Captain, 1962; Rear-Admiral, 1970; Vice-Admiral, 1972.

Tret'yak, Ivan Moyseyevich. Colonel General, USSR Army; Commander, Belorussian Military District, 1967- . Born in 1923 in Popovka, Ukraine. Volunteered for the Army in 1940. Attended Infantry Academy, 1940-41; General Staff War College. Commissioned in 1941. Served in the Soviet-German War, 1941-45. Commander, Infantry Battalion, 29th Guard Rifle Division, 1943; Commander, 93d Rifle Regiment, 1944-45; Commander, Baku Garrison, Transcaucasian Military District, 1966-67. Member, Communist Party of the Soviet Union. Hero of the Soviet Union; two Orders of Lenin; two Orders of Red Banner; Order of Kutuzov; Order of Aleksandr Nevskiy; two Orders of Red Star; and other orders and medals. Promoted to Major General, c. 1962; Lieutenant General, 1965; Colonel General, 1968.

Trewby, George Francis Allan. Vice-Admiral, British Royal Navy; Chief of Fleet Support, 1971- . Born July 8, 1917, in Simonstown, South Africa. Attended Royal Naval College, Dartmouth (King's Dirk, 1934); Royal Naval Engineering College, Keyham; Royal Naval College, Greenwich; Imperial Defence College, 1965. Commissioned in 1934. Served at sea in WW II. Commanding Officer, HMS *Sultan*, 1963-64; Captain of Naval Base, Portland, 1966-68; Assistant Controller (Polaris), Ministry of Defence, 1968-71. Chartered Engineer; Fellow of the Institution of Mechanical Engineers; Member of the Institute of Marine Engineers; Member of the Royal Institution of Naval Architects. Promoted to Captain, 1959; Rear-Admiral, 1968; Vice-Admiral, 1971.

Trimble, Robert F. Major General, United States Air Force; Director of Procurement Policy, Deputy Chief of Staff, Systems and Logistics, Headquarters, US Air Force, Washington, D.C., 1970- . Born July 26, 1924, Boligee, Alabama. US Military Academy, 1943-45; University of Michigan, MBA, 1951; Air Command and Staff College, 1959-60; Industrial College of the Armed Forces, 1965-66. Commissioned Second Lieutenant, US Army Air Corps, 1945. Combat duty in the Korean War. Chief, Field Services Division, Directorate of Procurement, Headquarters US Air Forces Europe, 1963-65; Chief, Aircraft and Major Equipment Buying Division, Ogden Air Materiel Area, Air Force Logistics Command, Hill Air Force Base, Utah, 1966-68; Military Assistant to the Deputy Assistant Secretary of the Air Force for Procurement, 1968-70. Legion of Merit; Air Force Commendation Medal with Oak Leaf Cluster; and other medals and awards. Promoted to Brigadier General, November 1, 1971; Major General, 1973.

Troup, John Anthony Rose. Vice-Admiral, British Royal Navy; Flag Officer Submarines, 1973- . Born July 18, 1921. Attended Royal Naval College, Dartmouth. Joined the Royal Navy in 1936. Served in submarines in WW II. Naval Assistant to First Sea Lord, 1959-61; Commander, 3d Submarine Squadron, 1961-63; Director of Naval Equipment, 1963-65; Captain of the Fleet (Home), 1965-66; Commander, HMS *Intrepid*, 1966-68; Flag Officer, Sea Training, and Commander, HM Naval Base Portland, 1969-71; Commander Far East Fleet, 1971-73.

DSC and Bar. Promoted to Captain, 1959; Rear-Admiral, 1969; Vice-Admiral, 1972.

Trowbridge, Richard John. Rear-Admiral, British Royal Navy; Flag Officer, Royal Yachts, 1970- . Born January 21, 1920. Studied at Imperial Defence College, 1966. Joined the Royal Navy as Boy Seaman in 1935; commissioned Sub-Lieutenant, Royal Navy, in 1940. Served at sea in WW II. Commander, Fishery Protection Squadron, 1962-64; Commander, HMS *Hampshire*, 1967-69. Extra Equerry to the Queen, 1970. Promoted to Captain, 1960; Rear-Admiral, 1970.

Trudinger, Lawrence Robert. Air Vice-Marshal, Royal Australian Air Force; Defence Medical Adviser and Chairman, Defence Medical Services Committee, 1967- . Director General, Medical Services, RAAF, 1963-67. CBE; ME.

Truly, Richard H. Lieutenant Commander, US Navy; NASA Astronaut, 1969- . Born November 12, 1937, Fayette, Mississippi. Georgia Institute of Technology, Bachelor of Aeronautical Engineering, 1959; US Air Force Aerospace Research Pilot School. Commissioned Ensign, US Navy, 1959. Fighter Squadron 33, aboard USS *Intrepid* and USS *Enterprise*, 1960-63; US Air Force Manned Orbiting Laboratory Program. NASA experience: Member, Support Crew, Apollo-Soyuz Test Project, July 1975.

Truong, Ngo Quang. Lieutenant General, Army of the Republic of South Vietnam; Commander I Corps/MR 1.

Tseng Ssu-yü. Lieutenant General, People's Liberation Army, People's Republic of China; Commander, People's Liberation Army Wuhan Units, 1967- . Born 1907. Studied at Red Army Military Academy. Joined Red Army, c. 1930; Chinese Communist Party, c. 1932. Participated in anti-Japanese guerrilla warfare; took part in Long March; fought in Civil War and Korean War. Staff, 1st Red Army, 1935; Chief, Political Branch, Infantry Regiment, 8th Route Army, 1938; Political Commissar, 8th Military Sub-District, 1941; Commander, 4th Column, North China People's Liberation Army, 1948; Headquarters, Shenyang Military Region, 1960; Deputy Commander, Shenyang Military Region, 1964; Chairman, Hupeh Provincial Revolutionary Committee, 1968; Member of Presidium, CCP Ninth National Party Congress, 1969; Member, Ninth Central Committee, 1969; Member of Tenth CCP Central Committee, 1973; Member of Presidium, Tenth National Party Congress, 1973. Order of August First; Order of Independence and Freedom; Order of Liberation; and other medals and awards.

Tseng Yung-ya. Major General, People's Liberation Army, People's Republic of China; Commander, Tibet Military Region, 1968-71. Born 1919, Kiangsi. Participated in anti-Japanese guerrilla warfare, 1937-45; took part in Long March; fought in Civil War. Leader of guerrilla detachment, Hopei, 1939; Commander, 14th Sub-district, East Hopei Military District, 1946; Commander 136th Division, 46th

Army, 1948; Deputy Commander, 46th Army, 1952; Commander, Hopei Military District, 1957; Commander, Military Forces, People's Liberation Army, Tibet, 1964-68; Chairman, Tibet Autonomous Regional Revolutionary Committee, 1968; Member Communist Party since 1931; Member of Presidium, Ninth National Party Congress, 1969; Alternate Member, Ninth Central Committee, 1969. Order of Independence and Freedom; Order of Liberation; and other medals and awards.

Tsui Chih-tao. Admiral, Navy of Republic of China; Administrative Vice Minister, Ministry of National Defense, 1970- . Born October 16, 1914, Hupeh. Studied at Chinese Naval Academy; Training Course, Kiel Fleet, German Navy; Naval Training Course, Miami, Florida, USA; Naval Tactics School, USA; National Defense College; Naval Amphibious Training Course, USA. Served in Sino-Japanese War; Chinese Civil War. Commander, Mine Squadron, 1952-54; Commander, Destroyer Squadron, 1955-59; Commander, Amphibious Force Command, 1959-61; Commander, Fleet Command, 1961-65; Deputy Commander in Chief, Chinese Navy, 1965-70. Promoted to Rear Admiral, 1955; Vice Admiral, 1959.

Tu, Le Van. Brigadier General, Army of the Republic of South Vietnam; Commander 25th Infantry Division.

Tuczapski, Tadeusz. Lieutenant General, Polish Army; Vice Minister of Defense and Inspector General of Territorial Defense, 1971- . Born September 23, 1922, in Lvov, Poland (now USSR). Lvov University, 1941-42; Officers Artillery School, 1944-45; General Staff War College, USSR, 1955-57. Served on Polish-German Front, 1945. Formerly Commander of Artillery Regiment and Artillery Brigade; Deputy Chief of Staff, Main Artillery Command, Polish Armed Forces; Commander, Artillery, Military District; Chief of Staff, Main Artillery Command, Polish Armed Forces; Deputy Chief of General Staff, 1962-65; First Deputy Inspector General of Training, Main Inspectorate of Training, 1965-68; Inspector General of Training, Main Inspectorate of Training, 1968-71, and Deputy Commander in Chief, Warsaw Pact Forces. Banner of Labor, II Class; Polonia Restituta; Cross of Valor; and other Polish and foreign orders and awards. Promoted to Major General, July 1957; Lieutenant General, 1963. Member of Polish United Workers Party, and Candidate Member of its Central Committee.

Tung, Nguyen Dinh. Senior Colonel, People's Army of Vietnam; Chief Justice, Central Military Court, 1967; Deputy Chief Justice, People's Supreme Court, 1967; Member, Mobilization and Militia Bureau, People's Army of Vietnam, 1966. Promoted to Senior Colonel, c. 1966.

Tural, Cemal. General, Turkish Army; Member, Supreme Military Council, 1969- . Born in 1929. Studied at Technical University, Istanbul. Formerly Commanding General, 2d Army; Commander in Chief Land Forces, 1964-66; Chief of Staff, 1966-69.

Turantayev, V.V. Colonel General, USSR Army. Served on the Soviet-German Front in WW II. Chief of Staff, Group of Soviet Forces in Germany, 1969-71. Member, Communist Party of the Soviet Union.

Turner, Myron George. Rear Admiral, Dental Corps, United States Navy; Commanding Officer, Naval Dental Center, Director of Dental Activities, Eleventh Naval District, and Staff Dental Officer, Naval Base, San Diego, California, 1971- . Born April 4, 1913, in McArthur, Ohio. Ohio State University, Dental College, Columbus, DDS, 1936; Postgraduate Course in Prosthetics, 1953-54; Naval Dental School, 1938-39, 1943. Commissioned First Lieutenant, Dental Corps, US Army, 1936; Lieutenant (j.g.), Dental Corps, US Navy, 1938. Served in the Pacific Theater in WW II. Depot Dental Officer, Marine Corps Recruit Depot, San Diego, 1966-68; Inspector General, Dental, and Assistant Chief, Dental Division, Bureau of Medicine and Surgery, 1968-70; Director of Dental Activities, Eleventh Naval District, San Diego, California, 1970-71. Various medals and awards. Promoted to Rear Admiral, July 1, 1965.

Turner, Stansfield. Vice Admiral, United States Navy; President, Naval War College, 1972- . Born in Highland Park, Illinois. Amherst College, Amherst, Massachusetts, 1941-43; US Naval Academy, 1943-46; Rhodes Scholar, Oxford University, 1947-50; Advanced Management Program, Harvard Business School, 1966. Commissioned Ensign, US Navy, in 1946. Served in the Korean War and the Vietnam War. Commanding Officer USS *Rowan* (DD782), 1962-63; Systems Analyst, Office of Asssistant Secretary of Defense (Systems Analysis), 1963-66; Commanding Officer USS *Horne* (DLG30), 1967-68; Executive Assistant and Naval Aide to the Secretary of the Navy, 1969-70; Commander Cruiser-Destroyer Flotilla EIGHT, 1970-71; Director, Systems Analysis Division, Office of the CNO, 1971-72. Promoted to Rear Admiral, May 1970; Vice Admiral, June 30, 1972.

Turner, Vernon R. Major General, United States Air Force; Director of Aircraft and Missiles, Office, Assistant Secretary of Defense (Installations and Logistics), 1969- . Born January 3, 1920, in Idalou, Texas. Texas Technological College; US Military Academy, 1940-43; University of Chicago, MBA, 1948; National War College, 1962-63; George Washington University, MA, International Affairs, 1963; Air War College, 1966. Commissioned Second Lieutenant, US Army Air Corps, 1943. Combat duty in the European Theater, WW II, POW. Division Director of Operations, Vandenberg Air Force Base, 1963-64; Faculty, Air War College, 1964-67; Commander, Air Force Data Systems Design Center, 1967-69; Deputy Assistant, Logistics Planning, Headquarters, US Air Force, 1967. Silver Star; Legion of Merit; and other Medals and Awards. Promoted to Brigadier General, April 1, 1969; Major General, March 1, 1972.

Tutarinov, I. Colonel General, USSR Army; Chief Representative, High Command Warsaw Pact in Hungary.

Served on the Soviet-German Front in WW II. Member, Communist Party of Soviet Union.

Tuzo, Sir Harry (Craufurd). Lieutenant-General, British Army; Commander, Northern Army Group, and Commander-in-Chief, British Army of the Rhine, 1973-   . Born August 26, 1917. Attended Wellington College; Oriel College, Oxford, BA, 1939, MA, 1970; Imperial Defence College, 1966. Commissioned in the Royal Artillery in 1939. Served in Europe in WW II. Commanding Officer, 3d Regiment, Royal Horse Artillery, 1960-62; Assistant Commandant, Royal Military Academy, Sandhurst, 1962-63; Commander, 51 Gurkha Infantry Brigade, 1963-65; Chief of Staff, British Army of the Rhine, 1967-69; Director, Royal Artillery, 1969-71; General Officer Commanding, and Director of Operations, Northern Ireland, 1971-73. KCB; OBE; MC. Promoted to Major-General, 1966; Lieutenant-General, 1971.

Tyurnev, P. Lieutenant General, USSR Army; Deputy Chief Representative, Warsaw Pact High Command in Czechoslovakia. Served on the Soviet-German Front in WW II. Member, Communist Party of the Soviet Union.

U

U, Tin. Brigadier, Burmese Army; Deputy Minister of Defense and Chief of the Burmese Army, 1972-   . Born c. 1925. Attended Rangoon University. Served in the Burma Independence Army in WW II. Formerly Commanding Officer of Strategic Regional Central Command. Member of the Secretariat of the Central Committee of the Burma Socialist Program Party.

Uchida, Katzutomi. Admiral, Japanese Self-Defense Force; Chief of the Maritime Staff, Defense Agency, Japan.

Urbanowicz, Jozef. General, Polish Army; Deputy Minister of National Defense for General Affairs, 1971-   . Born in 1916 in Orel, USSR. Merchant Marine School, USSR; General Staff War College, Warsaw, 1956-58. Served with Soviet Army, 1941-43, and then with the 1st Polish Army in the USSR, on the Soviet-German Front, WW II. Deputy for Political Affairs, 6th Infantry Regiment, and later 4th Infantry Division, 1943-45; Chief of Political Directorate, Polish Navy, 1945-52; Deputy Commander, Political Affairs, Border Troops; Deputy Commander, Air Force Political Affairs; Deputy Commandant, General Staff War College; Commandant, Military-Political College, 1958-60; First Deputy Chief, Main Political Directorate, 1960-65; Chief of Main Political Directorate, 1965-68; Deputy Minister of Defense and Chief of Main Political Directorate, 1968-71. Order of Sztandar Pracy; Cross of Grunwald; Virtuti Militari; Red Banner (USSR); and other Polish and foreign medals and awards. Promoted to Colonel, 1945; Major General, October 1958; Lieutenant General, 1970. Member of Polish United Workers Party and of its Central Committee.

Uribe Escandon, Humberto. Vice Admiral, Mexican Navy; Commander in Chief of the Mexican Navy.

Ursano, James Joseph. Major General, United States Army; Deputy Chief of Staff for Personnel, US Army, Pacific-Fort Shafter, Hawaii, 1972-   . Born April 13, 1921, Newark, New York. Niagara University, BS Degree, Natural Sciences; The Infantry School, Basic and Advanced Courses; The Adjutant General School, Advanced Course; US Army Command and General Staff College; US Army War College; Harvard University, MA Degree, Business Administration; George Washington University, MA Degree, International Affairs. Commissioned Second Lieutenant, US Army Reserve, 1943. Served in WW II and Vietnam War. Executive Officer, Office, Deputy Chief of Staff for Personnel, US Army, Europe and Seventh Army, 1967-68; Director of Personnel Systems, Office, Deputy Chief of Staff for Personnel, US Army, Washington, D.C., 1968-70; Commanding General, US Army Personnel Information Systems Command, and Director of Personnel Systems, Office, Deputy Chief of Staff for Personnel, US Army, Washington, D.C., 1970; Deputy Chief of Staff, Personnel and Administration, US Army, Vietnam, 1970-72. Distinguished Service Medal with Oak Leaf Cluster; Legion of Merit with two Oak Leaf Clusters; and other medals and awards. Promoted to Brigadier General, March 1, 1969; Major General, April 1, 1971.

Ushakov, Sergey Fyodorovich. Colonel General, USSR Air Force; First Deputy Chief of Staff, Soviet Air Force. Born in 1908 in Kalinin Oblast. Drafted into the Air Force in 1930. Attended Air Force Academy, c. 1931-c. 1934; General Staff War College, 1950s. Commissioned c. 1934. Served in the Soviet-Finnish War, 1939-41; Soviet-German War, 1941-45. Squadron Navigator, 746th Air Force Long Range Regiment, 1941-43; held several high positions on Air Force Headquarters Staff, and taught at Air Force War College; expert in Strategic Air Force Operations; Member, Communist Party of the Soviet Union. Hero of the Soviet Union; two Orders of Lenin; Order of Red Banner; Order of Red Star; and other Soviet and foreign orders and medals. Promoted to Lieutenant General, 1959; Colonel General, 1968.

Usman, Musa. Colonel, Nigerian Air Force; Military Governor, North East State of Nigeria, 1967-   . Born in 1940, in Enugu. Attended Military Training School, Zaria; Regular Officers Special Training School, Accra, Ghana; Officer Cadet School, Aldershot, England; US Army Infantry School, Fort Benning, Georgia. Member Nigerian Contingent, United Nations Peacekeeping Force, Congo; Commanding Officer, Nigerian Air Force, Kaduna Base.

V

Vadora, Julio. General, Uruguayan Army; Commanding General, Military Region IV.

Valencia Tovar, Alvaro. Major General, Colombian Army; Chief of Colombian Delegation, Inter-American Defense Board. Promoted to Major General December 16, 1971.

Valensuela, Carlos. Vice Admiral, Mexican Navy; Naval Headquarters, Mexico, 1973-   ; former Naval Attache, Embassy of Mexico, Washington, D.C.

Vallejo Vivas, Reinaldo. Rear Admiral, Ecuadorean Navy; Commander in Chief, Ecuadorean Navy.

Valo, Vasil. Colonel General, Army of Czechoslovakia; 1st Deputy Minister of National Defense, 1971-   . Born April 24, 1921, in Zadna, Ruthenia (now in USSR). Attended General Staff School, Prague, 1949-52; Voroshilov General Staff College, Moscow, 1960-62. Served in Soviet Army, then in 1st Czechoslovak Army Corps, WW II. Commander, Central Military District, 1968-69; Commander, Western Military District, 1969-71. Member of Czechoslovak Communist Party.

Valverde Vega, Fernando. Minister of Public Security, Costa Rica, 1970-   . Born June 5, 1901, San Ramon. Attended Colegio Evans. Vice President and Minister of Governance and Police, 1948; Ambassador in a Special Mission to the United Nations Food and Agriculture Organization, Rome, 1955; Minister of Public Security, 1955-57, 1970-date; Deputy in Legislative Assembly, 1962-66.

VanArsdall, Clyde James, Jr. Rear Admiral, United States Navy; Commandant, Twelfth Naval District, and Commander, Naval Base, San Francisco, California, 1972-   . Born July 22, 1913, in Indianola, Mississippi. US Naval Academy, 1930-34. Commissioned Ensign, US Navy, in 1934. Served Atlantic and Pacific Theaters, WW II. Head, Joint and International Plans Branch, Strategic Plans Division, Office of the CNO, 1960-62; Commander Destroyer Flotilla ONE, 1962-63; Chief of War Games Division, Plans and Policy Directorate, J-5, Joint Staff, Joint Chiefs of Staff, 1963-66; Commander South Atlantic Force/Commander Task Force EIGHTY-SIX, 1966-67; Commander Cruiser-Destroyer Force, US Atlantic Fleet, 1967-69; Deputy Chief of Staff, Joint Staff, Commander in Chief, US European Command, 1969-71; Commander Western Sea Frontier, 1971-72. Navy Cross; Distinguished Service Medal; Silver Star Medal; Legion of Merit with Gold Star; and other US and foreign medals and awards. Promoted to Rear Admiral, July 1, 1962.

Vanden Boeynants, Paul. Minister of National Defense, and Chairman of the Ministerial Committee of Economic and Social Coordination, Belgium, 1972-   . Born May 22, 1919, in Forest, Belgium. Studied at Saint-Michel College, Brussels, Belgium. City Counsellor of Brussels since 1952; Deputy-Mayor for Commerce and for the Public Properties of Brussels, 1952-58, and for Public Works, 1971-72; Minister of the Middle Classes, 1958-61; National Chairman of the Christian Socialist Party, 1961-66; Prime Minister,

1966-68; Minister of State, 1969. President of the professional organization of butchers.

van de Vijver, P.P. Rear Admiral, Royal Netherlands Navy; Flag Officer Naval Material.

Van Dyck, J. Commodore, Belgian Navy; Chief of the Navy General Staff, 1973-   . Born August 29, 1919, in Anvers. Attended Saint-Jean Berchmans College, Anvers; Senior School of Navigation; Royal Naval College, Greenwich; Artillery School, Chatham; Royal Navy Staff College, Greenwich; Tactical School, Woolwich. Commissioned Sub-lieutenant, British Royal Navy Reserve; transferred to Belgium Naval Force, 1946. Served on patrol craft and antisubmarine vessels in WW II. Commander, Minesweeping Center, Ostend, 1961-62; Deputy Chief of Staff to Commandant of the Benelux subzone from the English Channel to Den Helder, 1962-64; Chief of Ostend Maritime Command and Commandant of the Operational Group of the Naval Force, 1964-68; Deputy Chief of Staff (Plans) to the Allied Commander in Chief, Northwood (England), 1968-70; Inspector General, Belgian Naval Force, 1970-73.

Vannoy, Frank Wilson. Vice Admiral, United States Navy; Deputy Chief of Naval Operations (Plans and Policy), 1971-   . Born in Madisonville, Kentucky. University of Kentucky, Lexington, 1934-35; US Naval Academy, 1935-39; Naval War College, 1954-55. Commissioned Ensign, US Navy, in 1939. Served in the Atlantic and Central Pacific Theaters in WW II; amphibious operations in the Vietnam War. Commanding Officer, USS *Vermilion* (AKA-107), 1961-63; Commander Amphibious Squadron TEN, 1963-64; Head, Joint and International Plans Branch, Office of CNO, 1964-65; Commander Amphibious Training Command, Atlantic Fleet, 1965-66; Commander Amphibious Group ONE and later THREE, 1967-68; Deputy Director (Plans and Policy), J-5, Joint Staff Office, Joint Chiefs of Staff, 1968-70; Assistant Deputy Chief of Naval Operations (Plans and Policy), Office of the CNO, 1970-71. Legion of Merit with three Gold Stars and Combat "V"; Navy Commendation Medal; and other US and foreign medals and awards. Promoted to Vice Admiral, July 1, 1971.

Varenius, Bo Gerhard Otto. Major General, Swedish Royal Coast Artillery; Chief of Naval Staff, 1972-   . Attended Royal Navy Staff College; Royal National Defense College. Commanding Officer, Coastal Artillery, Gotland District, 1964-66; Chief of Staff, Military Command, Lower Norrland, 1970-72. Commander of the Royal Order of the Sword; and other medals and awards. Promoted to Major General, 1972.

Vargas Caballero, Luis E. Vice Admiral, Peruvian Navy; Minister of the Navy. Born February 10, 1916, in Tacna. Attended Naval School, 1934-39; Naval War College; Center for Advanced Military Studies. Commissioned in 1939. Commandant, Submarine Flotilla, 1964; Commander, Center for Naval Technical Instruction and Training;

Assistant Chief of Staff of the Navy; Chief of Staff of the Navy; Minister of Justice and Culture, 1968-69; Minister of Housing, 1969-72; Minister of the Navy and Senior Commander of the Navy. Orden Militar de Ayacucho; Cruz Peruana al Mérito Naval; Orden Gran Almirante Grau; Orden Cruz Peruana al Mérito Militar; Orden Cruz Peruana al Mérito Aeronáutico; Legion of Merit (USA); and other medals and awards from many nations. Promoted to Rear Admiral, January 1, 1968; Vice Admiral, January 1, 1972.

Vargas Sierra, Jose Manuel. General, Colombian Army; Chief of the Joint General Staff, 1970-   . Born September 28, 1921, Bogota. Military Cadets School; Regular General Staff Course; Advanced Studies Course, War College; Artillery and Staff Courses (USA). Commissioned January 1, 1941. Orden de Boyacá (Gran Oficial); Orden del Mérito Militar Antonio Ricaurte (Gran Oficial); orden Naval Almirante Padilla (Gran Oficial); Orden Militar Antonio Nariño (Gran Oficial); Orden Militar José Maria Cordoba (Gran Oficial); and other medals and awards, Colombian and from other nations. Promoted to Brigadier General, June 16, 1966; Major General, June 30, 1969; General, June 30, 1972.

Varon Valencia, Abraham Vicente. General, Colombian Army; Commanding General of the Armed Forces, 1971-   . Born November 11, 1920, Honda "Tolima." Military Cadet School; General Staff Course, War College; Infantry Course, Panama Canal Zone; Special Infantry Course, Chile; Orientation and Information Course (USA); Command and Staff School (USA). Commissioned December 16, 1940. Orden del Mérito Antonio Nariño (Gran Oficial); Orden Naval Almirante Padilla (Gran Oficial); Orden del Mérito José Maria Cordoba (Gran Oficial); Orden Militar 13 de Junio (Comendador); and other medals and awards, Colombian and from other nations.

Vashura, P.V. Lieutenant General, USSR Army; Chief, Political Directorate, Urals Military District, 1963-   . Served on the Soviet-German Front in WW II. Member, Communist Party of the Soviet Union.

Vasilev, G. K. Vice Admiral, USSR Navy. Served in the Soviet-German War (WW II). First Deputy Commander in Chief Pacific Fleet, 1964-72. Member, Communist Party of the Soviet Union.

Vasyagin, Semyon Petrovich. Colonel General, USSR Army; Chief, Political Directorate, Soviet Ground Forces, and Deputy Chief, Main Political Directorate, Soviet Army and Navy, 1967-   . Born in 1910. Drafted into Soviet Army in 1932. Studied at Senior Communist Party Institute, c. 1934-37; assigned to Army Political Work. Served in the Soviet-German War, 1941-45. Deputy Commander for Political Affairs, 60th Rifle Corps, Belorussian Front, 1944-45; Chief, Political Directorate Military District, and later Group of Soviet Forces stationed abroad, 1947 - c. 55; Deputy Commander for Political Affairs, Far Eastern Military District, 1955-57; Deputy

Commander for Political Affairs, Odessa Military District, 1958; Chief, Political Directorate, Group of Soviet Forces, Germany, 1958-67; Member, Communist Party of the Soviet Union, 1932-   ; Deputy to USSR Supreme Soviet. Two Orders of Lenin; three Orders of Red Banner; Order of Red Star; and other Soviet and foreign orders and medals.

Vaughan, Woodrow Wilson. Lieutenant General, United States Army; Deputy Commanding General, US Army Materiel Command, Washington, D.C., 1970. Born May 9, 1918, Woodford, Oklahoma. US Military Academy; The Quartermaster School, Advanced Course; US Command and General Staff College; Naval War College; Industrial College of the Armed Forces; Stanford University, MBA Degree, Business Administration. Commissioned Second Lieutenant in 1940. Served in WW II. Commanding General, US Army Natick Laboratories, Natick, Massachusetts, 1964-66; Assistant Director, Plans, Programs and Systems, Defense Supply Agency, Cameron Station, Alexandria, Virginia, 1966-67; Deputy Director, Defense Supply Agency, Cameron Station, Alexandria, Virginia, 1967-69; Commanding General, US Army Communications Zone, Europe, 1969; Commanding General, US Army Theater Army Support Command, Europe, 1969-70; Deputy Chief of Staff for Logistics, US Army, Europe, 1970. Distinguished Service Medal; Legion of Merit with Oak Leaf Cluster; Bronze Star Medal with two Oak Leaf Clusters; and other medals and awards. Promoted to Brigadier General, June 1, 1963; Major General, July 1, 1966; Lieutenant General, November 1, 1970.

Vazquez Maiztegui, Fernando. Rear Admiral, Argentine Navy; Naval Attache, Embassy of Argentina, London and The Netherlands.

Velasco Alvarado, Juan. Major General, Peruvian Army; President of Peru and Commander in Chief Peruvian Armed Forces, 1968-   . Born June 16, 1910, in Piura. Attended Cadets School. Previous positions include: Commanding General, 2d Light Division; Military Attache, Peruvian Embassy, Paris, France; Chief of Staff, 1st Military Region; Inspector General of the Army; Army Representative on Inter-American Defense Board; Chief of Staff, Army; Chairman, Joint Chiefs of Staff. Promoted to Colonel, 1955; Brigadier General, 1959; Major General, 1965.

Veth, Kenneth LeRoy. Rear Admiral, United States Navy; Commandant Fourth Naval District and Commander Naval Base, Philadelphia, Pennsylvania, 1968-   . Born September 29, 1911, in Minot, North Dakota. Minot State Teachers College, 1929-31; US Naval Academy, 1931-35; Naval War College, Strategy and Tactics Course, 1952-53. Commissioned Ensign, US Navy, in 1935. Served in the Pacific Theater and Southeast Asia Command in WW II; Vietnam War. Commander Destroyer Flotilla SEVEN, 1960-61; Commander Mine Force, Pacific, and Commander Naval Base, Los Angeles, 1961-64; Commander Antisubmarine Warfare Group THREE, 1964-65; Chief of Legislative Affairs, Navy Department, 1965-67;

Commander US Naval Forces, Vietnam, and Chief of Naval Advisory Group, US Military Assistance Command, Vietnam, 1967-68. Distinguished Service Medal; Legion of Merit (Navy) with Oak Leaf Cluster (Army); Bronze Star Medal (Army); Air Medal (Army); and other US and foreign medals and awards. Promoted to Rear Admiral, July 1, 1961.

Vien, Cao Van. General, Army of the Republic of South Vietnam; Chief, Joint General Staff.

Vigilione, Andrea. General, Italian Army; Chief of the General Staff, 1973-   . Born August 24, 1914, in Turin. Military Academy; Infantry School; Staff College. Combat duty in WW II. Commanding Officer, 76th Infantry Regiment, 1959-63; Commander, "Granatieri di Sardegna" Infantry Division, 1963-66; General Officer Commanding, "Folgore" Division, 1966-68; Deputy Commander, Central Military Region, 1968-71; Commander, Southern Military Region, 1971-72; Commander, Central Military Region, 1972-73. Bronze Medal; Cross for Military Gallantry; Promotion for War Merit; and other medals and awards.

Vinals-Carsi, Luis. Major General, Mexican Army; Military and Air Attache, Embassy of Mexico, Washington, D.C.; Chief of Mexican Delegation, Inter-American Defense Board; Chairman, Joint Mexican-United States Defense Commission. Date of Rank: November 20, 1971.

Vincent, Douglas. Major-General, Australian Army; Adjutant General, Australian Army, 1970-   . Attended Royal Military College, Duntroon; Imperial Defence College, 1964. Commissioned in December 1938. Served in the Middle East and Northwest Europe in WW II, and in the Vietnam War. Commander, Australian Army Force, Singapore, Malaya, 1962-63; Commander, 1st Task Force, 1965; Commander, 1st Division, 1966; Commander Australian Force in Vietnam, 1967-68; Head of Australian Joint Services Staff, Washington, D.C., 1968-70. CB; OBE.

Vinh, Nguyen Van. Lieutenant General, People's Army of Vietnam; Deputy Chief of Staff, People's Army of Vietnam; Alternate Member, Lao Dong Party Central Committee; Chairman, Reunification Department of Lao Dong Party Central Committee, 1964; Chairman, National Reunification Commission, 1960. Born in 1917 in Nam Dinh. Vice Minister of National Defense, 1959; elected Deputy to National Assembly, 1960; Member, Second National Assembly Standing Committee; Deputy, Third National Assembly and Third Standing Committee; Acting Chairman, National Assembly Standing Committee, and Chief of General Staff, 1966. Promoted to Major General, 1959.

Vinson, Wilbur Henry, Jr. Major General, United States Army; Commanding General, US Army Southern European Task Force and Support Group, 1973-   . Born October 10, 1924, at Fort Benning, Georgia. Attended US Military Academy; Artillery School, Basic and Advanced Courses; Command and General Staff College; National War College,

1965-66; University of Southern California, MS, Mechanical Engineering; University of Pittsburgh, 1968. Commissioned Second Lieutenant June 5, 1945. Served in the Vietnam War. Commanding Officer, 2d Battalion, 19th Artillery, then S-3, then Deputy Commander, Division Artillery, 1st Cavalry Division (Airmobile), US Army, Pacific-Vietnam, 1966-67; Chief, NIKE-X and Space Division, Office of the Chief of Research and Development, 1966-68; Commanding Officer, Division Artillery, then Assistant Division Commander, 2d Armored Division, Fort Hood, Texas, 1969; Commanding General, I Corps (Group) Artillery, Eighth US Army, US Army, Pacific-Korea, 1970-71; Director of Missiles and Space, Office of the Chief of Research and Development, US Army, 1971; Director of Plans and Programs and Deputy Chief of Research and Development (International Programs), Office of the Chief of Research and Development, 1971-73. Silver Star; Legion of Merit with four Oak Leaf Clusters; Bronze Star Medal with Oak Leaf Cluster; and other medals and awards. Promoted to Brigadier General, June 1, 1970; Major General, March 1, 1973.

Vischer, Johann Jacob. Lieutenant General, Swiss Army; Chief of the General Staff. Born 1914. Promoted to Lieutenant General, 1969.

Vlasov, N. Major General, USSR Army; First Deputy Commander, Northern Group of Soviet Forces, Poland, 1969-   . Served on the Soviet-German Front in WW II. Member of the Communist Party of the Soviet Union.

Vogt, John W., Jr. General, United States Air Force; Commander, US Support Activities Group, and Commander, Seventh Air Force (PACAF), 1973-   . Born in 1920. Yale University, BA; Columbia University, MA; Harvard School for International Affairs; Primary and Advanced Flying Schools, 1941-42. Commissioned Second Lieutenant, US Army Air Corps, in 1942. Combat duty in the European Theater, WW II; Vietnam War. Deputy Assistant Director of Plans, Office, Deputy Chief of Staff, Plans and Programs, Headquarters, US Air Force, 1960-63; Director, Policy Planning Staff, Office of Assistant Secretary of Defense, International Security Affairs, 1963-65; Deputy for Plans and Operations, Pacific Air Forces, 1965-68; Assistant Deputy Chief of Staff, Plans and Operations, Headquarters, US Air Force, 1968-69; Director for Operations, J-3, Joint Staff, Office of Joint Chiefs of Staff, 1969-70; Director, Joint Staff, Office of Joint Chiefs of Staff, 1970-72; Deputy Commander, Air Military Assistance Command, Vietnam, 1972-73. Distinguished Service Medal (Air Force Design) with Oak Leaf Cluster; Distinguished Service Medal (Army Design); Silver Star; Legion of Merit; Distinguished Flying Cross with four Oak Leaf Clusters; Bronze Star Medal; Croix de Guerre with Etoile de Vermeil; and other US and foreign medals and awards. Promoted to General, April 7, 1972.

Voloshko, G. Major General, Artillery, USSR Army; First Deputy Chief, Political Directorate, Moscow Air Defense

District. Served on the Soviet-German Front in WW II. Member, Communist Party of the Soviet Union.

Volynov, Boris Valentinovich. Colonel, USSR Air Force; Cosmonaut, 1959- . Born December 18, 1934. Attended Air Force Pilot School; Zhukovskiy Air Force Engineering War College; Cosmonaut Training Unit, 1959. Commissioned Second Lieutenant, Soviet Air Force, 1956. Fighter Pilot, 1956-59; Commander, Space Ship Soyuz-5. Hero of the Soviet Union; Gold Star Medal; Order of Lenin; Order of Red Banner; Order of Red Star; Pilot-Cosmonaut of the USSR; K. Tsiolkovsky Gold Medal of the USSR Academy of Sciences; and other medals and awards. Member, Communist Party of the Soviet Union since 1958.

Vredeling, Henk. Minister of Defense, The Netherlands, May 11, 1973- . Born November 20, 1924. Attended Agricultural University of Wageningen. Since 1956 Member of Parliament, Second Chamber. Member of European Parliament.

Vtorushin, L. Major General, USSR Army; Deputy Chief, Political Directorate, Siberian Military District. Served on the Soviet-German Front in WW II. Member, Communist Party of the Soviet Union.

Vu, Vuong Thua. Major General, People's Army of Vietnam; Deputy Chief, General Staff, 1955; Deputy Chief, General Directorate of Rear Services, 1970. Born in 1916 in Son Tay Province. Service in Chinese Army, 1945; Commander, 308th Division, 1950-54; Chairman, Military and Administration Committee of Hanoi, 1955; Member, Vietnam Fatherland Front, 1955; head of higher military school, Hanoi, 1959; Commander, Military Region Three, 1964; Political Commissar, Air Defence-Air Force Command, 1967. Promoted to Major General, 1950.

W

Wade, Horace M. General, United States Air Force; Vice Chief of Staff, United States Air Force, 1972- . Born March 12, 1916, in Magnolia, Arkansas. Magnolia Agricultural and Mechanical Junior College, 1934-36; Primary and Advanced Flying Schools, 1937-38; University of Arkansas, BS, 1948; Armed Forces Staff College, 1949; National War College, 1954-55. Commissioned Second Lieutenant, US Army Air Corps, 1938. Combat duty in the China-Burma-India and Middle Eastern Theaters, WW II; Vietnam War. Director of Personnel, Headquarters Strategic Air Command, 1955-59; Commander 4310th Air Division, Strategic Air Command, Nouasseur Air Base, Morocco, 1959-61; Deputy Commander, Eighth Air Force, 1961-62; Assistant, Deputy Chief of Staff, Plans and Programs, Headquarters USAF, 1962-63; Assistant, Deputy Chief of Staff, Plans and Operations, Headquarters USAF, 1963-64; Commander, Eighth Air Force, 1964-66; Deputy Chief of Staff, Personnel, Headquarters USAF, 1966-68; Commander in Chief, US Air Forces, Europe, 1968-69;

Chief of Staff, Supreme Headquarters Allied Powers Europe, 1969-72. Distinguished Service Medal with one Oak Leaf Cluster; Silver Star; Legion of Merit with two Oak Leaf Clusters; Distinguished Flying Cross; Air Medal with one Oak Leaf Cluster; and other medals and awards. Promoted to Brigadier General, September 1, 1955; Major General, August 1, 1959; Lieutenant General, December 1, 1964; General, July 31, 1968.

Wade, Ruthven Lowry. Air Vice-Marshal, British Royal Air Force; Assistant Chief of Air Staff (Operations), 1973- . Attended Cheltenham College; Royal Air Force College, Cranwell Air Force Staff College, 1953; Imperial Defence College, 1965. Commissioned in the Royal Air Force in 1939. Served in the United Kingdom and Mediterranean in WW II. Staff Officer, Air Headquarters, Malta; Commander, Bomber Command Station, RAF Gaydon, 1962-65; Air Executive to Deputy for Nuclear Affairs, SHAPE, 1967-68; Air Officer Commanding, No. 1 (Bomber) Group, Strike Command, 1968-71; Deputy Commander, Royal Air Force, Germany, 1971-73. CB; DFC. Promoted to Group Captain, 1960; Air Commodore, 1964; Air Vice-Marshal, 1968.

Waggener, John Garnett. Major General, United States Army; Commander, US Military Group, Argentina, 1972- . Born August 7, 1925, in Gideon, Missouri. Attended US Military Academy; Ground General School; Engineer School, Basic and Advanced Courses; Command and General Staff College; Army War College, 1967-68; Massachusetts Institute of Technology, MSCE, Civil and Nuclear Engineering. Commissioned Second Lieutenant June 8, 1948. Served in the Vietnam War. Commanding Officer, 307th Engineer Battalion, Dominican Republic, later Fort Bragg, North Carolina, 1965-67; Assistant Chief of Staff, G-3, 82d Airborne Division, Fort Bragg, North Carolina, 1967; Commanding Officer, 45th Engineer Group (Construction), US Army, Pacific-Vietnam, 1968-69; Chief of Combat Systems Support Division, Doctrine and Systems Directorate, Office of the Assistant Chief of Staff for Force Development, 1969-70; Deputy Director of Requirements and Procurement, US Army Materiel Command, 1970-72. Legion of Merit with two Oak Leaf Clusters; Air Medal (4 awards); and other medals and awards. Promoted to Brigadier General June 1, 1971; Major General August 1, 1973.

Wagner, Austin C. Rear Admiral, United States Coast Guard; Commander, 7th Coast Guard District, Miami, Florida, 1973- . Born May 24, 1919, New York. Lehigh University; US Coast Guard Academy, 1938-41. Commissioned Ensign, 1941. Served in Atlantic Theater, WW II. Commandant of Cadets, US Coast Guard Academy, 1964-67; Commanding Officer, Coast Guard Base, Governors Island, New York, 1967-70; Chief, Office of Boating Safety Headquarters, US Coast Guard, 1970-73. Navy Commendation Medal; WW II campaign medals and ribbons; and other medals and awards. Promoted to Captain, July 1, 1963; Rear Admiral, July 1, 1970.

Wagstaff, Jack Jennings. Major General, United States Army; Chief, Military Assistance Advisory Group, Germany, 1973-   . Born May 6, 1917, Salt Lake City, Utah. University of Oregon, BS Degree—Pre-Law; University of Oregon, LLB Degree—Law; Infantry School, Basic and Advanced Courses; U.S. Army Command and General Staff College; U.S. Army War College. Commissioned Second Lieutenant, U.S. Army Reserve, 1939. Served in WW II and Vietnam War. Commanding General, U.S. Army, Europe and Seventh Army Troops, U.S. Army Europe, 1966-68; Deputy Commander, U.S. Military Assistance Command, Thailand/Joint U.S. Military Advisory Group, Thailand, 1969-70; Deputy Commanding General, II Field Force, U.S. Army, Pacific-Vietnam, 1970-71; Commanding General, Third Regional Assistance Command, U.S. Military Assistance Command, Vietnam, 1971; Deputy Commanding General for Reserve Forces, Northern Area, Fifth U.S. Army, Fort Sheridan, Illinois, 1972-73. Distinguished Service Medal; Legion of Merit with Oak Leaf Cluster; Bronze Star Medal; and other medals and awards. Promoted to Brigadier General, November 26, 1966; Major General, March 8, 1969.

Wåhlin, Sten. Director General (equivalent to major general), Sweden; Director General, Defense Materiel Administration (FMV), 1968-   . Attended Artillery and Engineering Staff College, 1938; Royal National Defense College, 1965, 1971. Commanding Officer, Infantry Regiment No. 13, 1963; Chief, Army Ordnance Corps and Army Materiel Department, 1964-68. Commander of the Royal Order of the Sword; Commander of the Royal Order of the Northern Star; and other medals and awards. Member of the Royal Academy of Military Sciences. Promoted to Director General, 1968.

Wakeford, Richard Gordon. Air Vice-Marshal, British Royal Air Force; Director of Service Intelligence, Ministry of Defence, 1972-   . Born April 20, 1922. Attended Kelly College, Tavistock; Central Flying School, 1947; Imperial Defence College, 1969. Joined the Royal Air Force in 1941. Served in Flying Boats with Coastal Command in WW II; Malaya, 1952-58. Commander, the Queen's Flight, 1958-61; Directing Staff, Royal Air Force Staff College, 1961-64; Commander, Royal Air Force, Scampton; Senior Air Staff Officer, Headquarters, 3 Group, Bomber Command; Assistant Commandant (Cadets), Royal Air Force College, Cranwell; Commander, Northern Maritime Air Region, and Air Officer, Scotland and Northern Ireland, 1970-72. MVO; OBE; AFC.

Walker, Glenn David. Lieutenant General, United States Army; Assistant to the Chief of Staff for Training, Office, Chief of Staff, US Army, Washington, D.C., 1972-   . Born January 21, 1916, Woodworth, Louisiana. Mississippi College, BA Degree, Social Science; US Army Command and General Staff College; US Army War College; The National War College. Commissioned Second Lieutenant, US Army Reserve, 1941. Served in WW II and Vietnam War. Assistant Division Commander, 4th Infantry Division, US Army, Pacific-Vietnam, 1966-67; Special Assistant to

Chief of Staff, US Continental Army Command, Fort Monroe, Virginia, 1967; Deputy Chief of Staff for Military Operations and Reserve Forces, US Continental Army Command, Fort Monroe, Virginia, 1967-69; Commanding General, 4th Infantry Division, US Army, Pacific-Vietnam, 1969-70; Assistant Deputy Chief of Staff for Military Operations, US Army, Washington, D.C., 1970-71; Commanding General, I Corps (ROK/US) Group, US Army, Pacific-Korea, 1971-72. Distinguished Service Medal with Oak Leaf Cluster; Silver Star with Oak Leaf Cluster; Legion of Merit with two Oak Leaf Clusters; Distinguished Flying Cross; Bronze Star Medal; and other medals and awards. Promoted to Brigadier General, July 1, 1964; Major General, November 1, 1967; Lieutenant General, August 1, 1971.

Walker, Sam Sims. Major General, United States Army; Commanding General, 3d Infantry Division, US Army, Europe, 1972-   . Born July 31, 1925, in West Point, New York. Attended US Military Academy; Infantry School, Basic and Advanced Courses; Command and General Staff College; National War College, 1963-64; George Washington University, MA, International Affairs; Harvard University. Commissioned Second Lieutenant June 4, 1946. Served in the Vietnam War. Executive Officer, 3d Brigade, then Assistant Chief of Staff, G-3, then Commanding Officer, 2d Brigade, 1st Infantry Division, US Army, Pacific-Vietnam, 1966-67; Chief of Force Readiness Team, Force Planning and Analysis Office, Office of the Assistant Vice Chief of Staff, 1967-68; Army Fellow, Council on Foreign Relations, 1968-69; Assistant Division Commander, 82d Airborne Division, Fort Bragg, North Carolina, 1969; Commandant of Cadets, US Military Academy, 1969-72. Silver Star with Oak Leaf Cluster; Legion of Merit with two Oak Leaf Clusters; Distinguished Flying Cross; Bronze Star Medal; and other medals and awards. Promoted to Brigadier General, September 8, 1969; Major General, October 1, 1972.

Walker, Thomas Jackson. Vice Admiral, United States Navy; Commander Naval Air Force, US Pacific Fleet, 1971-   . Born August 6, 1916, in Edgartown, Massachusetts. Marion (Alabama) Military Institute; US Naval Academy, 1935-39; Flight Training Course, 1941-42; Postgraduate School, Ordnance Engineering Course (Aviation), 1943-44; Industrial College of the Armed Forces, 1955-56. Commissioned Ensign, US Navy, in 1939; designated Naval Aviator in 1942. Served in the Atlantic Theater in WW II; Vietnam War. Commanding Officer USS *Constellation*, 1961-62; Assistant Director, Aviation Plans Division, Office of the CNO, 1962-64; Naval Deputy, Joint Task Force TWO, 1964-66; Commander Carrier Division THREE, 1966-67; Deputy Commander for Plans and Programs, and Comptroller, Naval Air Systems Command, 1967-69; Commander Naval Air Systems Command, 1969-71. Legion of Merit; Bronze Star Medal; Distinguished Service Medal; Navy Commendation Medal with two Gold Stars and Combat "V"; and other US and foreign medals and awards. Promoted to Rear Admiral, July 1965; Vice Admiral, May 28, 1971.

Walking, Alec Ernest. Major-General, British Army; Deputy Master-General of the Ordnance, 1970-   . Born April 12, 1918. Keble College, Oxford, BA, Modern Languages, 1939; BA, Natural Science, 1949; Staff College, Quetta, 1944; Imperial Defence College, 1965. Commissioned in the Royal Artillery in 1940. Served in North Africa and Burma in WW II. Brigade Commander (Territorial Army), 1963-64; Deputy Commandant, Royal Military College of Science, 1966-68; Director-General, Artillery, 1969-70. CB; OBE.

Wallace, George Magoun, II. Major General, United States Army; Director, Inter-American Region, Office of the Assistant Secretary of Defense (International Security Affairs), 1973-   . Born January 15, 1924, in Washington, D.C. Attended US Military Academy; Artillery School; Infantry School; Command and General Staff College; Army War College, 1965-66; George Washington University, MS, International Affairs. Commissioned Second Lieutenant June 5, 1945. Served in the Vietnam War. Commanding Officer, 1st Battalion, 16th Infantry, later Task Force Commander, 1st Infantry Division, US Army, Pacific-Vietnam, 1966-67; Assistant Chief of Staff, G-3 of Task Force Oregon, US Army, Pacific-Vietnam, 1967; Commanding Officer, Advanced Individual Training Brigade, US Army Training Center, Infantry, and Fort Dix, New Jersey, 1967-68; Executive Officer, Plans and Policy Directorate, Joint Chiefs of Staff Organization, 1968-69; Director, J-3, US Southern Command, Quarry Heights, Canal Zone, 1969-72; Assistant Division Commander, 2d Infantry Division, US Army, Pacific-Korea, 1972; Holding Detachment, Office of the Chief of Staff, for duty as Chairman, SPANNER Study Group, Office of the Assistant Chief of Staff for Force Development, 1973. Silver Star; Legion of Merit with three Oak Leaf Clusters; Distinguished Flying Cross; Bronze Star Medal with V Device with two Oak Leaf Clusters; and other medals and awards. Promoted to Brigadier General, February 1, 1970; Major General, February 1, 1973.

Wallace, Kenneth Carroll. Rear Admiral, United States Navy; Deputy Director of Research, Development, Test and Evaluation, Office of the Chief of Naval Operations, 1972-   . Born July 30, 1920, in New London, Connecticut. US Naval Academy, 1939-42; Naval Post Graduate School, 1949-50; Massachusetts Institute of Technology, MS, Electrical Engineering, 1952; Army Command and General Staff College, 1957-58; Naval Nuclear Power School, 1965; Naval Nuclear Power Training Unit, 1965-66. Commissioned Ensign, US Navy, in 1942. Served in the Pacific Theater, WW II; Korean War; Vietnam War. Commanding Officer, USS *Long Beach* (CG(N)9), 1966-68; Military Assistant to Deputy Director (Strategic and Space Systems), Office of the Director of Defense Research and Engineering, Office of the Secretary of Defense, 1968-70; Commander Cruiser-Destroyer Flotilla TWELVE, 1970-72. Legion of Merit; Bronze Star Medal; and other US and foreign medals and awards. Promoted to Rear Admiral, August 1, 1968.

Walters, Vernon Anthony. Lieutenant General, United States Army; Deputy Director, Central Intelligence Agency, Washington, D.C., 1972-   . Born January 3, 1917, New York, New York. The Military Intelligence Training Center School. Commissioned Second Lieutenant, US Army Reserve, 1942. Served in WW II. US Army Attache, American Embassy, Rome, Italy, 1960-62; Defense Army Attache, American Embassy, Rio de Janeiro, Brazil, 1962-67; Defense Attache and Army Attache, American Embassy, Paris, France, 1967-72. Distinguished Service Medal with Oak Leaf Cluster; Legion of Merit with Oak Leaf Cluster; Bronze Star Medal; and other medals and awards. Promoted to Brigadier General, February 1, 1965; Major General, February 1, 1968; Lieutenant General, April 10, 1972.

Wang Hsi-ling. Rear Admiral, Navy of the Republic of China; Naval Attache, Chinese Embassy, Washington, D.C.

Wang Huai-Hsiang. Major General, People's Liberation Army, People's Republic of China; 1st Political Commissar, Kirin Military District, 1968-   . Participated in anti-Japanese guerrilla warfare, 1937-45; fought in Civil War. Formerly on Staff, Changchun Armed Force, People's Liberation Army; Chairman, Kirin Provincial Revolutionary Committee, 1968-   ; Member CCP Presidium, Ninth National Party Congress, 1969; Member, Central Committeee, 1969-   ; Member CCP Presidium, Tenth National Party Congress, 1973; Member, Tenth CCP Central Committee, 1973. Order of Independence and Freedom; Order of Liberation; and other medals and awards.

Wang Hui-ch'iu. Lieutenant General, Air Force of the People's Liberation Army, People's Republic of China; Deputy or Chief Political Commissar, PLA Air Force, 1969-   . Born 1911, Hunan. Attended Marxist-Leninist College, Moscow. Director, Political Department, 5th Army Corps, 2d Field Army; Deputy Director, Political Department, Kweichow Military District, 1950-52; Deputy Political Commissar, Kweichow Military District, 1952-55; Director, Political Department, PLA Air Force, 1955; Deputy Political Commissar, PLA Air Force, 1964-69; Member Presidium, 9th National Congress, 1959; Member Central Committee, 1969. Order of Liberation, 1st Class.

Wang Hung-k'un. Admiral, Navy of the People's Liberation Army, People's Republic of China; Deputy Commander and Political Commissar, Chinese Navy, 1950-   . Born in 1907 in Hupeh. Joined the Communist guerrilla forces in the Hupeh-Honan-Anhwei border area, c. 1919; Commander, 29th Regiment, Fourth Red Army, Oyüwan Base Area, 1931-32; Commander, 10th Division, Fourth Front Army, 1932-34; Commander, Fourth Red Army, 1934-c. 1936; Commander of one of the units, 129th Division, 1937-c. 1939; Political Commissar, South Hopeh Military District, 1939; Commander, West Shantung Military District, 1939-c. 1942; assigned to New Fourth Army, c. 1942-c. 1945; Deputy Commander, Shansi-Hopeh-Shantung-Honan Military Region, 1946-47; Commander, Sixth Column (battle group), Central Plains

Liberation Army, 1946-c. 1949; Commander, 17th Army Corps, Fourth Field Army, and Deputy Commander Hupeh Military District, 1949-1950; Member, Central-South Military and Administrative Committee, 1950-51; Member, Hupeh Provincial People's Government Council, 1950-54; Member, National Defense Council, 1954; Deputy to First, Second and Third National People's Congresses, 1954-59; Member, CCP Ninth Central Committee, 1959; Member of Tenth CCP Central Committee, 1973. Fought in Sino-Japanese War and the Civil War; took part in the Long March. Orders of August First, Independence and Freedom, and Liberation, 1st Class.

Wang Pi-ch'eng. Lieutenant General, People's Liberation Army, People's Republic of China; Commander, Kunming Military Region; Born c. 1912 in Hunan. Fought in Sino-Japanese War, the Civil War and the Korean War. Unit Commander, 1st Division, New Fourth Army, c. 1940-41; Commander, 2d Brigade, 1st Division, New Fourth Army, and Commander, 2d and then 3d Military Sub-Districts of Kiangsu-Chekiang Military Region, 1945; Commander, 6th Division, New Fourth Army, 1947; Commander, 6th Column (combat group based on the 6th Division), 1948; Vice Commander, 7th Army Group, Third Field Army, Hangchow, and Commander, 24th Army, 1949; Deputy Commander, then Commander, Chekiang Military District, 1949-c. 1953; Commander, 8th Army Corps, Third Field Army, Nanking, 1950; Member, Chekiang Provincial People's Government, 1951; commanded a Chinese People's Volunteers Force in Korea; Commander, Shanghai Garrison Command, 1955-61; Member, Shanghai Municipal People's Council, 1957-61; Commanding Officer, 1961, and Deputy Commander, Nanking Units, People's Liberation Army, 1961; Chinese Communist Party Member; Deputy, Third National People's Congress, 1964; Member of Tenth CCP Central Committee, 1973: Member of the Presidium, Tenth National Party Congress, 1973.

Wang Shu-Sheng. Senior General, People's Liberation Army, People's Republic of China; Vice Minister of National Defense, 1954-   . Born in 1905 in Hsiaokan, Hupeh. Attended Resist-Japan Military and Political College, 1936. Fought in Sino-Japanese War and the Civil War. Joined and later commanded guerrilla groups incorporated into the Communist Oyüwan Soviet and in Northwest Szechwan, early 1930's; Deputy Commander, Fourth Front Army, c. 1933-37; Commander, West Honan Military District, c. 1937-c. 1946; Member, Communist Central Plains Committee, 1939; Commander, First Column, Central Plains Military Region, 1946; Commander, Honan-Hopei Military Region, 1948-49; Deputy Commander and later Commander, Hupeh Military District, 1949-54; Member, Central-South Military and Administrative Committee, 1949-53; Member, Hupeh Provisional People's Government Council, 1949-55; Third Deputy Commander, Central-South Military Region, 1954; Director, General Ordnance Department, People's Liberation Army, 1956-c. 1959; Member, National Defense Council, 1954; Member, Hupeh Provincial Party Committee, 1955-68; Deputy, National People's Congress,

1954; Member CCP since 1927, Central Committee, 1956, 1969, 1973. Orders of August First, Independence and Freedom, and Liberation, 1st Class; Albanian Order of Guerrillas, 1st Class.

Ward, Norvell Gardiner. Rear Admiral, United States Navy; Commander Caribbean Sea Frontier, Commandant Tenth Naval District, and Commander Antilles Defense Command, 1970-   . Born December 30, 1912, in Indian Head, Maryland. US Naval Academy, 1931-35; Naval Submarine School, 1937-38; Armed Forces Staff College, 1952-53; National War College, 1957-58. Commissioned Ensign, US Navy, in 1935. Served in the Pacific Theater, WW II; Korean War; Vietnam War. Commander Submarine Squadron FOURTEEN, 1958-61; Head, Navy Plans Branch, Strategic Plans Division, Office of the CNO, 1962-65; Chief, Naval Advisory Group, US Military Assistance Command, Vietnam, 1965-67; Commander, Naval Forces, Vietnam, 1966-67; Commander Service Group THREE, 1967-68; Assistant Chief of Naval Operations (Safety), 1968-70. Navy Cross; Distinguished Service Medal; Silver Star Medal with two Gold Stars; Legion of Merit with four Gold Stars and Combat "V"; Bronze Star Medal with Gold Star and Combat "V"; and other US and foreign medals and awards. Promoted to Captain, June 1, 1954; Rear Admiral, August 1, 1963.

Ward, Sir Richard (Erskine). Lieutenant-General, British Army; Commander, British Forces, Hong Kong, 1970-   . Born October 15, 1917. Attended Marlborough College; Royal Military Academy, Sandhurst; Staff College, Camberley, 1944; Imperial Defence College, 1961. Commissioned in the Royal Tank Corps in 1937. Served with armored units in WW II and the Korean War. Staff of Chief of Defence Staff, 1962; Commander, 20 Armoured Brigade, 1963; General Officer Commanding, 1st Division, 1965-67; Vice-Adjutant-General, 1968-70. KCB; DSO and Bar; MC; Croix de Guerre with Palm; Chevalier, Order of Leopold II with Palm (Belgium); and other medals and awards. Promoted to Major-General, 1965; Lieutenant-General, 1970.

Ward-Harrison, John Martin Donald. Major General, British Army; Chief of Staff, Headquarters, Northern Command, 1970-   . Born April 18, 1918. Attended Staff College, South Africa, 1945; Imperial Defence College, 1965. Commissioned in the Suffolk and Norfolk Yeomanry in 1939. Served in the European Theater in WW II. Commander, 10th Royal Hussars (PWO), 1959-62; Colonel, General Staff, 1962-63; Brigadier, Royal Armoured Corps, E and S Commands, 1964; Deputy Commandant, Staff College, Camberley, 1966-68; General Officer Commanding, Northumbrian District, 1968-70. OBE, MC and Bar.

Warner, John W. United States Secretary of the Navy, 1972-   . Born February 18, 1927, Washington, D.C. Washington and Lee University, BS, Engineering, 1949; University of Virginia Law School, LLB, 1953. Enlisted in the Navy, 1944-46; Marine Corps Reserve, 1950-61;

commissioned Second Lieutenant, 1950; combat duty, Korean War. Special Assistant to the US Attorney, 1956-57; Assistant US Attorney, 1957-60; private law practice, 1960-69; Under Secretary of the Navy, 1969-72; Director of Ocean Affairs, 1971-   . Department of Defense Distinguished Public Service Medal.

Waters, Stanley C. Lieutenant-General, Canadian Armed Forces; Commander, Mobile Command, St. Hubert, Quebec, 1973-   . Born June 14, 1920, in Winnipeg. Attended University of Alberta; Canadian Army Staff College, Kingston, Ontario; US Marine Corps School, Senior Course, Quantico, Virginia (USA). Commissioned in the Canadian Army in 1942. Served in North Africa, the Aleutians, Italy, and Northern Europe in WW II. Director of Administration, Canadian Army Headquarters, 1963-64; Director of Training, Men, Canadian Forces Headquarters, 1964-65; Director of Training, Canadian Forces Headquarters, 1965-66; Commander 1 Canadian Infantry Brigade Group, Calgary, 1966-68; Chief of Staff, Operations and Training, Mobile Command Headquarters, St. Hubert, Quebec, 1968-70; Assistant Chief of Staff, Plans and Policy, SHAPE Headquarters, Casteau, Belgium, 1970-72; Deputy Chief of Defence Staff, Operations, Ottawa, 1972-73. Silver Star (USA) and other medals and awards. Promoted to Major-General, May 3, 1970; Lieutenant-General, September 1972.

Watkins, James H. Major General, United States Air Force; Deputy Director, Defense Mapping Agency, Department of Defense, 1972-   . Born June 28, 1919, in San Saba, Texas. Tarleton State College, Stephenville, Texas, 1937-40; US Military Academy, 1940-43; California Institute of Technology, 1948-50, MS, Electrical Engineering; Canadian National Defence College, Kingston, Ontario, 1964-65. Commissioned Second Lieutenant, US Army Air Corps, 1943. Combat duty in North Africa and Italy, ETO, WW II; Vietnam War. Deputy Commander, 3510th Flying Training Wing, 1963-64; Chief, Flying Training Division, Deputy Chief of Staff for Personnel, 1965-66; Secretary, Air Staff, 1966-68; Commander, 3510th Flying Training Wing, 1968-69; Deputy Chief of Staff, Operations, Air Training Command, 1969-71; Chief, Air Force Advisory Group, US Military Assistance Command, Vietnam (MACV), 1971-72. Legion of Merit with two Oak Leaf Clusters; Distinguished Flying Cross with two Oak Leaf Clusters; and other US and foreign medals and orders. Promoted to Brigadier General, 1969; Major General, September 1, 1971.

Watson, Philip Alexander. Rear-Admiral, British Royal Navy; Director General, Weapons (Naval), Ministry of Defence, 1970-   . Born October 7, 1919. Attended Senior Officers' War Course, 1966. Commissioned in the Royal Naval Volunteer Reserve in 1940; transferred to Royal Navy, 1946; qualified as Torpedo Specialist in 1943. Served at sea in WW II. Ship Department, Ministry of Defence, 1963-66; Commander, HMS *Collingwood*, 1967-69; Deputy Director of Engineering (Ship Department), Ministry of Defence, 1969-70.` MVO. Fellow

of the Institute of Electrical Engineers; Fellow of the Institute of Electronic and Radio Engineers. Promoted to Captain, 1963; Rear-Admiral, 1970.

Watt, James. Surgeon Vice-Admiral, British Royal Navy; Dean of Naval Medicine, and Medical Officer-in-Charge, Institute of Naval Medicine, Alverstoke, 1969-   . Born August 19, 1914. University of Durham, MB, ChB, 1938, ChM, 1949. Consultant in Surgery, Royal Naval Hospital, Haslar, 1963; Joint Professor of Naval Surgery, Royal College of Surgeons of England, and Royal Naval Hospital, Haslar, 1965; Chairman, Royal Navy Clinic Research Working Party, 1969. Queen's Honorary Surgeon, 1969. Fellow of the Royal College of Surgeons; Fellow of Royal Society of Medicine; Fellow, Association of Surgeons of Great Britain and Ireland; Fellow, Royal Society of Medicine. Promoted to Surgeon Captain, 1965; Surgeon Rear-Admiral, 1969; Surgeon Vice-Admiral, 1972.

Webb, Richard James Holden. Lieutenant General, Royal New Zealand Army; Chief, Defence Staff, New Zealand, 1971-   . Born December 1919, in Nelson. Attended Nelson College, Royal Military College, Duntroon, Australia; Middle East Staff College, Haifa; Artillery School, Fort Sill, Oklahoma (USA); Joint Services Staff College, Latimer, United Kingdom; Imperial Defence College, United Kingdom. Commissioned in 1941. Served in Middle East and Italy in WW II; and in the Korean War. Quartermaster General, NZ Army, 1967; Deputy Chief, General Staff, NZ Army, 1968-70; Chief, General Staff, NZ Army, 1970-71. Companion of the Bath; Commander of the British Empire; Legion of Merit (Commander). Promoted to Lieutenant General, 1971.

Weber, LaVern Erick. Major General, United States Army; Director, Army National Guard, Office, Chief of National Guard Bureau, Washington, D.C., 1971-   . Born September 3, 1923, Lone Wolf, Oklahoma. East Central State College, BS Degree, Education; The Infantry School, Advanced Course; US Army Command and General Staff College. Commissioned Second Lieutenant, 1948. Chief of Staff, 45th Infantry Division, Army National Guard, 1964-65; The Adjutant General, State of Oklahoma, 1965-71. Legion of Merit; and other medals and awards. Promoted to Brigadier General, November 18, 1964; Major General, December 28, 1967.

Wei Chung-liang. General, Air Force of Republic of China; Vice Chairman, Vocational Assistance Commission for Retired Servicemen, 1967-   . Born November 28, 1909, Kwangtung. Central Military Academy; Central Air Force Academy; Armed Forces Staff College; National War College. Served in Sino-Japanese War; Chinese Civil War. Formerly Commanding General, Air Service Command, 1949-54; Commandant, Air Command and Staff College, 1954-56; Director, Political Department, General Headquarters, Chinese Air Force, 1956-62; Commanding General, Training Command, Chinese Air Force, 1962-65; Administrative Vice Minister, Ministry of National Defense, 1965-66; Vice Chief of the General Staff, Ministry of National Defense, 1966-67.

Wei Kuo-ch'ing. First Political Commissar, Kwangsi Military District, 1964- . Born 1907, Tunglan Hsien, Kwangsi. Served in Sino-Japanese War; took part in Long March and the Civil War. Joined Nationalist Revolutionary Army, 1926; participated in Paise uprising, Kwangsi, 1929; Regimental Commander, Third Army Corps, c. 1933; Troop Commander, New Fourth Army, East-central China, c. 1938; Commander, 8th Brigade, Third Division, Kiangsu, 1941; Commander, 4th Division, and Commander Huaipei 1st Military Sub-District, 1944-45; Communist Representative to the Field Group at Hsu-Chou, Kiangsu, to supervise cease-fire agreement between Nationalist and Communist Forces, 1946; Commander, 2d Column (battle group), East China Field Army, 1946-49; Deputy Political Commissar, then Commissar, 10th Army Group, Third Field Army, 1949; Vice-Chairman, Foochow Military Control Commission and Mayor of Foochow, 1949; Deputy Political Commissar and Director of the Political Department, Fukien Military District, 1949-51; Commander, Public Security Forces, c. 1953; Member, National Defense Council, 1954; Deputy to First, Second, and Third National People's Congresses, and Member of Presidium, 1954-64; Member of Standing Committee, 1954-57; Vice-Chairman, State Council's Nationalities Affairs Commission, 1954-57; Governor, Kwangsi Province, 1955-58; Chairman of Kwangsi, 1958-68; Chinese Communist Party Member since 1930; First Party Secretary, Kwangsi Province, 1961, and First Political Commissar, Kwangsi Military District, 1964; Alternate Member, CCP Central Committee, 1956-69; First Secretary, Kwangsi Provincial Party Committee, 1962; Chairman, Kwangsi Revolutionary Committee, 1968- ; Member, CCP Ninth Central Committee, 1969; Member, Politburo, 1973; Member, CCP Tenth Central Committee, 1973; Member of Presidium, Tenth National Party Congress, 1973. Orders of August First, Independence and Freedom, and Liberation, 1st Class.

Weinel, John P. Vice Admiral, United States Navy; Assistant to the Chairman of the Joint Chiefs of Staff, 1972- . US Naval Academy, 1935-39; Flight Training Course, 1942; NATO Defense College; National War College. Commissioned Ensign, US Navy, in 1939; designated Naval Aviator in 1942. Served in the Pacific Theater, WW II; Korean War; Vietnam War. Director, Strategic Plans and Policy Division, Office of the CNO; Assistant Deputy Chief of Naval Operations (Plans and Policy), 1970; Director for Plans and Policy, J-5, the Joint Chiefs of Staff, 1970-72. Distinguished Service Medal with Gold Star; Legion of Merit twice; Air Medal; Navy Commendation Medal; and other US and foreign medals and awards. Promoted to Vice Admiral, 1970.

Weinkopf, Gustav. General of Artillery, Austrian Army; Director, Section II, Ministry of Defense, 1969- . Born July 10, 1914. Attended the Theresian Military Academy in Wiener Neustadt, 1934-37. Commissioned Second Lieutenant, Austrian Army, in 1937. Served in the German Army in WW II. Chief, Personnel Section, 1959-66; Chief, Personnel Group, 1966-69. Grosses Ehrenzeichen; Silbernes Ehrenzeichen; and other medals and awards. Promoted to Colonel, 1964; Brigadier, 1967; Major General, 1970; General of Artillery, 1971.

Weisner, Maurice Franklin. Admiral, United States Navy; Vice Chief of Naval Operations, 1972- . Born November 20, 1917, in Knoxville, Tennessee. University of Tennessee, 1936-37; US Naval Academy, 1937-41; Flight Training Course, 1942-43; National War College, 1958-59. Commissioned Ensign, US Navy, in 1941; designated Naval Aviator in 1943. Served in the Pacific Theater, WW II; Korean War; Vietnam War. Commanding Officer USS *Guadalupe*, 1960-61; Commanding Officer USS *Coral Sea*, 1961-62; Assistant Director for Captain Detail, Bureau of Naval Personnel, 1962-64; Director, Air Weapons System Analysis Staff, Office of the CNO, 1964-65; Commander Carrier Division ONE, 1965-67; Assistant Chief of Naval Personnel for Personnel Control, 1967-68; Deputy Chief of Naval Personnel, 1968-69; Commander Attack Carrier Striking Force, Seventh Fleet, and Commander Carrier Division FIVE, 1969-70; Commander Seventh Fleet, 1970-71; Deputy Chief of Naval Operations (Air Warfare), 1971-72. Distinguished Service Medal with Gold Star; Legion of Merit with Gold Star; Distinguished Flying Cross with Gold Star; Air Medal with five Gold Stars; Commendation Medal; and other US and foreign medals and awards. Promoted to Rear Admiral, December 1, 1965; Vice Admiral, July 9, 1969; Admiral, September 1, 1972.

Weitz, Paul Joseph. Commander, US Navy; NASA Astronaut, 1966- . Born July 25, 1932, Erie, Pennsylvania. Pennsylvania State University, BS, Aeronautical Engineering, 1954; US Naval Postgraduate School, MS, Aeronautical Engineering, 1964; Navy Flight Training School, 1955-56. Commissioned Ensign, US Navy, 1954; designated Naval Aviator, 1956. A-4 Tactics Instructor, VA-44, Naval Air Station, Jacksonville, Florida, 1956-60; Project Officer, VX-5, China Lake, California, 1960-62; VAH-4, Naval Air Station, Whidbey, Washington, 1964-66. NASA experience: Member, Support Crew, Apollo 12; Pilot, Skylab 2.

Weitzenfeld, Daniel K. Rear Admiral, United States Navy; Vice Commander, Naval Air Systems Command, 1971- . Born October 22, 1917, in Chicago, Illinois. US Naval Academy, 1935-39; Flight Training Course, 1942; Naval Postgraduate School, Annapolis; California Institute of Technology, MS, Aeronautical Engineering. Commissioned Ensign, US Navy, in 1939; designated Naval Aviator in 1942. Served in the Atlantic Theater, WW II. Ship Installations Officer, Bureau of Naval Weapons, 1964-66; Assistant Executive Director for Engineering, Naval Air Systems Command, 1966-67; Naval Air Systems Command Representative, Atlantic, 1967-69; Assistant Commander for Material Acquisition, Naval Air Systems Command, 1969-71. Promoted to Rear Admiral, July 1967.

Wells, David Charles. Rear Admiral, Royal Australian Navy; ANZUK Force Commander, Malaysia/Singapore, 1971- . Born November 19, 1918, in Inverell, New

South Wales. Attended St. Peter's College, Adelaide; Royal Australian Naval College; Imperial Defence College, 1965. Joined the Royal Australian Navy in 1933. Served at sea in WW II. Commanding Officer, HMAS *Voyager*, 1960-62; Royal Navy Exchange Service, and Deputy Director, Royal Navy Staff College, 1962-64; Commanding Officer, HMAS *Melbourne*, 1965-66; Commanding Officer, HMAS *Albatross*, 1967; Flag Officer-in-Charge, East Australian Area, 1968-70; Deputy Chief of Naval Staff, Australia, 1970-71. CBE. Promoted to Rear-Admiral in 1968.

Wen Yu-ch'eng. Lieutenant General, People's Liberation Army, People's Republic of China; Commander, Peking Garrison, District People's Liberation Army, 1968-   . Attended Red Army Military Academy. Joined Red Army in 1930, Chinese Communist Party in 1930. Participated in anti-Japanese guerrilla warfare; took part in Long March, the Civil War and the Korean War. Commander, 53d Regiment, New Fourth Army, 1941; Regimental Commander, Independent 5th Brigade, Shantung Column, 1942; Vice-Commander, Independent 5th Brigade, 1944; Vice-Commander, Independent Division, 1945; Commander, 10th Division, 4th Column, Northeast Field Army, 1947; Vice-Commander, then Commander, 41st Army, 1949-50; Chief of Staff, Canton Military Region, 1958-62; Vice-Commander, Canton Military Region, 1962-67; in charge of Communist Party Central-South Bureau, 1966; Deputy Chief of General Staff, Headquarters, People's Liberation Army, 1967; Member, Administrative Bureau, Military Affairs Committee, 1968; Member Presidium, CCP Ninth National Congress, 1969; Member, Central Committee, 1969. Order of August First; Order of Independence and Freedom; Order of Liberation; and other medals and awards.

Weschler, Thomas Robert. Rear Admiral, United States Navy; Commander Cruiser-Destroyer Force, US Atlantic Fleet, and Commander, Cruiser-Destroyer Flotilla TWO, 1971-   . Born December 21, 1917, in Erie, Pennsylvania. US Naval Academy, 1935-39; graduated with distinction but not commissioned in US Navy due to defective vision; Naval Postgraduate School, Ordnance Engineering Course, Annapolis, 1945-46; Massachusetts Institute of Technology, MS, 1946; Naval War College, 1950-51; National War College, 1962-63. Commissioned Ensign, US Naval Reserve, in 1940; Transferred to US Navy in 1946. Served in the Atlantic and Pacific Theaters, WW II; Korean War; Vietnam War. Commanding Officer USS *Montrose* (APA-212), 1963-64; Assistant Chief of Staff (Plans), Commander Amphibious Force, Pacific, 1964-65; Commander Amphibious Squadron THREE, 1965-66; Commander Naval Support Activity, Danang, Vietnam, 1966-67; Program Coordinator, Destroyer and Missile Destroyer Program, Office of the CNO, 1967-70; Commander Cruiser Destroyer Flotilla TWO, 1970-71. Distinguished Service Medal; Legion of Merit with two Gold Stars; Navy Commendation Medal; and other US and foreign medals and awards. Promoted to Rear Admiral, October 11, 1966.

West, Richard Luther. Major General, United States Army; Deputy Chief of Staff, Comptroller, US Army Forces Command, Fort McPherson, Georgia, 1973-   . Born January 8, 1925, in Ithaca, New York. Attended US Military Academy; Engineer School, Basic and Advanced Courses; Command and General Staff College; Industrial College of the Armed Forces, 1964-65; Princeton University, MS, Civil Engineering; George Washington University, MBA, Business Administration. Commissioned Second Lieutenant, June 5, 1945. Served in the Vietnam War. Chief, Office of Programming, later Executive Officer, Office of the Assistant Secretary of the Army (Financial Management), 1966-68; Commanding Officer, 79th Engineer Group, US Army, Pacific-Vietnam, 1968-69; Engineer, II Field Force, US Army, Pacific-Vietnam, 1969; Assistant, later District Engineer, US Army Engineer Division, Albuquerque, 1969-71; Comptroller, Continental Army Command, Fort Monroe, Virginia, 1971-73. Legion of Merit with Oak Leaf Cluster; Bronze Star Medal; Air Medal (3 awards); and other medals and awards. Promoted to Brigadier General, August 1, 1971; Major General, September 1, 1973.

Westin, Bo Lars Axel. Lieutenant General, Swedish Royal Coast Artillery; Commandant, Royal National Defense College, 1972-   . Attended Royal Navy Staff College, 1946-47; Royal National Defense College, 1958, 1966. Defense Attache, Swedish Embassy, Washington, D.C., USA, 1951-53; Deputy Chief, Defense Staff, 1965-68; Chief, Navy Staff, 1968-70; Chief, Defense Staff, 1970-72. Knight Commander of the Royal Order of the Sword; and other medals and awards. Member of the Royal Academy of Military Sciences; Member of the Royal Society of Naval Sciences. Promoted to Lieutenant General in 1969.

Wetherill, Roderick. Major General, United States Army; Commanding General, US Army Field Artillery Center, and Commandant, US Army Field Artillery School, Fort Sill, Oklahoma, 1970-   . Born January 19, 1918, Atlanta, Georgia. US Military Academy; The Field Artillery School, Basic and Advanced Courses; US Army Command and General Staff College; US Army War College. Commissioned Second Lieutenant, 1940. Served in WW II; and Vietnam War. Commanding General, XVIII Airborne Corps Artillery, Fort Bragg, North Carolina, 1965; Chief of Staff, XVIII Airborne Corps, Fort Bragg, North Carolina, 1966; Commanding General, 24th Infantry Division, US Army, Europe, later Fort Riley, Kansas, 1966-68; Assistant Deputy to the Commander for Civil Operations and Revolutionary Development Support, US Army Military Assistance Command, Vietnam, 1968-69; Commanding General, Delta Military Assistance Command, US Military Assistance Command, Vietnam, 1969-70. Distinguished Service Medal; Silver Star; Legion of Merit with Oak Leaf Cluster; Bronze Star Medal with Oak Leaf Cluster; and other medals and awards. Promoted to Brigadier General, September 1, 1963; Major General, August 1, 1966.

Wetter, Ernst. Major General, Swiss Air Force; Commander of the Division of Air Force and Antiaircraft Troops. Born in 1914.

Wey, Joseph Edet Akinwale. Vice Admiral, Nigerian Navy; Member, Supreme Military Council and Federal Executive Council, Nigeria, 1972- . Born March 7, 1918, in Calabar. Attended Ikot Ekprene and St. Patrick's College, Calabar. Commissioned Sub-Lieutenant, Engineer, Nigerian Navy, in 1956. Commanding Officer and Naval Officer in Charge, Apapa Naval Base, 1962-63; Chief of Naval Staff, 1963; Commander, Nigerian Navy, 1964-71; Commissioner for Establishments and Service Matters, 1971; Acting Commissioner for Labor, 1971. Promoted to Commander, 1962; Commodore, 1964; Rear Admiral, 1967; Vice-Admiral, 1971.

Weyand, Frederick Carlton. General, United States Army; Vice Chief of Staff, US Army, 1973- . Born September 15, 1916, Arbuckle, California. University of California, AB, Criminology; The Coast Artillery School, Advanced Course; The Infantry School, Advanced Course; US Army Command and General Staff College; Armed Forces Staff College; The National War College. Commissioned Second Lieutenant, US Army Reserve, 1938. Served in WW II and Vietnam War. Commanding General, 25th Infantry Division, US Army Pacific-Vietnam, 1966-67; Deputy Commanding General, later Commanding General II Field Force, US Army Pacific-Vietnam, 1967-68; Chief, Office of Reserve Components, US Army, Washington, D.C., 1968-69; Military Advisor, US Peace Delegation, Paris, France, 1969-70; Assistant Chief of Staff for Force Development, US Army, Washington, D.C., 1970; Deputy Commander, US Military Assistance Command, Vietnam, 1970-72; Commander, US Military Assistance Command, Vietnam, and Commanding General, US Army Vietnam, 1972-73; Commander in Chief, US Army Pacific, 1973. Distinguished Service Cross; Distinguished Service Medal with Oak Leaf Cluster; Silver Star; Legion of Merit with Oak Leaf Cluster; Bronze Star Medal with Oak Leaf Cluster; and other medals and awards. Promoted to Brigadier General, August 1, 1960; Major General, November 1, 1962; Lieutenant General, July 1, 1967; General, November 1, 1970.

Weymouth, Ralph. Vice Admiral, United States Navy; Director of Research, Development, Test and Evaluation, Office of the CNO, 1971- . Born May 26, 1917, in Seattle, Washington. US Naval Academy, 1934-38; Flight Training Courses, 1940-41; Naval Post Graduate School, 1946-48; Massachusetts Institute of Technology, MS, Aeronautical Engineering, 1948-49; Armed Forces Staff College, 1952; National War College, 1961-62. Commissioned Ensign, US Navy, in 1938; designated Naval Aviator in 1941. Served in the Pacific Theater, WW II; Korean War; Vietnam War. Assistant for Advanced Technology, Office of the CNO, 1964-65; Commander Iceland Defense Force, 1965-67; Commander Antisubmarine Warfare Group ONE, 1967-68; Commander Fleet Air Wings, US Atlantic Fleet, and Commander Fleet

Air Wing FIVE, 1968-70; Director of Navy Program Planning, Office of the CNO, 1970-71. Navy Cross; Legion of Merit with two Gold Stars; Distinguished Flying Cross with four Gold Stars; Air Medal with Two Gold Stars; and other US and foreign medals and awards. Promoted to Vice Admiral, January 1, 1971.

Whalen, Mark Alexander. Vice Admiral, United States Coast Guard; Commander, Pacific Area, and Commander 12th Coast Guard District, San Francisco, California, 1970- . Born October 8, 1913, Washington, D.C. Georgetown University; US Coast Guard Academy, 1933-37; Naval War College, 1958-59. Commissioned Ensign, 1937. Served in the Atlantic Theater, WW II. Chief, Operations Division, 3d Coast Guard District, New York, 1965-66; Chief of Staff, Headquarters, US Coast Guard, 1966-68; Commander Eastern Area and Commander 3d Coast Guard District, New York, 1968-70. Coast Guard Commendation Medal; Legion of Merit, Distinguished Service Medal; and other medals and citations. Promoted to Rear Admiral, July 1, 1966; Vice Admiral, October 14, 1972.

Wheeler, Sir (Henry) Neil (George). Air Chief Marshal, British Royal Air Force; Air Member for Supply and Organisation, Ministry of Defence, 1970- . Born July 8, 1917. Attended St. Helen's College, Southsea Hants; Royal Air College, Cranwell; Royal Air Force Staff College, 1943; US Army Command and Staff College, 1944; Imperial Defence College, 1961. Commissioned in 1937. Flew in Bomber, Fighter and Coastal Commands in WW II. Ministry of Defence, 1961-63; Senior Air Staff Officer, Headquarters, RAF Germany, 2d Tactical Air Force, 1963-66; Assistant Chief of Defence Staff (Operational Requirements), Ministry of Defence, 1966-67; Deputy Chief of Defence Staff, 1967-68; Commander, Far East Air Force, 1969-70. Aide de Camp to the Queen, 1957-61. KCB; CBE; DSO; DFC and Bar; AFC.

Wheeler, Kenneth Ray. Rear Admiral, Supply Corps, United States Navy; Commander, Naval Supply Systems Command, and Chief of the Supply Corps, 1970- . Born June 3, 1918, in Huntsville, Arkansas. University of California, Berkeley, BS, 1939; Naval War College, 1956-57; Harvard University Graduate School of Business Administration, 1964-65. Commissioned Ensign, US Naval Reserve, in 1939; transferred to Supply Corps, US Navy, in 1939. POW, Corregidor, WW II; served in the Korean War. Fleet Supply Officer and Assistant Chief of Staff for Supply, Staff of Commander in Chief, Atlantic Fleet, 1965-67; Director of Financial Services, Office of the Comptroller, Navy Department, 1967-69; Vice Commander, Naval Supply Systems Command, 1969-70. Legion of Merit with Gold Star; Bronze Star Medal with Gold Star and Combat "V"; and other medals and awards. Promoted to Captain, August 1, 1957; Rear Admiral, August 10, 1965.

White, Michael William Langtry. Air Vice-Marshal, British Royal Air Force; Principal Medical Officer, RAF Training

Command, 1971-   . Born March 6, 1915. St. Bartholomew's Hospital, MD, 1940; Staff College, 1955. DPH. Served in the Mediterranean Theater in WW II. Member, Royal College of Surgeons; Licentiate of the Royal College of Physicians, London, MFCM. Queen's Honorary Physician. Promoted to Air Vice-Marshal in 1971.

White, Peter. Rear-Admiral, British Royal Navy; Admiral Superintendent, HM Dockyard, Rosyth, 1971-   . Born January 25, 1919. Attended Dover College; Imperial Defence College, 1964. Staff positions in WW II. Deputy Director, Service Conditions and Fleet Supply Duties, Admiralty, 1961-63; Commanding Officer, HMS *Raleigh*, 1965-66; Principal Staff Officer to Chief of Defence Staff, 1967-69; Director-General, Fleet Services, 1969-71. CBE.

Whiteley, Peter John Frederick. Major-General, British Royal Marines; Chief of Staff, Headquarters, Allied Forces Northern Europe, Oslo, Norway, 1972-   . Born December 13, 1920. Bishop's Stortford College; Bembridge School; Ecole des Roches; Staff College, Camberley, 1954; NATO Defence College, 1968. Joined the Royal Marines in 1940. Served at sea and ashore in WW II. Instructor, Staff College, Camberley, 1960-63; Commanding Officer, 42 Commando, 1965-66; Colonel General Staff, Department of Commanding General, Royal Marines, 1966-68; Commander, 3d Commando Brigade, 1968-70; Major-General, Commando Forces, 1970-72. OBE. Member of the British Institute of Management.

Wick, Fritz. Major General, Swiss Army; Commanding General, 12th Mountain Division. Born in 1915.

Wickham, John Adams, Jr. Major General, United States Army; Military Assistant to Secretary of Defense, Washington, D.C., 1973-   . Born June 25, 1928, in Dobbs Ferry, New York. Attended U.S. Military Academy; The Infantry School, Basic and Advanced Courses; U.S. Army Command and General Staff College; Armed Forces Staff College; National War College; Harvard University, MPA, MA. Commissioned Second Lieutenant in 1950. Served in the Vietnam War. Commanding Officer, 5th Battalion, 7th Cavalry, 1st Air Cavalry Division (Airmobile), Pacific-Vietnam, 1967; Member, Nuclear Branch, later Short Range Branch, Strategic Plans and Policy Division, J-5, Joint Chiefs of Staff Organization, 1968-69; Commanding Officer, 1st Brigade, 3d Infantry Division, US Army, Europe, 1969-70; Member, Staff Group, Office of Chairman, Joint Chiefs of Staff, 1970-71; Deputy Chief of Staff for Economic Affairs, US Military Assistance Command, Vietnam, 1971-73; Deputy Chief US Representative, Four Party Joint Military Commission, Vietnam, 1973; Office of Assistant Vice Chief of Staff, US Army, 1973. Distinguished Service Medal; Silver Star with Oak Leaf Cluster; Legion of Merit with three Oak Leaf Clusters; Bronze Star Medal with V Device; Purple Heart; and other medals and awards. Promoted to Brigadier General, July 1, 1972; Major General, July 14, 1973.

Wier, James Arista. Major General, United States Army; Commanding General, Fitzsimons General Hospital, Denver, Colorado, 1969-   . Born August 27, 1916, Newberry, Indiana. University of Louisville, MD Degree; Medical Field Service School, Basic Course. Commissioned First Lieutenant, US Army Reserve, 1938. Served in WW II, Vietnam War. Director of Medical Services, 1st Logistical Command, US Army, Pacific-Vietnam, 1966; Commanding Officer, 44th Medical Brigade, US Army, Pacific-Vietnam, 1966; Staff Surgeon, US Army, Vietnam, US Army, Pacific-Vietnam, 1966-67; Commanding General, William Beaumont General Hospital, El Paso, Texas, 1967-68; Director of Staff, Office, Deputy Assistant Secretary of Defense (Health and Medical), Office, Deputy Secretary of Defense (Manpower and Reserve Affairs), Washington, D.C., 1968-69. Distinguished Service Medal; Legion of Merit; Bronze Star Medal; and other medals and awards. Promoted to Brigadier General, November 10, 1966; Major General, August 1, 1969.

Wildbolz, Hans. Lieutenant General, Swiss Army; Commanding General, 2d Army Corps. Born in 1912. Promoted to Lieutenant General, 1972.

Wilkins, John H. Major General, United States Air Force; Director of Plans and Hospitalization, Office of the Surgeon General, US Air Force, Washington, D. C., 1971-   . Born on July 25, 1921, in McAlester, Oklahoma. Johns Hopkins University, MD, 1945; Flight Surgeon Course and Wing Surgeon Course, Air Force School of Aviation Medicine, Brooks Air Force Base, Texas; Air War College, 1959-60. Commissioned in 1946. Commander, US Air Force Hospital, and Surgeon for 801st Air Division, Lockbourne Air Force Base, Ohio, 1963-65; Chief of the Plans and Management Division, then Deputy Director of Plans and Hospitalization, Office of the Surgeon General, Headquarters US Air Force, Washington, D.C., 1965-70; Command Surgeon, Aerospace Defense Command and North American Air Defense Command, Ent Air Force Base, Colorado, 1970-71. Legion of Merit with two Oak Leaf Clusters; and other medals and awards. Member of Aerospace Medical Association, American Medical Association, Association of Military Surgeons of the US, American College of Hospital Administrators; Society of Air Force Flight Surgeons, and the Air Force Association. Promoted to Brigadier General, December 31, 1970; Major General, 1973.

Wilkinson, Eugene P. Vice Admiral, United States Navy; Deputy Chief of Naval Operations (Submarine Warfare), Office of the CNO, 1972-   . Born August 10, 1918, Long Beach, California. San Diego State College, BS, 1938; US Naval Submarine School, 1941-42; Naval War College, 1957-58. Commissioned Ensign, US Navy, in 1940. Served on submarines in WW II. Commanding Officer, Guided Missile Cruiser USS *Long Beach*, 1961-63; Director, Submarine Warfare Division, Office of the CNO, 1963-66; Chief of Staff, Headquarters, US Forces, Japan, 1966-69; Commander Submarine Flotilla TWO, 1969-70; Commander Submarine Force, US Atlantic Fleet,

Submarine Operations Advisor for Polaris Operations Atlantic Command and Supreme Allied Command, Atlantic, Commander, Submarines Allied Command, and Commander Submarine Force, Western Atlantic Area, 1970-72. Silver Star; Distinguished Service Medal; Legion of Merit; and other medals and awards.

Wille, Fritz. Lieutenant General, Swiss Army; Commanding General, 3d Mountain Army Corps. Born in 1912. Promoted to Lieutenant General, 1972.

Williams, Allen H. Minister of National Defense, Liberia.

Williams, David. Rear-Admiral, British Royal Navy; Director-General of Naval Manpower and Training, 1972-   . Born October 22, 1921. Attended Royal Naval College, Dartmouth; US Naval War College. Served at sea in WW II. Naval Assistant to First Sea Lord, 1961-64; Commanding Officer, HMS *Devonshire*, 1964-66; Director of Naval Plans, 1966-68; Staff of Britannia Royal Naval College, Dartmouth, 1968-70; Flag Officer, Second in Command, Far East Fleet, 1970-72. Promoted to Rear-Admiral in 1970.

Williams, James Weldon. Rear Admiral, United States Coast Guard; Commander, 11th Coast Guard District, Long Beach, California, 1971-   . Born March 2, 1914, Farmersville, Texas. University of Texas, Austin, 1932-34; US Coast Guard Academy, 1934-38; Flight Training Course, 1942-43; Aircraft Maintenance Officer School, 1947-48; Air Force Base Institute of Technology, College of Industrial Administration, 1950-51. Commissioned Ensign, 1938; designated Coast Guard Aviator, 1943. Served in Atlantic Theater, WW II. Commanding Officer, Air Base Complex, Elizabeth City, North Carolina, 1964-66; Deputy Commander, Eastern Area, New York, 1966-67; Deputy Assistant Secretary, Administration, Office, Secretary of Transportation, 1967-70; Inspector General, US Coast Guard, 1970-71. Legion of Merit; WW II campaign service medals and ribbons; and other medals and citations. Promoted to Captain, October 16, 1959; Rear Admiral, May 1, 1967.

Williams, Joseph Warford, Jr. Rear Admiral, United States Navy; Commandant Eleventh Naval District and Commander Naval Base, San Diego, California, 1970-   . Born June 28, 1911, in Chicago, Illinois. US Naval Academy, 1929-33; Naval Submarine School, 1937; Naval War College, Senior Warfare Course, 1954-55. Commissioned Ensign, US Navy, in 1933. Served in the Pacific Theater, WW II; Vietnam War. Commander Military Sea Transportation Service, Eastern Atlantic and Mediterranean Area, 1961-62; Commander Military Sea Transportation Service, Pacific Area, 1962-64; Commander Naval Forces, Korea, and Navy Member, United Nations Military Armistice Commission, 1964; Commander Logistic Forces, US Seventh Fleet, 1964-65; Assistant Chief of Naval Operations (Training), 1965-66; Deputy Commander Submarine Force, US Atlantic Fleet, and Commander Submarine Flotilla TWO, 1966-67; Inspector General, US

Pacific Fleet, 1967-70. Navy Cross; Silver Star Medal; Legion of Merit with five Gold Stars; Bronze Star Medal and other medals and awards. Promoted to Rear Admiral, July 1, 1961.

Williams, Robert Ray. Lieutenant General, United States Army; Deputy Commander-in-Chief and Chief of Staff, U.S. Army, Pacific-Hawaii, 1972-   . Born June 30, 1918, Evanston, Wyoming. U.S. Military Academy; The Field Artillery School, Basic Course; The Artillery School, Advanced Course; Armed Forces Staff College; U.S. Army War College. Commissioned Second Lieutenant, 1940. Served in WW II and Vietnam War. Commander, U.S. Army Test and Evaluation Control Group, Fort Benning, Georgia, 1963-65; Assistant Division Commander, 2d Infantry Division, U.S. Army, Korea, 1965-66; Director of Army Aviation, Office, Assistant Chief of Staff for Force Development, U.S. Army, Washington, D.C., 1966-67; Commanding General, 1st Aviation Brigade, and Aviation Officer, U.S. Army, Pacific-Vietnam, 1967-69; Deputy Assistant Chief of Staff for Force Development, U.S. Army, Washington, D.C., 1969-70; Assistant Chief of Staff for Force Development, U.S. Army, Washington, D.C., 1970-72. Distinguished Service Medal with Oak Leaf Cluster; Legion of Merit; Distinguished Flying Cross with Oak Leaf Cluster; and other medals and awards. Promoted to Brigadier General, April 17, 1962; Major General, March 1, 1967; Lieutenant General, November 1, 1970.

Williamson, Ellis Warner. Major General, United States Army; Chief, Military Assistance Group, Iran/US Military Mission with the Iranian Army, 1971-   . Born June 2, 1918, Raeford, North Carolina. Atlantic Christian College, BA Degree, Education; The Infantry School, Advanced Course; US Army Command and General Staff College; Armed Forces Staff College; The National War College; George Washington University, MA Degree, International Affairs. Commissioned Second Lieutenant, Army National Guard, 1941. Served in WW II and Vietnam War. Commanding General, 173d Airborne Brigade, US Army, Pacific-Okinawa, later Pacific-Vietnam, 1963-66; Assistant Commandant, US Army Infantry School, Fort Benning, Georgia, 1966; Commanding General, US Army Training Center, Infantry, and Fort Polk, Louisiana, 1966-68; Commanding General, 25th Infantry Division, US Army, Pacific-Vietnam, 1968-69; Deputy Chief, Office of Reserve Components, US Army, Washington, D.C., 1969-71. Distinguished Service Cross; Distinguished Service Medal with two Oak Leaf Clusters; Silver Star with five Oak Leaf Clusters; Distinguished Flying Cross; Bronze Star Medal with three Oak Leaf Clusters; and other medals and awards. Promoted to Brigadier General, August 1, 1963; Major General, October 17, 1966.

Willison, Sir David (John). Lieutenant-General, British Army; Deputy Chief to Defence Chief (Intelligence), 1972-   . Born December 25, 1919. Attended Royal Military Academy, Woolwich; Imperial Defence College, 1966. Commanding Officer, 38 Engineer Regiment, 1960-63; Colonel, General Staff (MI/DI4), Ministry of

Defence, 1963-66; Brigadier, General Staff (Intelligence) Ministry of Defence, 1967-70; Brigadier, General Staff (Intelligence and Security)/Assistant Chief of Staff, G2, Headquarters, NORTHAG, 1970-71; Director of Service Intelligence, Ministry of Defence, 1971-72. KCB; OBE; MC.

Willoughby, Sir John (Edward Francis). Major-General, British Army; Advisor on Defence to Federation of Arab Amirates, 1968-71. Born June 18, 1913. Commissioned in the Middlesex Regiment in 1933. Served in the Pacific, USA, Burma and Europe in WW II, and in the Korean War. Chief of Staff, Land Forces, Hong Kong, 1961; General Officer Commanding, 48 Infantry Division (Territorial Army), and West Midland District, 1963-65; General Officer Commanding, Land Forces, Middle East Command, Inspector-General, Federal Regular Army of South Arabia, and Security Commander, Aden State, 1965-67. KBE; OBE.

Wills Olaya, Eduardo. Rear Admiral, Colombian Navy; Chief of Naval Operations.

Wilson, Alan Christopher Wyndham. Rear-Admiral, British Royal Navy; Senior Naval Member, Directing Staff, Royal College of Defence Studies, 1972-   . Born September 7, 1919. Attended St. Bee's, Cumberland; Imperial Defence College, 1969. Served at sea in WW II. Served on HMS *Ark Royal*, 1959-61; Admiralty, 1963-64; Staff of Flag Officer, Aircraft Carriers, 1964-66; Staff of Commander Far East Fleet, 1966-69; Head of British Defence Liaison Staff, Canberra, 1970-72.

Wilson, Alexander James. Major-General, British Army; Vice-Adjutant-General, Ministry of Defence, 1972-   . Born April 13, 1921. Winchester College; New College, Oxford, BA, Law; Army Staff College, 1950. Commanding Officer, 1st Battalion, XX Lancashire Fusiliers, 1962-64; Chief of Staff, 1964-66, and Acting Commander, 1965-66, United Nations Force in Cyprus; Commander 147 Infantry Brigade, 1966-67; Director of Army Recruiting, 1967-70; General Officer Commanding North West District, 1970-72. CBE; MBE; MC.

Wilson, Joseph G. Major General, United States Air Force; Assistant Deputy Chief of Staff, Plans and Operations, Headquarters US Air Force, 1972-   . Born April 13, 1921, in Richmond, Virginia. Virginia Polytechnic Institute, Blacksburg, Virginia; Army Air Corps Flying School, 1943-44; Air Command and Staff School, 1955; Army War College, 1959-60. Commissioned Second Lieutenant, US Army Air Corps, 1944. Combat duty with the Eighth Air Force, Europe, WW II; Vietnam War. Director, Tactical Control Systems, Deputy Chief of Staff, Operations, 1964-65; Chief, Headquarters, US Air Force Command and Control Evaluation Team, 1965; Commander, 8th Tactical Fighter Wing, 1965-66; Assistant Deputy Chief of Staff, Personnel, Tactical Air Command, 1966-67; Assistant Deputy Chief of Staff, Operations, Tactical Air Command, 1967-69; Commander, US Air Force Special Operations Force, 1969-70; Commander,

Nineteenth Air Force, 1970; Deputy Chief of Staff, Operations, Seventh Air Force, Vietnam, 1970-72; Deputy Chief of Staff, Plans, Headquarters, Pacific Air Forces, 1972. Distinguished Service Medal; Legion of Merit with two Oak Leaf Clusters; Distinguished Flying Cross with five Oak Leaf Clusters; and other US and foreign medals and awards. Promoted to Major General, June 1, 1970.

Wilson, Louis Hugh. Lieutenant General, United States Marine Corps; Commanding General, Fleet Marine Force, Pacific, 1972-   . Born February 11, 1920, Brandon, Mississippi. Millsaps College, BA, 1941; Officers Senior Course, Marine Corps Schools, 1954; National War College, 1961-62. Commissioned Second Lieutenant, USMCR, 1941. Served in Pacific Theater, WW II; Korean War; Vietnam War. Deputy Chief of Staff (Plans and Programs), Headquarters, Marine Corps, 1962-65; Assistant Chief of Staff, G-3, 1st Marine Division, 1965-66; Commander, 6th Marine Corps District, 1966; Legislative Assistant to Marine Corps Commandant, 1967-68; Chief of Staff, Fleet Marine Force, Pacific, 1968-70; Commanding General, I Marine Amphibious Force, 3d Marine Division, 1970-71; Deputy for Education, and Director, Education Center, Marine Corps Development and Education Command, 1971-72. Medal of Honor; Legion of Merit with two Gold Stars; and other US and foreign medals and awards. Promoted to Brigadier General, November 3, 1966; Major General, March 16, 1970; Lieutenant General, August 9, 1972.

Wilson, Louis L., Jr. Lieutenant General, United States Air Force; Inspector General, United States Air Force, 1971-   . Born January 10, 1919, in Huntington, West Virginia. US Military Academy, 1939-43; Flying School, 1942. Commissioned in 1943. Combat duty in the European Theater, WW II. Deputy Director, Operational Requirements and Development Plans, Headquarters USAF, 1964-68; Vice Commander, Headquarters Space and Missile Systems Organization, Air Force Systems Command, 1968-70; Commander, Space and Missile Test Center, Vandenberg Air Force Base, California, 1970-71. Distinguished Service Medal; Legion of Merit with one Oak Leaf Cluster; Distinguished Flying Cross, and other US and foreign medals and awards. Promoted to Brigadier General, September 1, 1966; Major General, August 1, 1969; Lieutenant General, September 1, 1971.

Wilson, Samuel Vaughn. Major General, United States Army; Deputy Director for Estimates, Intelligence Agency, 1973-   . Born September 23, 1923, in Rice, Virginia. Attended The Infantry School, Advanced Course; Command and General Staff College; Air War College, 1963-64; Defense Intelligence School, 1971. Commissioned Second Lieutenant, August 17, 1942. Served in WW II. Commanding Officer, 6th Special Forces Group (Airborne), 1st Special Forces, Fort Bragg, North Carolina, 1967-68; Special Assistant to Commanding General, US Army John F. Kennedy Center for Special Warfare, Fort Bragg, North Carolina, 1968-69; Director, Military Assistance School, US Army Institute of Military Assistance, Fort Bragg, North Carolina, 1969; Assistant Commandant, US Army Institute of Military Assistance, Fort Bragg, 1969-70; Assistant Division Commander, 82d Airborne Division, 1970-71; US Defence Attache, Moscow, USSR, 1971-73. Distinguished Service Cross; Distinguished Medal with Oak Leaf Cluster; Silver Star with Oak Leaf Cluster; Legion of Merit with Oak Leaf Cluster; Bronze Star Medal; and other medals and awards. Promoted to Brigadier General September 1, 1970; Major General July 14, 1973.

Winn, Charles Vivian. Air Vice-Marshal, British Royal Air Force; Air Officer Commanding, Scotland and Northern Ireland, 1972- . Born April 20, 1918. Attended Wycliffe College. Served in WW II. Chief of Plans and Operations, Far East, 1962-65; Director of Operations (Air), Ministry of Defence, 1965-68; Air Commander, Malta, 1968-71; Chief of Plans, SHAPE, 1971. CBE; DSO; DFC; Queen's Commendation for Bravery. Member, British Institute of Management.

Wisman, William Woodrow. Major General, United States Air Force; Special Project Officer, Static War, Headquarters, Supreme Headquarters Allied Powers, Europe, 1972- . Born May 30, 1918, in Augusta, Kansas. Ohio State University; Army Air Corps Flying School, 1940; Air Command and Staff School, 1948; Air War College, 1956-57. Commissioned Second Lieutenant, US Army Air Corps, 1940. Combat duty in the China-Burma-India Theater in WW II. Commander, 819th Strategic Aerospace Division, 1962-64; Deputy Director, Operations, National Military Command Center, Office of the Joint Chiefs of Staff, 1964-68; Deputy Chief of Staff, Plans and Programs, J-5, North American Air Defence/Continental Air Defense Command (NORAD/CONAD), 1968-72. Distinguished Service Medal, Legion of Merit, Distinguished Flying Cross; and other medals and awards.

Wolfe, William Roy, Jr. Major General, United States Army; Deputy Director for Counterinsurgency and Special Activities, J-3, Organization of the Joint Chiefs of Staff, 1973- . Born June 13, 1924, in Honolulu, Hawaii. Attended US Military Academy; Field Artillery School; Artillery School; Command and General Staff College; Armed Forces Staff College; Army War College, 1965-66; Army Civil Affairs School, 1967-68; Vanderbilt University, MA, Social Psychology. Commissioned Second Lieutenant June 5, 1945. Served in the Vietnam War. Commanding Officer, 1st Cavalry Division Artillery (Airmobile), US Army, Pacific-Vietnam, 1968-69; Chief of the Revolutionary Development Division, Office of the Special Assistant for Counterinsurgency and Special Activities, Joint Chiefs of Staff Organization, 1969; Deputy Commanding General, US Army, Alaska, and Commanding General, Fort Wainwright, Alaska, 1969-70; Chief of Staff, US Alaskan Command, 1970-72; Deputy Director of Operations, US Military Assistance Command, Vietnam, 1972. Legion of Merit with two Oak Leaf Clusters; Bronze Star Medal with V Device; Air Medal with V Device (12 awards). Promoted to Brigadier General December 1, 1969; Major General October 1, 1972.

Wolff, Herbert Eric. Major General, United States Army; Deputy Director for Signal Intelligence Operations, National Security Agency/Central Security Service, Fort George G. Meade, 1973- . Born May 24, 1925, in Cologne, Germany. Attended Rutgers University, BA, Psychology; University of Maryland, BS, Government and Politics; George Washington University, MA, International Affairs; Infantry School, Advanced Course; Command and General Staff College; Army War College. Commissioned Second Lieutenant May 1, 1945. Served in WW II and the Vietnam War. Deputy Assistant Commandant, US Army Infantry School, later Commanding Officer, US Army Training Center, Infantry, Fort Benning, Georgia, 1967-68; Deputy Commanding General, US Army Training Center, Infantry, and Fort Dix, New Jersey, 1968-69; Assistant Division Commander, 1st Infantry, US Army, Pacific-Vietnam, 1969-70; Commanding General and Senior Advisor, Capital Military Assistance Command, US Military Assistance Command, Vietnam, 1970; Commanding General, US Army Security Agency, Pacific, US Army, Pacific-Hawaii, 1970-72; Deputy Chief, Central Security Service, Fort George G. Meade, Maryland, 1972-73. Distinguished Service Medal; Silver Star with Oak Leaf Cluster; Legion of Merit with two Oak Leaf Clusters; Distinguished Flying Cross; Bronze Star Medal with V Device with three Oak Leaf Clusters; and other medals and awards. Promoted to Brigadier General August 1, 1968; Major General September 1, 1972.

Woodrow, Albert John. Major-General, British Army; General Officer Commanding, Wales, 1970- . Born June 3, 1919. Attended Sheffield University. Commissioned in the Royal Signals, 1940. Served in Europe and Burma in WW II. Commanding Officer, 1 Division, Signals, 1961-63; British Army Staff, Washington, D.C., USA, 1963-65; Commander, Training Brigade, Royal Signals, 1965-68; Director of Public Relations, Army, 1968-70. MBE. Member of the British Institute of Management. Promoted to Brigadier, 1965; Major-General, 1970.

Woods, Mark William. Rear Admiral, United States Navy; Commander Cruiser-Destroyer Force, US Pacific Fleet, 1972- . Born April 28, 1918, in Whitehall, Montana. University of Nebraska, 1936-38; US Naval Academy, 1938-41; Naval Postgraduate School, Annapolis; John Hopkins University, MS, Engineering, 1946-49; Naval War College, 1951-52. Commissioned Ensign, US Navy, in 1941. Served in the Pacific Theater, WW II; Korean War; Vietnam War. Executive Officer, Naval Ship Missile Systems Engineering Station, Port Hueneme, California, 1963-64; Commanding Officer, USS *Canberra* (CAG-2), 1964-66; Commander Cruiser-Destroyer Flotilla NINE, 1966-67; Vice Commander and later Commander, Naval Ordnance Systems Command, 1967-72. Silver Star Medal; Legion of Merit; Navy Commendation Medal with Gold Star; and other US and foreign medals and awards. Promoted to Rear Admiral, July 1, 1967.

Woolwine, Walter James. Lieutenant General, United States Army; Director for Logistics, Organization, Joint Chiefs of

Staff, Washington, D.C., 1971-   . Born January 26, 1919, Bluefield, West Virginia. US Military Academy; The Quartermaster School, Basic and Advanced Courses; Command and General Staff College; Industrial College of the Armed Forces; Harvard University, MBA Degree, Business Administration. Commissioned Second Lieutenant, 1941. Served in WW II and Vietnam War. Chief, Theaters Division, OPRED Office, later Deputy Director of Supply, US Army Materiel Command, Washington, D.C., 1966; Director of Procurement and Production, later Deputy Commanding General for Materiel Acquisition, US Army Materiel Command, Washington, D.C., 1966-69; Commanding General, 1st Logistical Command, later Assistant Deputy Commanding General for Materiel, Headquarters, US Army, Vietnam, 1969-71; Special Assistant to the Deputy Chief of Staff for Logistics, Office, Deputy Chief of Staff for Logistics, Washington, D.C., 1971. Distinguished Service Medal with Oak Leaf Cluster; Legion of Merit with Oak Leaf Cluster; Bronze Star Medal; and other medals and awards. Promoted to Brigadier General, January 1, 1967; Major General, November 1, 1968; Lieutenant General, August 1, 1971.

Worden, Alfred Merrill. Lieutenant Colonel, US Air Force; NASA Astronaut, 1966-   . Born February 7, 1932, Jackson, Michigan. US Military Academy, 1951-55; University of Michigan, MS degrees in Astronautical/Aeronautical Engineering and Instrumentation Engineering, 1963; Empire Test Pilots School, Farnborough, England, 1964-65; Aerospace Research Pilots School, 1965; Instrument Pilots Instructor School, 1963. Commissioned Second Lieutenant, US Air Force, June 1955. Pilot and Armament Officer, 95th Fighter Interceptor Squadron, 1957-61; Instructor, Aerospace Research Pilots School, 1965-66. NASA experience: Member, Support Crew, Apollo 9; Backup Command Module Pilot, Apollo 12; Command Module Pilot, Apollo 15. NASA Distinguished Service Medal; Air Force Distinguished Service Medal; Senior Pilot Astronaut Wings; City of New York Gold Medal; United Nations Peace Medal; City of Chicago Gold Medal; Air Force Association's David C. Schilling Trophy; Kitty Hawk Memorial Award; AIAA Haley Astronautics Award; Arnold Air Society's John F. Kennedy Trophy; Robert J. Collier Trophy; Order of Leopold (Belgium); New York Police Department St. George Association's Golden Rule Award; Honorary Doctorate of Astronautical Science, University of Michigan, 1971.

Worsley, Richard Edward. Major-General, British Army; General Officer Commanding, 3d Division, 1972-   . Born May 29, 1923. Attended Radley College; Imperial Defence College, 1968. Commissioned in Rifle Brigade in 1942. Served in the Middle East and Italy in WW II; Malaya, 1956-57. Commanding Officer, The Royal Dragoons, 1962-65; Commander, 7th Armoured Brigade, 1965-67; Chief of Staff, Far East Land Forces, 1969-71. OBE.

Wu Fa-hsien (Wu 'Wen-yu). Lieutenant General, People's Liberation Army, People's Republic of China. Born in 1914 in Kiangsi. Attended Red Army Military Academy. Joined Red Army, c. 1932. Participated in anti-Japanese guerrilla warfare; took part in Long March; fought in the Civil War. Political Commissar, 1st Army Corps, 1936; Commander, Military Unit, 1940; Political Commissar, 4th Field Army, 1949; Deputy Political Commissar and Director of Political Department, Kwangsi Military District, 1950-52; Member, Kwangsi Provincial Party Committee, 1950; Deputy Political Commissar, People's Liberation Army Air Force, 1952-55; Political Commissar, Headquarters, People's Liberation Army Air Force, 1957; Deputy Chief of General Staff, People's Liberation Army, 1968. Member of Chinese Communist Party since c. 1930; Member of Presidium, Member of Central Committee, and Member of Politburo, Ninth National Congress, 1969. Whereabouts since September 1971 unknown. Order of August First; Order of Independence and Freedom; Order of Liberation; and other medals and awards.

Wu Lieh. Major General, People's Liberation Army, People's Republic of China; Deputy Political Commissar, Public Security Force, 1972-   . Served in Sino-Japanese War and Chinese Civil War. Company Commander, State Political Defense Regiment, 1935; Regimental Commander, 2d Division, Public Security Forces, 1949-53; Commander, Peking Garrison District, 1960; Vice Commander, Public Security Forces, 1964; Deputy to 3d National Party Congress, 1964. Order of Liberation, 1st Class. Promoted to Major General, 1959.

Y

Yakubovskiy, Ivan Ignat'yevich. Marshal of the Soviet Union; First Deputy Minister of Defense and Commander in Chief, Warsaw Pact Forces, 1967-   . Born July 1, 1912, in Zaitsevo, Mogilev Oblast. Drafted into Soviet Army, 1932. Attended Military Academy, 1932-35; General Staff War College. Commissioned in 1935. Served in the Soviet-Polish War, 1939; Soviet-German War, 1941-45. Commander, 91st Tank Brigade, 1942-43; Deputy Commander, 6th Guards Tank Corps, 1944-45; Commander, Tank Division, 1945-46; Commander, Armored Troops, Carpathian Military District, 1952-53; Deputy Commander in Chief, Group of Soviet Forces, Germany, 1957-60; Commander in Chief, Group of Soviet Forces, Germany, 1960-65; Commander, Kiev Military District, 1965-67; Member, Communist Party of the Soviet Union, 1937-   ; Member, Communist Party Central Committee; Deputy to USSR Supreme Soviet. Twice Hero of the Soviet Union; three Orders of Lenin; four Orders of Red Banner; Order of Fatherland War; Order of Suvorov; Order of Kutuzov; Order of Red Star; and other Soviet and foreign orders and medals. Promoted to Marshal of the Soviet Union, 1967.

Yakushin, V.Z. Lieutenant General, USSR Army; Chief of Staff, Group of Soviet Forces in Germany, 1971-   . Served on the Soviet-German Front in WW II. Chief of Staff, Carpathian Military District, 1969-71; Member, Communist Party of the Soviet Union.

Yamanaka, Sandanori. Director General, Japanese Self Defense Agency, 1973-   . Formerly Director General, Prime Minister's Office.

Yamkovoy, B. Vice Admiral, USSR Navy; Chief of Staff, Black Sea Fleet, 1971-   . Served in the Soviet-German War, 1941-45. Member, Communist Party of the Soviet Union.

Yang Ch'eng-wu. Colonel General, People's Liberation Army, People's Republic of China; Member, National Defense Council. Born in 1912, in Ch'ang-T'ing, Fukien. Red Army Academy, 1936; War College, USSR. Joined Red Army, 1930. Anti-Japanese guerrilla warfare, 1937-45; took part in Long March; Civil War. Political Commissar, 4th Regiment, 2d Division, 1932-36; Commander, Shansi-Hopeh Military Sub-district, 1941; Commander, 5th Sub-district, West Hopeh Military District, 1942; Commander, Central Hopeh Military District, 1945; Commander, 1st Independent Division, 1947; Commander, Tientsin Garrison, 1949-53; Commander, 7th Corps, North China Military Region, 1949 ca. 1953; Commander, Army, Korean War, 1951; Chief of Staff and Deputy Commander, North China Military Region, 1954-55; Commander, Peking-Tientsin Garrison, 1955-56; Commander, Air Defense Force, People's Liberation Army, 1957-58; Deputy Chief of Staff, People's Liberation Army, 1959-66; Acting Chief of Staff, 1966-68. Member, Chinese Communist Party since ca. 1932; Alternate Member, Central Committee, CCP; Deputy to the National People's Congress. Order of August 1; Order of Independence and Freedom; Order of Liberation; and other medals and awards. Promoted to Colonel General, 1955.

Yang Te-chih. General, People's Liberation Army, People's Republic of China; Commander, Tsinan Military Region, 1958-   . Born in 1910 in Liling, Hunan. Studied Military Tactics at Nanking Military Academy, 1955. Joined Red Army, 1927. Served in Sino-Japanese War; Chinese Civil War; Korean War. Participated as soldier, then as officer, in various units and actions; participated in the Long March; Division Commander, Jehol-Liaoning Military Region, 1945; Commander, 1st Column, Shansi-Hopei-Chahar area, 1947; Commander, Army Group, 1947; Commander, 2d Army Corps, 1948; Commander, Ninghsia Military Region and Chairman Yinchuan Military Control Commission, 1949; Chief of Staff, Chinese People's Volunteers, 1951; Deputy Commander, CPV, 1953-54, Commander, 1954-55; Deputy Director, Political Department, CPV, 1954; Member, National Defense Council, 1954; 1st Vice Chairman, Shantung Provincial Revolutionary Committee, 1967; Member of Presidium, Ninth National Congress, and Member of Ninth Central Committee, 1969-   . Member of Presidium, Tenth National Congress, and Member of Tenth Central Committee, 1973-   . National Flag Medal, Democratic People's Republic of Korea; Guerrilla Medal, 1st Class, Albania; orders of People's Republic of China awarded in 1955.

Yang Yung. Lieutenant General, People's Liberation Army, People's Republic of China; Commander, Sinkiang Military Region, 1973-   . Commander, Peking Military Region until 1967. Member, Chinese Communist Party; Member of Tenth CCP Central Committee, 1973; Member of Presidium, Tenth National Party Congress, 1973.

Yao Chao-yuan. Major General, Air Force of Republic of China; Deputy Chief of the General Staff, Intelligence, Ministry of National Defense, 1972-   . Born July 17, 1918, Hopei. Air Force Academy; Command and General Staff College, Chinese Air Force; Flying Training Courses, USA; National Defense Research Institute. Served in Sino-Japanese War; Chinese Civil War. Wing Commander, 4th Tactical Fighter Wing, 1965-68; Deputy Commander, Air Force Combat Command, 1968-69; Assistant Deputy Commander, G/S, Operations, Ministry of National Defense, 1969-70; Superintendent, Air Force Academy, 1970-72.

Yariv, Aharon. Major General, Israeli Army; Assistant to the Chief of Staff, Israeli Army. Military Attache, Embassy of Israel, Washington, D.C., 1956-59; recently Chief of Israeli Military Intelligence.

Yefimov, Aleksandr Nikolayevich. Colonel General, USSR Air Force; First Deputy Commander in Chief, Soviet Air Force, 1969-   . Born February 6, 1923, Kantemirovka, Voronezh Oblast. Volunteered for the Air Force, 1941. Attended Air Force Academy, 1941-42; Air Force War College, 1948-51; General Staff War College, 1955-57. Served in the Soviet-German War, 1941-45. Flight and later Squadron Commander; Commander, various Air Force units; held major Air Force commands in the Baltic and Carpathian Military Districts; Member, Communist Party of the Soviet Union, 1943-   ; Deputy to the Ukrainian Supreme Soviet. Twice Hero of the Soviet Union; three Orders of Lenin; three Orders of Red Banner; Order of Fatherland War; Order of Red Star; and other Soviet and Foreign orders and medals. Promoted to Major General, 1960; Lieutenant General, c. 1968; Colonel General, 1970.

Yefimov, P.I. Colonel General, USSR Army; First Deputy Chief, Main Political Directorate, Soviet Army and Navy, 1958-   . Served on the Soviet-German Front in WW II. Order of Lenin; Order of Red Banner; and other orders and medals. Member, Communist Party of the Soviet Union.

Yegorov, Boris Borisovich. Soviet Cosmonaut, 1960-   . Born in 1937. Attended Moscow Medical Institute, MSc, Aviation and Cosmic Medicine. Physician, Voskhod-1 Spacecraft, 1964. Hero of the Soviet Union; Order of Lenin; Pilot-Cosmonaut USSR; and other medals and awards.

Yegorov, G.M. Admiral, USSR Navy; Commander in Chief, Northern Fleet, 1971-   . Born in 1920. Attended Frunze Naval School, 1941. Commissioned in 1941. Served as Submarine Officer, Baltic Fleet, in WW II. Chief of Staff, Northern Fleet, 1965-67; Deputy Commander, Soviet

Navy, and Director, Combat Training, 1967-71. Member, Communist Party of the Soviet Union. Promoted to Admiral, 1971.

Yegorovskiy. Colonel General, USSR Army. Served on the Soviet-German Front in WW II. Commander, Urals Military District until 1970; Member, Communist Party of the Soviet Union.

Yeh Chien-ying. Marshal, People's Liberation Army, People's Republic of China; Vice Chairman, Military Affairs Commission of Chinese Communist Party Central Committee, 1967-   . Born in 1899 in Mei-Hsien, Kwantung. Yunnan Military Academy, 1919; Red Army Military College, Moscow, USSR, 1928. Served in Sino-Japanese War; took part in Long March; The Civil War. Instructor, Whampoa Military Academy, Canton, 1924-25; Chief of Staff, First Army, Nationalist Revolutionary Army; Commander 21st Division, 1925-26; Commander 2d Division, 1926; took part in planning and participated in Nanchang uprising and the Canton insurrection, 1927; Chief of Staff, Central Revolutionary Military Council, 1932-33; Chief of Staff, Red First Front Army, 1933-35; drafted military plan for Long March; Chief of Staff, Red 3d Army Corps, 1935; during Sino-Japanese War (1937-45) served as Communists' top liaison official with Nationalists in Sian, Nanking, Hankow, Chungking, as well as Chief of Staff, 8th Route Army, 1937; Deputy Chief of General Staff, People's Revolutionary Military Council, 1946; Chairman, Canton Military Control Commission, 1949; Commander and Political Commissar, Kwangtung Military District, 1949; Secretary, CCP Canton Municipal Committee, 1949-52; Chairman of Kwangtung, 1949-55; Council Member, Sino-Soviet Friendship Association, 1949-54; Member, Overseas Chinese Affairs Commission, GAC, 1949-54; Vice Chairman, Central-South Military and Administrative Committee, Wuhan, 1940-54; Acting Commander, Central-South Military Region, 1952-54; Chief, Supervision Department, People's Liberation Army, 1954; Vice Chairman, National Defense Council, 1954; Member, First, Second, and Third National People's Congresses, 1954, 1959, 1965; Member of Presidium and Standing Committee; Member, Inspectorate of the Armed Forces, 1954-58; Commandant and Political Commissar, Academy of Military Science, Peking, 1958; Member, CCP Seventh Central Committee, 1945-56, Eighth Central Committee, 1956-69, Ninth Central Committee and Politburo, 1969; Member, Presidium, CCP Ninth National Congress, 1969; Vice Chairman, Presidium, Tenth National Congress, 1973; Vice President, Politburo, 1973. Orders of August First, Independence and Freedom, and Liberation, 1st Class.

Yeh Hsiang-chih. Lieutenant General, Army of Republic of China; Director, Intelligence Bureau, Ministry of National Defense, 1960-   . Born September 29, 1912, Shanghai. Educated at Meiji University, Tokyo, Japan. Deputy Chief, Security Bureau, Ministry of National Defense, 1946-49; Deputy Chief, Mainland Operations Office, Ministry of National Defense, 1950-52; Deputy Chief, later Chief, 2d

Section, Central Committee, Kuomintang, 1953-62. Author of *The Law of the National Socialist Party*.

Yen Chung-ch'uan. Major General, People's Liberation Army, People's Republic of China; Deputy Chief of General Staff, 1969-   . Fought in anti-Japanese guerrilla warfare, 1937-45 and in Civil War. Responsible Person, Preparatory Group, Kwantung Provincial Revolutionary Committee, 1967; Vice Chairman, Kwantung Provincial Revolutionary Committee, 1968-69; Chief of Staff, Canton Military Region, 1968-69; Alternate Member, Chinese Communist Party Central Committee, 1969. Order of Independence and Freedom; Order of Liberation; and other medals and awards.

Yen Fu-sheng. Lieutenant General, People's Liberation Army, People's Republic of China; Deputy Political Commissar, People's Liberation Army, Canton Military Forces, 1963-   . Attended Red Army Military Academy. Joined Red Army, 1927; Chinese Communist Party, 1927. Participated in anti-Japanese guerrilla warfare, 1937-45; took part in the Long March, and the Civil War. Political Commissar, 8th Route Army, 1938-41; Political Commissar, Northeast Field Army, 1948; Chief, West Hunan Administrative Office, 1950; Member, Hunan Provincial Party Committee, 1955; Political Commissar, Hunan Military District, 1960; Director, Political Department, Canton Military Region, 1961; Member, Standing Committee, Chinese Communist Party Committee, Canton Units, 1964; Vice Chairman, Kwangtung People's Committee Supporting Patriotic Compatriots in Hong Kong-Kowloon, 1967. Order of August First; Order of Independence and Freedom; Order of Liberation; and other medals and awards.

Yepishev, A.A. General of the Army, USSR Army; Chief, Main Political Directorate, Soviet Army and Navy, 1962-   . Born May 19, 1908, in Astrakhan. Studied at Mechanization and Armored Troops College. Served on the Soviet-German Front in WW II. Deputy Minister, State Security, USSR, 1951-53; First Secretary, Odessa Oblast Committee, Communist Party, 1953-55; Ambassador to Romania, 1955-61; Ambassador to Yugoslavia, 1961-62; Member, Communist Party of the Soviet Union, since 1962; Member, CPSU Central Committee, since 1964; Deputy to Supreme Soviet of USSR. Two Orders of Lenin; three Orders of Red Banner; three Orders of Red Star; Order of Bogdan Khmelnitskiy; and other orders and medals. Promoted to General of the Army, 1962.

Yershov, I. Lieutenant General, USSR Army; Chief of Staff, Kiev Military District. Served on the Soviet-German Front in WW II. Member, Communist Party of the Soviet Union.

Yigit, Orhan. General, Turkish Army; Commander, Turkish Gendarmerie Forces, 1972-   . Studied at Military Academy; Infantry School; War College. Formerly Commander of Special Courses, War College; Division Commander; Assistant Chief of Staff, for Personnel, to

Chief of General Staff; Commander, Army Corps; Member, Supreme Military Council. Distinguished Unit Award; and other medals and awards. Promoted to General, August 30, 1971.

Ylirisku, Otto E. Lieutenant General, Army of Finland; Commanding General Finnish Border Guards, 1970-   . Born April 29, 1918, Jyvaskyla, Finland. Attended Military Academy, 1938-39; War College, 1949-51. Served in Winter War; Continuation War. Staff Officer, Armored Brigade, 1953-54; Instructor, War College, 1954-58; Commanding Officer, Pohjanmaa Jaeger Battalion, 1958-62; Inspector of Infantry, General Headquarters, 1966-70. Cross of Freedom, 2d, 3d, and 4th Class with Swords; Order of Finland's White Rose, 1st Class; Commemorative Medals of Winter and Continuation Wars; German Iron Cross, 2d Class; and other medals and awards. Promoted to Lieutenant General, April 1, 1970.

Young, Alexander. Major-General, British Army; Commandant, Royal Army Ordnance Corps, 1971-   . Born February 22, 1915. Attended Daniel Stewart's College, Edinburgh. Served in BEF and War Office in WW II. Headquarters, Staff British Army of the Rhine, 1959-61; War Office Staff, 1961-64; Deputy Director of Ordnance Services, Eastern Command, 1964-65; Commander, COD, Bicester, 1965-67; Commander, United Kingdom Base Organisation, 1967-68; Director of Ordnance Services, Ministry of Defence, 1968-71. CB. Fellow of the British Institute of Management.

Young, John W. Captain, US Navy; NASA Astronaut, 1962-   . Born September 24, 1930, San Francisco, California. Georgia Institute of Technology, BS, Aeronautical Engineering, 1952; US Naval Test Pilot School, 1959. Commissioned Ensign, US Navy, 1952. Fighter Squadron 103, 1953-58; Test Pilot, Naval Air Test Center, 1959-62; Maintenance Officer, All-Weather-Fighter Squadron 143. NASA experience: Pilot, Gemini 1, March 23, 1965; Backup Pilot, Gemini 6; Command Pilot, Gemini 10; Backup Command Module Pilot, Apollo 7; Command Module Pilot, Apollo 10, May 18-26, 1969; Backup Spacecraft Commander, Apollo 13; Spacecraft Commander, Apollo 16, April 16-27, 1972; Backup Spacecraft Commander, Apollo 17; Responsibility for Space Shuttle Group of the Astronaut Office. Two NASA Distinguished Service Medals; two NASA Exceptional Service Medals; Manned Spacecraft Center Certificate of Commendation; Navy Astronaut Wings; two Navy Distinguished Service Medals; three Navy Distinguished Flying Crosses; Georgia Tech Distinguished Young Alumni Award, 1965, and Distinguished Service Alumni Award, 1972; Society of Experimental Test Pilots' Ivan C. Kincheloe Award; Honorary LLD, Western State University College of Law, 1969; Honorary Doctorate of Applied Science, Florida Technological University, 1970.

Young, Kendall S. Major General, United States Air Force; Air Deputy, Allied Forces Northern Europe, Oslo, Norway, 1973-   . Born January 14, 1920, Baltimore, Maryland.

Baltimore Polytechnic Institute; University of Maryland; Army Air Forces Flying School, 1942. Commissioned Second Lieutenant, US Army, 1941; received pilot wings and transferred to US Army Air Corps, 1942. Combat duty in North Africa, Italy, WW II; Vietnam War. Commander, 1370th Photo-Mapping Wing, 1963-65; Director of Plans, Deputy Chief of Staff, Operations, Headquarters, US Air Forces in Europe, 1965-66; Commander, 7101st Air Base Wing, Wiesbaden, Germany, 1966-67; Commander, 66th Tactical Reconnaissance Wing, England, 1967-68; Commander, 363d Tactical Reconnaissance Wing, 1968-69; Chief, Air Force Advisory Group, US Military Assistance Command, Vietnam (MACV), 1969-71; Deputy Chief of Staff, Plans, Headquarters, United States Air Forces, Europe, 1971-73. Distinguished Service Medal; Silver Star; Legion of Merit; Distinguished Flying Cross with Oak Leaf Cluster; and other US and foreign medals and awards. Promoted to Major General, August 1, 1971.

Young, Robert Paul. Major General, United States Army; Director of Military Construction, Office, Chief of Engineers, US Army, Washington, D.C., 1972-   . Born December 17, 1919, Mitchell, South Dakota. US Military Academy; US Army Command and General Staff College; US Army War College; Harvard University, MS Degree, Civil Engineering. Commissioned Second Lieutenant, 1942. Served in WW II and Vietnam War. Commanding Officer, Engineer Command (Provisional), US Army, Europe, 1966-67; Division Engineer, US Army Engineer Division, Huntsville, Alabama, 1967-70; Director of Construction, US Military Assistance Command, Vietnam, 1970-71; Commanding General, US Army Engineer Command, Vietnam, US Army, Pacific-Vietnam, 1971-72. Distinguished Service Medal with Oak Leaf Cluster; Legion of Merit with Oak Leaf Cluster; and other medals and awards. Promoted to Brigadier General, September 27, 1967; Major General, August 1, 1970.

Younger, Allan Elton. Major-General, British Army; Senior Army Member of the Directing Staff, Royal College of Defence Studies, 1972-   . Born May 4, 1919. Attended Royal Military Academy, Woolwich; Christ's College, Cambridge; Royal Military Academy, Sandhurst. Commissioned in Royal Engineers in 1939. Served in northwest Europe in WW II. Commander 36 Corps Engineer Regiment, UK and Kenya, 1960-62; Instructor, US Army Command and General Staff College, 1963-66; Member, Programme Evaluation Group, 1966-68; Chief Engineer, Army Strategic Command, 1968-69; Chief of Staff, Headquarters Allied Forces Northern Europe, Oslo, 1970-72. DSO; OBE; MA; Silver Star (US).

Younger, John William. Major-General, British Army; Director of Management and Support of Intelligence, 1973-   . Born November 18, 1920. Attended Royal Military College, Sandhurst. Commissioned Second Lieutenant in the Coldstream Guards in 1939. Served in the Middle East in WW II; POW. Assistant Quartermaster-General, Headquarters London District, 1961-63; Assistant Adjutant General, War Office, 1963-65;

Ministry of Defence, 1967-70; Director of Quartering (Army), Ministry of Defence, 1970-73. CBE. Promoted to Brigadier in 1967; Major General in 1971.

Yu Hao-chang. General, Army of Republic of China; Commander in Chief, Chinese Army, 1969- . Born April 14, 1918, Anhwei. Military Academy; Army War College; Armored School, USA; Command and General Staff College, USA; Senior Officers Amphibious Warfare Course and Senior Naval Officers Course. Served in Sino-Japanese War; Chinese Civil War. Deputy Commandant, Chinese Marine Corps, 1953-56; Division Commander, 1957-59; Chief of Staff, Kinmen Defense Command, 1959-61; Commanding Officer, VIII Corps, 1961-63; Chief of Staff, General Headquarters, Chinese Army, 1964; Commandant, Chinese Marine Corps, 1965-68; Vice Chief of the General Staff, Ministry of National Defense, 1968-69.

Yu Pak-chuan. General, Army of Republic of China; Commanding General, Armed Forces University, 1969- . Born 1910, Hongkong. Trained at Royal Military Academy, Sandhurst, England; The School of Artillery, Larkhill, England; The School of Antiaircraft Artillery, Biggin Hill, England; Chinese War College, Chungking; Command and General Staff College, USA. Barrister-at-Law, Inner Temple, England. Served in Sino-Japanese War and Chinese Civil War. Chinese Delegate to the UN Military Staff Committee; Deputy Commandant, Chinese War College, Taiwan; Vice Chief of the General Staff, Operations and Planning, Ministry of National Defense; Commander, 1st Corps, and Deputy Commander, Kinmen; Commander, 9th Corps, and Deputy Commander, Kinmen; Vice Chief of the General Staff, Ministry of National Defense; Personal Chief of Staff to the President, 1966-67; Chairman, JORC, Ministry of National Defense, 1967-69.

Yu Pe-sheng. Admiral, Navy of Republic of China; Vice Chief of General Staff, Ministry of National Defense, 1967- . Born September 7, 1913, Kiangsu. Studied at Chinese Naval Academy, 1934; Royal Naval College, United Kingdom, 1945; Armed Forces War University; Amphibious Course for Senior Foreign Officers, USA; National War College. Served in Sino-Japanese War; Chinese Civil War. Commander, Destroyer Squadron, 1959-61; Commander, Amphibious Force Command, 1961-65; Commander, Fleet Command, 1965; Deputy Commander in Chief, Chinese Navy, 1965-67. Author of *Research on the Deployment of Postwar Coastal Defense; Military Harbor Rehabilitation.*

Yu, San. General, Burmese Army; Deputy Prime Minister and Defense Minister of Burma and Chief of Burmese Armed Forces, 1973- . Born c. 1920. Attended Rangoon University; US Command and General Staff College. Served in the Burma Independence Army in World War II. Formerly head of a regional military command; Vice Chief of Staff for the Army prior to April 1972. Promoted to General, April 1972. Member of Secretariat of the Central Committee of the Burma Socialist Program Party.

Yuan Kuo-cheng. Lieutenant General, Marine Corps of Republic of China; Commanding General, Chinese Army Training and Combat Development Command, 1971- Born September 14, 1917, Anhwei. Training: Military Academy; Army Command and Staff College; Armed Forces Command and Staff College; Command and General Staff College, USA. Served in Sino-Japanese War; Chinese Civil War. Commanding Officer, 167th Regiment, 56th Division, Chinese Marine Corps, 1947-52; Commanding General, 1st Marine Division, Chinese Marine Corps, 1957-61; Commanding General, Fleet Marine Force, Chinese Marine Corps, 1963-67; Commandant, Chinese Marine Corps, 1968-71.

Yugov, K.V. Lieutenant General, USSR Army; Chief of Staff, Transbaikal Military District, 1969- . Served on the Soviet-German Front, in WW II. Member, Communist Party of the Soviet Union.

Yurpolskiy, I.I. Lieutenant General, USSR Army; Deputy Commander, Transcaucasus Military District. Served on the Soviet-German Front in WW II. Member, Communist Party of the Soviet Union.

Z

Zagala, Rafael G. Brigadier General, Philippine Army; Commanding General, Philippine Army. Born October 28, 1919, in Taal, Batangas. Attended Ateneo de Manila, BA Degree, 1941; Lyceum of the Philippines, BS Degree, Commerce, 1958; Military Police Course, MPCTS, Alabang, Rizal, 1945; Associate Advanced Infantry Course, Fort Benning, Georgia, USA, 1953; Associate Command and General Staff Course, Fort Leavenworth, Kansas, USA, 1963. Commissioned Second Lieutenant in 1941. Served in the Pacific Theater, WW II; Vietnam War. Recent duty includes Commandant, Ground Combat School, PATC; Commander, Tank Battalion, 1st Infantry Division; G3, Philippine Army, 1966; Commander, Security Battalion, PHILCAG, Vietnam. Military Merit Medal; Gold Cross; and other medals and awards.

Zagorianakos, Dimitrios J. Lieutenant General, Hellenic Army; Chief, Hellenic Army, 1972- . Born August 23, 1918, Githion of Laconia, Greece. Attended Military Academy; School of Artillery, Larkhill, England; Infantry School; Higher War College. Commissioned Second Lieutenant (artillery), 1939. Served in Albanian Campaign, 1940-41; Greece, Middle East, and Italy, WW II; Anticommunist War, 1944-49. G-3, Army Corps "B"; Divisional Artillery Commander; Chief of Staff, Army Corps "C"; Commander, Infantry Division; Commander, Army Corps "C", 1970-72. Promoted to Lieutenant General, 1970.

Zaira, E. Major General, Israeli Army. Formerly Naval, Military and Air Attache, Embassy of Israel, Washington, D.C.

Zais, Melvin. Lieutenant General, United States Army; Commanding General, Third U.S. Army, Fort McPherson, Georgia, 1972- . Born May 8, 1916, Fall River, Massachusetts. University of New Hampshire, BA Degree, Political Science; U.S. Command and General Staff College; Armed Forces Staff College; The National War College. Commissioned Second Lieutenant, U.S. Army Reserve, 1937. Served in WW II and Vietnam War. Assistant Division Commander, 1st Infantry Division, U.S. Army, Vietnam, 1966; Director of Individual Training, Office, Deputy Chief of Staff for Personnel, U.S. Army, Washington, D.C. 1966-68; Commanding General, 101st Airborne Division (Airmobile), U.S. Army, Vietnam, 1968-69; Commanding General, XXIV Corps, U.S. Army, Vietnam, 1969-70; Director for Operations, J-3, Organization of the Joint Chiefs of Staff, U.S. Army, Washington, D.C., 1970-72. Distinguished Service Medal with three Oak Leaf Clusters, Silver Star with Oak Leaf Cluster; Legion of Merit with two Oak Leaf Clusters; Distinguished Flying Cross with Oak Leaf Cluster; Bronze Star Medal, and other medals and awards. Promoted to Brigadier General, June 1, 1964; Major General, May 1, 1967; Lieutenant General, August 1, 1969.

Zaitsev, V. Major General, USSR Army; Chief Personnel, Rear Services (Logistics), Ministry of Defense. Served on the Soviet-German Front in WW II. Member, Communist Party of the Soviet Union.

Zakharov, M.N. Admiral, USSR Navy; Chief, Political Section, Naval War College, 1971- . Served in the Soviet-German War, 1941-45. Chief, Political Directorate, Pacific Fleet, 1957-71. Member, Communist Party of the Soviet Union.

Zapater Vantosse, Fernando. Rear Admiral, Peruvian Navy; Chief of the Naval Staff.

Zekri, Fuad. Rear Admiral, Navy of the Arab Republic of Egypt; Commander, Egyptian Navy, 1972-

Zheltov, A.S. Colonel General, USSR Army; Commandant, Lenin Military-Political College. Served on the Soviet-German Front in WW II. Member, Communist Party of the Soviet Union.

Zimmermann, Armin. Admiral, Navy of the Federal Republic of Germany; Inspector General of the Armed Forces (Bundeswehr) 1972- . Born December 23, 1917, Blumenau, Brazil. Attended Naval Officers School. Commissioned Ensign in 1939. Served in WW II in the Baltic and North Seas. Joined the Bundeswehr in 1956 with the rank of Navy Commander; Commander, North Sea Naval Forces; Commander of the Fleet, 1970-72.

Zimmermann, Edwin Julius, Jr. Rear Admiral, United States Naval Reserve; Commander, Naval Surface Reserve, Omaha, Nebraska, 1972- . Born February 25, 1918, in Wichita, Kansas. Southern Methodist University, Dallas, Texas, BS, Commerce, 1941; US Naval Reserve

Midshipmans School, Northwestern University, Chicago, Illinois, 1941-42; Fleet Sonar School, 1954. Commissioned Ensign, US Naval Reserve, in 1942. Served in the Atlantic and Pacific Theaters, WW II; Korean War; released from active duty 1946; returned to active duty, 1950. Commander Reserve Destroyer Squadron THIRTY-FOUR, 1965-66; Director, Naval Reserve Plans Division, Office of the CNO, and Assistant Deputy CNO (Naval Reserve), 1966-68; Deputy Commander, Naval Reserve Training Command, Omaha, Nebraska, 1968-70; Assistant Deputy Chief of Naval Operations (Naval Reserve), 1970-72. Various medals and awards. Promoted to Rear Admiral, July 1, 1967.

Zollikofer, Laurenz. Major General, Swiss Army; Commanding General, 6th Division. Born in 1913.

Zolotov, S. Lieutenant General, USSR Army; Chief, Political Directorate, Central Group of Soviet Forces, Czechoslovakia, 1969- . Served on the Soviet-German Front in WW II. Member, Communist Party of the Soviet Union.

Zubia, Eduardo. General, Uruguayan Army; Commanding General, Military Region II.

Zulu, Alexander G. Minister of Defense, Zambia.

Zumstein, Jörg. Major General, Swiss Army; Commanding General, 3d Division. Born in 1923.

Zumwalt, Elmo Russell, Jr. Admiral, United States Navy; Chief of Naval Operations, 1970- . Born November 29, 1920, in San Francisco, California. US Naval Academy, 1939-42; Naval War College, 1952-53; National War College, 1961-62. Commissioned Ensign, US Navy, in 1942. Served in the Pacific Theater, WW II; Korean War; Vietnam War. Commanding Officer USS *Arnold J. Isbell*, 1955-57; Bureau of Naval Personnel, 1957-58; Special Assistant for Naval Personnel, then Executive Assistant and Senior Aide to Assistant Secretary of the Navy (Personnel and Reserve Forces), 1958-59; Staff Officer, Office of the Assistant Secretary of Defense (International Security Affairs), 1962-63; Executive Assistant and Senior Aide to the Secretary of the Navy, 1963-65; Commander Cruiser-Destroyer Flotilla SEVEN, 1965-66; Director, Systems Analysis Division, Office of the CNO, and Deputy Scientific Officer to the Center for Naval Analyses, 1966-68; Commander Naval Forces, Vietnam, and Chief of the Naval Advisory Group, US Military Assistance Command, Vietnam, 1968-70. Distinguished Service Medal with Gold Star; Legion of Merit with Gold Star; Bronze Star with Combat "V"; Navy Commendation Medal with Combat "V"; and other US and foreign medals and awards. Promoted to Rear Admiral, 1965; Admiral, July 1, 1970.

Zvartsev, A. Lieutenant General, USSR Army; Chief of Staff, Turkestan Military District, 1969- Served on the Soviet-German Front in WW II. Member, Communist Party of the Soviet Union.

Zyryanov, P.I. Colonel General, USSR Frontier Troops; Commander in Chief, Soviet Frontier Troops. Served on the Soviet-German Front in WW II. Member, Communist Party of the Soviet Union.

Zyto, Albin. Major General, Polish Air Force; Deputy Chief of Main Political Directorate, Polish Armed Forces. Formerly Deputy Commander, Political Affairs, Operational Air Force, Poznan; Deputy Commander, Political Affairs, Air Force. Cross of Grunwald; Cross of Merit; and other Polish and foreign orders and awards. Member of Polish United Workers Party.

MILITARY LEADERS BY NATION

AFGHANISTAN

*Khan Mohammad Khan

ALBANIA

*Balluku, Beqir
†Dume, Petrit
†Hasko, Eris
 Hoxha, Vehbi
 Kidsyzi, Qazim
†Mati, Abdi
 Shydi, Tanush

ALGERIA

*Boumedienne, Houari

ARGENTINA

 Agosti, Orlando Ramon
*Aguirre Obarrio, Eduardo
†Alvares, Carlos
 Alvarez, José Angel
†Carcagno, Jorge Raul
†Fautario, Hector Luis
 Fuenterrosa, Eugenio
 Giavedoni, Ruben Paul
 Gomez Centurion, Luis Carlos
 Rey, Carlos Alberto
 Sartorio, Jorge José
 Vazquez Maiztegui, Fernando

AUSTRALIA

*Barnard, Lance H.
†Brogan, Mervyn Francis
 Castles, Bryan J.
 Cleary, Colin Garfield
 Crabb, Gordon John Branstone
 Douglas, Desmond Lloyd George
 Dovers, William John
 Dunstan, Donald Beaumont

 Eaton, Brian Alexander
 Fraser, Colin Angus Ewen
 Graham, Stuart Clarence
 Hassett, Francis George
 Hay, Robert Arthur
 Hennock, Keith Selwyn
 MacDonald, Arthur Leslie
 Mackay, Kenneth
 Morgan, David Archibald Stevenson
 Mussared, Brynmor Wheatley
 Pearson, Cedric Maudsley Ingram
†Peek, Richard Innes
†Read, Charles Frederick
 Rowland, James Anthony
 Smith, Sir Victor (Alfred Trumper)
 Stevenson, Hugh David
 Susans, Ronald Thomas
 Synnot, Anthony Monckton
 Trudinger, Lawrence Robert
 Vincent, Douglas
 Wells, David Charles

AUSTRIA

 Auswöger, Otto
 Foltin, Ferdinand
 Koiner, Gottfried
†Leeb, Anton
*Lütgendorf, Karl Ferdinand
 Obermair, Hubert
 Reichel, Ignaz
 Weinkopf, Gustav

BANGLADESH

†Haque, N.
†Khondker, A. K.
*Mujibur Rahman, Sheikh
 Rahman, Ziaur
†Safiullah, K. M.

BELGIUM

†Crekillie, Armand François Emile

†Debeche, Albert
 Donnet, Baron M.
†Roman, Pierre
*Vanden Boeynants, Paul
†Van Dyck, J.

BOLIVIA

†Adriazola Valda, Oscar
†Alcoreza Melgarejo, Carlos
 Alvarez Penaranda, Raul
 Carrasco Riveros, José
 Gallardo B., Enrique
*Mendieta, Jaime Florentino
†Pinto Telleria, Xavier
 Ruiz Velarde, Cesar
†Sanches, Eliado

BRAZIL

†Alcantara, Francisco Augusto Simas
 de
 Araripe Macedo, Joelmir Campos de
 Bentes Monteiro, Euler
†Bornes Fortes, Breno
 Correa, Samuel Augusto Alves
 Dantas Torres, Maurício
 da Silva, Paulo Victor
 de Magalhaes, Gualter Maria Menezes
†de Oliveira Figueiredo, João Baptista
 Espellet, Eddy Sampaio
 Geisel, Orlando
 Henning, Geraldo Azevedo
 Jannuzzi, Arnaldo de Negreiros
 Jordão, José de Carvalho
 Labarthe, Ramon Gomez Leite
 Leig, Victor Didrich
†Marques, Roberval Pizarro
 Mello de Almeida, Reynaldo
 Nunes, Adalberto de Barros
 Sampaio Fernandes, Octavio José

BULGARIA

 Atanasov, Nikola

*Signifies Minister of Defense; †signifies head of service or senior commander.

†Dobrev, Khristo
*Dzhurov, Dobri Marinov
†Semerdzhiev, Atanas
Transki, Stavcho

BURMA

†Dan, Thaung
†Tin, Thaung
†U, Tin
†Yu, San

CAMBODIA

†Nol, Lon
†Sarendy, Vong

CAMEROON

*Daoudou, Sadou
†Semengue, Pierre

CANADA

Boyle, Douglas Seaman
Brodie, Harry B.
Carr, William K.
Cloutier, Sylvain
†Dextraze, Jacques Alfred
Edwards, G. J. J.
Falls, Robert Hilborn
Garton, William Maris
Hull, A. Chester
Leslie, Edward Murray Dailzell
L'Heureux, L. J.
Lier, R. H.
Pickford, R. John
*Richardson, James
Stovel, Richard Carlton
Waters, Stanley C.

CENTRAL AFRICAN REPUBLIC

Banza, Alexandre
*†Bokassa, Jean Bedel

CHAD

†Malloum, Felix
*Tombalbaye, François

CHILE

*Carvajal Prado, Patricio

Eberhard, Luis
†Leigh Guzman, Gustavo
Mandujano, Galvarino
†Mendoza, Cesar
†Merino Castro, José Toribio
†Pinochet Ugarte, Augusto
Rodriguez Theodor, Ervaldo

CHINA, PEOPLE'S REPUBLIC OF

Chang Ta-chih
Chang T'i-hsueh
Chen Chang-feng
Ch'en Hsi-lien
Ch'en Jen Chi
Ch'en K'ang
Ch'en Shih-ch'ü
Ch'en Tsai-tao
Cheng Wei-shan
Ch'eng Shih-ch'ing
Ch'in Chi-wei
Ch'iu Hui-tso
Chung Han-hua
Han Hsien-ch'u
Hsiao Ching-kuang
Hsiao Hua
Hsieh Fu-chih
Hsieh Tang-chung
Hsien Heng-han
Hsu Hsiang-ch'ien
Hsü Kuang-ta (Hsü Hao)
Hsu Shih-yu
Huang Yung-sheng
K'ung Shih-ch'uan
Li Teh-sheng
Li T'ien-yu
Li Tsai-han
Li Tso-p'eng
Li Yuan
Liu Chien-hsun
Liu Hsien-ch'uan
Liu Hsing-yuan
Lung Shu-chin
Nieh Jung-chen
P'eng Shao-hui
Su Chen-hua
Su Yü
T'an Fu-jen
T'eng Hai-ch'ing
Ting Sheng
Tseng Ssu-yü
Tseng Yung-ya
Wang Huai-Hsiang
Wang Hui-ch'iu
Wang Hung-k'un
Wang Pi-ch'eng
Wang Shu-sheng
Wei Kuo-ch'ing
Wen Yu-ch'eng

Wu Fa-hsien (Wu Wen-yu)
Wu Lieh
Yang Ch'eng-wu
Yang Te-chih
Yang Yung
*Yeh Chien-ying
Yen Chung-ch'uan
Yen Fu-sheng

CHINA, REPUBLIC OF (TAIWAN)

Chang Kuo-ying
Chao Kwei-sun
Chen Ching-kun
†Chen I-fan
*Chen Ta-ching
Cheng Wei-yuan
†Chiang Kai-shek (Chiang Chung-
    cheng)
Chiang Wego Wei-kuo
Feng Chi-chung
Hua Shing-chuan
Huang Chieh
Huang Hsi-lin
Kao Kuei-yuan
†Lai Ming-tang
Lee Tun-chien
Lei Kai-shuen
Liu An-chi
Liu Yu-chang
Lo Yu-lun
Loo Chih-teh
Louie Yen-chun
Sun Chien-lin
†Sung Chang-chih
Tsui Chih-tao
Wang Hsi-ling
Wei Chung-liang
Yao Chao-yuan
Yeh Hsiang-chih
†Yu Hao-chang
Yu Pak-chuan
Yu Pe-sheng
Yuan Kuo-cheng

COLOMBIA

Alba, Jorge
Angarita, Agustin
†Calderon Molano, José Ramon
*Currea Cubides, Hernando
Diaz Osorio, Alfonso
Forero, José G.
†Herrera Calderon, Alvaro
†Parra Ramirez, Jaime
Valencia Tovar, Alvaro
†Vargas Sierra, José Manuel
†Varon Valencia, Abraham Vicente
Wills Olaya, Eduardo

COSTA RICA

*Valverde Vega, Fernando

CUBA

*Castro Ruz, Raul

CYPRUS

*Eoannides, George

CZECHOSLOVAKIA

Brabec, Antonin
Cepicky, Josef
†Cincar, Jozef
*Dzur, Martin
Faglic, Andrej
Gros, Alois
Horacek, Vaclav
Korbela, Martin
Kosmel, Eduard
Kuczera, Bohuslaw
Lomsky, Bohumir
Reindl, Jiri
Rytir, Otakar
Sadek, Frantisek
†Svoboda, Ludvik
Valo, Vasil

DAHOMEY

†De Souza, Paul Emile
*Kerekou, Mathieu
†Sinzogan, Benoit

DENMARK

†Blixenkrone-Moller, Otto
†Thostrup, Sven

DOMINICAN REPUBLIC

Amiama Castillo, Francisco A.
*Jimenez, Ramon Emilio, Jr.
†Logrono Contin, Manuel A.

ECUADOR

*Aulestia, Victor
Maldonado, Marco Aurelio
Ortega Ortega, Jorge

†Vallejo Vivas, Reinaldo

EGYPT, ARAB REPUBLIC OF

†'Ali, Ahmad Isma'il
Gamassi, Mohammed
al Hariri, Abdel Wahab
Mounir, A.
Sharif, Bashir
†al-Shazili, Sa'd al-Din Muhammad
   al-Husayni
†Zekri, Fuad

EL SALVADOR

Guzman, Carlos
*Romero, Carlos Humberto

ETHIOPIA

Desta, Iskender
*Gerbe, Kebede

FINLAND

*Gestrin, Lars Olof Kristian
Haaksalo, Magnus
Hallila, Allan T.
Halmevaara, Kai Y.
Halttu, Paavo Oskari
Helske, Esko
†Junttila, Paavo J.
Krogerus, Holger
Lehti, Olavi J.
†Leinonen, Kaarlo O.
Mielonen, Unto Oskar
†Pirhonen, Jouko K. E.
†Salmela, Eero J. V.
Sarmanne, Kai B.
Setälä, Erkki V.
Siilasvuo, Ensio
Sisto, Mikko J.
Sutela, Lauri J.
Ylirisku, Otto E.

FRANCE

Alibert, Pierre Leon Antoine
Aubiniere Lippmann, Robert Joseph
Avon, Maurice Antoine
Barthelemy, Maurice Louis
Bigeard, Marcel Maurice
†Boissieu Dean de Luigné, Alain de
Brasseur-Kermadec
†Cantarel, Emile Pierre Adrien
   Clement

Clotteau
*Debré, Michel
Delahouse, Paul
Gelinet, André
Grasset, Etienne de
†Grigaut, Claude
Jarry, Pierre
†Joybert, Marc de
†Maurin, François
Meltz, André
Patou, André
Rousselot
Sanguinetti, A. M. F.

GABON

†Boylingui, Nazaire

GERMAN DEMOCRATIC REPUBLIC

Brunner, Horst
Dickel, Friedrich
†Ehm, Willi
*Hoffman, Karl Heinz
Miehlke, Erich
Poppe, Helmut
Streletz, Fritz
Streubel, Johannes
Teller, Günther

GERMANY, FEDERAL REPUBLIC OF

Bennecke, Jürgen
Berkhan, Karl Wilhelm
†de Maiziere, Ulrich Karl Ernst
Ferber, Ernst
Fingerhut, Helmut
Hartwig, Paul
†Kühnle, Heinz
*Leber, Georg
Mann, Siegfried
Speigl, Matthaus
Steinhoff, Johannes
†Zimmermann, Armin

GHANA

*Achcampong, Ignatius K.
†Quaye, P. F.

GREECE

Alpsu, Osman

†Angelis, Odysseus
†Arapakis, Peter
 Mastrantonis, Michael
†Mitsanas, Thomas B.
 Papadopoulos, George
 Papanikolau, Alexander
 Petmezas, G.
†Zagorianakos, Dimitrios J.

GUATEMALA

 Rios-Montt, José Efraim
*Rubio, Fausto David

HAITI

*Nazaire, Breton

HONDURAS

*Galo Soto, Raül

HUNGARY

 Csémi, Károly
*Czinege, Lajos

INDIA

 Aurora, Jagjit Singh
†Bewoor, Gopal Gurunath
 Jacob, J. F. R.
 Kamath, V. A.
 Kohli, S. N.
 Krishnan, N.
 Kuruvila, E. C.
†Nanda, S. M.
*Ram, Jagjivan
 Sarma, S. H.

INDONESIA

†Anwar, Mohammed
 Bachri, Samsjul
 Judono, Subroto
 Kadir, L. M. Abdul
*Panggabean Maradem
 Soedardjo, Nichlany
 Soedarman, Soesilo
 Sudiono
†Sudomo, R.
†Suharto, T. N. J.
 Suprapto
 Suromihardjo, Suadi

IRAN

*Azimi, Reza
†Khatami, Muhammad
 Mobasser, Mohsen
†Moezzi, Muhammad
 Nassiri, Ne'motollah
 Nura'i, Abdollah
†Oveisi, Gholam Ali
†Rassai, Farajolla
 Sadri, Ja'afar-Qoli
 Sa'adatmand, Abol-Hassan

IRAQ

 Ghaidan, Saadoun
†Shanshal, Abdul-Jabbar
*Shebab, Hammad

IRELAND

*Donegan, Patric

ISRAEL

†Botzer, A.
*Dayan, Moshe
†Elazar, David
 Eyal, S.
 Gonen, Shmuel
 Gur, Mordechai
 Hod, Mordechai
 Hofi, Yitzhak
 Lior, Hisrael
 Magen, Klamam
 Yariv, Aharon
 Zaira, E.

ITALY

 Birindelli, Gino
 Ciarlini, Giannetto
 Cucino, Andrea
†De Giorgi, Gino
 Gambetta, Mario
†Henke, Eugenio
†Lucertini, Vincenzo
*Tanassi, Mario
†Vigilione, Andrea

IVORY COAST

*M'bahia Ble, Kouadio

JAMAICA

*Manley, Michel

JAPAN

†Hoshino, Seizaburo
 Ichinomiya, Mayuki
 Kunishima, Kiyonori
 Takenaka, Yoshio
 Uchida, Katzutomi
*Yamanaka, Sadanori

JORDAN

 Abu-Taleb, Fathi
 Jumian, Shafik
 Maita, Kasim Hassan
†Majali, Habis Rifiafan
†Shaker, Zaid Ben

KENYA

*Gichuru, James S.

KOREA, DEMOCRATIC PEOPLE'S REPUBLIC OF

*Choi, Hyon
†Kwon, Yu Chan

KOREA, REPUBLIC OF

 Cha, Su-Kap
 Chang, Bong Chun
†Han Sin
†Kim, Kyu Sop
†Lee, Byong Mun
 Oh, Yun-Kyong
†Ok, Man Ho
†Ro, Jae Hyun

KUWAIT

*al Sabah, al Salem

LAOS

†Abhany, Kouprasith
†Kindavong, Prince Sinthanavong
 Sisouk Na Champassak
*Souvanna Phouma, His Highness
 Prince

LEBANON

†Boustany, Emile Georges
Ghazi, Henry
Raphael, Antoine

LESOTHO

*Leabua, Jonathan

LIBERIA

*Williams, Allen H.

LIBYA

†Qaddafi, Muammar el

LUXEMBOURG

*Schaus, Eugene

MALAGASY

*Ramarolahy, Philibert

MALAYSIA

*Hamzah bin Haji Abu Samah, Datu
†Osman bin Tunku Mohd, Jewa
Rahman, Unku Ahmed bin Abdul
Salleh, Mohn Zain bin Mohd
Thanabalasingan, Dato K.

MALI

*Doukara, Kissima

MAURITANIA

*Diagana, Sidi Mohamed

MAURITIUS

*Ramgoolam, Sir Seewoosagur

MEXICO

Artigas Fernandez, Mario
Blanco-Peyrefitte, J.

Bravo Carrera, Luis M.
Chazaro Lara, Ricardo
*Cuenca Diaz, Hermenegildo
Gomez Ortega, Miguel A.
Ramos Ramirez, Angel
†Uribe Escandon, Humberto
Valensuela, Carlos
Vinals-Carsi Luis

MONGOLIA

*Dorj, B.

MOROCCO

*Benjelloun, Muhammad
†Kabbaj, Muhammad

NEPAL

*Kirti Nidhi Bista

NETHERLANDS

†Ijesselstein, G.
†Knoop, Joannes Henri
Kruimink, F. E.
Mastrigt, Harry van
Mommersteeg, J. A.
Peijnenburg, Gerard Henri Joan
   Marie
†Roest, Eric
Stemerdink, A.
van de Vijver, P. P.
*Vredeling, Henk

NEW ZEALAND

*Faulkner, Arthur James
†Pearce, Leslie Arthur
Robertson, John Fraser
†St. George, Douglas Fitzclarence
*Thorne, Edward Courtenay
Webb, Richard James Holden

NICARAGUA

Gutierrez-Rivera, Julio
*Sanchez, Heberto
†Somoza Debayle, Anatasio

NIGER

†Balla, Arabe Chawey
*Kaziende, Leopold

NIGERIA

Adebayo, Robert
Diete-Spiff, Alfred Papapreye
Ejoor, David Akpode
Esuene, Udoakaha Jacob
†Gowon, Yakubu
†Hassan, Usman Katsina
Johnson, Mobolaji Olufunso
†Katsina, Hassan U.
Kyari, Abba
Ogbemudia, Samuel Osaigbovo
Usman, Musa
Wey, Joseph Edet Akinwale

NORWAY

Braadland, Magne
Johannessen, Folke Hauger
*Kleppe, Johan
Mohr, Wilhelm
Petersen, Thorleif
†Skjong, Hans Sigurd
Storheill, Skule Valentin

PAKISTAN

†Ahmad, Hasan Hafeez
Ahmed, Aziz
Ahmed, Rashid
Ahmed, Syed Ghias Uddin
*Bhutto, Zulfikar Ali
†Chaudhry, Zafar Ahmad
Hall, Eric G.
†Khan, Tikka
†Rahim Khan, A.

PARAGUAY

*Cabello, Leodegar
†Caceres, Juan Antonio
Fretes Davalos, Carlos J.
†Gonzalez, Hugo
†Quiñónez, Vicente F.
†Stroessner, Alfredo

PERU

Amat y Leon Mujica, Manuel
Arce, José L.
Arrisueno C., Alfredo
Chamot Biggs, Jorge
Fortelia, Eduardo
†Gilardi Rodriguez, Rolando
*Mercado Jarrin, Edgardo

Meza-Cuadra, Aníbal
Paredes, A. Isaias
Schroth, Enrique
Vargas Caballero, Luis E.
†Velasco Alvarado, Juan
Zapater Vantosse, Fernando

PHILIPPINES

*Enrile, Juan Ponce
†Espino, Romeo C.
Ileto, Rafael M.
†Ramos, Fidel V.
†Rancudo, José L.
†Ruiz, Hilario M.
†Zagala, Rafael G.

POLAND

Antos, Stanislaw
Baranski, Wojciech
Baryla, Jozef
Chocha, Boleslaw
Cieslik, Jan
Czubinski, Lucjan
Czyzewski, Waclaw
Dysko, Edward
Dziekan, Tadeusz
Grudzien, Mieczyslaw
Hupalowski, Tadeuxz
Jagas, Waclaw
†Janczyszyn, Ludwik
*Jaruzelski, Wojciech Witold
Jasinski, Antoni
Kaliski, Sylwester
Kaminski, Josef
Koczara, Henryk
Kopijkowski, Wlodzimierz
Korzeniecki, Konstanty
Kufel, Teodor
Lancucki, Edward
Lozowicki, Longin
†Michalowski, Henryk
Michta, Norbert
Molczyk, Eugeniusz
Obiedzinski, Mieczyslaw
Obroniecki, Tadeusz
Oliwa, Wlodzimierz
†Paszkowski, Roman
Pietraszkiewicz, Hieronim
Pirog, Jan
Polanski, Wladyslaw
Rozlubirski, Edwin
†Sawicki, Florian
Sawczuk, Wlodzimierz
Skalski, Jerzy
Stebelski, Josef
Stryga, Michal

Studzinski, Zozislaw
Szpitel, Edward
Szydlowski, Zbigniew
Tuczapski, Tadeusz
Urbanowicz, Jozef
Zyto, Albin

PORTUGAL

Albert y Correia, Joae
*de SaVianna Rebelo, Horacio Jose
†Deslandes, Venancio
†Ornelas e Vasconcelow, Fernando
Pereira Crespo, Manuel
Pereira do Nascimento, Jose

RHODESIA

*Howman, John Hartley

ROMANIA

Dinca, Ion
†Ghoerghe, Ion
*Ionita, Ion
Logofatu, Georghe
†Martes, Grigore
Nicolescu, Mariu
Oprita, Constantin
Tirca, Sterian

RWANDA

*Habyarimana, Juvelnal

SAUDI ARABIA

al-Faris, Ibrahim Mohamed
*Saud, His Royal Highness Prince
 Sultan ibn 'Abd al-'Aziz al

SIERRA LEONE

*Stevens, Siaka Probyn

SINGAPORE

*Goh Keng Swee

SOMALIA

*Samater, Mohamed Ali
†Siyad Barre, Muhammad

SOUTH AFRICA

†Biermann, H. H.
Biernamm, S. C.
*Botha, Peter W.
†Johnson, J.
Terry Lloyd, M. R.

SPAIN

†Barbudo Duarte, Excmo. Sr. Don
 Enrique
Baturone Colombo, Excmo. Sr. Don
 Adolfo
Castañon de Mena, Don Juan
†Cuadra Medina, Mariano
Franco Ibarnegaray, Carlos
González López, Excmo. Sr. Don
 José R.
Guerrero Garcia, Miguel
Montel Touzet, Arturo
Murcia Rubio, Javier
Pascual Sanz, Ramiro
Perez de Eulate y Vida, Teodoro
Pita de Veiga y Sanz, Excmo. Sr. Don
 Gabriel
Salvador Diaz-Benjumea, Julio
Serrano de Pablo Jimenez, Luis

SRI LANKA

*Bandaranaike, Sirimavo Ratwatte
 Dias
†Hunter, D. V.

SUDAN

Ahmad, Mohammed al-Baqir
†Nimeiry, Gaafar Mohamed el

SWEDEN

Ahnfelt, Sigmund
†Almgren, Carl Eric
*Andersson, Sven Olof Morgan
Arvas, Dag Gustaf Christer
Clemedson, Carl-Johan
Eggert, Folke Gustaf
Eklund, Carl Gunnar
Grandin, Gunnar Emil
Hökmark, Anders Gösta
Holm, Karl Eric
Kierkegaard, Sören Christer Douglas
Liljestrand, Bengt
Ljung, Karl Hilmer Lennart
Ljung, Per Ove Poul

Ljunggren, Lars Rasmus Hunning
Löwenhielm, Fredrik
Lundmark, Karl-Gösta Olof
†Lundvall, Bengt Gustav Gottfrid
Neij, Arvid Hans Magnus
Nordlöf, Gunnar
Nordström, Kjell Alarik
Olin, Sven-Olof
Olson, Sven-Olof
Palmstierna, Nils-Fredrik
Personne, Nils Birger Valdemar
Peyron, Gustaf Fredrik Carl
Rasin, Bengt Göran
Rheborg, Rolf
Rosenius, Bengt
Rudberg, Per Y.
Simonsson, Nils Victor
Skoglund, Claes Gösta
Sköld, Nils Gunnar
Ståhl, Carl-Gustaf
†Stenberg, Dick
Swanstein, Stig Nils Sigvard
†Synnergren, Stig Gustaf Eugen
Thunborg, Anders I.
Varenius, Bo Gerhard Otto
Wählin, Sten
Westin, Bo Lars Axel

SWITZERLAND

Aeberhard, Alfred
Baumann, Hans
Bays, Marcel
Blocher, Rudolf
Bolliger, Kurt
Borel, Denis
Christe, Robert
de Chastonay, Bernard
de Courten, Harald
Gisiger, Louis
*Gnägi, Rudolf
Grossenbacher, Charles
Hauser, Hans
Hirschy, Pierre
Honegger, Ernst
Hüssi, Johann
Jeanmaire, Jean-Louis
Kaech, Arnold
Käser, Reinhold
Keller, Oskar
Lattion, Gérard
Lohner, Ernst
Maurer, Fritz
Messmer, Hans
Ochsner, Richard
Pittet, Oliver
Rapold, Hans
Rickenmann, Kurt
Reichlin, Georg

Roost, Hans
Senn, Hans
Schuler, Ernst
Stucki, Robert
Thiébaud, Jämes
Trautweiler, Hans
†Vischer, Johann Jacob
Wetter, Ernst
Wick, Fritz
Wildbolz, Hans
Wille, Fritz
Zollikofer, Laurenz
Zumstein, Jörg

SYRIA

*†Tlass, Mustafa

THAILAND

†Bamrungphong, Boonchai
Chaloryoo, Sa-Ngad
†Chandrubeksa, Boonchoo
Charusathiara, Prapass
Dawee, Chullasapya
Dhiradhamrong, Abhichart
Hiranyasthiti, Chote
Hongsakula, Marin
Kamol, Dejatunga
Kittikachorn, Thanom
Mayalarp, Surakij
Muangmanee, Siri
Patayakul, Samran
Ruchibhan, Chanien
Seniwong Na Ayudhya, Tawit
Sirigaya, Amorn
†Sivara, Kris
Thejatunka, Kamol
†Thomya, Cherdchai

TOGO

*Eyadema, Etienne Gnassingbe

TRINIDAD and TOBAGO

*Pitt, Basil M. P.

TUNISIA

†Essoussi, Mohamed el Habib Ben
   Mohamed Ben Brahim
*Farhat, Abdallah
†Jedidi, Bechir Ben Mohamed Ben
   Sadok

†Talbi, Azzeddine Bel El Abed Ben
   Abderrahman

TURKEY

Akin, Veichi
Akinci, Esref
Ayan, Ethem R.
†Batur, Muhsin
†Eyiceoglu, Celal
Firat, Hilmi
Kayacan, Kemal
†Sancar, M. Semih
Tural, Cemal
Yigit, Orhan

UGANDA

*†Amin, Idi

UNION OF SOVIET SOCIALIST REPUBLICS

*Grechko, Andrei Antonovich
Moskalenko, Kiril Semyonovich
Yakubovskiy, Ivan Ignat'yevich

USSR Army
Abramov, K.
Aganov, S. K.
Alekseyev, N. N.
Altunin, Aleksandr T.
Ambaryan, Kh.
Andryushchenko, V. K.
Anishchyk, G. S.
Antipov, P.
Ariko, G. I.
Arsiyev, Nikolay Aleksandrovich
Avseyenko, V.
†Babdzhanyan, A. Kh.
Balakirev, V.
Bashtanikov, N.
†Batitskiy, Pavel Fyodorovich
Bednyagin, A.
Belik, P. A.
Beloborodov, Afanasiy Pavlovich
Belonozhko, S. Ya.
Belónsov, G.
Beregovoy, Mikhail Timofeyevich
Bliznyuk, I.
Bobylev, S.
Bondarenko, F. M.
Borisov, G.
Boychenko, I.
Boyko, V. P.
Buchenko, V. I,
Chasha, I.

Chizh, V. F.
Danilov, W. A.
Dankevich, P.
Davidenko, V. I.
Debalyuk, A.
Dement'ev, V. T.
Dorinin, M.
Dragunskiy, David Abramovich
Druzhinin, M.
Druzhinin, V. V.
Dudur, I.
Dyatlenko, V. K.
Fomichev, M. G.
Frolenkov, M.
Frolov, A. A.
Ganeyev, K.
Gerasimov, I.
Glotov, M.
Golofast, G.
Golovnin, M. I.
Golushko, I.
Goncharov, V. A.
Goranskiy, I.
Gorban, V.
Gorbovskiy, D. V.
Gorchakov, Pyotr Andreyevich
Govorov, Vladimir L.
Grechko, S. N.
Grekov, V.
Gribkov, A.
Grigorev, M. G.
Grushevoy, K.
Gubin, I. A.
Gusakovskiy,
Ivonov, B.
Ivanov, B. A.
Ivanov, M. T.
Ivanov, S. P.
Ivanovskiy, Yevgeniy
Ivashutin, P. I.
Kalashnik, M. Kh.
Karpov, V. N.
Kazakov, M. I.
Kazalov, L.
Khalipov, I. F.
Kharchenko, V. K.
Khetagurov, Georgiy Ivanovich
Khomulo, M. G.
Khoreshko, G.
Klyuev, A.
Kolesnikov, A.
Kolesnikov, I. S.
Komarovskiy, A. N.
Kovalev, I. M.
Kozhanov, K.
Kozmin, Aleksander
Kremenskiy, S. I.
Kryukov, A.
†Kulikov, Victor G.
Kurkotkin, Semyon K.

Kurochkin, K.
Kuznetsov, Leonid Ivanovich
Lashchenko, Pyotr Nikolayevich
Lavriyenko, N.
Leont'ev, N.
Levchenko, N.
Levchenko, P.
Lezhepekov, V.
Likachev, B.
Liskov, V. I.
Litovtsev, D. I.
Lizychev, A.
Lukashin, P. T.
Lyashchenko, Nikolay Grigor'yevich
Lyashko, N. M.
Lyashko, Veniamin Ivanovich
Lykov, I.
Makarychev, Mikhail Ivanovich
Makarevskiy, B.
Maksimov, K.
Malashenko, E.
Maltsev, Y. Y.
Marchenko, Y.
Margelov, Vasiliy Filippovich
Marushchak, F.
Martynov, I.
Mayorov, A. M.
Mayorov, Ya.
Mazhayev, F. A.
Mazhorov, G. I.
Mednikov, I.
Mel'nikov, P.
Merimskiy, V.
Mishchenko, A.
Mosyaikin, V.
Nagibin, N.
Nachinkin, N. A.
Naumenko, Yu.
Nikitin, M.
Nikitin, Vasiliy Vasil'evich
Obaturov, G. I.
Ogarkov, Nikolay Vasilyevich
Okunev, V. V.
Olifirov, F. A.
Olnev, E.
Ovcharenko, I.
Ovcharov, A.
Parshikov, A.
Pashchuk, K.
†Pavlovskiy, Ivan Grigoryevich
Peredelskiy, G.
Petrenko, P.
Petronis, P.
Petrov, I. V.
Pikalov, V. K.
Pokryshkin, Alexandr Ivanovich
Ponomarev, M.
Popov, G.
Povaly, M. I.
Radziyevskiy, Aleksey Ivanovich

Radziyevskiy, S. I.
Repin, I. P.
Rosseykin, I.
Ryabov, Yu.
Salmanov, G.
Samokhodskiy, P. Ya.
Semenov, I.
Shaposhnikov, P.
Shavrov, I. E.
Shcheglov, Afanasiy Fyodorovich
Shchukin, N.
Shelepin, A.
Shevchenko, A. I.
Shirogov, K.
Shurupov, A. G.
Sidorov, M. D.
Sil'chenko, N. K.
Slipchenko, P. F.
Sokolov, I.
Sokolov, S. I.
Sorokin,
Sredin, G. R.
Stepanov, V.
Stepchenko, F. P.
Sulatskov, S.
Sysoyev, P.
Tankayev, Magomed Tankayevich
Tenishchev, I.
Tkachev, F.
Tolstikov, O. V.
Tolubko, Vladimir Fyodorovich
Tovma, Vsevolod S.
Tret'yak, Ivan Moyseyevich
Turantayev, V. V.
Tutarinov, I.
Tyurnev, P.
Vashura, P. V.
Vasyagin, Semyon Petrovich
Vlasov, N.
Voloshko, G.
Vtorushin, L.
Yakushin, V. Z.
Yefimov, P. I.
Yegorovskiy,
†Yepishev, A. A.
Yershov, I.
Yugov, K. V.
Yurpolskiy, I. I.
Zaitsev, V.
Zheltov, A. S.
Zolotov, S.
Zvartsev, A.
Zyryanov, P. I.

USSR Navy
Alekseyev, Vladimir Nikolayevich
Amel'ko, Nikolay Nikolayevich
Baranov, N. M.
Baturov, N.
Bevz, S.

Bochkarev, M.
Bondarenko, G. A.
Borzov, Ivan Ivanovich
Burlachenko, P. D.
Chernobay, G. K.
Chursin, Serafim Evgenevich
Globa, Ya. N.
†Gorshkov, Sergey G.
Grishanov, V. M.
Gulyaev, S. A.
Kasatonov, Vladimir Afanasievich
Khokhlov, Pyotr Il'ich
Khovrin, Nikolay Ivanovich
Khrenov, V. A.
Kichev, V.
Kosov, A.
Kotov, P. G.
Kudelkin, Ya. M.
Kulakov, Nikolay Mikhaylovich
Kuznetsov, G. A.
Kuznetsov, I. M.
Leonenkov, V. M.
Lobov, Semyon Mikhaylovich
Maslov, V.
Mikhailin, V. V.
Mironenko, Aleksandr Alekseyevich
Mizin, L. V.
Novikov, V. G.
Oleynik, G. G.
Orël, E. A.
Petelin, Aleksandr Ivanovich
Plekhanov, A.
Pochupaylo, Y. G.
Polekhin, B.
Rassokho, A. I.
Rudnev, I. S.
Savelev, F. I.
Sergeyev, Nikolay Dmitriyevich
Shabalin, A. O.
Shablikov, N. I.
Sizov, F. Ya.
Smirnov, N. I.
Sysoyev, V. S.
Tomashevskiy, A.
Vasilev, G. K.
Yamkovoy, B.
Yegorov, G. M.
Zakharov, M. N.

USSR Air Force
Antipov, A.
Borovykh, A. G.
Bugayev, Boris Pavlovich
Fedayev, N.
Gorelov, S.
Grishkov, N.
Ishchenko, F.
Koldunov, A.
Konstantinov, A.
Kulichev, I.

†Kutakhov, Pavel Stepanovich
Loginov, V.
Lysenko, V.
Melekhin, B.
Mironov, N. A.
Moroz, I. M.
Petukhov, N. V.
Polynin, F.
Savitskiy, V.
Shevchuk, V.
Silantyev, A.
Skubilin, V.
Sozinov, V.
Ushakov, Sergey Fyodorovich
Yefimov, Aleksandr Nikolayevich

USSR Air Force, Cosmonaut
Belyayev, Pavel Ivanovich
Beregovoy, Georgij Timofeyevich
Bykovsky, Valery Fyodorovich
Gorbatko, Viktor Vasiliyevich
Kamanin, Nikolai Petrovich
Khrunov, Evgeny Vasilievich
Leonov, Alexey Arkhipovich
Nikolayev, Andrian Grigorievich
Philipchenko, Anatoly Vasilievich
Popovich, Pavel Romanovich
Leonov, Alexey Arkhipovich
Shonin, Georgy Stepanovich
Tereshkova-Nikolayeva, Valentina
    Vladimirovna
Titov, Herman Stepanovich
Volynov, Boris Valentinovich
Yegorov, Boris Borisovich

UNITED KINGDOM

Gilmour, Ian
*Mason, Roy

British Army
Abraham, Sutton Martin
    O'Heguerty
Archer, Arthur John
Badcock, John Michael Watson
Baird, James Parlane
Bate, William
Beach, W. G. H.
Blacker, Sir Cecil (Hugh)
Blair, Chandos
Bowes-Lyon, (Francis) James (Cecil)
Bramall, Edwin Noel Westby
Britten, Robert Wallace Tudor
Buckland, Ronald John Denys Eden
Burnett, Edward John Sidney
Butler, Hew Dacres George
Butler, Sir Mervyn (Andrew Haldane)
Caldwell, Frank Griffiths
Carpenter, V. H. J.

Carroll, Derek Raymond
†Carver, Sir (Richard) Michael
    (Power)
Cattanach, Helen
Collin, Geoffrey de Egglesfield
Cooper, William Frank
Cowtan, Frank Willoughby John
Creasey, Timothy May
Cunningham, Hugh Patrick
Douglas-Withers, John Keppel
    Ingold
Dunbar, Charles Whish
Dye, Jack Bertie
Eugster, Sir Basil
Farrar-Hockley, Anthony Heritage
Fitzpatrick, Sir (Geoffrey Richard)
    Desmond
Ford, Robert Cyril
Fraser, Sir David (William)
Gibbon, Sir John (Houghton)
Gibbs, Sir Roland (Christopher)
Gilbert, Glyn Charles Anglim
Gould, John Charles
Gray, (Reginald) John
Hall, Kenneth
Harman, Jack Wentworth
House, David George
Howard-Dobson, Patrick John
Irvine, John
Irwin, Brian St. George
Jackson, Sir William Godfrey
    Fothergill
Janes, Mervyn
Jeffrey, Hugh Crozier
King, Sir Frank (Douglas)
Knutton, Harry
Lewis, Alfred George
Lewis, John Michael Hardwicke
Lyall Grant, Ian Hallam
McGhie, John
McKay, Alexander Matthew
McMeekin, Terence Douglas Herbert
Majury, James Herbert Samuel
Marshall, Roger Sydenham
Martin, Peter Lawrence de Carteret
Mitchell, Robert Imrie
Mogg, Sir John
Nolan, Eileen Joan
Page, Charles Edward
Pain, Horace Rollo Squarey
Pearson, Sir Thomas (Cecil Hook)
Phelps, L. T. H.
Purdon, Corran William Brooke
Read, Sir (John) Antony (Jervis)
Read, John Hugh Sherlock
Richardson, Thomas Anthony
Robertson, James Howden
Rogers, Norman Charles
Sawers, James Maxwell
Scott-Barrett, David William

Scott-Bowden, Logan
Scotter, William Norman Roy
Sharp, Sir John (Aubrey Taylor)
Somerville, Ronald Macaulay
Strawson, John Michael
Talbot, Sir Norman (Graham Guy)
Taylor, Sir Allan (Macnab).
Thomas, Sir (John) Noel
Tuzo, Sir Harry (Craufurd)
Walking, Alec Ernest
Ward, Sir Richard (Erskine)
Ward-Harrison, John Martin Donald
Willison, Sir David (John)
Willoughby, Sir John (Edward
    Francis)
Wilson, Alexander James
Woodrow, Albert John
Worsley, Richard Edward
Young, Alexander
Younger, Allan Elton
Younger, John William

Royal Navy
Anson, Sir Peter
†Ashmore, Sir Edward (Beckwith)
Ashmore, Peter William Beckwith
Begg, Sir Varyl (Cargill)
Binns, George Augustus
Blundell, Daphne Mary
Cruddas, Thomas Rennison
Dunlop, Colin Charles Harrison
Dymoke, Lionel Dorian
Easton, Ian
Eberle, James Henry Fuller
Empson, Sir (Leslie) Derek
Fell, Michael Frampton
Forrest, Ronald Stephen
Griffin, Sir Anthony Templer
    Frdderick Griffith
Griffin, Michael Harold
Hall, Geoffrey Penrose Dickinson
Hill-Norton, Sir Peter (John)
Hollins, Hubert Walter Elphinstone
Hunter, John
Jungius, James George
Leach, Henry Conyers
Lees-Spalding, Ian Jaffery
Lewin, Sir Terence Thornton
Lewis, Sir Andrew Mackenzie
Lewis-Jones, Robert Gwilym
Llewellyn, Jack Rowbottom
Lucey, Martin Noel
Lygo, Raymond Derek
McClintock, Cyril Lawson Tait
McIntosh, Sir Ian Stewart
McKaig, Sir (John) Rae
Mansfield, Edward Gerard Napier
Miller, Andrew John
Morgan, Brinley John
Morton, Anthony Storrs

Nixon, Harry Desmond
O'Connor, Anthony
†Pollock, Sir Michael (Patrick)
Pope, John Ernle
Power, Arthur Mackenzie
Raikes, Iwan Geoffrey
Raper, Sir (Robert) George
Robertson, Ian George William
Scott, William David Stewart
Shepherd, Charles William Haimes
Spickernell, Derek Garland
Tait, Allan Gordon
Templeton-Cotill, John Atrill
Treacher, John Devereux
Trewby, George Francis Allan
Troup, John Anthony Rose
Trowbridge, Richard John
Watson, Philip Alexander
Watt, James
White, Peter
Williams, David
Wilson, Alan Christopher Wyndham

Royal Air Force
Aiken, Sir John (Alexander Carlisle)
Allerton, Ord Denny
Ball, Alfred Henry Wynne
Barraclough, Sir John
Beamish, Cecil Howard
Beetham, Michael James
Betts, Charles Stephen
Bird, Frank Ronald
Bird-Wilson, Harold Arthur Cooper
Broom, Ivor Gordon
Browne, Charles Duncan Alfred
Bullen, Reginald
Button, Arthur Daniel
Cameron, Neil
Campbell, Ian Robert
Clementi, Cresswell Montagu
Coulthard, Colin Weall
Crompton, Roy Hartley
Crowley-Milling, Sir Denis
Davies, Alan Cyril
Dhenin, Geoffrey Howard
Dodd, Frank Leslie
Downey, John Chegwyn Thomas
Ducat-Amos, Barbara Mary
Durkin, Herbert
Evans, David George
FitzPatrick, David Beatty
Foxley-Norris, Sir Christopher (Neil)
Freer, Robert William George
Giddings, Kenneth Charles Michael
Griffiths, Arthur
Harbison, William
Harding, Ross Philip
Harland, Reginald Edward Wynyard
Hawkins, Desmond Ernest
Hazlewood, Frederick Samuel

Heward, Sir Anthony (Wilkinson)
Hoad, Norman Edward
Hodges, Sir Lewis (Macdonald)
Hodgkinson, Sir (William) Derek
Horsley, Beresford Peter Torrington
Hughes, Frederick Desmond
Humphrey, Sir Andrew (Henry)
Jackson, Ralph Coburn
Johnson, F. S. R.
Jolly, Robert Malcolm
Lamb, George Colin
Lawrence, John Thornett
Le Cheminant, Sir Peter (de Lacey)
Lock, Basil Goodhand
Lowe, Douglas Charles
Martin, Sir Harold Brownlow
    (Morgan)
Maynard, Sir Nigel Martin
Mellersh, Francis Richard Lee
Morris, Ronald James Arthur
Plumtree, Eric
Pringle, Sir Charles (Norman Seaton)
Robertson, William Duncan
Sidey, Sir Ernest (Shaw)
Sidney-Wilmot, Aubrey
Smallwood, Sir Denis (Graham)
Sowrey, Frederick Beresford
†Spotswood, Sir Denis (Frank)
Stack, Sir (Thomas) Neville
Steedman, Alexander McKay Sinclair
Sykes, William
Wade, Ruthven Lowry
Wakeford, Richard Gordon
Wheeler, Sir (Henry) Neil (George)
White, Michael William Langtry
Winn, Charles Vivian

Royal Marines
†Gourlay, Basil Ian Spencer
Kay, Patrick Richard
Loudoun, Robert Beverley
Macafee, John Leeper Anketell
Owen, John Ivor Headon
Whiteley, Peter John Frederick

UNITED STATES

Callaway, Howard H.
Clements, William P., Jr.
McLucas, John L.
Sanders, Frank
*Schlesinger, James R.
Warner, John W.

United States Army
Aaron, Harold Robert
†Abrams, Creighton Williams
Adams, Andrew Joseph
Albright, Jack Alvin

Almquist, Elmer Hugo
Antonelli, Theodore
Appel, John Glenn
Baer, Robert Jacob
Bailey, Mildred Caroon
Baldwin, Clarke Tileston, Jr.
Barfield, Thomas Harwell
Barnes, John Winthrop
Bautz, Edward, Jr.
Bayer, Kenneth Howard
Beatty, George Samuel, Jr.
Benade, Leo Edward
Bennett, Donald Vivian
Bennett, Warren Kennedy
Berry, Sidney Bryan
Blakefield, William Henry
Blanchard, George Samuel, Jr.
Bolling, Alexander Russell, Jr.
Bolton, Donnelly Paul
Bowers, Verne Lyle
Bradley, Omar Nelson
Brown, Charles Pershing
Burdett, Allen Mitchell, Jr.
Burke, William Alden
Burton, Jonathan Rowell
Caldwell, William Burns, III
Camm, Frank Ambler
Cantlay, George Gordon
Cassidy, Patrick Francis
Cassidy, Richard Thomas
Chapman, Curtis Wheaton, Jr.
Clarke, Frederick James
Clay, Frank Butner
Cleland, John Robin Davis, Jr.
Coats, Wendell John
Cobb, William Warren
Coffin, Robert Edmondston
Coleman, William Smith
Collins, Arthur Sylvester, Jr.
Conroy, Raymond Chandler
Cooksey, Howard Harrison
Cooper, Kenneth Banks
Corcoran, Charles Allen
Cowles, Donald Harry
Crawford, Albert Benjamin, Jr.
Crittenberger, Willis Dale, Jr.
Crizer, Pat William
Cunningham, Hubert Summers
Cushman, John Holloway
D'Ambrosio, Eugene Joseph
Daniel, Charles Dwelle, Jr.
David, Bert Alison
Davidson, Phillip Buford, Jr.
Davis, Franklin Milton, Jr.
Davison, Frederic Ellis
Davison, Michael Shannon
Deane, John Russell, Jr.
DePuy, William Eugene
Desobry, William Robertson
Dolvin, Welborn Griffin

Donley, Edwin I.
Dunn, Carroll Hilton
Dunn, John Murphy
Duquemin, Gordon James
Elder, John Howard, Jr.
Ellis, Vincent Henry
Emerson, Henry Everett
Ewell, Julian Johnson
Flanagan, Edward Michael, Jr.
Forbes, Robert Charles
Forrester, Eugene Priest
Foster, Hugh Franklin, Jr.
Foster, Ralph Longwell
Franklin, Wesley Charles
Fuller, Lawrence Joseph
Fulton, William Bennison
Fuson, Jack Carter
Galloway, James Vance
Gard, Robert Gibbins, Jr.
Garth, Marshall Bragg
Gettys, Charles Martin
Gibbons, James Joseph
Gleszer, Roland Merril
Godding, George Arthur
Goodpaster, Andrew Jackson
Graham, Daniel Orrin
Graham, Erwin Montgomery, Jr.
Graves, Ernest, Jr.
Greenlief, Francis Stevens
Greer, Thomas Upton
Gribble, William Charles, Jr.
Guthrie, John Reiley
Hall, Charles Maurice
Hallgren, Hal Edward
Hamlet, James Frank
Hay, John Hancock, Jr.
Hayward, Harold Ira
Heiser, Rolland Valentine
Hennessey, John Joseph
Higgins, Hugh Richard
Hightower, John Milton
Hill, L. Gordon, Jr.
Hodson, Kenneth Joe
Hollingsworth, James Francis
Hollis, Harris Whitton
Hoover, John Elwood
Hospelhorn, Cecil Walton
Huffman, Burnside Elijah, Jr.
Hughes, Carl Wilson
Hughes, Frederic John
Hutchin, Claire Elwood, Jr.
Hyatt, Gerhardt Wilfred
Jennings, Hal Bruce, Jr.
Johansen, Eivind Herbert
Johnson, Kenneth Lawson
Kalergis, James George
Kendall, Maurice Wesley
Kerwin, Walter Thomas, Jr.
Klingenhagen, John Louis
Knowles, Richard Thomas

Knowlton, William Allen
Koisch, Francis Paul
Kornet, Fred, Jr.
Kraft, William Russell, Jr.
Kroesen, Frederick James, Jr.
Lang, Clarence Joseph
Leahy, Osmund Alfred
Leber, Walter Philip
Lee, Richard McGowan
Lekson, John Stephan
Le Van, Cj
Lilly, Roger Merrill
Lotz, Walter Edward, Jr.
Mabry, George Lafayette, Jr.
McAlister, Robert Carter
McChrystal, Herbert Joseph, Jr.
McClellan, Stan Leon
McConnell, Richard Edward
McDonough, Joseph Corbett
McEnery, John Winn
McGiffert, John Rutherford, II
McGovern, Donald Hugh
McKeen, Chester M., Jr.
McLaughlin, John Daniel
McLeod, William Eugene
Maddox, William Johnston, Jr.
Maples, Herron Nichols
Marks, Sidney Michael
Marshall, Robert Creel
Matheson, Salve Hugo
Mayo, George, Jr.
Mellen, Thomas Wright
Meyer, Edward Charles
Meyer, Stewart Canfield
Mildren, Frank Thomas
Miley, Henry Augustine, Jr.
Milloy, Albert Ernest
Moncrief, William Henry, Jr.
Moore, Harley Lester, Jr.
Moore, Harold Gregory
Morris, John Woodland
Murphy, Raymond Patrick
Myer, Charles Robert
Neel, Spurgeon Hart, Jr.
Noble, Charles Carmin
Norton, John
Ochs, Elmer Raymond
Olenchuk, Peter George
Orr, Kenneth Dew
Ott, David Ewing
Palmer, Bruce, Jr.
Parfitt, Harold Robert
Parker, David Stuart
Parker, Harold Edward
Patton, George Smith
Pearson, Willard
Peers, William Raymond
Penney, Howard Wilson
Pepke, Donn Royce
Pezdirtz, Joseph Warren

Pickett, George Edward
Pieklik, Joseph Edward
Ploger, Robert Riis
Post, Alton Gustav
Potts, William Edward
Powers, Patrick William
Proudfoot, Robert James
Prugh, George Shipley
Putnam, George Washington, Jr.
Ramsey, Lloyd Brinkley
Rattan, Donald Volney
Raymond, Daniel Arthur
Rebh, George Anthony
Richards, Darrie Hewitt
Richards, Ralph Julian, Jr.
Rienzi, Thomas Matthew
Roberts, Elvy Benton
Roberts, J. Milnor, Jr.
Rogers, Bernard William
Rollins, Andrew Peach, Jr.
Roseborough, Morgan Garrott
Ross, Marion Collier
Rosson, William Bradford
Rowny, Edward Leon
Ryder, Charles Wolcott, Jr.
St. John, Adrian, II
Salter, Sylvan Edwin
Sammet, George, Jr.
Schrader, Henry Carl
Schulke, Herbert Ardis, Jr.
Seignious, George Marion, II
Seitz, Richard Joe
Seneff, George Phillip, Jr.
Shedd, William Edgar, III
Shoemaker, Raymond Leroy
Shoemaker, Robert Morin
Sidle, Winant
Simmons, Charles James
Singlaub, John Kirk
Smith, Albert Hamman, Jr.
Smith, DeWitt Clinton, Jr.
Smith, Edwin Howell, Jr.
Smith, Homer Duggins, Jr.
Smith, James Clifton
Smith, Robert Bruce
Sparrow, Herbert George
Spragins, Charles Echols
Starnes, William Love
Starry, Donn Albert
Stilwell, Richard Giles
Street, Oliver Day, III
Sumner, Gordon, Jr.
Sutherland, James William, Jr.
Sweeney, Arthur Hamilton, Jr.
Taber, Robert Clinton
Tackaberry, Thomas Howard
Talbott, Orwin Clark
Tarpley, Thomas McKee
Taylor, Leonard Burbank
Terry, Robert Davis

Thurman, John Royster
Tobiason, Orville Leroy
Ursano, James Joseph
Vaughan, Woodrow Wilson
Vinson, Wilbur Henry, Jr.
Waggener, John Garnett
Wagstaff, Jack Jennings
Walker, Glenn David
Walker, Sam Sims
Wallace, George Magoun, II
Walters, Vernon Anthony
Weber, LaVern Erick
West, Richard Luther
Wetherill, Roderick
Weyand, Frederick Carlton
Wickham, John Adams, Jr.
Wier, James Arista
Williams, Robert Ray
Williamson, Ellis Warner
Wilson, Samuel Vaughn
Wolfe, William Roy, Jr.
Wolff, Herbert Eric
Woolwine, Walter James
Young, Robert Paul
Zais, Melvin

United States Navy
Abbot, James Lloyd, Jr.
Adamson, Robert E., Jr.
Albrittain, John Warren
Anderson, Herbert Henry
Anderson, Roy Gene
Andrews, Burton Howell
Armstrong, Parker Broadhurst
Bagley, David Harrington
Bagley, Worth Harrington
Ballenger, Felix Pettey
Barrett, John Michael
Baughan, Robert Louis, Jr.
Baumberger, Walter Harlen
Bayne, Marmaduke Gresham
Behrens, William Wohlsen, Jr.
Beling, John Kingsman
Bell, Clarence Edwin
Bennett, Fred G.
Bergin, Daniel Edward
Beshany, Philip Arthur
Bloxom, Elliott
Bringle, William Floyd
Bulkeley, John Duncan
Burke, Julian Thompson, Jr.
Cagle, Malcolm Winfield
Calvert, James Francis
Carmody, Martin Doan
Cary, Freeman Hamilton
Cassell, George Louis
Charbonnet, Pierre Numa, Jr.
Christman, Thomas Jackson
Clancy, Albert Harrison, Jr.
Clarey, Bernard Ambrose

Cobb, James Outterson
Colbert, Richard G.
Cole, Philip Patten
Cook, Ralph Edward
Cooke, Edward William
Cooper, Damon Warren
Cosgrove, Paul F., Jr.
Cousins, Ralph Wynne
Cramer, Shannon Davenport, Jr.
Crawford, Earl Russell
Davies, Thomas Daniel
Davis, George Monroe, Jr.
Davis, John Blount, Jr.
de Poix, Vincent Paul
Dillon, John G.
Donaldson, James Carmichael, Jr.
Dowd, Wallace Rutherford, Jr.
Duerk, Alene Bertha
Enger, Walter Melvin
Erly, Robert Broussard
Esch, Arthur Gerald
Etter, Harry Stough
Faucett, Ralph Eugene
Flanagan, William Robert
Freeman, Mason B.
Gaddis, Walter Donald
Garrett, Francis Leonard
Gayler, Noel
Geis, Lawrence Raymond
Gilkeson, Fillmore Bolling
Gillette, Norman Campbell, Jr.
Grantham, Emery Arden
Guest, William Selman
Guinn, Dick Henry
Hadden, Mayo Addison, Jr.
Harlfinger, Frederick Joseph, II
Harnish, William Max
Hayward, Thomas Bibb
Harty, Harry Lafayette, Jr.
Heffner, Grover Chester
Heyworth, Lawrence, Jr.
Hildreth, James Bertram
Hill, Clarence Arthur, Jr.
Holloway, James Lemuel, III
Holmquist, Carl Oreal
Hooper, Edwin Bickford
Houser, William Douglas
Isaman, Roy Maurice
Jackson, David Henry
Johnson, Henry Joseph
Johnson, John Bell
Johnston, Means, Jr.
Jones, Frank Cox
Kauffman, Draper Laurence
Kidd, Isaac Campbell, Jr.
King, Jerome H., Jr.
Kossler, Herman Joseph
Lacy, Paul Lindsay, Jr.
Lambert, Valdemar Greene
Lascara, Vincent Alfred

LeBourgeois, Julien Johnson
Lee, Kent Liston
Lemos, William Edward
Long, Robert Lyman John
Longino, James Charles, Jr.
Lyness, Douglas Henry
McClellan, Thomas Rufus
McClendon, William Roger
McCuddin, Leo B.
Mack, William Paden
McManus, Philip Stanley
McMorries, Edwin Eliot
Marschall, Albert Rhoades
Maurer, John Howard
Michaelis, Frederick Hayes
Miller, George Harold
Miller, Gerald E.
Minter, Charles Stamps, Jr.
Moore, George Everett
Moore, Howard Shackleford
Moore, Sam Howard
Moorer, Joe Park
†Moorer, Thomas Hinman
Moran, William Joseph
Morrison, George Stephen
Osborn, James Butler
Pearson, Rufus Judson, Jr.
Peet, Raymond Edward
Plate, Douglas Caulfield
Price, Frank Hoblitzell, Jr.
Ramage, James David
Rapp, William Theodore
Reich, Eli Thomas
Rice, Joseph Enoch
Rickover, Hyman George
Riera, Robert Emmett
Rieve, Roland
Robertson, Horace Bascomb, Jr.
Rosenberg, Edwin Miller
Salzer, Robert Samuel
Schneider, Raymond John
Scott, John Alexander
Sell, Leslie Hale
Shear, Harold Edson
Shepard, Tazewell Taylor, Jr.
Small, Walter Lowry
Smith, John Victor
Smith, Levering
Sonenshein, Nathan
Staring, Merlin Howard
Suerstedt, Henry, Jr.
Sutherling, Elton Woodrow
Swanson, Leroy Vincent
Talley, George Clyde, Jr.
Tibbets, Joseph Bonaficld
Turner, Myron George
Turner, Stansfield
VanArsdall, Clyde James, Jr.
Vannoy, Frank Wilson
Veth, Kenneth LeRoy

Walker, Thomas Jackson
Wallace, Kenneth Carroll
Ward, Norvell Gardiner
Weinel, John P.
Weisner, Maurice Franklin
Weitzenfeld, Daniel K.
Weschler, Thomas Robert
Weymouth, Ralph
Wheeler, Kenneth Ray
Wilkinson, Eugene P.
Williams, Joseph Warford, Jr.
Woods, Mark William
Zimmermann, Edwin Julius, Jr.
†Zumwalt, Elmo Russell, Jr.

United States Air Force
Allen, James R.
Allen, Lew, Jr.
Allison, Royal Bertram
Anderson, Andrew B., Jr.
Anthis, Rollen Henry
Ascani, Fred J.
Bacalis, Paul N.
Bailey, James A.
Baker, Royal Newman
Bellamy, Jack
Bellis, Benjamin N.
Belser, Joseph H.
Bennett, Charles I., Jr.
Berg, William W.
Blank, Jonas L.
Blesse, Frederick C.
Blood, Gordon F.
Bolt, Jones E.
Boswell, Marion L.
Boylan, George S., Jr.
Braswell, Arnold W.
Bray, Leslie W., Jr.
Breedlove, James M.
Brett, Devol
Brown, George Scratchley
Brown, I. G.
Bryan, William E., Jr.
Burns, John J.
Campbell, Roland A.
Campbell, William Beverly
Carlton, Paul K.
Carson, Charles William, Jr.
Casey, Maurice F.
Catledge, Richard C.
Catton, Jack J.
Chairsell, William S.
Chapman, Kenneth R.
Chase, Levi R.
Cheney, James Spiers
Clark, Albert P.
Clay, Lucius D., Jr.
Cody, Joseph Julius, Jr.
Cole, Ray M.
Colladay, Martin G.

Collins, Harold Edward
Corbin, Thomas G.
Cragg, Ernest T.
Creech, Wilbur L.
Cross, Richard G., Jr.
Crow, Duward Lowery
Curtis, Gilbert L.
Darmstandler, Harry M.
Davis, Woodard E., Jr.
DeLonga, Peter R.
DeLuca, Joseph R.
Dempster, Kenneth C.
Dettre, Rexford H., Jr.
Dickman, Joseph Lawrence
Dietrich, William Allen
Dixon, Robert James
Dougherty, Russell Elliott
Dreiseszun, Abraham J.
Dupont, Rene G.
Eade, George J.
Edmundson, James Valentine
Elliott, Frank W., Jr.
Ellis, Billy J.
Ellis, Richard H.
Evans, Andrew J., Jr.
Evans, William John
Faver, Dudley Ervin
Felices, Salvador E.
Fish, Howard M.
Fleming, Lawrence J.
Frankosky, James O.
Furlong, Raymond B.
Galligan, Walter T.
Gamble, Jack K.
Gavin, Herbert J.
Gideon, Francis C.
Gillem, Alvan C., II
Ginsburgh, Robert N.
Giraudo, John C.
Glasser, Otto John
Glauch, Alden G.
Gould, Gordon T., Jr.
Gonge, John F.
Gossick, Lee V.
Graham, Gordon M.
Hails, Robert E.
Hamilton, Colin C., Jr.
Hansen, Homer K.
Hardin, Ernest C., Jr.
Hargrove, Clifford W.
Harrell, William S.
Hayes, William R.
Hedlund, Earl C.
Hendry, Augustus Mallory, Jr.
Henry, John Bailey, Jr.
Herring, John Henry, Jr.
Hill, James A.
Hill, James E.
Hoban, Richard M.
Holland, Ralph T.

Holm, Jeanne M.
Holt, William Harvey
Hombs, Roger
Hudson, Eugene L.
Hudson, John B.
Hughes, James D.
Huyser, Robert E.
Ireland, Clare T., Jr.
Jack, William A.
James, Daniel, Jr.
Johnson, George Marvin, Jr.
Johnson, Gerald W.
Johnson, Oris B.
Johnson, Warren D.
Jones, David C.
Jones, David M.
Jumper, Jimmy J.
Kearney, Lester T., Jr.
Keck, James M.
Keegan, George J., Jr.
Kent, Glenn A.
Kern, John R., Jr.
Kidd, John Burns
Kirkendall, James F.
Knight, James A., Jr.
Kucheman, Henry B., Jr.
Kullman, John R.
LeBailly, Eugene Bernard
Lewis, Homer I.
Lewis, Leo C.
Lewis, Oliver W.
Lightner, Lawrence Scott
Locke, John Langford
Loving, George G., Jr.
Lowe, Jessup D.
Lukeman, Robert Patrick
Lyon, Herbert A.
McBride, William P.
McBride, William V.
MacDonald, William R.
McGarvey, Billie J.
McGehee, Thomas Kendrick
McGough, Edward A., III
McKee, George H.
McLaughlin, George W.
McNabb, John M.
McNeff, Edward P.
McNeil, Travis R.
McNickle, Melvin F.
McPherson, John B.
Madsen, Frank M., Jr.
Maloy, Robert W.
Manor, Leroy J.
Marshall, Winton W.
Martin, Glen Webster
Meyer, John C.
Milton, Theodore R.
Minter, Charles F., Sr.
Mitchell, Newell Dwight
Moats, Sanford K.

Moench, John O.
Momyer, William Wallace
Moore, Otis C.
Moore, William Grover, Jr.
Morgan, Thomas W.
Murphy, John R.
Nash, Slade
Nelson, Douglas T.
Nunn, Donald G.
O'Connor, Edmund F.
O'Keefe, Timothy Francis
Paschall, James E.
Paschall, Lee M.
Patch, Paul F.
Patterson, Robert A.
Pattillo, Charles C.
Pattillo, Cuthbert A.
Patton, John S.
Pauly, John W.
Petit, Robert Lindsay
Phillips, Samuel C.
Philpott, Jammie M.
Pitts, William Frederick
Poe, Bryce, II
Price, Harold L.
Price, James L.
Pursley, Robert E.
Rafalko, Edmund A.
Ratkovich, Edward
Reilly, M. R.
Rhodarmer, Roger K.
Rhodes, George
Robbins, Jack Bonds
Robbins, Jay T.
Roberts, John W.
Robinson, Ray A., Jr.
Rogers, Felix M.
Rosencrans, Evan W.
Ross, Donald Henry
Russell, Austin J.
Russell, Kendall
Salisbury, Arthur G.
Schoning, William M.
Schultz, Kenneth W.
Scowcroft, Brent
Seith, Louis Theodore
Searles, Dewitt R.
Shaefer, Richard F.
Sherrill, James C.
Shiely, Albert R., Jr.
Shotts, Bryan M.
Sianis, Pete C.
Simokaitis, Frank J.
Simon, Henry
Sitton, Ray B.
Slay, Alton D.
Smith, Donavon F.
Smith, Foster L.
Smith, Howard P.
Smith, William Y.

Smith, Larry Allen
Smith, Robert Nelson
Snavely, William W.
Stapleton, Carl W.
Steel, Maxwell W., Jr.
Steffes, Eugene Q., Jr.
Steinkraus, Lawrence W.
Stewart, James T.
Stewart, Richard R.
Stoney, Roberts Paul
Sweat, Dale S.
Talbott, Carlos M.
Tallman, Kenneth L.
Tanberg, Lawrence F.
Terry, Roy M.
Teubner, Harold C.
Tighe, Eugene Francis, Jr.
Tkach, Walter Robert
Trimble, Robert F.
Turner, Vernon R.
Vogt, John W., Jr.
Wade, Horace M.
Watkins, James H.
Wilkins, John H.
Wilson, Joseph G.
Wilson, Louis L., Jr.
Wisman, William Woodrow
Young, Kendall S.

United States Marine Corps
Adams, Arthur Harvey
Anderson, Earl Edward
Armstrong, Alan James
Axtell, George Clifton
Barrow, Robert H.
Beckington, Herbert L.
Brown, Leslie E.
†Cushman, Robert Everton, Jr.
Dulacki, Leo J.
Dwyer, Ross T.
Elwood, Hugh McJunkin
Fairburn, Robert Randell
Fegan, Joseph Charles, Jr.
Fris, Edward Steve
Haynes, Fred E.
Hill, Homer Spurgeon
Hoffman, Carl W.
Jaskilka, Samuel
Johnson, William Gentry
Keller, Robert Prescott
Lahue, Foster Carr
McLaughlin, John N.
Metzger, Louis
Miller, Thomas H., Jr.
Olson, Harry C.
Poggemeyer, Herman, Jr.
Robinson, Wallace Hamilton, Jr.
Ryan, Michael Patrick
Simpson, Ormond Ralph
Snowden, Lawrence Fontaine

Spanjer, Ralph H.
Wilson, Louis Hugh

United States Coast Guard
†Bender, Chester R.
Benkert, William Michael
Bullard, Ross P.
Engel, Benjamin Franklin
Fletcher, Robert Rowland
Hayes, John Briggs
Heckman, Albert A.
Jenkins, William Ambrose
Johansen, Julian Elliott
McClelland, Joseph James
Moreau, James Walter
Morrison, William L.
Palmer, James Alexander
Pearson, Helmer Sheppard
Perry, Ellis Lee
Ratti, Ricardo Allen
Rea, William Freeland, III
Richmond, Chester Arthur, Jr.
Sargent, Thomas Reece, III
Scarborough, Robert Henry, Jr.
Scheiderer, Edward Donald
Siemens, Abe Harold
Siler, Owen Wesley
Steele, Joseph Rodgers
Thompson, Glenn Owen
Thompson, John Fawdrey, Jr.
Wagner, Austin C.
Whalen, Mark Alexander
Williams, James Weldon

United States Astronauts
Allen, Joseph P.
Bean, Alan L.
Bobko, Karol J.
Brand, Vance DeVoe
Carr, Gerald Paul
Cernan, Eugene A.
Conrad, Charles, Jr.
Crippen, Robert L.
Duke, Charles Moss, Jr.
England, Anthony Wayne
Engle, Joe Henry
Evans, Ronald E.
Fullerton, Charles G.
Garriott, Owen K.
Gibson, Edward G.
Haise, Fred Wallace, Jr.
Hartsfield, Henry W., Jr.
Henize, Karl G.
Irwin, James Benson
Kerwin, Joseph P.
Lenoir, William B.
Lind, Don Leslie
Lousma, Jack Robert
McCandless, Bruce, II
McDivitt, James A.

Mattingly, Thomas K.
Mitchell, Edgar Dean
Musgrave, Story
Overmyer, Robert F.
Parker, Robert Allan Ridley
Peterson, Donald H.
Pogue, William Reid
Roosa, Stuart Allen
Schmitt, Harrison H.
Schweickart, Russell L.
Scott, David R.
Shepard, Alan B., Jr.
Slayton, Donald K.
Stafford, Thomas P.
Swigert, John Leonard, Jr.
Thornton, William Edgar
Truly, Richard H.
Weitz, Paul Joseph
Worden, Alfred Merrill
Young, John W.

UPPER VOLTA

†Lamizana, Sangoule
*Traore, Daouda

URUGUAY

†Alvarez, Gregorio
†Chiappe Posse, Hugo
Cristi, Esteban
†Gonzalez, Victor
Groppi, Silvio E.
Jaume, José Pedro
Martini, Hugo
Olazabal, Conrado
Paladini, Dante
†Perez Caldes, José
Ravenna, Walter
Torres Negreira, Pedro
Vadora, Julio
Zubia, Eduardo

VENEZUELA

†Cardenas Ramirez, Lucio
Garcia Landraeta, Alfredo
Leal Torres, Homero Ignacio
Miliani Aranguren, Francisco
†Ordoñez, Luis Arturo
*Pardi Davila, Gustavo
Perez Leffmans, Armando José
Rosales, Francisco
†Seijas Villalobos, José Constantino
†Sucre Figarella, Juan Manuel

VIETNAM, DEMOCRATIC REPUBLIC OF (NORTH)

Can, Vu Van
Chiem, Vu Xuan
Dao, Le Quang
Do, Tran
Don, Nguyen
Dung, Van Tien
*†Giap, Vo Nguyen
Hai, Tran Quy
Hao, Song
Hieu, Tran
Hoa, Le Quang
Huu, Chinh
Kiet, Pham
Luong, Tran
Man, Chu Huy
Mau, Phan Ngoc
Nam, Nguyen Van
Nghia, Tran Dai
Nhan, Luong
Quang, Tran Van
Sam, Tran
Tan, Chu Van
Tan, Le Trong
Tai, Phung The
Thai, Hoang Van
Thao, Hoang Minh
Tho, Tran
Tra, Tran Van
Tung, Nguyen Dinh
Vinh, Nguyen Van
Vu, Vuong Thua

VIETNAM, REPUBLIC OF (SOUTH)

Cam, Tran Van
Cang, Chung Tan
†Chon, Tran Van
Dao, Le Minh
Di, Tran Ba
Giai, Do Ke
Hinh, Nguyen Duy
Hung, Le Van
Khanh, Nguyen Duc
*Khiem, Tran Thien
Lan, Bui The
Lich, Tran Quoc
Luong, Le Quang
Luong, Nguyen Van
Minh, Nguyen Van
†Minh, Tran Van
Nam, Nguyen Khoa
Nghi, Nguyen Vinh
Nhut, Tran Van
Niem, Phan Dinh
Tan, Nguyen Huu

c.1

DATE DUE			